T0389617

The Slavic Religion in the Light of 11th- and 12th-Century German Chronicles (Thietmar of Merseburg, Adam of Bremen, Helmold of Bosau)

East Central and Eastern Europe in the Middle Ages, 450–1450

General Editors

Florin Curta and Dušan Zupka

VOLUME 60

The titles published in this series are listed at *brill.com/ecee*

The Slavic Religion in the Light of 11th- and 12th-Century German Chronicles (Thietmar of Merseburg, Adam of Bremen, Helmold of Bosau)

Studies on the Christian Interpretation of Pre-Christian Cults and Beliefs in the Middle Ages

By

Stanisław Rosik

Translated by

Anna Tyszkiewicz

BRILL

LEIDEN | BOSTON

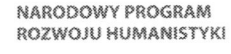 Preparation and translation of the publication financed under the program of the Minister of Science and Higher Education in Poland under the name "National Program for the Development of Humanities" in 2012–2014.

Cover illustration: The so-called "bear", ancient sculpture from around Strzegomiany near Mount Slęża (now at the top of the mountain), Stanisław Rosik.

Library of Congress Cataloging-in-Publication Data

Names: Rosik, Stanisław, author.
Title: The Slavic religion in the light of 11th- and 12th-century German
    chronicles (Thietmar of Merseburg, Adam of Bremen, Helmold of Bosau) : studies on the
    Christian Interpretation of Pre-Christian cults and beliefs in the Middle Ages / by Stanisław Rosik.
Description: Leiden ; Boston : Brill, 2020. | Series: East central and eastern Europe in the Middle
    Ages, 1450-1450, 1872-8103 ; volume 60 | Includes bibliographical references and index.
Identifiers: LCCN 2019056276 (print) | LCCN 2019056277 (ebook) |
    ISBN 9789004278882 (hardback) | ISBN 9789004331488 (nook edition)
Subjects: LCSH: Slavs—Religion--Sources. | Paganism—Europe,
    Eastern—History—Sources. | Europe, Eastern—Church history—Sources. |
    Thietmar, von Merseburg, Bishop of Merseburg, 975–1018. | Adam, von
    Bremen, active 11th century. | Helmold, approximately 1120-approximately 1177.
Classification: LCC BL930 .R674 2020 (print) | LCC BL930 (ebook) |
    DDC 299/.18—dc23
LC record available at https://lccn.loc.gov/2019056276
LC ebook record available at https://lccn.loc.gov/2019056277

Typeface for the Latin, Greek, and Cyrillic scripts: "Brill". See and download: brill.com/brill-typeface.

ISSN 1872-8103
ISBN 978-90-04-27888-2 (hardback)
ISBN 978-90-04-33148-8 (e-book)

Copyright 2020 by Koninklijke Brill NV, Leiden, The Netherlands.
Koninklijke Brill NV incorporates the imprints Brill, Brill Hes & De Graaf, Brill Nijhoff, Brill Rodopi,
Brill Sense, Hotei Publishing, mentis Verlag, Verlag Ferdinand Schöningh and Wilhelm Fink Verlag.
All rights reserved. No part of this publication may be reproduced, translated, stored in a retrieval system,
or transmitted in any form or by any means, electronic, mechanical, photocopying, recording or otherwise,
without prior written permission from the publisher.
Authorization to photocopy items for internal or personal use is granted by Koninklijke Brill NV provided
that the appropriate fees are paid directly to The Copyright Clearance Center, 222 Rosewood Drive, Suite 910,
Danvers, MA 01923, USA. Fees are subject to change.

This book is printed on acid-free paper and produced in a sustainable manner.

Contents

List of Figures and Map   IX

Introduction   1

1   *Interpretatio Christiana* of Old Slavic Religion as a Problem in Scholarly Reflection   10

   1   *Interpretatio Christiana* of Slavic Religion in Scholarly Opinions   10

     1.1   *Aleksander Brückner*   10

     1.2   *Erwin von Wienecke*   13

     1.3   *Stanisław Urbańczyk*   17

     1.4   *Henryk Łowmiański*   19

     1.5   *Leszek Moszyński*   23

     1.6   *On* Interpretatio Christiana: *Discussion Addendum and Summary*   25

       1.6.1   Christian Interpretation versus the Credibility of Sources on Slavic Religion   28

       1.6.2   *Interpretatio Christiana*: the Essence of the Phenomenon and Its Constituent Procedures   31

   2   Further Research Perspectives   32

2   The Religion of the Slavs in *Thietmar's Chronicle*   39

   1   Introduction: Thietmar of Merseburg and His Work   39

     Excursus: Saturn at the Wagrians (Widukind of Corvey, *Res gestae Saxonicae libri tres* III, 68)   54

   2   The Religion of the Slavs in Thietmar's Chronicle – Historiographical Analysis   56

     2.1   *The Holy Spring of the Tribe Glomače*   56

     2.2   *On Afterlife*   59

     2.3   *Slavic Religiousness in View of Bishop Boso's Mission*   72

     2.4   *Uprising of the Polabian Slavs* (983)   76

     2.5   *The* regnum ablatum *War between Mieszko* I *and Boleslav the Pious*   91

     2.6   *Radogošč*   93

       2.6.1   *Urbs tricornis, silva et mare* – Location of the Phanum   94

       2.6.2   *Dii manu facti*   99

       2.6.3   Svarožic – *deorum primus*   106

		2.6.4	*Ministri* 125

        2.6.4   *Ministri*   125
        2.6.5   The Oracle, Divinations and Auguries   128
        2.6.6   *Principalis monarchia*   133
        2.6.7   Oath of Peace   142
        2.6.8   Echo of the 983 Rebellion   144
    2.7   *Wigbert and* Zutibure   145
    2.8   *The Third War between Henry II and Boleslav the Brave: Ślęża Mountain and the Liutici Goddesses*   149
    2.9   *Hennil*   161
    2.10 *Reinbern and the Religion of Sea-Side Communities under Boleslav the Brave's Rule*   164
    2.11 *On Funeral Customs of the Slavs*   176
    2.12 *The Obodrite Pagan Reaction (1018)*   183
  3   The Religion of the Slavs in Thietmar's Chronicle – Closing Remarks   187

3   Adam of Bremen on Slavic Religion   197
  1   Introduction: Adam of Bremen and His Work   197
  2   The Religion of the Slavs in *Gesta Hammaburgensis ecclesiae pontificum* – Historiographical Analysis   212
    2.1   *Rethra*   212
    2.2   Iumne   226
    2.3   *The Revolt during the Pontificate of Libentius*   235
    2.4   *Gottschalks' Times and the Slavic Rebellion of 1066*   240
    2.5   *Rügen*   247
  3   The Religion of the Slavs in the Historical and Theological Vision of Adam of Bremen   249

4   *Helmoldi Cronica Slavorum* on Slavic Religion   256
  1   Helmold and His *Chronicle of the Slavs*   256
  2   The Religion of the Slavs in Helmold's Chronicle (Text Analysis)   265
    2.1   *Slavdom on the Threshold of the Oeuvre*   265
    2.2   *The First Wave of Christianization*   270
        2.2.1   Charlemagne, Anskar, and the Slavs   270
        2.2.2   The Rugians, Svantevit and the Legend of Corvey   273
    2.3   *The Second Revolution of the Wheel of History*   285
    2.4   *From Gottschalk Time Success to the 1066 Rebellion*   294
    2.5   *The Fourth High and Low Tide of Christianization*   299
        2.5.1   The Rans' Religion in the Description of Their Struggle with Henry the Obodrite Prince   300

CONTENTS VII

2.5.2   Vicelin – Difficult Beginnings of the Mission   303
2.5.3   On Slavic Rituals: Helmold I, 52   306
2.6   *The Last Ascent and Fall of the Polabian Mission*   323
2.7   *Towards Lasting Success of the Missionary Action*   326
2.7.1   Vicelin and Prove's Cult in Starigard   327
2.7.2   Count Adolf II and the Struggle with Idolatry   328
2.7.3   Helmold on a Journey with Gerold – a Treasury of Knowledge on Polabian Religion   330
2.8   *Epilogue: the Final Tackling of Rans and Their Cult*   355
3   The Slavic Religion in the "World" of Helmold's Work   368

Conclusions   383
1   On the Historical Stage   383
2   The Perspective of Theology and Culture Confrontation   386
3   *Argumentum ex interpretatione ...*   389

Bibliography   391
Index of Ancient Historical, Biblical and Mythical Figures   428
Index of Modern Authors   435

Figures and Map

Figures

1 Reconstruction of the Slavonic temple from Gross Raden (11th c.), Stanisław
   Rosik   101
2 The small bronze figure of a horse from Wolin (11th c.), Muzeum Regionalne im.
   Andrzeja Kaubego w Wolinie / The Regional Andrzej Kaube Museum in
   Wolin.   130
3 Mount Ślęża, Stanisław Rosik   150
4 The so called "bear", ancient sculpture from around Strzegomiany near Mount
   Slęża (now at the top of the mountain), Stanisław Rosik   156
5 The so called "sviatovid" from Wolin (9th c.), The Institute of Archaeology
   and Ethnology PAS, Centre for Medieval Archaeology of the Baltic Region in
   Szczecin, Stanisław Rosik   340
6 Cape of Arkona, Stanisław Rosik   362

Map

"Slavic tribes between Oder and Elbe in 10th–12th c.", Krzysztof Wachowiak
(University of Wrocław)   x

MAP 1   Slavic tribes between Oder and Elbe in 10th–12th c.
           KRZYSZTOF WACHOWIAK (UNIVERSITY OF WROCŁAW)

Introduction

Questioning Christian interpretation of the religion of the Slavs in the historiography of the Middle Ages has so far been treated in historical studies as a marginal issue, usually considered in the context of reflections on the credibility of the authors of the extant sources. The most extensive opinion on this matter was presented by Erwin von Wienecke,[1] who used the argument *ex interpretatione* for the purpose of proving that the literary images of Slavic beliefs and cults cannot be trusted in the reconstruction of the old religion, due to the fact that they were created according to a biblical model. In this way he tried to show that Slavdom did not actually reach the stage of polytheism and idolatry in its religious development. These theses were methodologically inspired by Herbert Achterberg's dissertation[2] analyzing *interpretatio Christiana* of the Germanic religion.

Achterberg deserves credit for making interpretations of pre-Christian native religions a valued research topic in and of itself. However, using his findings (a seemingly perfect comparative perspective) encounters major difficulties in the case of this work. The methodological basis for all of his reasoning is rather obsolete today. Nevertheless it should be emphasized that this scholar had influence on von Wienecke's concept, whose characterization was closely related to interpretations of the Slavic cults and beliefs constructed by the authors associated with the church, and thereafter became a reference point for other scholars' positions on this matter.

Despite the negation of this German scholar's hypercriticism in the matter of the development of Slavic beliefs and cults, the methodological aspect of his concept was in fact accepted, which suggests that the descriptions known from medieval historiography are just figments of their authors' imaginations, inspired by images drawn from the Christian tradition and the antique literary heritage. With such an assumption, the basic question was about the degree of distortion of the image of the old religion, due to the infiltration of this image by culturally unfamiliar elements. The discussion was dominated by an approach based in source-analysis, which was narrowed down substantially to

---

1 Erwin von Wienecke, *Untersuchungen zur Religion der Westslawen*, (Forschungen zur Vor- und Frühgeschichte) 1 (Leipzig: Harrassowitz, 1940), pp. 23 ff.

2 Herbert Achterberg, *Interpretatio Christiana. Verkleidete Glaubensgestalten der Germanen auf deutschem Boden*, (Form und Geist. Arbeiten zur germanischen Philologie) 19 (Leipzig: Hermann Eichblatt Verlag, 1930).

© KONINKLIJKE BRILL NV, LEIDEN, 2020 | DOI:10.1163/9789004331488_002

2   INTRODUCTION

the evaluation of the usefulness of the sources in studying pre-Christian Slavic
religious systems.

Furthermore, the overall evaluation of the consequences of the influence of
interpretatio Christana on the substance of the historiographical image of pre-
Christian cults and beliefs, determined *a priori*, accepted the scholar's assumptions regarding the development of a vernacular religion. However, this failed
to include a comprehensive study of the cultural context in which the description of the elements of this religion under investigation came to being. It is
still difficult not to notice that some of chroniclers' sources, respected for the
value of the information provided, were often ranked as being distinguished as
the interpretation of Slavic religions in terms of Christian theology, as well as
in terms of a sophisticated literary convention. Those observations became a
premise to propose[3] a postulate, to treat the issue of *interpretatio Christiana*
as a separate matter entirely. The concept of *interpretatio Christiana* should be
developed in research on the culture and intellectual life of the circles that created the basic written sources for studies of the Slavic religion. This is explored
in the present book.

A methodological approach for this type of study was in fact first prepared
in the field of social history, developed in the twentieth century, mainly by the
subsequent generations of historians representing the *Annales* School. Scholars
committed to reflecting on mentality (*mentalité*) posed a critical question –
which directly concerned *interpretatio Christiana* – regarding the ways of thinking about and experiencing individualities, which were conditioned by being
embedded in a particular epoch and a socio-cultural environment. This wide
area of investigation corresponds perfectly with research concentrated more
rigorously on the categories of culture, in which the then-vision of the world
was expressed.[4] Taking into consideration the value system which shaped the
world views of Christian authors writing about non-Christian religions, it is
important to mention the phenomenologically-inspired studies of the culture
of the European civilization that was formed in the Middle Ages.[5]

---

3 Stanisław Rosik, *Udział chrześcijaństwa w powstaniu policefalnych posągów kultowych u
   Słowian zachodnich* (Wrocław: Instytut Historyczny Uniwersytetu Wrocławskiego, 1995),
   pp. 84–91.

4 *E.g.* Aron Guriewicz [Gurevich], *Kategorie kultury średniowiecznej*, trans. Józef Dancygier
   (Warszawa: PIW, 1976) [orig. *Kategorii srednevekovoi kultury* (Moskva: Iskusstvo, 1972)].

5 For rather old works, but classics in this matter, see *e.g.* Christopher Dawson, *The Making
   of Europe: An Introduction to the History of European Unity* (London: Sheed and Ward, 1932);
   idem, *Formowanie się chrześcijaństwa*, trans. Józef Marzęcki (Warszawa: Instytut Wydawniczy
   PAX, 1987) [orig. *The Formation of Christendom* (New York: Sheed and Ward, 1967)]. For an alternative synthetic view based on "Europeanization" as a strategy of research, see especially
   Robert Bartlett, *The Making of Europe. Conquest, Colonization and Cultural Changes 950–1350*

INTRODUCTION

The aforementioned areas of investigation set the basic context of thought, which the issue of Christian interpretation of pre-Christian beliefs and cults is an integral part. It includes the ways of understanding, explaining, and representing those beliefs, as well as the topic of reading such religious phenomena in the terms of a foreign culture, evaluating them from the perspective of church doctrine, and finally acknowledging and appreciating their place and importance in the scene of presented history. The objects of analysis in the following study are particular historiographic pictures that constitute a shape of interpretation of Slavic religion, embedded in the "world of the text". The goal of this study, therefore, is to determine the social and cultural facts, as well as the work routines of the chronicler, all of which contributed to the creation of these pictures in a particular "here and now."

Substantial support for the investigation is provided by studies on medieval historiography and finally by studies on socio-cultural memory (*memoria*) in the Middle Ages. It was created and cultivated with regards to the historiographical works, which at the same time promoted a particular set of values by referring to specific events, often legendary, and the scenery in which they took place. An integral part of this investigation is a traditional element of studies on *interpretatio Christiana* – confronting medieval literary visions of Slavic beliefs and cults with the results of studies on the history of religion.

Anthropological approaches are also significant in the context of this study. On one hand, it is crucial to take into consideration the meaning of the specificity of present-day ways of discovering the world of medieval thought. This involves dealing with a problem of the so-called "cultural imputation" with regard to studying texts from several centuries ago. On the other hand, reaching beyond the strictly methodological reflection, it is vital to appreciate the historical research on perception of "the other," which has been developing rapidly over the past decades. In the cultural circle in which the chroniclers' descriptions of the cults and beliefs of the Slavs were created, the act of defining a religion as pagan set a perspective of its perception in terms of otherness or even hostility.

This may cause doubts about whether today's categorization of something as "pagan", and so forth, does not evoke an automatic prejudice against the religion under investigation. That includes not only its pejorative evaluation conditioned by church doctrine, but also its perception from outside, from the Christian point of view, or even from the standpoint of European civilization

---

(London: Allen Lane/Penguin Press, 1993) [Polish trans. *Tworzenie Europy. Podbój, kolonizacja i przemiany kulturowe 950–1350*, trans. Grażyna Waluga (Poznań: PTPN, 2003)].

that was shaped a millennium ago.[6] Elements propagating this point of view also condition – as a result of cultural imputation – the present-day researchers' reflections on the religion of the old Slavs. In order to reduce this phenomenon, especially with regard to pejorative evaluations, it is advised to use terminology alternative to the word "pagan."[7] Such examples include the phrases and words "pre-Christian," "native," or "primary." However, these terms are not flawless either.[8] For these many reasons, especially in research on the *Barbaricum* peoples' religions, maintaining diligence in using the aforementioned terminology, so as to reduce the scale of unintentional imputations and associations, is of key importance.[9]

The image of "pagans" and "paganism" in Christian circles during the Christianization of Europe has become the subject of separate studies on culture, especially ones inspired by phenomenology[10] and later also by

---

6   See Lech Leciejewicz, *Nowa postać świata. Narodziny średniowiecznej cywilizacji europejskiej* (Wrocław: Wydawnictwo Uniwersytetu Wrocławskiego, 2000; 2nd ed. 2007) [trans. *La nuova forma del mondo. La nascita della civiltà europea Medievale*, trans. Claudio Madonia (Bologna: Società editrice il Mulino, 2004)].

7   The terms "paganism" and "pagan" have been used in the following work especially in the context of quoting and analyzing medieval sources as immanent elements of their content, as well as in quotations from texts of the authors from the last two centuries – they used this terminology as synonymous to "pre-Christian" or "native", thus without an *a priori* intention of judging negatively the non-Christian religion. In terms of historiography in the 20th century, in Poland for example the usage of the aforementioned terminology was neutralized in terms of the worldview, and so it was in the primary version of the following dissertation published in 2000.

8   In reference to the Slavs, none of the terms above embody the fact of infiltration of some elements of Christianity into the sphere of their religion before Christianization. Moreover, the first of the terms still uses Christianity as the point of reference. Furthermore, defining Slavic religion as "native" may suggest that Christianity is a foreign phenomenon for modern Slavic nations, which favors ideological contestation of European cultural heritage due to the presence of an element of Christianity in it (this tendency is illustrated among others by reactivating the phantasmata, that rooted in the XIX-century Romanticism, in the debates on Polish identity in present-day Europe); see *e.g.* Maria Janion, *Niesamowita Słowiańszczyzna. Fantazmaty literatury* (Kraków: Wydawnictwo Literackie, 2007).

9   However, the clash between Christianity and paganism should be interpreted in this case not only in terms of theologically conditioned contradiction, but also in the categories of cultural border (because some elements of primary beliefs or cult presented in medieval sources could even go unrecognized as religious phenomena by the authors).

10 Especially see Hans-Dietrich Kahl, "Die ersten Jahrhunderte des missionsgeschichtlichen Mittelalters. Bausteine für eine Phänomenologie bis ca. 1050," in *Kirchengeschichte als Missionsgeschichte*, vol. 2: *Die Kirchen des früheren Mittelalters*, part 1, ed. Knut Schäferdiek (München: Kaiser, 1978), pp. 11–76.

INTRODUCTION

anthropology.[11] The reception of these findings in the fields of research on the religion of the Slavs and its interpretation is one of the more important goals pursued in this work. It is worth emphasizing that the present study focuses primarily on historiography, with respect to the distinctiveness of references made by particular authors to Old Slavic religion. The most essential elements in this research are a consideration of the writer's individual experience, the genesis of a given work, the environment in which it was created, and finally the goals pursued with such work (*causa scribendi*). Only this approach can reveal characteristics of motifs and the procedures that influenced the interpretation of the pre-Christian Slavic religion, culturally and theologically.

A decrease of interest in *interpretatio Christiana* in research on spiritual culture of the old Slavs, which could be observed in the last decades of the twentieth century, resulted from the resignation of a substantial group of scholars from a thesis about the late formation of Slavic polytheism. The *ex interpretatione* argument, which has so far been used to undermine the credibility of chroniclers writing about Slavic gods and idols, became less important in this area of study. The key role in this process was played by ethno-religious comparative studies, mainly in relation to Indo-European peoples (Georges Dumézil), supported by achievements of religious studies inspired by archaeology and phenomenology (Rudolf Otto, Mircea Eliade).[12] The core of the debate at the time was a conviction about the existence of some primordial, highly-unified religious system which would constitute the heritage of the pre-Slavic era, which would undergo progressive disintegration during and after the human migration at the beginning of the Middle Ages.

---

11   *E.g.* Lutz E. von Padberg, "Christen und Heiden. Zur Sicht des Heidentums in ausgewählter angelsächsischer und fränkischer Überlieferung des 7. und 8. Jahrhunderts," in *Iconologia sacra. Mythos, Bildkunst und Dichtung in der Religions- und Sozialgeschichte Alteuropas. Festschrift für Karl Hauck*, ed. Hagen Keller, Nikolaus Staubach (Berlin/ New York: De Gruyter, 1994), pp. 291–312; Christian Lübke, "Zwischen Triglav und Christus. Die Anfänge der Christianisierung des Havellandes," *Wichmann-Jahrbuch des Diözesangeschichtsvereins Berlin* (NF 3) 34/35 (1994–1995), pp. 15–35; Robert Bartlett, "From Paganism to Christianity in Medieval Europe," in *Christianization and the Rise of Christian Monarchy. Scandinavia, Central Europe, and Rus' c. 900–1200*, ed. Nora Berend (Cambridge: Cambridge University Press, 2007), pp. 47–72; Hans-Werner Goetz, *Die Wahrnehmung anderer Religionen und christlich-abendländisches Selbstverständnis im frühen und hohen Mittelalter (5.–12. Jahrhundert)*, vol. 1 (Berlin: Akademie Verlag, 2013), and in the wider context of cultural studies on the mythical origins of Slavic peoples see also especially Jacek Banaszkiewicz, *Polskie dzieje bajeczne Mistrza Wincentego Kadłubka* (Wrocław: Wydawnictwo Uniwersytetu Wrocławskiego, 1998).

12   One must emphasize, however, that the methodological standpoints of Eliade and of Dumézil have been criticized in the last decades.

6   INTRODUCTION

This explains the predilection of researchers on both sides of the argument about the genesis of Slavic polytheism to search for some elements of a community of beliefs (for example a hypothetical general Slavic god-sovereign of the heavens). The genesis of the occurrence of some of the common elements in mythologies and cults of remote groups of Slavs might be sought not only in the area of the presumed unity of pre-Slavic religion, but also in the intensification of contacts between communities belonging to this ethnicity. The latter of the two directions of research gained importance at the turn of the 21st century. This can be attributed primarily to the stage of discussion on the ethno-genesis of Slavs, in which it is taken into consideration that they might have formed an ethnic community no earlier than during the period of migrations between the 4th and 6th centuries AD.[13]

Whatever the result of this discussion will be, it is important to highlight that even if one supports the argument for the existence of an earlier proto-Slavonic community, one should not accept as an axiom the idea of the existence within its boundaries of some monolithic religious model that would prevent its particular component groups from participation in a wider circle of the Indo-European culture for over a thousand years (since the hypothetical disintegration of the Balto-Slavic community). Written sources, which are dated to a later period, reveal only the plurality of religious systems of Slavs connected with particular tribal organisms that exemplify certain analogies, as well as differences resulting from participation in multiethnic cultural circles. This is why it is important to take into account the possibility of the existence of such a situation before the aforementioned period of migration, which might have been the reason for the collapse of the alleged pre-Slavic unity.

Thus, the term "religion" featured in this work's title does not imply one regionally diversified religion for the whole of the Slavs. Rather, it merely points to a particular sphere of their social life., embracing a wide variety of phenomena that exemplify the attitude of those communities towards the sphere of *sacrum*. These include beliefs and cult practices in strict connection with magic.[14]

---

13   See especially Florin Curta, *The Making of the Slavs. History and Archaeology of the Lower Danube Region, c. 500–700*, (Cambridge Studies in Medieval Life and Thought: Fourth Series) (Cambridge: Cambridge University Press 2001); *idem*, "Tworzenie Słowian. Powrót do słowiańskiej etnogenezy," in *Nie-Słowianie o początkach Słowian*, ed. Przemysław Urbańczyk (Poznań/Warszawa: PTPN, 2006), pp. 27–55.

14   It is worth mentioning that in the views of religious scholars magic is usually juxtaposed with religion as relating to the cult of God/gods – *e.g.* Émile Durkheim, *Elementarne formy życia życia religijnego. System totemiczny w Australii*, trans. Anna Zadrożyńska, ed. Elżbieta Tarkowska (Warszawa: PWN, 1990) [orig. *Les formes élémentaires de la vie religieuse. Le systeme totémique en Australie*, (Paris: Alcan, 1912)]; Geo Widengren, *Religionsphänomenologie*, (Berlin: De Gruyter, 1969), p. 8; Anders Hultgård, "Runeninschriften und

INTRODUCTION

An important role is also played here by a reference to the sphere of laws and customs of the barbarians, with whom it constituted an integral unity.[15]

In the corpus of sources available for studying the religion of Slavs, each of the three chronicles selected for this particular research – those of Thietmar of Merseburg (d. 1018), Adam of Bremen (d. after 1081) and Helmold of Bosau (d. after 1177) – is of the same, primary importance as the lives of St. Otto of Bamberg, the *Gesta Danorum* by Saxo Grammaticus, the *Primary Chronicle* by Nestor the Chronicler, and possibly the *Chronicle of Bohemians* by Cosmas of Prague. Each of the works listed above constitutes a comprehensive source material for the issue of interpreting primary Slavic religion, and each of them could serve as the basis for a separate monograph. The method of analysis chosen for this study requires an analytical core comprising three monographic studies of particular chronicles (Chapters 2–4). The juxtaposition of the results of those analyses enables the formulation of general remarks summarizing their contribution to the studies on medieval interpretation of pre-Christian Slavic religion.

The first chapter lays a crucial groundwork by investigating the history of research on this topic, namely characterizing the scope and aspects of the selected problem, and formulating postulates that will enable verification of the previous findings and demarcation of a wider perspective of analysis. In this case the key role is played by empiricism, *i.e.* by the analysis of sources touching upon particular examples of the interpretation of primary religions, and taking into account the originality of the views of the medieval authors.

Runendenkmäler als Quellen der Religionsgeschichte," in *Runeninschriften als Quellen interdisziplinärer Forschung. Abhandlungen des Vierten Internationalen Symposiums über Runen und Runeninschriften in Göttingen vom 4.–9. August 1995*, ed. Klaus Düwel (Reallexikon der Germanischen Altertumskunde – Ergänzungsbände) 15 (Berlin/New York: De Gruyter, 1998), p. 725. However, in the practice of historical research such a theoretical model is often impossible to uphold due to a close relationship between magical and religious practices in the context of social life. Thus in the following study the reference to the sphere of religion of the old Slavic nations will be made with consideration of magic; such a concept of religion appears on the (*magna*) *pars pro toto* basis (like in *e.g.* Mircea Eliade, *Traité d'histoire des religions* (Paris: Payot, 1949)). Moreover, such resolution corresponds with the fact that in numerous instances various practices of magical character turn out to be expressions of religious cult. In such cases it is important to highlight the viewpoint of these scholars, who have included magic into the sphere of religion, see *e.g.* John Middleton, "Magic: Theories of Magic," in *The Encyclopedia of Religion*, vol. 9, ed. Mircea Eliade (New York/London: Macmillan Publishing Company, 1987), pp. 82–89; Bernd-Christian Otto, *Magie. Rezeption- und diskursgeschichtliche Analysen von der Antike bis zur Neuzeit* (Berlin: De Gruyter, 2011).

15 For an example of synthetic description of those issues see: Karol Modzelewski, *Barbarzyńska Europa* (Warszawa: Iskry, 2004).

On this basis alone has an attempt been made to draw conclusions. The comparative framework, important for this research procedure, emerges from the juxtaposition of works representing the same historiographical genre (*gesta*) and – perhaps even more importantly – written by representatives of the Saxon church milieu at the stage of its engagement with the conversion of Polabian Slavs.

Those narratives were written over the course of almost two centuries, which allows for identifying some of the more durable tendencies of their authors and their environment in approaching primary religions with a specific ethnic character. Interpretations of native Slavic beliefs are thus considered as socio-cultural facts, rooted in the historic *hic et nunc* existence of the chroniclers, demonstrating certain attitudes and judgements conditioned by ideas functioning within a culture, including the doctrinal element of Christianity. Its specific dimension is manifested in distinct textual images, petrified and unrepeatable owing to their authors' individual intentions (in addition to those of later copyists').

This book is an updated version of a doctoral dissertation published in 2000,[16] which in the succeeding few years gained an important context through the synthesis of Barbarian Europe by Karol Modzelewski,[17] and also through further research on the perception of "others" in German historiography on the 11th–12th centuries,[18] in addition to the contacts between Germany and

---

16   Stanisław Rosik, *Interpretacja chrześcijańska religii pogańskich Słowian w świetle kronik niemieckich XI–XII wieku (Thietmar, Adam z Bremy, Helmold)*, (Acta Universitatis Wratislaviensis. Historia) 144 (Wrocław: Wydawnictwo Uniwersytetu Wrocławskiego 2000). Cf. the review: Przemysław Wiszewski, "Rec. S. Rosik, Interpretacja chrześcijańska religii pogańskich Słowian w świetle kronik niemieckich XI–XIII w. (Thietmar, Adam z Bremy, Helmold), Wrocław 2000," *Sobótka* 57 (2002) 1, pp. 77–83, and gloss: Gerard Labuda, "O wierzeniach pogańskich Słowian w kronikach niemieckich z XI i XII wieku. Glosa do: Stanisław Rosik, Interpretacja chrześcijańska religii pogańskich Słowian w świetle kronik niemieckich XI–XII wieku – Thietmar. Adam z Bremy. Helmold, 'Acta Universitatis Wratislaviensis', nr 2235: Historia CXLIV, Wrocław 2000," in *Monumenta manent. Księga pamiątkowa dedykowana Profesorowi Tadeuszowi Białeckiemu w 70. rocznicę urodzin*, ed. Adam Makowski, Edward Włodarczyk (Szczecin: Wydawnictwo Naukowe Uniwersytetu Szczecińskiego, 2003), pp. 37–57.

17   K. Modzelewski, see above, footnote 15.

18   Volker Scior, *Das Eigene und das Fremde. Identität und Fremdheit in den Chroniken Adams von Bremen, Helmolds von Bosau und Arnolds von Lübeck*, (Orbis mediaevalis / Vorstellungswelten des Mittelalters) 4 (Berlin: Akademie, 2002); David Fraesdorff, *Der barbarische Norden: Vorstellungen und Fremdheitskategorien bei Rimbert, Thietmar von Merseburg, Adam von Bremen und Helmold von Bosau*, (Orbis mediaevalis / Vorstellungswelten des Mittelalters) 5 (Berlin: Akademie, 2005). See also Thomas Wünsch, *Deutsche und Slawen im Mittelalter* (München: Oldenbourg, 2008), p. 77.

INTRODUCTION

Slavdom itself in the Middle Ages.[19] "Stepping into the same river" after nearly fifteen years has allowed me to develop some analyses further and verify certain partial findings (at the level of subchapters).[20]

Results of the studies from the first edition of this dissertation have already been made available for a non-Polish audience in its German summary and several later publications.[21] However, the scope of those publications was rather limited. I would like to express my gratitude to Professor Florin Curta (University of Florida) for encouraging me to prepare a full, updated version of the work in English and for the invitation to publish it as a part of a series at the Brill Publishing House. I would also like to thank to Brill Publishing House for the kind and exemplary coordination of editorial works. Similarly, I am very grateful to Dr Bryan Kozik and Dr Gregory Leighton for the editing of the manuscript of this book. Translation into English was financed as a part of the National Programme for the Development of Humanities (project by the Ministry of Science and Higher Education in Poland).

---

19   Christian Lübke, *Fremde im östlichen Europa. Von Gesellschaften ohne Staat zu verstaatlichten Gesellschaften (9.–11. Jahrhundert)* (Köln/Weimar/Wien: Böhlau 2001); *idem*, "Pogańscy Słowianie i chrześcijańscy Niemcy. Tożsamości mieszkańców Połabszczyzny w VIII–XII w.," in *Bogowie i ich ludy. Religie pogańskie a procesy tworzenia się tożsamości kulturowej, etnicznej, plemiennej i narodowej w średniowieczu*, ed. Leszek P. Słupecki (Wrocław: Chronicon, 2008), pp. 73–84.

20   Important methodological inspiration and substantial contribution in the form of detailed research results in the modernized edition was the research on social and cultural memory (*memoria*) – in practice mainly hagiography – of St. Otto of Bamberg in the 12th c., within which the postulated continuation of studies on interpretation of the religion of the Slavs, which was declared in the first version of this study, was largely conducted, see: Stanisław Rosik, *Conversio gentis Pomeranorum. Studium świadectwa o wydarzeniu (XII wiek)* (Wrocław: Chronicon, 2010).

21   See: Rosik, *Interpretacja*, pp. 354–363; *idem*, "Rudes in fide gentilium populi … Fortdauer der Anzeichen des Heidentums zur Zeit der Christianisierung der Slawen im Lichte der deutschen narrativen Quellen des 11. und 12. Jahrhunderts," *Questiones Medii Aevii novae* 7 (2002), pp. 45–76; *idem*, "Greeks and Romans in pagan Wolin. Integrating the Barbarians into the collective memory of the Latin West at the time of the conversion of the Slavs," in *Rome, Constantinople and Newly-Converted Europe, Archaeological and Historical Evidence*, vol. 1, ed. Maciej Salamon *et al.* (Kraków/Leipzig: GWZO / Rzeszów: Instytut Archeologii Uniwersytetu Rzeszowskiego / Warszawa: IAE PAN, 2012), pp. 195–201.

CHAPTER 1

Interpretatio Christiana of Old Slavic Religion as a Problem in Scholarly Reflection

1 *Interpretatio Christiana* of Slavic Religion in Scholarly Opinions

The problem of the Christian interpretation of the primary religions of the Slavs arose at the time of positivistic criticism of the first historical reconstructions of their cults and beliefs. The research question was specified as *interpretatio Christiana* in 1939 by the German scholar Erwin von Wienecke, however it was suggested somewhat earlier, although it was not named so and was understood in a slightly different way. The foundations for all views on the subject until today were laid as early as the time of Aleksander Brückner's studies.

1.1 *Aleksander Brückner*

In Aleksander Brückner's studies on the religion of the Slavs, there were *a priori* assumptions that prompted his skepticism in relation to the value of medieval sources and later chronicles.[1] Having realized a conflict between his own research results and the information in written sources, Brückner adopted the stance that the authors – starting with late antique Procopius of Caesarea and ending with Jan Długosz (Joannes Dlugossius) and his successors – actually did not provide details of the essence of Slavic religious beliefs. They were satisfied with, or sometimes had to be satisfied with, using commonplace opinions based on two conventions of cultural and literary interpretation of the elements of primary Slavic religions: a Classical antique one and a medieval Christian one. Such ideas were used many times to support the argumentation of the author of "Mitologia słowiańska" [The Slavic Mythology], and they were formulated most clearly on the pages of "Mitologia polska" [The Polish Mythology], when he made an attempt to explain the genesis of Joannes Dlugossius's *Olympus*.

---

1 A bumper issue of Aleksander Brückner's works *Mitologia słowiańska i polska*, [The Slavic and Polish Mythology] edited with an introduction by Stanisław Urbańczyk (Warszawa: PWN, 1985), which encompasses: "Wierzenia i stosunki rodzinne," in *Encyklopedia polska* AU, vol. 4 (Kraków, 1912), p. 148–187; *idem, Mitologia słowiańska* (Kraków, 1918); *Mitologia polska. Studium porównawcze* (Kraków, 1924); "Mythologische Thesen," trans. Stanisław Urbańczyk, in *Archiv für Slavische Philologie* 40 (1926), pp. 1–21; "Ludy bałtyckie. Pierwotna wiara i kulty," in *Polska, jej dzieje i kultura*, vol. 1, ed. Stanisław Lam (Warszawa, 1929), pp. 4–50.

INTERPRETATIO CHRISTIANA OF OLD SLAVIC RELIGION

The Old Polish pantheon was to be born in the quiet refuge of canon Joannes's chamber filled with vellums. How then was he to find information about Polands' deities five centuries after the baptism of Poland? "Easily" – replies Brückner – "since every idolatry was a work of one and the same Satan, who caught people in his snares; the same happened everywhere; Greek gods were the same as the Roman ones; Athena – Minerva, Ares – Mars, and so the Polans also had their Mars, Pluto, Venus and Jupiter, like the Romans, only they would be given their own Polish names."[2] In such a way he explained the medieval *interpretatio classica*; however, he was of another opinion with reference to Procopius, an erudite of the late Antiquity: "Procopius scorned the Slavs like dogs, he did not scrutinize the matter confining himself to an Old Greek cliché."[3]

From the perspective of later discussion, the editor of Brückner's works stated that discerning Satan's acts in the Slavic religion, and more generally explanations based on a Christian point of view, have referred to *interpretatio Christiana* occurring next to a classical point of view.[4] It seems, however, that this conflicted with Brückner's concept in which the "Roman contribution" in the case of medieval hagiography became an integral part of Christian interpretation. It was used independently in Ancient times, the evidence of which may be Procopius's "cliché". He referred to ancient Classical tradition taught in schools, in which a typical interpretation was based on the essence of mythology presenting gods as personifications of the forces of nature.[5]

---

2   Brückner, *Mitologia słowiańska i polska*, p. 222, it can be added that according to Brückner, Joannes Dlugossius took names of Polish gods from folk songs; cf. also to other places: *ibidem*, p. 37: Dlugossius's testimony is worthless, which "results from his views on paganism spreading in the Middle Ages and even later. An act of one devil, invented for the perdition of humankind, it is uniform, the same gods which were worshipped in antiquity were also worshipped by all pagans, including ours; only their names changed depending on time and place." In addition to this, contrary to Cosmas, who used ancient names, Dlugossius adopted national terminology; *ibidem*, p. 217, it is stated that Cosmas could not know any Czech god and used classical names; later it was emphasized that in Pomerania *interpretatio Romana* all too frequently replaced native names (Pluto is mentioned instead of – maybe Veles, Mars appeared regularly; cf. *ibidem*, p. 255). *Ibidem*, p. 227: the so called *interpretatio Romana, i.e.* the "Roman lecture" – as it was pointed out by Brückner – was conducted also in antiquity with reference to Celtic and German gods, however, Dlugossius connected Roman gods with non-existing ones, and next Maciej of Miechów floundered much further in the same direction.

3   *Ibidem*, p. 257; and *ibidem*, p. 334: "a cultured Greek would never even dream of collecting information about Slavic religion; he would do with a rhetorical template. His information is false and carries no meaning".

4   Both of them had a distorting influence on accounts of medieval chroniclers on Slavic religion. See: Brückner, *Mitologia słowiańska i polska*, p. 222 (editor's note).

5   *Ibidem*, pp. 46 and 173; cf. footnote 3 in this chapter.

Apart from the "Roman interpretation" (*interpretatio Romana*), the aftermath of finding works of the devil in the Slavic religion, according to Brückner, was the derivation of Slavic gods from Christian saints and other historical figures. A good example is St. Vitus, who was to become Svantevit, or Veles, who was presented as St. Balazs, and other deities, *e.g.* the ones introduced by famous rulers.[6]

Lastly, Brückner took note of the influence of biblical templates on the construction of descriptions of Slavic religion.[7] In this respect he polemicized with Evgeniĭ Anichkov, who even earlier pointed out that Rus' chroniclers copied the biblical images[8] (first and foremost with the "The Philosopher's Speech" from *Povest' vremennich let*[9]), showing more confidence however in the content of their works related to the development of Slavic beliefs and cults.

---

6 *Ibidem*, pp. 35 f., he decisively rejected origination of the cult of Svantevit of Rügen from St. Vitus, a patron of missionary monks from Corvey; similarly to the cult of Volos in Rus' which originated from St. Balazs, considering both of these concepts as ideas of medieval priests. "Bringing down pagan gods to supposed saints (...) resembles only bygone euhemerism taken over by Rus' chroniclers and scribes from Greek sources, as they were convinced (...) that paganism was the same everywhere and worshipped Hellenic or Rus' gods". However, in an old apocryphal "The Home Going of Mary" he indicates an example in which Rus' gods were translated as former dignitaries: Perun in Greece, Chors in Cyprus, "Troian" – Roman Emperor. It can also be added that even *Powiest' wriemiennych let* [*Tale of Bygone Years*] in "The Philosopher's Speech" under the year 986, it presents the idea of pagan gods originating from people (see footnote 9 in this chapter). For a discussion on "euhemeric" genesis of Svantevit see chapter IV below. The role of "euphemerism" in the church interpretation of Germanic pantheons was discussed by Achterberg, *Interpretatio Christiana*, pp. 171 ff.

7 Brückner, *Mitologia słowiańska i polska*, p. 174. Brückner compares Procopius's information with Helmold of Bosau *Chronicle of the Slavs* (I, 84) (especially the problem of the "god of gods"), claiming that "if in this Procopius's testimony, a school-like cult of Jupiter god of thunder was recaptured, in Helmold's work the influence of Christianity is apparent."

8 *Ibidem*, p. 184, Brückner persistently claimed that the evolution of Rus' beliefs outlined in "The Philosopher's Speech" came only from Christian tradition. However, E. Anichkov presented another opinion, his contribution to the discussion was putting emphasis on two schemes: the first of them referred to the *Book of Deuteronomy* (Deut 7:5), where there is a description of overthrowing pagan altars, breaking idols or burning groves, the other one is a theological qualification based on a reflection on the *Epistle of St. Paul to the Romans* (Rom 1:25) and discusses preference for putting the creation above the Creator. The author observed both schemes in "The Philosopher's Speech" and saw stages of the development of pre-Christian religions in them, see Evgeniĭ Anichkov, *Jazyčestvo i drevnaia Rus'* (Petersburg Tip. M.M. Stasiulevicha, 1914), pp. 105–126, especially 106, 111, 114. Also Boris A. Rybakov, *Jazyčestvo drievnich slavyan* (Moskwa: Nauka, 1981), pp. 10 f., in such periodization in "The Philosopher's Speech" has perceived a reflection of real processes preserved in folk memory, however, presented according to a model borrowed from Greek and Egyptian mythology.

9 For the right passage of "The Philosopher's Speech" see *Povest' wremennich let*, part 1, text and translation, trans. Dmitriĭ S. Likhachev, Boris A. Romanov, ed. Varvara P. Adrjanova-Peretc (Moskva/Leningrad: Izdatelʹstvo Akademii Nauk SSSR, 1950) [further: PVL], p. 64, under the

INTERPRETATIO CHRISTIANA OF OLD SLAVIC RELIGION

To sum up Brückner's findings, it is worth emphasizing three types of observed consequences of theological assumptions in explanations of Slavic beliefs: 1) the so-called Roman lecture; 2) origination of Slavic gods from people – saints or important dignitaries ("euhemerization"); 3) inspiration taken from biblical images in cult and belief descriptions. It should be noted that the scholar did not bother about images directly diabolising Slavic gods in terms of language (*diabolus, daemon, etc.*), which became a subject of later in-depth analyses of other scholars. Regarding the method used by him in reconstructing pre-Christian Slavic religion, the study of specific terms did not play a leading role. Undoubtedly he took inspiration from the language of medieval sources when he was establishing the criteria of an interpretation of non-Christian religion in them; however, the dependence of these narratives on the language of the Bible did not have the force of a decisive argument for him, as was the case for hyper-critics of the idea of Slavic polytheism, led by E. von Wienecke.

1.2 *Erwin von Wienecke*

The author of "Untersuchungen zur Religion der Westslawen" (1939), Erwin von Wienecke, excluded the formation of polytheism among the Slavs even in the final phase of the development of their native religion, reducing it to the level of primeval demonolatry. However, this view is in flagrant contradiction with medieval written sources, and resultingly in Wienecke's work reflections on the way these medieval works were created. These are of profound significance to his work. They were inspired by Herbert Achterberg's treatise, which is a detailed source study of semantic fields of terms used in descriptions of the Germanic religion. A parallel analytical trend in this case took elements of cult and belief as its starting point, and then followed images and names that those elements acquired in church writers' texts.

Achterberg's central consideration was the group of Latin terms *diabolus, daemon,* and the German *unholde* (evil spirit). The author also studied forms of interpretation taken by Christianity from Greek and Roman mythology. To summarize source analyses, Achterberg first characterized *interpretatio*

---

year 6494 [986] it was noted that: "They were divided into seventy one peoples and they left for various countries and each of them developed their own traditions. According to the devil's teachings, they made offerings to groves, sources and rivers, and so they did not know God. (...) Later the devil caused even more insanity among people and they started to make idols – wooden, copper, some other marble, golden or silver ones; they bowed to them, brought their sons and daughters to them and made offerings of them, and the whole earth was defiled. The first idolater was Seruch, he made idols to worship the dead: idols of dead emperors, heroes and magicians as well adulteresses."

Christiana in comparison with *interpretatio Romana*, reducing the former to diabolisation and demonisation, while the latter was supposed to come down to identifications of pantheons of various peoples as in the model known from the ancient civilisation of the Mediterranean. Regarding the matter of the old authors' credibility, Achterberg stated that medieval sources did not show actual indications of the Germanic religion, but only presented its interpreted characters.[10]

Although these judgements may seem quite categorical, they do not give comprehensive characteristics of the phenomenon of *interpretatio Christiana*, and thus they do not allow unquestioned conclusions to be drawn about the substantial content of the testimonies of the pre-Christian religion. Wienecke (inspired by Achterberg's work) did not take this danger into account and undertook an attack on the credibility of old historiographers of the Slavic religion.[11] The key claim for him was that, when in the Middle Ages non-Christian cults and beliefs were described using expressions deriving from the language of antique and Christian literature, one should not automatically assume that they conceal true information about the development level of the Slavic religion. A monk creating in the refuge of his cell an image of the hostile *sacrum* had at his disposal not only antique and biblical vocabulary, but also stereotypical images and prototypes of paganism taken from the *Vulgate*.[12] Hence the German scholar advanced a thesis that while Tacitus was able to describe primary cults without statues and temples, medieval authors were no longer able to do so.

Thus, words found in antique writings, such as '*statua*,' '*effigies*,' or '*templum*,' *a priori* became typical expressions used in medieval descriptions of Slavs' native religion. Von Wienecke, however, rejected the possibility that these common expressions and schemes cover real forms of cult religion, and he did so on the basis of an analysis of St. Otto of Bamberg's miracle, described by three of his biographers.[13] Out of gross exaggeration he claimed that an error made

---

10   Achterberg, *Interpretatio*, pp. 169–176. The author emphasizes that diabolisation of the non-Christian *sacrum* did not result only from a missionary method, but mainly from the church doctrine. From among other ways to explain the genesis of pagan gods in a Christian perspective, Achterberg picks two: reducing them to fallen angels and euhemerization. Finally, however, all interpretation measures were to focus on the kingdom of darkness and its ruler. Cf. *e.g.* Fraesdorff, *Der barbarische Norden*, pp. 207 f.

11   The discussion below was based on Wienecke, *Untersuchungen*, pp. 23–29.

12   *Ibidem*, p. 24.

13   This case was considered a model and normative example of writers' interference in the real image of primary religions. Contradictions occurring in particular accounts, according to Wienecke, result from various degrees of using the Life of St. Martin by Gregory of Tours, which was considered the only source of information of Otto's hagiographers.

INTERPRETATIO CHRISTIANA OF OLD SLAVIC RELIGION 15

in earlier searching in Slavic religious studies (*i.e.* before 1939) was the uncritical acceptance of clichés and expressions functioning in the church literary tradition. To prove how detrimental this was to the credibility of medieval authors, he quoted a few examples from Rus' and also from western Slavic lands.[14]

Lastly von Wienecke emphasizes that the first commandment for a monk in his monastic cell was a sentence from the Book of Exodus (20:4): "Thou shalt not make to thyself a graven thing." Hence it was necessary to imagine the cults treated as pagan following Biblical patterns (*i.e.* with statues), because otherwise the sense of the commandment in the word of God would be contested. In this way of thinking the existence of statues was to be automatically connected with temple objects, the treasury and offerings, *etc.* The use of stereotypical collocations by medieval authors was to result in creating images of Slavic religion separated from its historical reality.[15] In a later part of his argument, von Wienecke notes that in this case, not only was the use of biblical terminology important, but also the way the essence of non-Christian beliefs

---

14 E. Wienecke focused on showing that terminology used in particular texts was evidently of Biblical origin (*e.g.* Helmold's *ambitum fani, reverentia, etc.*) and thus it cannot certainly refer to the Slavic religion. In a description of the Rus' idolatry in the *Chronicle of Nestor* (about Vladimir placing in 980 a statue of Perun and other deities on a hill, see PVL, under the year 6488 [980], p. 56) he found the "Devil" which undoubtedly is proof of *interpretatio Christiana*. Wienecke thought it was possible that the whole place came from an ecclesiastical interpretation for the purpose of creating a foundation legend for St. Basil's church. Similarly, the "Philosopher's Speech" under the year 6494 [986] seemed suspicious to him (see footnote 9 in this chapter), where a reference to Psalm 106 and Psalm 115 was noticed. These gold and silver images, according to Wienecke, were to be transferred from the Bible to a description of the heavily gilded Frey temple in Uppsala (also Redigast's temple in Rethra) by Adam of Bremen; Ebo's comments on Triglav's image (II, 13 and III, 1) and even Knytlingasaga (deity's gold moustache). According to Wienecke, the most determining Biblical place for medieval descriptions was: The Second Book of Chronicles (2 Chr 15:17; 28:4) and The First Book of Kings (1 Kgs 2:7). The same image was built by legends about saints: the Monk of Prüfening (III, 10) is a nearly word for word copy of a fragment of Gregory of Tours's Book I *De virtutibus S. Martini* (Otto's miracle is Martin's miracle); a similar influence was exerted on St. Otto's hagiographers by Sulpicius Severus.

15 E. von Wienecke claimed that sanctities personified in nature were to obtain the name *fanum*, and due to the fact that there were usually no shrines (*fanum*) without deities' images, only using this name was to assume their existence, hence it usually occurs in sources in the form of an expression *fanum cum idolis*; following this thought von Wienecke concluded that in minds steeped in Biblical thought, the very existence of paganism presupposed the presence of idolatry: hence the word *deus* automatically gained its counterparts *idolum, simulacrum, statua, effigies*. Biblical patterns are, among others, The First Epistle of St. Paul to the Thessalonians and *Psalms* (Ps 115:4–7 and Ps 135:15–17).

was understood in the spirit of views from the Holy Bible.[16] The author also emphasizes the presence of the element of terror in medieval descriptions of pagan deities (*terribili visu*) which, according to him, is also of Biblical origin.[17]

In this most extensive statement on the interpretation of the Slavic religion in the medieval historiography or hagiography, von Wienecke followed Achterberg in the classification of literary terms and motifs along two lines: a Classical one – the so-called *interpretatio classica antiqua (graeca vel Romana)*; and the Christian one – the so-called *interpretatio Christiana*. Von Wienecke perceived mechanisms of both interpretations as uniform. Just like Greeks or Romans in ancient times were able to find their own pantheon under different names in Germanic or Celtic beliefs, medieval monks reduced Slavic deities to Christian *antisacrum*.

The occurrence of these trends in the same descriptions – according to von Wienecke – makes it necessary to consider them as a whole, because the mentality of chroniclers was the product of a monastic school, where a synthesis of the Classical antique and Christianity took place. All interpretation efforts made in the Middle Ages were defined by von Wieneckeas *interpretatio ecclesiastica*. This idea introduces chaos because, especially with reference to the Middle Ages, the differentiation proposed by the researcher between the adjectives 'church' and 'Christian' is artificial, and without an additional definition it does not carry much information.[18] Thus this postulate was ignored by scholars, who interchangeably use both names in practice.[19]

The comments on the church interpretation made by Wienecke at the start of his work influenced later sections of his book. In this interpretation, possible confirmation of polytheism in sources was considered as a consequence of Biblical influences. Radical characters of these theses evoked negative criticism.[20] Most of the statements connected with temples and statues,

---

16 *E.g.* the Second Epistle of St. Paul to the Corinthians (2 Cor 6:15): "And what concord hath Christ with Belial?" inspired the Letter of St. Bruno and Herbord's description (III, 7), which according to von Wienecke casts doubt on these reports.

17 *E.g.* Ps 115 and 135; The Book of Esther (Esth 15:9).

18 In Wienecke's understanding *interpretatio Christiana* means Biblical, patristical, hagiographic, liturgical or encompassing monastic rules. However, medieval Christianity, as perceived by monastic scribes, was a compact culture system based on worldview uniformity, in which there were linguistic and thought structures, including literary ones related to antique times. This way of thinking was presented by A. Brückner and combined the so-called Roman lecture with Christian thought.

19 *E.g.* Gerard Labuda, "Rec. E. Wienecke, Untersuchungen zur Religion der Westslawen, Leipzig 1939," *Slavia Occidentalis* 18 (1947), p. 462.

20 As early as 1941 Thede Palm in *Zeitschrift für slavische Philologie*; see Špiro Kulišić, *Stara Slovenska religija u svietlu novijih istraživanja posebno balkanoloških* (Sarajevo: Akademija

INTERPRETATIO CHRISTIANA OF OLD SLAVIC RELIGION   17

especially polycephalic ones, were rejected, and – it is worth emphasizing –
they were rejected even before discovery of the first archaeological findings,
the interpretation of which discredited these concepts.[21] What is more interesting is that no attack was undertaken on von Wienecke's statements related
to the essence of *interpretatio ecclesiastica* mechanisms, but only on the way
of argumentation in which it becomes the only (and additionally negative)
criterion of an chronicler's credibility.

1.3   *Stanisław Urbańczyk*

In his "Religia pogańskich Słowian" [The Religion of Pagan Slavs] (Kraków
1947),[22] S. Urbańczyk introduced the metaphorical concept of "glasses" to the
discussion on Christian interpretation, which were used by medieval scribes
when observing the world of pre-Christian beliefs. The notion encompasses ways of "deforming reality" resulting from "limitations of human nature"
which "finds it hard to objectively observe events and so define them." These
medieval interpretational efforts were understood by Urbańczyk in accordance with von Wienecke's views, although not with such skepticism about
the substance of sources. However, the key role in the justification of the very
occurrence of *interpretatio Christiana* was to be played by a conviction that in
the Middle Ages "paganism was thought to be identical in all times and on all

---

     nauka i umjetnosti Bosne i Hercegovine, 1979), p. 180. G. Labuda, as above, criticised
     Wienecke's conclusions from the Brückner's point of view. It seems that Wienecke, al-
     though he voiced numerous objections directed at Brückner's works, accusing them of
     not being sufficiently critical, did not read them in detail. Additionally, other polem-
     ics with von Wienecke were conducted by Stanisław Urbańczyk, "Rec. E. Wienecke,
     Untersuchungen zur Religion der Westslawen der Westslaven. Leipzig 1940. Forschungen
     zur Vor- u. Frühgeschichte. 1," *Rocznik Slawistyczny* 16 (1948), pp. 40–56; Bruno Meriggi,
     "Il concetto del Dio nelle religioni dei popoli Slavi," *Ricerche Slavistiche* 1 (1952), pp. 166–
     167; Raffaelle Pettazzoni, *Wszechwiedza bogów*, trans. Barbara Sieroszewska (Warszawa:
     Książka i Wiedza, 1967) [orig. *L'onniscienza di Dio* (Torino, 1955)], pp. 244–236; cf. Alois
     Schmaus, "Zur altslawischen Religionsgeschichte," *Saeculum* 4 (1953), p. 209.

21   It is worth mentioning that development of research – especially archaeological – on the
     Baltic Slavs changes the context of views which were discussed for decades in terms of
     E. von Wienecke theses. See below, pp. 29 f.

22   Religious studies of S. Urbańczyk were published in a joint publication: Stanisław
     Urbańczyk, *Dawni Słowianie. Wiara i kult* (Wrocław/Warszawa/Kraków: Ossolineum,
     1991), which includes: supplemented edition *idem, Religia pogańskich Słowian* (Kraków,
     1947); *idem*, "Wierzenia plemion prapolskich," in *Początki państwa polskiego, Księga
     tysiąclecia*, vol. 2, ed. Kazimierz Tymieniecki *et al.* (Poznań 1962, pp. 137–153); *idem*, "O
     rekonstrukcję religii pogańskich Słowian," in *Religia pogańskich Słowian, Sesja naukowa w
     Kielcach*, ed. Karol Strug (Kielce, 1968), pp. 29–46; *idem*, "Wierzenia dawnych Słowian", in
     idem, Dawni Słowianie, pp. 143–165 (not printed earlier).

lands."[23] Being in contact with historical sources today, one may not always be sufficiently sensitive to reveal the action of these interpretation "glasses" because one is used to Christian and antique notions. Only reading the works of Arabic authors allows one to become aware of this type of interpretation.

S. Urbańczyk did not focus on emphasizing the dependence of medieval texts on the Bible and Christian literature in his examples, yet occasionally he emphasized episodes which were to show the essence of pagan cults in a theological perspective.[24] However, in an opinion given later, he speaks about an "interpretation filter" which one should always take into account when evaluating sources, and this filter is a Christian interpretation which "saw an embodiment of the Satan in pagan beliefs."[25] He presents a similar position in the introduction to A. Brückner's works: "... frequently medieval authors no longer could or had no skills to reach information about non-Christian beliefs, as they could see paganism through Christian theologians' glasses or the angle of Greek and Roman mythology (the so called *interpretatio Christiana* and *interpretatio classica Romana*). Both were false. *Interpretatio Christiana* requested them to see everywhere the influence of the devil and stupidity. A perfect example of *interpretatio Romana* is a description of Polish paganism by Długosz [Joannes Dlugossius]."[26]

This idea does not precisely define co-occurrence rules for both interpretations. Earlier attempts to solve this problem – let us remember – were undertaken by von Wienecke by introducing the notion of *interpretatio ecclesiastica*. In this situation S. Urbańczyk, although adopting A. Brückner's basic assumption about "one paganism" in the minds of medieval clergy, did not derive the "Roman interpretation" of the Slavic religion from theological premises, and he supported Wienecke's view of double-track tradition – *i.e.* the tradition

---

23   Urbańczyk, *Dawni Słowianie*, p. 14. *Ibidem*, p. 156, there is information about foreign names of demons penetrating into the Slavic culture from the preaching of sermonisers who are convinced that there is only one paganism in the whole world, and so they pommel non-existing forms of cults, customs and beliefs there.

24   *E.g. ibidem* p. 14: "when the Satan in a form of a swarm of flies came out form a pagan idol, or when a pagan priest died leaving a terrible smell".

25   *Ibidem*, p. 125.

26   *Ibidem* p. 201. Similarly in "Wierzenia dawnych Słowian" [Beliefs of ancient Slavs] first published in 1991: "In the way of presenting what was seen or heard, chroniclers depended on their knowledge of the Bible and Greek and Roman mythology, they willingly used phraseology borrowed from these sources, and Slavic 'gods' were given foreign names, *e.g.* Jupiter, Diana, Venus, Ceres, Apollo, Hephaestus, *etc.* They saw Slavic relation as if through foreign glasses (the so called *interpretatio ecclesiastica, classica, romana*)" – *ibidem*, p. 144.

INTERPRETATIO CHRISTIANA OF OLD SLAVIC RELIGION   19

that embodied ancient Roman (or Greek) interpretation in addition to the Christian one – in the presentation of primary religions.

Furthermore, S. Urbańczyk also indicated that it was possible that medieval authors sometimes had correct information based on their own experience connected with the Slavic religion, and resigned from presenting it for various reasons, such as saving expensive writing materials, low significance relative to the main plot of the work, and lastly awareness that their addressees knew the matter very well and did not need any additional information.[27] These general comments prove that the matter of credibility of medieval authors cannot be viewed from a one-sided perspective: "Usually it is hard to tell how much truth is hidden under borrowed phraseology. In the assessment of such places and generally the assessment of sources, there are significant differences between scholars."[28]

The statements of this Slavist show the permanence of his stance over a period of a few decades, and the simultaneous mining for new shades of the influence of the interpretation filter. Methodological views, although referring only to a general evaluation of sources, were applied in work on reconstruction of particular expressions of Slavic religion.[29]

1.4   *Henryk Łowmiański*

"Medieval written sources on Slavic religion are not only scarce but also their content is deficient, and in addition to this, they were written by not always very well informed authors who as a rule were averse to it."[30] This opinion of H. Łowmiański was to justify a rather particular – although in fact not far from von Wienecke's procedure – way of using written sources in the overall construction of the vision of the Slavic religion.

Łowmiański introduced to his work a number of notions inspired by phenomenological (and psychological) religious studies,[31] however, in his method of work on a text, he is much closer to an older positivist trend. He did not share G. Dumézil's conviction that polytheism was formed as early as the Indo-European community period. However, he proposed a notion of prototheism as the most appropriate one to define the development level of the early Slavs'

---

27   *Ibidem*, p. 123.

28   *Ibidem*, p. 144.

29   *E.g. ibidem*, p. 57: aversion to paganism or its non-understanding were to have influence on Thietmar to attribute the Slavs a conviction that everything was over at the moment of death. See below, p. 59.

30   Henryk Łowmiański, *Religia Słowian i jej upadek* (*w. VI–XII*) (Warszawa: PWN, 1979), p. 62.

31   See *ibidem*, pp. 9 ff. (chapter: *Prolegomena*).

beliefs. He argued for a a cult of personified heaven, which is the beginning of the first of gods ascending in the system of primeval polydoxy.[32]

Thus the majority of the Slavs were never to achieve the level of polytheism, and only in confrontation with Christianity were Rus' and, first of all, the Elbslavs to create their own gods. As a result, descriptions of the Slavic religion refer to at least three groups of phenomena – polydoxy, prototheism and polytheism (magic could also be included). Thus the question arises: to what extent are descriptive conventions adequate to show this state? Theoretical indications appear in this respect in a few places in Łowmiański's basic treatise "Religia Słowian i jej upadek (w. VI–XII)" ["Religion of Slavs and its decline (6th–12th c.)"] and allow one to compile a rather coherent approach to the problem.

The task of revealing the original character of the old religion, and thus eliminating secondary influences on its literary image, is complicated by "a reef which is hard to go around" in the form of imprecise source data, which is explained by Łowmiański in a different manner than von Wienecke. Deformations of the Slavic religion's image were to have been created "not so much because of incorrect observations, but more because of descriptions formulated using wrong methods. Errors in the methods were a consequence of two main reasons: 1) a ready-schematic image of the system of pagan beliefs which deformed the Slavic reality in the opinion of the Christian clergy, thanks to which descriptions of these beliefs are available; 2) a mixture of data in descriptions, some information was taken from real observation and some transferred from literature not reflecting the reality."[33] These general rules became a very useful tool in the elimination of source data discrepant with Łowmiański's stance on the development of beliefs and cults among the Slavs.

To put all phenomena encompassed by the sources in order, the scholar referred to the stages of development of pre-Christian religion from "The Philosopher's Speech" (theoreticians' of *interpretatio Christiana* favourite text) and using two biblical schemes indicated by Anichkov. The first of them referred to Deuteronomy (7:5) and characterised idolatry, *i.e.* – in Łowmiański's perspective – polytheism; the other one, from the Epistle of St. Paul to the Romans (1:25), based on the idea of prioritising creation over the Creator, was transferred to the basic layer of Slavic beliefs – polydoxy. The latter is reflected in the cult of groves, rivers, and wells, while polytheism corresponds with the

---

32   On hypothetical prototheism of the Slavs: *ibidem*, p. 31 ff., especially 37, and to sum up 398 f., cf. Jadwiga Bogdanowicz, *Religie w dziejach cywilizacji* (Gdańsk: Wydawnictwo Uniwersytetu Gdańskiego, 1995) pp. 43 ff.

33   Łowmiański, *Religia*, pp. 131 f.

INTERPRETATIO CHRISTIANA OF OLD SLAVIC RELIGION

"more serious error" – making marble, wooden, copper and gold statues as well as the offering of one's own children.[34]

Contrary to Anichkov, who saw two stages in the development of beliefs shown in medieval sources with both of these biblical schemes, Łowmiański attributed both of these trite images to one historical reality. In his research proposal the alleged interpretation scheme imputed to medieval authors caused "the deformation of the image of Slavic religion in an amplification sense, *i.e.* in the direction of polytheism, however, it did not limit richness of beliefs transmitted in the old literature: it is exactly the magic for which there was no place in the scheme, that is represented here in the abundance of facts. Hence sources, regardless of the scheme, allow all four polydoxy areas to be learned: cult of nature, cult of the dead, magic and demonology. (...) The image of polydoxy is blurred only by careless literary methods blurring borders between actual beliefs and literary borrowings, noted down in literature including own speculations or even fables told by the authors."[35]

However – to continue Łowmiański's thought – "in credible sources a small group of cult objects taken from nature was reflected, and these were some phenomena of great significance for a farming community (the sun and fire) and visible settlements of demons, places to make offerings in the form of waters, groves and stones. In any case a direct cult of the last category cannot be excluded. Zoolatry cannot be certainly traced in sources. There was a special respect for oxen due to their extensive use in farming."[36] Furthermore the scholar claimed that the cult of nature was so evident in the sources because it was decisively hostile to the Christian worldview, and disapproval of the clergy resulted in stigmatising its expressions (although only the most glaring ones, not all of them). However, a smaller interest of medieval historiographers in Slavic beliefs related to life after death was to be justified by a certain concurrence of notions related to the human soul and Christian beliefs, which did not lead to as strong a confrontation of viewpoints.[37]

---

34   *Ibidem*, p. 130. See above, pp. 12 f., footnote 9. On Anichkov's work see p. 12, footnote 8.

35   *Ibidem*, p. 133. Cf. *ibidem*, p. 136: "A view typical of Christian literature, that the 'cult of creation' was a characteristic feature of the pagan worldview, requests special caution in evaluation of the credibility of information on this area of beliefs, whose descriptions were in danger of being deformed by trite amplifications." The case of Rus' could have been misleading, there occurred polytheism (= cult of gods) and polydoxy (= cult of nature) so the scheme reflected reality, however, due to the fact that demons were called "gods" there – according to Łowmiański – some lower rank spirits were counted as gods by the Rus' writers by mistake (see *ibidem* p. 132).

36   *Ibidem*, p. 139.

37   *Ibidem*.

A general view from H. Łowmiański's findings is worth quoting literally: "The fact of the victory of Christianity over Greek and Roman polytheism (idolatry), similarly to the polytheistic paganism scheme in a biblical account, did not remain indifferent to formulation of Christian sources related to the religion of these pagans who, at the moment of their baptism, practiced polydoxy. The clergy was inclined to identify this polydoxy with polytheism and introduce to source information appropriate expressions amplifying the reach of polytheism beyond the circle of ancient civilisation, which misled later researchers."[38] However, optimism on the matter of possibly capturing the (alleged) amplification mentioned in this opinion, *i.e.* an polytheistic "insertion," during analysis of the sources is based on the researcher's *a priori* assumption related to the development of Slavic beliefs.

Without entering into a discussion of the substance of the achieved results, one should take note of one research procedure. The crucial fact is that the key proposed by Łowmiański, based on the semantic capacity of the word "creation," raises serious doubts. Firstly, the biblical context of the idea of *creaturam anteponere Creatori* does not authorise the reader to understand "creation" only in the four cult areas – nature, the dead, magic, and demons – listed by the scholar, but it directly refers to the worship of images (idols) – characteristics of polytheism. In this spirit the phrase occurs in Latin historiography of the Middle Ages.[39]

Secondly, H. Łowmiański agreed with von Wienecke that expressions such as *ydolum* and *ydolatria* may mean primary cults in general and do not constitute a decisive criterion in specifying whether they encompass statues typical of polytheism.[40] This thesis is confirmed, *e.g.* on the basis of Czech sources, where the notion of idol was used to describe nature-related objects and demons. In consequence of these findings, an argument is advanced that there was no polytheism in the area of Bohemia and Poland.[41] Nevertheless, in considerations of the descriptions of the Northern Polabia, he voiced no doubt on the actual presence of statues and temples in this area. On the other hand, however, he rejected the real existence of temples and statues in Kołobrzeg (exactly: in "Salsa Cholbergiensis"), contemporary to the famous temple in Radogošč, described in the same terms by the same author, *i.e.* Thietmar of Merseburg.[42]

---

38   Henryk Łowmiański, "Politeizm słowiański," *Przegląd Historyczny* 75 (1984) 4, p. 657.

39   See below, p. 89.

40   Łowmiański, *Religia*, p. 166, footnote 418.

41   *Ibidem*, pp. 204 ff., especially 208, where "Homiliary of Opatovice" is discussed.

42   See below, pp. 165 ff.

INTERPRETATIO CHRISTIANA OF OLD SLAVIC RELIGION

It is, therefore, not hard to notice that H. Łowmiański did not pay excessive attention to the specificity of sources and the erudition of their authors. So the strength and edge of the argument derived from Christian interpretation in his research depended on *a priori* assumptions, which is confirmed in a few other particular examples of his analysis of these sources.[43] Regardless of its apparent arbitrariness, H. Łowmiański's stance on Christian interpretation of Slavic religion in medieval historiography means significant progress in research methodology in relation to E. von Wienecke's findings.[44] Łowmiański drew attention to the fact that not all interpretation schemes have equally deforming influence on the image of primary cults and beliefs. Some elements taken from literature are not treated as Christian or Roman interpretation, but are considered "purely literary expressions".[45]

1.5   *Leszek Moszyński*

The view of Leszek Moszyński on the Slavic religion – expressed in the 1990s – deviates from comparative studies in this field, increasingly popular at that time.[46] The scholar doubts the precision of medieval source data related to the pre-Christian religion of the Slavs. Although he does not refer directly

---

43   *E.g. Ibidem*, p. 158, on the basis of a reference in a Rus' chronicle from the 11th c.: "these are not gods, only wood" H. Łowmiański claimed that people there did not imagine statues made of any other material but wood, which allows one to eliminate all figures made of other materials than wood from Slavic lands. Later, *ibidem*, p. 180, in a story about a pagan priest pretending to be a god and threatening pagans that they would lose crops after christening, Łowmiański claims that the narration about this mystification truly is an example of missionary propaganda, however, this fabrication shows a general conviction about the protective role of gods. However, he denies that a reference from a sermon by John Chrysostom about idolators, who make offerings to the moon (see *ibidem*, p. 99) was based on historical facts. Similarly according to Łowmiański "euhemerism" in Rus' writings is only a literary reminiscence (see *ibidem*, p. 125).

44   Łowmiański, *Religia*, p. 166: "Wienecke's criticism was one-sided and did not differentiate trite content from the description of specific facts, which were quite numerous in these accounts."

45   This is a stance on a reference made by Cosmas about worshipping Roman deities by Czech distant ancestors, *ibidem*, pp. 204 f.

46   However, even today it is hard to consider this position obsolete, taking into consideration that the skeptical attitude to the reception of comparative models developed in the 20th c. persisted among the historians of the Slavdom (recently Dariusz A. Sikorski, *Kościół w Polsce za Mieszka I i Bolesława Chrobrego* (Poznań: Wydawnictwo Naukowe UAM, 2011), pp. 62 ff.). However, this trend functions as an alternative for a more common affirmation for the achievements of anthropology, structural analysis and religious studies comparatistics, which at the current stage of research does not mean slavish adherence to Dumézil's schemes criticised by the said skeptics.

to the notion of *interpretatio Christiana*, he decisively enters the area defined by this term.

According to L. Moszyński, the old Slavs were to worship the only God (the so called *sv̨ętъ Bogъ*), who was called Svarog by the people living on the Vistula and Perun by the people living on the Dnieper; they did not know polytheism, neither did they know statues and temples. Old Slavic demonology was poorly-developed and it gained more body later, *i.e.* during contacts with neighbouring peoples. Concurrence of Łowmiański's views is partly based on different premises (*e.g.* Celtic influences are considered significant).

Moszyński questioned the existence of an Old Slavic mythology claiming that "the scholars up to now [*i.e.* 1995 – sic!] were not critical enough using premises from medieval texts and did not take into account the then literary convention. The medieval clergy fighting with the remains of the old Slavic religion presented it according to the scheme they knew from the Old Greek and Old Roman religion. Frequently they created fictitious theonims themselves (*e.g.* Joannes Dlugossius) and sometimes they collated all names of deities they knew from various sources (*e.g.* Hegumen Nikon, the author of the so-called Nestor's Chronicle). The medieval custom of substituting original names with native ones in translations should also be taken into consideration. In such cases numerous mistakes were made (*e.g.* glosses in the Malalas Chronicle). The same method was used even by St. Hieronymus in his translations of the Acts of the Apostles".[47]

Consequently L. Moszyński warned against using the very name "paganism" or "pagan" with reference to various forms of the religious life of the Slavs, because in his opinion they *a priori* evoke categories typical of ancient Mediterranean religions. Such extreme cautiousness may raise doubts,[48] but it markedly shows the problem of limitations in learning about the past, indicated earlier, which result from influences of contemporary culture on researchers. It is impossible to agree with the above general assessment of the previous scholars with reference to their lack of criticism, not only due to the rather nonchalant generalization, but also because of not taking into account at least the relevant debate over *interpretatio Christiana*.

The negative assessment of the cognitive value of the medieval sources to Slavic religion in the works of L. Moszyński refers mainly to theonims, and

---

47 Leszek Moszyński, *Die vorchristliche Religion der Slaven im Lichte der slavischen Sprachwissenschaft* (KölnWeimar/Wien: Böhlau, 1992), p. 127; cf. *idem*, "Współczesne metody (etymologiczna i filologiczna) rekonstruowania prasłowiańskich wierzeń," *Światowit* 40 (1995), p. 108.

48 See above, footnote 28 in this chapter.

INTERPRETATIO CHRISTIANA OF OLD SLAVIC RELIGION   25

consequently brings negation of the existence of Old Slavic polytheism and
mythology. Admittedly a reconstructed procedure of substituting biblical
and antique names with native ones, which was a binding convention, is an important finding in research on the mentality of the medieval authors. However,
attribution of this pattern (one may speak here of *interpretatio mythologica*) to
the generality of authors writing about the Slavic religion should be verified on
the basis of analyses of particular texts.

1.6   *On* Interpretatio Christiana: *Discussion Addendum and Summary*

In the research on the religion of the early Slavs, the 20th c. witnessed a
strengthened conviction that the way religion was presented in medieval
sources was conditioned by worldview-related prejudices of the authors –
ideological hostility, negative emotions, confidence that the circle treated as
pagan was culturally inferior. Apart from the above-mentioned scholars, this
view was shared by a number of researchers interested not only in the religion
of the Slavs (*e.g.* Z. Rajewski,[49] G. Rytter[50]), but also in the history of their culture and social life (*e.g.* J. Herrmann,[51] Z. Váňa[52]). Usually they only expressed

---

49   Zdzisław Rajewski, "Święta woda u Słowian – źródła, rzeki, jeziora," *Slavia Antiqua* 21
      (1974), p. 111: "The value of the documentary basis is varied, *e.g.* there are accounts of me-
      dieval chroniclers, who as followers of the new faith and its arduous propagators, did not
      understand much from the essence of pagan beliefs and interpreted them in a Christian
      convention, avoiding, as one would assume, detailed descriptions, not to become spokes-
      men of 'devil's affairs'."

50   Grażyna Rytter, "O badaniach nad prasłowiańską terminologią religijną," *Slavia
      Occidentalis* 43 (1986), pp. 129–134: "… accounts of German missionaries and chroniclers
      (possibly except for Thietmar) on paganism in Polabia are not free from subjective and
      emotive assessment." It is surprising in this case that Thietmar was considered an excep-
      tion (especially in the light of analysis in the further part of this work).

51   *Die Slawen in Deutschland. Geschichte und Kultur der slawischen Stämme westlich von Oder
      und Neiße vom 6. bis. 12. Jahrhundert*, ed. Joachim Herrmann (Berlin: Akademie-Verlag
      1985), p. 322: "Für diese Chronisten war die heidnische Religion eine zutiefst feindliche
      Ideologie und ihre Vertreter und Anhänger die ärgsten Widersacher, die man zu über-
      winden trachtete. Ihre Erzählungen und Berichte stehen daher ganz in diesem Anliegen,
      d. h. sie geben ein Bild der heidnischen Religion, das der christlichen Interpretation
      unterliegt."

52   Zdeněk Váňa, *The world of the ancient Slavs*, trans. Till Gottheiner (London: Orbis, 1983),
      pp. 82 f., claims that when the Slavs "did appear on the scene, civilized Europe was already
      Christian and was not greatly interested in or showed an understanding of the spiritual
      life of barbarians, whom they viewed with condescension and with the sole aim of bring-
      ing them at the earliest possible date into the Christian community. Contemporary evi-
      dence is not always of equal value; apart from reliable reports by eyewitnesses there is
      often second- or third-hand information with various degrees of distortion. Later chroni-
      clers, remote in time and thought from the pre-Christian period, added many facts, and

26   CHAPTER 1

a general opinion that medieval writers made a subjective assessment of primary religions, without taking deeper interest and attempting to understand their essence.[53] Thus, in such context the negative approach to the historical value of narrative sources is not surprising.

A. Brückner and E. von Wienecke supported the view that assumes medieval authors' usage of clichés and literary borrowings instead of referring to the actual phenomena of the spiritual culture of the pre-Christian Slavs. A similar opinion was expressed by H. Łowmiański, who emphasized, however, that some of these borrowings – exactly the ones which distort the picture of beliefs – appear as a result of disdain for primary cults. S. Urbańczyk stated that aversion to Christianity was the reason for devising fictional facts and contenting themselves with superficial, unverified information. This leading trend in reflection on *interpretatio Christiana* of the Slavic religion assumes the occurrence of information in sources, which would indicate more advanced development than was actually the case in the tribal world.

However, it is worth mentioning that in this debate one can find alternative explanations for the influence of clerical authors' worldviews on the shape of sources on Slavic religion, hence the conviction that templates used to present religion actually made it more impoverished in the light of the sources than it really was (*e.g.* W. Dziewulski).[54] W. Hensel even claimed that chroniclers intentionally "primitivized" the described beliefs and cults of the Slavs by denying that they possessed even some traits of polytheism in areas where it occurred from the beginning of the Middle Ages.[55] A polemicized view was

---

      even invented them when they misunderstood popular customs". Similarly – although
      with emphasis on diabolisation and stronger deformation by *interpretatio Christiana* than
      Romana – Zdeněk Váňa, *Svět slovanských bohů a démonů* (Praha: Panorama, 1990), p. 26.

53   This very general discussion is very accurately summarised in the opinion expressed by
      Tadeusz J. Horbacz, Zbigniew Lechowicz, "Archeologia a poznawanie religii," *Z otchłani
      wieków* 47 (1981) 3, p. 179, who assumed "lack of objectivity" of written sources, which
      "even at the stage of their creation were burdened with subjectivity resulting from different culture, worldview and negative emotional attitude of the authors writing about
      the religion of the Slavs". Cf. also *e.g.* Alfonso M. di Nola, "Slavi," in *Enciclopedia delle
      Religioni*, ed. Mario Gozzini, vol. 5 (Firenze: Vallecchi, 1973), col. 1138; Andrzej L. Miś,
      "Przedchrześcijańska religia Rugian," *Slavia Antiqua* 38 (1997), p. 105.

54   Władysław Dziewulski, *Postępy chrystianizacji i proces likwidacji pogaństwa w Polsce
      wczesnofeudalnej* (Wrocław/Warszawa/Kraków: Ossolineum, 1964), p. 9, used the argument *ex interpretatione Christiana*, to prove the conviction that the pre-Christian religion
      of the Slavs was not inferior in comparison with the spiritual culture of German peoples
      in terms of richness of cult forms and beliefs.

55   Witold Hensel, *U źródeł Polski średniowiecznej* (Wrocław/Warszawa/Kraków: Ossolineum,
      1974), pp. 225 f.: "On one hand they did not have much orientation in the environment
      in which they happened to be, and on the other hand, they did not look approvingly at

INTERPRETATIO CHRISTIANA OF OLD SLAVIC RELIGION   27

expressed by H. Łowmiański, who thought in turn that chroniclers showed a lack of interest in some "lower" forms of cults and beliefs, which did not attract their attention because they were insignificant in the perspective of confrontation with the church doctrine.[56]

S. Urbańczyk considered the possibility of another justification for the fragmentary nature of source data related to the Slavic religion. Apart from a lack of more profound interest in hostile religion, restrictions resulting from themes of works and their genre characteristics, or even economical treatment of the material which was used for writing (high costs of vellum production), the Slavist also took into account the possibility that in some clerical circles knowledge about Slavic cults and beliefs was quite considerable, and hence being a commonly known subject it was often neglected.[57] This supposition seems well-founded, especially in the case of authors from dioceses interested in missions among the Slavs. The remains of Slavic beliefs accounted for

---

old pagan practices. They put a lot of energy into showing that forms of old pagan religious cult were incredibly primeval and primitive." This view is supported by a conviction that the Slavs believed in personified deities even earlier than in the 10th c., which was formed on a general Indo-European culture base (compare earlier references to the work by Georges Dumézil, *Les dieux des Indo-Européens* (Paris, 1952) in: Witold Hensel, *Polska przed tysiącem lat* (Wrocław/Warszawa: Ossolineum, 1960), p. 193).

56   Łowmiański, *Religia*, p. 62, footnote 122, based on findings connected with *interpretatio Christiana*, polemicises with W. Hensel's opinion in the following way: 1) medieval authors did not know how to differentiate between pagan primitive and developed cults; they were generally qualified as abominable superstitions (*superstitiones abominabiles*); 2) it was thought that a regular element of a pagan cult was worshipping idols, so paganism maintained the traditional name idolatry, worshipping idols, which is now called polytheism; it is not possible that polytheism was deliberately concealed; 3) medieval authors (Thietmar, Adam of Bremen, Helmold, Saxo) are the ones who have presented a lot of information about pagan gods, their names and temples. Widukind speaks about Saturn and does not hesitate to compare Slavic polytheism with well-developed Roman polytheism. Even if Czech authors (Christianus, hagiographers, Cosmas) did not write about local gods, this was not because they wanted to keep silent on the matter of names but because of a lack of data. The first and second point actually discredit Hensel's thesis on efforts made by clergy scribes to make the Slavic religion look primitive, however, the third one was dictated by an *a priori* assumed thesis that there was no polytheism outside Elbslavs and Rus', while one should remember that authors writing about figures of gods referred to cults contemporary to them or quite close in time, whereas in Poland and Bohemia the official, public pre-Christian cult at Cosmas or in Gallus Anonymous's times had not existed for a long time. Moreover, Cosmas attributing Greek and Roman deities to the Czech, does not do it to devise gods in general (cf. Łowmiański, *Politeizm słowiański*, p. 657) but more to dignify the early history of his people with an ancient overtone. Thus it is hard to draw conclusions on the historical value of the studies on the religion of the Slavs in his work on this basis.

57   S. Urbańczyk, *Dawni Słowianie*, p. 123.

by them, *e.g.* as a curiosity or testimony of stupidity, could enter the pages of chronicles, yet they had been disguised in a costume of biblical or antique literary convention, which was not so poor to be unable to depict various dimensions of faith and cult.[58]

According to the general opinion of scholarly research on the topic, negative attitudes toward the Slavic *sacrum* resulted in the selection of thematic motifs in medieval historiography, and sometimes a decrease in the informers' credibility (which is explained below). The gap between the historical reality of the Slavic religion and its image in sources grew even more due to cultural distinctiveness between the contemporary circles of *Barbaricum* and *Christianitas*.

1.6.1   Christian Interpretation versus the Credibility of Sources
          on Slavic Religion

Conclusions about the Christian interpretation of primary religions became a key premise for justifying the positions of Slavic religion researchers concerning the credibility of the authors of medieval sources. The most extreme hypercritical view in this matter was expressed by E. von Wienecke, and it was based on a conviction that clerical writers did not have direct contact with the non-Christian *sacrum*. To describe it they had to work with only remote echoes of its existence, because for theological reasons the image of the Slavic religion in their works was to be nothing more than a multiplication of biblical models.

A less radical stance was taken over twenty years earlier by A. Brückner, who assumed that descriptions of Slavic beliefs and cults were a mosaic of historical truth and literary borrowings, which could be used in places where information was missing, realizing that religions treated as paganism were the same everywhere. A similar point of view was represented half a century later by H. Łowmiański, who thought that in addition to "purely" literary borrowings in the sources, there are also accounts about Slavic religion with mostly true information, regardless of biblical or ancient stylization of the narration. He assumed that interpretational schemes used by medieval chroniclers did not always collide with facts. Following this way of thinking – similarly to his contemporary Boris A. Rybakov – H. Łowmiański even took into account the accuracy of speculation presented at the beginning of the 20th c. by E. Anichkov, who in "The Philosopher's Speech" from *Nestor's Letopis* (PVL) wanted to find a picture of consecutive stages in the evolution of the Slavic religion put in the perspective of biblical categories.[59]

---

58   Rosik, *Udział*, pp. 89 f.
59   See above, footnote 9 in this chapter.

INTERPRETATIO CHRISTIANA OF OLD SLAVIC RELIGION 29

There is a similar discussion of the significance of allegorical and symbolical motifs, especially motifs surrounding numbers, related to the Slavic *sacrum* in the medieval historiography. Various instances of this debate[60] show that the confluence of a given detail from a source on Slavic religion with a passage in the Bible or with a motif from Classical mythology, and even more so the appearance of a symbolic number universally exploited in the sacral context, is not a sufficient premise to question the credibility of source data. This coincidence could result from the use in the descriptions of some symbolical or allegorical elements from the cultural circle of Christianity or ancient Greeks or Romans based on associations with native elements of Slavic cult and beliefs.

The factor that supported the occurrence of these associations was the community of elements of the world of religion emphasized on a universal scale,[61] especially with regard to Indo-European peoples, thanks to comparative and anthropological studies. Thus it is not accidental that Aleksander Gieysztor – inspired by G. Dumézil's concepts – on the pages of the already foundational work, "Mitologia Słowian" [Mythology of Slavs] (1982), undertook to develop an apology for chroniclers who had been accused by the positivists of distorting facts due to favouring the Christian interpretation.[62] Leszek P. Słupecki referred to Gieysztor's methodological standpoint in a monograph of Slavic sanctuaries, and he questioned, for example, the views assuming that Thietmar of Merseburg's information about temples in Pomerania, east of the

---

60   *E.g.* Jerzy Strzelczyk, "Rec. Festschrift für Walter Schlesinger, Bd. II, herausgegeben von Helmut Beumann (Mitteldeutsche Forschungen, Bd. 74/II), Böhlau Verlag, Köln-Wien 1974," *Studia Historica Slavo-Germanica UAM* 5 (1976), p. 202, in the discussion on the central temple of the Liutici in Thietmar's and Adam of Bremen's descriptions, indicated that it could not be excluded that allegorical and symbolical motifs (including numbers) appeared in this case by association with credible data, which was available to the chroniclers. The said scholar was rather reserved in his attitude to R. Schmidt's concept negating their credibility with reference to details in the descriptions of Radogošč/Rethra exactly due to the occurrence of literary borrowings and symbolical motifs. See below, p. 221.

61   The existence of elements of this common religious world is perfectly emphasized in the works of M. Eliade. The key element in this reflection trend is universality of symbols in shaping forms of religious life, see Leszek Kołakowski, "Mircea Eliade: religia jako paraliż czasu," in Mircea Eliade, *Traktat o historii religii*, trans. Jan Wierusz-Kowalski (Łódź: Opus, 1993), pp. i–vi.

62   Aleksander Gieysztor, *Mitologia Słowian*, ed. Aneta Pieniądz, introduction Karol Modzelewski, afterword Leszek P. Słupecki (Warszawa: Wydawnictwo Uniwersytetu Warszawskiego, 2006 [1st ed. 1982]), pp. 45, 110 *et passim* (when taking into account the way the scholar had treated medieval written sources in his investigations).

30   CHAPTER 1

Oder (Odra) River, was a cliché and was not true in the reality of the 10th and 11th centuries.[63]

The panorama presented here, of model exemplifications of the approaches of researchers working on material from the religion of the Slavs to the credibility of medieval authors, shows that an element of key significance in the assessment of the influence of Christian interpretation on the cognitive value of sources is the nature of methodological assumptions in research proceedings. This is especially evident in the choice the religious studies methodologies and the different attitudes toward arguments from other disciplines, such as archaeology, linguistics and ethnography. It is essential that the basis for conclusions on this issue was the analyses of particular places in texts which were suspected of "deformations" of the old Slavic reality.

Treatment of some source information about Slavic religion as credible, in practice, meant assuming that its Christian interpretation (or ancient Classical one) occurred in only some parts of the works of medieval historiographers, or – which better depicts the essence of this issue – that there are places in their texts in which the interpretation of these types is indefinable. However, even with reference to passages in which there is no doubt about its influence on the shape of the source, sometimes there are marked discrepancies in the assessment of its credibility.[64] In the context of these observations, special attention should be paid to these efforts, which lead to defining the relations between the source image of primary religion and its reality, recognized in the light of historical or archaeological research.

Although these investigations were undertaken in a very one-sided manner, because they referred only to possible "deformation" of past fact in the medieval literature, they have already allowed some basic findings to be made. It is especially important that it was established that using literary, biblical or antique schemes in descriptions of phenomena regarded as paganism did not always mean deformation of the image of Slavic beliefs and cults. Apart from this, one should take into account the occurrence of detailed information

---

63   Leszek P. Słupecki, *Slavonic Pagan Sanctuaries* (Warsaw: IAE PAN, 1994), p. 201. One should also take note of works in which all names of ancient deities occurring in descriptions of the pre-Christian Slavdom are uncritically accepted and treated as *interpretatio Romana vel graeca* of native supernatural creatures, see *e.g.* Adam Wirski, "Bóstwo morskie pogańskich Pomorzan," in *Krzyżowcy, kronikarze, dyplomaci*, (Gdańskie studia z dziejów średniowiecza) 4 (Gdańsk: Wydawnictwo Uniwersytetu Gdańskiego, 1997), pp. 309–327.

64   A clear example for this matter is a discussion about Helmold's information (I, 84) on hierarchisation of the Slavic pantheon (an image of "god of gods" and his subordinate deities); see below pp. 345 ff. Comp. also comments on "The Philosopher's Speech" discussed above, see pp. 12 f., 20f.

about those beliefs and cults as purely literary genesis. Observation of these detailed investigations created premises for reflection on the essence of the *interpretatio Christiana* phenomenon and definition of its constituent procedures of the explanation and presentation of Slavic religion.

1.6.2   *Interpretatio Christiana*: the Essence of the Phenomenon and Its
          Constituent Procedures

The basic mode of understanding the interpretation of the Slavic religion in different variants – Christian, ancient Classical, or "mythological" (in the way it was understood by L. Moszyński) – which was determined in the research conducted in the 20th c., encompasses the conviction that medieval sources, instead of content reflecting the reality of the given primary religion, showed images borrowed from antique and Christian literature. This view was presented by A. Brückner, and its extreme version was expressed by E. von Wienecke, who assumed that the interpretation layer completely substituted information or made it impossible to conduct scientific reconstruction. Such an extreme position did not even earn the recognition of H. Łowmiański, who represented a similar research perspective in terms of hypercriticism but took into account *stricte* literary genesis of only some information.[65] Hence in the other instances one should take into account a possible genesis of textual references to Classical antique and Christian traditions on the basis of interrelation with credible data on the Slavic religion.

S. Urbańczyk offered another way of looking at the *interpretatio Christiana*; he referred to a pictorial notion of "glasses" or "filter", which would deform the image of the religion of the Slavs, but in numerous cases its impact was beyond perception (also due to the existence of the community of modern notions about religion and the ones present in the mental culture of the Middle Ages). Such a metaphorical phrase allows the entirety of phenomena constituting Christian interpretation of primary cults and beliefs to be encompassed, and refers mainly to the mentality of medieval authors.

Thought patterns attributed to medieval authors in descriptions of the Slavic *sacrum* – diabolisation, "euhemerization", substitution of biblical and ancient names with native ones as part of a fixed scheme, filling gaps in information with literary borrowings, *etc.* – together create quite a rich catalogue.

---

65   Let us remember that this scholar assumed a different impact of *interpretatio Christiana* with reference to various spheres of pre-Christian religion and such a proposal of reconstruction of a writing procedure allowed him to *a priori* justify assumption on the development of beliefs and cult of the Early Slavdom. The growing number of archaeological sources and better use of comparatistics in studies on religious research outdated this position (and particularly E. von Wienecke's ideas).

32   CHAPTER 1

Its particular elements do not constitute one harmonious entity, which leads
to a postulate of reaching deeper into the mental and spiritual culture of of
the Middle Ages. The strict subject of research in this case is its textual manifestation. The research so far has allowed basic systematization of information
about the Slavic religion to be established.

The qualification of that information enables one to distinguish: 1) literary
borrowings which have nothing in common with historical reality; 2) literary
borrowings related to facts based on association; 3) images of cults and beliefs
presented in biblical convention or referring to antique literature (*e.g.* paraphrases, *etc.*); 4) reality of the religion of the Slavs interpreted only at the level
of Latin or Greek. It is easy to observe that in fact the whole image of pre-
Christian religion in Church sources is interpreted on the basis of worldview,
culture, and language.

Biblical and antique infiltration can be found at several levels of text
structure: 1) language (words, phraseology);[66] 2) paraphrases, quotations;[67]
3) templates in the presentation of the arrangement of *sacrum* recognized as
pagan and the definition of its nature;[68] 4) general convention of description –
saturation with emotive elements, assessment of paganism, *etc.*; 5) text motifs
such as commentaries – frequently illustrated with reference to the Bible and
Church literature – or descriptions of events (usually in a miraculous setting).

2   **Further Research Perspectives**

In the research conducted so far, findings on the medieval mechanisms of *interpretatio Christiana* of the native religion of the Slavs have been determined
by the method of source analysis, in which the decisive role has been played by
typology of phenomena according to biblical or patristic "archetypical" structures. However, making use of the *ex interpretatione* argument in evaluating the
credibility of the sources (or the authors, in fact) resulted from criticism typical of positivism, which had to be based on a certain *a priori* thesis related to
the form of Slavic beliefs and cults.

This is why one should, all the more, appreciate the decision to increase
the value of Christian interpretation "as such" in the framework of research

---

66   First of all, typical expressions, *e.g.* Slavic gods – demons, devils (*e.g.* Svarožic associated
      with the devil); religion of the Slavs: polytheism, polydoxy and its objects – *ydolatria,
      idola, templa, fana* etc. One should remember about the contribution of antique notions
      (including mythological ones) in medieval Christian thought.
67   *E.g.* see footnote 16 in this chapter.
68   *E.g.* "euhemerization" – see above; cf. di Nola, "Slavi," col. 1147.

INTERPRETATIO CHRISTIANA OF OLD SLAVIC RELIGION

on the perception of primary religions at the time of the early medieval Christianization of Europe. Works by H.-D. Kahl, B. Wavra, L.E. von Padberg, or R. Bartlett offer a clear turn in thinking about the Middle Ages, which explains the way pre-Christian *sacrum* was perceived from the perspective of notions fixed in the epoch's mentality, focusing mainly on the categories of Christian doctrine.[69]

The possibility of confronting the dependent relationship between a literary fact in the source and a "reconstructed" historical one can indeed provide significant knowledge about cultural processes. This yields insight into a singular phenomenon of reception of particular information about the Slavic religion and its explanation by a chronicler.[70] However, the inability to define clearly and precisely to which beliefs and cults the text refers constitutes only a constraint for the spectrum of the investigations in the discussed area, but does not preclude their keeping. The mere appearance of references to the sphere of spiritual culture of the early Slavs in the texts is itself of fundamental relevance to the study.

An attempt to maximize the range of the consideration of the diversity of ways of medieval interpretation of their religion is connected with the postulate of reaching outside the scope defined in the existing studies in relation to the term *interpretatio Christiana* (or *classica Romana vel graeca*). It is important to take into consideration not only the situations in which the elements of Slavs' religion presented in the sources were not recognized by the chroniclers as phenomena of a religious character, but also those whose descriptions do not involve pejorative connotations (for example due to the literary convention or the method of the realization of the text's ideological program).

---

69   Kahl, "Die ersten Jahrhunderte," p. 37–42, shared Achterberg and Wienecke's opinion on the nature of *interpretatio Christiana*, he also adds a euhemeric motif; however – what is essential – he located the very phenomenon of interpretation in the context of discussion on mission ideology as an element of a consistent system encompassing theological justification of particular missionary procedures. This starting point for the discussion on *interpretatio Christiana* turns out to be optimum, because exactly in this intellectual environment of antiquity and the Middle Ages the discussed phenomenon was born (the very reality of primary religions does not much influence on its theological assessment). Cf. Brigitte Wavra, *Salzburg und Hamburg Erzbistumsgründung und Missiospolitik in karolinischer Zeit* (Berlin: Duncker & Humblot, 1991), pp. 15 ff. The goal of L.E. von Padberg's study is to show the mutual image of Christians and pagans in the Early Middle Ages – see Padberg, "Christen und Heiden," pp. 291–312. See also above, p. 5, footnote 11.

70   It would be more appropriate to say "historiographic", however, because of work on medieval historiography, the term "historiographic fact" is not used here, not to cause any notion-related confusion.

Furthermore, various manifestations of Christian interpretation of Slavic cults and beliefs found in the chronicles were not only the effect of their author's reflection, but also – provided that the descriptions were not fictitious to the core – accomplishments of their protagonists who, thanks to described actions, tendencies, and recalled opinions. These expressed certain attitudes towards the Slavic religion and provided premises for its evaluation from a theological perspective. In such cases, special attention must be paid to Christian cult activities, gestures, and rituals, the meaning of which refer to the sphere of spiritual confrontation with the *sacrum* treated as hostile or pagan. Analysis of symbols and allegories is of key importance here as well, including the (conditioned by the theology) performative (creative) function of liturgical signs and services in the cultural dimension, especially in relation to the spectacular activities performed by the missionaries to defeat the primary cults.

Thus the form of the textual vision of Slavic religion was influenced by a combination of various kinds of factors belonging to the socio-cultural environment of the author. This vision was also formed by his attitude toward individuals, communities, institutions, and events he knew from experience or from oral or written records that proved worth commemorating in the pages of a historical work.[71] In such a case, the activities of the writer belonged to the process of shaping the memory (*memoria*) that took place in particular environments, in this case in German church circles, but also – especially in case of Thietmar – among the elites gathered around the monarch.[72]

In defining the aforementioned space of memory it is necessary to include the social[73] and the cultural dimension,[74] especially taking into account the

---

[71] It is important here to take into consideration not only individuals and social organization forms (within the monarchy, Church *etc.*) but also the set of rules regulating the social life and on the other hand some rituals and practices, mainly liturgical, important for expression of the attitude towards paganism.

[72] See Lutz E. von Padberg, "Geschichtsschreibung und kulturelles Gedächtnis. Formen der Vergangenheitswahrnehmung in der hochmittelalterlichen Historiographie am Beispiel von Thietmar von Merseburg, Adam von Bremen und Helmold von Bosau," *Zeitschrift für Kirchengeschichte* 105 (1994), pp. 156–177.

[73] Maurice Halbwachs, "The Social Frameworks of Memory," in *idem, On collective memory*, trans. Lewis A. Coser (Chicago: The University of Chicago Press, 1992 [orig. ed. 1925]), pp. 35–191.

[74] For inspiring comments on this issue see: Otto Gerhard Oexle, "Obcowanie żywych i umarłych. Rozważania o pojęciu >>memoria<<", trans. Marian Arszyński, in Otto Gerhard Oexle, *Społeczeństwo średniowiecza. Mentalność – grupy społeczne – formy życia* (Toruń: Wydawnictwo UMK, 2000), pp. 55–57. At this point the author highlights the insufficiency of relying only on the sociological aspect in characterization of the collective memory, criticizing the findings of M. Halbwachs (see above, footnote 73 in this chapter).

INTERPRETATIO CHRISTIANA OF OLD SLAVIC RELIGION

contribution of historical reflections visible in commemorative activities,[75] which resulted, among other things, in the development of the contemporary historiography.[76] Information that functioned in this memory space was of course only fragmentarily reflected in chronicles or annals, but it is vital to remember that at the time it was, at least partially, common knowledge. However, to some extent it was an expression of the author's personal point of view through which he presented his opinion on the local disputes and made a creative contribution to the debate.

It should be emphasized that "the *causa scribendi* of a historiographer working in the 11th–15th centuries was not a dialogue with undefined posterity – the public that required news and entertainment – or the will to save objectively described events from oblivion. It instead was meant to influence the thoughts and activities of his contemporaries, specific people, environments, communities and social groups. At that time historiography was used mainly for parenesis – teaching contemporaries through historical *exempla* or documentation prepared for interim practical goals."[77] A typical task of the historiography of the time was the interpretation of events according to some general rules, which enabled the portrayal of some meaning of those events in a moral and theological perspective, primarily with reference to the world of the Bible.

Incorporating the history of the community, monarchy, dynasty, or institution (such as a metropolis or a bishopric) into the common past existing in the cultural sphere of the *Christianitas* circle was also an important element in the composition of historiography, especially in the cases of threads involving legends containing references to ancient Romans, Greeks, and other nations. The Slavs and their native religion became an element of a thusly constructed narrative of the history that involves also some information about the events and phenomena contemporary to the writers.

---

75 *Ibidem.* Consideration of historical reflection on characteristics of the collective memory in the context of discussion on Halbwachs's concept is also suggested by Paul Ricoeur, *Pamięć, historia, zapomnienie*, trans. Janusz Margański (Kraków: Universitas, 2006), pp. 157 f.

76 This characteristic feature of the chroniclers' work is well exemplified by Thietmar's accidental comment on a fragment commemorating Archbishop of Magdeburg Walthard (d. 1012) as an "epitaph engraved not in stone" (VI, 75). It is important to mention the topical declarations of Helmold of Bosau, who explained the reasons of their literary work; see further, pp. 260 f.

77 Edward Potkowski, "Problemy kultury piśmiennej łacińskiego średniowiecza," *Przegląd Humanistyczny* 3 (1994), p. 34. There is also literature on pragmatic writing related to medieval historiography. See also *e.g.* Franz-Josef Schmale, "Mentalität und Berichtshorizont, Absicht und Situation hochmittelalterlicher Geschichtsschreiber," *Historische Zeitschrift* 226 (1978) 1, pp. 5 ff.; Jerzy Topolski, *Metodologia historii* (Warszawa: PWN, 1984), p. 66.

Due to their individual erudition and writing skills they were able to influence their own environment, although their mentality did not function in isolation from the mental background of the social groups to which they belonged.[78] While observing the chronicler's personal attitude towards paganism as a whole and to its particular representations on the basis of the sources, an analysis should consider not only the originality of the literary vision but firstly the fact of the author's belonging to a defined intellectual milieu, an ethnic community within a monarchy and the Church. Placement in such a context determined the shape of the so-called cultural imputation as a complex factor that influenced the perception of the world of the Slavs, which was, to varying degrees, strange to the chroniclers.

At the same time, one should take into account the existence of the completely conscious reflection of chroniclers as erudites and theologians or politicians, placing Slavic religion in the "world of the text" with respect for the pragmatic goals (*causa scribendi*) of his work. Thus relations (mostly confrontation) between Christianity and paganism in the sphere of *sacrum* in the analyses below will be traced not only with reference to Church issues but also political issues integrated with them. However, it should also be emphasized that Christianity and paganism are treated not only in categories of ideological and worldview juxtapositions, but also as different cultural systems, participating in a community resulting from the fact that both circles are set in a universal area of human activity and its cultural heritage.

For that reason the working definition of the discussed notion of Christian interpretation in the light of medieval historiography, proposed here, refers to the very notion of "interpretation" understood as the entirety of phenomena which contributed to the perception, understanding, and explanation of the phenomenon of the Slavic religion by its medieval historiographers. The subject of the research will be notions, views, assessments, symbols, allegories, opinions (with particular attention to stereotypes and literary *topoi*, which saturate various literary works),[79] literary borrowings taken out of con-

---

78 The issue of such dependence of an individual on the sphere of collective imagination (representation) belongs to the fundamental issues researched by social history in the xx-century, especially within the standards defined by the *Annales* circle.

79 For the matter of stereotypical opinions ("group judgements") see *e.g.* Zbigniew Bokszański, *Stereotypy a kultura* (Wrocław: Wydawnictwo Uniwersytetu Wrocławskiego, 2001); Jacek Schmidt, "Funkcje i właściwości stereotypów etnicznych. Refleksje teoretyczne," in *Wokół stereotypów Niemców i Polaków*, ed. Wojciech Wrzesiński, (Acta Universitatis Wratislaviensis. Historia) 79 (Wrocław: Wydawnictwo Uniwersytetu Wrocławskiego, 1991), pp. 5–11; Andrzej Feliks Grabski, *Polska w opiniach obcych X–XII w.* (Warszawa: PWN, 1964), pp. 5 f.; Modzelewski, *Barbarzyńska Europa*, pp. 18 ff.

text, commentaries (also historiographic concepts *implicite* included in literary action), and finally information about rituals, gestures, and activities of Christians (*e.g.* missionaries) in the historical substrate being the object of literary description and reflecting attitudes toward paganism.

On the other hand, such a consideration will comprise the ways that these semantic unities function within the text. This will permit the learning of automatic reactions and fixed routes followed by medieval thought with reference to the Slavic *sacrum*. This explains the fundamental importance of the examination of the texts' language in the analyses presented below. In the following study some space has been devoted to characterization of the emotional tone of particular descriptions and other issues in the area of social history, in the second half of the 20th c., defined with the category of collective psychology.[80] Nowadays this area of research is usually attributed to historical anthropology, and more precisely to the problem of the "the other."[81] The dynamic development of this trend in medieval studies during the last decades favours the intensification of reflection on the interpretation of Slavic religion. At this point it is important to enumerate some syntheses of the issue of the so-called "barbarians", as well as studies on mutual cross-references of the Slavs and the Germans, and also the perceptions of others based on German chronicles from the 11th and 12th centuries.[82]

Thus, the aforementioned contexts of research undertaken in this study are nowadays more often placed in the area of historical anthropology[83] and cultural history,[84] at the same time moving away from social history whose foundations can be traced back to Émile Durkheim. However, these changes in the general tendencies within the studies on culture and social life do not

---

80   For a general look at these issues see *e.g.* Bronisław Geremek, "Umysłowość i psychologia zbiorowa w historii," *Przegląd Historyczny* 53 (1962) 4, pp. 629–643; Paweł Lewicki, "O psychologii historycznej," *Kwartalnik Historyczny* 82 (1975) 3, pp. 584–592.

81   A good example of popularization of this trend of research within the humanities nearly three decades ago are Todorov's studies – see: Tzvetan Todorov, *Nous et les Autres. La Réflexion française sur la diversité humaine* (Paris: Seuil, 1989).

82   See above, pp. 7–9, footnotes 15, 18, 19, and also *e.g.* Andrzej Pleszczyński, *Niemcy wobec pierwszej monarchii piastowskiej (963–1034). Narodziny stereotypu. Postrzeganie i cywilizacyjna klasyfikacja władców Polski i ich kraju* (Lublin: Wydawnictwo UMCS, 2008); cf. *idem, The Birth of a Stereotype: Polish Rulers and Their Country in German Writings, c. 1000 A.D.*, (East Central and Eastern Europe in the Middle Ages, 450–1450) 15 (Leiden: Brill, 2011).

83   See *e.g.* Richard van Dülmen, *Historische Anthropologie. Entwicklung, Probleme, Aufgaben* (Köln/Weimar/Wien: Böhlau, 2000).

84   See *e.g.* Peter Burke, *What is Cultural History?* (Oxford: Polity Press, 2004); cf. *idem, Historia kulturowa. Wprowadzenie*, trans. Justyn Hunia (Kraków: Wydawnictwo Uniwersytetu Jagiellońskiego, 2012).

revolutionize the perception of the issue of medieval interpretation of Slavic cults and beliefs, since it has its own history. A critical reflection offers some new directions for further research where references to a historic phenomenon of beliefs and cults of pre-Christian, "barbarian" communities are of key importance.

The value of this approach used in this study does not only lie in the source criticism. Above all it contributes to recognition of particular cases of interpretation of the spiritual culture of the Slavs, whose final expressions are found in the chronicles.[85] After a general, introductory presentation of each of the three sources, i.e. the chronicles of Thietmar, Adam of Bremen, and Helmold of Bosau, there will be presented in individual monographic chapters devoted to each of the texts an exegesis of subsequent passages, related in diverse ways to the matters of Slavic *sacrum*. The most important part of these analyses will be the consideration of the intratextual references, which will allow to respect the postulate of treating the "world of the text" as one, coherent presentation of the world and to highlight the specificity of each of the author's views of the interpretation of Slavic religion.[86]

Thus, the phenomenon recalled in the title of this work will be treated not only with reference to the culturally and doctrinally conditioned behaviors and views based on Christian doctrine, but also as a fact existing in the sphere of cultural memory of the author's environment. Observation of particular cases of interpretation of Slavic cults and beliefs in the texts will allow the indication of variable and nonvariable elements of the Saxon Church *milieu* in the attitude towards the spiritual culture of the Slavs at the stage of their Christianization between the 10th and 12th centuries.

---

85   In face of petrification of the corpus of medieval written sources, the possibilities of research on the religion of the Slavs is constantly increased by the development of archeological research. General development of thought in religious studies is also of importance here. The "canonical" compilation of written sources collected by *Fontes historiae religionis Slavicae*, ed. Karl H. Meyer, Fontes historiae religionis 4 (Berlin: De Gruyter, 1931) lacks the passage from William of Malmesbury's chronicle which, however, was used in the 1930s by Pettazzoni, *Wszechwiedza*, p. 507, as a source on the religion of the Liutici (see below, p. 129, footnote 403). See also Michał Łuczyński, "*Herberti De miraculis* as a source to the history of religion of western Slavs," *Studia Mythologica Slavica* 16 (2013), pp. 69–77.

86   See *e.g.* Paul Ricoeur, *Język, tekst, interpretacja*, trans. Piotr Graff, Katarzyna Rosner (Warszawa: PIW, 1989).

CHAPTER 2

The Religion of the Slavs in *Thietmar's Chronicle*

1   Introduction: Thietmar of Merseburg and His Work

Thietmar, the Bishop of Merseburg and an excellent chronicler, was born on 25 July 975 into a family of eastern German counts, which enabled him to become acquainted with issues related to the Slavs from early childhood.[1] His father Siegfried, from the Saxon Walbeck family, participated in the battles of Cidini in 972 (with the Polish ruler Mieszko I), Tanger River (983), and Brenna (990) with the Polabian Slavs. The chronicler's great grandfathers on the side of both his mother and father not only bore the same name – Lothar – but were also both killed by the Slavs in the battle of *Lunkini* (Lenzen) in 929. Thietmar was the third – after Henry and Frederick – of Siegfried and Kunigunde's sons (his mother came from the Stade family), and he also had some younger siblings: Siegfried, Bruno, and Oda, as well as a half-brother named Willigis.

Family matters, which Thietmar was so sensitive about, did not go favourably for him and finally he witnessed the extinction of the Walbeck family, which was related to the Ekkehardinger family from Meißen, Saxon margraves from the Northern March or the Austrian Babenbergs. The chronicler's older brothers, who chose the knightly career, were not outstandingly successful in the elite of the Holy Roman Empire (Germany). However, Thietmar himself and two of his brothers who became priests were more successful. Siegfried became the Bishop of Münster, and Bruno became the Bishop of Verden. Villigis, born out of wedlock, became only a monastery prior in Walbeck. Oda married

---

1   For Thietmar's biographic details and his education, see Helmut Lippelt, *Thietmar von Merseburg. Reichsbischof und Chronist* (Mitteldeutsche Forschungen) 72 (Köln/Wien: Böhlau, 1973), pp. 46–137; Marian Zygmunt Jedlicki, "Wstęp," in *Kronika Thietmara* [*Thietmari Chronicon*], Latin and Polish text, ed. and trans. Marian Zygmunt Jedlicki (Poznań: Instytut Zachodni, 1953), pp. i–xxxi; Werner Trillmich, "Einleitung," in *Thietmari Merseburgensis Episcopi Chronicon*, Latin and German text, ed. and trans. Robert Holtzmann/Werner Trillmich, Ausgewählte Quellen zur deutschen Geschichte des Mittelalters 9 (Darmstadt: Wissenschaftliche Buchgesellschaft, 1992), pp. ix–xiii; David A. Warner, "Introduction: Thietmar, bishop and Chronicler," in *Ottonian Germany. The Chronicon of Thietmar of Merseburg*, trans. and ed. David A. Warner (Manchester/New York: Manchester University Press, 2001), pp. 1–64; Kerstin Schulmeyer-Ahl, *Der Anfang vom Ende der Ottonen. Konstitutionsbedingungen historiographischer Nachrichten in der Chronik Thietmars von Merseburg* (Berlin: De Gruyter, 2009), pp. 6–26; Fraesdorff, *Der barbarische Norden*, pp. 135–138.

© KONINKLIJKE BRILL NV, LEIDEN, 2020 | DOI:10.1163/9789004331488_004

count Goswin of Valkenburg, but Thietmar was not particularly happy about it. He emphasized his aristocratic background on numerous occasions,[2] and his admiration for his ancestors corresponds with the contemporary trend to privatize church institutions in Germany (the so-called proprietary church, Germ. "Eigenkirchen").[3]

Thietmar received a rudimentary education (the ability to read and write) when he was staying with his aunt Emnilda, the canoness in Quedlinburg. His next teacher was abbot Rikdag 990–1005 in the Magdeburg Monastery of St. John of the Mountain, where he was moved as a 12-year old boy. The decisive influence on his erudition and literary education occurred during the years he spent at the cathedral school in Magdeburg (the best in eastern Germany), where he worked under the supervision of masters Ekkehard "the Red" and later Geddo (d. 1016). His unusual proficiency in quoting memorized fragments of the Bible (which is confirmed by insignificant deviations from the original text) could have been an effect of his intellectual formation in a monastery school. In the matter of his knowledge of patristics, it is hard to judge: he mentions Tertullian only once and quotations from St. Gregory the Great prevail over those of St. Augustine of Hippo, with seven and three quotations of each, respectively.

Such a prevalence of quotations from Gregory's paraenetic works over Augustine's literary legacy, in which universalist ideas form a critical dimension of his perspective in viewing world history, corresponds with the way Thietmar distributed emphasis in his presentation of the role of the empire and the Church on the scene of history. The chronicler focused particularly on Germany's eastern politics, a history of the local church network, and on current pastoral tasks, while matters related to the expansion of the Empire and Christendom across the world occupy a less significant place in his work. A particular kind of canon was created in the characteristics of this chronicler's mentality, in which he is confronted with his friend from the Magdeburg school, and also a distant relative, St. Bruno of Querfurt. However, as years

---

2 Because he was high-born he allegedly did not show particular diligence in some church services (*e.g.* he did not like confessing), Lech A. Tyszkiewicz, "Rec. Helmut Lippelt, Thietmar von Merseburg. Reichsbischof und Chronist. Mitteldeutsche Forschungen, Bd. 72, Böhlau Verlag, Köln-Wien 1973 s. 245, 2 ilustr.," *Studia Historica Slavo-Germanica UAM* 5 (1976), p. 204.

3 These private monasteries and churches were places in which memory of dead ancestors was especially cultivated, frequently they were buried there and it was a place where prayers were offered for them; this part devoted to the dead is treated as a reminiscence of their still pre-Christian cult (see Lippelt, *Thietmar von Merseburg*, pp. 5–16, especially 14 f.). It is worth also taking into consideration the influence of Christian eschatology on the genesis of this post-mortem care for the deceased.

THE RELIGION OF THE SLAVS IN THIETMAR'S CHRONICLE   41

went by differences in their political and ecclesiastical views caused them to
grow apart.

In about 997 Bruno joined the court chaplaincy of the Emperor Otto III.
He later devoted his life to contemplation as an eremite and finally started
evangelization of the *Barbaricum* countries.[4] Thietmar, on the other hand, did
not share Bruno's support for Otto III's line of politics. His later sympathy with
Henry II thus became something natural. Furthermore, the ascetic and mystical trend which had permeated the spiritual landscape of Western Europe
(in large part thanks to the Benedictines) was not very popular in Thietmar's
church environment centered in Magdeburg. This trend influenced the missionary vocations of figures like St. Adalbert of Prague and St. Bruno, who
undertook to evangelize the peoples of *Barbaricum* using methods similar to
the ones presented in the New Testament, even to the point of martyrdom.
However, Thietmar did not hide his admiration for their attitude, and there
are also instances in which he shared Bruno's views, especially when it comes
to his moral assessment of events and decisions of rulers or church hierarchs.[5]

Taking into consideration the different social and political contexts in which
Thietmar and Bruno had to act helps explain the dissonance between their
views, despite being former schoolmates. These differences are well illustrated
by the attitude of both clergymen to Otto III's concept of *renovatio imperii
Romanorum*, which corresponded with Bruno's activity even after the emper-
or's death. A significant element in this political endeavor was increasing the
importance of Slavdom, or more strictly speaking its then leader, Boleslav the
Brave, to one of the Empire's pillars.[6] Thietmar (at least on the pages of his

---

4   Lippelt, *Thietmar von Merseburg*, p. 118; Jerzy Strzelczyk, *Apostołowie Europy* (Warszawa:
    PAX, 1997), p. 210; *ibidem*, p. 210–22; see also Friedrich Lotter, "Christliche Völkergemeinschaft
    und Heidenmission. Das Weltbild Bruns von Querfurt," in *Early Christianity in Central and
    East Europe*, ed. Przemysław Urbańczyk, vol. 1 (Warsaw: Semper, 1997), p. 163–174. For bio-
    graphic and bibliographic indications on Bruno of Querfurt see: *Bruno z Kwerfurtu. Osoba –
    dzieło – epoka*, ed. Marian Dygo, Wojciech Fałkowski (Pułtusk: Wydawnictwo Akademii
    Humanistycznej im. Aleksandra Gieysztora, 2010); and lately Miłosz Sosnowski, "Kilka
    uwag o chronologii życia i twórczości Brunona z Kwerfurtu," *Roczniki Historyczne* 82 (2016),
    p. 63–78.
5   See below, pp. 89 f., 104 f., 107–109, 159.
6   Literature related to the concept of *renovatio imperii Romanorum* is extensive, especially
    the period of celebrations connected with the 1000th anniversary of the council Gniezno
    (1000) brought a revival of research on this issue, it was a part of a wider programme of
    commemorating the thought and achievement of Otto III and his peers. See *e.g.* Jerzy
    Strzelczyk, *Otton III* (Wrocław: Ossolineum, 2000); Roman Michałowski, *Zjazd gnieźnieński.
    Religijne przesłanki powstania arcybiskupstwa gnieźnieńskiego* (Wrocław: Wydawnictwo
    Uniwersytetu Wrocławskiego, 2005). It is worth emphasizing in this debate a skeptical trend
    which contradicts the overly idealistic evaluation of Otto's programme implementation in

work) expressed his regret over this fact as he supported an earlier concept of the Empire reaching the times of Otto I.

The archdiocese of Magdeburg, established by Otto in the 960s, undertook the Christianization of the Polabian tribes as a mission that was strictly dependent on the renovated Roman empire. The propagation of Christianity, *i.e.* introduction of the Kingdom of God in a theological sense, in practice meant extending the influences and structures of the Empire and the related Church network at the same time. This concept of mission introduced in Polabia was completely accepted by Thietmar.[7] However, it is hard to assess on this basis whether he thought it was the best way for Christianization to be used, including in relation to other missionary areas in the countries of the *Barbaricum*. He focused on the tasks set before the Magdeburg environment in which he grew up and lived the life of a clergyman.

Thietmar started his career as prior of the monastery in Walbeck in 1002, which he obtained after negotiations with his paternal uncle Lothar (this simony was the reason for his compunction). Yet, before his priestly ordination he was promoted to the canon of Magdeburg. From 1004 Tagino, the Archbishop of Magdeburg, was Thietmar's protector and friend, who ordained him a priest in the same year. Being a metropolitan's protégé, at the age of 34, Thietmar reached the top of his clerical career. On 24 April 1009 he became Bishop of the Merseburg Diocese of the Magdeburg suffragan bishopric, revived in 1004 after 23 years of non-existence. Thietmar became a member of the top elite (*principes*) in Germany, and it should be noted that Merseburg was the place of royal conventions. The city was also a starting point for the German expansion to the east. Thietmar probably participated in wars with Boleslav the Brave, and he must have witnessed Polish and German negotiations more than once. He developed an independent view on the Empire's politics in the east,[8] however, his contribution to the Empire's policy was not significant.[9]

As a bishop, he focused on regaining the property of the Merseburg diocese, which after its revival in 1004 had been reduced in relation to its

---

political practice, see *e.g.* Gerd Althoff, *Die Ottonen: Königsherrschaft ohne Staat*, (Urban-Taschenbücher) 473 (Stuttgart: Kohlhammer, 2005), pp. 181–192.

7 For more information see pp. 77 ff.

8 It is worth remembering that there was a custom of awarding official state positions to church dignitaries, it was started by Charlemagne and was characteristic for the "Ottonian system" – Lippelt, *Thietmar von Merseburg*, pp. 34–45; Althoff, *Die Ottonen*, pp. 234–239.

9 Lippelt, *Thietmar von Merseburg*, pp. 116–118, 197; cf. Tyszkiewicz, "Rec. Helmut Lippelt," p. 205.

THE RELIGION OF THE SLAVS IN THIETMAR'S CHRONICLE 43

original territory.[10] This required a lot of work and energy that included forging documents.[11] However, Thietmar was successful in this field in part thanks to the favourable attitude of the monarch. It even seems that he considered the well-being of the diocese more important than his family matters.[12] On the pages of his chronicle he showed care for the morality of Christians and observing Canon Law, and most certainly he did not try to avoid pastoral duties, which is confirmed by the passages of his chronicle containing elements of catechesis and moralization.[13] A part of his diocese also encompassed Sorbian peoples, which brought him face to face with the issue of Christianization. Although he had some knowledge of the Slavic language, missionary duties were not of primary importance to him.[14]

Thietmar died at a relatively young age on 1 December 1018, and until the last days of his life he continued writing the *Chronicle* that he had started six years earlier. The original of the chronicle dictated by Thietmar, with his original notes – the so-called Dresden Manuscript – was mostly destroyed during the bombing of Dresden in 1945. This loss is compensated by its facsimile made in 1905.[15] Nowadays we also have access to the 14th c. transcript of the so called Corvey recension of Thietmar's *Chronicon*, made in the Abbey of Corvey

---

10   The history of the Merseburg Diocese covering the period from its establishment in 968, through its dissolution in 981 and reconstruction which started in 1004, and was continued with Thietmar's participation, see Lippelt, *Thietmar von Merseburg*, pp. 90–115, and also: Gerard Labuda, *Fragmenty dziejów Słowiańszczyzny zachodniej*, vol. 3 (Poznań: Wydawnictwo Poznańskie, 1975), pp. 184 f., 194; *idem*, "Merseburg," in sss, vol. 3, pp. 196 f.

11   Lippelt, *Thietmar von Merseburg*, pp. 94 f., 104, 114, emphasizes that the motif of document forging conducted by Thietmar was conviction that the claims were legitimate. Similarly, this biased attitude to the then statesmen on the pages of the chronicle resulted from the main goal of Thietmar's work, which according to him, was compensation for damage done to the bishopric. See also Tyszkiewicz, "Rec. Helmut Lippelt," p. 205; Strzelczyk "Thietmar," in sss, vol. 6, p. 74.

12   Jedlicki, "Wstęp," p. xxvi, ensuring achieving the goal, which was maintaining the king's favour, he explains Thietmar's resignation from asserting the chapter's rights related to the election of archbishop after Walthard's death, and the candidate was the chronicler's cousin – Theodoric. Lippelt, *Thietmar von Merseburg*, pp. 127–129, moreover he proves that Thietmar supported the canonical election of bishops and only supernatural signs (*e.g.* king's dreams) helped him to accept such a significant role of the ruler in appointing church positions.

13   Lippelt, *Thietmar von Merseburg*, p. 120.

14   Lippelt, *Thietmar von Merseburg*, p. 118; J. Strzelczyk, "Thietmar," pp. 74 f. Thietmar wanted to show off his knowledge of the Slavic language more than his real knowledge of this language allowed, however, there is concrete evidence that he managed to use the language of the Slavic population in his diocese. See below pp. 74, 151.

15   Available on-line: http://www.mgh-bibliothek.de/digilib/thietmar.html [access: 15.04 .2018].

44   CHAPTER 2

Monastery in about 1120. The text includes some amendments and interpolations (currently it is kept in the Royal Library of Brussels).[16]

In the prologue to the work, the chronicler stated that his aim was to describe the lives and customs of Saxon rulers as well as the fortunes of "our"
(Saxon) Church and its pastors.[17] The cornerstone in the narrative structure
are the legendary beginnings, *origines*, of Merseburg. Then he connected this
episode with the first victories of Saxon duke Henry I, from 919 the king and
founder of the Liudolfing dynasty.[18] The presentations of the reigns of the dynasty's consecutive representatives establishes the main axis of the narrative,[19]
in which the chronicler also included further key events from the history of
the Merseburg Diocese, its temporary decommissioning (981) and restitution
(1004), and combined this first event with a theological and moral explanation
of its consequences, *i.e.* the misfortunes striking the Ottonian Empire.[20] Hence
it is not accidental that for a long time in the research on Thietmar's *causa
scribendi* there have been conjectures that his aspiration was ensuring a lasting
place in history for the diocese, or even an argument in fighting for revindica-
tion of the lands which were not regained after the restitution.[21]

However, the motifs evident in the written work of Thietmar seem to be
more complex. On the one hand, his work is an extensive commentary on the
politics of the imperial rulers and their neighbours, and it contains a moral
assessment of their attitudes and actions, and even current affairs.[22] In the
work written *cum ira et studio* one can observe the attitude of an experienced
politician and fighter for Church rights,[23] who used his writing as a weapon
to influence the environment of the imperial elite. However, on the other
hand the *memoria* (commemoration) trend seems to be equally important in
Thietmar's work. It focuses on the German rulers, particular Church dignitaries

---

16   For manuscripts, publications and translations of Thietmar's Chronicle see Jedlicki,
      "Wstęp," p. xxxvi ff.; Trillmich, "Einleitung," in *Thietmari Merseburgensis Episcopi
      Chronicon*, p. xxviii ff.

17   Thietmar I, [Prologus], p. 3.

18   Thietmar I, 1–3. It is worth mentioning that there was a discussion among scholars re-
      lated to the order of writing particular books, see Jedlicki, "Wstęp," p. xxxi f. and Trillmich,
      "Einleitung," in *Thietmari Merseburgensis Episcopi Chronicon*, p. xxiv.

19   The matter of Thietmar's personal attitude to the particular rulers of the Saxon dynasty
      was extensively discussed by Lippelt, *Thietmar von Merseburg*, pp. 138–192; Schulmeyer-
      Ahl, *Der Anfang*, pp. 49–212.

20   See below, pp. 76, 85, 89 f.; relatively recently on this matter Schulmeyer-Ahl, *Der Anfang*,
      pp. 246–308.

21   Jedlicki, "Wstęp," p. xxxiv.

22   *E.g.* the relations between Henry II with Boleslav the Brave, see below pp. 158 f.

23   Strzelczyk, "Thietmar," p. 75.

THE RELIGION OF THE SLAVS IN THIETMAR'S CHRONICLE   45

and distinguished, powerful figures (including his ancestors) or the rulers of
neighbouring countries. The chronicler does not keep away from digressions,
some of which are excellent, refined monuments cut in words.

A very accurate term to describe the character of these digressions entwined
in the main narration is an "epitaph engraved not in stone but in heart's memory," which appears in the story about Archbishop of Magdeburg Walthard.[24]
Especially in these descriptions one can observe the promotion of particular
values and models of behaviour that are attributed by Thietmar to (individual?) characters.[25] In his approach to rulers and distinguished clergymen, he applied the *aurea mediocritas* principle.[26] The chronicler willingly shares his life
experience and knowledge with the reader-addressee,[27] and he proves himself
to be a keen observer in descriptions of the peoples who were strange to him.
He paid special attention to political and missionary issues using every opportunity to include his own commentary. Although he read a lot, he did not consider it too important to transfer faithfully the information that he gained, and
he also interpreted that information in his own way.[28] Thus *curiositas* seems to
be quite an important motif that inspired Thietmar. He took delight in including various bits of trivia and curiosities,[29] including the ones related to the
supernatural nature.[30]

In this context it is worth emphasizing that these types of phenomena
played an important role in the religiosity of the bishop of Merseburg, as he
strongly believed in demons and dreams.[31] Morover it should be emphasized
that Thietmar showed good intuition for ecclesiology.[32] Similarly to the cases

---

24   Thietmar VI, 75.
25   See below, *e.g.* on Reinbern.
26   Lippelt, *Thietmar von Merseburg*, pp. 193–202, especially 201. Tyszkiewicz, "Rec. Helmut
     Lippelt," p. 206.
27   Thietmar I, [Prologus], presents Thietmar's successor at the bishop's post as the addres-
     see of the work.
28   *Ibidem*, p. xxvii.
29   Trillmich, "Einleitung," in *Thietmari Merseburgensis Episcopi Chronicon*, p. xxvi; Adam
     Krawiec, "Sny, widzenia i zmarli w kronice Thietmara z Merseburga," *Roczniki Historyczne*
     69 (2003), pp. 33–48; *idem*, "Do czego służą duchy – o pragmatyce niezwykłości
     w Kronice Thietmara z Merseburga," in *Causa creandi. O pragmatyce źródła historyczne-
     go*, ed. Stanisław Rosik, Przemysław Wiszewski (Wrocław: Wydawnictwo Uniwersytetu
     Wrocławskiego, 2005), pp. 463–472.
30   Also non-Christian ones, see below, pp. 58 f.
31   Cf. Lippelt, *Thietmar von Merseburg*, p. 121.
32   This observation is well illustrated by Thietmar VIII, 6: "Omnis homo, flos agri, debet a
     matre ecclesia prius renasci in innocenciam salvatoris Christi ..." (trans. D.A. Warner in:
     Ottonian Germany, p. 365: "All mortals, like the flowers of the field, must first be reborn
     into the innocence of Christ the Saviour through the mother church").

of other contemporary erudites, in Thietmar's text the theological reflection was developed through references to the Bible and the liturgy, for both ideas and particular images and quotations. This thought is rather raw and scanty, however, as there is an abundance of hidden senses under such phrases, allegories, and symbols that can be revealed by speculative theology and expressed in the language of philosophy.

From a literary perspective Thietmar's chronicle did not receive a high assessment, but this ought to be seen as evidence of its author's undoubtable historical talent.[33] Digressions which spoil the continuity of the main narrative and have a negative effect on its literary value, from the historical point of view, contain very important material. One should also emphasize the chronicler's careful choice of vocabulary, regardless of stylistic shortcomings.[34] He also made his own – not terribly successful – attempts at poetry. Among the Classical authors Thietmar placed Horace, Virgil, and Ovid at the helm. Quotations from the works of Persius, Lucan, Martial, Terentius, Juvenal, Statius or the so-called Dion Cato are far less common in his writing. Perhaps he only knew of their works indirectly through excerpts he read at school. He additionally referred to Macrobius Ambrosius Theodosius. Regarding the Christian writers, apart from the already mentioned St. Augustine, Tertullian and Gregory the Great, he quoted Prudentius and Isidore of Seville. The crumbs of Greek occurring here and there in the chronicle do not convince us that Thietmar knew this language. They only confirm the Byzantine influences in the contemporary Latin.

In older parts of the chronicle there appears information taken from the German annals, and mainly from *Res gestae Saxonicae* by Widukind of Corvey. Apart from this, the chronicler used documents (the history of Merseburg, Magdeburg, Walbeck), quoted the resolutions of the Synod of Dortmund (1005), and it is evident that he knew written records related to Magdeburg, Halberstadt, and the Lower Saxony monasteries (Berge, Corvey, Helmstedt, Nienburg). According to Werner Trillmich, it is possible to prove that he knew also the obituary books from Merseburg, Magdeburg, and Lüneburg. *The Annals of Quedlinburg* were useful for the chronicler in his work on books I–IV and VI. One can also find in Thietmar's work some individual borrowings from

---

33   Thietmar's education is discussed by Jedlicki, "Wstęp," p. xv ff.; Trillmich, "Einleitung," in
       Thietmari Merseburgensis Episcopi Chronicon, p. xxv ff.; Lippelt, *Thietmar von Merseburg*,
       pp. 71–87.

34   Jedlicki, "Wstęp," p. lii.

THE RELIGION OF THE SLAVS IN THIETMAR'S CHRONICLE   47

hagiographies and the biographies of rulers. However, it is doubtful whether he knew the Chronicle of Regino of Prüm.[35]

Thietmar's literary sources play only a minor role when one looks at his entire work.[36] He knew many issues from experience. Some main actors on the political scene certainly informed him personally, such as Emperor Henry II, Archbishops Walthard and Tagino, as well as other dignitaries, including some of his own relatives.

Thietmar's work falls into the *gesta* genre, which was a trend in historiography growing in popularity in the 11th c. Its characteristic feature was close relation to a particular nation, territory or institution.[37] However, there is also a place for the world of great politics and the problems of the universal Church, whose stage more than once is Rome or even Constantinople. The history of German rulers and their subjects was entwined in this narration with the history of neighbouring countries, with Slavic matters clearly emphasized (*e.g.* 78 out of 429 chapters of the chronicle refer to Poland).[38]

Already in earlier historical science many scholars had a high regard of Thietmar's credibility as well as the data related to the history of the Slavs from the 10th c. to 1018 presented in his work.[39] On the other hand, it was demonstrated over half a century ago that he took from his home some preconceived notions about the Slavs and that he was generally averse to them.[40] Furthermore, it has been argued that the basic criterion for his evaluation of the Slavs was their submissive or rebellious behaviour towards the Emperors. Some scholars have tried to blame it on Thietmar's belief in the German ideology of *Drang nach Osten*,[41] which effected in his negative opinion about Otto III's

---

35   Strzelczyk, "Thietmar," p. 75. Trillmich, "Einleitung," in *Thietmari Merseburgensis Episcopi Chronicon*, p. xxvi.

36   Trillmich, "Einleitung," in *Thietmari Merseburgensis Episcopi Chronicon*, p. xxv.

37   *E.g.* B. Kürbis, "Więź najstarszego dziejopisarstwa polskiego z państwem," in *Początki Państwa Polskiego. Księga Tysiąclecia*, vol. 2, ed. Kazimierz Tymieniecki *et al.* (Poznań: PWN, 1962) p. 219.

38   It was already observed by Leon Koczy, "Thietmar i Widukind (z powodu nowych wydań obu pisarzy)," *Kwartalnik Historyczny* 50 (1936) 2, p. 659.

39   Lech A. Tyszkiewicz, "Motywy oceny Słowian w Kronice Thietmara," in *Studia z dziejów kultury i ideologii poświęcone Ewie Maleczyńskiej*, ed. Roman Heck, Wacław Korta, Józef Leszczyński (Wrocław: Ossolineum, 1968), s. 105.

40   *E.g.* Jedlicki, "Wstęp," p. xxvi.

41   Erich Donnert, "Dannyje niemieckich istočnikov rannego srednevekovja o slavyanach i programma vostočnoj ekspansii u Tietmara mierzeburskogo," *Sredniye Veka* 27 (1965), pp. 26–39; a similar point of view was taken by Donnert also in other works, *e.g. idem*, "Die frühmittelalterlich-deutsche Slawenkunde und Thietmar von Merseburg," *Zeitschrift für Slawistik* 9 (1964), pp. 77–90.

politics.[42] This "German" point of view has also been attributed to Thietmar in the case of missionary ideas about which he was taught at school, and therefore his views were contrary to St. Bruno's "universalistic" program.[43] In the context of how modern historiography has regarded Thietmar, it is not surprising that some scholars have tried to prove Thietmar's aversion to the Slavs by referring to fragments of his chronicle where, for example, he mentioned *Sclavorum conspirata manus*.[44]

The shortcomings of presenting Thietmar's attitude toward the Slavs in these ways were indicated in 1968 by Lech Tyszkiewicz, who emphasized that the chronicler wrote about them as an ethnic group only where there were no completely consolidated states (Liutici, Obodrites), while in reference to Bohemia, Poland, and Rus', he was mainly interested in their rulers. Hence it is a mistake to transfer the negative assessment of these individuals to the people (their subjects), especially given that the chronicler devoted so much attention to them. The author presents numerous examples denying such one-sided assessment of Slavs on the pages of the chronicle, only to conclude finally that the chronicler was highly objective and that there was no uniform stance on the Slavs as a whole.[45] For Tyszkiewicz, "it becomes clear that the motif behind the assessment of the Slavs in Thietmar's Chronicle could not be nationalism or even an ordinary sense of ethnic strangeness." Instead, loyalty to the Church or to the state and the religious factor first and foremost characterized Thietmar's assessment of the Slavs.[46]

Further discussion in the last two decades has deviated even more from the anachronisms in which the modern political ideologies influenced or even determined the reflection (*e.g.* a reference to the *Drang nach Osten* concept coined in the 19th c.), to strongly appreciate the so-called anthropological factor. More precisely, the chronicler's approach to the Slavs was defined to a large extent in terms of approach to the "other." It manifested itself, for instance, in Thietmar's aforementioned pejorative judgements and the usage of stereotypes. In this case not only ethnic, but also religious strangeness is taken into account.[47] It closely corresponds with the subject of this

---

42   Marian Zygmunt Jedlicki, "Poglądy prawno-polityczne Thietmara. Przyczynek do badań nad świadomością prawną wschodnioniemieckich feudałów na przełomie X i XI wieku," *Czasopismo prawno-historyczne* 5 (1953), p. 54.

43   Koczy, "Thietmar i Widukind," pp. 660 f.

44   Donnert, "Dannyje," p. 32; cf. Thietmar III, 17.

45   Tyszkiewicz, "Motywy," pp. 110 ff. and 118.

46   *Ibidem*, p. 117. The priority of church matters in Thietmar's hierarchy of values was discussed earlier *e.g.* by Koczy, "Thietmar i Widukind," pp. 663 f.

47   For the issue of the perception of the Slavs in Thietmar's chronicle on the basis of the original version of this study, see Stanisław Rosik, "*Rudes in fide gentilium populi* ... Fortdauer der Anzeichen des Heidentums zur Zeit der Christianisierung der Slawen im Lichte der

THE RELIGION OF THE SLAVS IN THIETMAR'S CHRONICLE   49

work, and in particular instances these phenomena are the subject of analyses as one of the dimensions of Thietmar's assessment of the religion of the Slavs.

However, in this case, precisely defining the place attributed by Thietmar to the cults and beliefs of the Slavs in the narrative, as well as the qualification of phenomena in the cultural and theological interpretation, is of key importance. He drew its categories from Christian literature, and mainly from the Bible. It was treated in accordance with contemporary principles as a record of senses hidden at a few levels of interpretation, and each of them was a carrier of revealed cognition.[48] The allegorical method especially allowed views, phenomena, or events from the biblical world to become universalized, so as to express an essential knowledge useful in a theological interpretation of the history of humankind.[49] It was particularly relevant for the contemporary historiography, because the substantive trend in this field of literacy saw the described history as a continuation of biblical events in which God's plan of salvation is implemented.[50]

In Thietmar's work one can observe a conviction that God continuously intervenes in the fate of individuals and societies led by their rulers, a characteristic which is especially clear in the pages of the Old Testament.[51] It is

---

deutschen narrativen Quellen des 11. und 12. Jahrhunderts," *Questiones Medii Aevii novae* 7 (2002), pp. 45–76; and next strictly in accordance with the trend to juxtapose the "familiar" with the "strange" see Scior, *Das Eigene und das Fremde*, and Fraesdorff, *Der barbarische Norden*, who separated in his analysis the ethnic and religious otherness.

48   Stanisław Wielgus, *Badania nad Biblią w starożytności i w średniowieczu* (Lublin: Towarzystwo Naukowe KUL, 1990), pp. 75–123, especially 114–119; cf. John H. Hayes, "A history of Interpretation," in *Mercer Commentary on the Bible.* ed. Watson E. Mills, Richard F. Wilson (Macon, Georgia: Mercer University Press), pp. 27 ff.

49   The source of the allegorical explanation of the Bible is the Alexandrian historical-allegorical school, which was used by St. Augustine. "History from his perspective is a certain universal process of creation of the humankind by God and Christ, a chain of human situations and the resultant of the rational beings' actions which this way or another implement the universal plans of God." – Czesław Bartnik, "Augustyńska historiologia," *Vox Patrum* 8 (1988), p. 796. This way of working with the Bible was undertaken by Medieval historiography. Cf. André Vauchez, *Duchowość średniowiecza*, trans. Hanna Zaremska (Gdańsk: Marabut, 1996) [orig. *La spiritualité du Moyen Âge occidental VIII–XIII* (Paris, 1975)], pp. 144 f.

50   Padberg, *Die Christianisierung Europas im Mittelalter* (Stuttgart: Reclam, 1998), p. 188; Schulmeyer-Ahl, *Der Anfang*, p. 100.

51   *E.g.* Thietmar II, 12. Widukind of Corvey also worked in this way – see Hagen Keller, "Machabaeorum pugnae. Zum Stellenwert eines biblischen Vorbilds in Widukinds Deutung der ottonischen Königsherrschaft," in *Iconologia sacra. Mythos, Bildkunst und Dichtung in der Religions- und Sozialgeschichte Alteuropas. Festschrift für Karl Hauck*, ed. Hagen Keller, Nikolaus Staubach, (Arbeiten zur Frühmittelalterforschung) 23 (Berlin/New York: de Gruyter, 1994) pp. 417–437.

worth quoting a historian of spirituality with reference to this medieval vision of history: "God does not allow events to take place against justice, before he sends His punishment, he gives various warning signs, uses elements and stars, resorts to visions and miracles. Everyone should carefully follow them and notice them in time."[52] In the case of Thietmar's particular attention paid to the moral-theological assessment of his characters' behaviour on the stage of history, it turns out to be generally similar to St. Augustine's thought, which was fundamental in the historiography of the Middle Ages. However, it is hard to talk here about any particular inspiration from the concept of *civitas Dei* created by this Father of the Church.[53] The main reason for this is that in the historiology of the Merseburg bishop, the biblical idea of the kingdom of Christ is of key significance.[54]

Already in the *Prologue* Thietmar prays to Christ as the "kings' adornment" and ruler of empires: "Christe, decus regum, moderator et imperiorum, / Propiciare tuo cum commisis sibi regno ..."[55] A striking feature of this expression seems to be the idea of an "entrustment" of a given community to a ruler (*commisi sibi*, "entrusted to him"), *i.e.* Christ in this case. This theological image becomes a model in the earthly dimension as well. Hence, for example, Otto I's victory in the Battle of the Lech River (955), according to Thietmar, was a reason for joy for all the Christians, *i.e.* "omnis christianitas," however, the most joyful ones were those entrusted to the king: "maximeque regi commissa."[56] In this context one can observe "entrusting" to a particular ruler, or in the case of the Germans (Saxons) a particular community, as a part of a whole which is *Christianitas*.

This image corresponds well with the term *vicarius Dei* applied to the ruler of Germany – not only the king, but also the emperor – which indicates the idea of representing God.[57] Hence in this perspective the monarch becomes the head of the people unified in the spiritual dimension. Under his control

---

52   Vauchez, *Duchowość*, p. 45. Cf. *e.g.* Thietmar I, 27.

53   See Bartnik, "Augustyńska historiologia."

54   For the idea of the Kingdom of God in the Ottonian epoch in Germany see *e.g.* Reinhart Staats, "Missionsgeschichte Nordeuropas. Eine geistesgeschichtliche Einführung," in *Rom und Byzanz im Norden. Mission und Glaubenswechsel im Ostseeraum während des 8.–14. Jahrhunderts*, vol. 1, ed. Michael Müller-Wille (Stuttgart: Steiner, 1997), p. 25.

55   Thietmar, Prologus.

56   *Ibidem*, II, 10.

57   *Ibidem*. See also Thietmar VI, 1: "vicarium suimet in terris"; cf. I, 26: "reges nostri et imperatores summi rectoris vice in hac peregrinatione prepositi". Hence the ruler's duty to be involved in Church matters, and the guarantee of good rule were ruler's virtues and observing moral principles in which his election was manifested, see *e.g.* Thietmar I, 26; VI, 11; VII, 8; V, 17. See Dariusz Prucnal, "Władca chrześcijański w Kronice Thietmara biskupa

THE RELIGION OF THE SLAVS IN THIETMAR'S CHRONICLE   51

there were also bishops, which was characteristic for the so-called Ottonian system in Germany. However, Thietmar clearly indicates a limitation of this authority: the emperor – even together with the pope, the Roman Synod, and the metropolitan bishop – did not have the right to raise his hand against the existence of a bishopric and its property. This view was expressed on a matter which was of paramount importance for him, *i.e.* the liquidation of the bishopric in Merseburg at the synod in Rome in 981. A chain of misfortunes which, in his interpretation, affected the people and institutions responsible for that fact, was an expression of heavenly punishment for this attack on "Christ's sheepfold."[58]

In Thietmar's perspective, a bishopric fully represented Christ and his people (allegorical "bride"), and those who did harm to this institution, even Christians, in the theological perspective became enemies of God himself.[59] Thus it is not accidental that with reference to bishops, as representatives of Christ, the term "entrust" (*committere*) of a community of people is used in the chronicle, just like in the case of the monarch.[60] In this case even the very concept of empowerment of *civitates* ("cities") is significant, particularly indicating capitals, the most important centres, which achieved their prime historical development owing to the establishment of a bishopric in them. So, the chronicler emphasized that until 981 Merseburg "was governed liberally" ("liberaliter dominabatur"), and therefore the liquidation of the local bishopric was an attack on its rightful liberty (*libertas*).

The achievement of such a high status by a given centre, *civitas* or *urbs*, was a consequence of particular historical circumstances and events, which again was perfectly presented by the Merseburg example. The choice of the future bishopric capital was mainly based on its Roman origins, legendary in this

---

Merseburskiego," *Roczniki Humanistyczne* 44 (1996) 2, pp. 5–6, 18, 23. See also Lippelt, *Thietmar von Merseburg*, p. 35, 186; Warner, "Introduction," pp. 16 ff.

58   The one who inspired this trespass, archbishop of Magdeburg Gisiler, was compared to a "mercenary" who was a denial of Christ the "good shepherd" in the evangelical parable. See below, pp. 85 ff.

59   The name Christ's "bride" (sponsa) was used by Thietmar to refer to cathedral churches (see later, pp. 105 f). The then theology of the particular Church was very advanced. See *e.g.* Paul P. Gilbert, *Wprowadzenie do teologii średniowiecza*, trans. Tytus Górski (Kraków: WAM, 1997 [orig. *Introduzione alla teologia medioevale*. Roma, 1992]), p. 63.

60   See *e.g.* Thietmar II, 28; Stanisław Rosik, "*Romanorum prepotens imperator augustus* und *valentior sibi in Christo domnus apostolicus* in der Chronik Thietmars von Merseburg," in *Inter laurum et olivam*, ed. Jiří Šouša, Ivana Ebelová, (Acta Universitatis Carolinae – Philosophica et Historica 1–2 (2002), Z pomocných věd historických) 16 (Praha: Nakladatelství Karolinum, 2007), pp. 373–378.

case.[61] The Mars-related etymology of the city name was enriched by a Slavic element added by Thietmar, for he emphasized that for the local inhabitants, it was "the middle" (Slavonic *mese*, today it means: balk) of their oecumene. Finally, the complete promotion of the city was due to the actions of representatives of the Liudolfing dynasty, which were highly praised by the chronicler. Its founder Henry I managed to successfully unite the territories adjacent to Merseburg that had belonged to various lords.[62] The bishopric was founded by Otto I, and in this way he fulfilled an oath made to God to ensure for himself the victory in the Lech River battle (955).[63]

In Widukind of Corvey's narration, composed after his military success, Otto I gained the *imperator* title thanks to his army's acclamation.[64] However, Thietmar did not take this motif from his predecessor's work, and instead connected Otto's obtainment of the emperor's dignity to his coronation in Rome. This was exactly the city which in his narrative bestows the dignity of the emperor.[65] Moreover the pope leading the Roman Church cannot be judged by anyone else but God.[66] In this context the position of the emperor is ancillary to the Holy See, which is expressed in the title of the defender of St. Peter's Church or of St. Peter himself. Thus, it is not accidental that, according to Thietmar, Otto I was punished for raising his hand against Pope Benedict V by a plague that devastated the imperial army.

The universalist idea of Rome is significantly demonstrated on the pages of the chronicle through the coexistence of two main pillars of the contemporary social order: priesthood (*sacerdotium*) and monarchy (*imperium/regnum*).[67] In the chronicle, Rome, the Romulus city[68] serving as the capital

---

61   The city was to be named by the Romans ("ex Romulea gente") who used the word Mars due to his military virtues and victories.

62   Thietmar I, 2–3.

63   *Ibidem*, II, 10.

64   *Widukindi res gestae Saxonicae – Widukinds Sachsengeschichte*, Latin and German text, ed. and trans. Paul Hirsch, Albert Bauer, Reinhold Rau, Ausgewählte Quellen zur deutschen Geschichte des Mittelalters 8 (Darmstadt: Wissenschaftliche Buchgesellschaft, 1971) [further: Widukind], III, 49. Similarly earlier Henry I became an emperor in this chronicle (I, 39) after his victory over the Hungarians in the Unstrut battle (931).

65   Thietmar II, [Prologus]: "Imperatorem fecit sibi Roma potentem / Hunc ..." (cf. trans. D.A. Warner in: *Ottonian Germany*, p. 88: "Rome made this powerful man her Emperor ...").

66   Thietmar II, 28.

67   The ruler of the Roman Empire has the leading role among Christian rulers who manifest their support for the Holy See and also their political position with the payment of the so called St. Peter's denar (cf. *e.g.* Thietmar VI, 92).

68   Thietmar VII, 71: "arca Romulea".

THE RELIGION OF THE SLAVS IN THIETMAR'S CHRONICLE   53

of St. Peter's Church, turns out to be the "capital of all cities,"[69] and, just as in case of Merseburg, it was a model by which to define the status of the other *civitates* raised to the bishopric rank. Thus, the monarch's role is protecting the old liberty of such cities and respecting the inviolability of the Church located in them.

In summary, in the literary world created by Thietmar, the Kingdom of God is present on at least a few levels. The lowest one is the diocese, and the Merseburg bishopric is crucial for the entire narrative. At a higher level there is the monarchy, fundamental for the construction of the whole chronicle narration, as it constituted the history of the Liudolfing kingdom and the related church network. The chronicler's ties with this milieu are expressed in the "our" (*nostri*) category when he was referring to the Saxons. The highest level in the social dimension is that of *Christianitas*, the unity which is centred on Rome, and in which political practice means variously shaped relations between political organisms and the papacy as well as the empire.

However, with full respect for the institutional hierarchy in his world, the chronicler was able to reprove the decision of the superior power, which was justified with a reference to the higher moral order determined by a relation to Christ both in the social and individual dimension. It is depicted well in his interpretation of the liquidation of the bishopric of Merseburg. Thietmar defended the well-being of the diocese and treated it as a qualitatively complete representation of a mystical community whose head was Christ. Hence it is not accidental that the rights of the diocese or, in other words, its freedom (*libertas*), were inviolable in the chronicler's opinion, even though it was only an element in the Liudolfing monarchy structure and it was subordinate to the Magdeburg metropolis. The infringement of these rights resulted in the earlier mentioned misfortunes that affected the people making such decisions and the institutions benefitting from them.

In this literary context pagans could become a tool used by the heavens as an instrument of punishment, which did not change the fact that they remained enemies of Christ and Christian community in general. Their religion and perceived idolatry ensured this. Because of them, according to the contemporary theological arguments, the space of social life became open to the *antisacrum*. These powers were hostile to the world and mankind and, according to Thietmar, they were also manifested in a social circle already treated as Christian. They were evoked especially by sin. By nature, they were diabolic creatures, powers of the eternal chaos revolting against the Creator, and in the

---

69   *Ibidem*, VII, 71. It is characteristic that the Roman emperor in the East (Byzantine) is
       called the Constantinople or Greek emperor by Thietmar (II, 15).

54   CHAPTER 2

accompanying cosmological dimension one has to outline here the widest horizon of the chronicler's reflection on the religion of Slavic peoples.

References to this sphere of beliefs and cults appear throughout the whole of Thietmar's work, from the first to the last page, and usually they do not constitute individual entities, such as a very precious excurse about the Liutici cult concentrated in and around Radogošč. In this situation an optimal solution seems to be the presentation of analyses of particular records in the order of their appearance in the narrative. The research conducted in this way on particular cases with respect to the interpretation of Slavic religion will be summarized at the end of this chapter.[70] This chain of analyses will be preceded by an excurse devoted to the *Deeds of the Saxons* by Widukind of Corvey. It is the source of information used most extensively by Thietmar and, also highly important, it includes the information about the presence of a "Saturn" idol at the Elbslavs.

Excursus: Saturn at the Wagrians (Widukind of Corvey, *Res gestae Saxonicae libri tres* III, 68)

Widukind of Corvey[71] presented the capitulation of a certain stronghold (most likely Starigard/Oldenburg) of the Wagrian tribe to Margrave Hermann Billung in 967, writing a few years after this event.[72] The chronicler mentioned that among the loot from the stronghold there was a copper figure of Saturn, which was used by Hermann to offer the people an extraordinary show.[73] Was it because nobody expected to find a Roman idol among the Slavs? E. von Wienecke

---

70   The chronicle translated and edited by M.Z. Jedlicki (1953) was used in the research, it was based on R. Holtzmann's edition which in turn used the Dresden Manuscript (see above, p. 39, footnote 1, and p. 43, footnote 15). It is worth mentioning an edition of the chronicle edited by W. Trillmich (*Thietmari Merseburgensis Episcopi Chronicon*), and it was also published its English translation in 2001 by D.A. Warner, see: *Ottonian Germany*; see above, p. 39, footnote 1.

71   Widukind's work marks the beginning of the German (Saxon) historiography, the Slavs are treated grudgingly in it and they are attributed stereotypical, pejorative epithets. See *e.g.* Jerzy Strzelczyk, "Widukind," in SSS, vol. 6, pp. 423 f.; Rudolf Buchner, "Einleitung," in Widukind, pp. 3–10; Lech A. Tyszkiewicz, "Sasi i inne ludy w dziejach saskich Widukinda z Korwei," in Acta Universitatis Wratislaviensis. Historia 23 (Wrocław: Wydawnictwo Uniwersytetu Wrocławskiego, 1974), pp. 23 ff.

72   Henryk Łowmiański, *Początki Polski*, vol. 5 (Warszawa: PWN, 1973), p. 285, footnote 926; Lech Leciejewicz, *Słowianie zachodni* (Wrocław/Warszawa/Kraków: Ossolineum, 1989), p. 193.

73   Widukind III, 68: "urbis predam suis militibus donavit, simulacro Saturni ex aere fuso, quod ibi inter alia urbis spolia repperit, magnum spectaculum populo prebuit" (the victorious leader "gave the loot from the city to his soldiers, [and] offered a great spectacle

THE RELIGION OF THE SLAVS IN THIETMAR'S CHRONICLE   55

considered this object to be an ancient relic, which indicated that idolatry was strange to the Slavs.[74] H. Łowmiański argued, however, that the idol was an object of the Wagrian cult, and a surprising element was its cultic function as a new phenomenon in Polabia.[75]

The existence of idolatry in Polabia in the second half of the 10th c. should be considered possible and not necessarily a *novum*.[76] Despite that, it is not known whether this statue was an object of the Slavic cult or an example of accumulation of treasures by the stronghold's inhabitants. One way or another, the use of the word *simulacrum* in the case of Widukind acquires a pejorative theological qualification as the chronicler identified it with *daemonium*,[77] a deity or idol. For him worshipping such objects was an antithetical to faith in Christ.[78] Similarly the very appearance of the Roman god was related to the sphere of cult that Widukind considered an error in the doctrinal perspective (*error*), which is indicated in his commentary on the presentation of pre-Christian rites performed by the Saxons.[79] Moreover, their deities were presented by the chronicler in the *interpretatio Romana vel graeca* convention,[80] which corresponds with a legend claiming that Saxons were of Greek origin.[81]

In the case of "Saturn" among the Wagrians, it is difficult to dispute the intention of attributing the Roman religious beliefs to the Slavic reality due to

---

      to the people thanks to an image of Saturn cast in bronze which he obtained along with other spoils from the city"). Cf. Słupecki, *Slavonic Pagan Sanctuaries*, p. 67.

74   Wienecke, *Untersuchungen*, p. 179. The "Saturn" figure was considered as imported from Rome also by Włodzimierz Szafrański, *Prahistoria religii na ziemiach polskich* (Wrocław/ Warszawa/Kraków: Ossolineum, 1987), p. 363.

75   Łowmiański, *Religia*, pp. 169 f. stated that in accordance with the concept he supported assuming the creation of Polabian polytheism not earlier than in the 10th–11th c.

76   The existence of statues and temples in Polabia from at least the 10th c. is properly documented. See *e.g.* Gieysztor, *Mitologia*, pp. 230–241; Leciejewicz, *Słowianie*, p. 115; Słupecki, *Slavonic Pagan Sanctuaries*, pp. 86 ff., 108 f.; *idem*, "Einflüsse des Christentums auf die heidnische Religion des Ostseeslawen im 8.–12. Jahrhundert: Tempel – Götterbilder – Kult," in *Rom und Byzanz im Norden. Mission und Glaubenswechsel im Ostseeraum während des 8.–14. Jahrhunderts*, vol. 2, ed. Michael Müller-Wille (Stuttgart: Steiner, 1997), p. 182–184; Sebastian, Brather, "Mehrköpfige Gottheit," in *Reallexikon der germanischen Altertumskunde*, vol. 19, ed. Johannes Hoops (Berlin/New York: De Gruyter, 2001), pp. 503–505; *idem*, *Archäologie der westlichen Slawen. Siedlung, Wirtschaft und Gesellschaft im früh- und hochmittelalterlichen Ostmitteleuropa* (Berlin/New York: De Gruyter, 2001), pp. 322–325. See also below pp. 172–176.

77   Widukind III, 65: "simulacra vero daemonia esse et non deos testatus est".

78   *Ibidem*: "... Christum deum solum colendum decrevit, idola respuenda subiectis gentibus imperat ..."

79   Widukind I, 12: *error paternum*.

80   *Ibidem*.

81   Widukind I, 2, presents Saxons as descendants of Alexander the Great army dispersed all over the world.

56   CHAPTER 2

the silence of other sources on this matter. It does not in the least, however, decrease the probability of the thesis that here the chronicler applied *interpretatio Romana* of some Slavic deity,[82] *e.g.* a god of fertility.[83] It is worth taking into consideration that the Saxons could have considered the Slavic idol to be a Roman one by mistake. If this was the case, it would be a cause of surprise, either because it was found among the Slavs or because it was worshipped by them. Each of the solutions discussed here supports a hypothetical interpretation of the spectacle (*spectaculum*) arranged by the margrave for his people, not only to present the figure of "Saturn" in public but also to conduct a ritual form of annihilation of idolatry.[84]

2   The Religion of the Slavs in Thietmar's Chronicle –
         Historiographical Analysis

2.1   *The Holy Spring of the Tribe Glomače*
Even on the threshold of Henry I's history, which constitutes the body of the first book of the *Chronicle*, Thietmar hints at the world of the Slavic *sacrum* in the description of the military expedition of the then Saxon duke to the country of Daleminzi also called Glomače.[85] The chronicler explained the latter name – used by the Slavs (while the former was used by the Germans) – by referring to a certain spring:

---

82   Urbańczyk, *Dawni Słowianie*, p. 187; Łowmiański, *Religia*, pp. 62, 170; Tyszkiewicz, *Sasi*, p. 35.

83   H.V. Ackenheil, *Gottheiten und Kultstätten in und um Oldenburg in Wagrien: archäoglottische Studien über germanisches und slawisches Heidentum* (Hamburg: Fotodruck an der Uni, 1983), p. 51; Erich Hoffmann, "Beiträge zur Geschichte der Obodriten zur Zeit der Nakoniden," in *Zwischen Christianisierung und Europäisierung. Beiträge zur Geschichte Osteuropas in Mittelalter und früher Neuzeivol. Festschrift für Peter Nitsche zum 65. Geburtstag*, ed. Eckhard Hübner, Ekkehard Klug, Jan Kusber (Stuttgart: Franz Steiner Verlag, 1998), p. 27. Ackenheil, *Gottheiten*, p. 33, proposed to interpret "Saturn" and god of Wagrians named Prove as different forms of the same highest divinity, however, according to Helmold, no statues were put up for Prove so the idea raises doubts; cf. *Helmoldi presbyteri bozoviensis Cronica Slavorum*, ed. Bernhard Schmeidler, MGH SSrerGerm in usum scholarum (1937) [further: Helmold], I, 84.

84   In the mid-12th c. Ebo of Michelsberg defined the rituals of the elimination of idols in Polabia as *spectaculum* (see: *Ebonis Vita S. Ottonis Episcopi Babenbergensis*, ed. Kazimierz Liman, Jan Wikarjak, MPH n.s. 7/2 (1969) [further: Ebo], III, 10) however this is not a strong premise in the interpretation of this term in the discussed passage of Widukind's work.

85   It took place in 912 at the latest. See: Gerard Labuda, "Henryk I," in SSS, vol. 2, p. 201; *idem, Fragmenty dziejów Słowiańszczyzny zachodniej*, vol. 1 (Poznań: Wydawnictwo Poznańskie, 1960), p. 249.

THE RELIGION OF THE SLAVS IN THIETMAR'S CHRONICLE   57

Glomač "is a spring located no more than two miles away from the Elbe,
which [*i.e.* Glomač] itself gives birth to a swamp, [and] often produces marvels
as the inhabitants claim and as it has been confirmed by many eyewitnesses.
When a good peace is going to profit the natives, and that soil bears[86] its fruit,
it [Glomač] is covered with wheat, oats, and acorn and makes joyful the souls
of the neighbours who often gather at it. When, however, a ferocious tempest
of war advances, it forecasts the future event with [a sign of] blood and ashes.
Every inhabitant, although with dubious hope, reveres and fears this [spring]
more than the churches."[87]

Thus, the spring was a "reliable sensor informing the people in its care about
any change of fate."[88] Due to the presented type of divination signs, in relation
to the source one should take into account the occurrence of a fertility and an
abundance cult, which generally corresponds to findings referring to aquatic
hierophany.[89]

Worship of springs, which was characteristic for the Slavs at the time of
Christianization, is not surprising.[90] A bog surrounding the holy spring of

---

86   The right analogies to explain the meaning "(non) mentitur" in this case seem to be some
      passages in *Biblia Sacra juxta Vulgatam Clementinam. Editio Electronica*, ed. Michaele
      Tvveedale (London, 2005) [further: Vulgate], *e.g.* Hab 3:17: "mentietur opus olivæ" or
      Hos 9:2: "vinum mentietur eis".
87   Thietmar I, 3: "Glomuzi est fons, non plus ab Albi quam duo miliaria positus, qui unam de
      se paludem generans, mira, ut incolae pro vero asserunt oculisque approbatum est a mul-
      tis, sepe operatur. Cum bona pax est indigenis profutura, suumque haec terra non men-
      titur fructum, idem tritico et avena ac glandine refertus, laetos vicinorum ad se crebro
      confluentium efficit animos. Quando autem seva belli tempestas ingruerit, sanguine et
      cinere certum futuri exitus indicium premonstrat. Hunc omnis incola plus quam aeccle-
      sias, spe quamvis dubia, veneratur et timet".
88   Jacek Banaszkiewicz, "Źródło Głomacz i jego rajska okolica," in *Viae historicae. Księga ju-
      bileuszowa dedykowana Profesorowi Lechowi A. Tyszkiewiczowi w siedemdziesiątą rocznicę
      urodzin*, ed. Mateusz Goliński, Stanisław Rosik, (Acta Universitatis Wratislaviensis.
      Historia) 152 (Wrocław: Wydawnictwo Uniwersytetu Wrocławskiego, 2001), pp. 407–414.
89   See Słupecki, *Slavonic Pagan Sanctuaries*, pp. 165 f.; moreover the author conjectures on
      the basis of comparative premises that the marshland surrounding Glomač was the place
      of offerings. See also Szafrański, *Prahistoria*, p. 321.
90   The cult of waters among the Slavs is also mentioned by Procopius of Caesarea in the
      first preserved information about their religion from the mid-6th c. – see: Procopius
      Caesariensis, *De Bellis* 7.14.1, see Procopius Caesariensis, *Opera Omnia*, vol. 2: *De Bellis libri
      V–VIII*, ed. Jakob Haury (Leipzig: Teubner, 1963), p. 357; cf. *Testimonia najdawniejszych
      dziejów Słowian. Seria grecka, zeszyt 2. Pisarze z V–X w.*, ed. Anna Brzóstowska, Wincenty
      Swoboda (Wrocław/Warszawad/Kraków: Ossolineum, 1989), pp. 60 f. (strictly speaking,
      this information concerns Antes and Sclavenes).

Glomač[91] only strengthened the natural impression of *sacrum* inaccessibility. The very name Glomač (*Glomuzi*) has eponimic nature, and due to the location of the tribe's original abodes near a spring, and possibly also its particular usefulness in everyday life of the local people, it can be assumed that the spring was the embodiment of tutelary supernatural forces taking care of Glomače public life.[92] However, the genesis of the name of this tribe is most certainly related to the very fact of settlement near a stream (analogically to tribal names originating from rivers, such as the Vislane or Moravians).[93] Taking into account Thietmar's information that Glomač is located not more than two miles away from the Elbe, the cult area in question is hypothetically located near the town Lommatzsch in the Meissen district.[94] Yet, it is only a speculation.

The observation that each of the local inhabitants worshipped and feared ("veneratur et timet") the spring and the bog surrounding it much more than the churches stemmed from pastoral practice and care. It is not accidental that the chronicler lamented over the uncertainty of hope ("spes quamvis dubia") rested by Slavs in this source of supernatural power. It is essential that Thietmar did not question the occurrence of the miraculous element (*mira*) in the case of this aquatic hierophany, which was the reason for its worship by the local inhabitants.[95] However, the claim that the spring was worshipped more than churches does not mean the latter ones were not important in the

---

91 Accepted here reconstruction of the name of the venerated spring as Glomač can cause discussion – see: Urbańczyk, *Dawni Słowianie*, pp. 78, 115; D.A. Warner in: *Ottonian Germany*, p. 68, footnote 11.

92 Gieysztor, *Mitologia*, p. 216; L. Leciejewicz, ">>In Pago Silensi vocabulo hoc a quodam monte ... sibi indito<<. O funkcji miejsc kultu pogańskiego w systemie politycznym Słowian Zachodnich doby plemiennej", *Sobótka* 42 (1987) 2, p. 132; it is supported in the further part of narration: "Et haec provincia ab Albi usque in Caminizi fluvium porrecta vocabulum ab eo trahit dirivatum." – Thietmar I, 3.

93 Creation of the tribal name of the Glomače originating from the sanctuary of Glomač was supposed by *e.g.* Hansjürgen Brachman, "Zur religiösen Vorstellungwelt der sorbischen Stämme an Elbe und Saale," *Studia Onomastica* 5 (1987), p. 51; Leszek P. Słupecki, "Ślęza, Radunia, Wieżyca. Miejsca kultu pogańskiego Słowian w średniowieczu," *Kwartalnik Historyczny* 99 (1992) 2, pp. 13 f.; *idem*, *Slavonic Pagan Sanctuaries*, p. 176. For the discussion on the name of country and tribe with consideration of the role of the river in their etymology (on the example of Glomače and Ślężanie) see below in this chapter p. 150.

94 Jerzy Nalepa, "Głomacz," in SSS, vol. 2, p. 111; *idem*, "Głomacze," in SSS, vol. 2, p. 111; Leciejewicz, ">>In Pago", p. 128: Altlommatsch, near Meissen; Słupecki, *Slavonic Pagan Sanctuaries*, p. 165; Andrzej Wędzki, "Gana," in SSS, vol. 2, p. 79. According to scholars near the spring there was the capital of the tribe – Gana, devastated during the 928/929 fights (it was hypothetically identified with the Burgberg stronghold).

95 This ascertainment remains in agreement with the Early Christian tradition in which pagan miracles were associated with peculiarities, performances, and was treated as a "wonder", and at the same time, as it was emphasized by St. Augustine, these unusual

THE RELIGION OF THE SLAVS IN THIETMAR'S CHRONICLE 59

life of the Daleminzi, which suggests that they practiced religious syncretism (dual faith).

2.2   *On Afterlife*

Thietmar – having mentioned the death of his great grandfathers in the Battle of Lenzen in 929[96] – continued his story with a very clear message: "That no one faithful to Christ may doubt the future resurrection of the dead, but rather proceed to the joy of blessed immortality, zealously, and through holy desire ..."[97] After referring to a number of miraculous events confirming the existence of the afterlife,[98] the chronicler finished the digression with a didactic and at the same time apologetic argument on the matter.[99] Here, among his adversaries, were also the Slavs: "to the illiterate, and especially to the Slavs who think that everything ends with the temporal death, I say these things announcing the certainty of the resurrection and future remuneration for the quality of merits to all faithful."[100] A subsequent argument on types of souls, aimed at persuading readers that the afterlife exists, was taken by the chronicler from St. Gregory's *Dialogues.*[101]

By citing this authority, Thietmar did not hide his conviction of his own erudition and defined his mission as a teacher: he claimed he was a "whetstone" which does not sharpen himself but sharpens iron. He used this Horatian metaphor with an explanation that he did not want to become a "mute dog" when

---

  signs attributed to pagan deities obliged people to worship them, see Marian Rusecki, *Cud w myśli chrześcijańskiej* (Lublin: Towarzystwo Naukowe KUL, 1991), pp. 55–58.

96 Thietmar I, 10.

97 Trans. D.A. Warner in: *Ottonian Germany*, p. 75; cf. Thietmar I, 11: "Ut nullus Christo fidelium de futura mortuorum resurrectione diffidat, sed ad beatae immortalitatis gaudia anhelanter per sancta proficiscatur desideria ..."

98 Thietmar I, 11–13. Cf. Schulmeyer-Ahl, *Der Anfang*, pp. 75 f. The concept treating manifestation of the deceased as the proof of soul immortality was borrowed by Thietmar from Book IV of Gregory the Great's *Dialogues* – see Thietmar, p. 23, footnote 67; cf. Berthold Altaner, Alfred Stuiber, *Patrologia. Życie, pisma i nauka Ojców Kościoła*, trans. Paweł Pachciarek (Warszawa: Instytut Wydawniczy PAX, 1990) [orig. *Patrologie: Leben, Schriften und Lehre der Kirchenväter* (Freiburg, 1966)], p. 611.

99 This part of narration follows the same scheme as the New Testament, in which proclaiming creeds of faith was connected with descriptions of miracles confirming them.

100 Thietmar, I, 14, p. 23: "inlitteratis et maxime Sclavis, qui cum morte temporali omnia putant finiri, haec loquor, certitudinem resurreccionis et pro qualitate meriti futurae remunerationis firmiter indicens cunctis fidelibus". This place is an interesting example of the chronicler's autocreation as a bishop and teacher (however, it is difficult to assume reading the word "loquor" that he addressed his work to the illiterate and the Slavs). See also Schulmeyer-Ahl, *Der Anfang*, p. 104.

101 Gregory the Great, *Dialogi*, IV, 3 – see: Thietmar, p. 23, footnote 67.

60   CHAPTER 2

views contradicting the church doctrine were spread around the world.[102] This
comparison to a dog is far from any reference to paganism in this case,[103] and
one has to take into account here the whole phrase "mute dog" (*mutus canis*),
which in the Bible – it is not mentioned in the editions of the chronicle –
denotes lazy prophets who are not faithful to their vocation. This was the
meaning in which it appeared in patristic literature as well.[104] In this context
the phrase "mute dog" used by Thietmar means a bishop who neglects teaching his people.[105]

Listing the Slavs among *inlitterati* that opposed one of the fundamental
dogmas of the ecclesiastical *credo* at yet another instance confirms Thietmar's
conviction that the Slavs were unruly by nature and difficult to convert.[106] Yet,
claiming that they questioned the afterlife has raised discussions among scholars for generations. However, there is one issue on which scholars all agree:
with the available information, it is not possible to prove that the Slavs had
no belief in the afterlife.[107] The principal premise in this matter is the very

---

102   Thietmar I, 14: "Etsi ego fungar vice cotis, ferrum et non se exacuentis, tamen, ne muti
      canis obprobrio noter ..."; cf. Horace, *De arte poetica*, v. 304 – see Thietmar, p. 23, footnote
      66; Lippelt, *Thietmar von Merseburg*, p. 82.

103   For *canes* as a topos in medieval literature with reference to the Slavs, see below pp. 291 f.

104   Unworthy shepherds are mentioned in the Book of Isaiah (Isa 56:10), which is mentioned
      also by St. Ambrose see: Dorothea Forstner, *Świat symboliki chrześcijańskiej*, trans. Paweł
      Pachciarek, Ryszard Turzyński, Wanda Zakrzewska (Warszawa: PAX, 1990) [orig. *Die Welt
      der christlichen Symbole* (Innsbruck, 1977)], pp. 293 f.

105   Forstner, *Świat*, pp. 293 f.

106   *E.g.* Thietmar, I, 4, when he mentions fire which was to miraculously appear at the place
      of the martyrdom of Aaron the bishop of Würzburg and his companions, he emphasizes
      that "sanctos Dei martires hos esse nec Sclavi dubitant", which makes us realize that ex-
      actly the Slavs, in the chronicler's view, are a good example of people who are stubborn
      and oppose the Christian religion. Similarly when he discusses Boso's missionary efforts
      (see below, pp. 73–75) he stressed their futility in the face of the ill will of the people to be
      converted. One could ask if the chronicler's aversion to the Slavs, emphasized especially
      when describing their opposition to Christianization, is not supported by treating them
      as rebels against the Empire or even by the author's personal grudge. Mentioning Slavic
      lack of faith in the resurrection is a part of an argument directly preceded by information
      about a fight of the Polabian Slavs against their dependence on the Empire, in which both
      of Thietmar's great-grandfathers died.

107   At the current stage of the discussion it is certain that the Slavs believed in the soul's life
      after man's death but a clear difference between the soul and body was no longer clear
      (Stanisław Bylina, *Człowiek i zaświaty. Wizje kar pośmiertnych w Polsce średniowiecznej*
      (Warszawa: Upowszechnianie Nauki-Oświata "UN-O", 1992), p. 8). The soul was associ-
      ated with something invisible (waft, wind) abiding in connection with the body or as its
      apparition (invisible copy of the deceased). It could appear in the world of the living as
      a phantom, *e.g.* as a double of the deceased and also as a ghost, or at last – following the
      ethnographic material – animals (insects, birds, *etc.*), see Kazimierz Moszyński, *Kultura*

THE RELIGION OF THE SLAVS IN THIETMAR'S CHRONICLE   61

universality of the conviction that it existed (usually in relation to the afterlife of souls) and the significance of these views in religious systems on a
world scale.[108]

Thus one may either say that the chronicler made a mistake, or tried to explain what made him give such an opinion with a very probable assumption
that he had knowledge of the notions of uneducated classes of people in his
environment.[109] Therefore, scholars have focused on understanding the reason
for why Thietmar treated Slavic beliefs in such a way, especially considering his
Christian worldview. Secondly, scholars have wondered which particular Slavic
(native) views could be interpreted by the chronicler in such a radical way,
which was very accurately described by Stanisław Urbańczyk half a century
ago, who claimed that Thietmar's opinion "was caused either by his resent for
paganism or by the difference between Christian and pagan views."[110]

The basis for this very general assessment was also formed by the views of
outstanding pioneers of Slavic studies. For example, Lubor Niederle claimed
that Thietmar's intention was to show that the Slavs did not believe in the resurrection and recompense for this life.[111] However, Aleksander Brückner went
even further in his speculations and suggested that Thietmar, by attributing
the Slavs' faith in the death of the soul, meant their "own" Slavic soul, and not
the immortal "Christian" soul.[112] This idea was rightly questioned by Henryk
Łowmiański, who noted that the chronicler clearly explained the Church's doctrine of one soul in every person in the above mentioned reference to Gregory
the Great's treatise.[113]

On the other hand, in the message "cum morte temporali omnia (...) finiri"
("everything ends with the temporal death"), Łowmiański himself wanted to
find a reflection of the archaic Indo-European faith substrate, or more precisely

---

ludowa Słowian, vol. 2, part 1 (Warszawa: Wiedza Powszechna, 1967 [1st ed. 1936]), on soul
by the index.

108   "The cult of the ancestors was so common everywhere that the Slavdom would be a peculiar island requiring explanations" – Urbańczyk, *Dawni Słowianie*, p. 57 [first edition
1947]. The author referred here to Czech and Polish medieval historiography. See also
Bylina, *Człowiek*, pp. 7 f.; idem, *Kultura ludowa Polski i Słowiańszczyzny średniowiecznej*
(Warszawa: Mazowiecka Wyższa Szkoła Humanistyczno-Pedagogiczna, 1999), pp. 12 f.

109   One should take into account that Thietmar working as a priest of the Sorbian people
understood their speech and knew their views from first-hand experience, see above.

110   Urbańczyk, *Dawni Słowianie*, p. 57.

111   Lubomír Niederle, *Život starych Slovanů*, vol. 2, part 1 (Praha: Bursík & Kohout, 1924),
pp. 38 f.; the same Kazimierz Tymieniecki, *Społeczeństwo Słowian Lechickich* (Lwów: K.S.
Jakubowski, 1928), p. 39.

112   Brückner, *Mitologia słowiańska i polska*, p. 174.

113   Łowmiański, *Religia*, p. 142.

62   CHAPTER 2

faith in the "live corpse" (*defunctus vivus*),[114] which was to manifest itself after death until its body was decomposed. However, this idea seems mistaken – the "living corpse" has an element of life, so in this case not everything is finished. Moreover, the appearance of the deceased in this part of the work[115] was used as proof of the soul's immortality, thus it is hard to defend the position that Thietmar understood the phenomena in any other way in the case of possible faith among the "illiterate" (including the Slavs).[116]

A. Gieysztor has offered a different approach: "the conceptual range of the spirit and soul among the Slavs is wide: beside soul-self and soul-life, *i.e.* breath, so definitions of the state of one's own psychological awareness and life force, there is the soul-phantom. It is an image – an apparition, a nightmare or shadow, a copy of a man when he was still alive, in reference to the deceased he was called more directly a 'dead man' (in Polish: with compassion as the word "nieboszczyk" originally means "unfortunate", "not rich"). After death this image disappears in the wind, but it can return, eat and drink, and eventually

---

114   On the same matter *e.g.* Moszyński, *Kultura*, pp. 588 and 655; Edward Potkowski, *Dziedzictwo Wierzeń pogańskich w średniowiecznych Niemczech. Defuncti vivi* (Warszawa: Wydawnictwo Uniwersytetu Warszawskiego, 1973), p. 7 *et passim.*; see also Urbańczyk, *Dawni Słowianie*, pp. 114, 159; Sergey A. Tokarev, *Pierwotne formy religii i ich rozwój*, trans. Mirosław Nowaczyk (Warszawa: Książka i Wiedza, 1969) [orig. *Rannie formy religii i ikh razvitie* (Moskva, 1964)], p. 169. In the development of beliefs, the motif of a "living corpse" was to precede a conviction of the existence of a paradigm of the world of the dead in the form of the Greek Hades or the Biblical Sheol.

115   See Thietmar I, 12.

116   Thus H. Łowmiański's argument loses its topicality (*Religia*, p. 142), its goal was explanation of the alleged antinomy in the text of Thietmar's chronicle, who in another place mentions that Slavic widows were killed to "follow their husbands" meaning following them to the world of the dead. H. Łowmiański claimed that "a critique of Thietmar's text allows the recognition of two contradicting pieces of information: 1) about the death of the soul with the body, 2) about survival of the soul after the death of a body. Only the latter has wide, independent of Thietmar, support in sources, however this does not mean that the first one did not reflect Slavic beliefs." To clarify the way both of these concepts functioned in the culture of old Slavs, Łowmiański proposed a solution based on taking into consideration the evolution of beliefs. And so the conviction of the "living corpse" was to be set in the oldest layer while a view of separation of the fate of the decomposing body and the soul migrating to the beyond was to represent a later stage of beliefs. Rus' sources prove that souls of the dead stayed in the living world, and one should remember that there was an alternative place for souls in the underworld kingdom of the dead. This is why possibilities of parallel functioning of both of these views on the afterlife in the environment of the newly Christianised Slavs should not be questioned, however, at the same time it is not possible to verify the idea that both views were taken into account by Thietmar (at least for the reason that there are no premises that he tried to explain these kind of subtleties in the presentation of religious images which were strange to him).

THE RELIGION OF THE SLAVS IN THIETMAR'S CHRONICLE   63

depart to the beyond where it dwells."[117] The world of the dead, which was
most probably ruled by Veles, was to be achieved by souls after crossing a far-
away river, which was confirmed in burial customs.[118] Concluding this part of
his considerations, Gieysztor made one more attempt to explain the sense of
the chronicler's statement: "There was a common uncertainty among the Slavs
connected with the place where souls abide after death; in the old Rus' this
place was called 'nevedomaja strana' [*i.e.* unknown land – S.R.]. Thietmar of
Merseburg even supposed that the Slavs thought that 'the worldly death was
the end of everything.'"[119]

   Stanisław Bylina also noticed that there are numerous indications that the
reconstructed reality of the Slavic world of the dead was far from being coherent and consistent,[120] which is in opposition to widely held views on religion
in general.[121] In this situation one should take into account the possibility of
changes in views concerning the afterlife of souls during the decline of pre-
Christian religion among the Slavs, and the "unknown" or "foreign country"
(*nevedomaja* or *čužaja strana*) known from Rus' may be a trace of the disappearance of the original spatial images of the beyond.[122] However, the very
existence of the remains of Slavic beliefs and images of the afterlife in sources

---

117   Gieysztor, *Mitologia*, p. 259; see also Moszyński, *Kultura*, pp. 584 ff.
118   Moszyński, *Kultura*, pp. 597 f. emphasizes that the Slavs knew about a universal view
      (America, Asia, Europe) that in the limits of the worldly universe there were rivers.
      Because of this image there was a custom of building footbridges over a stream in Belarus
      or a belief in crossing a ford after death. In Rus' and the Balkans there was also the Charon's
      obol motif (*ibidem*, p. 655). Łowmiański, *Religia*, pp. 69 f. claims, however, that the motif
      of the peripheral river across which souls of the deceased had to go paying "an obol", first
      reached the southern Slavs and later the northern Slavs, which solves the riddle of its
      origin, after Christianization, because in the 10th c. linen patches were used to pay, and
      not ore. One cannot exclude, however, that reception of antique mythology was based on
      a native custom which was only modified. This indicates that there was possibly a native
      belief in the underworld kingdom from the Lithuanian myth of Sovi, which according to
      A. Brückner (Aleksander Brückner, *Starożytna Litwa. Ludy i bogi. Szkice historyczne i mito-
      logiczne*, ed. Jan Jaskanis (Olsztyn: Pojezierze, 1979), pp. 65 f. and 70 f.) received the Slavic
      form of the underworld, inhabited by ancestors called *vele* (sing. *vel*), a grey, dark world
      without green, sun and living people. See also Bylina, *Kultura*, pp. 16–19.
119   Gieysztor, *Mitologia*, p. 252; cf. Bylina, *Kultura*, p. 15. Łowmiański, *Religia*, p. 142, concludes
      similarly: "... Thietmar's enigmatic remark about another obligation of the soul in future
      life without even an explanation, proves no clear idea of this world, and thus lack of inter-
      est in it." However, referring the remark on "other obligation of the soul" to the Slavs does
      not seem right – see below, pp. 69 f.
120   Bylina, *Człowiek*, p. 31.
121   Being a system, religions usually consistently describe the world and the beyond.
122   Stanisław Bylina, "Problemy słowiańskiego świata zmarłych. Kategorie przestrzeni i
      czasu," *Światowit* 40 (1995), pp. 9–12.

64   CHAPTER 2

suggests that some time ago they were a part of consistent systems. However, their structure must have turned out to be so weak in confrontation with Christianity that it was nearly completely destroyed,[123] leaving only a trace in the folk culture after Christianization.[124]

In the scholarly attempts to reconstruct the model of the Slavic world of the dead, there is a striking dominance of its pessimistic visions.[125] Even A. Brückner, while making a comparative study with religion among the Balts, saw the Slavic underworld called the *nawia* as the domain of shadows, "without the sun and warmth, without food or drink ...," which was ruled by Veles. The deceased ancestors allegedly appeared among living ones in the spring and autumn, to be fed, washed, and kept warm ...[126] Such a vision of the afterlife makes it a kind of imitation of earthly life and is connected with the existence of an opinion that there were contacts between both worlds.[127]

Searching for analogies to the Slavic world of the dead, Brückner's contemporary – Mikołaj Rudnicki, indicated the heritage of the Ancient Hellada: "This compliance must represent the Indo-European belief which is very old and in contrast to the Germanic one: the Lechitic, or Slavic beyond is sad and empty, without food and drink, without sun and warmth, similar to

---

123   The poor development of Slavic eschatology, which was considered a fact on the basis of written sources, was seen as the reason for easy, as devoid of strong competition, reception of faith in God's judgement, salvation or eternal perdition, brought by Christianity (Łowmiański, *Religia*, p. 360).

124   Similarly Bylina, *Człowiek*, p. 31.

125   In the scholarly debate on the Slavic world of the dead in the Arabic source of Ibn-Fadlan about burial customs of Rus' people it was taken into account that they had an optimistic vision of the beyond as heaven. This evidence was thought to be an isolated case not creditworthy due to the fact that the Slavs were attributed elements of eschatology which was strange to them, see Łowmiański, *Religia*, p. 143; Bylina, *Człowiek*, p. 14. It was indicated that at best there was a possibility that this heaven-related element was more archaic and referred to the Indo-European myth, in which one of the gods tends souls of the dead in a meadow (one should remember here the role of cattle in the life of the early medieval Slavs) – see *idem*, *Problemy*, pp. 16 f. At the current stage of discussion the Slavic identification of the then Rus' raises significant doubts (see Władysław Duczko, *Viking Rus: Studies on the Presence of Scandinavians in Eastern Europe*, (The Northern World, v) 12 (Boston/Leiden: Brill, 2004)), thus usefulness of this source in research on the religion of the Slavs is decreasing. Even if one assumes that at that stage the Rus' people were Slavicised, it is highly probable that their eschatological imagery was not changed and they even permeated to Slavic circles in which they existed.

126   Brückner, *Mitologia słowiańska i polska*, pp. 53, 259; see also under, p. 65, footnote 129. H. Łowmiański shared this view in *Religia*, p. 144.

127   S. Bylina strengthened this thesis in reference to various dimensions of life (family, society) furthermore extending source documentation by adding folk sources. Bylina, *Człowiek*, pp. 21 ff.

THE RELIGION OF THE SLAVS IN THIETMAR'S CHRONICLE 65

the Greek Elysium. The Germanic world of the dead has a different nature and contains other, non-Indo-European imagery elements."[128] In this interpretation, making offerings to the dead does not support the thesis of the wellbeing of the world beyond or the afterlife, and – to the contrary – it proves that the deceased in the kingdom of Nyja (identified with Pluto), located on the peripheries of the cosmos, did not have any reward for their earthly life and needed offerings made by their descendants.[129]

Death in this perspective equates to the Slavic word 'nycie' – disappearance, drying out, perishing, dying.[130] According to K.T. Witczak, exactly "this type of image related to the fate after death among the Polabian Slavs is confirmed at the beginning of the 11th c. by the German chronicler Thietmar, when he writes that the Slavs believe that life ends after death. There is no need to negate it (...), or interpret it in any extreme way that the Slavs did not have any imagery of the world of the dead."[131] Such an assessment seems to be really close to Thietmar's text, but there is a question about the completeness of its conformance. The source, regardless of interpretation and whether it is extreme or not, clearly states that the Slavs thought that the death of earthly life was the end of everything.

---

128   Mikołaj Rudnicki, "Bóstwa lechickie," *Slavia Occidentalis* 5 (1926), p. 383; cf. Krzysztof T. Witczak, "Ze studiów nad religią Prasłowian. Część 2: Prapolska Nyja a grecka Enyo," *Slavia Occidentalis* 51 (1994), p. 126 f.

129   Cf. Urbańczyk, *Dawni Słowianie*, pp. 158 f. It is possible that instead of the whole property, only a coin was put into a grave – Józef Kostrzewski, *Kultura prapolska* (Poznań: Instytut Zachodni, 1947), pp. 330 f., although this custom should more probably be identified with ancient Greek or Roman infiltration in folk beliefs at the time of the Christianization of the Slavs.

130   Witczak, "Ze studiów," p. 126 (the author referred here to Rudnicki's research conducted in 1930s, speculating on connections between the Greek Enyo and the alleged old Polish Nyja). Brückner, *Mitologia słowiańska i polska*, p. 149, indicated an analogy in Lithuanian mythology where there was information on *vele* (ancestors) headed by Veles the ruler of *navia* – a shady place where *vele* abode. *Ibidem*, p. 259: "In their [*i.e. vele* – S.R.] underworld there was no sun or warmth, no food or drink, so ancestors' spirits would appear in spring and autumn to be washed, heated, fed and given a drink; the ones who neglected this were exposed to vindictive wrath. This grey state of shadows, which was maybe ruled by Veles, was called *navia*; collective name *navie* meant specters." *Navia* corresponds with imagery of afterlife – 'unava', 'unynie', 'nyć' means 'longing, boredom, tiredness'; cf. Urbańczyk, *Dawni Słowianie*, pp. 116, 159. The motif of the "living corpse" belongs to this trend, it would visit living people searching for lost people and property. Although in this case the end of human existence would be connected with the final decomposition of the body and would rather be a more archaic conviction than the mythology it preceded and maybe partly gave rise to.

131   Witczak, "Ze studiów," p. 127.

66   CHAPTER 2

It is noticeable that in the scholarly discussion about Thietmar's opinion
there is a need to find a grain of truth, with a simultaneous assumption that
its literal meaning is unacceptable.[132] That is why the basic postulate coming
from the previous attempts at exegesis directs the research to "the author's
world," so as to find in this area an explanation for why such opinions could
be expressed by the chronicler. The basic indication in this case was the worldview controversy between the elites and large groups of illiterate and uneducated people (*inlitterati*). It was exactly them to whom, *expressis verbis*, the
chronicler attributed the opinion that the end of earthly life was the end of
everything.

In the definition of the premises that influenced Thietmar's opinion,
the marking of the social range of these *inlitterati* in his account is of key
importance.[133] In the Middle Ages, in Western Europe the term *illiterate* – also
called *idioti, simplices, rudes* – were used to refer to a great majority of the society, which was confronted with a relatively small group of literate people, *i.e.*
literati who were usually clergymen.[134] It is important to mention that the *illiterati* encompassed not only those who were actually illiterate but also those
who could not prove their high erudition. This is why some clergy were also
considered *illiterati*.[135]

However, in the case of Thietmar's analyzed reference, this model of social
division is not fully adequate, because marking a boundary between *litterati*

---

132   The knowledge on the matters related to death in the religion of the Old Slavs can be
       extended by analysis of burial rites and objects left in graves; for reflection on burial rites
       and objects found in graves see Leciejewicz, *Słowianie*, pp. 117 ff. and also below pp. 176 ff.

133   H. Łowmiański (*Religia*, pp. 141) mentioned that among skeptics questioning the afterlife
       there were also Germans, however, the skeptics were mainly the Slavs. This direction in
       reflection turns attention away from the chronicler's intention, who focuses mainly on
       the circle of *inlitterati* and views functioning in it, and not on ethnic relations.

134   See *e.g.* Cf. Ernst Robert Curtius, *Literatura europejska i łacińskie średniowiecze*, trans.
       Andrzej Borowski (Kraków: Universitas, 1997) [orig. *Europäische Literatur und lateinisch-
       es Mittelalter* (Bern, 1948)], p. 31; Jacques Le Goff, *Kultura średniowiecznej Europy*, trans.
       Hanna Szumańska-Gross (Warszawa: Volumen, 1994) [orig. *La civilisation de l'Occident
       médiéval* (Paris, 1964)], p. 17. See also: Herbert Grundmann, "Litteratus – illiteratus," *Archiv
       für Kulturgeschichte* 40 (1958), pp. 1–65.

135   For example Cosmas of Prague accused Boleslaw II the Pious's brother, Strachkvas
       (Kristián), that he represented such attitude: he knew the alphabet but neglected theolo-
       gical studies. *Cosmae Pragensis Chronica Boemorum*, ed. Bertold Bretholz, MGH SSrerGerm
       n.s. 2 (1923) [further: Cosmas], I, 30. "A real literate person was *sacris litteris eruditus* – he
       knew sacral literature, especially the *Bible*" – Jerzy Dowiat, "Krąg uczony i jego instytucje,"
       in *Kultura Polski średniowiecznej X–XIII w.*, ed. Jerzy Dowiat (Warszawa: PIW, 1985), p. 252,
       the autor refers in this context to Cosmas's sentence, I, 22: "sacris litteris erudita" (about
       Mlada – Boleslaw II the Czech's sister). Cf. Herbert Grundmann, "Litteratus – illiteratus,"
       pp. 3 f.

and *inlitterati* (*illitterati*) is not connected with belonging to the clergy or having the ability to read, but rather the basic criterion in this respect was participation in the culture of the written word (the *Bible* and literature read at schools). It could also be only listening (*e.g.* sermons in church) and as a result accepting the rudiments of the church doctrine.[136] Thus scripture and oral tradition were identification signs of opposing worldviews, while individual ability or inability to read was not a sole determining factor of belonging to one of them.[137]

In the light of Thietmar's work, the pastoral activity of teaching the truths of the Christian faith was considered a panacea for the ignorance of the "illiterate."[138] The chronicler did not mention there the pre-Christian genesis of the views he opposed. It must have been obvious for him – he himself had to face the challenge of converting Sorbs tribes, just as the members of his own diocese and his predecessors did.[139] He also witnessed the renaissance of native cults among his neighbours in the North-Polabian (Elbslavs) territories. However, in neither case did the chronicler treat the Slavs as pagans, which was due to the peculiarity of the contemporary missionary theology, shown in other places of his work; in that interpretation *e.g.* the Elbslavs rebelling against the Empire were considered apostates-pagans.[140]

---

136 For "oral literacy" see *e.g.* Edward Potkowski, *Książka i pismo w średniowieczu. Studia z dziejów kultury piśmiennej i komunikacji społecznej* (Pułtusk: Akademia Humanistyczna im. Aleksandra Gieysztora, 2006), p. 23 f. (there is also literature on the matter).

137 It is worth mentioning that oral tradition elements occur very often in works written by medieval erudites, which is very important for the reconstruction of pre-Christian and folk beliefs. Meanwhile radical opposition of the literate circle and the "folk" one occurring in earlier studies, *a priori* eliminated this direction of research, because one did not expect such traces in church culture works – see: Padberg, "Geschichtsschreibung," p. 177; cf. Staats, "Missionsgeschichte Nordeuropas," pp. 13, 30.

138 This conviction must have also been reinforced by reading the Bible, *e.g.* the Book of Hosea (Hos 4: 6).

139 Mentioning the soul's fate after death by Thietmar may be a reflection of a pre-baptismal catechesis, which he gave himself or recommended to be given in the territory of his diocese. The pre-baptismal catechesis encompassed truths recommended by St. Augustin in *De catechizandis rudibus*: soul immortality, judgement, reward and punishment, Holy Trinity, the Saviour and the Last Judgment. It is clearly seen that these issues encompass the afterlife of man. See *e.g.*: Zygmunt Sułowski, "Pierwszy Kościół polski," in *Chrześcijaństwo w Polsce. Zarys przemian 966–1979*, ed. Jerzy Kłoczowski (Lublin: Towarzystwo Naukowe KUL, 1992), p. 31 f.; cf. Marian Rechowicz, "Początki i rozwój kultury scholastycznej (do końca XIV wieku)," in *Dzieje teologii katolickiej w Polsce*, ed. Marian Rechowicz, vol. 1: *Średniowiecze* (Lublin: Towarzystwo Naukowe KUL, 1974), p. 24; Jerzy Wolny, "Z dziejów katechezy," in *Dzieje teologii katolickiej w Polsce*, ed. Marian Rechowicz, vol. 1: *Średniowiecze* (Lublin: Towarzystwo Naukowe KUL, 1974), p. 169.

140 See below, pp. 80 f., 160 f. (footnote 528).

68   CHAPTER 2

By including the Slavs in the circle of *inlitterati* in the passage, Thietmar did not refer to this kind of categorization, but he appreciated confrontation in the dimension of mental culture. His attitude toward the *inlitterati* reflects influence of a mental trend, still up-to-date in the 9th–11th c. in monastic circles, which grew from the experience of propagators of Christianity who acted in earlier times in the Germanic territories. These missionaries promoted a system of values in a context where knowledge was transferred orally, and where paganism, tribal community and the world of nature were in opposition to the higher valued literacy, Christianity, and culture that was created with strong participation of the clergy.[141]

Moreover, in openly confronting the views of the "illiterate," Thietmar indirectly indicated that even after the abolition of tribal power structures and the related institution of cults (which was taking place in his times in southern Polabia), the other carriers of pre-Christian culture were still alive, with oral tradition playing the leading role. Hence the eradication of pre-Christian religious views from social space could take place, just like in the passage, not under the banner of confrontation with paganism or demonic powers, but counteracting the ignorance related to fundamental truths of the Christian credo.

Thus in attempting to explain the genesis of Thietmar's statement about the Slavs – *omnia (putant) finiri etc.* – one should first take into account the Christian doctrine on life after death, which was considered normative by the author.[142] An important element in this way of reasoning was automatic connection between the afterlife and immortality, whose threshold is the judgement of merits (or sins) and resurrection. This way of thinking was strange to non-Christianized people or those having only very superficial knowledge of the dogmas of the new religion.

The discussed passage, when read with consideration for ecclesiastical or theological categories, clarifies two matters: 1) the Slavs do not believe in repayment after death for what they did in their lifetime and 2) they do not believe

---

141   Françoise Hiraux, "Les vitae des évangelisateurs, schema de projects et de quotidiennetés," in *La vie quotidienne des moines et chanoines réguliers au Moyen Age et Temps modernes, Actes du Premier Colloque International du L.A.R.H.C.O.R. Wrocław – Książ, 30 novembre–4 decembre 1994*, vol. 2, ed. Marek Derwich (Wrocław: Institut d'histoire de l'Université de Wrocław, 1995), pp. 425–438; see also Padberg, "Christen," pp. 291 f. This trend becomes visible in the chronicles of Adam of Bremen and Helmold, where the mission ideology is of major significance – see below, pp. 241, 255, 257, 294.

142   Thietmar I, 14: "... haec loquor, certitudinem resurreccionis et pro qualitate meriti futurae remunerationis firmiter indicens cunctis fidelibus" ("... I say these things announcing the certainty of the resurrection and future remuneration for the quality of merits to all faithful").

THE RELIGION OF THE SLAVS IN THIETMAR'S CHRONICLE   69

in resurrection. In fact there is consensus among scholars when it comes to
both of these matters, as they assume that pre-Christian Slavs did not believe
that moral merits of the deceased influenced their life after death,[143] and furthermore, especially in the light of comparative studies, there are the premises
to claim that Slavs did not have any concept of resurrection as well.[144]

Additional information about Slavic beliefs in Thietmar's work may be a
part of a theological commentary used as argumentation against them,[145] such
as St. Gregory's reasoning about souls recalled by the chronicler.[146] "For there
are three [kinds of] souls which do not begin equally and do not end simultaneously. The first one [is that] of the incorporeal angels which exists with them
without beginning and end; the second one [is that] of the humans which begins with them but does not partake of the end, since it is immortal and, as
some heathens think, it does not have that function in the future which [it
has] in our age; the third kind are the souls of cattle and birds which experience the equal share in fate with body both with regard to the beginning and
end."[147] Thus a question arises of which of the quoted statements should show
the absurdity of the views of Slavs.

H. Łowmiański treated them as these *quidam gentiles*, who think that
"in the afterlife their souls have another role (*officium*) than in earthly life."[148]
Following this line, Łowmiański faced the necessity of defending his stance by
speculating that on the pages of the chronicle very near to each other, there are
two contradictory views: the first about the annihilation of the soul by death
and the second about its continuing existence in the afterlife. To explain this
paradox, he proposed to find references to the two different layers of Slavic

---

143 *E.g.* Bruno Meriggi, "Die Anfänge des Christentums bei den Baltischen Slaven," in
     Annales Instituti Slavici 6 (1969–1970): *Das heidnische und christliche Slaventum*, vol. 2
     (Wiesbaden: Harrassowitz, 1970), p. 49; Łowmiański, *Religia*, p. 235; Urbańczyk, *Dawni
     Słowianie*, p. 158; Bylina, *Człowiek*, p. 42.

144 The idea of resurrection as an element of a new eschatological reality, characteristic for
     Christianity, does not find its counterpart in the circle of Indo-European peoples' beliefs
     (and thus also the Slavic ones before Christianization) referring to cyclical reintegration
     of the cosmos.

145 Even A. Brückner tried to use this commentary, however, to no success, which is shown in
     further discussion of scholars – see above.

146 Lippelt, *Thietmar von Merseburg*, pp. 82 f.

147 Thietmar I, 14, p. 23: "Tres namque sunt animae, non equaliter incipientes nec simul
     finientes. Prima angelorum incorporeorum, quae cum eis est sine inicio et termino; II
     hominum, quae cum eis sumit exordium, sed in fine non habens participium, namque
     inmortalis est, et ut quidam gentiles opinantur, in futuro non habens hoc offitium, quod
     in hoc seculo; tercia species est animae pecudum et volatilium, quae cum corpore parem
     inicii finisque sortitur equalitatem".

148 As in footnote 113 in this chapter.

70   CHAPTER 2

beliefs in both places of the chronicle. Such a hypothesis is doubtful, however, because it breaks the logical coherence of the chronicler's account: the statement taken from the *Dialogues* is a commentary on the view that everything ends with the end of temporary life, including also the life of a soul, hence it is hard to think that information about its role (*officium*) after death could relate to the Slavs.[149] Thus the question of which part of the quoted commentary refers to their specific beliefs remains unanswered, and an interesting possibility of the hypothetical reply is provided by a reference to a third type of souls mentioned in St. Gregory's commentary.

If, according to the Slavs, death was to mean the total annihilation of human existence, then one has to assume, that from their perspective in terms of the afterlife, people did not differ from animals whose souls were to finish their lives at the time of their earthly death. The very proclamation of the death of the soul is presented in this case by the chronicler's alleged deduction based on an encounter with a belief that there is no significant difference between animal and human souls.[150] For comparison it is worth referring at least to the account of Master Vincent, called Kadłubek, confirming that the Prussians believed in the transmigration of souls which could emigrate to animal bodies.[151] Thus it is also possible that similar images were not alien in the Slavic world.[152]

However, whether Thietmar encountered such pagan views on the soul cannot be unambiguously determined, especially since the simple explanation of a hypothetical "animalization" of human existence may be not a reference to Slavic beliefs so much as reaching toward the collection of views functioning in the chronicler's intellectual environment. Most certainly the radical view that a lack of knowledge of the Creator reduces the human being to an animal state was not strange to him.[153] When elaborating on these kinds of speculation, one should not forget that they ascend to at least the third floor of

---

149   Thietmar did not define the view of the illiterate as typical of paganism because – as it was rightly thought by H. Lippelt – he perceived *quidam gentiles* as educated non-Christian ancient authors. See Lippelt, *Thietmar von Merseburg*, p. 83.

150   Basic arguments related to the so-called primitive cults encompass the view that their followers do not see a clear difference between an animal, human or divine creature, and the animal creature seems to them to be the basic form – Durkheim, *Elementarne formy*, p. 61.

151   *Magistri Vincentii dicti Kadłubek Chronica Polonorum*, ed. Marian Plezia, MPH n.s. 11 (Kraków: Polska Akademia Umiejętności, 1994), IV, 19. Cf. Szafrański, *Prahistoria*, p. 407.

152   This is possibly supported by zoomorphism of the human soul in Slavic imagery, deduced from contemporary folk beliefs (the human soul was to have a material form of a bee or a bird, although it could also be a misty apparition in white). See Urbańczyk, *Dawni Słowianie*, p. 158.

153   This view occurs in sources from this epoch, see *e.g.* Ebo II, 1.

THE RELIGION OF THE SLAVS IN THIETMAR'S CHRONICLE   71

hypothetical constructions, which resemble a house of cards given such scarce
source information.

Hence there is no other choice but to assume that these suggestions are
a moderately successful interpretation, and so, in this situation one should
first of all consider the possibility that none of the presented variants of the
fate of souls in St. Gregory's commentary were mentioned as a counterpart of
the view imputed by Thietmar of the *inlitterati*. This entire argument could be
the chronicler's reply to their stance as part of a literary creation of his own
image as a bishop and teacher, so as to cultivate the intellectual fallow land
on the same basis as writing on a *tabula rasa*. However, he asked a question
about the fate of man in the afterlife first and foremost from the perspective of
Christian eschatology (judgment, heaven, hell *etc.*), and in this light the Slavic
views could be relatively easily reduced to a conviction that the earthly death
"ends everything."

In this respect, the visions of the Slavic world of the dead painted as the sad
kingdom of Nyja or Veles, a place for souls which were turned into shadow-
phantoms by death and meant disappearance ("nycie", "leaving for nawia",
etc.), could have turned out to be inspirational for the chronicler, which is indicated by the earlier discussed findings of historians of religion.[154] Another
inspiration – certainly less dependable as a hypothesis explaining the genesis
of the discussed Thietmar's information – could be the possible Slavic views
treating the fate of humans and animals in the afterlife in the same way. One
should also take into account a possible crisis of Slavic eschatology, especially
at the time of contact and confrontation with Christianity, the result of which
could be the earlier mentioned uncertainty about the afterlife.[155]

In summary, all these opinions hypothetically pertain to the sphere of beliefs that were interpreted by Thietmar, acting as a representative of the circle
of written culture (*litterati*), as confirming death as the end of all things. Such
a verdict is the effect of the chronicler's theological reflection assessing native Slavic views from the perspective of Christian teachings. Hence, the very
information provided by Thietmar (although laconic and referring to patristic thought) provides more information about his mentality than about pre-
Christian religion. Moreover, the applied category *inlitterati* (but not pagans)
in Thietmar's account indicated a special model of viewing the Slavs. They

---

154   A justification for making grave gifts and also suicides or killings of Slavic wives at their
      husbands' funerals, confirmed by Thietmar, most certainly was based on a Slavic belief
      in a need for support for the deceased in the beyond, however, not in the least heavenly
      ones. See above p. 178.

155   Which is illustrated by the already mentioned motif of *nevedomaja strana* in Rus', *i.e.* an
      unknown country, see before, p. 63.

72   CHAPTER 2

were seen as participants in an environment which co-created the extensive
"illiterate" group in the whole society subdued to Christian power. This view
was created in a particular perspective, as a result of a focus on the Slavic people living in contemporary Germany, and certainly the Magdeburg metropolis
in which the bishop of Merseburg worked.[156]

2.3   Slavic Religiousness in View of Bishop Boso's Mission

Thietmar did what he heralded in the *Prologue* of his chronicle: he described
the lives and achievements of the bishops of Merseburg, which in two cases –
Boso (d. 970) and Wigbert (d. 1009)[157] – resulted in source material that reveals the attitude of the Slavs as they underwent conversion. The first of the
above-mentioned passages, devoted to Boso,[158] casts light on Slavic religiosity
(although it does not inform directly about cult practices).

Boso was to be characterized with exceptional ardour in evangelization of
the Slavic people entrusted to him: "He, in order to teach those entrusted to
him more easily, wrote down the Slavic words and ordered them to chant *Kyrie
eleison* while explaining its usefulness to them."[159] As one can see, Boso not
only explained to the Slavs the benefits of the rites of the new faith, but also
tried to do so in their language. A precise definition of the scope of activities
this missionary was involved in is disputable.

The most optimistic position was taken by researchers who agreed with
Marian Zygmunt Jedlicki's explanation that "Boso wrote the word of God in a
Slavic language."[160] However, a more certain statement seems to be a decision
not to deviate too much from the literal meaning of the text and remained
confined to the opinion that Boso wrote particular Slavic words ("Slavonica
scripserat verba") in a form of a glossary useful in catechesis. Another option
was the recording of particular prayers (especially liturgical ones).[161]

---

156   A different model of such a particular view resulting in comprehensive characteristics
       of Slavic religiosity is observed in Helmold's chronicle. The author uses the Christians –
       Slavs juxtaposition (*Christiani – Slavi*), see below, pp. 363, 383 f.
157   See below, pp. 145 ff.
158   Thietmar II, 36–37.
159   *Ibidem*, II, 37: "Hic ut sibi comissos eo facilius instrueret, Sclavonica scripserat verba et
       eos kirieleison cantare rogavit exponens eis huius utilitatem".
160   Thietmar II, 37 (in the Polish translation, p. 100).
161   Franz Zagiba, *Das Geistesleben der Slawen im Frühen Mittelalter* (Wien/Köln/Graz: Böhlau,
       1971), pp. 123, 141 ff., attributes to Boso extensive activity related to Slavic texts; see also:
       Karlheinz Hengst, "Slawische Sprachstudien im Mittelalter im sächsisch-thüringischen
       Raum," *Zeitschrift für Slawistik* 37 (1992) 3, pp. 397–406; Lübke, *Fremde*, p. 73; Wojciech
       Mrozowicz, "Początki kultury pisma na Słowiańszczyźnie zachodniej," in *Słowiańszczyzna
       w tworzeniu Europy (X–XIII/XIV w)*, ed. Stanisław Rosik (Wrocław: Chronicon, 2008),

THE RELIGION OF THE SLAVS IN THIETMAR'S CHRONICLE   73

For Thietmar, Boso was an example to follow. It is highly probable that the above discussed polemic on the afterlife with the views of people referred to as *inlitterati* (mainly the Slavs) is an echo of the chronicler's catechetical activity – trying to follow in the footsteps of Boso and his preaching. He also learned the Slavic speech in a way which enabled him to make contacts in this language and teach in the environment of the Sorbs staying in his diocese.

This inspires the question about the activity of Thietmar's predecessor and whether the activity took place among already baptized people or whether its goal was leading them to baptism. Both of these options are possible. Thietmar informs that Boso, before becoming a bishop, acted in "the East" – probably also in benefices which belonged to the church in Merseburg – and this mission evidently led to the baptism of people living in church demesne or at least in areas encompassed by the church network.[162] Thus, being a bishop, Boso could continue the (supposed) earlier activity and then his catechesis would also lead to baptism.

The religious mentality of the Sorbs was visible in their reaction to Boso's efforts, who wanted them to memorize and repeat *Kyrie eleison*. In the Christian religiosity of the time, this formula was attributed miraculous, nearly magic power.[163] Hence it is of no surprise that the *Kyrie* was introduced as an elementary prayer, and the measure of its popularity and significance is visible in the fact that after its development it was transformed into native songs, *e.g.* the Czech "Hospodine, pomiluj ny" (God have mercy).[164] According to Thietmar, the Slavs did not appreciate the priest's efforts and especially the benefits related to singing *Kyrie*: "The fools to [their] wickedness jeeringly changed it to

---

pp. 29–42; Dariusz A. Sikorski, *Początki Kościoła w Polsce* (Poznań: Wydawnictwo PTPN, 2012), pp. 263 ff.

162   Thietmar II, 36: "Beneficium autem omne, quod ad aecclesias in Merseburg et in Mimenlevo positas ac ad Thornburg et Kirberge pertinens fuit, antequam ordinaretur, optinuit. Et quia is in oriente innumeram Christo plebem predicacione assidua et baptismate vendicavit, inperatori placuit eleccionemque de tribus constituendis episcopatibus ei dedit, Misnensis, Citicensis atque Merseburgiensis."

163   This was confirmed in the 13th c. by Durandus, see Paweł Sczaniecki, *Służba Boża w dawnej Polsce* (Poznań/Warszawa/Lublin: Księgarnia św. Wojciecha, 1962), p. 52. Various situations in which *Kyrie* was used were documented by Thietmar himself: IV, 20 – when fatally ill; IV 22, p. 175 – in joy after withstanding a siege. See also Jerzy Woronczak, *Studia o literaturze średniowiecza i renesansu* (Wrocław: Wydawnictwo Uniwersytetu Wrocławskiego, 1993), p. 77.

164   *Bogurodzica*, ed. Jerzy Woronczak *et al.* (Wrocław: Ossolineum, 1962), p. 10; Woronczak, *Studia o literaturze*, p. 79. Cf. Leciejewicz, *Słowianie*, p. 213.

ukrivolsa which means in our language: an alder stands in the bush, while they were saying: 'So said Boso' when he [actually] had said it differently."[165]

Although in the replacement of the words *Kyrie eleison* with "ukrivolsa", Thietmar saw maliciousness and the sneering of dull-witted people, the possibilities here for interpretation are much greater. The deformation of the sound *Kyrie* in the Slavic environment was not uncommon and not in the least malicious. If one refers to "Krlessu," mentioned by Cosmas of Prague regarding the events of the year 968,[166] sung by the Czech people, and also the famous "kierlesch" sung by Poles not only during the battle of Grunwald/Tannenberg (1410) but also as early as the mid-13th c. during the battle of Iaroslav with the Rus' dukes, one may also assume that among Slavs catechised by Boso, *Kyrie* received its own special shape, *i.e.* "ukrivolsa," without any perverse intention.[167]

However, adoption of this stance means deviation from the chronicler's opinion (or that of his informers) and requires finding certain adaptations to strange cult activity in the behaviour of the Slavic people. Undoubtedly in this kind of environment, open to magical practices, the prayer *Kyrie* could have been thought to be an incantation and its repetition a mantic practice. This view is supported by the simultaneous repetition of the apposition that such a way of prayer was ordered by Boso, which would be the guarantor of its effectiveness and an intermediary to the sphere of the *sacrum*. Another way of reasoning suggests that the Slavs could fear the wrath of their native deities, and so they added the name of the one who told them to do so.[168] This anxiety could be explained by the phenomenon of double faith, where apart from the new God there was still respect for the efficiency of the activity of earlier deities.[169]

The above interpretations are rather disputable, and there is a strong alternative for them in the opinion of the chronicler himself, which was commented

---

165 Thietmar II, 37, p. 101: "Qui vecordes hoc in malum irrisorie mutabant ukrivolsa, quod nostra lingua dicitur: aeleri stat in frutectum, dicentes: 'Sic locutus est Boso', cum ille aliter dixerit". Cf. Lübke, *Fremde*, p. 73.

166 Cosmas I, 23; see *e.g.* Woronczak, *Studia o literaturze*, pp. 78 f.; Lübke, *Fremde*, p. 73. It is worth emphasizing that the Czech chronicler attributed the creation of the *Krlessu* form to "simple and benighted", while the duke's entourage was to sing "Chrystus kenaido". This allows the assumption that garbling of prayers was, as results also from Thietmar's note, a typical example of the attitude characteristic of uneducated people and treated as a sign of stupidity.

167 Sczaniecki, *Służba*, pp. 51 f.; Woronczak, *Studia o literaturze*, p. 80.

168 In an essayistic perspective, this way of reasoning was undertaken by Zofia Kossak-Szczucka, Zygmunt Szatkowski, *Troja Północy* (Warszawa: Instytut Wydawniczy PAX, 1986), p. 69.

169 Dziewulski, *Postępy*, p. 62.

THE RELIGION OF THE SLAVS IN THIETMAR'S CHRONICLE   75

on in a significant way by P. Sczaniecki: "However, the Slavs did not like this chant and so they garbled it, so it did not make any sense. This does not surprise anyone who developed the right judgement on the tactless behaviour of the Merseburg apostles. Apart from this, one should take into account that the Slavs were attached to their own religious songs. Thus, resistance was unavoidable, especially given that the new teachings were demanding and hard to understand, and its songs too simple and monotonous."[170]

When summarizing these remarks on the description of Boso's activity, one should emphasize that it provides a particular image of the mentality of the Slavs and inspires further investigation of the motifs of the garble of the word *Kyrie*. Moreover, in the precept to repeat the prayer with the missionary's name, one finds an effort to include Boso within the sphere of the *sacrum*, so that he would become a mediator ensuring contact with the so far strange Christian God.[171] One should also take into account the possibility of "familiarizing" the strange (Christian) *sacrum* and the Slavic practice associated with it by attempting to identify some sense (in relation to the very words) in a formula so unclear in its original wording.[172]

This search does not go beyond the sphere of speculations, and so it is still worth emphasizing the conviction of the chronicler that Christian prayers were treated by Slavs with a sneer and a lack of understanding. This confirms a common view that the historiographers of the time showed an aversion to paganism and did not make any effort to understand its essence (at least to start polemic, as it was the case at the time of early-Christian apologetics). However, the case of Boso denies the schematic judgment, so common in 20th c. studies,

---

170   Sczaniecki, *Służba*, p. 50.

171   Similarly in the next century, representatives of the conquered Polabian tribes were to have made an apotheosis offer to the victorious Henry the Lion, so that as their god he could serve his God (see Helmold 1, 84). For discussion see below, pp. 351 f.

172   The possible occurrence of this phenomenon is indicated by an interesting contribution made by Leszek Moszyński, "Staropołabski teonim Tjarnaglofi. Próba nowej etymologii," in *»Tgolí chole Mestró«. Gedenkschrift für R. Olesch*, ed. Renate Lachmann *et al.* (Köln/Wien: Böhlau, 1990), pp. 33–39, especially p. 38, and although the proposed historical background of identification of West Slavic god's name "Tjarnaglofi" with "Thorn-headed" (in Polish: "Cierniogłowy") Christ raises doubts (the author supported this reasoning with an rather indefensible hypothesis put forward by H. Łowmiański on the mechanism of the birth of polytheism not earlier than in 928 as a result of unsuccessful Christianization; for the discussion on the matter see below, pp. 173–176), the etymology and hypothetical mechanism of the behaviour of Christened people certainly deserve attention. Reconstruction of this "other" side of history, *i.e.* the image of Christianity in the eyes of Christened pagans was earlier discussed by *e.g.* Padberg, "Christen," pp. 310–312.

76   CHAPTER 2

that missions in Slavic countries were conducted by priests who did not know the native language of local people.[173]

The activity of the above-mentioned predecessor of Thietmar was the second fundamental stage of Christianization distinguished in connection with St. Augustine's thoughts on missions in the Early Middle Ages – that was leading the entirety of people to voluntary reception of the new teachings and baptism after liquidation of institutional paganism (this was the first of these stages).[174] This type of missiological concept became the subject of debate among scholars on the character of the insurgency of the Polabian Slavs against the rule of the Empire (specifically, the Saxons) in 983.

2.4 Uprising of the Polabian Slavs (983)

The great insurgency of the Polabian Slavs against the Empire in 983 became, in Thietmar's narration, one of the main links in a chain of misfortunes that affected the empire in the times of Otto II as a result of the liquidation of the Merseburg Diocese in 981.[175] According to the chronicler, the direct reason for the uprising[176] was repression of the Slavic peoples paying tribute to the empire by the Margrave of the Northern March Theodoric (d. 985): "The peoples who accepted Christianity paid tribute to kings and emperors, but

---

173   It is essential that this view was based on the theological interpretation of the pagan religion attributed to the clergy. See *e.g.* Jerzy Dowiat, *Chrzest Polski* (Warszawa: Wiedza Powszechna, 1960), pp. 33 f.

174   See *e.g.* Hans-Dietrich Kahl, *Heidenfrage und Slawenfrage im deutschen Mittelalter. Ausgewählte Studien 1953–2008*, (East Central and Eastern Europe in the Middle Ages, 450–1450) 4 (Leiden/Boston: Brill, 2011), pp. 466 f.; *Storia della chiesa*, vol. 4: *Il primo Medievo (VIII–XII secolo)*, ed. Hubert Jedin (Milano: Jaca Book, 1969), p. 318; Rechowicz, "Początki," pp. 20 ff., especially 22 f.

175   See *e.g.* Schulmeyer-Ahl, *Der Anfang*, p. 246 ff. and also below pp. 89 f., footnote 235.

176   Thietmar III, 17–19. For facts see Gerard Labuda, "Powstania Słowian połabskich u schyłku X wieku," *Slavia Occidentalis* 18 (1947), pp. 153–200. Joachim Herrmann, "Der Lutizenaufstand 983. Zu den geschichtlichen Voraussetzungen und den historischen Wirkungen," *Zeitschrift für Archäologie* 18 (1984) 1, pp. 9–17; Wolfgang H. Fritze, "Der slawische Aufstand von 983 – eine Schicksalswende in der Geschichte Mitteleuropas," in *Festschrift der Landesgeschichtlichen Vereinigung für die Mark Brandenburg zu ihrem hundertjährigen Bestehen 1884–1984*, ed. Eckart Henning, Werner Vogel (Berlin: Landesgeschichtliche Vereinigung für die Mark Brandenburg, 1984), pp. 9–55; Lorenz Weinrich, "Der Slawenaufstand von 983 in der Darstellung des Bischof Thietmar von Merseburg," in *Historiographia Mediaevalis. Studien zur Geschichtsschreibung und Quellenkunde des Mittelalters. Festschrift für Franz-Josef Schmale zum 65. Geburtstag*, ed. Dieter Berg, Hans-Werner Goetz (Darmstadt: Wissenschaftliche Buchgesellschaft, 1988), p. 77–87; Kazimierz Myśliński, *Polska wobec Słowian połabskich do końca wieku XII* (Lublin: Wydawnictwo UMCS, 1993), pp. 54 ff.; recently: Paweł Babij, *Wojskowość Słowian Połabskich*, vol. 1 (Wrocław: Chronicon, 2017), pp. 136–138.

THE RELIGION OF THE SLAVS IN THIETMAR'S CHRONICLE   77

as they suffered from duke Theoderic's arrogance, they unanimously took up arms breaking the law."[177] Owing to the publication of the Polish version of the chronicle, a view of its interpreter was widespread that Theodoric's "pride" or "arrogance" (*superbia*) in this context would mean "lawlessness," which was expressed in the oppression of Slavic peasants.[178] However, this type of interpretation disregards the sententious trend which was crucial in Thietmar's work: in his opinion pride was the reason for military defeats, fall of kingdoms, and internal wars.[179]

A more extensive debate was incited among historians by Thietmar's claim that the insurgence of the Veleti, from that moment called the Liutici, took place after the Christianization of these people ("suscepta christianitate").[180] The basis for the chronicler's claim did not have to be any mass conversion on the scale of the whole tribe,[181] because a characteristic feature of missions in Central Europe in the 10th c. was addressing evangelization first of all to the governing elites, and their conversion meant that the whole country was

---

177   Thietmar III, 17: "Gentes, quae suscepta christianitate regibus et inperatoribus tributarie serviebant, superbia Thiedrici ducis aggravate presumpcione unanimi arma commoverant."

178   Jedlicki, "Poglądy," p. 46. The same in the Polish translation of Thietmar III, 17, p. 130.

179   See Thietmar VI, 10; VI, 99; VIII, 23. See also Schulmeyer-Ahl, *Der Anfang*, pp. 285, 291, 302. These chronicler's opinions are in harmony with a wider context of medieval morality, in which *superbia* is indicated as the main and very typical "class-related" sin of feudal lords. Georges Duby, *Czasy katedr. Sztuka i społeczeństwo 980–1420* (Warszawa: PIW, 1986) [orig. *Le temps des cathédrales, l'Art et la Société*, 980–1420 (Paris 1976)], p. 72; Prucnal, "Władca chrześcijański," p. 8.

180   The appearance of the name "Liutici" was an expression of the transformation which took place in the social and political life of the Veleti tribes. Its consequence turned out to be the formation of a supra-tribal community concentrated around the sanctuary in Radogošč that expressed its identity with this new name – *e.g.* Christian Lübke, "The Polabian Alternative. Paganism between Christian Kingdoms," in *Europe around the year 1000*, ed. Przemysław Urbańczyk (Warszawa: DiG, 2001), pp. 379–389; Tomasz Skonieczny, "Od Wieletów do Luciców. W sprawie zmiany tożsamości plemion wieleckich u schyłku X wieku," in *Populi terrae marisque. Prace poświęcone pamięci Profesora Lecha Leciejewicza*, ed. Marian Rębkowski, Stanisław Rosik (Wrocław: Chronicon, 2011) pp. 83–91; Jarosław Sochacki, "Związek Lucicki – między Polską a Cesarstwem do 1002 r.," *Slavia Antiqua* 47 (2006), pp. 26 ff.; Felix Biermann, "Zentralisierungsprozesse bei den nördlichen Elbslawen," in *Zentralisierungsprozesse und Herrschaftsbildung im frühmittelalterlichen Ostmitteleuropa*, ed. Przemysław Sikora, (Studien zur Archäologie Europas) 23 (Bonn: Habelt Verlag, 2014), p. 175.

181   According to Łowmiański, *Religia*, pp. 261 f. the expression "suscepta christianitate" means "mass Christianization", and this is why he accused Thietmar of a lack of credibility, see also below.

considered Christian.[182] However, in the case of the Veleti, before 983 there was most probably no conversion even of the tribal elders.[183] This view is supported not only by a lack of sources, but also by the very success of the rebellion raised in the same year, as well as by the prime of the native cult.

Thus, it should be assumed that the information about the previous Christianization by the insurgent Liutici shows the German clergy's perspective on the dissemination of Christianity, and not so much the advancement of individual conversions of the Slavic people or their positive attitude to the new religion. From this perspective, it was essential to first extend imperial control and the related church network units to areas of the *Barbaricum*. Thus, achieving of expansionist political goals created good conditions for missionary activity. However, it did not mean that such an action would be undertaken.

In an earlier debate among historians, especially Polish ones, the German clergy of the 10th c. was accused of a lack of ardour in the conversion of Slavs, contenting themselves with the establishment of new bishoprics and tributes received by the empire, lay lords, and clergy.[184] It was also taken into account that decisions on undertaking missions were postponed due to the hatred of the Slavic people toward the new rule and its institutions, leaving nobody to want to exacerbate these tones by forcing baptism among the invaded people. This left the matter of mass Christianization to the efforts of clergymen whose

---

182 On the basis of this Thietmar presents the situation in Poland in the times of the first Piasts, he treated this country as a Christian one (see below, pp. 176 f). In this context it is worth mentioning a classical opinion of Aleksander Gieysztor, "Przemiany ideologiczne w państwie pierwszych Piastów a wprowadzenie chrześcijaństwa," in *Początki Państwa Polskiego Księga Tysiąclecia*, vol. 2, ed. Kazimierz Tymieniecki *et al.* (Poznań: PWN, 1962), p. 165: "The Church was interested in the conversion of elites which were treated as *pars pro toto* also because personal experience of individuals was not as important for it as the **mass awareness** [emphasis – S.R.] of large groups of baptized people who were controlled by external discipline. The pressure of political power shaped the intended group attitudes not infrequently using *ad terrorem* measures, as was shown by Thietmar in Poland in the times of Boleslav the Brave. According to the Church, it aroused special responsibility of the ruler for the salvation of his people, without which his own salvation would not be possible". Imputing in the above statement "large groups of baptized people" the phenomenon of "mass awareness" as opposed to "personal experience of an individual" is a certain identification mark of the research methodology which today is rather obsolete.

183 H. Łowmiański, as in footnote 181 in this chapter; Aleksander Gieysztor, "Bemerkungen zur Apostasie in Zentral- und Osteuropa im 10. und 11. Jahrhundert," *Zeitschrift für Archäologie* 18 (1984), p. 5.

184 *E.g.* Kazimierz Tymieniecki, "Państwo polskie w stosunku do Niemiec i cesarstwa średniowiecznego w X wieku." *Początki Państwa Polskiego. Księga Tysiąclecia*, vol. 1, ed. Kazimierz Tymieniecki *et al.* (Poznań: PWN, 1962), p. 290.

THE RELIGION OF THE SLAVS IN THIETMAR'S CHRONICLE   79

activity was often considered exceptional – *e.g.* Boso or Wigbert – or the "natural flow of events."[185]

This type of speculation is marked by (and radicalized by) the trauma of the Second World War – a social debate on the "eternal" hostile attitude of Germans toward the Slavs, in the context of which a view expressed by H. Łowmiański seems to be even stronger, namely that Thietmar's information on the Christianization of the Veleti before 983 was a cliché.[186] As a matter of fact, the chronicler was to focus only on the imposition of tributary obligations on the Slavic tribes, and only this fact was to predetermine whether they were considered Christian.[187]

This kind of opinion suggests that the chronicler intended to distort reality. However, he wrote for an audience that could discover any confabulation – witnesses of the described events were in fact still alive – so at least for this reason it is worth questioning the intentions attributed to him, and undertaking a search for an alternative explanation for the particular words used to describe the acceptance of Christianity by the Liutici before their rebellion in the 10th c. A compelling perspective is created in this case by a reference to research on the role of the empire in the intellectual milieu of the chronicler and especially in the missiological reflections of the time.

It is worth remembering that Thietmar – analogically to St. Augustine's thought, in which *sacerdotium* and *imperium* are two pillars of *civitas Dei* in an earthly dimension – depicts the monarchy (imperial or royal power) as a representation of Christ's kingdom in the temporal world. This is why even the very inclusion of particular peoples by the imperial authority and the related church structures, in the opinion of church circles, made them subjects of the Kingdom of God,[188] which in certain situations did not have to be connected to the advancement of individual conversion, as is indicated in the chronicle.

---

185   *E.g. ibidem*, and also: Łowmiański, *Religia*, pp. 262 f.; Jan Śrutwa, "Diecezje Pomorza Zachodniego (Diecezja Wolińska a później Kamieńska) między związkami z Gnieznem, Magdeburgiem i bezpośrednią zależnością od Stolicy Apostolskiej," *Szczecińskie Studia Kościelne* 2 (1991), p. 33. For information on mass Christenings of the Slavic people conducted by Boso also in areas where there had already existed a lasting Church network, see above pp. 72 f.

186   Łowmiański, *Religia*, pp. 261 f.

187   H. Łowmiański developed this thought referring not only to Thietmar's data, but also to Wipo's work created in the mid-11th c., in which before the rebellion in 983, the Liutici were considered as semi-Christians (*semichristiani*) and after the rebellion as pagans: "it seems that *semichristiani* are the pagans who pay tribute, and those who stopped doing so are qualified as *pagani*" – *ibidem*, p. 262, footnote 675.

188   It is worth emphasizing that the Christianization of the Slavs, *de facto* funding the Magdeburg metropolis on their lands, was one of the merits which, according to Thietmar,

80   CHAPTER 2

This in turn depended on the specifics of the missionary theology of the time, according to which the preaching of good news and the encompassing of new peoples by the Christian community was interpreted at two levels: first as the Christianization of whole nations (*gentes*), and second regarding the particular people creating them.[189] Thietmar's description certainly refers to the former and so he means all *gentes*,[190] in which "later, instead of veneration for Christ and his fisherman venerable Peter, manifested veneration for the devil's heresy."[191]

This emphasis on worship of Christ and St. Peter in the theological aspect completes the image of inclusion of the Veleti tribes to the *Christianitas* circle, which forms a basis for treating them as apostates after their rebellion. Although in the discussed passage this term is not used to refer to them, mentioning this categorization with regard to Liutici's attitude is justified in a wider context of the work (an analogy to a similar pagan reaction among the Obodrites), and also in terms of Wipo's testimony created in the next generation. This author of the *Gesta* of King Conrad II, when he mentioned these events, referred not only to the apostasy of the Liutici, but also to their

---

 justified the imperial title bestowed upon Otto I in 962, although it is hard to speak about personal conversion of the people subdued in 955. See Lübke, "Zwischen Triglav," p. 25. For missions in the Ottonian times with consideration for military aspects see Padberg, *Die Christianisierung*, pp. 150–153.

189 Wavra, *Salzburg und Hamburg*, p. 15. The summary information provided by Adam of Bremen, that after the battle of Lenzen in 929 "… baptizatusque est totus gentilium populus, ecclesiae in Sclavania tunc primum constructae" ("… and the whole pagan people was baptized and churches were built then in Slavdom for the first time") should be understood in the same spirit – cf. *Magistri Adam Bremensis Gesta Hammmaburgensis Ecclesiae Pontificum*, ed. Bernhard Schmeidler, MGH SSrerGerm in usum scholarum (1917) [further: Adam], II, 5 (see also below p. 209). The concept of conversion of whole peoples was created in reference to the order to preach the holy gospel given in the *Vulgate*: *docete omnes gentes*. Nota bene, this expression loses the sense of the original, Greek text: "make the disciples of all nations", however, it perfectly well presents the key postulate of the medieval missionary doctrine to evangelise all groups of people, thus "teaching and christening all nations".

190 *Gens* in this context is not only a political or ethnic category, it also has theological connotations, which was prejudged by the influence of the *Vulgate* on the understanding of such notions as *gens*, *populus* and *natio* in the Middle Ages, see Benedykt Zientara, "Populus – gens – natio. Z zagadnień wczesnośredniowiecznej terminologii etnicznej," in *Cultus et cognitio. Studia z dziejów średniowiecznej kultury*, ed. Stefan K. Kuczyński *et al.* (Warszawa: PWN, 1976), p. 677; *idem*, *Świt narodów europejskich* (Warszawa: PIW, 1985), pp. 20 ff. See also below, p. 208, footnote 54.

191 Thietmar III, 17: "Vice Christi et piscatoris eiusdem venerabilis Petri varia demoniacae heresis cultura deinceps veneratur …" On Peter the Apostle as Christ's Fisher see the Gospel According to St. Luke (Lk 5:10); cf. Forstner, *Świat*, p. 297.

THE RELIGION OF THE SLAVS IN THIETMAR'S CHRONICLE   81

complete return to paganism: "quique olim semichristiani, nunc per apostati-
cam nequitiam omnino sunt pagani" ("Those former semi-Christians, due to
their apostatic evilness, are completely pagan now").[192]

Wipo wrote in the 40's of the 11th c., *i.e.* in the times when the third generation of the Liutici enjoyed freedom from Saxon domination, so he had
certainty that the results of the rebellion begun in 983 were lasting. However,
the quotation from his chronicle makes one realize that even the complete
repaganisation of the Liutici, in the environment of the Saxon clergy, did not
change the fundamental assessment of the consequences of their earlier subjection to the empire and the related Church organisation.[193] However, it is
striking in that they are called here *semichristiani* ("half-Christians"), which
would indicate insufficient individual conversion,[194] ignored in Thietmar's
perspective based on the level of *gentes*.

The use of the expression *varia demoniacae heresis cultura* to define the religion of the Liutici by the chronicler from Merseburg presents it as an error
in faith, caused by demonic, devilish powers. According to H.D. Kahl, even the
very occurrence of the notion of heresy in the assessment of this flourishing
paganism became a precondition for the thesis that because the Liutici were
treated as apostates, Thietmar refused them the right to complete rejection
of the Christian community.[195] Thus, following this way of thinking, he would
treat them as heretics but not as pagans. Analogies with such treatment of heretics could be searched for not only in the late Middle Ages, but also in the late
antique Roman Empire.[196]

The latter direction of comparison is especially significant for Kahl's concept, in which it is essential that the Liutici were treated not as pagans, but
as evil, false Christians. On this basis, according to the mentioned scholar,

---

192   Wipo, *Gesta Chuonradi II*, ed. Harry Bresslau, MGH SSrerGerm in usum scholarum (1915),
       33, p. 52.
193   The memory of this original Church organisation in the northern Polabia, established in
       the 10th c., was preserved until the times of the next Christianization of these lands in the
       12th c.; a good example here is the presentation of Havelberg in the hagiography of
       St. Otto of Bamberg in the 50's of the 12th c. (see Ebo III, 3).
194   The expression *semipagani*, half-pagans, functioned in a similar way and expressed the
       idea that wide masses of people included in the Christian circle for a few generations
       were Christianised only to a small extent (a good example is what Cosmas I, 4, wrote
       about the attitude of Czech rural people in the 12th c., see also below, pp. 149, 152).
195   Kahl, *Die ersten Jahrhunderte*, p. 52. In this way of reasoning, the notions of heresy seem
       the most significant, and it referred to the rejection of the earlier accepted Christian re-
       ligion, *i.e.* apostasy, because according to the Church doctrine no deed could cancel bap-
       tism, even repudiation of religion.
196   *E.g.* Gieysztor, *Bemerkungen*, pp. 5–7.

Thietmar's contemporary St. Bruno of Querfurt was to agitate to start a mission war against these people, referring to the rule coined by St. Augustine "compellere intrare!" – "force them to enter (the Church)."[197] It is important that initially this rule did not refer to the pagans, Jews, or the "fallen" (*lapsi*), but only to schismatic Christians (strictly speaking the Donatists) who strived for the destruction of the Roman Church organization in Africa by force.[198] Hence the primary sense of the rule of *compellere intrare* was calling for re-Catholicisation, and this is the way in which H.D. Kahl wanted to understand it in the works of St. Bruno referring to the Liutici, on the assumption that he recognized them as apostates.[199]

When H. Łowmiański undertook polemics with this perspective, he regarded it, in association with the principle of *compellere intrare* based on the thought of St. Augustine, as inadequate in terms of the missionary activity in Polabia, and he emphasizes that the political pressure (tribute) was not accompanied by forced baptism. This polemic is misguided. H.D. Kahl's idea was an indication of an ideology promoted by St. Bruno and not the actual state of the mission among the Liutici. This is only the first issue, however, H. Łowmiański went further: he examined the understanding of this traditional formula and found two stages of action in it: *compellere* – the forceful invasion of the pagan territory – and *intrare* – peaceful introduction of these people to Christianity.[200] In this way, using **one** principle, he created two principles which in reality did not exist. These speculations should be mentioned however, due to their reception in the debate on the missions among the Slavs.[201]

Regardless of the rather wide acceptance of H.D. Kahl's concept in the historical debate, it should be noted that at the current stage of discussion its weak points are being emphasized. The life of St. Adalbert (*vita altera*), written by St. Bruno, indicated that forcing pagans – and not only apostates – to accept Christianity was shown as the essential role of rulers since the time of Constantine the Great. This raises doubts, as it would mean that in writing this letter to Henry II, which is fundamental to the debate, Bruno changed his mind

---

197 The rule was coined on the basis of an allegorical interpretation of an evangelical parable (cf. Lk 14:23) about a feast in which any people met in the streets were forced to participate.

198 Stanisław Kowalczyk, "Filozofia pokoju św. Augustyna," *Vox Patrum* 8 (1988), p. 855.

199 See Kahl, *Compellere intrare*, p. 173. The Letter to King Henry II, written in about 1008, is of basic importance here, in the letter St. Bruno ordered the ruler of Germany to withdraw from a military alliance with the Liutici and make them join the Church. See below, pp. 107 f.

200 Łowmiański, *Religia*, pp. 261 ff.

201 Recently *e.g.* Janion, *Niesamowita Słowiańszczyzna*, pp. 15 f.

THE RELIGION OF THE SLAVS IN THIETMAR'S CHRONICLE   83

and narrowed the principle of *compellere intrare* only to apostates.[202] This departure from the principle of St. Augustine's concept was characteristic in the wider context of this epoch.[203]

In the context of these findings, and returning to Thietmar's passage that was discussed earlier, one should revise the view that defining the Slavic return to paganism as heresy ("haeresis cultura") is strictly connected with recognizing them as apostates, not pagans. It is hard to speak here about such a correlation. Since Thietmar did not mention individual conversion in the case of the Liutici, it is difficult to consider at all the impossibility of the obliteration of baptism, as was the case when it came to typical heretics and apostates in Late Antiquity or the High Middle Ages; the discussed passage of the chronicle refers only to the level of *gentes*.

Thietmar based his laconic description of the situation, which occurred as a consequence of the Slavic uprising in 983, on the rule of juxtaposition of grace and sin and, more precisely, the antithesis of the worship of Christ accompanied by St. Peter and demonic heresy. However, in the same sentence he mentioned that this turn of events was favoured not only by pagans, but also by Christians.[204] Thus, parallel to the above-mentioned theological qualifications, a division between pagans and Christians also appears here. Perforce apostasy or heresy is outlined in this context as transition to the side of paganism,[205] which is in accordance with the information from Wipo's work on the total repaganisation of the Liutici as a result of their "apostatic evilness" (*apostatica nequitia*).

That Thietmar claimed that this change praised pagans along with Christians nowadays sounds very enigmatic and has provoked various speculations. Over half a century ago Gerard Labuda proposed to treat this place as an indication that only a part of the rebellious Polabian Slavdom was Christened, while the root of the rebellion was in a part concentrated around the sanctuary and the assembly in Radogošč. In this conception, the Christians happily returning to paganism were Slavs burdened with tributes and duties to the Empire and

---

202   Roman Michałowski, "Król czy misjonarz? Rozumienie misji w X/XI w.," in *Bruno z Kwerfurtu. Osoba – dzieło – epoka*, ed. Marian Dygo, Wojciech Fałkowski (Pułtusk: Wydawnictwo Akademii Humanistycznej im. Aleksandra Gieysztora, 2010), pp. 140–142, pays particular attention to this. The author emphasizes the terminological concurrence of the expression of a mission war with the pagans in the Letter to King Henry and the Life of St. Adalbert in the form of *compelle intrare* ("force [them] to enter").

203   *E.g.* Le Goff, *Kultura*, p. 158; Vauchez, *Duchowość*, p. 11.

204   *Ibidem*: "et flebilis haec mutatio non solum a gentilibus, verum etiam a christianis extollitur."

205   It is hard not to first of all see the Liutici in the mentioned pagans, see below.

Church institutions.[206] However, due to the weakness of the contemporary Church network and the lack of evidence for individual conversion among the Veleti before 983, any attempts to find the Christian part of their community in Thietmar's reference does not seem sufficiently justified. Considering the fact that the Liutici, after the renouncement of the power of the Empire, were recognized by the chronicler as pagan (*gentiles*), it seems doubtful that he would still treat some of them as Christians when he describes their joy at rejecting Christianity.

This is why it is worth considering the idea put forward by, among others, Lech Leciejewicz, that the Slavic rebellion could have made the Saxon lords happy as it offered them an excuse for raiding lands which were previously protected by the imperial power.[207] This concept outlines the divergence between the interests of the German Church and wealthy secular lords for whom the Christianization of the eastern frontiers of the Reich was not a favourable course of action because of the peace that it brought to these areas. According to this interpretation, Thietmar would stigmatise the military actions whose goal was only plunder without establishment of the imperial and Church authority, and from the theological perspective the expansion of Christ's kingdom.

The above attempts to solve this riddle refer to the supposed interests of groups that have been constructed in various ways (the oppressed Slavic people, Saxon lords craving for more plunder). Especially in the case of the chronicler's interpretation of history however, one should also consider the influence of non-economic reasons for the presentation of such an inexplicable attitude of these Christians. When Thietmar referenced it, he may have wanted to allude to other attitudes and views that are not clearly expressed in his chronicle, perhaps held by some of the participants in the debate on the evaluation of these dramatic events in the environment of the Empire[208] or even its Christian neighbours.

The fact that in the intellectual context this debate exceeded the area of profits and losses measured in a social and economic perspective is confirmed not only in further passages of Thiemar's chronicle, but also in the hagiographic work of Bruno of Querfurt. The latter is the author of the earliest source which explains the genesis of the Slavic rebellion in theological dialectics, referring

---

206 Labuda, "Powstania Słowian," p. 174. *Idem, Fragmenty*, vol. 1, p. 226, footnote 92 (similarly Słupecki, "Einflüsse," p. 178).

207 Leciejewicz, *Słowianie*, p. 164.

208 Lübke, "Zwischen Triglav," p. 26, claims that the pagan attack turned mainly against the clergy and the secular members of the elite of the Empire, but not against particular Christian believers.

THE RELIGION OF THE SLAVS IN THIETMAR'S CHRONICLE   85

to the motif of being penalized for a transgression of the contemporary elite of
the Christian world.

An important circumstance that induced the Slavic rebellion in 983 was
Otto II's involvement in Italy and the weakening of his political position as
a result of the defeats he suffered there.[209] Meanwhile the chronicler, using a
digression in his narration, disrupted the chronology of events[210] by locating
the description of the Slavic rebellion just after the story of the liquidation
of the bishopric in Merseburg in 981. It was the consequence of Gisiler the
Archbishop of Magdeburg's wickedness, extensively presented by Thietmar,
and supported by the emperor and the synod in Rome where the decisions on
this matter were made. Thus what happened in Polabia in 983 was considered
God's punishment for liquidation of the Merseburg diocese, which was also
claimed *expressis verbis* by the chronicler in the sentence introducing the account of these events,[211] and moreover when he referred to his father's dream,
in which they were anticipated as the coming "rain" of God's punishment.[212]

It was to become a fact only three days later, on the 29th of June, as this
is the date claimed by the chronicler to be the beginning of the Slavic rebellion. It was also the Feast of St. Peter the Apostle, which corresponds with
the earlier reference to the rejection of not only Christ but also of St. Peter. In
Thietmar's description the first brunt of the rebellion fell on Gisiler's metropolis, or more strictly speaking on its subordinate dioceses in Brandenburg and
Havelberg, the cathedrals of which were devastated. The account of the events
first emphasizes the damage to the Church and evokes an impression that the
pagans showed their intense hatred and satisfied their greed by looting Church

---

209   However, it is not very probable that they would turn out to be the only decisive factor
      in the Veleti decision on starting the war, as then Thietmar, who had good orientation
      in the situation, would not decide to use false – and so also weak – argumentation sup-
      porting his views, see: Labuda, "Powstania Słowian," pp. 169 f.; *idem, Fragmenty*, vol. 1,
      pp. 222 f., 226. However, a view expressed some time ago by Koczy, "Thietmar i Widukind,"
      p. 659, that "liquidation of the Merseburg bishopric in 981 was the best proof that the
      Empire sacrificed the missions among the Slavs at the cost of the Italian affairs" is widely
      exaggerated.
210   For chronology of the rebellion and other events at that time, see Labuda, "Powstania
      Słowian," pp. 167 ff.; *idem, Fragmenty*, vol. 1, pp. 210 ff., and especially p. 215–217; Babij,
      Wojskowość, pp. 136 f. For the Obodrite leader Mstivoy and his possible participation in
      the rebellion in 983, see Labuda, *Fragmenty*, vol. 1, pp. 217–222, 300, and also Bernhard
      Friedmann, *Untersuchungen zur Geschichte des abodritischen Fürstentums bis zum Ende
      des 10. Jahrhunderts* (Berlin: Duncker & Humblot 1986), pp. 259–272. See also above p. 76,
      footnote 176.
211   Thietmar III, 16: "Sed quae res destruccionem hanc subsequerentur, lector, attende!"
212   Thietmar III, 17. This "rain" sent to the righteous and unrighteous is a reference to the
      Gospel (Mt 5:45).

86   CHAPTER 2

property, which is the reason for a very pejorative assessment of their behaviour by the chronicler, who used the expression *avari canes* in his description.[213]

The concept of presenting these events as punishment for the decisions made in Rome in 981 remains in accordance with the information placed just after the description of the Slavic rebellion. This section referred to a raid by the Czechs – *de facto* from 987 – who attacked the diocese in Zeitz. They were yet another assailant of the Merseburg diocese. Later the chronicler writes about looting the St. Lawrence Monastery in Kalbe,[214] adding a theological explanation of the reasons for the defeat: "Our wrongdoings caused our fear and made their spirit stronger."[215] It is striking that the chronicler feels solidarity in the guilt and sense of defeat with the losing Saxons, which probably results directly from the fact that his relatives were involved in the conflict.[216] In this way the motif of God's punishment administered for sins exceeds the matters related to the liquidation of the bishopric of Merseburg, but this city still does not lose its significance in this context. Suddenly, there was a twist of action on the literary stage of history, and the wave of pagan success was stopped by a miraculous intervention from heavens, namely St. Lawrence the patron saint of the Merseburg diocese.

These plots will be developed in another story dedicated to the raid of the Obodrite duke Mstivoy who attacked Hamburg, although it most certainly did not have much to do with the rebellion in 983.[217] Thietmar combines a description of a town fire with a miraculous event: in the middle of the flames a

---

213 Thietmar III, 17 called Slavic plunderers who defaced the corpse of Bishop Dodilo "greedy dogs" (*avari canes*). It does not seem that this expression was restricted only for the Slavs because the same phrase was used by Thietmar (IV, 25) when he refers to Danes (cf. *e.g.* Fraesdorff, *Der barbarische Norden*, pp. 243 f.). For the topical expression *canes* strictly referring to the Slavs see below pp. 237, 289 f. In earlier historiography this emphasis on the greediness of the Slavs expressed in plundering churches, was considered an indication that the reason for their mutiny was economic oppression and mainly the tithe (see *e.g.* Labuda, *Powstania Słowian*, pp. 161, 173). In the light of this research speculations of this type do not seem justified: Thietmar's significant interest in devastations of church facilities is conditioned mainly by his particular interest in the religious aspect of these dramatic events.

214 It was the ancestral monastery of Saxon margraves, see *e.g.* Friedman, *Untersuchungen*, pp. 260 f.

215 Thietmar III, 18: "nostra etenim facinora nobis formidinem et his suggerebant validam mentem".

216 One should especially emphasize the participation in fights with the rebellious Slavs of the chronicler's father, count Siegfried.

217 Most probably Mstivoy's attack of Hamburg took place a few years later, see Labuda, "Powstania Słowian," pp. 169, 192 f.; Babij, *Wojskowość*, p. 139. See also below, pp. 235 f.

THE RELIGION OF THE SLAVS IN THIETMAR'S CHRONICLE 87

golden right hand appeared from heaven to lift and save the relics of saints.[218] The chronicler emphasizes that the miracle happened in a place where a bishopric formerly had been located,[219] and this in a sense connected Hamburg with Merseburg, which had also lost the rank of bishopric capital.[220] Thus this moment that stoked the chronicler's empathy could have influenced his will to show appreciation for Hamburg in the pages of the chronicle by mentioning this miracle, but it would not be his only motivation.

The admiration of the army for this supernatural intervention in the narrative was accompanied by fear of the Obodrite duke, Mstivoy, who ultimately became insane, which seems a trite motif in descriptions of people who stood out against God.[221] However, when shortly before his death he was sprinkled with holy water – most certainly as a form of exorcism – he reacted by shouting that he was being burnt by St. Lawrence,[222] which referred to an earlier description of the Slavic raid of the monastery in Kalbe, which had this saint as its patron. Mstivoy's insanity and his abandonment to the fate of demonic powers, in the perspective of the chronicle, appears to be punishment for the destruction of the said monastery[223] as a display of vengeance from God himself and his saint.[224]

The chronicler did not mention the fact that the Obodrite duke participated in the raid that devastated Kalbe. He attracted the revenge of God, and especially St. Lawrence, only for his role in the community of those who assailed

---

218   Thietmar III, 18; cf. Schulmeyer-Ahl, *Der Anfang*, p. 298. For the symbolic meaning of the "hand of God" (*manus Dei*) as a sign of supernatural custody, see *e.g.* Forstner, *Świat*, pp. 352 f.; Le Goff, *Kultura*, p. 164.

219   Thietmar III, 18: "ubi sedes episcopalis quondam fuit".

220   For information on moving the capital to Bremen see below, p. 205.

221   Possibly it is a motif inspired by the Bible – *e.g.* the Book of Isaiah (Is 19:14) in Vulgate: "miscuit in medio eius spiritum vertiginis"; cf. also Helmold II, 100: God confused the minds of the Slavs and they were defeated in the battle.

222   The fact that Mstivoy underwent church rites indicates that he did not reject Christianity, and even if he did, it was for a short time. The very burning down of Hamburg, and – as one can assume from the information on the fate of the mentioned relics of saints – the local church, is not identical with apostasy.

223   Thietmar's information about the revenge taken by St. Lawrence on Mstivoy can be an argument to support the view that he participated in the raid of the monastery in Kalbe, however, it is hard to take any definite decisions only on this basis – see M.Z. Jedlicki in: Thietmar, p. 133, footnote 103; Adam Turasiewicz, *Dzieje polityczne Obodrzyców. Od IX wieku do utraty niepodległości w latach 1160–1164* (Kraków: Nomos, 2004), p. 105; Jerzy Strzelczyk, *Bohaterowie Słowian Połabskich* (Poznań: Wydawnictwo Poznańskie, 2017), p. 181.

224   There is a similar situation in Thietmar V, 12 – here the chronicler claims that it was God himself to punish the Alamans with death, because they destroyed the church in Strasbourg – cf. *e.g.* Prucnal, "Władca chrześcijański," p. 12.

the Church, the core of which was the rebellious Slavs from 983. In this context it is especially worth remembering St. Lawrence's special role as protector of Merseburg. The cathedral in this town was dedicated to him, and the bishopric there was founded by Otto I out of gratitude for victory over a dozen years earlier in the battle on the Lech River (955).[225] Hence Thietmar created an image of the patron saint of his own diocese as an intercessor ensuring the effective protection for the Saxons in the time of war.

The description of the supernatural intervention from Hamburg and the reminiscence of Mstivoy's defeat in Thietmar's narration are a prelude to the change of fate for the endangered Christian world.[226] It was brought about by the battle of the Tanger River (983), which was preceded, however, by[227] a schematic picture of the immense devastation of the whole area of the Slavs' rebellion and further emphasis on the power of rebellious tribes: "By the time the Slavs had burned and pillaged all the burgs and villages as far as the river Tanger, there were more than thirty bands of warriors on foot and horseback. Without sustaining any losses and aided by their gods, they did not hesitate to ravage the rest of the region, as their blaring trumpets preceded them."[228] It is worth turning attention to the support offered to the Slavs by their gods: they were preceded by trumpeters,[229] so these gods were idols or most certainly banners of gods, the so called "stanice" (sing. "stanica"), which are called gods by the chronicler following biblical examples.[230]

Thus, Thietmar sketched an image of the earthly confrontation of spiritual powers, which becomes especially expressive when juxtaposed with the later part of the narration where he described the Saxon counteroffensive. The Saxon leaders and army gathered to resist the Slavs before the decisive battle, which was to take place on Saturday, and underwent the necessary spiritual preparations: "They all attend to mass; making their bodies and souls

---

225   It is emphasized by Thietmar II, 10.

226   Thietmar III, 18.

227   Thietmar III, 19.

228   Trans. D.A. Warner in: *Ottonian Germany*, p. 142; cf. Thietmar III, 19: "Desolatis tunc omnibus preda et incedio urbibus ac villis usque ad aquam, quae Tongera vocatur, convenerunt e Sclavis peditum ac equitum plus quam XXX legiones, quae sine aliqua lesione residua quaeque suorum auxilio deorum tunc devastare non dubitarent, tubicinis precedentibus."

229   So Thietmar outlines an image of a march headed by idols, whose arrival is announced by the sound of trumpets. However, it is worth taking into account that these were the trumpets of war, hence their sound should not necessarily be related to some religious rites.

230   For more information see pp. 105 and 157.

THE RELIGION OF THE SLAVS IN THIETMAR'S CHRONICLE   89

stronger with the heavenly sacrament."[231] Their victory was celebrated in the
Saxon camp on Sunday, the day which is specially predisposed for celebration
of triumph, and was also interpreted theologically as an appropriate day for
overcoming evil powers.

The Battle of the Tanger River actually stopped the military progress of
the Slavs, but scholars rightly doubt whether it was such a spectacular Saxon
victory[232] as was claimed by Thietmar. In the success of the Christian side he
saw a miraculous sign from God: "Praised is God by the victors in all miraculous deeds and the truthful words of Doctor Paul were confirmed: 'There is no
prudence, no force, no counsel [that can succeed] against the Lord.'"[233] The
chronicler finished the passage with a classic *interpretatio Christiana* perspective of the Slavic cult, whose essentialized idolatry was putting creation above
the Creator: "Abandoned were those who at first decided to reject God and
who foolishly placed the hand-made and completely meaningless idols over
their creator."[234]

This completed the historical narrative of the direct consequences of the
liquidation of the Merseburg bishopric, with the respect to the theological
perspective. In the light of Thietmar's narrative the consequences were most
significant for the German church, starting with the suffragan dioceses of the
Magdeburg metropolis, which corresponds with the fact that Archbishop
Gisiler was considered the main culprit of the "freedom" (*libertas*) of the
Merseburg attack. In this way the chronicler created his own interpretation
of a common perspective, which was not new for the imperial elites, and explained the eruption of the Slavic rebellion as punishment for the liquidation
of the Merseburg diocese. He did not copy Bruno of Querfurt's concept, who
only about a dozen years earlier indicated that Emperor Otto II should take
the main burden of guilt in this case, and his sin offended not so much God
himself, but St. Lawrence as the patron of the bishopric in Merseburg.[235]

---

231   Thietmar III, 19: "missam omnes audiunt, corpus animamque caelestii sacramento muni-
       unt". See also Schulmeyer-Ahl, *Der Anfang*, pp. 293, 298.
232   For the battle of Tanger see *e.g.*: Labuda, *Powstania Słowian*, pp. 154, 157; Babij, *Wojskowość*,
       p. 137.
233   Thietmar III, 19: "Laudatur a victoribus in cunctis Deus mirabilis operibus, approbaturque
       veredicus Pauli doctoris sermo: 'Non est prudentia, neque fortitudo nec consilium adver-
       sus Domine'". It is important to mention that this is not St. Paul's thought but the *Book of
       Proverbs* (Prov 21:30). See also Schulmeyer-Ahl, *Der Anfang*, p. 293.
234   Thietmar III, 19: "Derelicti sunt, qui prius Deum spernere presumpserunt idolaque manu-
       facta et prorsus inania creatori suo stulto preposuerunt." Cf. Rom 1:25.
235   See *Sancti Adalberti Pragensis, episcopi et martyris Vita altera auctore Brunone Querfurtensi*,
       ed. Jadwiga Karwasińska, MPH n.s. 4/2 (1969) [further: Vita Adalberti II], 10, 12; see *e.g.*

Thietmar, in appreciation for the prominent role of Gisiler, places the emperor among the secondary culprits in this matter, without offering him any absolution however. When the narritive of the chronicle returns to the Italian issues and to the events of the year 982, the motif of punishment for Otto recurs. After a battle of Cotrone in Calabria where he was defeated by the Saracens, he was to admit: "Because of my sins I have fallen into this misery."[236] The conventional tone of this confession can support the thesis that the chronicler did not necessarily refer strictly to the Merseburg affairs, and he more probably expressed a general, not very favourable assessment of Otto's rule.

It is difficult, however, to find in the chronicle a sin committed by this emperor that would be bigger than the liquidation of the diocese of Merseburg. Hence, as an alternative possibility, one should take into account that according to Thietmar even the defeat at Cotrone started a string of misfortunes that fell on the empire after the memorable synod in Rome in 981, and the one that followed was the Slavic rebellion, which is laconically mentioned again by the chronicler, this time chronologically, stating its date *expressis verbis*: 983.[237] However, the fact that he earlier decided to devote such an extensive digression regardless of chronology, strongly supports the view that he not only had a ready image of the theological and moral interpretation of the consequences of the liquidation of the Merseburg diocese (it was convergent with the one presented by St. Bruno earlier), but also that this image was considered "canonical" by himself in the environmental debate in which he participated.

The description of the rebellion of Polabian Slavs in 983 provides rich material for research on the Christian interpretation of Slavic religion. In terms of theological assessment, there are prominent categories – such as apostasy, demonic heresy, and vain idolatry – connected with the typical focus on valuing idols (*idola*) more than the Creator. Moreover, in this part of the narration paganism constitutes an important factor on the stage of history. On one hand it embodies forces hostile to Christ and his followers, defeated in military action thanks to explicit supernatural support (God, St. Lawrence). On the other hand, pagans are a passive tool of God's punishment. The chronicler's emotiveness also becomes visible – "greedy dogs" *etc.* Thus, there is striking agreement in the negative assessment of primary religion from the theological

---

Michał Tomaszek, "Brunon z Kwerfurtu i Otton II: powstanie słowiańskie 983 roku jako grzech cesarza," *Kwartalnik Historyczny* 109 (2002) 4, pp. 5–23.

236   Thietmar III, 21: "peccatis meis id promerentibus ad hanc veni miseriam."

237   *Ibidem*, III, 24. This information is an additional note from *Annales Quedlinburgenses* and could have appeared after completing the first version of Thietmar's work, see W. Trillmich in: *Thietmari Merseburgensis Episcopi Chronicon*, ed. Trillmich, p. 113, footnote 93.

THE RELIGION OF THE SLAVS IN THIETMAR'S CHRONICLE   91

perspective and its destructive role in the history of the Empire and the related Church network as well as among the Saxons themselves.

2.5 *The* regnum ablatum *War between Mieszko I and Boleslav the Pious*

In a description of the military conflict (hypothetically dated to 990) between Poland and Bohemia,[238] supported by the Liutici, Thietmar confirmed that the latter made human offerings.[239] When the already defeated Czech ruler, Boleslav the Pious, was on his way back home, he came across a stronghold whose name was not mentioned by the chronicler, "and without any resistance of its inhabitants, he seized it and its lord, whom he gave to the Liutici for beheading. Without delay they sacrificed him to their tutelary gods in front of the gates of the city."[240] This laconic information was not supported with any theological commentary, and in terms of vocabulary was primarily neutral (apart from the expression *dii*, which automatically recalled negative connotations related to paganism).

The testimony about a Slavic human offering is not surprising, and there is a high probability that the use of the expression *decollere* to indicate the type of death can be interpreted not only as killing in general but, literally, as beheading. Sources confirm that Slavic deities were offered cut heads (*e.g.* Adam of Bremen,[241] the Letter of Bruno of Querfurt to King Henry II),[242] for

---

238   Czech Boleslav II the Pious wanted to regain some "dominion taken away from him" ("regnum sibi ablatum") by Polish Mieszko I, most often it is hypothetically located in the territories of Silesia or Lusatia. The date of 990 was proposed on the basis of a record in Czech historiography from the 12th c. claiming that this was the year when the Czechs lost Niemcza (Nimptsch), and the strongholds bearing this name were located in Silesia (see below, p. 149) and in Lusatia. The discussion about it has been continued for generations and is not over yet. On this matter, see *e.g.* Lech A. Tyszkiewicz, "Przyłączenie Śląska do monarchii piastowskiej pod koniec X wieku," in *Od plemienia do państwa. Śląsk na tle Słowiańszczyzny Zachodniej*, ed. Lech Leciejewicz (Wrocław/Warszawa: Volumen, 1991), pp. 120–152; cf. Stanisław Rosik, "The formation of Silesia (to 1163). Factors of regional integration," in *The long formation of the Region Silesia (c. 1000–1526)*, ed. Przemysław Wiszewski, (Cuius regio? Ideological and Territorial Cohesion of the Historical Region of Silesia (c. 1000–2000) 1) (Wrocław: Publishing House Wydawnictwo eBooki.com.pl, 2013), pp. 54 f.

239   A description of these events Thietmar, IV, 11–13. See Labuda, *Fragmenty*, vol. 1, pp. 298 f.; Myśliński, *Polska wobec Słowian*, pp. 40 f.; Babij, *Wojskowość*, pp. 138, 241 f.

240   Thietmar IV, 13, p. 163: "et hanc [scil. urbem – S.R.] cum domino eius, urbanis nil repugnantibus, acquisivit eundemque Liuticis ad decollandum dedit. Nec mora, diis fautoribus haec ostia ante urbem offertur".

241   See below, p. 244.

242   The Letter of Bruno see below, p. 107, footnote 320; see below pp. 244–246, where there is also more information about the Slavic custom of offering a cut off head.

92   CHAPTER 2

which the nearby Scandinavian analogies can also be relevant.[243] Thietmar's
information also indicates that offerings were made not only in sanctuaries,
but also *ad hoc*.[244] It seems interesting in this situation that a Christian ruler
offered a Christian as an offering to Liutician deities. It is possibly that he had
the commander of the occupied stronghold executed in this way, a style of the
pagans' own invention.[245]

For the chronicler, the religious dimension of this execution is obvious, and
in this situation it is surprising that his reaction was so indifferent. It could
possibly be explained by Boleslav's achievement in other areas. The Polish side
of this conflict was supported by the Saxons, who on their way to this war happened to be in a dangerous situation themselves and could not count on Polish
ruler Mieszko I's help. In this situation Boleslav the Pious not only reached an
agreement with them, but also stopped the Liutici from immediately chasing
them, which allowed them to safely reach Magdeburg. The Bohemian prince
turned out to be the benefactor of the Saxons, among whom was the chronicler's father, and so the chronicler could resign from condemning his alliance
with pagans or their offering.[246]

However, the Liutici themselves, when their pursuit of the Saxons was presented, were called *infideles*[247] by Thietmar, and this term was most certainly

---

243   *E.g.* according to Adam IV, 27: "... ex omni animante, quod masculinum est, novem capita
      offeruntur ..." ("... of every living creature, which is male, nine heads are offered ..."). Cf.
      Anders Hultgård, "Från ögonvittnesskildring till retorik: Adam av Bremens notiser om
      Uppsalakulten i religionshistorisk belysning," in *Uppsalakulten och Adam av Bremen*, ed.
      Anders Hultgård (Nora: Nya Doxa, 1997), p. 32.

244   Leszek P. Słupecki, "Archaeological Sources and Written Sources in Studying Symbolic
      Culture (Exemplified by Research on the Pre-Christian Religion of the Slavs)," in *Theory
      and Practice of Archaeological Research*, vol. 3, ed. Stanisław Tabaczyński (Warsaw: IAE
      PAN, 1998), p. 339.

245   After making a human offering, mentioned according to this passage, the Liutici decided
      to return home, which became a reason for the speculation that a ritual murder was in
      this case accompanied by divination which predestined the decision of Liutici leaders
      (such opinion was expressed by Babij, *Wojskowość*, pp. 242 f.).

246   This special care shown by Thietmar, also as a bishop, for "our" (*nostri*) people is discussed
      by Lippelt, *Thietmar von Merseburg*, p. 121.

247   Thietmar IV, 13. In the Polish translation of this passage of the chronicle M.Z. Jedlicki
      used the word "wiarołomny", *i.e.* "unfaithful" in the meaning of "treacherous", for *infideles*,
      which in the context was to indicate that the Liutici broke their obligation not to attack
      the Saxons released by Boleslav. However, in the chronicle there is no testimony for such
      obligation of the Liutici, there is only a request made to them by the Czech ruler not to
      chase the Saxons. The renewal of the Czech-Veleti alliance in this situation, contrary to
      the suggestion of the Polish translator, did not have to mean a ban on chase Saxons.

THE RELIGION OF THE SLAVS IN THIETMAR'S CHRONICLE   93

used – similarly to other places in the work devoted to these tribes[248] – to
refer to their religious attitude. This happend exactly in the most extensive
discourse devoted to their cult and beliefs, as well as to social and political
organisation of the Liutici, in which the central place was taken by the famous
capital in Radogošč.

2.6   *Radogošč*

The account in Thietmar's chronicle of the participation of the Liutici in the
war with Boleslav the Brave, in which they supported Henry II, provides an opportunity to explore Radogošč.[249] It is a good example of a very capable political intuition among the Liutici, since they knew how to use conflicts between
their Christian neighbours to their own benefit.[250] They joined the German
expedition that started in September 1005 on the day before crossing the Oder
(Odra) River and – as was mentioned by the chronicler – "they followed their
gods that went at the front."[251] He meant here images of gods carried in front
of the army.[252] The lack of a more extensive comment on these idols is compensated by the author's introduction to the description of the sanctuary in
Radogošč:

"Although I shudder to say anything about them, nevertheless, in order that
you, dear reader, may better understand the vain superstition and meaningless
worship of this people, I will briefly explain who they are and from whence they
have come."[253] So Thietmar recoiled from presenting the pagan religion, but

---

248   See *e.g.* Thietmar VI, 25. This category was used on the pages of the chronicle more often,
        it turns out to be ambiguous but in the case of Liutici adequate for apostasy suggested by
        the chronicler. H.-D. Kahl emphasizes that in the Middle Ages the word *infideles* was used
        to refer to non-Christians (Jews and pagans) as well as heretics, "false Christians". Kahl,
        Die ersten Jahrhunderte, pp. 46 f.

249   For the matter of the Empire-Liutici alliance and the expedition in 1005 see Labuda,
        Fragmenty, vol. 3, p. 187; Myśliński, *Polska wobec Słowian*, pp. 83 ff.; Grzegorz Domański,
        "Problem plemienia (?) Nice," in *Słowiańszczyzna w Europie średniowiecznej. Księga
        pamiątkowa dla Lecha Leciejewicza*, vol. 1: *Plemiona i wczesne państwa*, ed. Zofia
        Kurnatowska (Wrocław: IAE PAN, 1996), pp. 61 ff.; Babij, *Wojskowość*, pp. 144–147.

250   Zygmunt Sułowski, "Sporne problemy dziejów Związku Wieletów-Luciców," in
        *Słowiańszczyzna Połabska między Niemcami a Polską. Materiały z konferencji nau-
        kowej zorganizowanej przez Instytut Historii UAM w dniach 28–29 IV 1980 r.*, ed. Jerzy
        Strzelczyk (Poznań: Wydawnictwo UAM, 1981), p. 163; cf. Piotr Bogdanowicz, "Co można
        wydedukować z Kroniki Thietmara? Ważny fragment z dziejów panowania Bolesława
        Chrobrego," *Nasza Przeszłość* 10 (1959), pp. 71–111; Babij, *Wojskowość*, p. 144.

251   Thietmar VI, 22: "deos suimet precedentes subsequuti".

252   *E.g. ibidem* VII, 64.

253   Trans. D.A. Warner in: *Ottonian Germany*, pp. 252 f.; cf. Thietmar VI, 23: "Quamvis
        autem de hiis aliquid dicere perhorrescam, tamen, ut scias, lector amate, vanam eorum

94   CHAPTER 2

he would present evidence of the Liutici trespassing against Christian faith –
superstition (*superstitio*) – and the vain nature of their cult practice, and therefore his words are not groundless. He presented not only the famous sanctuary
but also gave a comprehensive view of the religious life of these tribes.

The chronicler did not reveal from whom he received the information about
the Liutici religion, however it is possible that he received it from the Liutici
themselves because he could contact them directly due to their relations
with Henry II and his retinue. Another possible circle of informers could be
the Saxons, as they participated in both fights and alliances with Liutici. In
Thietmar's environment it was natural that various opinions about the Liutici
cult would be spread, and he constructed its image on the basis of such views,
not only to satisfy his reader's curiosity of the strange world but also to show
the role of the pagans on the stage of history.[254]

The apostrophe to the "beloved reader" – the successor of the bishop's
throne[255] – is an indication of the categories of thought in which this excurse
will be presented. Thietmar addressed this part of the narration to a clergyman
representing a mindset similar to his own. He did not need to build argumentation on the essence of idolatry, and could directly show the image of the pagan
cult and beliefs interpreted from the theological and literary point of view.

2.6.1   *Urbs tricornis, silva et mare* – Location of the Phanum
"In the land of Redars there is a city [urbs] called Radogošč" – are the words
which start the excurse about the famous capitol of Liutici – "with three cor-
ners and three gates, surrounded by a great forest, untouched by inhabitants
and treated as holy. Two gates stand open for all incomers; the third one is the
smallest and opens eastwards, showing a path that leads to a lake which is situated nearby and truly horrible in appearance."[256]

The term *urbs*, similarly to *civitas*, is used by Thietmar to refer to fortified
centres of power,[257] not necessarily related to economic functions (such as

---

         supersticionem inanioremque populi istius executionem, qui sint vel unde huc venerint,
         strictim enodabo".
254   On the role of this excurse in the Thietmar's chronicle see also Schulmeyer-Ahl, *Der
         Anfang*, p. 135.
255   See above, p. 45, footnote 27.
256   Thietmar VI, 22: "Est urbs quaedam in pago Riedirierun Riedegost nomine, tricornis ac
         tres in se continens portas, quam undique silva ab incolis intacta et venerabilis circumdat
         magna. Duae eiusdem portae cunctis introeuntibus patent; tercia, quae orientem respicit
         et minima est, tramitem ad mare iuxta positum et visu nimis horribile monstrat."
257   Stanisław Rosik, "O 'rozpoznawaniu' civitas w świecie słowiańskich plemion (tzw. Geograf
         Bawarski a łacińskie przekazy z XI–XII w.). Uwagi do dyskusji nad kształtowaniem się
         pojęcia grodu," in *Funkcje grodów w państwa wczesnośredniowiecznej Europy Środkowej.*

THE RELIGION OF THE SLAVS IN THIETMAR'S CHRONICLE   95

trade and crafts). However, in this case he did not use a term that would emphasize the centre of military functions (*e.g. castrum, munimentum*), but he uses the same terms as in the case of Merseburg or Rome.[258] Thus the example of Radogošč forms the premise that the word *urbs* or *civitas* was used by the chronicler to refer to centres of political and religious life, even in the circle of the tribal, pre-Christian communities.[259]

The location of Radogošč is a widely discussed problem and until today there is no definitive solution on this matter. A very significant premise in this case is a reference to the description of the central Liutici temple in Adam of Bremen's work written half a century later. The author used the name Rethra to refer to the centre where the temple was located, and he presented topographic data different from that provided by Thietmar.[260] Thus treating Rethra and Radogošč as one and the same centre is only a hypothesis, although the most probable solution, and this is why both chroniclers' accounts were usually and not accidentally treated jointly as searching for the famous centre of Liutici cult; altogether they have resulted in nearly twenty different proposals.[261]

      Społeczeństwo, gospodarka, ideologia, ed. Krystian Chrzan, Krzysztof Czapla, Sławomir Moździoch (Głogów/Wrocław: Wydawnictwo Instytutu Archeologii i Etnologii PAN, 2014), pp. 37–42. For discussion on the matter see also *e.g.*: Marie Bláhová, *Evropská sídliště latinských pramenech obdobi raného feudalismu* (Praha: Karolinum, 1986), pp. 88–93; Sébastien Rossignol, "Civitas in Early Medieval Central Europe – Stronghold or District?," *The Medieval History Journal* 14 (2011), 1, pp. 71–99.

258   Rome was recognized by Thietmar (VII, 71) as "capud [sic!] omnium urbium".

259   There will soon be more information on the political and religious significance of Radogošč, see pp. 128 ff., 133 ff.

260   Adam II, 18; for more information see below, pp. 212 ff.

261   Numerous suggested locations of Radogošč/Rethra are shown on the maps in: Słupecki, *Slavonic Pagan Sanctuaries*, p. 59; Jerzy Strzelczyk, *Mity, podania i wierzenia dawnych Słowian* (Poznań: Rebis, 1998), p. 196. For a long time C. Schuchardt's view was dominant, it located Radogošč on a hill, Castel Hill near Feldberg on Feldberg Lake (on the basis of excavation work from 1922), Carl Schuchhardt, *Arkona, Rethra, Vineta. Ortsuntersuchungen und Ausgrabungen* (Berlin: H. Schoetz & Co, 1926). The hypothesis was rejected as a result of control research conducted by J. Herrmann, which showed that there were no traces of a 10th–11th c. temple and stronghold in this place, see Joachim Herrmann, "Feldberg, Rethra und die wilzischen Höhenburgen," *Slavia Antiqua* 16 (1969), pp. 33–35, 68. However, a construction which was hypothetically considered a temple was discovered in this area (*ibidem*, pp. 65 f.); it was not located at the top of a hill, but on one of the eastern hillsides going down to the lake, in a place separated with a moat. The Feldberg stronghold existed in 7th–9th c. (*ibidem*, pp. 59 f.), so even then it was possible to date the existence of Slavic temples covered with roofs on the basis of the conducted identification (see Gieysztor, *Mitologia*, p. 226). It is worth mentioning that E. von Wienecke, found an analogy between "three-horned" Radogošč and three hills (Slavic "głowa" [head]), from which the name and shape of the Szczecin (Stettin) idol Triglav derived, hence he located Radogošč in Szczecin. For discussion on the matter see Evamaria

96   CHAPTER 2

Thietmar's account shows that the location of the "three-horn town" ensured quite well the inviolability of this holy place – it was surrounded by
virgin forest (*silva*) and lake (*mare*) waters from all sides.[262] The forest is presented as a place venerated (*venerabilis*) by local people and also untouched
(*intacta*). A path leading to the lake, mentioned in the text, can also be a hypothetical premise that allows ascertaining of aquatic cults practiced near
the lake.[263] The picture of the forest surrounding Radogošč, outlined by the
chronicler evokes an impression of eeriness, which is only strengthened by
an element of looming terror in a reference to the lake (*visu nimis horribile*).
Thietmar created a similar atmosphere in his description of the sanctuary of
the Glomače, which allows this emotional element of terror and eeriness to be
recognized as a specific way of presenting the pagan *sacrum* by this author.[264]
The three-horn shape of the stronghold and a reference to three gates to
enter this place provokes researchers to speculate on the sacral and symbolic
significance of these topographic details. *Nota bene*, later Adam of Bremen
described the cult centre of the Redarians differently: he emphasized the existence of nine gates.[265] Roderich Schmidt, discussing the lack of clarity in

---

Engel, "Der Beitrag der Mediävistik zur Klärung des Rethra – Problems," *Slavia Antiqua*
16 (1969), pp. 95–98; Roderich Schmidt, "Rethra. Das Heiligtum der Lutizen als Heiden-
Metropole," in *Festschrift für Walter Schlesinger*, vol. 2, ed. Helmut Beumann (Köln/Wien:
Böhlau, 1974), pp. 366 f., 372–380; Lothar Dralle, "Rethra. Zu Bedeutung und Lage des redarischen Kultortes," *Jahrbuch für die Geschichte Mittel- und Ostdeutschlands* 33 (1984),
pp. 48–61; Słupecki, *Slavonic Pagan Sanctuaries*, pp. 51 ff.; Rainer Szczesiak, "Auf der Suche
nach Rethra! Ein interessantes Kapitel deutscher Forschungsgeschichte," in *Siedlung,
Kommunikation und Wirtschaft im westslawischen Raum: Beiträge der Sektion zur slawisch-
en Frühgeschichte des 5. Deutschen Archäologenkongresses in Frankfurt an der Oder, 4. bis
7. April 2005*, ed. Felix Biermann, (Beiträge zur Ur- und Frühgeschichte Mitteleuropas) 46
(Langenweißbach: Beier & Beran, 2007), pp. 313–334.

262   Leszek P. Słupecki, "Wykopaliska słowiańskich świątyń," *Mówią Wieki* (1991) 11, p. 34, emphasizes that, except for Garz ("Carentia") in Rügen, all known Slavic temples were under
water (river, sea, lake), which indicates that sanctuaries were formed in such a way that
they would reflect the elements of the universe. The author referred here to M. Eliade's
studies showing an archetypical, mythical image of the world (*imago mundi*), in which
gods dwelled on high mountains surrounded by the primordial ocean.

263   Some image of them is given by Thietmar in his earlier account on Glomače, see above p. 57 ff.

264   This spirit of terror is also present in further lines of this description, *e.g.* Thietmar emphasizes such elements as scary looking helmets or wild animals' horns (beasts). One
should remember that E. Wienecke claimed that the element of terror was a typical sign
of *interpretatio Christiana* see above, p. 16.

265   In Rethra – Adam II, 21; see below, p. 212 f. Moszyński, *Kultura*, pp. 713 f., emphasizes
that in the Slavic symbols of numbers, number three and its multiplicity were especially
important, which can be helpful in the interpretation of the sanctuary topography in the
11th c.

THE RELIGION OF THE SLAVS IN THIETMAR'S CHRONICLE   97

this information about Radogošč (identifying it with Rethra), claimed that the triangular shape of the town did not reflect the real topography of this cult centre, and it was only a conception by the chronicler who wanted to provide symbolic sense through spatial arrangement.[266] An additional argument supporting such a hypothetical view, in Schmidt's opinion, is the possibility of association of the adjective *tricornis* defining the shape of the city with wild animals' horns (Latin *cornus*, pl. *cornua*), which – according to Thietmar – were used as building materials in the construction of the temple there (see below). For the horn was a symbol of power, ferocity, and anti-sacral forces,[267] it in this case would go to the topography in the chronicler's narrative as a symbolic element: Svarožic's capital would have "triple" power to oppose a triune God, just like polytheistic triads (*e.g.* the trinity form Uppsala known from the work of Adam of Bremen).[268]

Due to the ubiquity of the trinity element in shaping sacral and social space in the lives of Indo-European communities, including Slavic ones, it is hard to doubt Thietmar's credibility on the sole basis of symbolic associations related to the Radogošč *urbs*.[269] This is why R. Schmidt's argumentation is hardly verifiable. However, somehow incidentally, as a thought experiment,[270] it shows that Thietmar created an image highly prone to symbolic interpretation, which is a characteristic element of contemporary literary conventions. On one hand it harmonised the narration by referring to symbolic numbers,[271] and on the other hand this sensitivity to symbols – not only numerical ones – made the authors emphasize these types of motifs in descriptions, or even build a

---

266 Schmidt, "Rethra," pp. 378 ff. The author mentions in his argumentation the rich in symbols description of Rethra presented by Adam of Bremen (see below, pp. 212 ff.), to make his readers cognizant of the special climate in descriptions of pagan metropolises, however, one can hardly agree that Thietmar's account on Radogošč is as "contaminated" with conventional motifs as Adam of Bremen's passage about Rethra (see below, pp. 220 f.).

267 Forstner, *Świat*, pp. 255, 328.

268 Schmidt, "Rethra," pp. 387 ff. See also Fraesdorff, *Der barbarische Norden*, pp. 243 f., and below, p. 218.

269 Strzelczyk, *Rec. Festschrift*, p. 202.

270 If such associations come to the mind of a researcher after centuries, one may justifiably assume that similar "more profound" senses were also found in this text by a reader contemporary to the author, more open to >>symbolic thinking <<, and what is more the author himself composed the text meaning to evoke such associations as a gate to various symbolic and allegorical interpretations. This type of reading falls into text interpretation canons typical for the mentality of that epoch. For more information on the rules of text interpretation with regard for the classical form of the "four senses" see *e.g.* Hayes, "A history of Interpretation," pp. 27 ff.; Teresa Michałowska, *Średniowiecze* (Warszawa: PWN, 2006), pp. 18 f.

271 For the symbolic importance of number three see Forstner, *Świat*, p. 43.

98   CHAPTER 2

certain game of associations strengthening the presence of certain elements
in the climate of the narrative (here *e.g.* the terror thanks to the introduction
of similarly sounding words: *tricornis – cornua bestiarum*).

In the light of Thietmar's chronicle, Radogošč was first of all a cult centre,
which is confirmed by the very fact that a temple was erected there. As a matter of fact, it was a very elaborate one: "There is nothing more in it than a wood-
en shrine, built with great artistry, which instead of foundations was supported
on horns of various wild beasts."[272] The "beast's horns," which according to the
chronicler were used as the foundation of the temple, are usually interpreted
as foundation offerings, assuming that he meant not only the horns of wild
animals but rather whole skulls;[273] and this supports an attribution of this element of the building to apotropaic significance.[274] However, even without this
hypothetical interpretation, and only on the basis of the already mentioned
symbolic horn, one can interpret the use of wild animal horns as magical protection for the sanctuary.

However, it is worth emphasizing the expression "pro basibus sustentatur,"
which indicates basing the whole structure on the said "beast horns,"[275] which
in the case of the assumption that these are horns of wild animals does not
seem very probable for construction related reasons. Hence one should take

---

272 Thietmar VI, 23: "In eadem est nil nisi fanum de ligno artificiose compositum, quod pro
     basibus diversarum sustentatur cornibus bestiarum". In reference to the description of
     Radogošč it was ascertained that pre-Christian temples erected for the Western Slavs were
     built by specialist carpenters, *e.g.* Witold Hensel, *Słowiańszczyzna wczesnośredniowieczna*
     (Warszawa: PWN, 1987) p. 243.

273 The prevailing opinion is that the wild animals' horns mentioned by Thietmar are foun-
     dation offerings, see Hensel, *Słowiańszczyzna wczesnośredniowieczna*, p. 520; Szafrański,
     Prahistoria, p. 364. Rich material (including illustrations) on foundation offerings in
     Silesia has been recently presented by Bogusław Gediga, "Chrystianizacja i utrzymywanie
     się przedchrześcijańskich praktyk kultowych na Śląsku," in *Słowiańszczyzna w Europie
     średniowiecznej. Księga pamiątkowa dla Lecha Leciejewicza*, vol. 1: *Plemiona i wczesne
     państwa*, ed. Zofia Kurnatowska (Wrocław: IAE PAN, 1996), pp. 159–167. However, there
     are also other proposed solutions of this puzzling question: Urbańczyk, *Dawni Słowianie*,
     p. 74, who claims that beams were tied with natural hooks made of trimmed branches of
     some beams which resembled animal horns. Teresa Kiersnowska, Ryszard Kiersnowski,
     Życie codzienne na Pomorzu wczesnośredniowiecznym (Warszawa: PIW, 1970), p. 54, took
     into account both branched logs and foundation offerings.

274 Such interpretation is supported by an analogy in folk magic observation, in which ani-
     mal heads had apotropaic significance, Jerzy Dowiat, "Pogląd na świat," in *Kultura Polski
     średniowiecznej X–XIII w.*, ed. Jerzy Dowiat (Warszawa: PIW, 1985), p. 180.

275 Thus Brückner, *Mitologia słowiańska i polska*, p. 299), apposed this detail with a tradi-
     tional story about a witch living in a "chicken-legged hut".

THE RELIGION OF THE SLAVS IN THIETMAR'S CHRONICLE   99

into account the confabulation or even amplification[276] used by either the
chronicler's informants or himself. It is possible that Thietmar wanted to emphasize this motif as architectural detail for its symbolic meaning. In this way
in his literary vision the holiest sanctuary of the Liutici was based on a symbolic embodiment of ferocious and destructive powers of the underworldly –
in the Christian understanding, devilish – nature.

By emphasizing that in Radogošč there is only a temple, Thietmar indicated
that it was a strictly cultic location. The fortifications surrounding it were not
only understood in military terms, but also as indicating a holy place,[277] or
even the holiest place. Even the forest surrounding the famous *urbs* was to remain untouched and was worshipped by the Liutici. Thus one may put forward
a hypothesis that when speaking about Radogošč, the chronicler refers to a
wider sacral space, a holy grove located near the lake (which here also had the
nature of hierophany, which will be referred to later), where assemblies and
the oracle, mentioned by the chronicler later in his narration, operated. The
centre of this sacred area was the cult stronghold with the temple.[278]

2.6.2   *Dii manu facti*

The chronicler further describes the décor and equipment in the temple, starting with information on the decorations of the external walls: "As it appears
to the observers, its outer walls are decorated with various images of gods and
goddesses, carved in a marvellous manner."[279] Painted sculptures or effigies
on walls are also confirmed in other sources related to the Slavic religion.[280]

---

276   This supposed amplification could respond, for instance, some bones being in fact remains of animal sacrifices, especially skulls with horns. Same archaeological analogies
that could support this interpretation have been found in Scandinavia, for instance, at
Borg in Östergötland, where a small house interpreted as a cultic building was discovered, and a lot of bones (75 kilos) around it (see: Ann-Lili Nielsen, "Rituals and power.
About small buildings and animal bones from late Iron Age," in *Old Norse Religion in Long-
Term Perspectives: Origins, Changes, and Interactions: an international conference in Lund,
Sweden, June 3–7, 2004*, ed. Anders Andrén, Kristina Jennbert, Catharina Raudvere (Lund:
Nordic Academic Press, 2006), pp. 243–247).
277   Słupecki, *Archaeological Sources*, p. 340.
278   A certain analogy in this case is Prove's holy grove in the Wagrians land described by
Helmold, where also judgments were made. Holy oaks dedicated to the deity were sur-
rounded by a palisade and the holy grove was located in the forest, see below, pp. 332 f.
279   Thietmar VI, 23: "Huius parietes variae deorum dearumque imagines mirifice insculptae,
ut cernentibus videtur, exterius ornant."
280   *Herbordi Dialogus de Vita S. Ottonis Episcopi Babenbergensis*, ed. Kazimierz Liman,
Jan Wikarjak, MPH n.s. 7/3 (1974) [further: Herbord], II, 32; Saxo Grammaticus, *Gesta
Danorum / The History of the Danes*, ed. Karsten Friis-Jensen, trans. Peter Fisher, vol. 1–2
(Oxford: Clarendon Press, 2015) [further: Saxo], XIV, 39, 2.

On the basis of these accounts, a thesis was formed that a special style was developed in the construction of Slavic temples, their characteristic feature being wall reliefs.[281] However, on the basis of available sources, the incidence of this style should be restricted to the Polabian and Pomeranian area, and one should also take into account a more extensive, non-Slavic cultural context influencing its formation, taking especially into account Scandinavian infiltration. The way such effigies looked is potentially shown in the older cultic buildings discovered in Gross Raden, in which the walls were made up of rows of decorated, anthropomorphic pillars with heads.[282]

Placing the above mentioned effigies on external walls of temples raised doubts among some scholars about whether they showed images of gods.[283] However, one can speculate that they illustrated mythical content[284] by combining earthly and supernatural creatures in one vision.[285] In such a case Thietmar could generally consider this iconography as images of gods and goddesses,[286] but on the other hand it is worth not conceding his credibility without these types of speculations and additions. Effigies of idols, which were

---

281   Łowmiański, *Religia*, p. 176.

282   Słupecki, "Wykopaliska," pp. 29 f.; *idem*, "Słowiańskie posągi bóstw," *Kwartalnik Historii Kultury Materialnej* 41 (1993), p. 43. Cf. Ewald Schuldt, *Gross Raden. Ein slawischer Tempelort des 9./10. Jahrhunderts in Mecklenburg* (Berlin: Akademie-Verlag, 1985), pp. 35–49. It is worth adding that the board from Ralswiek (probably a relic of a temple) was similar to pillars from Gross Raden and had a clearly visible outline of a human face and bust, there were also traces of three colours of paint, which confirms Herbord's information about painting sculptures on the temple walls. See also: Słupecki, "Słowiańskie posągi," p. 63; *idem*, "Archaeological Sources," pp. 343 f. At the end of the 90's of the 20th c. Sławomir Moździoch, "Społeczność plemienna Śląska w IX–X wieku," in *Śląsk około roku 1000*, ed. Edmund Małachowicz, Marta Młynarska-Kaletynowa (Wrocław: Polska Akademia Nauk, 2000), pp. 42 ff., interpreted a sculptured plank discovered nearly half a century earlier in Ostrów Tumski in Wrocław, among remains of a wooden construction (which was considered a temple from the period of the pagan reaction in the 30's of the 11th c.) as an object analogous to pillars from Gross Raden and hence an anthropomorphic one.

283   Brückner, *Mitologia słowiańska i polska*, p. 190. Urbańczyk, *Dawni Słowianie*, p. 74, claims that the same thing happened in Ancient Greece, however, there gods constituted artistic motif, which is very hard to prove in the Slavdom.

284   Leszek P. Słupecki, "Świątynie pogańskich Pomorzan w czasach misji świętego Ottona (Szczecin)," *Przegląd Religioznawczy* (1993) 3, p. 28.

285   It is worth referring to the description of a temple of Triglav in Szczecin (Stettin) written by Herbord (II, 32), according to whom wall figures outside and inside the temple were to present people and animals (including birds).

286   The basis for considering them divine images by a medieval theologian could be a reference to the Bible, where there is a statement that pagans exchanged the glory of the immortal God for images of mortal creatures: people, birds and animals – see Rom 1:23.

THE RELIGION OF THE SLAVS IN THIETMAR'S CHRONICLE

FIGURE 1   Reconstruction of the Slavonic temple from Gross Raden (11th c.)
STANISŁAW ROSIK

the main hierophany (or one of them) for a given community, could have been made after all, which will be explained later in more detail.

Thietmar claims that in the temple "stand gods, made by hand, with their names carved, frighteningly dressed in helmets and armours. Among them the first one is named Svarožic who is worshipped above others by all the pagans."[287] The context of this statement convincingly demonstrates that he meant the idol called Svarožic, which was the prominent figure among the all other idols. Most certainly their military equipment was real, not sculpted.[288] Placing numerous figures inside the temple is not confirmed in other sources on the Slavic religion, apart from maybe Adam of Bremen who also wrote about the central temple of the Liutici.[289] On the other hand a certain analogy can be

---

287   Thietmar VI, 23: "dii stant manu facti, singulis nominibus insculptis, galeis atque loricis terribiliter vestiti, quorum primus Zuarasici dicitur et pre caeteris a cunctis gentilibus honoratur et colitur".

288   For comparison there are Scandinavian statues which were dressed in apparels and jewellery, which was emphasized by Słupecki, "Słowiańskie posągi," p. 64.

289   Adam II, 21. Discussion and possible doubts on the existence of numerous statues in Rethra described by Adam of Bremen, see below, pp. 217 f.

found in Rus': in Nestor's chronicle there is information that in Kiev there were statutes of the Rus' pantheon, including Perun.[290]

Describing the statues inside the temple as "hand-made gods" – *dii manu facti*, and locating the outside images of gods and goddesses – *deorum dearumque imagines*, begs the question of how the chronicler viewed the Slavic images of deities. Did he try to emphasize differences in the way they were treated by pagans by using these two different terms? How in this context should one refer to the terms *deus* and *dea* referring to divine images taken by the Liutici for the war?[291]

The expression (*dii*) *manu facti* refers also to the biblical texts of both the Old and the New Testament. A classical example of the use of this phrase is Psalm 115 (*Vulgate*: 113).[292] However, in the discussion on Thietmar's information on making images of gods and goddesses (*deorum dearumque imagines*), it is worth also recalling an episode described in the Acts of the Apostles about protests against St. Paul in Ephesus, initiated by a certain Demetrius in defence of the local Artemis cult. He manufactures little temples used as amulets and complained that the Apostle "avertit multam turbam dicens quoniam non sunt **dii, qui manibus fiunt** [emphasis – S.R.]." The commotion was deescalated by a state official who said: "Viri Ephesii, quis enim est hominum, qui nesciat Ephesiorum civitatem cultricem esse magne Dianae et simulacri a Iove delapsi."[293]

These last words lead to the conclusion that the famous statue was the embodiment of the goddess herself for her worshippers, a specific materialized "here and now" miraculous phenomenon. Hence its images were made. Identification of a deity with its image took place in a particular cult centre and was related to a particular object, which constituted hierophany. Thus Thietmar, who had been surrounded by biblical images since his childhood, had a ready view on the subject of not only theological interpretation of idols, but also how they were viewed by idolaters themselves (certainly this opinion is taken from the New Testament and so it is an exemplification of *interpretatio*

---

290 PVL, under the year 6488 [980].

291 *E.g.* Thietmar VI, 22.

292 Ps 115:4 (Vulgate: Ps 113:12): "simulacra gentium (...) opera manuum hominum" (according to *Septuaginta*) or "idola gentium (...) opus manuum hominum" (according to the Hebrew Bible). See also in Vulgate: Ba 6:50–51: "... quia non sunt dii sed opera manum hominum" (this chapter in the tradition was called also *Epistula Jeremiae*).

293 Act 19:26 and 35 (http://www.vatican.va/archive/bible/nova_vulgata/documents/nova-vulgata_nt_actus-apostolorum_lt.html). Quoting this story in its Latin version on the basis of the *Vulgate*, allows a closer look at Thietmar's mentality. A striking element is the *interpretatio Romana* of the Old Greek religion visible in the *Vulgate*, *e.g.* Artemis became Diane.

THE RELIGION OF THE SLAVS IN THIETMAR'S CHRONICLE   103

biblica of the idol cult in ancient times). Although it is impossible to prove that it was exactly this episode in the New Testament that inspired the description of the temple in Radogošč, it is important to invoke it as an analogy in the perception of the pagan *sacrum*.

In Thietmar's chronicle perspective, pagans worship particular, material embodiments of divinity[294] and not only idols; in a similar way they venerate elements of the landscape, such as mountains (*mons* in *pagus Silensi*) or a grove (*lucus Zutibure*).[295] This opinion of the chronicler could have been to some extent inspired by his knowledge of his contemporary Slavic cults. One should also take into account the mentality of these tribal communities manifested in their attitude toward cult objects found in temples and worshipped elements of the natural world, *i.e.* treating them as personifications of divine powers and creatures. An analogy in this case is readily formed by observing the duration of such structure of thought in the later Slavic folklore.[296]

Coming back to Thietmar's narrative, as a synonym for "dii manu facti" one should recognize the term *idola*, which was used in the above discussed passage on the Slavic rebellion (983) in reference to the canon defining the essence of the pagan cult as *creaturam anteponere creatori*, which is present in the Bible. In this theological judgement one should see the main inspiration for reducing pagan gods to hand-made objects. However, this way of thinking did not exclude the chronicler's references to religious images of the Liutici themselves: or to the examples similar to the discussed episode from the Acts of the Apostles, or to the Liutici myths treated analogically with ancient mythology. Both proposed variants correspond well with the expression *imagines deorum dearumque*, with reference to sculptures on the external walls of the temple.

Thus it is not surprising that in Thietmar's work there were also particular functions of pagan deities, such as *dii fautores*,[297] for which biblical analogies can also be drawn.[298] However, in this respect the reference to ancient mythologies that confirmed *expressis verbis* in the chronicle was equally important.[299]

---

294   For such a concept in Helmold's work see below, p. 378.
295   This "materialistic" outlook on the pagan cult is present even in *interpretatio biblica* of the pagan *sacrum* (see also: Wis 13) and is also expressed by Thietmar.
296   Religious images were often called gods by Slavic peasants who even whipped them if their prayers were not heard. The name 'god' was also used to refer to the sun, moon, fire or even living people: sorcerers. See Moszyński, *Kultura*, p. 707.
297   See above, p. 91.
298   *E.g.* in the episode from the Acts of the Apostles (Act 28:4) pagans mention the goddess of vengeance.
299   *E.g.* Thietmar on Pluto (VIII, 3), on Mars (VIII, 27).

104 CHAPTER 2

In the description of Radogošč such expressions indicating the character of the deities worshipped there are missing, but there is no doubt as to their military competence due to military equipment worn by idols. The fact that the statues collected in the temple personified the Liutici pantheon is supported by the information that each of the idols had its name carved in the temple.

If this detail was not produced in either the chronicler's or his informer's imagination, which is supported by suspiciously strong similarity among the names purportedly engraved on the sculptures in churches,[300] one should take into account the fact that the names were recorded in the runic, Latin, or even Old Slavic alphabet.[301] It is hard to solve this problem, especially because Thietmar could also in a literary way create (confabulate) the description in accordance with the model of ancient temples in the Mediterranean region, so as to emphasize the essence of the trespass of the apostatic Liutici, *i.e.* their return to polytheism as the ancient form of denial of the monotheistic cult of the Creator. Deities' names are a mark allowing recognition of a personal reality to serve as the addressee of a pagan cult, and so it was not accidental that they played an important role even in the ancient practice of *abrenuntiatio diaboli*, during which people would repudiate a particular deity. Its cult was treated in the theological interpretation as being open to the power of *antisacrum*, which is in accordance with a view presented in the Bible, directly identifying pagan deities with demons.[302]

The same rule was followed when Bruno of Querfurt directly called Svarožic a devil – "diabolus Zuarasici."[303] Similar diabolization or demonization of the Liutici *sacrum* can also be observed in Thietmar's chronicle, when in later lines of the discourse he called the Liutici idols "demons' statues" (*simulachra*

---

300   The information about inscriptions is very suspicious for Urbańczyk, *Dawni Słowianie*, p. 65; Kiersnowska, Kiersnowski, *Życie codzienne*, p. 54, also doubt their existence. A general statement on following church models was made by Leciejewicz, *Słowianie*, p. 193. A possibility of such borrowings was accepted also by Słupecki, "Einflüsse," pp. 180 f., who made a reservation, however, that the very idea of the temple among the Slavs was formed on a native basis.

301   Słupecki, "Einflüsse," pp. 178 f., made a supposition that the Slavs became familiar with scripture during the first Christianization and after the pagan reaction used this skill to name statues. Earlier Dralle, "Rethra," p. 42 f., claimed that inscriptions were made in the Old Slavic alphabet due to Czech influences in Polabia – cf. Jerzy Strzelczyk, "Tysiąclecie powstania Słowian połabskich 983–1983. Naukowe rezultaty jubileuszu," *Studia Historica Slavo-Germanica* 14 (1988), p. 258.

302   See *e.g.* Ps 96:37 (Vulgate: Ps 95:37); cf. 1 Cor 10:20.

303   *Epistola Brunonis ad Henricum regem*, see below, pp. 107 f.

THE RELIGION OF THE SLAVS IN THIETMAR'S CHRONICLE   105

demonum).[304] However, in this case one should take into account that he either shared Bruno's view treating deities as devils (see below), or he did not go
so far in this identification and only mentioned that actually the pagan cult
was dedicated to demons, since he was convinced that gods were only a creation of the deceived human mind.[305]

The last sentence connected with the interior decoration of the temple provides information about the gods' war banners (so called stanice) placed there
and carried by infantry during war expeditions: "Their banners are never removed from here, unless they are needed for an expedition – in such case footsoldiers carry them."[306] There was also a widely held view that Thietmar, in
other places of his chronicle when presenting the war theatre, calls them gods
and goddesses. However, it is not possible to exclude that not only banners,
but also other cult statues, were taken to war expeditions. In descriptions of
Liutici expeditions the term *deus* or *dea* refers to an idol, a worshipped object,[307]
but due to a very special literary convention another semantic aspect is also
evident.

The chronicler showed predilection to present *sacrum* objects as mystical
items that occurred on the historical stage. It is perfectly visible in his creativity in the way he treated cathedral churches as "Christ's bride" (*sponsa Christi*),
thus having the building embody or even personify this mystic being which is
the Church community in ecclesiological reflection, presented as a bride dedicated to Christ.[308] In this line of reasoning, the earthly, material reality and the

---

304   In the notions of Christianity there is an organic relation between an idol and demons,
      see below (p. 219), however, here one should emphasize that Thietmar knew the etymology of the 'demon' written by Isidore of Seville (Thietmar I, 24) and the context of his
      work shows that he does not restrict the activity of fallen spiritual creatures only to the
      pagan cult. Thus the expression *simulachra demonum* indicates a strictly theological category, not referring directly to Slavic beliefs.

305   1 Cor 10:20 can be interpreted in the same way.

306   Thietmar VI, 23: "Vexilla quoque eorum, nisi ad expeditionis necessaria, et tunc per
      pedites, hinc nullatenus moventur."

307   Ps 96:5 (Vulgate according to Septuaginta Ps 95:5): "dii gentium daemonia".

308   When mentioning the consecration of these buildings, Thietmar speaks directly about
      the consecration of "the bride of Christ" by the hands of the bishops gathered there (*e.g.*
      Thietmar VI, 60: "Peracta in civitate Bavenbergensi aecclesia maiore, cum natalicius regis
      dies esset [et XXXV. iam inciperet annus], II. Non. Mai omnis primatus ad dedicationem
      istius aulae ibidem congregatur; et sponsa haec Christi per manus [Iohannis patriarchae
      de Aquileia et aliorum plus quam XXX episcoporum] consecratur"; cf. trans. D.A. Warner
      in: *Ottonian Germany*, p. 278, VI, 60: "When the cathedral in the city of Bamberg had been
      completed, all the leading men of the realm gathered there on 6 May, the king's thirty-
      fifth birthday, to participate in its consecration. Patriarch John of Aquileia and more than
      thirty other bishops undertook the consecration of this bride of Christ"). The image of the

106   CHAPTER 2

spiritual reality are immanently connected with a particular place and material condition.[309]

On the historical stage created by Thietmar, the Liutici "gods" function in an analogous way. Their "unutterable fury" (*ineffabilis furor*) is calmed by offerings made to them.[310] They also lead the Liutici army, thus personifying antisacral powers adverse to Christ's kingdom. In Svarožic's image and the other "dii manu facti" surrounding it in the Radogošč temple, one can find similarities to a vision well known from the New Testament presenting Satan leading a community of demons. However, this is not an undisputable basis for the view that this biblical archetype was imprinted on the chronicler's description in the shape of the topical demons' *princeps*,[311] which is worth considering in a wider context of research on the religion of the Slavs.

2.6.3 Svarožic – *deorum primus*

Thietmar did not describe how idols were distributed in the Radogošč temple, however the phrase, "among them [*i.e.* gods – S.R.] the first one is named Svarožic who is worshipped above others by all the pagans"[312] is a premise for placing the idol of Svarožic in the central part of the sacral space. However, lack of information about at least the number of other idols makes it difficult to draw further conclusions.[313] As a possible context for any speculations in this matter, one should take into account the image of the triad of idols in Uppsala described by Adam of Bremen, according to whom Thor, leading the

---

      mystic wedding of God and the community of his people (as his bride) finds its model in
      the Old Testament and becomes the basic idea for the Song of Songs.

309   For more information on this matter, see S. Rosik, "Sponsae Christi oraz dii manu facti
      w Kronice Thietmara. Elementy konwencji dziejopisarskiej w służbie historiologii," in
      *Viae historicae. Księga jubileuszowa dedykowana Profesorowi Lechowi A. Tyszkiewiczowi
      w siedemdziesiątą rocznicę urodzin*, ed. Mateusz Goliński, Stanisław Rosik, (Acta
      Universitatis Wratislaviensis. Historia) 152 (Wrocław: Wydawnictwo Uniwersytetu
      Wrocławskiego, 2001), pp. 415–421.

310   Thietmar VI, 25.

311   See Mt 12, 24; Mk 3:22; Lk 11:15; Adam of Bremen expressis verbis referred to this New
      Testament image in the description of Rethra, see below, p. 253.

312   Thietmar VI, 23: "... quorum primus Zuarasici dicitur et pre caeteris [diis – S.R.] a cunctis
      gentilibus honoratur et colitur".

313   In the other 11th and 12th c. descriptions of Slavic temples in the Polabia and Pomerania
      area, usually the presence of only one idol in them was emphasized (Rethra, Szczecin,
      Arkona – see below, pp. 217, 338, 357 ff.), however, it is impossible to completely exclude
      that there were not more of them, especially if one takes into account smaller, portable
      idols, whose existence was confirmed in the hagiography of St. Otto of Bamberg (see: Ebo
      II, 13; III, 1. Cf. Rosik, *Conversio*, pp. 290 ff., 355 f.).

THE RELIGION OF THE SLAVS IN THIETMAR'S CHRONICLE 107

pantheon, had his throne located in the middle of the temple.[314] Similarly, in "Carentia" (probably Garz) in Rügen, according to Saxo Grammaticus, at the time of the Danish invasion of the island there was a cult facility dedicated to the triad of deities led by Rugievit, but their statues were not located under one roof.[315] Another model of sanctuary spatial organization, referring to a larger group of idols, was proposed on the basis of archaeological exploration of supposed open cult places in the eastern Slavdom: a statue of the major deity was presumably surrounded by a circle of images of more or less significant figures in the pantheon.[316]

On the basis of the discussed information it is hard to define the reach of Svarožic's cult precisely. Taking into account the fact that the description refers to this particular sanctuary, the phrase "all pagans" (*cuncti gentiles*[317]) should apply mainly to the Liutici, although one should also take into account their neighbours, respecting their political influences and the authority of the oracle in Radogošč.[318] This assessment remains in agreement with the *Letter of Bruno of Querfurt to King Henry II*, which was most probably[319] written not more than a decade earlier and in which Svarožic was presented as a personification of the devil leading the Liutici. At that time the German ruler had an alliance against Poland with these tribes, and the famous missionary in his letter criticized this alliance.[320] An adequate passage in this epistolography gives an excellent example of Christian interpretation of paganism, developed with

---

314   Adam IV, 26.

315   Saxo XIV, 39, 39.

316   Słupecki, *Slavonic Pagan Sanctuaries*, pp. 120 ff.; Rosik, *Udział*, p. 91. Possibly this arrangement was used in the embodiment of the pantheon in Rus', according to PVL, established by Vladimir the Great on a hill in Kiev in 980; see above, p. 102, footnote 290.

317   Thietmar VI, 23.

318   It is a reference to Thietmar's account horizon, which does not exclude the possibility of Svarožic's cult in other Slavic countries, *e.g.* in Rus', which will soon be discussed in this chapter.

319   It is worth remembering that the oldest preserved manuscript with Bruno's letter comes from the second half of the 11th c. (see *e.g.* Sosnowski, "Kilka uwag," p. 65), so one should mention here a certain shadow of doubt related to which was its author or whether its content was the same as the original.

320   From Bruno's letter to Henry II (*Epistola Brunonis ad Henricum regem*, ed. Jadwiga Karwasińska, MPH n.s. 4/3 (1973), pp. 101 f.): "Ut autem salva gratia regis ita loqui liceat: bonumne est persequi christianum et habere in amicitia populum paganum? (...) Non credis peccatum, o rex, quando christianum caput, quod nefas est dictu, immolatur sub daemonum vexillo?" ("May I be allowed to say without losing royal favor: is it good to persecute a Christian [people] and cultivate friendship with pagan people? Don't you believe, my king, that it is a sin to give a head of a Christian – this shall not even be spoken about – as a sacrifice under demonic banners?"). About Bruno's letter see *e.g.* Wojciech Fałkowski, "List Brunona do króla Henryka," in *Bruno z Kwerfurtu. Osoba – dzieło – epoka,*

reference to the antithetical relationship between Christ and Belial, known already from the Second Epistle of St. Paul to the Corinthians:

"What is the agreement of Christ and Belial? What is the comparison of light and darkness? How is it possible for the devil Svarožic to meet the prince of the holy, yours and ours, St. Maurice? How can the holy lance and diabolic banners that feast on human blood touch their foreheads?"[321] Thus in theological and moral categories, Bruno evaluated political activity of the German king, and in the cascade of antitheses there is a striking hierarchy of entities in which Svarožic, as a personification of the devil, turned out to be subject to Belial.

In relation to this ruler of darkness, the Liutici god was somewhat analogous St. Maurice, the leader of saints and the Christian community in the empire circle (defined by Bruno as "vester et noster"), in terms of his relation to Christ. Hence it is not accidental that the last tier of the antithesis is determined by symbols of power playing a special role in the context of war expeditions: the Holy Lance (of St. Maurice) and blood-thirsty, devilish signs, Liutici banners. In this way the spiritual confrontation dimension taking place "here and now," in the theatre of a particular war, was emphasized.

Similarly Thietmar, after completing the excurse about Radogošč, stresses that the forces of the Liutici and the Empire set off against Poland had leaders who were "unequal" or "differing from each other" ("inparibus ducis"), which most certainly was a reference to war emblems carried in front of the allied armies, *i.e.* idols and the Holy Lance. However, there is doubts about the interpretation of Svarožic's character and status, and whether the chronicler shared this view, according to which he belonged to the same rank as devils serving Belial. He presented Svarožic as the first among gods (deities) whose cult was, in his opinion, a false alternative to Christ's religion.

In the world of the Bible known to him from reading, prophets and apostles struggled with polytheistic cults that had one major god (*e.g.* Baal, Ephesian Artemis). In biblical interpretation of these creatures, mythological motifs related to them are of minor significance, and the main message is the confrontation of their cult with monotheism. Particular polytheistic religious systems, in this perspective, are outlined as subsequent historical manifestations of evil spiritual powers, which supports a trend to assume that pagan deities are personifications of demons. A model image of this sphere of *antisacrum*

---

ed. Marian Dygo, Wojciech Fałkowski (Pułtusk: Wydawnictwo Akademii Humanistycznej im. Aleksandra Gieysztora, 2010), pp. 179–207.

321 "»Quae conventio Christi ad Belial?« quae comparatio luci ad tenebras? quomodo conveniunt Zuarasiz diabolus, et dux sanctorum vester et noster Mauritius? qua fronte coeunt sacra lancea et, qui pascuntur humano sanguine, diabolica vexilla?" – Bruno's letter to Henry II (*Epistola Brunonis*, pp. 101 f.); cf. 2 Cor 6:15.

THE RELIGION OF THE SLAVS IN THIETMAR'S CHRONICLE   109

in Christian tradition found its place in synoptic gospels mentioning Satan's dominion as the ruler (*princeps*) of demons.[322]

This model image of the "demons' princeps" was used by Adam of Bremen in his presentation of the cult of Redigast (Radogost), who was often identified with Svarožic.[323] In reference to Thietmar's information discussed here however, one should conclude that it was only a general archetypal model of presenting creatures hostile to God in a hierarchical way: one of them leads all other deities/demons. It is important to emphasize that this model had determined the above-mentioned biblical images as well as the historiographical visions of the Liutici religion in the 11th c., developed under their influence.

In the light of Thietmar's account, Svarožic is presented in a different way than in the interpretation of St. Bruno's letter, and one can say that he is an antithesis of Christ himself. Although the Bishop of Merseburg did not diabolize Svarožic in his description, he presented his cult in a theological perspective as open to the activity of demonic power led by Satan (also in accordance with an expression used in another place of the chronicle calling idols *simulacra demonum*). Thus, it is not surprising that Thietmar, without dwelling too much on Svarožic's abilities, directed attention to his name itself.[324] The role of the major deity of the Liutici on the historical stage is unambiguous: embodiment or even personification of powers hostile to Christ and his believers. In this perspective, it seems natural that the chronicler considers the universal abilities of this deity to be obvious following biblical examples of God's opponents.[325]

In this situation one should consider the possibility that this historiographic image of Svarožic's domination in the Liutici pantheon to a large extent was an effect of the influence of Christian interpretation of their *sacrum*. Similarly

322   See above, footnote 311 in this chapter.

323   See below p. 213.

324   It is also worth taking into account – as the context of Thietmar's pastoral activity, which influenced his attitude to the Slavic sacrum – that at the time of introducing Christianity, clergy involved in missionary activity perforce had to pay attention to names of native deities, due to their significance in exorcist practice, especially in baptismal rites, during which evil spirits and cults of particular deities were repudiated. More general information about exorcisms and their historical development can be found in *e.g.* Bogusław Nadolski, *Liturgika*, vol. 3 (Poznań: Pallotinum, 1992), pp. 249–253.

325   Hence, a model used by Thietmar to define Svarožic and other deities' competences in the first instance would be not referring to ancient mythology but rather Christian demonology, which is additionally confirmed in another place by calling Slavic statues *simulachra demonum* (see pp. 104 f.). A demon must have been perceived by the chronicler as a spirit omnicompetent (although not almighty), which is also supported by quoting Isidore of Seville' etymology of the word 'demon' as "omniscient" (Thietmar I, 24: "daimon, id est omnia sciens"); see W. Trillmich in: *Thietmari Merseburgensis Episcopi Chronicon*, ed. Trillmich, p. 28, footnote 74.

110   CHAPTER 2

it is worth reflecting on the problem of the high level of militarization in the
Radogošč pantheon, which is indicated by Thietmar's statement that all gods
in the Radogošč sanctuary were equipped with fearful helmets and armour.[326]
Thus a question arises of whether this emphasis on military attributes, and
also of abilities, is not a result of a literary creation of the scene of described
events. Or perhaps the military functions of the deities actually came to the
fore due to a very special situation in which the Liutici Federation was formed
and functioned.

A key indication in searching for the answer to this question is Svarožic's
name.[327] Etymologically Svarožic means "Svarog's son" or possibly "little
Svarog," and this assessment extends the geographical circle of these inqui-
ries. Svarog appears in Rus' historiography, more precisely in PVL, in which he
was identified on the basis of *interpretatio classica graeca* with Hephaestus.[328]
Information about him appears only in the final redaction from the second
decade of the 12th c. and it is a gloss in a passage borrowed from an early
Byzantine chronicle by John Malalas (*Chronographia*), in which there is also
Svarog's son called Dazbog,[329] identified with Helios.[330] H. Łowmiański made

---

326   War attributes were usually assigned to deities of seaside Slavic tribes, *e.g.* Svantevit,
       Rugievit or Iarovit – see *e.g.* Miś, "Przedchrześcijańska religia," p. 108; Strzelczyk, *Mity*,
       pp. 84, 174, 209; Rosik, *Conversio*, pp. 419 ff. Indirect information about the character of
       the Liutici god could be included in a comparison made in the letter of Bruno to Henry II:
       Christ – Belial and devil Svarožic – St. Maurice. Gieysztor, *Mitologia*, p. 170, claimed that
       the fact that the Radogošč god was in opposition to the patron saint of chivalry was the
       basis to conclude he had war competences. It is worth adding here that on the basis
       of this passage in the letter of Bruno a Slavic pseudo-deity called Belial was born (see:
       Urbańczyk, *Dawni Słowianie*, p. 187), which offers some explanation as to how far it was
       possible not to take into account the Christian interpretation during the research on
       Slavic beliefs.

327   It was reconstructed, let us remember, on the basis of the lection: *Zuarasizi* (Thietmar VI,
       23) and *Zuarasiz* in the letter of Bruno to Henry II (as in 321 in this chapter).

328   Brückner, *Mitologia słowiańska i polska*, p. 44, questioned accuracy of the identification of
       Svarog with Hephaestus occurring in PVL (cf. Moszyński, *Kultura*, p. 504), but it was only
       the beginning of the debate, see under footnotes 330, 337 in this chapter.

329   The name Dazbog was explained as 'god the giver' by F. Miklosich as early as the 19th c.,
       see Leszek Moszyński, "Prasłowiański panteon w słowniku etymologicznym i Lexiconie
       Franciszka Miklosicha," *Studia z Filologii Polskiej i Słowiańskiej* 31 (1993), p. 165, and also by
       Urbańczyk, *Dawni Słowianie*, p. 180; Kulišić, *Stara Slovenska religija*, pp. 41 f., 160–162, 173;
       Boris A. Rybakov, *Jazyčestvo drevnej Rusi* (Moskva: Nauka, 1987), p. 440. See also Strzelczyk,
       Mity, pp. 198 f.

330   PVL, under the year 6622 [1114]. This information was accepted without reservations
       by *e.g.* Pettazzoni, *Wszechwiedza*, pp. 220–223, who considered it *interpretatio slava*
       of Egyptian gods: Svarog-Feost, *i.e.* Hephaestus, who in John Malalas's Greek origi-
       nal was euhemeristically presented as one of the first Egyptian kings. Even Brückner,

THE RELIGION OF THE SLAVS IN THIETMAR'S CHRONICLE   111

an attempt to show that initially the all-Slavic, in his opinion, cult of Svarog
was not known in Rus' at the time of Christianization, and the discussed information (also referring to Dazbog) in fact was to apply only to the mythology of
southern Slavdom. However, the arguments for this conclusion are based on
excessively unstable ground.

The basis for Łowmiański's argument[331] is a conviction that the glosses in
PVL – about this deity were interpolations in the Slavic translation (from the
10th–11th c.) of John Malalas's chronicle, taken over to PVL (under the year
1114) in the third redaction (according to Shachmatov from 1118). The argument is formed in the following points: 1) Rus' sources do not know Svarog
apart from a borrowing from Malalas's work, which is surprising given a rather
large number of sources; similarly, Dazbog appears in them only twice: in PVL
and "The Tale of Igor's Campaign" (however, here probably it is also literary
genesis); 2) Rus' sermons do remain silent on the matter of these deities (the
name "Svarožic" in Rus' sermons refers only to fire); 3) Rus' historiography from
the 12th–13th c. does not know names of deities taken from colloquial language; 4) the environment in which the identification of Svarog and Dazbog
with Hephaestus and Helios occurred in glosses to John Malalas's work must
have known these Slavic deities, their origin and abilities. Meanwhile in Rus'
around 1118 (when the third edition of PVL was completed) the name Svarog
was considered strange since an additional gloss was written by the author of
the Rus' chronicle to the already existing glosses in the Slavic translation of
John Malalas's work, which included information that Svarog was a name used
by Egyptians. In another place he even added that penalties established by
Feost (Hephaestus) influenced the decision of giving him the name "Svarog."
Hence in Rus', Svarog was considered an Egyptian deity, which is why it could

---

Mitologia słowiańska i polska, p. 49, proposed to see the Sun in Svarožic (i.e. little Svarog),
considered – as Svarog's son – Dazbog, assuming at the same time that somewhere else he
was called Triglav, Svantevit or Iarovit. Łowmiański, Religia, pp. 98 f. expressed, however,
views opposing those of A. Brückner, who connected Svarog with great fire and Svarožic
with small fire, Łowmiański asked rhetorically: what fire does Sun originate from, since
it is the biggest one? Thus Hephaestus, in a gloss would be identified with Svarog not
because he meant fire, and because he was blacksmith, but because he was Dazbog-sun's
father. Hence, according to H. Łowmiański, the author of the gloss knew that Dazbog
was Svarog's son, and this is why, without hesitation, he called Hephaestus Svarog as he
was Helios's father. Malalas, being Syrian, probably knew the Egyptian version of the
myth of Hephaestus (Ptah) as Helios's father, and even this version – in the hypothesis of
H. Łowmiański – was connected with the Slavic mythology by the author of the glosses to
Malalas's work; in this concept the glosses were introduced to it in the Bulgarian environment (for the discussion related to this see below, footnote 332 in this chapter).

331   Łowmiański, Religia, pp. 92–96.

be concluded that Slavic mythological glosses must have found their way into John Malalas's chronicle, not in Rus', but at the stage of working on a translation of this chronicle in Bulgaria (and this environment was the place where Feost was identified as Svarog – without Egyptian references); 5) moreover the Bulgarian origin of the glosses is supported by the fact that Dazbog was called "Svarog's son" in them and not Svarožic. Dazbog – as Svarog's son – should be called "Svarožic" in the whole of the northern Slavdom, but not among the Bulgarians, because in Bulgaria the suffix -*itjo when creating a patronimicum was forgotten; Jakobson's argument that in Rus' there was a custom to call a person according to their father's name should be rejected here because this custom came later, and in the 10th–12th c. was only the patronimicum created; 6) the last argument against the Rus' provenance of the gloss is the fact that in an earlier – by half a century – version of PVL, Nikon did not mention Svarog when presenting Vladimir's pantheon encompassing mainly Rus' deities, thus as early as the mid-11th c. this deity was not remembered in Kiev, which gives authorization to delete it from the East Slavic pantheon.

Although the conviction – that a Slavic translation of Joannes Malalas's chronicle created in Bulgaria existed – adopted as the starting point for this argumentation was based on a wider discussion among scholars, it turned out to be only speculation, and thus further argumentation on its basis understandably leads to controversies.[332] Regardless, it is worth undertaking a detailed polemic with H. Łowmiański's view not only because of the implausibility of his claims, but also because the arguments based on it enter the realm of reflection on source studies and encompass proposals of definitions of thought that condition the creation of accounts about Slavic religion. This is critical in the discussion of its interpretation. The order of the polemic refers to the order of the H. Łowmiański's thesis:

1) the literary genesis of the appearance of Dazbog in Rus' sources is only an allegation, and to build further conclusions based on it is extremely risky; 2) Rus' sermons raised the problem of worshipping demons during the time of Christianization, and the cult of higher deities at the time of the so-called dual-faith could be losing its strength, this is why: 3) Svarog did not have to be present at all in colloquial language any more, and the similarity of his name to fire-'Svarožic' is a double-edged argument: calling fire 'Svarožic' could be a relic of an earlier cult addressed to a god; 4) recognising Svarog as an Egyptian god could indicate that at the time of Christianization the native cult and mythology in Rus' became an element of a new narration in the culture related to

---

332   It is strongly emphasized by Banaszkiewicz, *Polskie dzieje*, p. 134.

THE RELIGION OF THE SLAVS IN THIETMAR'S CHRONICLE   113

origines (monk-chroniclers could refer to this deity as a relic of outmoded my-thology, using it as a motif in the creation of a literary vision of the beginnings of society). Secondly it is worth taking into account the possibility that the discussed identification is *interpretatio slavica* of the Egyptian religion, *e.g.* in Rus' sources in the apocryph "*Хождение Богородицы по мукам*" ["Descent of the Mother of God into Hell"] there is information about the human origin of Rus' gods, they were "dignitaries, Perun in Greece, Chors on Cyprus, Troian was the emperor of Rome ...";[333] similarly Ordericus Vitalis wrote that the Liutici worshipped Thor and other Scandinavian deities, which must have been *interpretatio germanica* of Slavic Gods; 5) the name "Dazbog" has an independent etymology,[334] the power of which could be more attractive than the word "Svarožic" originating from his father's name, possibly being used in parallel to this deity – silence of sources, *i.e.* the fact that in this case patronimicum did not occur, can hardly be a strong argument in this discussion; 6) the lack of Svarog in Vladimir's pantheon described in PVL (981) can be explained mainly by the specifics of the religious reform conducted by him. With an eye to the significance of the Scandinavian element in the genesis of Rus', one should not be surprised in this case with the privileged position of the major deity – presumably Svarog's place was taken over by Perun, "ruler of thunder," following the model of the Nordic Thor. In this case it is possible to consider other speculations[335] similarly, as with reference to Svarožic, having noticed his absence in Vladimir's pantheon, one wonders whether at that time Svarožic could still be a non-anthropomorphised sacral phenomenon.[336] However, this absence can better be explained by *e.g.* a functional analysis: Perun's privileged position meant taking away a possibility to develop the cult of god Svarožic – he was also militant and agrarian (possibly identified with Svarog or Dazbog). In conclusion: the thesis of Svarog and Dazbog's absence in the area of social and cultural memory in Rus' in the 11th c. at the present stage of discussion cannot stand criticism.

In the perspective of a functional analysis, the identification of Svarog with Hephaestus also raises doubts among scholars,[337] while the identification

---

333   See: Brückner, *Mitologia słowiańska i polska*, p. 36.

334   See footnote 329 in this chapter.

335   See later, pp. 115 ff.

336   Urbańczyk, *Dawni Słowianie*, p. 151.

337   Gieysztor, *Mitologia*, pp. 171 ff., ascertained that identification of Svarog with Hephaestus – the god of fire and metalworking, and his son Dazbog with Helios – the god of sun, seems to be a downright reversal of hierarchy and descent. This and not any other adaptation of Greek characters' names to Slavic deities was to decide on the specifics of

114   CHAPTER 2

of Dazbog with Helios does not,[338] and this solar mythological explication
is used in attempts to define Svarog's real place in the Slavic pantheon –
as indentified with the mysterious "god of gods,"[339] but with doubts[340] – and
to justify Svarožic being treated as Dazbog's counterpart, or even identified
with him. Accepting this solution means questioning the thesis, supported by

---

erudition of the translator of this passage of Malalas's work. At the same time A. Gieysztor
thought that in this case it was not very probable that the Baltic myth about a blacksmith
forging the sun had any influence. Similarly Łowmiański, *Religia*, pp. 98 f., questioned the
sense of taking into account a reference to the Lithuanian myth about a blacksmith who
forged the sun in the analysis of the information discussed here, claiming that this motif
was a Finnish borrowing and was neither known in Slavic nor in Greek mythology.

338   Brückner, *Mitologia słowiańska i polska*, p. 33. See also A. Gieysztor, *Mitologia*, pp. 175, 179.
      See also above footnote 330 in this chapter.

339   Łowmiański, *Religia*, pp. 98 f. put forward his own concept of the development of Slavic
      beliefs: Svarožic's father was Svarog-sky representing an element of the Indo-European
      so-called prototheism. In the 11th c. Svarog was forgotten in the eastern Slavdom, and
      only Svarožic was worshipped, or more precisely three Svarožics: fire, Dazbog-Sun, moon.
      Łowmiański doubted if the south Slavic pantheon had more than three gods, because
      fire-Svarožic in Rus' was not the proper anthropomorphic god, he was a deified element
      similar to Hephaestus, before he turned into a divine blacksmith. The same referred to
      Dazbog and the moon, they could be deified celestial bodies. If Dazbog turned out to be
      an anthropomorphic deity, it would be the only trace of prototheism transformed into
      polytheism. According to Łowmiański, Svarog (and in other places Perun) are two differ-
      ent transformations of the original Indo-European deity of the sky. Hence Svarog would
      be identical with Helmold's (1, 84) "god of gods" (see below, p. 348).

340   Gieysztor, *Mitologia*, pp. 171–175, only partly shared position discussed here. In his po-
      lemic with Łowmiański, Gieysztor emphasized that the existence of Svarog and his son
      was proof that theogonic thought existed among the Slavs, although it is ignored by schol-
      ars representing naturistic primitivisation of their beliefs (*e.g.* postulating *e.g.* equating
      Svarožic with fire and Dazbog with the sun, taking into account the needs of the agrarian
      society as background of this phenomenon). According to Gieysztor, the cult of nature
      expresses human experience in searching for connections between the macrocosm and
      the microcosm (*i.e.* a human being), while in beliefs myth is projected on nature. The
      scholar found comparative material in the triple concept of fire in the Vedas referring to
      three functions: earthly, atmospheric (thunder) and heavenly (sun); he found an analo-
      gous division in the Roman religion. Gieysztor emphasized, however, that in the case of
      Indo-European mythologies, it does not seem that the Sun replaced a sovereign deity – it
      was more of the eye of the sky or the eye of the sovereigns of the world, Mitra and Varuna.
      However, if in Rus' there was a view that Svarog was Dazbog's father and Svarožic was fire,
      then firstly they – *i.e.* Dazbog and Svarožic – are identical, secondly their father is the fire
      of a higher order, *i.e.* the Sun. Hence Svarog is not the god of the sky at all, he is a deity
      so distinguished and close to the sovereigns of sky that sometimes he could even cover
      them. Then, however, Svarog would not be the "god of gods" (according to Helmold 1, 84).
      However, it is not easy to agree with the last statement – see below, pp. 347 f.

THE RELIGION OF THE SLAVS IN THIETMAR'S CHRONICLE   115

A. Brückner,[341] that Svarog was identical to Svarožic, based on an explanation
that the latter was a diminutive form of the former.[342]

Regardless of the view adopted on the matter, it is worth emphasizing that
the condition of medieval sources related to studies on the cult of Svarožic creates an exceptional opportunity to confirm the existence of a deity worshiped
in the east and west of the Slavdom.[343] Attempts made to explain this fact by
migration of the cult from Radogošč to Rus' or the other way around have remained only speculations,[344] which can hardly compete with better justified
searches in the studies on transformations of Slavic religion that took place
over centuries. In this perspective one can perceive Svarožic as the original
"fire spirit," known in this form in Rus', which turned into a god in Radogošč.
However, an alternative view seems equally worthy of attention, as it claims
that at the time of Christianization in Rus', the significance of Svarožic de-
clined and he had the status of a demon.[345]

At the root of this perspective there is a historical dispute about the genesis
of Slavic polytheism that has lasted for generations.[346] It is assumed that a cult
of numerous gods was characteristic of the Slavs from the beginning of their
existence (due to Indo-European heritage). However, there are also more skeptical interpretations, which generally accept the development of polytheism
only in Rus' and Polabia and not earlier than in the 10th c.[347] At the beginning
of the formation of the pantheon in this trend of hypothetical investigation
there was to be only one deity, identified with the "demiurge of the thunder-
bolt" mentioned in the mid-6th c. by Procopius of Caesarea, and worshiped

341   Brückner, *Mitologia słowiańska i polska*, pp. 338 f. Brückner assumed that the author of
      the gloss consciously chose for the name "the son of Svarogs" for Dazbog, because ex-
      actly Svarožic was Svarog. Cf. Moszyński, *Kultura*, pp. 240, 503; Pettazzoni, *Wszechwiedza*,
      p. 223; Urbańczyk, *Dawni Słowianie*, pp. 107, 180, 191.

342   Gieysztor, *Mitologia*, pp. 171, claimed that in the case of the name Svarožic: patronym or a
      diminutive, the question should be solved with a comparative analysis which indicates a
      filial relation.

343   Urbańczyk, *Dawni Słowianie*, pp. 27, 106; Gieysztor, *Mitologia*, p. 171. *Ibidem*, pp. 175 f., here
      referring to Ibn Rosteh and Al Gardezi testimonies on the matter of common worship of
      fire among the Slavs; see also Strzelczyk, *Mity*, p. 199.

344   Wienecke, *Untersuchungen*, pp. 261 f. claimed that Svarožic came to Radogošč from Rus'.
      Earlier Jagić assumed the opposite direction of this borrowing; cf. Brückner, *Mitologia
      słowiańska i polska*, p. 114; Pettazzoni, *Wszechwiedza*, p. 221.

345   Urbańczyk, *Dawni Słowianie*, pp. 27 f., 192.

346   Fundamental shaping of positions on this matter took place in the 70's and 80's of the
      20th c., which is well depicted in a comparison of synthetic studies by H. Łowmiański
      (*Religia*) and as an alternative A. Gieysztor (*Mitologia*), whose theses were referred to by
      Andrzej Szyjewski, *Religia Słowian* (Kraków: WAM, 2003). See earlier, pp. 19–28.

347   For more information on this matter see pp. 174 f.

by the Sclavenes and Antes.[348] The existence of the other Slavic deities mentioned in the earliest sources, especially in relation to Rus', in the case of these
research positions is treated with great caution. An essential element for the
skeptical arguments on this matter turns out to be a reference to interpretations of paganism in the culture (especially literary culture) of the Christian
circle, which is clearly depicted by Leszek Moszyński's reflections on the *Tale of
Bygone Years* (PVL) passage in his dissertation on pre-Christian religion of the
Slavs, written more than twenty years ago.[349]

Moszyński emphasized that this place in the chronicle refers to a mythological episode (from Homer's poetry), in which Helios discovered Aphrodite's
unfaithfulness, and the motif was recalled as an apology of monogamy.
According to a procedure known from translations of the Bible (*e.g.* that of
St. Hieronymus's), the translator introduced native names instead of antique
theonims. Hephaestus – as the one "called God by the Egyptians" – was identified with Svarog, whose existence did not raise any doubts according to
Moszyński. However, the same author treated the origin of Dazbog in quite a
different way, and he considered his name not to be a theonim but a wrongly
read greeting in the Christian environment (*dadjъ Bogъ!*). Such a way of thinking strictly corresponds with the fundamental thesis of the dissertation, which
refuses to admit the presence of Pre-Slavic and Slavic polytheism and mythology on the threshold of the Middle Ages. The only Slavic god was to be called
Svarog or Perun and was to be a transfiguration of the original and the only
sovereign of heavens (**svętъ Bogъ*), and was to associate with Hephaestus not
as a specific theonim but appellatively as a general symbol of the god. On the
other hand, the occurrence of the erroneous identification of Dazbog – in this
concept of a pseudo-deity – with Helios, should be explained in this way of
thinking by the absence of other higher supernatural creatures worshipped by
pre-Christian inhabitants of Rus'.

The most significant aspect of justification for this refutation of the existence of mythology and a pantheon of the early Slavs is an assumption that in
the assessment of the development of their spiritual culture, antique images
of the *sacrum*, including anthropomorphization, were the norm.[350] However,
in the case of investigations related to "barbarian" communities, such restrictions of the research questionnaire raise doubts. Firstly, cults were always

---

348   See above footnote 90 in this chapter.
349   Moszyński, *Die vorchristliche Religion*, pp. 3–16, 127. Detailed analyses of L. Moszyński de-
       cisively exceed the signalled here general outline.
350   For more information about it see earlier, pp. 13 ff., 19 ff.

THE RELIGION OF THE SLAVS IN THIETMAR'S CHRONICLE   117

accompanied by myth.[351] Secondly, anthropomorphization of *sacrum* is not an indispensable factor in the creation of the image of the world of gods and making its representations.[352] This is why, even if one shares a hypothetical view on the development of anthropomorphous divine representations under the influence of contacts with the circle of Christian civilization, it is impossible to impute automatically a lack of gods to early Slavdom. Thus, regarding their appearance in sources as a result of *interpretatio Christiana* (or *mythologica*) is based on *a priori* assumptions. At the current state of research it is only one of the hypothetical possibilities.

It is essential, however, that even a position which is so saturated with skepticism about the existence of the Slavic pantheon – correspondingly with a similar position expressed earlier by H. Łowmiański[353] – did not lead to a questioning of Svarog's leading role in the cult of Old Slavs. This correlates with an analysis of the account under the year 1114 in PVL by Jacek Banaszkiewicz,[354] who regarded Svarog as a "cultural hero" and sovereign ruler. He was a god who established the fundamentals of civilization that acted for the benefit of the community. He is accredited with technical progress (blacksmithing craft) and is accompanied by his legislative activity leading to the advancement of a primitive group of subjects to the level of a properly shaped community.[355] The motif of defending monogamy, present in this passage, in the light of this

---

351   Gieysztor, *Mitologia*, p. 25.
352   Rosik, *Udział*, pp. 71–83 and 99 f. It is worth adding that Tacitus mentioned that the highest Germanic god was worshipped in the form of a post, however, he did not refuse him divine nature due to this fact. This observation is even more important if one remembers that this Roman historian confirmed that Germans worshipped the most probably anthropomorphous figure of goddess Nerthus – see Publius Cornelius Tacitus, *Germania*, Latin and German text, ed. and trans. Eugen Fehrle (München: Lehmanns, 1935), 40, pp. 46–48. Cf. *e.g.* Stanisław Piekarczyk, *Religia Germanów*, in *Zarys dziejów religii*, ed. Józef Keller (Warszawa: Iskry, 1988), pp. 501 f. Thus anthropomorphisation of the sacrum sphere is a sufficient argument for development of a system of myths, however, its absence cannot negatively predestinate in this matter. Even the very occurrence of the symbolic treatment of elements of nature (*e.g.* through their cult) is a sufficient premise to confirm the presence of mythical images, and in this case not only source materials confirming this type of phenomena are of key importance, but also references to various methods used in religious studies (*e.g.* comparative analysis or phenomenological inspiration).
353   See earlier footnote 339 in this chapter.
354   Banaszkiewicz, *Polskie dzieje*, pp. 132 ff. who holds the position that Slavic mythological glosses were inserted into fragments of Malalas's chronicle at the time when in Rus' this text was used to create compiled historical compendia (13th c.).
355   *Ibidem*, p. 140.

interpretation is presented as a particular expression of protection of the inviolability of the established social order.

J. Banaszkiewicz's detailed argumentation, and especially his comparative analysis, allowed Svarog to be placed in a wide context of Indo-European mythology systems, which in turn support the thesis on dynamic development of beliefs in Slavic societies.[356] Thus one should take into account the possibility that literary borrowings in their presentation were adjusted to the needs of expressing native, mythical beliefs. This view is also supported by the occurrence of rather associative identification of representatives of ancient pantheons with Slavic deities, without respect for their original place in the ancient system of mythology – a good example of which is the interpretation of sovereign Svarog as Hephaestus, who did not enjoy such a high position.[357]

In the light of this research trend, the power of arguments that support considering Helios Dazbog as a pseudo-deity fades; it can be predestined neither by "infection" (as it was embellished) of the account with a borrowing from antique classics, nor by the very etymology of the theonim, however interesting L. Moszyński's proposal seems.[358] Thus there is a growing likelihood of the occurrence of theogonic motifs related to Svarog in the mythology of not only Eastern but also, by analogy, Western Slavs, which is essential in the discussion about the Liutici Svarožic.

---

356   An attempt of systematising this material dispersed in various traditions was undertaken by Szyjewski, *Religia*, pp. 101 f., for more information see p. 119.

357   Nota bene, W. Szafrański observed that if one assumes that the "religious system was an obvious reflection of social and economic reality, then this reconstructed myth about the divine blacksmith, who forged the sun, offers an excellent example of a projection of relation in the human environment onto the heavenly sphere in a situation when on the threshold of statehood, the well known is the well exposed role of rich blacksmiths usurping secular and religious power" (see W. Szafrański, *Religie światowe i religie Słowian*, (Religioznawstwo) 3 (Warszawa: Wyższa Szkoła Nauk Społecznych, 1983) p. 28; cf. *idem*, *Prahistoria*, pp. 14 f.). However, does the role of blacksmiths, in the case of the Rus' gloss, reflect "real" historical processes, or is it only a cultural (or literary) fact explaining mythical *origins*, this is impossible to decide on the basis of analysis of the PVL text. On the other hand, it is worth taking into account the connection between fiery Svarog and blacksmithing. Gieysztor, *Mitologia*, p. 103, emphasized that in the Iron Age there was a transformation of a deity rolling stone thunders at the mythical blacksmith, known also in Slavic folklore; in the etymology of **kovati* (forge) one can hear an Old Iranian blacksmithing deity Kave, and also Baltic Perkun's alternate name *Akmenis Kalvis* means stone blacksmith. Also Svarog's name can be associated with forging together red-hot iron. See also Pettazzoni, *Wszechwiedza*, pp. 221 f.

358   It is sufficient to assume that the divine name originating from a greeting (see above) was the effect of tabooisation of the original theonim.

THE RELIGION OF THE SLAVS IN THIETMAR'S CHRONICLE   119

The metrics of the name Svarog reach the Proto-Indo-European language substrate, from which originated the Old Indian core *svar-* (Old Iranian *hwar*), meaning radiance, light (of heaven) and sun.[359] This etymology corresponds with a proposed explanation of the name of "Rarog" (saker falcon), a mythical bird with glowing eyes, as a name taboo of Svarog.[360] Another less convincing idea is that Svarog was the god of the moon, called a horn by the Slavs (*e.g.* Polish "róg"), which would be confirmed by the theonim suffix '-rog.'[361] It is also emphasized that there is a connection between this theonim and fire, however, here the indication is the name Svarožic, as this was the word used to refer to fire in Rus' and the one people prayed to.[362]

According to A. Brückner the name Svarožic originates from fire understood as "fighter" or "bickerer,"[363] because 'swarzyć się' means 'quarrel or bicker' and the sound of wood crackling in fire would sound similar and resembles this activity. Such etymology is highly disputable, hence Kazimierz Moszyński proposed a more dependable one based on a saying connected with a thunder from Polesie: "Boh svarycsa" (God is upset), explaining that 'swarzyć się' (bicker) meant 'be upset', 'punish.'[364] Another solution is "forge two hot pieces

---

359 Moszyński, *Kultura*, p. 504; Pettazzoni, *Wszechwiedza*, p. 221; Urbańczyk, *Dawni Słowianie*, pp. 29, 191. Gieysztor, *Mitologia*, p. 172, complete these etymologies with V. Machek's reference to an Indian nickname of Indra – *svaraj*. Cf. Strzelczyk, *Mity, podania*, p. 199.

360 Exactly Gieysztor, *Mitologia*, pp. 177 f., claims after Jakobson that the name of the bird with glowing eyes among the Balts and Slavs: 'raróg', 'raroh', 'raragas' can be a taboo of the name of Svarog, which is supported by an analogous structure of the word; another indication in the matter, according to A. Gieysztor, is a mythical motif, in which Indra turns into a falcon in a fight with Vritra.

361 V. Pisani's view was critically presented by Kulišić, *Stara Slovenska religija*, pp. 171 f., 190. Moreover, in the description of Radogošč, Thietmar means animal horns in the foundation of the temple. This concept can result from inspiration derived from the "horn" motif sounding in the name Svarožic. An association between the shape of this architectural detail and horns could be the chronicler's *licenctia poetica*, as he knew the Slavic language (it is hard to assess how well); another possibility is that it was a Liutici invention in the building of the temple, taking into account symbolical associations evoked by the name of their deity. However, all these thoughts are only unverified speculations.

362 It is confirmed in Rus' by *The Word of Christolubec* (14th c.) – Urbańczyk, *Dawni Słowianie*, pp. 27, 150 f.; Strzelczyk, *Mity*, p. 199. The direction of this fiery interpretation of Svarog was determined as early as the 19th c. by Pavol Jozef Šafárik followed by Franz Miklosich (see Moszyński, *Prasłowiański panteon*, p. 170).

363 Brückner, *Mitologia słowiańska i polska*, p. 338.

364 Moszyński, *Kultura*, p. 505, emphasizes analogies to Zeus *maimaktes* – irascible, outraged; cf. Urbańczyk, *Dawni Słowianie*, p. 29.

120   CHAPTER 2

of iron," *i.e.* 'zwarzyć' (while '-og' is a suffix meaning a person who does this activity).[365]

In the research of the religious practices of the Early Slavs, all these associations or etymologies are of some value. It is not a matter of artificial attempts to attribute to one mythical character all activities and attributes associated with a term used to denote him, but putting emphasis on the significance of a symbolic, and thus myth-creating character of divine names. By way of association they could be a carrier of many, although not necessarily original, senses. However, from the perspective of theogonic research on the Svarog–Svarožic line, the most significant question is exactly related to the earliest connotations of both theonims, in which the motif of heavenly light and fire is so strong.

This situation brings about an analogy to Greek mythology in which origination of fiery Hephaestus from heavenly Zeus is also expressed in the filial relation,[366] however the analogy does not refer to the meaning in cult; Svarožic is outlined as the major deity worshipped by the Liutici, hence in this context he would replace the heavenly sovereign. Therefore it is not accidental that in the discussion on this matter there arises a model perspective of the Slavic theology, coined by Helmold (1, 84), who presented an image of a heavenly "god of gods," controlling only heavenly matters, while the earthly ones are entrusted to other gods, his blood relatives. Moreover, their significance was to depend on how closely they were related to him and thus by what share they represent his divinity.

In this light Svarožic can be regarded as an emanation of Svarog, and the closeness in origin as indicated by the relation between their names explains well his rank in the Radogošč pantheon. In fact, this Liutici god would be only one of these kinds of emanations of heavenly light and fire (Svarog) in Slavdom, and being hierophanies, they would usually assume a particular shape like the sun or fire located in various places (even in a cereal drying chamber[367]). These emanations, frequently strictly connected with a particular dimension of human existences, were closer to people than the heavenly source of their origin,[368] which did not disappear from mythologies but lost its priority in cult.

---

365   Urbańczyk, *Dawni Słowianie*, pp. 191 f. It is worth remembering that Brückner, *Mitologia słowiańska i polska*, p. 44, rejected "zwarzanie" (forging) of ore (by a blacksmith) and also Indian "Svarga" – "heaven" as an indication in the etymology of the name Svarožic.

366   Moszyński, *Kultura*, p. 505.

367   Urbańczyk, *Dawni Słowianie*, p. 191.

368   This can be proven by such local names Swarożyn, Swaroszyn, Swarzędz, although they could have derived directly from 'swarzyć' (bicker) without any sacral context, see Urbańczyk, *Dawni Słowianie*, p. 192. On the other hand Gieysztor, *Mitologia*, p. 172, where

THE RELIGION OF THE SLAVS IN THIETMAR'S CHRONICLE 121

In the case of the Liutici, the domination of Svarožic in the pantheon, clear in the light of written sources, bears hallmarks of henotheism. Thus the question arises of whether the tendency for such dominance in the sphere of the *sacrum* by one deity in the pantheon was the result of changes in the Slavic religion at the time of stronger confrontation with Christianity, and in consequence an attempt to strengthen the native religion through reconstruction of mythology following the example of monotheism. Alternatively, perhaps henotheism had a characteristic feature of Slavic beliefs since the beginning. In this matter a significant premise turned out to be the account of Procopius of Caesarea, who confirms the existence of the one god of the Sclavenes and Antes in the 6th c., who would dominate the pantheon throughout its formation from its very inception.[369]

However, such a position does not result directly from the source,[370] the contents of which are more conducive to the conviction that the Byzantine chronicler perceived the beliefs of peoples in polytheistic categories, and in addition to which, in a very special way, he only emphasized the character who resembled best the ancient mythological sovereign of the heavens who commanded thunder, such as Zeus or Jovi. Finally, one has to conclude that the view that assumes that the genesis of henotheism among the Slavs dated back to at least the 6th c. AD was based on *a priori* assumptions in the matter of the evolution of their beliefs, and more precisely a conviction that the Early Slavs did not know the concept of a deity at all. Due to the fact that in the current state of discussion, such a concept has a clear alternative, which is discussed above, the occurrence of a henotheistic tendency among the Slavs can be most certainly confirmed at the stage of intensified attempts of their Christianization (from the 10th c.).

However, in this hypothetical case there should be discussion of a trend leading to henotheism and not the phenomenon of henotheism in the strict sense of this term, because in relation to the Rus' and the Liutici in Thietmar's times, the medieval sources confirm only the domination of one of the gods

---

he emphasizes the significance of toponomastics in the research on Svarožic and indicates after Jakobson that such names as Twarożna Góra in Czech can be taboo.

369 A classic example of this kind of position is the concept of the so-called Slavic protothe-ism promoted by H. Łowmiański, which is referred to by L. Moszyński – see above, pp. 19 f.

370 It is worth emphasizing after Procopius's critical editions that there are two versions of the passage about the "lightning demiurge": 1) θεον ενα – "one god" (no information about others, however, no denial of their existence); 2) θεων ενα – "one of the gods"; see e.g. *Testimonia najdawniejszych dziejów Słowian*, p. 86 f. For more information see below, p. 346.

122   CHAPTER 2

over the representatives of the pantheon,[371] who did not lose the attribute of
divinity however. In the changing political and social situation in Polabia in
the 11th c., particular tribes introduced into the public cult the worship of one
of the gods as the patron of a given community, which is especially depicted
in the sources from the 12th c.[372] However, it is hard to consider this situation
as henotheism *sensu stricto*, because it did not mean the negation of the existence of other gods (*e.g.* neighbours' gods), and only meant public worship of
only one god of a particular tribe.

   A better term for this phenomenon seems to be monolatry. Its development,
similarly to the earlier henotheistic trend, was related to the accumulation of
various functions by the deity aspiring for leadership of the pantheon. Thus
Svarožic combines military characteristics with the competence of controlling atmospheric phenomena indicated in the symbolism of light and fire.[373]
Taking into consideration his leading role among the other gods in Radogošč,
an association with Perun is formed, but from the perspective of the functional
analysis, Perun is first of all Svarog's counterpart.[374] This is why it seems safer

---

371   Pettazzoni, *Wszechwiedza*, pp. 222 ff. stated that Dazbog was not as close to Svarog as
      Svarožic, and additionally if one assumes based on silence in the sources, that the west-
      ern Slavs did not know Svarog in the 11th c., he concluded that the evolution of the Slavic
      religion in the east led to the domination of the meteorological Perun (although traces
      of Svarog are also clear here), while in the west the solar Svarog-Svarožic became the
      sovereign. This is the way in which Pettazzoni viewed the civilizational distinctiveness
      between the East and the West of the Slavdom. Similarly Łowmiański, *Religia*, p. 97, ex-
      pressing a conviction about the existence of three southern Slavdom deities: the demi-
      urge of lightning = Perun, Dazbog and Svarog, claimed that in the Balkans – according
      to Procopius's testimony – initially only Perun was worshipped and Svarog appeared
      there in connection with the later colonisation of the Western Slavdom by the tribes of
      Croatians, Obodrite, and Serbs in the 6th c. The co-occurrence of the cult of Perun and
      Svarog in the same areas, according to this concept, was to be an expression of coexis-
      tence of two settlement trends, and not any evidence of polytheism. However, this way of
      thinking raises doubts related to the proposed way of confirmation in the sources of the
      cult of Svarog in the Balkans, and also the concept of the occurrence of the so-called pro-
      totheism among the Slavs and late development of polytheism among them (see above).
372   Helmold, hagiography of St. Otto of Bamberg, see below, pp. 306 ff., 338, 365. See also
      Rosik, *Conversio*, p. 264.
373   Gieysztor, *Mitologia*, pp. 177 f.: in Polabia the cult of Svarožic as the god of war requires
      adoption of the view that one of the fire properties – thunder in the atmosphere or fire
      causing destruction in the earthly environment – could evoke associations with ritual
      bonfires used to scare away hostile, supernatural forces.
374   Urbańczyk, *Dawni Słowianie*, p. 192, thought it was possible that after accepting the Slavic
      etymology of Svarog one could perceive him as a substitute name for *e.g.* Perun.

THE RELIGION OF THE SLAVS IN THIETMAR'S CHRONICLE

to support the view that Svarožic took over roles originally reserved for the said heavenly sovereigns.[375]

On the other hand, the analogy derived from Rus' sources, or more precisely a comparison with Dazbog, would indicate a possibility that the Liutici Svarožic is also responsible for the agrarian sphere. The power of this hypothetical assessment is enhanced by another analogy that is closer geographically, namely Svantevit, the major deity of the Rugians, who patronized war but was also worshipped as the god of harvest.[376] However, this type of agrarian role in the case of Svarožic was possibly not marked initially, and rather became visible only at a later stage of the evolution of his cult in the direction of henotheism or even monolatry, which was likely already referred to by Adam of Bremen.

The major Liutici god in his work is called Redigast, the name which initially was probably Svarožic's nickname and related to a particular cult centre located – important in this case – in the land of Redars. Therefore, Redigast primarly would be the patron of this tribe and the appearance of this theonim would be evidence of the already mentioned formation of cults for god-patrons of particular tribes[377] or centres in Polabia. In the cult and attributes of a few of these major deities one can see elements characteristic for Svarožic, such as warriorhood,[378] but also fire connotations, or more precisely associations with the sun. They are evoked for example by the symbolism of gold, of which Redigast's statue was made, or by the four faces of Svantevit of Arkona.[379]

This tendency to increase the significance of the solar element in the cult of the Polabian Slavs, the influence of which should be taken into account also

---

375 Gieysztor, *Mitologia*, p. 175: Svarožic-Dazbog would be an atmospheric god (which would overlap with Perun's competences) as well as the role of an offering fire and home. Three types of fire overlap with one another in the Indian pantheon, hence it makes sense to state that Svarožic was a diminutive form of Svarog, and not only a patronymic.

376 Saxo XIV, 39, 4–5; cf. Urbańczyk, *Dawni Słowianie*, pp. 110, 154. See also further, p. 313.

377 Urbańczyk, *Dawni Słowianie*, pp. 148 f., surmised that multiplicity of names does not necessarily denote multiplicity of gods (there may be local nicknames, taboos). Another view presented by this scholar holds that a nickname could be the beginning of a new god.

378 A characteristic shared by gods of the Polabian and Pomeranian tribes is belligerence; according to the sources they resemble a ruler, who participates in a war leading his battalions (according to Saxo XIV, 39, 7, Svantevit had a squad of 300 horsemen). See *e.g.* Vladimír Procházka, "Organisace kultu a kmenove zřizeni polabsko-pobaltskych slovanů," in *Vznik a počatki slovanů* 2 (Praha: Nakladatelství Československé akademie věd, 1958), p. 152; Babij, *Wojskowość*, pp. 265 f.

379 See below, pp. 212 ff., 364 f.

in the case of Svarožic,[380] is part of a broad comparative perspective,[381] which is understandable on account of the universality of the cult of the sun in the history of world religions. One should remember that at the twilight of the pre-Christian epoch, in the Roman world in the *sacrum* hierarchy it was possible to observe the promotion of solar deities in the form of *Sol Invictus* (Mitra, Heliogabal), which corresponded with aspirations to consolidate power in the empire accompanied by moving emphasis in the sphere of the cult to active powers, able to represent centralization better and, in the case of threats, also signifying redemptive trends in a mythological dimension.

It is worth taking into account that in the Polabian circle, on a similar basis, Slavic native beliefs and institutions, threatened by the expansion of Christianity and its political exponents, went through an evolution in which striving for consolidation of power was accompanied by appreciation of the solar element in the religious sphere. As emphasized by Mircea Eliade, the solar cult was highly developed only in societies characterized by advanced political organization. Hence its elements did not last long in Africa, Australia, or Melanesia, while they enjoyed popularity in Asia, Ancient Europe, Egypt (where it dominated), and among American peoples only in highly developed societies in Peru and Mexico.[382]

Coming back to the world of the Slavs, it is worth turning attention in this context to the fact that in Rus', in the light of information in PVL, Vladimir's reform in 980 significantly increased the rank of solar deities – Dazbog and Chors.[383] A solar attribute: a golden moustache, was worn even by Perun holding primacy over the Rus' pantheon.[384] However, it was him, the heavenly ruler of thunder (and not any counterpart of Helios), who turned out to be the most attractive as a patron of the ruleship for the duke; this choice must have been

---

380   A comparative argument on this matter is identification of Dazbog (Svarožic) with Helios, see Gieysztor, *Mitologia*, pp. 171 f.; cf. Kulišić, *Stara Slovenska religija*, pp. 237 f. See above pp. 110 f.

381   It is worthy to mention that the occurrence of solar cult has been discussed also in nearer to Western Slavs comparative context, *i.e.*, Scandinavian one, recently, see *e.g.* Andreas Nordberg, *Fornnordisk religionsforskning mellan teori och empiri. Kulten av anfäder, solen och vegetationsandar i idéhistorisk belysning*, (Acta Academiae regiae Gustavi Adolphi) 126 (Uppsala: Kungl. Gustav Adolfs akademien för svensk folk kultur, 2013); Anders Andrén, *Tracing Old Norse Cosmology. The world tree, middle earth, and the sun in archaeological perspectives*, (Vägar till Midgård) 16 (Lund: Nordic Academic Press, 2014), p. 117 ff., 164 ff.

382   Mircea Eliade, *Traktat o historii religii*, trans. Jan Wierusz-Kowalski (Łódź: Opus, 1993) [orig. *Traité d'histoire des religions* (Paris: Payot, 1949)], p. 127.

383   Moreover Vladimir the Great himself was associated with a later tradition of the tsar-sun. For more information see Rybakov, *Jazyčestvo drevnej Rusi*, p. 438–454.

384   PVL under the year 6488 [980].

THE RELIGION OF THE SLAVS IN THIETMAR'S CHRONICLE   125

influenced by Scandinavian trends and traditions in Rus' at the time with an
inspiring (at least due to the Varangian entourage of the ruler) warlike cult
of Thor.

Among the Liutici however, electing the solar and fiery deity descending
from Svarog to lead the pantheon corresponded with the agrarian character of
these societies, and a very special role of the assembly there. An oracle was of
key importance in its functioning, however, and in a comparative context it is
presented as a domain of solar deities. One can suppose that elevating Svarožic
or Svantevit's position to the leading one in the Liutici or Rugians' cult resulted
from aspirations to consolidate power in agrarian communities around the
assembly and temple, with the oracle installed there.[385] It was controlled by
priests. Therefore, it is also worth taking into consideration how their aspirations were fulfilled in the introduction of elements of theocracy (hierocracy)
in the social and political life as a possible engine of cultic transformation.

2.6.4   Ministri

Thietmar's reference to the ordination of priests by local inhabitants in
Radogošč attracts the special attention of scholars involved in the discussion
on how such a group of cultic officials came into existence in communities of
the Early Slavs.[386] The prevailing view holds that there is only certainty in this
matter with reference to the Polabian and Pomeranian area and not earlier
than the 10th c.[387] The exceptional position of priests – or actually the temporary cultic leaders – in the Liutici society was emphasized by the fact that they
remained sitting during offerings while all other participants of these rites had

---

385   Recently on the matter of these consolidation processes from the archaeological perspec-
       tive see: Biermann, *Zentralisierungsprozesse*, pp. 157–194.
386   Thietmar VI, 24: "Ad haec curiose tuenda ministri sunt specialiter ab indigenis constituti".
387   *E.g.* Łowmiański, *Politeizm, passim*; Kiersnowska, Kiersnowski, *Życie codzienne*, p. 34;
       Urbańczyk, *Dawni Słowianie*, p. 120, who emphasized that the priests were characterised
       by special outfits and long hair and beards (in Rügen). This author also repeats the view
       that formation of priesthood in the Polabian and Pomeranian native religion area was
       influenced by Christian models. This speculation can hardly be verified, and the informa-
       tion given by Thietmar about Radogošč does not help here either: functions of *ministri*
       there were different from responsibilities of the Christian clergy at that time. Searching
       for possible Christian inspiration in the appearance of Radogošč priests, one should refer
       to eremitism, however, it seems that it will be significantly more dependable to look for
       the genesis of these *ministri* in internal development mechanisms of the cults systems
       of the Elbslavs. See also *e.g.* Kazimierz Wachowski, *Słowiańszczyzna Zachodnia* (Poznań:
       Wydawnictwo Poznańskiego Towarzystwa Przyjaciół Nauk, 2000 [1st ed. 1903]), pp. 94,
       162 f.; Miś, "Przedchrześcijańska religia," pp. 136 f.

126   CHAPTER 2

to stand.[388] Taking into account the fact that the Liutici made offerings during war expeditions,[389] it is worth recognizing the possibility that some of the priests went to war with images of deities taken from the temple to accompany the military forces.

The fact that the temple was located deep in the forest does not seem to indicate that priests from Radogošč were in constant contact with the Liutici community, in contrast to priests from Arkona or Szczecin (Stettin). However, this does not mean that the temple in Radogošč had weaker political influence: the *ministri* interpreted divinations related to politics and also had the temple treasury of the whole tribal federation at their disposal.[390] When considering the Liutici political system, which according to Thietmar was not ruled by one leader ("dominus non presidet ullus"), one should take into account the possibility of a ruling system that evolved towards theocracy, which is indicated especially in later work of Helmold.[391]

However, this type of tendency meant strengthening the role of the assembly,[392] at which priests' votes (oracle) were significantly weighted, and at the same time in this case of the shaping of the ruling system, they were important in counteracting the formation of monarchic structures. On the other hand, there is no sufficient evidence to speculate that among the Liutici

---

388   Thietmar VI, 24: "Qui cum idolis immolare seu iram eorundem placare conveniunt, sedent hii, dumtaxat caeteris asstantibus …".

389   See above, pp. 91 f.

390   Leciejewicz, *Słowianie*, p. 132. *Ibidem*, p. 194, the author mentions the strong influence of priests (thanks to performed rituals) on the whole community as they were considered members of the wealthy elite; similarly Dralle, "Rethra," p. 41, assuming the presence of theocratic forms of power ("quasikönigliche Oberherrschaft") among the Veleti with reference to the capital in Radogošč, *ibidem*, pp. 37–39. See also Piotr Boroń, *Słowiańskie wiece plemienne* (Katowice: Wydawnictwo Uniwersytetu Śląskiego, 1999), p. 88.

391   See below pp. 302 f., 359, 374. The reasons for the growing significance of Radogošč, according to Dralle, "Rethra," pp. 43–47, are found in its significance during the Slavic rebellions (983, 1018). Native cults played a unifying role in the political association.

392   A wider context of the discussed reference, Thietmar VI, 25: "… Liutici (…) dominus non presidet ullus. Unanimi consilio ad placitum suimet necessaria discucientes, in rebus efficiendis omnes concordant", indicates that the main institution of the Liutici power was the assembly (cf. *e.g.* Jedlicki, "Poglądy," p. 68). It is not denied by Klaus Zernack, *Die burgstädtischen Volkversammlungen bei den Ost und Westslaven. Studien zur verfassungsgeschichtlichen Bedeutung des Veče* (Wiesbaden: Harrasowitz, 1967), pp. 208–215, although he emphasizes that in the light of written sources, the problem of the Liutici political system in the 11th c. seems quite complex: control of the supraregional community shows characteristics of an assembly (veche), however, it is concentrated around the political and religious centre in Rethra. For more information on the Slavic tribal assembly including Thietmar's data see Boroń, *Słowiańskie wiece*, pp. 7–105, especially 70, 82–84, 88. See also Fraesdorf, *Der barbarische Norden*, p. 140.

THE RELIGION OF THE SLAVS IN THIETMAR'S CHRONICLE 127

there was a priestly rule in the strict sense of this term. The very theocracy to which one can refer here, only in the dimension of sacral interpretation of the social order, is the situation in which Svarožic is presented as a mystical sovereign of a multi-tribal federation concentrated around his temple in Radogošč.[393]

The special significance of this place is also confirmed by locating there the group of these *ministri*, while some tribal sanctuaries in Polabia probably had to settle for only one priest.[394] It is characteristic that Thietmar refers to the priests in Radogošč as *ministri*, and not *sacerdotes*, *flamines* or *pontifices*, as they were called in later sources. These specifics of the terminology became a pretext for speculations related to a different status and responsibilities of cult servants in Radogošč in comparison with their Polabian or Pomeranian counterparts known from descriptions written in the 12th c.[395]

However, the said use of the term *ministri* seems to be clarified by the specifics of Thietmar's way of working and his precision in selecting words. He depicted Radogošč cultic leaders exactly as idols' servants and stewards of god's secrets and this range of roles is perfectly indicated in the term *minister*, especially with reference to the cult in the temple which was isolated from everyday tribal life. Such terms as *sacerdotes* or *pontifices* are used by the chronicler to refer to Christian clergy, priests, and hierarchs functioning every day in a

---

393   The role of Svantevit in Rügen is interpreted similarly, see below, p. 322. According to Kiersnowska, Kiersnowski, *Życie codzienne*, p. 168: "Among the Veleti Svarožic completely substituted a duke", however, this statement seems oversimplified as it does not take into account the overriding role of the assembly in the practice of governing the Liutici community.

394   *E.g.* Prove in Starigard according to Helmold I, 69.

395   Łowmiański, *Religia*, p. 233, insisted on calling the Liutici *ministri* "servants", to distinguish them from priests who were to be formed in the next decades. In Łowmiański's reasoning this speculation is yet another argument for the later development of the Polabian polytheism and its strict relation to formation of tribal statehood. In the temples of particular tribes there would be only one servant (like a priest in Arkona according to Saxo Grammaticus). The link preceding *ministri* in the chain of transformations in the institution of the Slavic cult were to be sorcerers or kin leaders. The concept raises doubts because its main premise, *i.e.* the term *minister* was interpreted without appropriate consideration for Thietmar's writing convention, yet in a way which supported H. Łowmiański's a priori judgements on the evolution of the Slavic religion. For information on Old Slavs' priests see *e.g.* Zdzisław Rajewski, "Pogańscy kapłani-czarodzieje w walce klasowej we wczesnym średniowieczu," *Wiadomości Archeologiczne* 39 (1975), pp. 503–509; Kulišić, *Stara Slovenska religija*, pp. 207 ff.; Urbańczyk, *Dawni Słowianie*, p. 120; *idem*, "Kapłani pogańscy," in sss, vol. 2, p. 371; Słupecki, *Slavonic Pagan Sanctuaries*, pp. 44, 68, 81 f., 161; Sven Wichert, "Die politische Rolle der heidnischen Priester bei den Westslaven," *Studia Mythologica Slavica* 13 (2010), pp. 33–42.

128   CHAPTER 2

wider social circulation, similarly to the pagan priests in Pomerania, Polabia, or Rügen known from 12th-c. sources.

The appearance of the term *ministri* in Thietmar's work harmonizes with the original literary convention, in which he presented subjects acting on the historical stage. In the chronicler's projection the main inhabitants of the temple stronghold were not priests, understood as agents between people and the *sacrum* sphere, but rather gods identified with idols. The main opponents of Christ and his followers in the picture outlined in this way are idols and demonical powers related to them, and not the priests serving them. It is different in the 12th-c. sources where in the Polabian and Pomeranian zone pagan priests were attributed as the main driving force in the opposition against Christianization and were thought to be leaders of the people.[396]

2.6.5   The Oracle, Divinations and Auguries
Divination rituals practiced by priests (*ministri*) in Radogošč, according to Thietmar, were started with the murmuring of mysterious words and the kicking of the ground which was related to casting lots, possibly in a dance.[397] Leszek P. Słupecki interpreted the kicking of the ground in a convincing way. He assumed that it was a ritual offering access to chthonic powers – an analogy to the discovery of the Centre of the Universe (omfalos), which was to precede casting lots and was known from the Oracle of Delphi.[398]

After casting lots and covering them with green grass there was time for hippomancy: "the horse that they consider to be the largest among others and worship as sacred they humbly lead over spearheads of two crossing spears stuck in ground."[399] So when the priests revealed the lots which they had used

---

396   It should be added that numerous analogies between the cult in Szczecin or Arkona and presented by Thietmar in Radogošč prove that the social rank of priests in all these centres was not as varied as was presented by scholars supporting their positions by an analysis of differences in names used to refer to these servants of the cult in Thietmar's chronicle and 12th c. sources – *e.g.* H. Łowmiański, see footnote 395 in this chapter.

397   Thietmar VI, 24: "... invicem clanculum mussantes terram cum tremore infodiunt, quo sortibus emissis rerum certitudinem dubiarum perquirant". For comparative material about Germanic cleromance see Leszek P. Słupecki, *Wyrocznie i wróżby pogańskich Skandynawów. Studium do dziejów idei przeznaczenia u ludów indoeuropejskich* (Warszawa: IAE PAN, 1998), pp. 103 ff.

398   Słupecki, *Wyrocznie*, pp. 144 f.

399   Thietmar VI, 24: "Quibus finitis cespite viridi eas operientes, equum, qui maximus inter alios habetur et ut sacer ab his veneratur, super fixas in terram duarum cuspides hastilium inter se transmissarum supplici obsequio ducunt". The spear divination has a certain analogy with a Roman rite of burying Mars's holy spears in his in the Regia building: peace

THE RELIGION OF THE SLAVS IN THIETMAR'S CHRONICLE 129

earlier, with the divine animal they repeated the augury.[400] Only the results of both divinations allowed them to take a positive decision on the planned initiative: "If the same omen appears in both cases, it is carried out in fact. Otherwise, the unhappy folk reject it."[401]

The horse as a sacred animal among the Slavic tribes was known also to other medieval authors – like the hagiographers Otto of Bamberg, Saxo Grammaticus,[402] and likely also William of Malmesbury[403] – and similarly a divination practice connected with leading an animal between spears. In this context it is worth adding that *Annales Augustani* under the year 1068 state directly that the Slavs possessed "a horse, which they worshipped as god in Rethra."[404] However, attributing treating an animal like a deity to the Liutici seems like an element aimed at ridiculing their beliefs.[405] A comparative

---

    or war prophecies were made based on observation whether the spears were moved – see Gieysztor, *Mitologia*, p. 129.

400   Thietmar VI, 24: "... premissis sortibus, quibus id exploravere prius, per hunc quasi divinum denuo auguriantur."

401   Trans. D.A. Warner in: *Ottonian Germany*, p. 253; cf. Thietmar VI, 24: "Et si in duabus hiis rebus par omen apparet, factis completur; sin autem, a tristibus populis hoc prorsus omittitur."

402   For hippomancy and hippolatry in the hagiography of Otto of Bamberg and Saxo Grammaticus's chronicle, see Słupecki, *Wyrocznie*, pp. 146–150; Rosik, *Conversio*, pp. 268–271. In the context of this discussion, one should also remember about archaeological findings which were to prove the presence of the horse in the Slavic cult. See *e.g.*: Szafrański, *Prahistoria*, pp. 370 f.

403   William of Malmesbury, *Gesta regum Anglorum: The History of English Kings*, vol. 1, ed. Roger Aubrey Baskerville Mynors, Rodney M. Thomson, Michael Winterbottom (Oxford: Clarendon Press, 1998) 2.189) information refers to the oracle of the Liutici or the Rans (Rujani). It was not included in the collection of source texts edited by K.H. Meyer, which can be explained by its poor reception in studies on the Slavic religion; in this context it was taken into account by Pettazzoni, *Wszechwiedza*, p. 507, and recently also R. Zaroff and L.P. Słupecki – see Leszek P. Słupecki, "Posłowie," in Gieysztor, *Mitologia*, pp. 340 f.

404   *Annales Augustani*, ed. Georg Heinrich Pertz, MGH SS 3 (1839), under the year 1068, p. 128: "... equum quem pro deo in Rheda [*i.e.* Rethra – S.R.] colebant".

405   This presumption corresponds with a wider context of occurrence of the discussed here evaluation of "pro deo", namely the information that the conqueror of Rethra, bishop Burchard, not only took a horse but also rode it – hence symbolically – tamed the alleged Slavic "deity".

FIGURE 2   The small bronze figure of a horse from Wolin (11th c.)
THE REGIONAL ANDRZEJ KAUBE MUSEUM IN WOLIN

material showing the role of the horse in rituals practiced in Szczecin and Arkona indicates that it was an attribute of the major god,[406] but it was not a deity.[407]

---

406   Gieysztor (*Mitologia*, p. 129) mentioned referring to the cult in Arkona on Rügen, that horse was not a sacrificial animal, it was one of the power symbols of a deity, in which in a comparative perspective one can observe a reference to a Vedic truth: the horse belongs to Varuna. Taking into account heavenly and possibly also solar connotations of Svarožic's cult, assume that the divination horse in Radogošč was white, similarly to solar Svantevit, and contrary to Triglav's black horse in Szczecin (whose coat colour would correspond with the characteristic chthonic genesis of this deity). In comparative research on Slavic hippomancy it is emphasized that according to Tacitus the Germans also practiced white horse divinations (cf. Tacitus, *Germania*, 10). Similarly also in ancient mythologies, horses of this coat colour were used by Ahura Mazda, Zeus and Helios. See Pettazzoni, *Wszechwiedza*, p. 218; Gieysztor, *Mitologia*, p. 129. See also a comparative material in: Słupecki, *Wyrocznie*, pp. 129–154, particularly 146; Vladas Žulkus, "Heidentum und Christentum in Lituanien im 10.–16. Jahrhundert," in *Rom und Byzanz im Norden. Mission und Glaubenswechsel im Ostseeraum während des 8.–14 Jahrhunderts*, vol. 2, ed. Michael Müller-Wille (Stuttgart: Steiner, 1997), pp. 144 f.
407   See *e.g.* Urbańczyk, *Dawni Słowianie*, p. 88.

THE RELIGION OF THE SLAVS IN THIETMAR'S CHRONICLE   131

This does not change the fact that the holy horse was distinguished in all surroundings as a manifestation of supernatural forces, and thus it was not treated only as a cult "tool" (like pieces of wood used in divinations).[408] Hence one should take into account that the Latin terminology used in descriptions does not allow us to show precisely the categories of defining *sacrum* by pre-Christian Slavs. The very qualification of divergence between *sacer* and *pro deo* however, opens more opportunities for research. A more precise term used by Thietmar, which shows both the holiness of an animal and its worship, does not mean that the animal belonged to the fellowship of gods.

Actually, it is worth adding that the expression "pro deo" does not require the Liutici thinking that an animal is a deity but indicates rather that in general instead of (*pro*) any god or even Christian God considered to be the only one, they worship the horse. This interpretation of the premise from *Annales Augustani* shows even more clearly that there was a trend to ridicule paganism in Christian circles using stereotypical judgments about worshipping the creation rather than the Creator.

Having presented divinations, let us return to Thietmar's narrative where there is a premise about another kind of prognostic used by the Liutici to predict the future. The chronicler quotes a legend from times immemorial about a particular sign heralding a civil war. It was a boar[409] emerging from a lake near Radogošč, with white tusks brightened by foam at its mouth, which perpetrated horror while rolling in mud.[410] In the chronicler's assessment this story alone forms evidence that old tales were full of various errors.[411] Nevertheless,

---

408   Pettazzoni, *Wszechwiedza*, p. 218, claimed that exactly thanks to its numinal and divine character the horse was able to offer divinations expected from this animal, correcting and perfecting earlier indications provided by casting lots.

409   To make this premise stronger, it seems worthy to stress that boar also played an important part in pre-Christian religious and military sphere in neighbouring Scandinavian circle, see Heinrich Beck, *Das Ebersignum im Germanischen: Ein Beitrag zur germanischen Tier-Symbolik*, (Quellen und Forschungen zur Sprach- und Kulturgeschichte der germanischen Völker. Neue Folge) 16 (Berlin: De Gruyter, 1965), pp. 47, 56–69; Olof Sundqvist, *Freyr's Offspring. Rulers and Religion in Ancient Svea Society*, (Acta Universitatis Upsaliensis. Historia Religionum) 22 (Uppsala 2002).

410   Thietmar VI, 24: "si quando his seva longae rebellionis assperitas immineat, ut e mari predicto aper magnus et candido dente e spumis lucescente exeat seque in volutabro delectatum terribili quassatione multis ostendat". From the perspective of the history of historiography, it is worth emphasizing that there were attempts to "rationally" explain the said motif of the boar, such as Rajewski, "Święta woda," p. 115: "The boar with bright, white tusks emerging form the lake in Radogošč, could be mountainous waves during a moonlit night."

411   The chronicler introduces this motif in his work with the following words: "Testatur idem antiquitas errore delusa vario …" (cf. Thietmar VI, 24). This multiple error in this expression can be also interpreted in the context of erroneous religious convictions or pagan myths.

the image of a boar in the story inspired a search in the area of mythology to discover the symbolism of this animal. A. Gieysztor mentioned that in the Slavdom the boar was a subject of an apotropaic cult (evidence for which is provided by a boar's skull with tusks pushed into a trunk of an old oak from the Dnieper River). Tusk charms protected from maledictions and originated myths, one of which was the basis for the legend reported by Thietmar.[412]

The boar emerging from a lake in the night was an image which in the Slavic cultural sphere evoked lunar symbolism,[413] for which one can find interpretation in the mythological presentation of Svarožic.[414] However, it is difficult to accept the idea that this boar was an embodiment of the Liutici god,[415] although it can likely be described as his attribute. However, the very threatening apparition of *sacrum* can be connected with its roles during times of war. This direction of interpretation would indicate – according to the above-mentioned A. Gieysztor's observation – that the old legend discussed here treats the boar as an embodiment of tutelary powers surrounding the Liutici.

However, it is worth suggesting in this case an alternative way of solving the riddle of this mythical scene. Namely, by referring to the symbolism of water as eternal chaos and the settlement of destructive powers of the universe, which is also indicated in the element of terror emphasized by Thietmar in the description of the lake in Radogošč.[416] This boar would be an embodiment of destructive powers present in a very sensitive area such as a civil war.[417] The

---

412   Gieysztor, *Mitologia*, p. 265.

413   Marek Cetwiński, Marek Derwich, *Herby, legendy, dawne mity* (Wrocław: KAW, 1989), p. 91. Lunar associations would be evoked by boar's tusks.

414   An indication here could be not only the very symbolism of light in the night sky: moon was also associated with a "horn" resounding in the theonym "Svarožic" (it is clearer in "Svarog", see above p. 119).

415   It was proposed by Janina Rosen-Przeworska, "Celtycka geneza niektórych wątków wierzeniowych i ikonograficznych u Słowian zachodnich," in *Słowiańszczyzna Połabska między Niemcami a Polską. Materiały z konferencji naukowej zorganizowanej przez Instytut Historii UAM w dniach 28–29 IV 1980 r.*, ed. Jerzy Strzelczyk (Poznań: Wydawnictwo UAM, 1981), p. 265.

416   Similar symbolism is represented by waters (*mare*) in an episode Thietmar devoted to Reinbern's activity (see below, p. 167).

417   According to Tomasz Skonieczny, ">>Testatur ... si quando his seva longae rebellionis assperitas immineat<< – dociekania nad przekazem Thietmara (VI, 24) o normach regulujących zachowanie ładu wewnętrznego w obrębie Związku Lucickiego," in *Orbis Hominum: Civitas, potestas, universitas. W kręgu badań nad kształtowaniem cywilizacji w wiekach średnich*, ed. Mateusz Goliński, Stanisław Rosik, (Scripta Historica Medievalia) 5, (Wrocław: Chronicon, 2016), pp. 61–74, this myth was created in the context of particular threat of disintegration of the Liutici federation due to the multi-tribal and

THE RELIGION OF THE SLAVS IN THIETMAR'S CHRONICLE   133

very prophetic image of the beast emerging from water would find its analogy in an earlier description of the Glomač spring, where the appearance of blood and ash in its water would herald a coming war.[418]

2.6.6   *Principalis monarchia*

Concluding the information about Radogošč, Thietmar outlines a cult of the Liutici tribes that deserves special attention: "There are as many temples as there are regions in this lands, and particular statues of demons that are worshipped by the infidels, among which [temples] the aforementioned city stands as superior."[419] This raises the question of to what extent the model of territorial organization of the cult, quoted in this passage, is congruent with the reality of the contemporary Slavic communities. It is certainly a vision of a bishop based on known to him models of organization of the Christian world, which is indicated in the very expression "principalem tenet monarchiam" in the presentation of sovereignty of Radogošč over the other cult centres.

It is worth paying attention to the fact that in this passage the expression "templa (...) inter quae civitas" is used, hence situationally, in terms of meaning, the words *templum* and *civitas* are at the same level. This unequivocally orients the description of the social and institutional reality with the sacral sphere. Thus, in the description, one can find an analogy to church organization: the centre (*civitas*) that is the seat of the diocese exercises authority over churches in various towns. However, in connection with the fact that in the discussion on the religion of the Elbslavs conducted so far, it is taken into account that the cult organization of the Liutici followed church models, and it is worth considering that Thietmar's information could be taken at face value in research on Polabia in the 10th–11th c.

A proposal in this trend of research was formulated in the most complete way by H. Łowmiański, who claimed on the basis of the quoted passage that

---

non-monarchic structure. Actually the civil war at the end of the 6th decade of the 11th c. brought the Liutici power to an end.

418   See above, p. 57.

419   Thietmar VI, 25: "Quot regiones sunt in his partibus, tot templa habentur et simulacra demonum singula ab infidelibus coluntur, inter quae civitas supramemorata principalem tenet monarchiam." Assuming that temples were not very common even in Polabia, the discussed *templa* is interpreted as various types of cult places – from holy groves through cult circles to roofed temples, see Urbańczyk, *Dawni Słowianie*, p. 79. Małgorzata Kowalczyk, *Wierzenia pogańskie za pierwszych Piastów* (Łódź: Wydawnictwo Łódzkie, 1968), p. 28, assumed that *templa* mentioned by Thietmar were simply groves and becks. However, this type of extension of the meaning of the word *templum* causes the loss of specifics of the chronicler's narration.

"each tribe has a temple in which there is worshipped an image of a deity."[420] Thus this author interpreted the word *regiones* as tribal territories. Based on a conviction that in each of these tribal temples there was only one idol, he juxtaposed their arrangement with the capital in Radogošč, in which Svarožic is surrounded by other *dii manu facti*. As a result the scholar adopted a position that to reconcile both pieces of information – synthetic (*i.e.* "Quot regiones ... etc.*") and detailed (*i.e.* the description of Radogošč) – "one has to assume that Svarožic was surrounded in the temple by other tribal gods, *i.e.* that the main temple contained the Liutici or Polabian pantheon."[421]

In this way it would be possible to find grounds for the thesis that the development of the pantheon, and hence polytheism, among the Polabian Slavs took place not earlier than in the 10th c. A stimulus for this change would be contact with the Christian world: both confrontational but also peaceful. According to H. Łowmiański then, "the cult of tribal gods overlapped the traditional polydoxy."[422] Therefore, in the light of this concept, tribal gods were called to existence exactly at the stage of consolidation of the Liutici Federation, which is essential in response to the ideological and political pressure of Christendom.

---

420   Łowmiański, *Religia*, p. 171. The author appreciated Thietmar claiming that he "did not restrict himself to presenting occasional records of the Liutici polytheism, but outlined also its synthetic image". A condition of this way of presenting the issue is a silent assumption that the expression *in his partibus* refers exactly to the Liutici territories and not to any wider area.

421   Łowmiański, *Religia*, p. 171.

422   The Liutici pantheon in Radogošč was perceived in reference to tribal territories even earlier, and the presented gods were to be patrons of particular tribes. Hence, *e.g.* Dowiat, *Chrzest*, p. 24, assumed that the unification of tribes required respect for territorial gods and in this way a hierarchy was built with one of them as the hegemon (the same Jerzy Gąssowski, "Między pogaństwem a chrześcijaństwem," in *Wierzenia przedchrześcijańskie na ziemiach polskich*, ed. Marian Kwapiński, Henryk Paner (Gdańsk: Wydawnictwo Muzeum Archeologicznego w Gdańsku, 1993), pp. 13 f.). On the other hand, Łowmiański, *Religia*, p. 170, connected the formation of polytheism with paganism fighting the pressure of Christianity, however, he perceived bringing deities into being as a reply to practical people's needs (following the Christian model), and not only political symbolism. He acknowledged that the heavenly Svarog and his subordinate tribal patrons were worshipped in Radogošč, and the whole pantheon in his opinion was created following the pattern of respect towards God and saints in Christianity. This concept was a polemic with an earlier idea created by Brückner, *Mitologia słowiańska i polska*, p. 35, who on the basis of inscriptions related to particular idols in Radogošč (see above pp. 101, 104), assumed that the sanctuary was established under the influence of Scandinavian patterns. This cultural borrowing, in Brückner's opinion, resulted in only temporary strengthening of paganism and so it is hard to consider Radogošč as a good indication for the reconstruction of the Polabian and Pomeranian model of cult.

THE RELIGION OF THE SLAVS IN THIETMAR'S CHRONICLE   135

The key question in this debate is the issue of the genesis of tribal gods. They
are confirmed in 11th and 12th c. sources,[423] and thus an assumption that they
existed in the 10th c. should certainly receive attention. The fact, which is obvious in the light of Thietmar's work, that Svarožic was a patron of the Redars,
does not necessarily mean that he was not worshipped by representatives of
other tribes as the common heritage of Polabian (or even generally Slavic)
beliefs from the time before the formation of the Liutici community around
Radogošč. Thietmar's record does not include information on what particular
deities were worshipped in temples in *regiones* and at best it can be assumed
that these *templa* were major cult places of particular tribes. Actually the term
regio is used by Thietmar to refer to tribal territories in presentation of the
Polabian area.[424] However, it is worth emphasizing that in a wider context of
the work the term *regio* refers also to whole countries, or on the other hand,
smaller territorial units concentrated around a particular centre.[425]

This semantic variant of *regio* corresponds with a view, which is a quite well
settled in the debate on Thietmar's information discussed here, that these *regiones* with temples were territories connected with particular strongholds as
their centres. The ground for this proposal is a conviction that as early as the
first decades of the 11th c., decentralization of tribal organization took place,
and so the cult was concentrated in the local power centres.[426] This image with

---

423   Leciejewicz, *Słowianie*, p. 114, discusses their occurrence at the end stage of Old Slavic
      religion.

424   *Regiones* mentioned by Thietmar (VI, 25) were considered tribal territories *e.g.* by
      Wachowski, *Słowiańszczyzna*, p. 66; Lech A. Tyszkiewicz, "Podziały plemienne i problem
      jedności Słowian," in *Słowiańszczyzna Połabska między Niemcami a Polską. Materiały z
      konferencji naukowej zorganizowanej przez Instytut Historii UAM w dniach 28–29 IV 1980
      r.*, ed. Jerzy Strzelczyk (Poznań: Wydawnictwo UAM, 1981), p. 127. It is worth remember-
      ing that Thietmar interchangeably used the terms '*pagus*', '*regio*', '*provincia*' to refer to
      tribal territories (of *e.g.* the Dalemici or Milceni) – *ibidem*, p. 116; cf. Lech A. Tyszkiewicz,
      "Plemiona słowiańskie we wczesnym średniowieczu," in *Słowiańszczyzna w Europie
      średniowiecznej Księga pamiątkowa dla Lecha Leciejewicza*, vol. 1: *Plemiona i wczesne
      państwa*, ed. Zofia Kurnatowska (Wrocław: IAE PAN, 1996), p. 48.

425   *E.g.* Merseburg, see Thietmar I, 2.

426   Like in Herrmann, "Feldberg, Rethra," pp. 67–69; *idem, Siedlung, Wirtschaft und gesell-
      schaftliche Verhältnisse der slawischen Stämme zwischen Oder/Neisse und Elbe* (Berlin:
      Akademie-Verlag, 1968), pp. 159 ff. Cf. Eike Gringmuth-Dallmer, Adolf Hollnagel,
      "Jungslawische Siedlung mit Holzidolen auf der Fischerinsel bei Neubrandenburg,"
      Ausgrabungen und Funde 15 (1970), p. 230. The same in Lech Leciejewicz, "Główne prob-
      lemy dziejów obodrzyckich," in *Słowiańszczyzna Połabska między Niemcami a Polską.
      Materiały z konferencji naukowej zorganizowanej przez Instytut Historii UAM w dniach
      28–29 IV 1980 r.*, ed. Jerzy Strzelczyk (Poznań: Wydawnictwo UAM, 1981), pp. 174 ff. The au-
      thor recognized a temple and a stronghold known from excavation work in Gross Raden
      as a typical example of a link in a chain of sanctuaries mentioned by Thietmar.

136   CHAPTER 2

reference to the Liutici can be confirmed not earlier than in the 12th c. in the
hagiography of Otto of Bamberg, in which early town centres are presented as
places where temples were built for local communities.[427]

However, in Thietmar's times, dozens of years before the disintegration of
the Liutici unity, it is hard to assume that sanctuaries intended for the whole
tribes would disappear. It should be taken into account that there was coexistence of cult places at various levels of social life. This solution is supported
by a comparative indication from Helmold's chronicle when he presents the
Wagrian land in the 12th c., where apart from a sanctuary of the patron-deity
of the Wagrians – Prove – he also mentions the existence of the stronghold
temple.[428] Moreover, one should also take into account the existence of cult
places even at the level of neighbourly communities.[429]

It seems that Thietmar's intention was primarily emphasizing the universal
occurrence of sanctuaries "in these parts," and not detailed lists that included
the precise numbers of temples. Similarly, treating the expression "simulachra
demonum singula" as confirmation of locating in each temple only one idol
seems an overly restrictive interpretation. In this context it is worth recalling
the phrase "singulis nominibus," which was used in the description of statues
of deities in Radogošč, to emphasize the meaning of the adjective 'singulus'
used by Thietmar and indicating not so much the number of names but rather
their uniqueness and privacy. Hence A. Brückner's decision to translate "quod
regiones (*etc.*)" as: "they have as many tiny countries as temples and worship
particular [emphasis – S.R.] demonic idols."[430]

However, even support for the interpretation, assuming that there was only
one idol in each temple, will not allow the character (and even more so names
or roles) of deities embodied by them to be defined. In the interpretation of
Thietmar's information, the emphasis of dedication of these sculptures to demons is of key significance. Hence the admission of this theological interpretation of paganism is in harmony with the expression *infideles* ("infidels"), used
in this context to refer to its followers. In this perspective it is hard to decide
whether the term "demons" refers to particular deities or more generally to an
antisacral addressee of idolatry understood in this way by Christians.

427   In Wolgast and Gützkow, see Ebo III, 7–11; cf. Rosik, *Conversio*, pp. 418–434.
428   See below, p. 345.
429   *E.g.* Leciejewicz, *Słowianie*, p. 115.
430   Brückner, *Mitologia słowiańska i polska*, p. 46.

THE RELIGION OF THE SLAVS IN THIETMAR'S CHRONICLE   137

Due to the fact that Thietmar used the expression *dii* to refer to idols, it seems more probable that he did not identify gods with demons.[431] Therefore he outlined an image in which "these parts" are controlled by demonic idolatry, and there are no direct references to the nature of the worshipped divine persons in the perspective of Slavic mythology. Building on such a basis a multi-layer hypothesis that *templa* in particular regions were dedicated to one tribal patron is evidence that *a priori* views in reflection of the development of the Slavic religion are very strong. Moreover, the idea to summarize these gods to create a supra-tribal pantheon concentrated around Svarožic in the temple in Radogošč was based on weak premises.[432]

Thus, resigning from this concept based on such weak grounds, one should take into account a premise included in Thietmar's claim that Svarožic was worshipped by all pagans (verbatim "cuncti gentiles"). Although the context shows that he means the idol from Radogošč, universality of this cult can indirectly indicate that it was not strictly related to only one place. There are no sufficient grounds for the thesis that the process of shaping tribal patron deities known from the 11th and 12th c. was advanced enough to claim that Svarožic was only the deity of the Redars – to the contrary, it is still possible to find references to Svarog on his behalf to a more general and original tradition of Slavic beliefs.

If one decides to exercise this option there will be two variants to consider: 1) Svarožic would originally be the sovereign of local pantheons of tribes that next belonged to the Liutici Federation; 2) Svarožic, being known among Liutici tribes would dominate local pantheons after their political and religious

---

431   For a discussion on the matter see above, p. 109. Nota bene, Thietmar showed good orientation in Christian demonology, *e.g.* on numerous occasions he described a mystical experience of his characters in which they were attacked by evil spirits; see also Thietmar I, 23, p. 34.

432   In H. Łowmiański's proposal the Liutici pantheon encompassed only gods with the same competences and at the same time the ones with the highest positions. The idea of creating such a federation of gods as an allegory of relations between Polabian tribes has its counterpart in attempts to explain the occurrence of polycephalism among seaside gods (Triglav, Svantevit) as an expression of tribes merging into larger organisms and melting together of their tribal unicephalic patrons into one figure with a few heads. This view was expressed by *e.g.* Włodzimierz Antoniewicz, "Religia dawnych Słowian," in *Religie świata*, ed. Eugeniusz Dąbrowski (Warszawa: Instytut Wydawniczy PAX, 1957), pp. 369–371; Dowiat, *Chrzest*, p. 27. This attempt to explain the polycephalism of Slavic statues of gods does not withstand criticism (see Rosik, *Udział*, pp. 57, 67 f. and see below, pp. 340 ff.), which indirectly influences the assessment of the proposal explaining a large number of idols in Radogošč as a result of activity of an analogous mechanism connected with the unification of tribes.

unification around Radogošč. In one way or another in the 11th c., as a result of progressing disintegration of cults in Polabia, Svarožic's place in cult would be taken by patron gods of particular tribes.[433]

It is worth emphasizing that although the proposal presented here in two variants is based on a premise in Thietmar's narration, the method of reasoning largely constructs a space about which sources keep silent. This is why it is still worth taking into account an alternative solution, assuming that the cult of the Radogošč sovereign was disseminated as an "all-federation" cult of mainly Liutici tribes, and maybe also their neighbours, which was a parallel cult in relation to worship addressed to native pantheons, connected with each of the above mentioned *regiones* temples.

To sum up this general outline of hypothetical findings about the reality of Slavic beliefs and cults related to the summary image of the Polabian network of temples discussed above, one should emphasize that Thietmar, talking about the ruling of the "principal monarchy" (*principalis monarchia*) by Radogošč, formed a theological perspective that showed the primacy of this idolatry centre over other centres. In this perspective, along with Svarožic, according to the chronicler, *primus deorum*, becoming also a counterpart of *princeps demonum*, the major Liutici temple becomes the capital of all Christ's enemies.

In the way it was treated by Liutici – to continue reading Thietmar's chronicle – there is a striking similarity to biblical motifs related to Jerusalem, such as greeting the Holy City and offering gifts: "They salute this [city] on their way to war, on their victorious return they worship it with proper gifts; and what sacrifice they shall make by the hands of servants [of the temple] that will be pleasant for gods they find out by drawing lots and [prophecies with a use of] a horse, as I have already mentioned. Their [gods'] unspeakable fury can be tamed by human and cattle blood."[434] Certainly there is no basis to exclude the possibility that the premise about greeting Radogošč refers to

---

433 Leciejewicz, *Słowianie*, pp. 215 ff., especially 222. It cannot be excluded that some gods who substituted in cult the universally worshipped Svarožic initially were his various, local hypostases, like we already know from the description written by Adam of Bremen Redigast (see above, pp. 212 ff.). A. Brückner even suggested that the names of Polabian and Pomeranian deities, such as Svantevit, Triglav and Iarovit are only local names of Svarožic (cf. Strzelczyk, *Mity*, p. 199 f.). However, this view seems oversimplified and one should take into account that the mythologies and cult of the above mentioned deities were formed in a longer process of various overlapping motifs and symbols (*e.g.* the chthonic one in the case of Triglav, which is discussed below).

434 Thietmar VI, 25: "Hanc ad bellum properantes salutant, illam prospere redeuntes muneribus debitis honorant, et quae placabilis hostia diis offerri a ministris debeat, per sortes ac per equum, sicut prefatus sum, diligenter inquiritur. Hominum ac sanguine pecudum ineffabilis horum furor mitigatur."

THE RELIGION OF THE SLAVS IN THIETMAR'S CHRONICLE   139

a Liutici custom, similarly to offering gifts, on the basis of which it is assumed that in the temple there was a treasury.[435]

The information is dominated by references to war issues and in this context, it is repeated that there were offerings made by priests and divinations (drawing lots, divination using horses). Especially if one remembers that the "wordless wrath" of the Liutici gods would fade thanks to offerings, not only animal but also human,[436] the conviction of their irascible nature is strengthened. This oversaturation of the description with a military element corresponds with the wider context of Thietmar's narration, in which the excurse devoted to Radogošč was placed, *i.e.* an account of the events of war.

However, when it comes to the major tribal sanctuary (with reference to the Redars), there is no information about other areas of collective life, apart from military issues, which were entrusted to divine powers that encourage reflection. It is interesting to examine to what extent this situation is related to the fact that this subject was discussed in this particular part of the work, and how real such "militarization" of a cult place in the social and political reality of Northern Polabia actually was at that time. In considerations connected with this problem, comparative material in sources related to Rügen in the 12th c. seems inspiring.[437]

The island was a place with coexisting power centres which competed and cooperated with each other at the same time – priestly power (assembly) in Arkona and the duke's power in "Carentia" (Garz?), where alternative theological systems were formed. Svantevit was a god from Arkona with universal powers, and because of this he transgressed the area of activity of martial Rugievit worshipped in "Carentia". A statue of Rugievit with seven faces and eight swords was located in a separate temple. In close proximity there were two more temples based on the same model: containing one polycephalic statue closed in a roofed sacral area. They were dedicated to five-faced Porenut and Porevit.[438]

Jacek Banaszkiewicz proposed to interpret these three gods analogically to the divine triad worshipped in the Uppsala temple, thus locating "Carentia" in

---

435   See above, footnotes 390 and 434 in this chapter. An analogy can be found in confirmations of keeping precious objects in temples in Szczecin (see *Die Prüfeninger Vita Bischof Ottos I. von Bamberg nach der Fassung des Großen Österreichischen Legendars*, ed. Jürgen Petersohn, MGH SSrerGerm in usum scholarum (1999) [further: Vita Prieflingensis], II, 11–12) or Arkona in narrative sources, see below, pp. 300 f.

436   For more information of human offerings in the context of Adam's reports see below pp. 244 ff.

437   Saxo Grammaticus XIV, 39, 3; 39, 39–40; cf. above footnote 326 in this chapter.

438   For polycephalism of Slavic idols and attempts to interpret it in studies on the Slavic religion see below, pp. 338 ff.

140   CHAPTER 2

a group of political power centres with pre-Christian cult places, a good example of which was also Kiev in the times of Vladimir the Great.[439] However,
Porevit and Porenut, when accompanying the major Rugievit, do not correspond with deities accompanying Thor in his pantheon in Uppsala in terms of
their function and position. However, they "follow a few regularities characteristic for the Dioskouri."[440]

Advantages of interpreting the triad of deities from "Carentia" in this way
are worth emphasizing, especially in the context of the already mentioned rivalry between this centre and Arkona. This was due to a weaker position of
this type of twin characters in mythologies in comparison with the gods. Since
Rugievit was their sovereign, he would not share his authority with them and
instead he would keep all the power to himself. He thus became an alternative
to the omnipotent Svantevit.[441] The choice of Rugievit with his military attributes to be the duke's patron shows the significance of military issues in the
legitimization of superior authority.

In this context such strong militarization of the pantheon in Radogošč would
indicate that in this stronghold there was not only a religious but also a political power centre of the federated Liutici. However, due to the fact that they
did not have one ruler controlling them, and at the same time the assembly
with significant contribution from the priests (the oracle) played the leading
role in governance,[442] the collation with Arkona gains more significance in a
comparative analysis. The sovereign worshipped there also possessed military
attributes, related to the already mentioned symbolism of superior authority.

---

439   Jacek Banaszkiewicz, "Pan Rugii – Rugiewit i jego towarzysze z Gardźca: Porewit i
      Porenut (Saxo Gramatyk, Gesta Danorum, XIV, 39, 38–41)," in *Słowiańszczyzna w Europie
      średniowiecznej. Księga pamiątkowa dla Lecha Leciejewicza*, vol. 1: *Plemiona i wczesne
      państwa*, ed. Zofia Kurnatowska (Wrocław: IAE PAN, 1996), pp. 75–82.

440   The positive character Porevit would find his antithesis in Porenut, which is supported
      by the proposed etymology of 'Porenut' as one who 'needs support' derived from '-por'
      (power) + 'nud' (like Old Polish meaning of "nuda" – boredom, German "Not" – need,
      pressure), which puts him in opposition to 'Porevit' as the 'Lord of power'. According to
      Saxo Grammaticus (XIV, 39, 41), both deities had five faces each, however, Porenut had
      one face on his chest, which suggests his inferiority in comparison with Porevit, who had
      all his faces on his head – see *ibidem*, p. 81.

441   Rugievit – being related to the ducal power alternative to Svantevit – was the god control-
      ling the whole universum (he had seven faces, which symbolically shows the completeness
      of his control, *e.g.* over the whole three-sector and four-direction cosmos), however –
      as was mentioned by Banaszkiewicz, "Pan Rugii," p. 81) – similarly to Thor or Perun, he
      delegated some of his activities to other supernatural creatures. However, other gods were
      not chosen, as this would deprive the sovereign of his omnicompetence, and dioskurs
      were selected as they were less significant and yet more universal in their activity (usually
      they would excel in the third function according to the Dumézil model).

442   See above, pp. 128 ff.

THE RELIGION OF THE SLAVS IN THIETMAR'S CHRONICLE 141

Due to these analogies one can speculate that Svarožic – similarly to Svantevit – could also experience in Radogošč other types of worship than those related to war (such as that from the Redars themselves). However, it seems equally probable that giving preeminence to the cult in Radogošč by military elements was a fact, because this stronghold was created to locate only the temple there and not to perform other functions typical of a settlement, such as activities related to agriculture or fairs,[443] where a harvest festival would be a natural phenomenon.

Another striking matter, similarly to Arkona, is the supra-tribal significance of Radogošč. It is worth mentioning here that according to Helmold, the Redars themselves were proud of the fact that they possessed such a famous temple – most certainly located in Radogošč, or a new one continuing its functions described by Thietmar[444] – who interpreted this as a title to become leaders of the Liutici. Therefore, the famous temple added splendour to them and political significance, not the other way around.

Hence the primacy of Radogošč in comparison with other temples is mainly explained by an exceptionally high effectiveness of hierophany in the opinion of its worshippers. However, even if in the other Liutici temples Svarožic was also worshipped, there are no premises to claim that they formed a network affiliated with the one in Radogošč and were dominated by its rule,[445] especially

---

443 The thesis results precisely from Thietmar's record, however, one should remember that in Adam of Bremen's description of Rhetra, which is hypothetically identified with Radogošč, one can observe premises indicating an urban and not only cult character of this centre, see below, p. 223.

444 See below, p. 295.

445 Procházka, "Organisace," p. 166, assumed that the presence of other Svantevit's temples in Rügen, mentioned by Saxo Grammaticus, meant that there was a system of Arkona's filial sanctuaries. Procházka used the same expression to refer to the Liutici organisation, where Svarožic was to have his filial temples in regions (*regiones*) or possibly local deities dominated by Svarožic were worshipped in them. However, even if one accepts this hypothesis with reference to Rügen, treating it as an analogy to Liutici raises doubts due to differences in the systems of the compared communities. In the case of the multi-tribal Liutici structure, implementation of the centralist policy through Radogošč would be significantly more difficult than in the case of Arkona in reference to one tribe, *i.e.* the Rans. Moreover, an important mechanism in the unification of the cult system on the island, assumed in this hypothesis, was to be the realisation of theocratic ambitions of Svantevit's priests competing with the ducal power. Meanwhile in the case of the Liutici Federation, it is hard to speak about such strong centralisation of power over the whole society, hence there was no social or political power able to conduct such a religious reform. However, it is worth emphasizing that the very idea of claiming that Svantevit's temples in Rügen were subordinate to the major sanctuary in Arkona raises doubts: since the deity was the major patron of the tribe, it could be worshipped in various parts of the island without any top-down decision to introduce cult made by priests from the major temple.

142   CHAPTER 2

in view of the fragile basis of the thesis on formation of temples and idolatry among the Polabian Slavs at the end of the 10th c. at the earliest.

It is hard to prove that the Liutici federation organization required a centralist religious system (imitating the church system).[446] It seems more probable that Radogošč, just like Arkona later, superseded other cult centres and took the initiative in organizing anti-Christian resistance.[447] Thus although Radogošč was not the duke's dwelling place or any other type of centre permanently controlling the Liutici, it was a place where the most important political decisions related to them and sometimes also to their neighbours were made.

It is not surprising that this supra-tribal authority in Thietmar's perspective was called "principalis monarchia". It should be emphasized, however, that the chronicler interpreted this situation in a very special way by reducing it only to a strictly religious sphere, presented from the perspective of theological evaluation of paganism, which resulted in a schematic picture of all temples dominated by Radogošč and the cults followed in them as a reality of idolatry and demons related to idols without any local nuances.

2.6.7   Oath of Peace

Further verses of Thietmar's work introduce readers to the social and political life of the Liutici.[448] At the end of this part there is information about a ritual peace settlement, which was formed with a reference to an archaic and universal symbolism of shaking the right hand and handing over a wisp of hair with grass.[449] The discussion about the significance of these symbols in a peace settlement gave rise to a proposal of explanations based on the grounds of political and religious behaviours.[450] A. Brückner suggested that the hair

---

446   Which clearly results from Adam of Bremen's chronicle – see below, p. 225.

447   However, from the perspective of a few centuries these were only ephemerides, which could not face the power of new ideological (Christian) systems becoming increasingly stronger in the whole of Central Europe. Leciejewicz, *Słowianie*, p. 193. Cf. Gerard Labuda, "Wytworzenie się wspólnoty etnicznej i kulturalnej plemion Słowiańszczyzny Połabskiej i jej przemiany w rozwoju dziejowym," in *Słowiańszczyzna Połabska między Niemcami a Polską. Materiały z konferencji naukowej zorganizowanej przez Instytut Historii UAM w dniach 28–29 IV 1980 r.*, ed. Jerzy Strzelczyk (Poznań: Wydawnictwo UAM, 1981), pp. 21 f.

448   According to this passage there was no single ruler above them and no single method used by them to reach a joint agreement during the assembly, which was their basic organ of power. For more information see, *e.g.* Modzelewski, *Barbarzyńska Europa*, pp. 364 f.; see also Boroń, *Słowiańskie wiece, passim*.

449   Thietmar VI, 25: "Pacem abraso crine supremo et cum gramine datisque affirmant dextris."

450   Jacob Grimm, *Deutsche Rechtsalterthümer*, 4th ed., Leipzig 1899, pp. 154–157, 191, 201–202, established that the right hand was a symbol of power (for the Slavs and Germans), and shaking hands meant strengthening the agreement by joining the power of both sides for better guarantee. On the other hand, handing over a wisp of hair was to mean readiness

THE RELIGION OF THE SLAVS IN THIETMAR'S CHRONICLE   143

was an offering to a deity[451] and most certainly a chthonic one, referring to an
analogous example of a custom in Rus' where oaths were taken to Veles. On the
basis of the Lithuanian name of turf – "velena,"[452] this pioneer in Slavistics concluded that underneath (under turf or grass) there is the kingdom of "vele" –
forefathers (Old Slavic "dziady"), ruled by Veles.[453] Hence, in the proposed
interpretation, the guarantor of the undertaken obligation would be a representative of the underworld.

It is characteristic, however, that in the second half of the 12th c., Helmold,
confirming the cult character of Slavic oaths, mentioned that the calling of
gods as guarantors was excluded and it was only possible to refer to elements
of nature (trees, stones).[454] This is why it is worth taking into consideration
that, possibly in the custom described by Thietmar, it was not so that some deities' sanctions were mentioned, but there were references to the symbolism –
maybe indicated also by grass motifs – of the underworld, which would engulf
the one who failed to keep his word. According to Saxo Grammaticus, on a
similar basis the Rugians threw a stone into water when taking an oath, wish-
ing that a perjurer would die this way.[455]

Next Thietmar adds that it was easy to bribe the Slavs and make them break
an agreement. This supports the view that there was a depreciation of the significance of concluded agreements which would be in accordance with the already mentioned ban on swearing an oath to gods. In the opinion of the Slavs,
breaking a promise could result in a wrath of gods with the whole community.
However, taking into account that in archaic communities elements of nature
were treated as emanating with sacral power, it would be hard to assume that
oaths sworn to them were devoid of any supernatural sanction in the opinion
of Slavs. Leaving it unnoticed by Christian authors is not surprising given their
mentality.

Thietmar himself, when mentioning the motif related to oaths of peace,
was far from the conviction that the described gestures could significantly
strengthen the concluded agreement. He wrote about this ritual to illustrate

---

for slavery because of not performing an agreement, while the ritual handing over of grass
from a battlefield was a sign of readiness to give the victor one's territory. Cf. M.Z. Jedlicki
in: Thietmar VI, 25, p. 351, footnote 126.

451 Brückner, *Mitologia słowiańska i polska*, p. 269.
452 *Ibidem*, p. 149.
453 The reference to Veles (or turn to non-personified underworld spheres) as a guarantee of
oaths remains in agreement with A. Brückner's opinion that the Slavs did not take oaths
to the Sun like other peoples – see *ibidem*, pp. 145, 269.
454 See below, pp. 354 f.
455 Saxo XIV, 25, 2; cf. Brückner, *Mitologia słowiańska i polska*, p. 145.

144   CHAPTER 2

his view of the exceptional perversity of the Liutici. This is clearly confirmed in
the introductory sentence to the description of the discussed ritual, especially
in the context of the information about the ease with which pagans would go
back on their word to fulfil an agreement because of corruption: "Although
infidels and unstable themselves, of others they demand stable and durable
faithfulness."[456]

2.6.8   Echo of the 983 Rebellion

In summary of the passage devoted to the Liutici there is a deploration and
warning: "Such warriors, once our servants, now free because of our wickedness, came with their gods for the purpose of supporting the king. Dear reader,
avoid both their society and their cult! Rather, hear and obey the mandates
of divine scripture! If you learn and commit to memory the faith declared by
Bishop Athanasius, the things that I have recounted above will rightly appear
meaningless to you."[457] The liberation of the Liutici from the German yoke is
read by Thietmar as a punishment for the iniquity of their earlier lords. At the
same time, it is striking that it is emphasized that pagans came to rescue the
Saxons in "such company" ("tali comitatu"), most certainly meaning Liutici
deities.

The Bishop of Merseburg saw a real threat to the Christian faith in contacts
with pagans, so he exhorted his readers to avoid mixing with the Liutici and
their cult and to give ear to recommendations of "divine scriptures," most
probably the Bible. However, patristic works cannot be excluded as a possibility. The crown argument for the valueless character of the described pagan rites
was to be a confrontation of the information presented by Thietmar with the
symbol of faith attributed to St. Athanasius. Yet on another occasion within the
chronicle a reference to "scriptures" becomes a determinant of the supremacy
of the Christian faith over the religion of the Slavs.[458]

---

456   Thietmar VI, 25: "Infideles ipsi et mutabiles ipsi inmutabilitatem ac magnam exigunt ab
      aliis fidem". In accordance with this opinion of the chronicler Kiersnowska, Kiersnowski,
      Życie codzienne, p. 152, emphasize that oath guarantees were not treated seriously; be-
      guiling enemies was an ordinary military procedure and the one who was deceived was
      considered a fool.

457   Trans. D.A. Warner in: *Ottonian Germany*, p. 254; cf. Thietmar VI, 25: "Hii milites, quon-
      dam servi nostrisque iniquitatibus tunc liberi, tali comitatu ad regem auxiliandum pro-
      ficiscuntur. Eorum cum cultu consorcia, lector, fugias, divinarum mandata scripturarum
      auscultando adimple: et fidem, quam Athanasius profitebatur episcopus, dicens memo-
      riterque retinens, haec, quae supra memoravi, nil esse probabis veraciter." See also Goetz,
      Die Wahrnehmung, p. 229.

458   Similarly to attributing the "illiterate" (*inlitterati*) the conviction that everything ends
      with worldly death, see above p. 59 ff.

THE RELIGION OF THE SLAVS IN THIETMAR'S CHRONICLE   145

An echo of the bishop's tirade condemning the idolatry of the Liutici still resounds after this digression in a newly started description of a march of the German and Liutici army. Thietmar emphasizes that in a camp on the Bóbr (*Pober*) River there were even "under uneven leaders the unequal troops."[459] This stress on inequality between leaders and the troops must be the result of an earlier juxtaposition of paganism and Christianity.[460] Thus the chronicler refers to the fact that the covenant between Henry II and the Liutici resulted in a worldview conflict in the Saxon environment. Although there are no words so typical of St. Bruno of Querfurt about the community between Christ and Belial, the theology in the assessment of these events is the same.[461]

2.7   *Wigbert and* Zutibure

Having abandoned descriptions of wars between the Empire and Poland, Thietmar returned to the thread of the activity of the Merseburg bishops, focusing on Wigbert (1004–1009), which was an opportunity to document the cult of the holy grove in the Chutici land.

The predecessor of the chronicler, "with his tireless preaching managed to dissuade those who were entrusted to him from the superstition of idle error; also the grove called *Zutibure*, worshipped as God and untouched since the ancient times, he cut out to the roots and built a church dedicated to St. Romanus in its place."[462] In the image one can observe the basic stages of missionary action: teaching and persuading the local community to reject paganism, later the so-called *abrenuntiatio diaboli, i.e.* elimination of a pagan cult place (in this case a grove) in the dimension of collective life, and also the establishment of a new sacral order in the public sphere by building a church.

---

459   Thietmar VI, 26: "inparibus ducibus inequales turmae". Jedlicki's suggestion (*ibidem*, footnote 129) that this expression emphasizes that the troops progressed under various leaderships – *i.e.* with Christian and pagan emblems, seems disputable in a literal sense. It is also possible to take into account the antithesis of Christ/St. Maurice and gods, or "get back on earth" and indicate a lack of equality in the commands of both allied armies (such assessment would definitely be burdened with religious and cultural issues).

460   Quite a common view – see Strzelczyk, *Mity*, p. 197.

461   About St. Bruno's letter, see above, pp. 107 f.; cf. Schulmeyer-Ahl, *Der Anfang*, p. 134. However, the thesis that the alliance between the Empire and the Liutici "meant formal equality of the religion of the Polabian Slavs" (see: Piotr Bogdanowicz, "Zjazd gnieźnieński w roku 1000," *Nasza Przeszłość* 16 (1962), p. 135) should be considered as exaggerated.

462   Thietmar VI, 37: "predicacione assidua comissos a vana superstitione erroris reduxit, lucumque Zutibure dictum, ab accolis ut Deum in omnibus honoratum et ab evo antiquo numquam violatum, radicitus eruens, sancto martiri Romano in eo ecclesiam construxit."

The name used to refer to the grove *Zutibure* is jointly translated by scholars as "Święty Bór" ("Holy Forest").[463] This etymologically proves that one deals here with a coniferous forest, resinous, or potentially a wetland (peloids).[464] In Polish folklore there is a forest demon called 'borowiec', 'borowy', or 'boruta,'[465] which allowed Leszk P. Słupecki to emphasize the demonic trace of the very name 'bór.'[466] The word "święty" ('holy') originally had a wider semantic range identified with force, power, and also sacral power.[467]

According to M.Z. Jedlicki there was a statue or a temple from which divinity radiated in the surrounding grove.[468] This speculation does not seem necessary given the possibility of directly personifying the *sacrum* in elements of nature, among which the tree is deeply rooted in the mythology of numerous peoples.[469] For the tree was not to be worshipped, but rather the sacral reality symbolized by it.[470] According to L. Moszyński it was a hypothetical, primordial god of the Old Slavs, the alleged *svętъ Bogъ* (Holy God), and the name of the grove turns out to be a typical example of metonymy: *svętъ borъ* ("holy grove") occurs instead of *borъ svętajego Boga* ("forest or grove of the holy God"). Even distancing oneself from the idea of the Old Slavic only god, it is worth not excluding from the field of hypotheses an interpretation of the name of this place based on substitution of the original sacral name.[471]

No information about the destruction of the statue or the temple in the holy grove of the Chutici was used by H. Łowmiański to support the thesis of the complete absence of such objects in southern Polabia.[472] The effectiveness of his arguments are diminished by the fact that the *Zutibure* cult was completed at the time of Christianization, so it is hard to support the opinion that possible temple institutions or tribal nature could survive until these times.

---

463   Thietmar, p. 368 (editor's footnote).
464   The etymology of "bór" – see Aleksander Brückner, *Słownik etymologiczny języka polskiego* (Warszawa: Wiedza Powszechna, 1957), p. 36; Urbańczyk, *Dawni Słowianie*, p. 157.
465   Urbańczyk, *Dawni Słowianie*, according to index.
466   Słupecki, *Slavonic Pagan Sanctuaries*, p. 162.
467   Urbańczyk, *Dawni Słowianie*, p. 193.
468   Thietmar, p. 369, editor's footnote 191.
469   An excellent analogy is the holy grove of Prove, a Wagrian deity, see below, p. 330.
470   This motif is developed by Gieysztor, *Mitologia*, pp. 219 f., who added that trees had healing properties, not only as cult objects but also as places where the demonic or deified sacrum not only appeared but also remained (the same: Herbord II, 32).
471   It is also worth mentioning that in the 18th c. an alleged Slavic deity was recorded – *Zuttibor, Svitibor, i.e.* "Święty Bór" ("Holy Grove") (see Strzelczyk, *Mity*, p. 194). It is a very weak trace to support the possible personification of the grove/'bór' (maybe a tree) in the form of a deity, as long as the mechanism of creating this pseudo-deity in a legend in any way matched the real thought processes from centuries earlier.
472   Łowmiański, *Religia*, p. 168.

THE RELIGION OF THE SLAVS IN THIETMAR'S CHRONICLE

Moreover, it cannot be excluded that idolatry existed on a smaller scale in the form of small figures kept at homes, *etc.*

Scholars jointly support the location of *Zutibure* near Lützen – today Scheiktbar – proposed by F. Kurze.[473] In this context, Jacek Banaszkiewicz's proposal deserved attention, which suggested conducting a model interpretation of the Chutici ecumene as a political, territorial, and religious unit with two power poles. The other centre – apart from the holy grove – was Merseburg, located only twenty kilometers away, which according to Thietmar was called "Mese" – slav. "miedza" (balk), the centre, by the inhabitants of the country.[474]

An analogic example would be the land of the Wagrians, with Starigard and Prove's grove mentioned by Helmold in the 12th c.[475] Similarly, in the case of the Glomače one can indicate Gana as their capital centre and their main sanctuary in the form of the Glomač spring and its flood plain. This comparative context supports the view that the holy grove was the main place of tribal cult for the Chutici,[476] however it is impossible to exclude an alternative solution that it was a holy sainthood only for some neighbouring communities living in the tribal domain already included in the German monarchy.

There are a few issues regarding the interpretation of Slavic cults from the perspective of Christianity that require further research. First of all, the claim that Wigbert, thanks to his persistence in the teaching the Slavs entrusted to him, discouraged them from *vana superstitio erroris* should be analyzed. This qualification of the pagan cult depicts it as a pernicious superstition resulting from an error, blindness. A measure of this "error" is the chronicler's claim that the grove had been untouched since ancient times, and "it was worshipped like God in every respect" ("ut Deum in omnibus honoratum").[477] It is hard to reject the impression that in this comparison there is an emphatic tone, however this does not exclude the conviction of its leading role in the religious life of the local community.

The very comparison of the grove cult with worshipping God corresponds with the stereotypical view that pagans worshipped the creation instead of the Creator (cf. Rom 1:25). In this context the information that Wigbert turned the grove into a church fits well as he, in a way, re-established the right order from the biblical perspective. The possibility cannot be excluded that precisely this missionary procedure could prompt the chronicler to the idea of comparison

---

473 M.Z. Jedlicki, see Thietmar, p. 369, footnote 191; Słupecki, *Slavonic Pagan Sanctuaries*, p. 161; L. Leciejewicz, "»In Pago," p. 128; *Die Slawen in Deutschland*, p. 310.

474 Thietmar I, 2, p. 5.

475 Banaszkiewicz, *Polskie dzieje*, pp. 421f.

476 *E.g.* Tyszkiewicz, "Podziały plemienne," p. 128.

477 Thietmar VI, 37.

148   CHAPTER 2

between the worship of the holy grove and the cult of God in Christianity.[478] However, on the other hand, one should take into account the strong attractiveness of hierophany in the form of a grove for the Slavs.[479]

The attachment of the Slavs to open cult spaces could be based on archaic Indo-European convictions, such as those mentioned by Tacitus with reference to the Germans. They were to think that it is not appropriate to close divine entities in temple walls.[480] If the Slavs shared this opinion, then the appearance of a new social and mythological impulse in the genesis of their temples should be appreciated.[481] Thus, maintaining archaic forms of open cult spaces did not necessarily have to mean an evolutionarily lower – pre-polytheistic – phase of religiosity. It does certainly support the thesis that a variety of cultic modes were in place. This was even observed by Helmold (I, 52) a century and a half later.

478   There are more examples of similar continuation of using a cult place from pre-Christian times by erecting a church in the Polabian and Pomeranian Slavdom. In the light of excavation work in Starigard/Oldenburg on the Wagrian land, such were vicissitudes of the cult place from the 8th/9th c. to the 10th/11th c.: first halls were placed there, they were used for representative and sacral functions; after a duke's baptism, they were replaced with a church which was probably demolished by rebelled Slavs and later an idol was placed there under the open sky, it was a place for making offerings, see below, p. 333, footnote 349, and also Słupecki, *Slavonic Pagan Sanctuaries*, pp. 108 f.; Strzelczyk, *Mity*, p. 211; Padberg, *Die Christianisierung*, p. 182. The very idea to replace cult objects with each other partly reminds about the recommendations of pope Gregory the Great (d. 604) to adapt pagan temples for the needs of the newly introduced Christianity (see *Gregorius Melito Abbati in Franciis*, in: *Gregorii I papae Registrum epistolarum*, vol. 2: *Libri VIII– XIV*, ed. Ludwig M. Hartmann, MGH Epp 2 (1899), XI, 56, p. 331; cf. *e.g.* Bolesław Kumor, "Praktyka misyjna Kościoła w X w.," *Nasza Przeszłość* 69 (1988), p. 23). For discussion on this matter see *e.g.* Sikorski, *Kościół w Polsce*, pp. 78 ff.

479   S. Urbańczyk ascertained that until the late, decadent phase of the pre-Christian epoch, the Slavs used rather archaic groves as the main places to make offerings and worship gods; groves had the same role for them as churches for Christians. This is why when sources mention temples, they can mean cult groves – see: Urbańczyk, *Dawni Słowianie*, pp. 121, 137, 160. However, at the current stage of research there are no reasons to doubt the existence of Slavic temples in the times when their written confirmations were created, hence the idea that holy groves were confused with a temple does not seem sufficiently justified.

480   Tacitus, *Germania*, 10 (p. 12); cf. Jerzy Gąssowski, "Kult religijny," in *Mały słownik kultury dawnych Słowian*, ed. Lech Leciejewicz (Warszawa: Wiedza Powszechna, 1988), p. 578.

481   The problem deserves further discussion, see p. 175.

THE RELIGION OF THE SLAVS IN THIETMAR'S CHRONICLE   149

2.8   The Third War between Henry II and Boleslav the Brave: Ślęża Mountain and the Liutici Goddesses

A description of the third stage of the struggle between Henry II and Boleslav the Brave brings a digression about the cult of Ślęża Mountain (718 msl). It returns to the motif of the German-Liutici alliance, in which the non-Christian religion becomes a component of complex political reality.[482] In the presentation of military actions in 1017, Thietmar mentions that the imperial army reached the castle town of Niemcza (Germ. Nimptsch), about which he said: "For it is situated in the *Silensi* land, whose name was given after some very high and grand mountain; due to its quality [*i.e.* attributes, character] and magnitude, when cursed paganism was venerated here, the mountain was highly worshipped by the inhabitants."[483]

The literature connected with the "Silesian Olympus" – raised about half a kilometre above the surrounding plane – is very rich,[484] and archaeological work can still bring unexpected revelations, which can be proven by results of the last decades.[485] There are also other cult places of this type in the Western Slavdom,[486] which makes Ślęża less exceptional than some earlier scholars wanted to admit. This mountain or possibly also its whole massif[487] was treated as a mythical centre of the country, which is indicated in

---

482   See *e.g.* Lübke, *Fremde*, p. 276, and above pp. 107 f.

483   Thietmar VII, 59: "Posita est autem haec in Pago Silensi, vocabulo hoc a quodam monte nimis excelso et grandi olim sibi indito; et hic ob qualitatem suam et quantitatem, cum execranda gentilitas ibi veneraretur, ab incolis omnibus nimis honorabatur."

484   For extensive scientific discussion on the prehistoric and early Medieval past of Ślęża see Wacław Korta, *Tajemnice góry Ślęży* (Katowice: Śląski Instytut Naukowy, 1988). See also Marta Młynarska-Kaletynowa, "Ślęża (2)," in SSS, vol. 5, pp. 564–566; Lech Leciejewicz, ">>In Pago," *passim*; Słupecki, "Ślęża," *Kwartalnik Historyczny* 99 (1992) 2, pp. 3–15; *idem*, *Slavonic Pagan Sanctuaries*, p. 172–176; Andrzej Mierzwiński, *Ślężańska układanka* (Wrocław: Chronicon, 2007); Stanisław Rosik, "Mons Silensis – axis mundi. Góra Ślęża między historią a fenomenologią," in *Sacrum pogańskie – sacrum chrześcijańskie. Kontynuacja miejsc kultu we wczesnośredniowiecznej Europie Środkowej*, ed. Krzysztof Bracha, Czesław Hadamik (Warszawa: DiG, 2010), pp. 179–192. See also footnotes 485 and 509 in this chapter.

485   Grzegorz Domański, *Ślęża w pradziejach i średniowieczu* (Wrocław: IAE PAN, 2002).

486   Cosmas (I, 4) provides general information on the cult of mountains and hills among Czech peasants. The main analogy to the Ślęża cult, albeit controversial in terms of detailed findings, is Łysiec in the Świętokrzyskie Mountains.

487   Sacral significance of neighbouring peaks: Wieżyca and Radunia supports location of cult circles there – Bogusław Gediga, *Śladami religii Prasłowian* (Wrocław: Ossolineum, 1976) p. 145.

150   CHAPTER 2

FIGURE 3   Mount Ślęża
             STANISŁAW ROSIK

the connection between its name and the ethonym of Ślężanie (Silensi).[488]
Similar to Thietmar's information about the Glomače (see above) bearing the
name of their holy spring, the land of the Silensi also received its name after
a holy place. However, an alternative idea about the etymology of the Silensi
land has strong premises in historical science, namely that the name comes
from the Ślęza River,[489] or possibly the general characteristics of this wet and
marshy land.[490]

Thietmar's work is not enough to solve this controversy, because he created it at the time when this mountain and river had an eponimic name for
the Ślężanie,[491] and their name was written as Sleenzane as early as the mid-
9th c. (or the beginning of the 10th c.) in the so called Bavarian Geographer.[492]

---

488   See e.g. Stanisław Rospond, "Ślężanie," in sss, vol. 5, pp. 566 f.; Słupecki, "Ślęza," pp. 13 f.;
      cf. idem, Slavonic Pagan Sanctuaries, pp. 172 ff.; Dušan Třeštik, Mýty kmene Čechů (7.–10.
      století) (Praha: Nakladatelství Lidové nowiny, 2003), p. 76. For a critical discussion of this
      matter see: Rosik, Mons Silensis – axis mundi, p. 183–185.
489   Jürgen Udolph, "Der Name Schlesiens," Jahrbuch der schlesischen Friedrich-Wilhelm-
      Universität zu Breslau 38/39 (1997–1998), pp. 15–18.
490   Rosik, "The formation," pp. 55–61.
491   Thietmar did not explicitly mention the name of the mountain, which is known from
      the sources from the 12th c. – see e.g. Codex Diplomaticus nec non epistolaris Silesiae,
      vol. 1: 971–1204, ed. Karol Maleczyński (Wrocław: Wrocławskie Towarzystwo Miłośników
      Historii, 1951), No. 22, p. 54: Mons Silencij.
492   Descriptio civitatum et regionum ad septentrionalem plagam Danubii, ed. Bohuslav
      Horák, Dušan Trávníček, in iidem, Descriptio civitatum et regionum ad septentrion-
      alem plagam Danubii (t. zv. Bavorský geograf), "Rozpravy Československé Akademie
      Věd" 66 (1956) 2, pp. 2–3; about Bavarian Geographer see: Henryk Łowmiański, "O

THE RELIGION OF THE SLAVS IN THIETMAR'S CHRONICLE   151

Therefore the very naming of the land surrounding the mountain took place in times immemorial even for Thietmar and, similarly to contemporary historians, he was doomed to validate his own speculations; one should also remember, that his etymologies in their scholarliness did not deviate from other similar attempts in his epoch. It was essentially guesswork based on associations of names and observations of the current state of affairs.[493]

Thietmar gives particular reasons, for which the mountain was to be worshipped: the original ones were *granditas* and *qualitas*, magnitude and "quality" – certainly the height – which provided inspiration for religious experience. These qualities made Ślęża a natural hierophany. In the case of Thietmar's narration there is striking emphasis on these features.[494] The qualities of the peak allowed for an analogy to the biblical formulae of describing holy mountains.[495] Thus the question arises whether in the explanation of the

---

  pochodzeniu Geografa bawarskiego," *Roczniki Historyczne* 20 (1951/1952), pp. 9–23; Jerzy Nalepa, "O nowszym ujęciu problematyki plemion słowiańskich u Geografa Bawarskiego. Uwagi krytyczne." *Slavia Occidentalis* 60 (2003), pp. 9–63; Sébastien Rossignol, "Überlegungen zur Datierung des Traktates des sog. Bayerischen Geographen anhand paläographischer und kodikologischer Beobachtungen," in *Der Wandel um 1000. Beiträge der Sektion zur slawischen Frühgeschichteder 18. Jahrestagung des Mittel- und Ostdeutschen Verbandes für Altertumsforschungin Greifswald, 23. bis 27. März 2009*, ed. Felix Biermann, Thomas Kersting, Anne Klammt, (Beiträge zur Ur- und Frühgeschichte Mitteleuropas) 60 (Langenweissbach: Beier & Beran, 2011), pp. 305–316.

493 In a few places in his chronicle Thietmar uses wrongly justified or (or dictated by *licentia poetica?*) explanations of the genesis of names: *e.g.* erroneously derived Magdeborn (*Medeburu*) from "mel prohibe" (11, 37) or – maybe as an intentional rhetorical figure – the name of Merseburg from Mars (1, 2). These attempts as well as name translations in other places (*e.g.* "Belgor" – "White Mountain" – into *Mons Pulcher* – "Beautiful Mountain", see: Thietmar VI, 56) show that Thietmar based explanations of toponomastics on not very good knowledge of the Slavic language and at the same time showed his own invention; certainly a similar – this time successful – attempt is association of the name *Nemzi (i.e.* Niemcza) with "Niemcy" – Germans. See *e.g.* Strzelczyk, *Thietmar*, p. 75.

494 Even mountain tops in the Alps were not described with this type of terms emphasizing their size, see Stanisław Rosik, "Gdy góra Ślęża przerosła Alpy ... Uwagi w sprawie recepcji kultury słowiańskiej w kręgu łacińskim (na przykładzie funkcjonowanie etymologii w tekstach do XII w.)," in *Źródła kultury umysłowej w Europie środkowej ze szczególnym uwzględnieniem Górnego Śląska*, ed. Antoni Barciak (Katowice: Instytut Górnośląski, 2005). p. 109; cf. Thietmar VI, 4.

495 The phrase "mons excelsus et grandis" corresponds with biblical word-clusters (cf. *mons excelsum – e.g.* Mt 4:8; Mt 17:1; Mk 9:1; Lk 4:5; or Rev 21:10: "in montem magnum et altum"), however, it should be emphasized that in the *Vulgate* the neuter gender was used to refer to a mountain (mons), hence it hard to speak here about direct correspondence between both texts, one should rather take into account the appearance of a common universal idea of presenting a holy mountain in both narratives, *i.e.*, Bible and Thietmar's work.

152   CHAPTER 2

reasons for the Ślęża cult the chronicler referred to any native Slavic tradition
or whether he based it on universal views functioning until today.[496]

The question of whether Ślęża was worshipped like gods (*i.e.* anthropomor-
phised creatures) cannot be solved. The vocabulary used by Thietmar suggests,
however, that there was a difference, since in relation to statues he uses the
verb *colere*. This does not undermine the rank of the cult of this mountain with
reference to idols, which is supported by the fact that in the above discussed
passage on the Holy Grove (*Zutibure*) the same verb was used as in the case   .
of Ślęża only with a comment – which is essential – that this grove was "ut
Deus (...) honoratus." Similarly to the case of Svarožic in Radogošč, the words
"honoratur et colitur" are used.[497] Thus the tenor of his message supports the
view that the mountain was deified, however, it is hard to state definitively
the extent to which it was an expression of the theological interpretation
of the pagan *sacrum*, or how it referred to the attitude of Ślęża worshippers.

It is worth remembering – as a comparative premise – that Cosmas of Prague
attributed the making of offerings to mountains and hills to Czech peasants
even in the 12th c.[498] This is a geographically close confirmation of Thietmar's
information about worshipping the mountain as such by the Slavic people.
This statement is supported by the findings of phenomenological religious
studies.[499] In this case, on the other hand, the hypothesis of an addressed
preexisting cult dedicated to the mountain itself is becoming more and more
probable in the light of anthropological and religious conceptions developed
in the recent years, especially in the context of the research on local societies. They highlight the fact that, within the scope of interpretation of people's
attitudes towards the sacred objects, that the justified is a resignation from a
model that implies a sharp dichotomy between the material and the immaterial, and an appreciation of materiality as a basic way of defining the presence
of a supernatural or mystical element while simultaneously a resignation from
treating the material sphere as just a sign.[500]

---

496   An extreme conjecture that Thietmar devised the very fact of the mountain cult on the
      basis of an association of the name of the country and the mountains seems improbable,
      taking into account that he wrote in and for the environment in which it was not difficult
      to verify this information.
497   See above, p. 106.
498   Cosmas I, 4: "ille montibus sive collibus litat."
499   *E.g.* Tomasz Węcławski, *Wspólny świat religii* (Kraków: Znak, 1995), p. 67.
500   These observations are also worth applying to interpretation of other objects of Slavic
      cult, described by Thietmar as for example *dii manu facti* ("hand-made gods") in
      Radgoszcz or the banners called goddesses (see above, p. 105, and under p. 157). For the
      "material turn" in the anthropological and religious studies see among others: Daniel
      Miller, "Materiality: An Introduction," in *Materiality*, ed. Daniel Miller (Durham/London:

THE RELIGION OF THE SLAVS IN THIETMAR'S CHRONICLE · 153

The hypothetical conclusion that Ślęża was a mythical centre of the ecumene favours using the idea of *axis mundi* in interpretation. The peaks of mountains are sometimes drowned in clouds, resulting in the perception of a cosmic mountain that combines the three spheres of the world: heaven, earth and underworld. Furthermore, the fact that not only Ślęża, but also the second and third highest mountains in the same massif are surrounded by stone walls, was considered to be evidence of its prehistoric cult. This fosters an association that this phenomenon of the landscape was the mythical mountain of the Slavs, *i.e. Triglav*, whose three tops correspond with the aforementioned three sectors of the cosmos.[501]

However, in the case of Ślęża there are no traces of a pre-Christian mythology in medieval sources that would resemble the motifs similar to those related to Triglav in Slovenia. Only in some medieval legends it is confirmed that it was treated as an exceptional place: the beginnings of an important abbey in Wrocław were associated with it, namely the Regular Canons on Piasek Island (Germ. Sandinsel),[502] or even the Piast dynasty itself. It was a tradition created in the Late Middle Ages and related to its Silesian branch. For Ślęża was perceived as the "Silesian Mountain," even in the 16th c., although then another name became common as it was related to the town of Sobótka,[503] located at the foot of the mountain (German: Zobtenberg, Polish: Sobótka). The current name of the mountain, "Ślęża," was officially introduced after Lower Silesia

---

Duke University Press Books, 2005), pp. 1–50; Matthew Engelke, "Material Religion," in *The Cambridge Companion to Religious Studies*, ed. Robert A. Orsi (Cambridge: Cambridge University Press, 2012), pp. 209–229; Richard M. Carp, "Material Culture," in *The Routledge Handbook of Research Methods in the Study of Religion*, ed. Michael Stausberg, Steven Engler (London: Routledge, 2014), pp. 474–490.

501   The second highest mountain top, Radunia, on which remnants of a burial ground from the times of the Lusatian culture were found, was associated with the underworld sphere, the world of the dead, by Słupecki, *Slavonic Pagan Sanctuaries*, pp. 175 f. However, it is hard to speak here about any continuity of this phenomenon until the times of Ślężanie (the burial ground attributed to them is located at the foot of Ślęża near the village Będkowice), Domański, *Ślęża w pradziejach*, p. 102.

502   Ślęża was the place where according to legendary tradition the convent of regular canons from Wrocław was originally located at the beginning of the 12th c., however, the only certain thing is the existence of its prepositure at the foot of the mountain. Passing the ownership of the Ślęża Massif to the monks is interpreted as striving for elimination of the relics of the native cult (*e.g.* Korta, *Tajemnice*, pp. 303 f.); this conjecture does not have any confirmation in sources.

503   The town was named after Saturday (Polish "sobota"), most likely because it was a fair day in this place. In the case of Radunia, L.P. Słupecki (*Slavonic Pagan Sanctuaries*, pp. 175 f.) referred to the relation between its name and "Radunitsa," *i.e.* East Slavic rites performed to worship the dead.

154   CHAPTER 2

became a part of Poland in 1945. It refers to the expression (*mons*) *Slenz*,[504] present in the earliest records of the mountain's name in 13th c. documents.

These early records of the name of the mountain, including the *mons Silentii* version, confirm Thietmar's information about its connection with the name of Ślężanie's land, which in the 12th c. referred to a wider area, namely Silesia, which was a province of the Piast state with its capital of Wrocław. For generations historians have debated a potentially earlier integration of the inhabitants of the Silesian land during the tribal period, exactly around the Ślężanie.[505] According to these hypotheses, Ślęża enjoyed a supra-tribal cult.[506] However, the premises on which these hypotheses are based are controversial, which is why the possibility of the occurrence of the supra-tribal Ślęża cult should be based first of all on appreciation of its value as hierophany, worth supralocal fame (like Radogošč).[507]

In the scholarly debate the cult of Ślęża often is associated to stone figures found on its slopes and thereabouts.[508] Some of them were created not earlier than in the 12th–13th c. AD, however, the most discussed ones are those whose dating is uncertain (*e.g.* the so called bear or monk); they are hypothetically, albeit not without dispute, connected with prehistorical art, *e.g.* Celtic.[509] It is hard to prove that their stay in this area until the period of Ślężanie was

---

504   It is worth emphasizing that on the Lusati-Veleti border an analogous name of a mountain appeared: Zlensgor, confirmed already in the 12th c. The name can be derived from '*slęg-' – 'damp', 'wet', and specifically from ponds surrounding this mountain (there is no river nearby); see: Jerzy Nalepa, "Ślęża Góra na pograniczu wielecko – łużyckim," *Onomastica* 2 (1956), pp. 318–322.

505   *E.g.* Lech A. Tyszkiewicz, "Plemiona słowiańskie we wczesnym średniowieczu," in *Słowiańszczyzna w Europie średniowiecznej Księga pamiątkowa dla Lecha Leciejewicza*, vol. 1: *Plemiona i wczesne państwa*, ed. Zofia Kurnatowska (Wrocław: IAE PAN, 1996), pp. 51 f.

506   *E.g.* Słupecki, "Ślęża," p. 14.

507   Rosik, "The formation," pp. 50 f.

508   They have fascinated scholars for over three centuries, see: Gottfried Heinrich Burghart, *Iter Sabothicum. Ausführliche Beschreibung einiger An. 1773 und die folgenden Jahre auf den Zobten = Berg gethanen Reißen / Wodurch sowohl Die natürliche als historische Beschaffenheit Dieses In Schlesien so bekannten und Berühmten Berges Der Welt vor Augen geleget wird, Mit Kupffern* (Breslau/Leipzig: Michael Hubert, 1736) as they are an inseparable element of the discussion on the mythical significance of Ślęża in the 19th–21st c.

509   *E.g.* Bogusław Gediga, "Monumentalna rzeźba >>mnicha<< ślężańskiego w świetle >>sztuki situl<<," in *Problemy epoki brązu i wczesnej epoki żelaza w Europie Środkowej. Księga jubileuszowa poświęcona Markowi Gedlowi w sześćdziesiątą rocznicę urodzin i czterdziestolecie pracy w Uniwersytecie Jagiellońskim.* ed. Jan Chochorowski (Kraków: Oficyna Cracovia, 1996), pp. 187–201; Domański, *Ślęża*, p. 92. Even if this identification is right, it is worth emphasizing that the crosses carved in them were earlier interpreted as solar cult signs while at the current stage of research they are considered border marks. They were carved most probably in the 12th–13th c. in connection with the division of the territorial

THE RELIGION OF THE SLAVS IN THIETMAR'S CHRONICLE   155

marked by the continuity of the cult. However, it is possible that these ancient sculptures were found and adapted by Slavs to their cult. The chance that the same had occurred with their German predecessors should also not be excluded. Nevertheless, these conjectures cannot be verified.

However, it is worth emphasizing that the very occurrence of cult objects on the mountain is not necessary to state that the mountain was worshipped. Certainly, their presence can indicate that it was treated as a holy place, yet in the case of Ślężanie one should first take into account the cult of the mountain itself. It is possible that the cultic objects and idols related to it would make another branch of their religious system.[510] In the context of the aforementioned information provided by Cosmas of Prague in the 12th c. referring to neighbouring Bohemia, which had been Christianized earlier, it is hard to suppose that the cult of Ślęża mountain, in the times of Boleslav the Brave nearly a century earlier, disappeared. However, Thietmar's narration indicates that this is exactly what happened, which is explained by the fact that he considered this country as Christianized at the moment it was encompassed by the diocese network as a part of a Christian monarchy, and at the same time he concentrated on the fate of the milieu strictly connected to the ruling elite of the Piast monarchy.[511]

The etymology of the name of this land, derived from the cult mountain, amplifies the role of paganism in its past, which will collide in the next verses with the heroic and manifestly Christian attitude of the defenders of Niemcza located nearby, who put a cross forward against the attacking pagans.[512] It seems significant that nearby in the text there is information that Niemcza was

---

ownership of the Ślęża Massif between the Canon Regular Abbey in Wrocław and the duke of Silesia, see: Korta, *Tajemnice*, pp. 193–233, 343 f.

510   Over twenty years ago on the Ślęża slope near the village – Będkowice, relics of a building related to Ślężanie were discovered near a small pond. The object is hypothetically interpreted as a sanctuary (like the one in Radogošč), see: Domański, *Ślęża*, p. 103.

511   A common view on Thietmar holds that he wrote about the cult related to Ślęża as if it was contemporary to the events of 1017. It was supported by a mistake in this place of the Polish translation of his chronicle (from 1953), which states that the mountain was worshipped due to its magnitude and predestination, as pagan rites were performed there. However, the text does not mention the "predestination" of the mountain for practicing cult there; yet Thietmar states that this cult of the mountain took place "there" (*ibi*), most certainly "in pago Silensi", where in the past (as it is indicated at least by the form of the verb *veneraretur* / "was venerated" together with "posita est" / "it is situated") the "damned paganism". Therefore the conviction that Thietmar's record *expressis verbis* confirms performing pagan rites on the mountain or, going even further in these speculations, the existence of a sanctuary there (*e.g.* Domański, *Ślęża*, pp. 103 f.), seems not well justified.

512   Thietmar VII, 60: "Ex parte gentili crucem sanctam erigebant eiusdem auxilio hos vinci sperababant" (cf. trans. D.A. Warner in: *Ottonian Germany*, p. 350: "Against of the pagans they erected the holy cross, hoping to conquer them with its help").

156   CHAPTER 2

FIGURE 4   The so-called "bear", ancient sculpture from around Strzegomiany near Mount
            Ślęża (now at the top of the mountain)
            STANISŁAW ROSIK

THE RELIGION OF THE SLAVS IN THIETMAR'S CHRONICLE   157

established by people who are defined by Thietmar as "nostri" (certainly meaning the Slavic name for the Germans "Niemcy").[513] The castle town turned out
to be a bulwark of Christianity, and such presentation of the course of events
shows the besiegers and the emperor himself in a bad light. This unfavour-
able impression is strengthened by words of admiration for the combat virtues
and courage presented by the Niemcza inhabitants, demonstrating the atmosphere among participants in this expedition.[514]

In the same spirit, the information about the fate of the divine images of the
Liutici becomes clear in the account of these events referenced by the historiographer of Merseburg after the unsuccessful siege of Niemcza was concluded.
Although the imperial forces managed to defeat the Polish military forces in
the Czech lands, "the Liutizi returned to their homeland in an angry mood
and complaining about the dishonour inflicted upon their goddess. One of
Margrave Herman's retainers had thrown a rock at a banner which bore her
image. When they attempted to cross the swollen waters of the Mulde, near the
burg Wurzen, they lost yet another image of their goddess and a most excellent
band of fifty *milites*."[515]

Images of goddesses on banners ("in vexillis"), the so called stanice, evoke
an association with the Letter of Bruno of Querfurt to King Henry II, in which
diabolica vexilla are juxtaposed to the Lance of St. Maurice, and hence most
certainly were carried in front of the army.[516] These military banners enjoyed
such respect of the Liutici that Thietmar did not hesitate to treat them explicitly as goddesses.[517] It is possible to observe a way, very characteristic for
this author, of understanding pagan *sacrum*. A. Brückner's explanation that a
motif behind the assumption that military banners were goddesses was due to
the fact that the noun is feminine – 'stanica.'[518] This claim fails to build confidence because Thietmar did not show any knowledge of this Slavic word, and
he used the Latin word *vexillum*, which is not feminine. Thus, it is possible to

---

513   Thietmar VII, 59.
514   They were definitely concerned about charges which were so clearly formulated in
       St. Bruno's letter. See footnote 429 in this chapter.
515   Trans. D.A. Warner in: *Ottonian Germany*, p. 353; cf. Thietmar VII, 64: "sed Liutici re-
       deuntes irati dedecus deae suimet illatum queruntur. Nam haec in vexillis formata a
       quodam Herimanni marchionis socio lapide uno traiecta est; et dum hoc ministri eius
       imperatori dolenter retulissent, ad emendationem XII talenta perceperunt. Et cum iuxta
       Vurcin civitatem Mildam nimis effusam transire voluissent, deam cum egreio L militum
       comitatu alteram perdidere." See also Babij, *Wojskowość*, pp. 146 f.
516   Christian Lübke, "Religion und ethnisches Bewusstsein bei den Lutizen," *Światowit* 40
       (1995), p. 85. See above, pp. 105 f.
517   Brückner, *Mitologia słowiańska i polska*, pp. 48, 51, 154, 190, 201, 336.
518   *Ibidem*, p. 154.

assume that the chronicler had some specific information about worshipping goddesses by the Liutici.[519]

Thietmar, although he mentioned their existence twice, did not go any further in his description to express condemnation for paganism explicitly. However, the very fact that he mentioned an attack on Liutici sacred objects is a form of rehabilitation of the German reputation, because it shows that the alliance with the "infidels" was not positively accepted by particular subjects of the emperor. Similarly, the information about the loss of the military banner and fifty excellent Liutici soldiers in the currents of the Mulda River introduces a pessimistic note to the narrative, and the very event could be interpreted as a twist of fate indicating the adversity of Providence. The chronicler's moderation in showing antipathy towards pagans somehow corresponds with a commentary to the last of these events; namely that some Liutici, perceiving the loss of the goddess and soldiers as bad fate, wanted to withdraw from the alliance with Henry II to which they were encouraged by "bad" people ("malorum instinctu").[520] Using the word "bad" to refer to this type of instigators clarifies the chronicler's position in this matter: loyalty to the emperor is his priority, even if his political line is offensive in the religious sphere.

The chronicler did not hesitate to show in an appropriate selection of the presented events (destruction of the Liutici goddesses) that the Liutici remained Christ's enemies, however – given their alliance with the emperor – he did not say it directly. It is important that in a wider context of the description of this war, the emperor and his allies do not enjoy Christ's grace. In the light of Thietmar's narration, that is given to the Polish side. It seems that emphasis on the fact that Boleslav, after the imperial forces withdrew from

---

519 L.P. Słupecki ("Archaeological Sources," p. 356) in the discussion on the Liutici goddesses referred to the figure of the so called twins from Fischerinsel, well-known from excavations. This author considered this image as a presentation of the Dioskouri creatures and emphasized that among Indo-European peoples they were accompanied exactly by female deities. Such archaic origin of female deities was opposed by L. Moszyński ("Staropołabski teonim," p. 39), who claimed that "in the Old Slavic language there was no original feminine formation ending with -a such as Latin *dea*, Greek θεα." The formation *bogyńi* is relatively new. The author considered the appearance of these goddesses a Christian influence (cult of Mother of God) on Slavic beliefs. However, one should take into account that a cult of particular deities, which gained feminine features, superseded the appearance of a general term defining them. Hence one should not exclude the shaping of goddesses' cult in the Slavic environment without the inspiration of Christian beliefs. However, taking into account the current state of the discussion on the ethnogenesis of the Slavs, thus a possibility that this ethnos was formed later than it was assumed in the model 20th-century concept of the Early Slavs, it is also hard to use the Pre-Slavic language as a strong argument in this debate.

520 Thietmar VII, 64.

THE RELIGION OF THE SLAVS IN THIETMAR'S CHRONICLE   159

Niemcza, "rejoiced in Lord and shared his earthly happiness with his soldiers," is not accidental.[521] Joy "in the Lord", which was assigned to him shows which side was taken by Christ in this case.[522] The emperor himself and his people do not represent evil powers here (only the Liutici do[523]), yet they suffered tremendous losses, in which the chronicler perceives consequences of their earlier faults.[524]

One can only speculate whether the said crime (*crimen*) was exactly this alliance with the Liutici. Nevertheless, it can be observed that the chronicler at best painfully accepted the necessity of this alliance. He emphasized the unwillingness of the Saxons to tolerate Slavic idols, and at the same time highly assessed the attitude of Boleslav's people in the religious dimension, at the time of their fight with the Liutici. Remembering his earlier regrets about the German-Liutici alliance,[525] one can assume that at least to some extent he shared the view so clearly expressed in the Letter of Bruno of Querfurt to King Henry II on the iniquity of his cooperation with pagans against the Christian neighbour. Taking into account earlier information from Thietmar about Boleslav the Brave, one should emphasize a distinct softening of the chronicler's opinion about this character.

It is possible that it happened partly under the influence of current events, such as the end of the conflict between Boleslav and the empire, sealed with the peace treaty of Bautzen in January 1018 and his marriage with the Saxon princess Oda.[526] Nevertheless the fundamental significance of attributing the

---

521   *Ibidem*: Boleslav "laetatur in Domino militibusque congaudet in seculo".

522   Emphasis on the "joy in the Lord" in the case of Boleslav deserves special attention, given that in the description of his first war with Henry, the chronicler saw in the Polish ruler only a personification of evil powers, which were tamed by the ruler of the empire to the joy "in God" of those who were close to him – Thietmar VI, 11: "Letantur in Deo familiares regis, corruptique tristantur fautores adulterini ducis" (cf. trans. D.A. Warner in: *Ottonian Germany*, p. 245: "While the kings supporters rejoiced in God, the corrupt supporters of the false duke were saddened"). What is more, in the neighbourhood of the quoted place he is referred to as a "roaring lion" (see Thietmar VI, 10) and a "venomous snake" (VI, 12), which in biblical tradition has connotations hostile to humanity and Christ – see: 1 P 5:8 and *e.g.* Is 27:1; Rev 12:9. Cf. Pleszczyński, *Niemcy*, p. 168.

523   Cf. Thietmar VI, 26.

524   Thietmar VII, 64: "Facta est haec expedicio ad perniciem hostis; sed crimine nostro multum lesit victoribus nostris." (cf. trans. D.A. Warner in: *Ottonian Germany*, p. 353: "This expedition was undertaken in order to annihilate the enemy, but it also inflicted wounds on us, the victors, because of our sin"). So the participants of this expedition are considered victorious by Thietmar, however, rather contrary to the quoted facts.

525   See pp. 144 f.

526   It is worth reminding that the chronicle was created over several years at earliest from 1012 and the chapters discussed here in the last months of chronicler's life as he died in 1018.

"joy in the Lord" to the Polish ruler after saving Niemcza is the fact that he belonged to the *Christianitas* community. Due to the offense of his opponents, Boleslav gained the favour of the heavens, and this assessment corresponds with a particular situation from the war theatre: these were his subjects to turn out to be the vanquishers of pagans, whose idolatry was an exceptional spiritual threat in the chronicler's perspective. Such an attitude towards paganism was an inalienable element of the system of values professed by the chronicler. Hence, a possible change of the political situation does not necessarily have to be taken into account in the explanation of his attitude to Boleslav, noticeable in the light of this passage.

An additional bond between Thietmar's Saxon environment and the community under Boleslav's rule is built by the element of a common past: his subjects defended the stronghold founded by "our people" according to the chronicler. Hence his hostility toward paganism manifested in the discussed passage makes him closer to Boleslav and his entourage in a context wider than only the described events, namely in the community of religion and culture (collective memory).[527] So it is not surprising that the chronicler, presenting the Liutici as the enemy of the holy cross during the military action, simultaneously distinguishes them clearly as "the pagan part" (*pars gentilis*). It can be vividly said that "damned paganism" ("execranda gentilitas"), in the light of the chronicle belonging to the past of the *Silensi* land, had returned thanks to the allied forces of the Liutici and the emperor.[528]

---

527 In the context of these observations it seems to lopsided to claim that in Thietmar's imagination the borderline between the Christian circle (*Christianitas*) and the pagan North and Eastern Europe, in the confines of which there would be Slavdom, including Poland and Rus', was of fundamental significance. This was the ascertainment of Fraesdorff, *Der barbarische Norden*, pp. 141 f., who argued that both countries were located in this zone by referring to Thietmar's information about the conflict between Boleslav the Brave and Vladimir the Great. According to this scholar the chronicler exhorted the "whole Christianity" to pray for the end of exactly this war. This view seems questionable because the conflict for whose ending *omnis christianitas* was to pray, was a civil war in Rus' fought for the heritage of the deceased Vladimir (it is indicated by additional quotation of the biblical phrase of the divided kingdom, cf. Lk 11:17). The conflict was related to Poland only indirectly, and also in the light of the above analyses of the description of the events "in pago Silensi" in 1017, it is hard to consider Boleslav's monarchy a part of the one – alternative to *Christianitas* – zone encompassing also Rus' (in the opinion of the chronicler after all also a Christian one), and even more so the pagan North. In the case of Thietmar's work >>the presented world<< is more complex than the said model assumed it to be.

528 In the light of the said terminology – *gentilitas* and *pars gentilis* – the Liutici even being apostates were still called *gentiles*, which contradicts the thesis (se *e.g.* by Fraesdorff, *Der*

THE RELIGION OF THE SLAVS IN THIETMAR'S CHRONICLE   161

2.9   *Hennil*

Thietmar, in a digression about his homeland, complained that its inhabitants seldomly attended churches and did not care about visiting their priests, yet they worshiped house deities with offerings, and depended strongly on their support.[529] An example of such a deity was Hennil, whom the chronicler associated with a cult object, namely a shepherd's staff (*baculum*) bearing this name, at the end of which there was a hand holding an iron ring. A shepherd would go around houses with it greeting those who opened the door and saying: "Watch out, Hennil, watch out!" to receive a small treat in return.[530]

The goal of this folk ritual was to ensure divine care. However, somehow defiantly, the story about Hennil in a wider context proves that hostile supernatural phenomena occur precisely because of these kind of practices. The idolatry of the local people contributed to manifestations of spectres, bogeys, or any other evil powers led by the "enemy" (Satan) in this area.[531] Thus, this time the motif of a spiritual threat caused by idolatry was not directly connected with the activity of evil powers in a cultic place or sanctuary, but in a wider territorial and social dimension.

The chronicler castigated Hennil's cult, quoting verses from the Psalms to prove its stupidity: "The idols of the heathens are the works of men, and so on ... Similar to those are all who make and put their trust in them."[532] A reference to the authority of the written word remains in contrast to an attribution of the condemned ritual to uneducated peasants. The chronicler emphasizes that Hennil's help was summoned using *rustica lingua*.[533] A biblical concept of pagan divinity, understood as a creation of human hands, was used in this case

---

  barbarische Norden, pp. 229 ff.; Goetz, *Die Wahrnehmung*, pp. 58 f.) that Thietmar used this expression only to refer to believers of original paganism, none apostates.

529 Thietmar VII, 69: "domesticos colunt deos multumque sibi prodesse eosdem sperantes hiis inmolant".

530 *Ibidem*: "... in cuius sumitate manus erat unum in se ferreum tenens circulum, quod cum pastore illius villae, in quo is fuerat, per omnes domos has singulariter ductus, in primo introitu a portitore suo sic salutaretur: 'Vigila, Hennil, vigila!' – sic enim rustica vocabatur lingua –; et epulantes ibi delicate".

531 *Ibidem*. An example of these phenomena is a story of a certain woman from Thietmar VII, 68.

532 Trans. D.A. Warner in: *Ottonian Germany*, p. 356; cf. Thietnar VII, 69: "Simulacra gentium opera hominum et caetera. Similes illis fiant facientes ea et confidentes hiis". Cf. Vulgate, Ps 113:12,16.

533 Thietmar VII, 69. In the discussed passage, yet another time on the pages of Thietmar's chronicle, it is possible to find juxtapositions of the culture of literate and illiterate people.

162   CHAPTER 2

to categorize a religious phenomenon not from the native Slavic circle, but
occurring in the environment already encompassed by (a not very efficient)
Christian ministry, but practicing, *de facto*, dual faith.

A supposition that Thietmar meant Slavs as worshipers of Hennil was the
cutting edge of research on their mythology in the 19th c.[534] However, since
the time when Aleksander Brückner criticized this position,[535] there remains
skepticism towards this line of inquiry. Regardless of the decision of whether
Hennil's worshippers were Slavic or Saxon people, the usefulness of this information for further research on paganism is undisputable.

A popular view holds that the deity called Hennil did not exist at all, and
in reality Thietmar's information refers only to an ordinary shepherd stick
used in some kind of ritual, which was wrongly and precipitately taken for
a deity by the chronicler.[536] However, this definition of the problem raises a
doubt even in its assumption, because it does not take into account the specifics of Thietmar's interpretation of idolatry, namely the fact that he regularly

---

534   Adam Naruszewicz, *Historia narodu polskiego*, vol. 2 (Leipzig: Breitkopf & Hertel, 1836),
      pp. 53 f., assumed that "Hennilus" was "Honiło" or "Gonidło" who was a god of guards. On
      the other hand Teodor Narbutt, *Dzieje starożytne narodu litewskiego*, vol. 1: *Mitologia lite-
      wska* (Vilnius: A. Marcinowski, 1835), pp. 110 f., referred to Lithuanian folklore on the basis
      of Maciej Stryjkowski's account (16th c.), to find in Hennil "Goniglis", a deity of shepherds,
      in whose name one can hear "gonić" (chase). In reference to these ideas Ignaz Johann
      Hanusch, *Die Wissenschaft des slavischen Mythus* (Lemberg/Stanislawow/Tarnow: Johann
      Milikowski, 1842), pp. 369 ff. assumed that the god mentioned by Thietmar was a tutelary
      deity of shepherds among Czechs and Sorbs and was called Honidlo, Honilo, Gonidło (lit.
      Goniglis's counterpart) and was associated with a shepherd custom of going round hous-
      es and giving gifts to one another. Then Jacob Grimm, *Deutsche Mythologie*, vol. 2 (Berlin:
      Ferdinand Dümmlers Verlagsbuchhandlung, 1876), p. 625, derived the name Hennil from
      Polish "hejnał" in the meaning of red sky in the morning and a song worshipping the ris-
      ing sun. According to Theodor Siebs, "Beiträge zur deutschen Mythologie," *Zeitschrift für
      Deustche Philologie* 24 (1892), p. 148, Hennil is a dimunitive of Henno – god of death, and
      later the waking light and spring (= Wodan). M.Z. Jedlicki in: Thietmar, p. 566 f., footnote
      463, supported Hanusch and Grimm's theses, however, this position was criticised (see foot-
      note 535 in this chapter). Hennil's place in the discussion on Slavic religion was solidified by
      K.H. Meyer, who decided to include a reference to him in the basic collection of source
      texts for research on Slavic religion (see *Fontes historiae religionis Slavicae*, pp. 11, 20). See
      also Strzelczyk, *Mity*, p. 79.
535   Brückner, *Mitologia słowiańska i polska*, p. 191, rejected the ideas of the Lithuanian
      Goniglis, Hungarian "hajnal" or "goniti-honiti" ('chase') – see above footnote 534 – assum-
      ing that Hennil definitely was a German name. Hennil's place in the Germanic mythology
      was supported by Dziewulski, *Postępy*, p. 6, and also Łowmiański, *Religia*, p. 201, without
      exceeding A. Brückner's findings.
536   Urbańczyk, *Dawni Słowianie*, p. 187; cf. *idem*, "Pseudobóstwa," in sss, vol. 4, pp. 405 f.;
      Strzelczyk, *Mity*, p. 79.

THE RELIGION OF THE SLAVS IN THIETMAR'S CHRONICLE   163

connects the notion of gods (*dii*) with material creations of human hands, idols.[537] A synonym for these "gods" is *simulachra gentium* called a human work and evoked in the discussed passage after a verse from a psalm.[538]

It is worth adding that in the Old Testament descriptions of idolaters are directly attributed to the worshipping of wood or a stick, hence Thietmar had at his disposal theological arguments against narrowing the notion of *simulacrum* to anthropomorphic representations.[539] In the context of these observations it should be stated that the presentation of Hennil as an object, a material thing, is related to the specifics of the theological interpretation of a particular cult object. In this situation the usefulness of the information discussed here in finding a solution to the problem of whether this name in the environment of the worshippers of this idol referred to a spiritual creature, a tutelary deity, or only a fetish, is significantly decreased.[540] Thus, the realm of hypothetical solutions to this riddle broadens.

The area left for speculations based on Thietmar's record is narrowed when the goal of assuming supernatural care from the described ritual is defined. Not only the content of the wandering shepherd, but also the shape of the carried cult object, indicate a reference to this kind of sacral power. The symbolism of a stick, a hand and a ring are connected with providing care and protection.[541] Therefore one can find an attribute of the tutelary deity called Hennil in this set,[542] or alternatively – taking into account the specifics of treatment of magic objects – assume that the fetish was given a specific name.

As an analogy to the "house gods" mentioned by Thietmar, it is possible to indicate *penates* mentioned by Helmold a century and a half later.[543] In this research perspective it should be assumed that Hennil's cult did not have a

---

537 Hence there one should not speak here of a mistake, as Brückner wanted to, but as conscious treatment (on the basis of theological interpretation of sacral phenomena) of material cult objects as pagan gods. For the matter of the term "dii manu facti", see above, p. 102.

538 Ps 138.

539 *E.g.* Hos 4:12.

540 Tadeusz Seweryn, "Figury kultowe," in SSS, vol. 2, pp. 55 f., assumed that Hennil was a tutelary fetish.

541 A shepherd's staff and hand universally mean power and care, protection, see *e.g.* Forstner, *Świat*, pp. 351ff.; in folk rituals a ring protected from diseases and various misfortunes (see *ibidem*, p. 423). Kulišić, *Stara Slovenska religija*, p. 158, quoted comparative material from folk culture to confirm this opinion, additionally he interpreted the stick and the ring as attributes of underworld and moon divinities.

542 M.Z. Jedlicki in: Thietmar, p. 566, footnote 162.

543 *E.g.* Leciejewicz, *Słowianie*, pp. 91 f. Cf. Procházka, "Organisace," p. 152; Gieysztor, *Mitologia*, pp. 270 ff., especially 237 f.

164   CHAPTER 2

wide reach, but rather it was localized to the local population, and in the case of the possible origin of this name from the name of some ancestor, a lack of its clear etymology would not be surprising. Finally coming back to the assumption that this "house god" was a pseudo-deity, it is worth considering – as an alternative to considering it a fetish – Thietmar's potential mistake in wrongly assuming that the name "Hennil" was the theonym.

Leszek Moszyński proposed to find in it a diminutive form of the Old German 'hano' or rooster, which, being a symbol of vigilance, would be called in a spell used by the shepherd going from one house to another.[544] On the other hand, Gerard Labuda claims that the alleged theonym, theonym, was in fact the greeting: "hey-no!" deformed in writing, which was used to remind a host to be alert.[545] Both of these quite recent concepts prove that for over two centuries of debates aimed at solving Hennil's puzzle, the most important factor still remains scholars' ingenuity – however, without much hope for a trustworthy verification of its effects.

2.10   Reinbern and the Religion of Sea-Side Communities under Boleslav the Brave's Rule

Thietmar, furthering his narrative, makes a digression devoted to the ruler of Rus', Vladimir the Great, who does not enjoy Thietmar's favour. He interwove his story with that of Reinbern's, who in the year 1000 was nominated as the suffragan bishop of the Gniezno metropolis, the Bishop of "Kołobrzeg Salt" (*Salsae Cholbergiensis episcopus*).[546] He was sent to Rus' accompanying the Polish ruler Boleslav the Brave's daughter, who married Sviatopolk, Vladimir's son. When the young ones were accused of plotting against Vladimir, and as a result were imprisoned, Reinbern was put in prison as well, where he died in about 1013.[547] In his narration the chronicler made him a martyr, who in the heavens above could scorn the threats of his persecutor, and who in his life followed ascetic ideals, similarly to Bruno of Querfurt, who was so highly assessed by the chronicler.[548]

---

544   Leszek Moszyński, "Hennil Thietmara – apelatyw czy teonim, germański czy słowiański?," *Onomastica Slavogermanica* 22 (2002), p. 46.

545   Labuda, "O wierzeniach," [2003], p. 51; [2012], p. 210.

546   Thietmar IV, 45.

547   In 1015 at the latest because he died before Vladimir's death which is dated to this year.

548   Thiemar (VII, 72) about Reinbern: "Vigiliarum et abstinenciae ac silencii assiduitate corpus suum affligens cor ad speculum divinae contemplacionis infixit", and about Bruno (*ibidem* VI, 94): "Dehinc ob lucrum animae laborem subiit diverse ac grandis viae, castigans corpus inedia et crucians vigilia"; cf. Stanisław Rosik, "Reinbern – Salsae Cholbergiensis ecclesiae episcopus," in *Salsa Cholbergiensis. Kołobrzeg w średniowieczu*, ed. Lech Leciejewicz, Marian Rębkowski (Kołobrzeg: Le petit Café, 2000), p. 86.

THE RELIGION OF THE SLAVS IN THIETMAR'S CHRONICLE 165

This mortification of the flesh with fasting and sleeplessness of his characters was explained by Thietmar by their involvement in the propagation of Christianity. Although Reinbern – contrary to Bruno – acted in the area where the diocese was legally established, he in fact had to eradicate native cults and introduce Christianity starting from scratch, which is expressed by the chronicler in a game of metaphors and symbols: "Destroying the shrines of idols he burnt them and – after throwing four stones anointed with holy chrism into the sea inhabited by demons and clearing it with holy water – for the glory of the Almighty God he has planted a new sprout on a tree that had not brought any fruit yet, that is, among an extremely foolish people he founded cultivation of holy preaching [the word of God]."[549]

The succinctness of this reference does not facilitate determination of the territorial reach of these activities. A detailed location of Reinbern's abode – associated with Kołobrzeg (Germ. Kolberg), or more precisely the salinas located there – most certainly was not on the Baltic Sea but a few kilometres away from the coast, most probably in the stronghold on the Parsęta River, in today's Budzistowo.[550] The people entrusted to him lived in the Baltic part of Boleslav the Brave's dominion that stretched between the Vistula and the Oder. However, Reinbern's activity was most certainly focused on the local main centres as agencies of the Piast rule, and additionally it is hard to expect that it

---

549 Thietmar VII 72: "Fana idolorum destruens incedit et, mare demonibus cultum inmissis quatuor lapidibus sacro crismate perunctis et aqua purgans benedicta, novam Domino omnipotenti propaginem in infructuosa arbore, id est in populo nimis insulso sanctae predicacionis plantationem eduxit".

550 The occurrence of the quoted by Thietmar: "Salsa Cholbergiensis" in *Annales Magdeburgenses* under the year 996 as *Salzcolberch* (see *Annales Magdeburgenses*, ed. Georg Heinrich Pertz, MGH SS 16 (1859), p. 159), indicates that in the Saxon environment the name of the bishop's abode was connected with salt (Lat. *salsa*, German *Salz*) and a mountain (German *-berg*). However, the 12th-century versions of the spelling of the name Kolberg (*e.g. Cholbreg, Colubrega*) indicate that the this "-berg"/"-berch" conceal the Slavic 'brzeg' (a coast), therefore in the term used by Thietmar to refer to the bishopric headquarters, it is most certainly possible to find "sól/solec koło brzegu" ("salt/salted [place] near a coast"). Until the 12th c. this two-word toponym would have been transformed into a one-barrelled name (which can be compared with the example of Wieliczka in Małopolska, which initially also was made of two words: "Wielka Sól" (*Magnum Sal*)) – see Lech Leciejewicz, "Kołobrzeg – siedziba biskupa Reinberna w 1000 roku," in *Memoriae amici et magistri. Studia historyczne poświęcone pamięci Prof. Wacława Korty (1919–1999)*, ed. Marek Derwich, Wojciech Mrozowicz, Rościsław Żerelik (Wrocław: Instytut Historyczny, 2001), pp. 39 f.; *idem*, Marian Rębkowski, "Uwagi końcowe. Początki Kołobrzegu w świetle rozpoznania archeologicznego," in *Kołobrzeg. Wczesne miasto nad Bałtykiem*, ed. Lech Leciejewicz, Marian Rębkowski, (Origines Polonorum) 2 (Warszawa: Trio, 2007), p. 302.

would reach the mouth of the Oder.[551] It seems natural that these missionary activities encompassed mainly the bishopric headquarters and the surrounding area. In light of the analyses presented below, this was also the place where one should locate the ritual of water consecration described by Thietmar.

After the annihilation by fire of idolatrous temples,[552] and hence also the performance of *abrenuntiatio diaboli* in the dimension of social life,[553] the chronicler mentions Reinbern's purification of the sea, which was a dwelling place for demons, by throwing into it four stones anointed with chrism and sprinkling it with holy water. Connecting the said evil spirits with paganism is not directly confirmed in the source,[554] although the ritual itself, if one assumes the historicity of this event, was unavoidably aimed at the cult addressed to the *sacrum* of the sea, which was a natural phenomenon in the case of the seaside community.[555]

However, one should extend the field of research in the case of the genesis of the demonization of the sea element in Thietmar's work. It is worth paying attention to innertextual references to show the specifics of his way

---

551   Even if, as sometimes hypothetically some form of the ruleship of the first Piasts reached this place, it is hard to assume that in populated and politically strong centres, such as Wolin or Szczecin, such radical missionary procedures, as the ones described by Thietmar would be used.

552   This way of eliminating idolatry takes its models from the Old Testament, see *e.g.* Deut 7:25; 1 Macc 5:44 and 68. However, it is hard to analyse the destruction of temples and statues with fire only as purposeful following biblical examples.

553   See *e.g.* Marian Rechowicz, "Chrzest Polski a katolicka teologia misyjna we wczesnym średniowieczu," *Ruch Biblijny i Liturgiczny* 19 (1966), pp. 67–74; for a more extensive discussion on this practice, see later, p. 357.

554   It is only speculation whether the rite performed by Reinbern could possibly be referred to particular deities either as a result of their diabolisation as an effect of *interpretatio Christiana* or due to didactic reasons related to neophytes. One should also consider in this context general references of Reinbern's act to the pre-Christian "sea religion" (see Czesław Deptuła, "Sakralne wartościowanie morza a problem integracji Pomorza z Polską we wczesnym średniowieczu," *Summarium* 4/24 (1975) [1978], pp. 164–173, esp. pp. 165, 168).

555   In the case of seaside people, treating the sea as hierophany is highly probable, which is also argued by a psychologising trend in religious studies reflection on the birth of a new cult in reference to the numinosum category. Rudolf Otto reflected in this term a feeling of weirdness, delight and fear marked with ambivalence, which overwhelms the human mind in the case of the majesty of the sea, desert or the sky, becoming the beginning of religious experience and cult, see Rudolf Otto, *Świętość. Elementy racjonalne i irracjonalne w pojęciu bóstwa*, trans. by Bogdan Kupis (Wrocław: Thesaurus Press, 1993) [orig. *Das Heilige: Über das Irrationale in der Idee des Göttlichen und sein Verhältnis zum Rationalen* (Breslau: Trewendt & Granier, 1917)], p. 32–34 *et passim*. The full scale of this kind of experience of phenomena in the shaping of religious life forms is analysed by the phenomenology of sacrum, see Gerardus van der Leeuw, *Phänomenologie der Religion* (Tübingen: J.C.B. Mohr, 1933); Eliade, *Traité d'histoire des religions*.

THE RELIGION OF THE SLAVS IN THIETMAR'S CHRONICLE   167

of composing the description of the spaces of manifestation for anti-sacral power. In Reinbern's episode one can see an analogy to the earlier description of Radogošč, and particularly the model collation of *fanum – mare*. It is worth remembering that Thietmar mentioned the presence of an area of water (*mare*) near the temple with idols that was an area of a particular hierophany: a boar coming out of it was a signal of the approaching civil war.[556]

Thus, this beast is a mythical sign of destructive forces acting against the ecumene, which in turn corresponds to the interpretation of the sea as a habitat of powers hostile to people and annihilated by Reinbern. This parallel becomes more expressive with regard to the fact that the chronicler used the same term *mare* to refer to a lake in his description of Radogošč,[557] and to waters, most certainly the Baltic, in the Kołobrzeg episode.[558] However, in the latter case it is not mentioned that *fana* were located near water and this is why both descriptions can only be connected at a textual level by the occurrence of motifs of a temple with idols and an area of water in the characteristics of the *sacrum*, or rather, *antisacrum* topography.

In this perspective, it is worth emphasizing that in Christian symbolism, the sea as the boundary of the cosmos symbolises the eternal chaos: a centre of destructive forces tamed by the Creator and withheld from harming the world.[559] Thus the rituals performed by Reinbern were to lead to the elimination of the power of demons both in the dimension of human society (*fana idolorum*) and also the natural world. It is thought-provoking that it was the latter dimension to be privileged in the introduction of Christianity. The chronicler *expressis*

---

556   See above, p. 132.

557   This is not a sufficient premise for the hypothetical location of Radogošč at the seaside, because this idea is not furthered by its location in the inland country of the Redars (for their abodes and the location of Radogošč see *e.g.* Gerard Labuda, "Redarowie," in SSS, vol. 4, pp. 477 f.; Jerzy Strzelczyk, "Radogoszcz," in SSS, vol. 4, pp. 450 f.).

558   The term *mare* in Thietmar's chronicle refers to both the sea (sea *e.g.* Thietmar II, 15, p. 67; III, 21, p. 137) and the lake (*e.g.* Thietmar II, 20, p. 71, where there is the term "Salsum mare", *i.e.* Salty Lake), which can be due to the confluence of the terms for these two types of basins (a lake and a sea) in his native language (in today's German it can be captured as a relic, comp. *die See, der See*). This is why it is worth considering the possibility that the ritual attributed to Reinbern referred to a lake (the same in the English translation of *Thietmar's Chronicle*; see *Ottonian Germany*, p. 358). However, the sea as the cult space of Reinbern's activity is indicated first of all by the very significance of this element in the spatial organisation of the ecumene and for the local community (salt and fish), as well as the fact that as hierophany it overwhelmed the power of all other nearby waters, see Rosik, *Conversio*, pp. 24 f.

559   The sea symbolises the powers of the eternal chaos, the magnitude of forces destructing the world which were tamed by God, see *e.g.* Job 38:8; cf. Forstner, *Świat*, pp. 65 f. Moreover, it should be added that in patristics salty waters are an image of the abyss of this world and its dangerous powers (see *ibidem*, pp. 133, 426).

168   CHAPTER 2

verbis claimed that the Bishop of "Kołobrzeg Salt" implanted ("eduxit") "a new branch on a tree which did not bear fruit," *i.e.* the "cultivation of holy proclamation," by purifying ("purgans") the sea.

The key role in the explanation of this image is played by the interpretation of the ritual of throwing stones into the briny sea. Anointing them with chrism means consecrating the space taken away from evil spirits, encompassing it with the grace order.[560] Their number, four, refers to the symbolism of the universum, the cosmos based on four cardinal points, which in connection with their anointment[561] allows the fact that they were thrown into the habitat of demons as an aspiration to stop the devastating activity of powers hostile to the world to be seen.[562] At the same time it represented the establishment of the new order, the order of the rule of Christ.[563] It is essential that the maritime element also embodied the sphere of the life-giving forces of the Christianized community. Fish and salt were the basis of its existence and even affluence. Similarly, the sea itself served as a communication artery. Hence, Reinbern could have intended to ensure the care of the new *sacrum* for the seaside community, or even to make them aware of this state.[564]

---

560   It is possible to metaphorically define the sense of this ritual as a "baptism" of the sea (cf. Deptuła, "Sakralne wartościowanie," pp. 165 f.), which shows its character better than the purely exorcistic interpretation. In the trend of purification and sanctification of the matter, Reinbern's ritual was interpreted numerous times, see *e.g.* Jan Kracik, "Chrzest w staropolskiej kulturze duchowej," *Nasza Przeszłość* 74 (1990), pp. 189–190; Jürgen Petersohn, "Der Akt von Gnesen im Jahre 1000 und die Errichtung des Bistums Salz-Kolberg. Zur historischen Substanz eines Jubiläums," *Baltische Studien* NF 87 (2001), p. 33.

561   The stone and chrism generally indicate the symbolism of Christ, and the chrism (oil) itself the order of grace – see Forstner, *Świat*, pp. 126–130, 172–174. An especially useful example of the interpretation of Reinbern's gesture is the treatment of a stone as weapons against evil and connecting it semantically with Christ himself (see *ibidem*, pp. 129 f.).

562   A clear picture of this kind of destructive power appears in the vision of prophet Daniel, in which four beasts come out of the sea defeated by the appearance of the "Son of Man" (Dan 7), a figure considered a prototype of Christ. The number of beasts indicates that the overcome threat was related to the whole universum. Thanks to the four stones, Reinbern's gesture has similar meaning, their anointment is to call the power of Christ to tame the chaos posing danger to the four cardinal points of the world. One can also read it this way that these four stones are the fundament of the ecclesial community, given the symbolism of the stone and anointment related to Christ (see above, footnote 561) as the fundament of the new Church (see Rosik, "Reinbern," pp. 95–107).

563   Forstner, *Świat*, pp. 125–127: in biblical tradition the stone was a symbol of God as the unconquered stronghold and also a sign of refraining the primordial see – the early beginning of the creation, which is worth emphasizing in the context of these investigations.

564   In search for the sense of the discussed ritual is worth taking into account the possibility of occurrence of a certain type of dialogue between Reinbern and the views of the converted people, which was aimed at making them realise the annihilation of the power

THE RELIGION OF THE SLAVS IN THIETMAR'S CHRONICLE   169

The interpretation of the Reinbern's ritual proposed here refers its elements
to the cultural context which conditioned both the very creation of the account and also the described activities – assuming that they were not *stricte*
literary construct. The significance of the symbols and ideas circulating in the
author's intellectual milieu were taken into account as well as the conditions
of the seaside community. However, these kinds of premises do not permit
anything further than the general conviction that behind the action of the
"Kołobrzeg Salt" Bishop there could be some sophisticated theological speculation (*e.g.* references to particular places in the Bible) prepared for this occasion. It is possible but it was not indispensable.

First of all one should take into account the creative (performative) function of signs in cult activities: a rite establishes and brings about a particular
reality.[565] The specifics of communication at the level of a symbol, which >>by
nature<< refers to numerous senses,[566] are elements of fundamental significance to consider. However, the development of a particular theological lecture explaining the importance of these kinds of activities (*e.g.* in preaching)
is somehow secondary and is not indispensable for considering them effective.

Hence, the fundamental theological goal of the ritual presented by Thietmar
is the introduction of the rule of Christ on the scale of the whole ecumene, and
by doing so establishing the basis for implantation of Christianity in this seaside community. It is demonstrated to be a passive element on the historical
stage, like a tree tended by a gardener's hand or a new crop. At the basis for the
use of this rhetoric it is possible to find a way of perceiving the Christianization
of a given country as the establishment of institutional order, which in this

---

of earlier worshipped supernatural forces, but first of all to manifest that God has taken
control of the sea. In this way the care of the new sacrum would visibly encompass the
neuralgic area for the seaside people's functioning: the sea element which ensured its
wellbeing but was also a sphere of various threats. Fear of losing the basis of their existence in the case of people devoid of the possibility of maintaining their native sacrum
could form a serious obstacle in opening to Christianity, which was taken into account in
the then circle of its propagators among pagans. St. Bruno of Querfurt mentions that the
Prussians, after defiling the holiness of their cult grove by St. Adalbert, were to fear there
would be no crops and that their animals would not be fertile (see Vita Adalberti II, 25).
According to biographical sources, similar problems occurred to Otto of Bamberg during
his Pomeranian-Liutician missions in the 12th c. (see Ebo III, 8).

565   See *e.g.* Bogusław Nadolski, *Liturgika*, vol. 1 (Poznań: Pallotinum, 1989), p. 20.
566   See *e.g.* Paul Ricoeur, ">>Symbol daje do myślenia<<", trans. Stanisław Cichowicz, in
       Paul Ricoeur, *Egzystencja i hermeneutyka. Rozprawy o metodzie*, ed. Stanisław Cichowicz
       (Warszawa: De Agostini, 2003), pp. 62–80.

170   CHAPTER 2

case precedes the change in the mentality of converted people and also shapes the perception of their community.[567]

It is not accidental that the people entrusted to Reinbern are not shown as pagan and attached to its native religion and customs, but are only hard to teach, blunt, or stupid. The expression "insulsus" used in this case etymologically means also without taste or more particularly without salt. Thus, the selection of this epithet harmonizes with Reinbern's expression "presul Salsae Cholbergiensis" – Bishop of the "Kołobrzeg Salt." It is worth emphasizing this confluence not only as a kind of play on words,[568] but also – taking into account the evangelical connotations of salt as a symbol of the presence of Christianity in the world – as a particular susceptibility of this passage to the allegorical interpretation typical of this epoch.[569] Hence in this lack of salt one can find a rather sophisticated, poetic expression of interpretation of the attitude of the people being converted.

When trying to determine its location in the institutional context, it is worth remembering, for comparison, the situation known to Thietmar from Polabia, where pre-Christian sanctuaries were still used on lands already controlled by bishoprics.[570] However, in the chronicler's optics these lands were no longer pagan due to the fact that they were encompassed by the network of the Church. Hence, Reinbern, also fighting idolatry and teaching people who were certainly not baptized, at the same time formally took care of them as his diocesans. This status was gained by the inhabitants of the seaside province of Boleslav the Brave's monarchy under the decisions of the Council of Gniezno (1000) upon the establishment of a metropolis there and the subjugation of three suffraganies to it. The one which was entrusted to Reinbern determined

---

567 See above, pp. 80 f.

568 Helmut Holzapfel, *Reinbern. Pierwszy biskup Pomorza*, trans. Ignacy Jeż (Koszalin: [Printed] Niepokalanów, OO. Franciszkanie, 1980) [orig. *Reinbern. Pommerns erster Bischof* (Würzburg: Echter, 1975)], pp. 22, proposed to find in the word *insulsus* an ironic allusion to *Salsa Cholbergiensis*, however, confining to this ascertainment seems insufficient due to the symbolical and allegorical significance of the salt motif in the then literary culture (see footnote 569 in this chapter).

569 The evangelical term used to denote Christ's followers as the "salt of the earth" (cf. Mt 5:13) finds its antinomy in the image of "unsalted" (*insulsus*) people thanks to Reinbern accepting "holy teaching". For more information on the variety of salt symbolism, referring to *e.g.* smartness of the mind or purification from evil, and so able to cast light on the interpreted Thietmar's narration, see Forstner, *Świat*, pp. 131–133.

570 See above, pp. 57 ff., 145 f.

THE RELIGION OF THE SLAVS IN THIETMAR'S CHRONICLE   171

the eastern part of the northern border of the contemporary Christian influence that was concentrated around Otto III's empire.[571]

Hence the ritual presented by Thietmar is depicted as one of the elements
in establishing a new order on the borderland of the ecumene, not only by
encompassing this land in the diocese but also on the basis of subduing – as
it was understood in the theological perspective – to Christ's rule the neighbouring sea element (which was also life-giving for native people). Such cult
action must have taken place at the initial stage of Reinbern's activity as a
bishop and it seems natural that it was located near his abode in the "Kolberg
Salt." By nature it would have a singular character contrary to dismantling
sanctuaries (*fana idolorum*) which were more numerous on the scale of the
country.

It is impossible to determine indisputably how long Reinbern's activity on
the Baltic Sea lasted. On the basis of Thietmar's record about his chaplain, accompanying Boleslav the Brave during his stay in Prague in 1004,[572] a hypothesis was formulated that maybe this was the time of the fall of the bishopric
in "Kołobrzeg Salt" as a result of pagan reaction.[573] However, Reinbern's possible participation in the military expedition of the monarch to whom he was
subject would not have been surprising in those times. Thus, the final possible
date of leaving his dioceses is determined by the said expedition to Rus'. At the
same time, it is impossible to exclude that even then the results of his mission-

---

571   For the concept of Otto III's *renovatio imperii Romanorum* and the significance of the
      Council of Gniezno encompassed by this concept, see Johannes Fried, "Die Erneuerung
      des Römischen Reiches," in *Europasmitte um 1000. Beiträge zur Geschichte, Kunst und
      Archäologie*, vol. 2, ed. Alfred Wieczorek, Hans-Martin Hinz (Stuttgart: Theiss, 2000),
      pp. 738–744; and above, p. 41.

572   Thietmar VI, 33. Another event taken into account in the hypothetical dating of the fall
      of the Kolberg Diocese is the arrival of Wolin (*Livilni*) envoys before the King of Germany
      Henry II in about 1007, to oppose the political plans of Boleslav the Brave. This action of
      the Wolin inhabitants against the Polish ruler was treated as a premise that Polish control
      over Pomerania was rejected, and Wolin was a part of it. However, there is a weakness in
      this research proposal, namely the fact that it is based on a hypothetical conviction that
      Poland controlled this town and that this control was so strong – which raises a funda-
      mental doubt – that it prevented the inhabitants of this town from independent political
      activity. This way or another, one should take into account that it is possible that the
      involvement of Boleslav the Brave in wars with Henry II led to the weakening or the fall of
      Polish authority over the Baltic lands and perhaps in consequence only after a few years
      after 1000 Reinbern's Christianization action conducted there was stopped.

573   See Władysław Kowalenko, "Kołobrzeg," in SSS, vol. 2, p. 447. See also Lech Leciejewicz,
      "Die sozialen und politischen Voraussetzungen des Glaubenswechsels in Pommern," in
      *Rom und Byzanz im Norden. Mission und Glaubenswechsel im Ostseeraum während des
      8.–14 Jahrhunderts*, vol. 2, ed. Michael Müller-Wille (Stuttgart: Steiner, 1997), p. 170.

ary activity did not have to be destroyed. The final *terminus ad quem* in this matter is determined by the crisis of the Piast Monarchy in the 30's of the 11th c., after which Pomerania became independent.[574] Its Christianization in the 12th c. sources is presented as work *in cruda radice*, which indicates that the diocese of the "Kołobrzeg Salt" turned out to be an ephemeride.

Contrary to the optimism expressed in the laconic description of Reinbern's activity, one has to assume that his activity brought rather moderate results in fighting pre-Christian cults. The scale of his achievements was even decreased by attempts of 20th-c. historians, who in general questioned the burning of temples of idols (*fana idolorum*) by the "Kołobrzeg Salt" Bishop, or more precisely the very possibility of his struggle with idolatry.[575] These historians, including H. Łowmiański who rendered considerable services in this respect, supported reducing its area of occurrence among the Western Slavs to Northern Polabia and the Baltic islands.[576] It is certainly possible to defend Thietmar's credibility by referring to the genesis of his information about Reinbern.[577] However,

---

574   It is worth emphasizing that the earliest testimony of the name of the Pomeranians dates back to 1046, and their formation as a geographical and social space is treated as a relic of the fact that earlier they were the Piast Monarchy province. Hence, using this ethnic name in Reinbern's times can raise doubts. See *e.g.* Ulf Stabenow, "Die Entstehung der Pomoranen," in *Slawen und Deutsche im südlichen Ostseeraum vom 11. bis zum 16. Jahrhundert. Archäologische, historische und sprachwissenschaftliche Beispiele aus Schleswig-Holstein, Mecklenburg und Pommern*, ed. Michael Müller-Wille, Dietrich Meier, Henning Unverhau (Neumünster: Wachholtz, 1995), pp. 127–148; Jan M. Piskorski, *Pomorze plemienne. Historia – Archeologia – Językoznawstwo* (Poznań/Szczecin: Sorus, 2002), pp. 30 ff.

575   Thede Palm, *Wendische Kultstäten. Quellenkritische Untersuchungen zu den letzten Jahrhunderten slavischen Heidentums* (Lund: Gleerupska Universitetsbokhandeln, 1937), p. 26, claimed that in this case the expression '*idolum*' is only a template of Christian interpretation.

576   The final argument of H. Łowmiański (*Religia*, pp. 167 f.) on the matter of the absence of temples and statues among Pomeranians living east of the Oder is the conviction that St. Otton of Bamberg did not come across them, especially while his activity took place over one hundred years before Reinbern's mission. It should be mentioned that it is *ex silentio* arguing, and additionally it does not take into account the fact that the specifics of this stage of narration of Otto's hagiographers (cf. Vita Prieflingensis II, 19–20; Ebo II, 18; Herbord II, 38–40) connected with his activity in Pomerania is brief, which does not further go into such details as in *e.g.* well developed episodes connected with Szczecin or Wolin (cf. Vita Prieflingensis II, 5–19; Ebo II, 7–13, 15; Herbord II, 24–37).

577   *E.g.* Słupecki, "Wykopaliska," p. 28, indicated that Reinbern's activity was probably very well known in Germany and Thietmar wrote about events contemporary to him. To strengthen this conviction, it is worth emphasizing that Reinbern came from Hassegau, located in the Merseburg diocese ruled by the chronicler, which obliged his interests even more in the direction of his compatriot. Information on this matter was most certainly

THE RELIGION OF THE SLAVS IN THIETMAR'S CHRONICLE   173

due to the fact that the attack was based on *a priori* assumed views on the matter of the development of the Slavic religion, it is worth focusing exactly on these assumptions.

In Łowmiański's argument, the line of the Oder achieves the rank of a border between polytheism and the lower stages of the development of Slavic beliefs and cults.[578] The development of polytheism was to be possible only in areas which were temporarily encompassed by the Church network in the 10th c., and the metric for this form of beliefs was the use of figural representations of deities. Yet, he took into account the possibility that Reinbern destroyed the Perynia type sanctuaries (bearing this name after the town Perynia located near Novgorod). According to archaeological reconstruction, this kind of a cultic place consisted of poles forming an oval shape surrounding a post located in the centre.[579]

At the same time, H. Łowmiański did not consider these objects as "regular temples."[580] Does it mean, however, that these types of sanctuaries did not deserve the name *fana idolorum*? The word *fanum*, and whether it could define an open cult space, are up for dispute. Another cases in which Thietmar used this word do not confirm such a possibility.[581] Nevertheless, the semantic range of the word *fanum* is sufficiently extensive to encompass the case of an open sky sanctuary, especially if one takes into account the general nature of

---

taken by Thietmar directly or indirectly from the chaplain of the Kolberg bishop, whom he mentions in his presentation of the events from 1004 (see above, footnote 572).

[578] To hypothetically limit the area of occurrence of polytheism in Polabia to its northern part, Łowmiański, *Religia*, pp. 168 f., quoted Thietmar's information on the matter of the southern part of Polabia, where sacrum was embodied in Glomač spring and its pool or the Holy Grove (*Zutibure*), and not temples with idols. This argument is derived from the silence of the source, and in addition H. Łowmiański disregarded a very important problem: the cult places of Sorbian and Lusatian tribes described by Thietmar functioned already at the time when the empire took control of this land and the related diocese organisation was introduced, therefore there was no place for public idolatry in this social context. It was more difficult to eradicate the cult of natural hierophanies so no wonder they survived longer.

[579] The hypothetical cult place in Perynia was discovered in 1908. In Western Pomerania some analogic cult places were discovered, *e.g.* two such places were discovered in Trzebiatów in 1931–1933, see *e.g.* Gieysztor, *Mitologia*, pp. 224 ff. Horbacz, Lechowicz, "Archeologia a poznawanie religii," p. 182, negated the qualification of the sanctuaries in Trzebiatów and one in Mielno as the Perynia type of sanctuary, however, they did not question the cult character of these places. Later excavation work proved the existence of similar objects in Rus', Bohemia and Poland.

[580] Łowmiański, *Religia*, p. 168.

[581] See Thietmar VI, 23.

174   CHAPTER 2

the discussed premise.[582] Nonetheless there is no doubt as to the possibility of using the word "idol" (*idolum*) to refer to posts in Perynia-type sanctuaries, especially in the *interpretatio Christiana* perspective, because even nonanthropomorphic sacral objects deserved such qualification, especially in the worldview of the medieval theologian.

Hence it is possible to defend Thietmar's credibility even only on the basis of the results of research on the religion of the Slavs, taken into account by H. Łowmiański on the assumption that polytheism – understood in the model from the Mediterranean Classical Antiquity circle and so connected with the temple cult and anthropomorphic idols – did not reach the Kołobrzeg salinas. Nonetheless, is it not an excessive multiplication of existences? It is worth first of all paying attention to the fact that the very concept of assuming a lack of "regular temples" in Pomerania in about the year 1000 results mainly from the general theory of evolution of the Slavic religion. The element of key significance here is the conviction that the lack of statues and temples was generally of common Pre-Slavic heritage, and only in Rus' and Polabia (and Rügen) these objects were formed because of external influences.

The fundamental premise in this case is the statement that in the Pre-Slavic language there is no separate expression to denote a statue or a temple, which would prove that before the period of migration, the Slavs did not have them.[583] However, in such argumentation, it would be necessary to assume that in the language of the forming Slavdom, separate terms for these objects were reserved, and they were excluded from everyday vocabulary. This assessment seems quite probable in the case of theonyms. It should still be noted that this is decisively less probable when it comes to the general terms that characterize the cult. Here an expression common also for the sphere of profanum could be sufficient, which is indicated in the term "kącina"/"kontina"/ *contina* (Slavic temple in Pomerania),[584] which owing only to the controversial custom – because it conditioned a pretension from the Romantic epoch – still

---

582   Filipowiak, "Słowiańskie wierzenia," p. 19. The author supports the hypothesis about open (in an analogy to Perynia) cult place in Kolberg.

583   Urbańczyk, *Dawni Słowianie*, pp. 61, 121 f., 160 f.; Łowmiański, *Religia*, p. 230; Hanna Popowska-Taborska, *Wczesne dzieje Słowian w świetle ich języka* (Wrocław/Warszawa/ Kraków: Ossolineum, 1991), p. 115; Moszyński, *Die vorchristliche Religion*, pp. 115–117. A polemic argument put forward by Leszek Bednarczuk, "W co wierzyli Prasłowianie? (W świetle badań prof. Leszka Moszyńskiego nad przedchrześcijańską religią Słowian)," *Kieleckie Studia Filologiczne* 10 (1996), p. 27, states that the fact that the statues and cult building preserved in the Slavdom had to have their names is not sufficient because no such objects evidently belonging to the "Pre-Slavic" culture were found.

584   See *e.g.* Vita Prieflingensis II, 11; Herbord II, 30–32.

THE RELIGION OF THE SLAVS IN THIETMAR'S CHRONICLE   175

functions in current studies on the Slavic religion as a typical term for a pre-Christian temple.[585]

On the other hand, it should be emphasized that at the current stage of the debate on the ethnogenesis of the Slavs – or more particularly while taking into account the concept of the formation of this ethnic community not earlier than in the 4th–6th c. AD with essential contribution of migration and acculturation[586] – the very assumption that originally there was to be a general Slavic community of terms referring to the sphere of cult, seems insufficiently justified. Because in the case of strengthening the cultural ties which brought the final formation of this ethnical community, it was exactly the religious sphere which strongly cultivated more archaic traditions and so it could not be made uniform, especially at the level of terminology.[587] Therefore in particular parts of the Slavdom, cult objects could have different names, which allows one to question the (alleged) exceptionality of this ethnos in comparison with other Indo-European peoples, expressed in pre-polytheistic >>primitivism<< of religious life forms.

Thus in verification of Thietmar's information about the existence of *fana idolorum* in Reinbern's diocese, the element of fundamental significance is the assessment of the development of the forms of social life which would support the development of a sacral infrastructure exceeding natural hierophanies.[588] In this respect, although Kołobrzeg was less populous, it can be compared with

---

585   Etymologically "kącina" refers to a roofed building; see *e.g.* Słupecki, *Slavonic Pagan Sanctuaries*, pp. 12 f. It is the same with statues, in the case of which general Slavic terms could be "słup" (post) or "bałwan" (idol); these names inform about the shape of objects but in some situations they were also cult objects, see Gieysztor, *Mitologia*, p. 230. The author also hypothetically proposed a general Slavic term for an idol – 'modła'. Cf. Słupecki, "Słowiańskie posągi," p. 36; *idem, Slavonic Pagan Sanctuaries*, p. 200.

586   See above, p. 6.

587   Stanisław Rosik, "Cień wieży Babel na pomorskich kącinach. O niepokornej służbie metafory w badaniach nad początkami Słowiańszczyzny i jej kultury duchowej," in *Mundus hominis – cywilizacja, kultura, natura. Wokół interdyscyplinarności badań historycznych*, ed. Stanisław Rosik, Przemysław Wiszewski, (Acta Universitatis Wratislaviensis. Historia) 175 (Wrocław: Wydawnictwo Uniwersytetu Wrocławskiego, 2006) pp. 401–408.

588   One of the most significant factors in this case is adapting cult forms to ways of human existence, especially in larger settlements, where such "domestication" of sacrum ensured more efficient access to it in everyday life. The key matter in this reflection on this process is the postulate of changing the paradigm of the description of the process genesis: departure from a discussion on the Slavs borrowing idols and temples from another culture to indicate how over centuries particular communities co-created multi-ethnic culture circles, in which idolatry was practiced. Another issue is the question about the scale and conditions of its development in particular tribes or centres (here the examples of the Wagrians is especially interesting as they practiced idolatry in their capital Starigard, but also had assembly (veche) by the holy grove dedicated to their god Prove, see below, pp. 333 f).

176   CHAPTER 2

the centres at the mouth of the Oder.[589] Hence the occurrence of idolatry or
even roofed temples, albeit only in this stronghold or its close neighbourhood,
fits the boundaries of probability,[590] especially when taking into account the
wider context of cultural contacts of coastal Slavic communities with neighbouring Scandinavia.[591]

This is why undermining Thietmar's credibility in the matter of Reinbern's
activity on the basis of general, abstract theories – besides being conditioned
by controversial methodological assumptions – fails to be convincing. An anti-
dote for the research procedure under question here is a turn to source analysis, which on the basis of the discussed episode allows for an appreciation of
not so much the content for research on the Slavic religion but rather the artistry of the chronicler as an interpreter of history and the pagan elements on
its stage.

2.11   *On Funeral Customs of the Slavs*

Discussing customs of Mieszko I's subjects, Thietmar mentioned a funeral rite:
"In the days of his father [*i.e.* Boleslav the Brave's – S.R.], when he still embraced heathenism, every woman followed her husband on to the funeral pyre,
after first being decapitated."[592] The ritual of body burning was seen as a typical
procedure for pre-Christian times and so it was described rather schematically.
However, in accordance with Thietmar's vision in which he presented Mieszko
as the originator of the conversion of all the people subjugated to him,[593] the

---

589   Szczecin or Wolin. However, it is worth taking into account in this comparison with
        Kolberg also centres in Liutici lands converted by Otto of Bamberg in the 12th c., they
        were less populated than the metropolises at the Oder mouth, which also had their tem-
        ples. See above footnote 427.

590   See *e.g.* H Hermann Bollnow, *Studien zur Geschichte der pommerschen Burgen und Städte
        im 12. und 13. Jahrhundert* (Köln/Graz: Böhlau, 1964), p. 93; Słupecki, *Slavonic Pagan
        Sanctuaries*, p. 70.

591   In Scandinavia pre-Christian cultic buildings or "temples" have been found by archae-
        ologists in recent years, for instance in Uppåkra, Scania, and Borg, Östergötland (see:
        Lars Larsson, Karl-Magnus Lenntorp, "The Enigmatic House," in *Continuity for Centuries:
        A Ceremonial Building and its Context at Uppåkra, Southern Sweden*, ed. Lars Larsson,
        (Uppåkrastudier) 10 (Stockholm: Almqvist & Wiksell International, 2004), pp. 3–48;
        Nielsen, "Rituals and power," pp. 243–247).

592   Thietmar VIII, 3, p. 583: "In tempore patris sui [*i.e.* Boleslav the Brave's – S.R.], cum is
        [Mieszko I – S.R.] gentilis esset, unaquaeque mulier post viri exequias sui cremati decol-
        lata subsequitur."

593   Therefore in Thietmar's perspective (IV, 56) Mieszko's individual conversion as the "head"
        (*caput*) resulted in attracting the community of his subjects considered as "defective
        members" (*membra debilia*): "... innatae infidelitatis toxicum evomuit et in sacro baptis-
        mate nevam originalem detersit. Et protinus caput suum et seniorem dilectum membra

THE RELIGION OF THE SLAVS IN THIETMAR'S CHRONICLE

ritual took place prior to his baptism. It should be emphasized, however, that in the light of archaeological discoveries, the cremation of dead bodies was still conducted in some parts of Piast lands until the 12th c., which makes the value of this testimony for research on the progress of the Christianization of Poland rather controversial.[594]

However, in analysis of Thietmar's information it is worth taking into account the specifics of perception of conversion as encompassing a given country within the Church network.[595] As a result, customs treated as pagan formally lost their raison d'être in public life, and this is the sphere of life the chronicler refers to, emphasizing in this context the religious affiliation of the ruler. Furthermore, for Thietmar the identifier of a pagan reality was not so much the ritual of cremation, but rather the drastic information about killing a wife so she would share her husband's fate after death. The occurrence of this practice is confirmed in earlier sources, and in the case of Thietmar's account doubts are raised in relation to the presumably conventional use of the participle *decollata*, because in Byzantine and Arabic descriptions there is information about strangling (hanging).[596]

---

     populi hactenus debilia subsequuntur et nupciali veste recepta inter caeteros Christi adoptivos numerantur."

594   See, *e.g.* Andrzej Janowski, *Groby komorowe w Europie środkowo-wschodniej. Problemy wybrane* (Szczecin: IAE PAN, 2015), pp. 81 ff. However, on the other hand it should be emphasized that inhumation became common on some lands under the rule of the first Piasts even before Christianity became their official religion, see below.

595   See above, pp. 79 f.

596   A catalogue of written sources was created by Helena Zoll-Adamikowa, *Wczesnośredniowieczne cmentarzyska ciałopalne Słowian na terenie Polski*, part 1: *Źródła* (Wrocław/Warszawa: Ossolineum, 1975), pp. 282 ff. First of all see *Mauricii Strategicum* 11, 6–7, in: *Testimonia najdawniejszych dziejów Słowian*, p. 138. Ibn Rosteh, *Kita_b al-A'la_q an-nafi_sa*, the Arabic text and its Polish translation, in *Źródła arabskie do dziejów Słowiańszczyzny*, vol. 2, part 2, ed. and trans. Tadeusz Lewicki (Wrocław/Warszawa/Kraków/Gdańsk: Ossolineum, 1977), p. 37. The author considered the accuracy of this description convincing that the account is a result of the observation of an eye-witness of a suicidal death of a Slavic wife (see *ibidem*, p. 113, footnotes 204, 205), however, given how late the manuscripts forming the basis of this edition were, it is hard to fully share this optimism. Helena Zoll-Adamikowa, Helena Zoll-Adamikowa, *Wczesnośredniowieczne cmentarzyska ciałopalne Słowian na terenie Polski*, part 2 (Wrocław/Warszawa: Ossolineum, 1979), pp. 191 f., supports the view that the widow hanged herself before cremation, considering Thietmar's *decollata* as a general term used to describe a dead person, not necessarily beheaded. *Ibidem*, pp. 244 ff., an attempt to reconstruct the whole cremation funeral and all related celebrations. See also Władysław Łosiński, "Z dziejów obrzędowości pogrzebowej u północnego odłamu Słowian zachodnich w świetle nowszych badań," in *Kraje słowiańskie w wiekach średnich. Profanum i sacrum*, ed. Hanna Kóčka-Krenz, Władysław Łosiński (Poznań: PTPN, 1998), pp. 473–483.

Such a custom, occurring in various cultural spheres, indicates that there was a conviction that an afterlife existed and that a wife should accompany her husband on his journey.[597] Two concepts are apparent here as a hypothetical explanation for this custom. The first one assumes that the world of the dead was organized in the same way as the human world,[598] and the other one that it is a dark place, empty and lonely and urging a dead man to be accompanied by his wife.[599] It is possible that this practice was to prevent a dead man from visiting, and also frightening, those who were still alive to seek their relatives whom they had parted because of death.[600]

Cremation as such indicates that there was a conviction that the soul existed as an immaterial element, independent of the body. This concept, supported by faith in the purifying power of fire, can justify the basic sense of the ritual.[601] The fact that the Western Slavs departed from it should be associated

---

597 Herodotus of Halicarnassus mentioned it referring to the Thracians; ethnology also offers examples, see *e.g.* Gediga, *Śladami*, p. 169.

598 This concept of the Slavic afterlife corresponds with references to ritual joy during funerals, which indicates faith in the beginning of new life and happiness that god had mercy for the dead – see Zoll-Adamikowa, *Wczesnośredniowieczne cmentarzyska*, part 2, pp. 236 f; for more information on these reactions to cremation – see also *ibidem*, p. 195 ff. The information about joy can also be found in Arabic sources, claiming that the soul leaves the burnt body to go to a better world (see Tadeusz Lewicki, "Obrzędy pogrzebowe Słowian w opisach podróżników i pisarzy arabskich," *Archeologia* 5 (1952–1953), pp. 122–154); the same matter, see above, pp. 64, 71.

599 See above pp. 64 f.

600 Gediga, *Śladami*, p. 170. Gieysztor, *Mitologia*, pp. 259 ff., indicated the double role of funeral rituals and the cult of the dead: prevention of unwanted visits of soul-phantoms or summoning them at the right time, for which he quotes a number of historical testimonies (Arabic, Byzantine, Czech and Polish sources) and finally ethnographic data from the Slavdom and neighbouring peoples. This ambivalent attitude to the dead corresponds with the findings of Bronisław Malinowski, *Szkice z teorii kultury* (Warszawa: Książka i Wiedza, 1958), p. 422 ff. in which he appreciates the emotional element in the ideology of funeral rituals. The cult of the dead reveals a certain duality of feelings: love and mourning related to the loss clash with abhorrence for the corpse and fear of his/her spirit; see also Zoll-Adamikowa, *Wczesnośredniowieczne cmentarzyska*, part 2, pp. 235 f.

601 According to Gediga, *Śladami*, pp. 116 f., cremation of corpses – possibly following the trail of popularisation of copper and bronze from the Near East – was accepted all over the territory of Poland at the time of the Lusatian culture based on an archaic conviction that fire was sacred and justification of this mythological custom would be a job for priests. See also Zoll-Adamikowa, *Wczesnośredniowieczne cmentarzyska*, part 2, pp. 240 f. The cult of fire was connected with cremation even earlier by M. Cabalska, who related its appearance among the Slavs, similarly to the ritual wife's death and joy accompanying funerals, to Hinduistic influences (see Maria Cabalska, "Głos w dyskusji," in *Religia pogańskich Słowian. Sesja naukowa w Kielcach*, ed. Karol Strug (Kielce: Muzeum Świętokrzyskie, 1968), pp. 113–117). However, there was no considerable justification for this speculation. B. Gediga raised the question of the connection between the cult of the Sun with ritual cremation (see Gediga, *Śladami*, p. 115). A connecting motif of solar beliefs

THE RELIGION OF THE SLAVS IN THIETMAR'S CHRONICLE   179

with progress in the introduction of Christianity among them, although it occasionally disappeared earlier.[602] As was observed by Stanisław Bylina, at the
final stage of Slavic religion, cremation was no longer "a necessary condition of
ensuring the deceased fortunate existence." This supports the thesis that there
were significant transformations in the system of beliefs, through which cremation consequently lost its ideological importance. It is symptomatic that it
is not mentioned in medieval sources as a practice contended with at the time
of the Christianization of the Slavs.[603]

Thietmar did not make any critical remarks connected with cremation
either and, what is more essential in the case of his account, neither did he
condemn the cruel rite of killing widows. This is very well explained by the
fact that in this part of his work the parenetic trend can be observed: the reference related to this Slavic custom became for the chronicler a springboard
to a tirade about the corruption of morals related to marital faithfulness in
the Christian environment. The impunity of his contemporary trespassers is
juxtaposed with the strict Law of Moses, and earlier also with the "shameful
and wretched penalty" ("turpis et poena miserabilis"), such as the mutilation
and sophisticated humiliation that was practiced with reference to harlots in
the times when Mieszko was pagan.[604] With regard to men who perpetrated
licentiousness, similar practices in terms of cruelty and public revilement were
still maintained by Boleslav the Brave, which is presented in an earlier chapter
of the chronicle.[605]

This type of drastic punishment was accepted by Thietmar as a necessary
reformatory measure for the subjects of the Piast monarchy: "The populace
must be fed like cattle and punished as one would a stubborn ass. Without

---

with the funeral cult could be a mythical view that the sun took the soul to the underworld, because the sun itself, reaching lower spheres of the world does not perish, it only
sets. Cf. Leciejewicz, *Słowianie*, p. 117.

602 Helena Zoll-Adamikowa, "Głos w dyskusji," *Nasza Przeszłość* 69 (1988), pp. 182–184; *eadem*,
"Modele recepcji rytuału szkieletowego u Słowian wschodnich i zachodnich," *Światowit* 40
(1995), pp. 174–184. J. Gąssowski emphasizes that for many peoples inhumation evidently
appeared before Christianity was introduced (*e.g.* in West and Central Pomerania it was
certainly present as early as the 10th c.) and the *a priori* assumption that inhumation
burials occurred on Polish lands after the baptism of Mieszko I, leads to paradoxical conclusions that settlement groups dated to the 8th c. did not have burial grounds at all (see
Jerzy Gąssowski, "Archeologia o schyłkowym pogaństwie," *Archeologia Polski* 37 (1992),
pp. 137 f.). Therefore one should take into account the possibility of changes in Slavic
burial rituals before the beginning of the mission on their lands. However, the very burial
ritual even in pre-Christian times could be a Christian infiltration. See also Łowmiański,
Religia, p. 317; Janowski, *Groby komorowe*, pp. 81 ff.

603 Bylina, *Problemy*, pp. 10 f.

604 Thietmar VIII, 3, p. 583.

605 *Ibidem*, VIII, 2.

severe punishment, the prince cannot put them to any useful purpose."[606] The chronicler's reference to similarity with animals, which must be tamed, in the context of severe punishment for sexual offences leads to an association with a very common view at that time that sexual chaos was befitting for cattle. Introduction of order in this sphere, in the contemporary mentality, indicated the existence of *cum lege et rege* community.[607] In the same spirit, Boleslav, apart from new church customs[608] and especially fasting,[609] firmly maintained the native tradition of counteracting sexual freedom, which was willingly accepted by the Bishop of Merseburg: "In her [*i.e.* Oda's] husband's [*i.e.* Boleslav] kingdom, the customs are many and varied. They are also harsh, but occasionally quite praiseworthy."[610] In this context, the information about kill-

---

606 Trans. D.A. Warner in: *Ottonian Germany*, pp. 361 f. Thietmar VIII, 2: "Populus enim suus more bovis est pascendus et tardi ritu asini cąstigandus et sine poena gravi non potest cum salute principis tractari." Cf. *e.g.* B. Kumor, *Praktyka misyjna*, p. 33 f.; Fraesdorff, *Der barbarische Norden*, pp. 247 f.; Andrzej Pleszczyński, Joanna Sobiesiak, Karol Szejgiec, Michał Tomaszek, Przemysław Tyszka, *Historia communitatem facit. Struktura narracji tworzących tożsamości grupowe w średniowieczu* (Wrocław: Chronicon, 2016), pp. 200 f.

607 Banaszkiewicz, *Polskie dzieje*, pp. 142–149.

608 Thietmar VI, 92, p. 449, confirms that Boleslav the Brave, having committed sins, studied church canon law himself to see what penance efface sins, which proves that following legal standards was one of the basic indicators of faith; see Gieysztor, "Przemiany ideologiczne," p. 166; Prucnal, "Władca chrześcijański," pp. 23 f.

609 Thietmar VIII, 2, mentions that in Boleslav the Brave's Poland breaking the meat eating ban after Tempus Septuagesimæ was punished with the knocking out of teeth, which is justified by the chronicler with the specifics of the beginnings of implanting "God's law": "Lex namque divina in hiis regionibus noviter exorta potestate tali melius quam ieiunio ab episcopi instituto corroboratur" (cf. trans. D.A. Warner in: *Ottonian Germany*, p. 362: "The law of God, newly introduced in these regions, gains more strength from such acts of force than from any fast imposed by the bishops"). It is worth mentioning that these methods were used to introduce Lent which was longer than usual and it lasted nine weeks, which additionally shows the exceptional rigourism of the Christianization action promoted by the Polish ruler; see Roman Michałowski, "Post dziewięciotygodniowy w Polsce Chrobrego. Studium z dziejów polityki religijnej pierwszych Piastów," *Kwartalnik Historyczny* 104 (2002) 1, pp. 5–39. It is worth remembering that according to Thietmar (IV, 56), Dobrava was to prevail upon Mieszko I to accept baptism exactly by breaking the ban on eating meat during Lent. This was a premise for speculation that Thietmar emphasized the extraordinarily severe fasting in Poland exactly in connection with Dobrava's trespass, however, it is impossible to decide whether there is only a possible association in the chronicler's mind or some particular remembrance about this event in the environment of the early Piast monarchy, which resulted in the specifics of fasting. The very motif of Mieszko's conversion by Dobrava is realisation of the topos of *mulier suadens*, which supports considering the discussed question first of all in the mental and literary culture area.

610 Trans. D.A. Warner in: *Ottonian Germany*, p. 361; cf. Thietmar VIII, 2: "In huius sponsi regno sunt multae consuetudines variae; et quamvis dirae, tamen sunt interdum laudabiles." However, these severe punishments introduced by Boleslav the Brave differed from what was recommended in penitentials. In newly converted Christian countries the role

THE RELIGION OF THE SLAVS IN THIETMAR'S CHRONICLE   181

ing wives instead of evoking disgust for being so drastic, expresses a model of
marital faithfulness.

The fact that Slavic relations were selected as a sort of ideal belongs to a
more extensive cultural context. The medieval Latin historiography, especially
from the 10th c., brings a conviction of the "toughness" of the Slavs, with a simultaneous positive assessment of their marital morality exactly related to a
wife's suicide during the funeral customs of her husband.[611] The earliest confirmation of the topos of self-immolation of a wife on her husband's pyre in the
Latin circle was recorded by the Anglo-Saxon, Winfrid-Boniface: "With such
passion do they share martial love that after her husband dies, a woman does
not want to live any longer. A woman is considered praiseworthy when she
puts herself to death with her own hand and burns herself on one pyre with
her husband."[612] In this case, similarly to the one described by the Merseburg
chronicler, this motif occurs in the context of information about the unusual
strength of faithfulness and love in marriage.

---

of the ruler was also to teach his subjects their religious duties. A model in this respect
was Charlemagne, and Thietmar, who certainly being aware of this tradition, praised
Boleslav the Brave's brutality, see Aleksander Gieysztor, "Ideowe wartości kultury polskiej
w w. X–XI. Przyjęcie chrześcijaństwa," *Kwartalnik Historyczny* 67 (1960) 4, p. 933; cf. *idem*,
"Przemiany ideologiczne," pp. 163, 165; see also Prucnal, "Władca chrześcijański," pp. 12
f., 23. This approval for strict standards gave rise to a variety of scholars' associations.
E.g. Lippelt, *Thietmar von Merseburg*, p. 195, finds in them confirmation of the chronicler's conservatism in which he is like Tacitus in accusing his contemporaries of a corruption of morals. For him the "golden age" was in Otto I's times which was also the time
of Mieszko's pagan rule. On the other hand Kahl, *Die ersten Jahrhunderte*, p. 57, claimed
that in Thietmar's eyes, Boleslav the Brave's activity is praiseworthy as it meant imposing
discipline in the Church spirit of *compellere intrare*. See also: Fraesdorff, *Der barbarische
Norden*, pp. 247 f.; Pleszczyński, *Niemcy*, p. 34; cf. *idem*, *The Birth of a Stereotype*, p. 31;
Goetz, *Die Wahrnehmung*, p. 198.

611   Lech A. Tyszkiewicz, "Slavi genus hominum durum," in *Wokół stereotypów Niemców
i Polaków*, ed. Wojciech Wrzesiński (Acta Universitatis Wratislaviensis. Historia) 114
(Wrocław: Wydawnictwo Uniwersytetu Wrocławskiego, 1993), pp. 8, 11–13. The topical
character is connected here not only to wives' suicides, but also *duritia* of the Slavs discussed by L.A. Tyszkiewicz in reference to the characteristics of these people written by
Widukind (II, 20) and available in earlier sources.

612   *Bonifatius una cum aliis episcopis Aethelbaldum regem Mercionum ad virtutem revocat*, in:
S. Bonifatii et Lulli Epistolae, ed. Wilhelm Gundlach, Ernst Dümmler, MGH Epp 3, Epp
Merovingici et Karolini aevi 1 (1892), Ep. 73, p. 342, or: *S. Bonifatii et Lulli Epistolae*, ed.
Michael Tangl, MGH Epp sel 1 (1916), Ep. 73, p. 150: "tam magno zelo matrimonii amorem
mutuum observant, ut mulier viro proprio mortuo vivere recuset. Et laudabilis mulier
inter illos esse iudicatur, quia propria manu sibi mortem intulerit et in una strue pariter
ardeat cum viro suo"; cf. Brückner, *Mitologia słowiańska i polska*, p. 63; Tyszkiewicz, "Slavi
genus," p. 8.

182   CHAPTER 2

Opinions related to the cognitive value of this and other topoi in studies on the pre-Christian customs of the early Slavs are divided, however, it is hard not to agree with the opinion of Lech A. Tyszkiewicz, that "even the biggest stereotypes were formed on some factual substrate, hence common opinions in antique, Byzantine and western European historiography of the Slavs were based on certain reality connected with their true character."[613] Therefore references to wives committing suicide at their husbands' funerals can be considered as a form of emphasizing one of the characterological features of Slavic peoples, which once it was observed, became a part of a fixed set of views about them.

This does not mean that it was a common practice, at least due to the fact that there are few double graves that have been excavated in Slavdom.[614] Jerzy Dowiat concluded that "we read in sources about living Slavic widows often enough to decisively reject the idea of forcing them to die together with their husbands." This author is more supportive of the view that more likely one of the female slaves, and not the wife, was burnt on a funeral pyre to accompany the deceased.[615] The same view was expressed by Helena Zoll-Adamikowa, however, she did not exclude that a wife's suicide occurred as well and was "certainly the consequence of complex impulses first of all of a social nature and possibly also for more emotional reasons."[616]

The multiplication of the topos discussed here could result from following in the footsteps of earlier authors and therefore also typical erudite preparation of contemporary authors. When writing about the Slavs, they used clichés and common views (although not completely groundless ones) to exemplify their own opinions.

---

613   Tyszkiewicz, *Slavi genus*, p. 5. Similarly Zoll-Adamikowa, *Wczesnośredniowieczne cmentarzyska*, part 2, p. 170. L.A. Tyszkiewicz's opinion is a polemic against B. Zašterová's position (cf. Bohumila Zášterová, "Les Avares et les Slaves dans la Tactique de Maurice," *Rozprawy Československé Akademie Věd* 81 (1971), pp. 3–82), who considered this type of schematic opinion as deprived of any substantial value in research on Slavic customs.

614   Urbańczyk, *Dawni Słowianie*, p. 61; Gediga, *Śladami*, p. 168; Bylina, *Człowiek i zaświaty*, p. 21. Some of these double burials were an effect of unfortunate events in which both spouses lost their lives, see *e.g.* Anna Wrzesińska, Jacek Wrzesiński, "Amor et mors – wczesnośredniowieczne groby podwójne," in *Viae historicae. Księga jubileuszowa dedykowana Profesorowi Lechowi A. Tyszkiewiczowi w siedemdziesiątą rocznicę urodzin*, ed. Mateusz Goliński, Stanisław Rosik, (Acta Universitatis Wratislaviensis. Historia) 152 (Wrocław: Wydawnictwo Uniwersytetu Wrocławskiego, 2001), pp. 435–444.

615   Jerzy Dowiat, "Normy postępowania i wzory osobowe," in *Kultura Polski średniowiecznej X–XIII w.*, ed. Jerzy Dowiat (Warszawa: PIW, 1985), p. 312.

616   Zoll-Adamikowa, *Wczesnośredniowieczne cmentarzyska*, part 2, p. 190. The authoress emphasized that the sources did not report any psychological pressure of the environment, which could lead to suicides among female Slavs, contrary to the customs of the Germanic Heruli (Procopius's testimony).

THE RELIGION OF THE SLAVS IN THIETMAR'S CHRONICLE   183

2.12   *The Obodrite Pagan Reaction (1018)*

The continuation of the Liutici plot, and at the same time the last confirmation of their activity in the pages of Thietmar's chronicle, is the information about their attack on the Obodrite duke Mstislav in 1018. According to the chronicler, the assault was their revenge for the Obodrite absence at the German and Liutici's expedition against Boleslav the Brave a year earlier.[617] It can also be explained by the fact that Henry II goaded the Liutici to punish the Obodrite duke for disobedience.[618]

However, this is only speculation and it seems more certain that the chronicler's intention was to show that Mstislav failed at his obligation, which makes the Liutici a tool used by the heavens, similarly to the description of the rebellion in 983 with reference to the Saxons. This plot remains in the shadow of the predominant narrative. It is striking that the assessment of the Liutici in this case is much stricter than earlier; this time the chronicler was not bound by their alliance with the empire.

Mstislav, beset by his enemies, was forced to leave the country, especially since the Liutici invasion – according to Thietmar, "in evil always consentaneous"[619] – was supported by the rebellious subjects of the duke. More precisely, "by the local people, rebellious against Christ and their own sovereign."[620] Thus, their rebellion against the duke's power turned out to be simultaneously an insurgency against Christ, and together with the Liutici invasion it was quite negatively assessed as an abhorrent trespass (*abominabilis*

---

617   Thietmar VIII, 5. See Turasiewicz, *Dzieje polityczne*, pp. 120 ff.; Babij, *Wojskowość*, p. 148.

618   *E.g.* Stanisław Zakrzewski, *Bolesław Chrobry Wielki* (Lwów: Ossolineum, 1925), p. 291; cf. Turasiewicz, *Dzieje polityczne*, p. 121. Quite different opinion was expressed by Sułowski, *Sporne problemy* p. 163, he perceived the attack of the Obodrite as a continuation of the Liutici activity from the times of their alliance with the empire, which weakened Boleslav the Brave's influences on their lands and fuelled the war which was also devastating for the Saxons. The Liutici took advantage of the exhaustion of the Christian antagonists after a long war and they attacked the stranded Obodrite duke themselves by sparking off a rebellion of his subjects. In the light of this interpretation the Liutici Federation is presented as an entity pursuing long term, consistent policy of weakening Christian influences in Polabia, by using any possible opportunity. Attributing to the Liutici this type of planned activity seems unverifiable, to say the least, and it is contradicted by their stable cooperation with the Germans, which by definition did not foster the plans of native cults' restitution in Polabia. For a more pertinent choice of the direction in searching for the genesis of the war in the growing Obodrite–Liutici antagonism based on political and religious differences see M.Z. Jedlicki in: Thietmar, VIII, 5, p. 587, footnote 26. Another possibility which should be taken into account is the idea that the attack was agreed on between the Liutici and the internal opposition of Mstislav (see below).

619   Thietmar VIII, 5: "in malo semper unanimes".

620   *Ibidem*: "per indigenas Christo seniorique proprio rebelles".

praesumptio). It is worth taking into account here that the Liutici attack took place in agreement with the internal opposition against Mstislav, for which the non-monarchic rule of the Liutici could also be an attractive option, along with a return to native beliefs and cults.

The chronicler mentions that the events took place "in the month of February which the heathen venerate with rites of purification and obligatory offerings. The month takes its name from the god of hell, Pluto, who is also called Februus."[621] The expression referring to worship given to the month, practiced by the pagans in the form of offerings and gifts, would indicate that it was a holy time, but the context of this information does not define which pagans are meant, only the ancient Roman ones or, more universally, any pagans.

Therefore, it should be taken into account that in this passage the chronicler was possibly referring to celebrations which in his culture had been interpreted as – since ancient times – related to Pluto, but in fact were known in his own time,[622] *e.g.* the Slavic cult of the dead, in which the idea of the underworld was significant. The idea to find a reference in Thietmar's "Pluto" to a similarly named Slavic deity however, *e.g.* Pereplut known from Rus',[623] can hardly be verified and is very difficult to explain from the perspective of the chronicler's erudition.[624]

---

621   Trans. D.A. Warner in: *Ottonian Germany*, p. 364. Thietmar VIII, 5: "Haec abominabilis presumptio fit mense Februario qui a gentilibus lustracione et muneris debiti exhibicione venerandus ab infernali deo Plutone, qui Februus dicitur, hoc nomen accepit."

622   In the Polish translation of the chronicle by M.Z. Jedlicki (see Thietmar, p. 586) appears the statement that "pagans worship February" by propitations, purification offerings and due gifts, which support the considered possibility. However, the version proposed by the translator deviates from the Latin text, in which the context of using gerundivum *venerandus* can also refer to the past.

623   Kulišić, *Stara Slovenska religija*, p. 148. For "Pereplut" see Urbańczyk, *Dawni Słowianie*, p. 183.

624   Firstly, there are no other confirmations for such a literary procedure in Thietmar's chronicle. Secondly, Roman deities functioned in it either in the explicit context of ancient Roman or Greek religions, or as a metaphor, for which there are good examples related to Mars: the first of these trends is depicted in the legend about the beginnings of Merseburg (I, 2) and the other one a reference to the civil war in the territory of the Netherlands (1018), Thietmar VIII, 27: "... Mars sevit in viscera, quod in perpetuum plangit mater aecclesia" (cf. trans. D.A. Warner in: *Ottonian Germany*, p. 380, VIII, 27: "... Mars raged among us in a fashion that mother church would forever lament"). On the other hand one should turn attention to the above discussed way in which Thietmar used a quotation from *Dialogues of Saint Gregory the Great*: the way the expression "quidam gentiles" functions in this case does not allow to clearly state whether it refers to a particular pagan environment in the Late Antiquity or a certain fraction of pagans which could still exist in the chronicler's times (see above, pp. 69 f.).

THE RELIGION OF THE SLAVS IN THIETMAR'S CHRONICLE   185

Provided that it is possible that the chronicler referred here to pagan customs, including the customs of the Polabian Slavs – although this is hardly probable – then one should take into account that *interpretatio Romana* could have some influence here, and a good comparative example would be the statue of Saturn, mentioned by Widukind of Corvey, which was looted by the Saxons after they conquered Starigard (Oldenburg), the major Wagrian centre in 967.[625]

In this case the very emphasis on particular pagan practices related to Pluto, especially in the context of the ancient tradition, strengthens the significance of the spiritual element hostile to Christianity, especially in the atmosphere of a description of a war. This could be understood in the context of the information that war started in February, during which since ancient times idolatry had flourished in a gloomy dimension related to death. The same climate accompanies further lines of this description presenting the triumph of paganism: "Then, all of the churches, dedicated to the honour and service of Christ, were wasted by fire and other forms of destruction. Even worse, the image of the crucified Christ was mutilated and the worship of idols was preferred to that of God."[626]

The devastation of churches and the symbolical cutting off of the image of the Holy Cross was to accompany the introduction of the cult of idols which were put above God, which, for yet another time on the pages of the chronicle, refers to the idea of *creaturam anteponere creatori*.[627] The mind (*mens*) of the Wagrians and Obodrite hardened in their obstinacy against God like "Pharaoh's heart."[628] Delivery of these people from slavery, following the Liutici, meant regaining political freedom, but at the same time departure from "the best Father and the noblest Lord" and the rejection of the "sweet yoke of Christ" to accept the "burden of devil's rule,"[629] which – according to the chronicler – was to be deplored by Christians and led them to plead with Christ so that this change would not be lasting.[630]

---

625 See above, pp. 54 f.

626 Trans. D.A. Warner in: *Ottonian Germany*, p. 364; cf. Thietmar VIII, 5: "Tunc omnes aecclesiae ad honorem et famulatum Christi in hiis partibus erectae incediis et destructionibus aliis cecidere et, quod miserabillimum fuit, imago Crucifixi truncata est cultusque idolorum Deo prepositus erigitur ...".

627 Following the model of the Epistle of St. Paul to the Romans (Rom 1:25); cf. Thietmar III, 19.

628 Thietmar VIII, 5: "... ut cor Faraonis ad haec induratur" – cf. Exod 7:13; Mt 11:30.

629 Thietmar VIII, 5: "... cervicem suam suavi iugo Christi excussam oneroso diabolicae dominacionis ponderi sua sponte subdiderant, meliori prius patre ac nobiliori domino in omnibus usi".

630 *Ibidem.*

186   CHAPTER 2

In the next chapter the chronicler developed the motif of the apostasy of
the Slavs being considered as *gens apostata*.[631] These events could appear to
their contemporaries to anticipate the near end of the world and the Last
Judgement, but the chronicler reassuringly does not share this opinion, referring to the authority of St. Paul:[632] "Let no faithful heart despair because of this
misfortune, or believe that the Day of Judgement is fast approaching since,
according to Paul's truthful admonition, one should not speak of such things
prior to the discord and cursed arrival of the Antichrist. Nor should there be
any sudden unrest among Christians, since their unanimity and stability ought
to be the highest."[633]

These passages did not attract the attention of researchers studying the religion of the Slavs too strongly, and actually their vagueness did not contribute
to the progress of its reconstruction. However, from the perspective of studies
on the interpretation of paganism, the usefulness of these chapters should be
very highly assessed. Similar to the description of the rebellion of the Polabian
Slavs in 983, they are a perfect example of the theological interpretation of
history conducted by the Bishop of Merseburg, which becomes clear after a
summary view of this material.

The basic classification of the pagan religion at the level of the word – *cultus
idolorum* – is connected to pejorative assessments of the character and attitudes of its followers: "in malo semper unanimes" ("always unanimous in evil")
regarding the Liutici or rebels (*rebelles*) against the worldly rule and Christ
himself in the case of Obodrite supporting apostasy. A striking element, indicating the unity of paganism in ancient times and contemporary to Thietmar,
is the reference to Pluto-Februus in the description of the time of these stormy
events. Another noteworthy element was a series of images taken from the
Christian tradition used in the interpretation of these events and attitudes of
Slavs: cutting off the Cross (*i.e.* image of the crucified Christ), putting idolatry
above the cult of the real God, Pharaoh's hardened heart like in the Book of

---

631   *Ibidem*, VII, 6: "Bernardus (…) apostatae istius gentis (…) episcopus …"
632   It is possible to find here a reference especially to 2 Thess 2:1 ff., which becomes even more
       probable due to Thietmar's clear reference to this text very near to this place, in: Thietmar
       VIII, 3, thus a little earlier (cf. 2 Thess 2:8).
633   Trans. D.A. Warner in: *Ottonian Germany*, p. 365; cf. Thietmar VIII, 6: "Nullius fidelis cor
       ob hanc infelicitatem in aliquam desperacionem veniat vel diem iudicii appropinquare
       dicat, quia secundum veredici ammonicionem Pauli ante dissensionem et Antichristi ex-
       ecrabilem adventum non debet e talibus aliquis oriri sermo nec inter christocolas subita
       venire commocio, cum eorundem unanimitas esse debeat in summis stabilitas." See also
       Schulmeyer-Ahl, *Der Anfang*, p. 174.

THE RELIGION OF THE SLAVS IN THIETMAR'S CHRONICLE   187

Exodus, rejection of the "sweet yoke" of Jesus only to accept devil's oppression or departure from "the best Father and the noblest master." Finally, the Slavic rebellion earned itself the name of apostasy; however, in the comment of the Bishop of Merseburg, it was not the final one as is understood in the Revelation.

3   The Religion of the Slavs in Thietmar's Chronicle – Closing
          Remarks

The original paganism of the Slavs in Thietmar's times in the literary perspective of his work belongs to the past. Evidence for this can be found primarily for Poland (the cult of Ślęża Mountain and burial ceremonies connected with killing widows). However, the cults of the Polabian tribes, so dynamic in his times, were treated by him as paganism resulting from apostasy, and due to this, even more worthy of condemnation.

Thietmar did not perceive ties to Christianity only in a personal dimension, but also as a dependence of particular communities, *gentes*, on Christian power, and especially the empire. In this way, regardless of the degree of advancement of personal conversion in these communities, which were being converted at that time, the very rebellion against the supreme power of Christian monarchy gained the dimension of apostasy. This is confirmed in the interpretation of the rebellion of the Liutici (983) who, according to Thietmar, rejected not only the dependence of the emperor but also the rule of Christ and St. Peter. Similarly, the Obodrite and Wagrians who rebelled against their duke (1018) were symptomatically defined by this author as "Christo seniorique proprio rebelles" ("rebellious against Christ and their own sovereign"), and also as *gens apostata*.

However, in places where the rule of the Christian monarchy and the related diocesan organization were not overthrown, people were not treated as pagan even when they practiced idolatry or worshiped sanctuaries embodied in nature. This refers to both communities in which Christianity was newly implanted (the diocesans of Reinbern or Chutici worshipping the holy grove of *Zutibure*) and communities encompassed by evangelization activity, but practicing "dual faith" (*e.g.* the Glomaci visiting the holy spring more often than churches, or worshippers of the "house god" called Hennil).

In this situation people under the care of bishops, even if they were at the stage prior to accepting Christianity, were treated as uneducated (even simplistic or stupid, like in *e.g.* the episode related to Reinbern), requiring a lot of catechetical effort, but at the same time no longer called pagan. Yet they can commit sins typical of pagans, which is shown in the reproach directed to Hennil's worshippers that they do not know *The Psalms of David*: "Simulacra gentium opera hominum (*etc.*)." However, the context of the narration indicates that Thietmar stigmatizes common ignorance in the matters of the Christian doctrine accompanied by idolatry among the inhabitants of the area of Walbeck.

The chronicler has a structured approach to Church Teaching: he indicates that literacy is the foundation for proclaiming the Christian faith from generation to generation. The Bible, *credo* of St. Athanasius, the works of the Church Fathers, *etc.*, are all critically important. "Scriptures" in Thietmar's perspective bring the essential knowledge of paganism in the light of theology, which is however, to a large extent detached from the historical substrate perceived from the perspective of the current state of research on the religion of the Slavs. *Inlitterati* form the dominant category in his assessment of pre-Christian or being Christianized Slavs, defining wide social circles at that time, which did not participate in the written culture and the knowledge and values that it brought.

A clear example of using the measure of the Church doctrine to the native views of Slavs is the view that "cum morte temporali omnia (...) finiri" ("everything ends with the temporal death"). The question about afterlife in relation to the Slavs, asked from the perspective of the Christian *credo*, remains in a vacuum: they do not respect judgement for their sins or resurrection, and possibly – not much however, because the fragments of *The Dialogues* of St. Gregory the Great quoted by the chronicler are only a trace in this issue – they do not see the difference between the fate of people and animals after death. Similarly conditioned by a religious mentality, the reactions of the Polabian people to the efforts of Bishop Boso to teach them to sing *Kyrie* (hypothetically: undertaking mantic practices, fear of the wrath of previous gods, a will to use Boso's authority as an agent between them and God, an attempt to camouflage their native beliefs) was read as a malicious mockery of prayer – which can also hardly be excluded – and at the same time as signs of stupidity.

The same measure is used by Thietmar (III, 19) to assess the attitudes of the Slavs who are presented as pagans (apostates); he emphasizes that they treated idols irrationally ("stulto"), *i.e.* they put the creation above the Creator (cf. Rom 1:25). The chronicler declares his abhorrence of the Liutici idolatry and viewed contact with them and their cult as dangerous (VI, 25: "Eorum cum cultu consorcia, lector, fugias ..." – "Avoid, reader, any connections with them or their cult ..."). These threats can be prevented by learning the Church

THE RELIGION OF THE SLAVS IN THIETMAR'S CHRONICLE   189

doctrine, however, the Bishop of Merseburg does not start a polemic with particular views of pre-Christian Slavs, as was the case in the early Christian apologetics. To ridicule their attitude, it was enough to qualify it as stupidity and sin, which in essence involved "putting the creation above the Creator."

In this perspective, the juxtaposition of paganism and Christianity in Thietmar's work is subdued to the supreme contradiction between the "faithful" and the "unfaithful" to God: (*christi*)*fideles* – *infideles*. Unfaithfulness certainly characterizes pagans or apostates in the social dimension, yet in theological assessment as such it has an universal nature, because it refers to every man due to his sinful nature; Thietmar expresses this view speaking about "the poison of innate unfaithfulness" (*innatae infidelitatis toxicum*), which a man can reject through baptism.

For Thietmar the world is essentially – like in the Bible or patristics (especially St. Augustine's thought) – a stage on which there is an ongoing struggle between good and evil. Nonetheless, this confrontation refers also to phenomena in nature, and a good example here is the description of Reinbern's activity when he performed the ritual of expelling demons from the sea, hence attempting to use Christ's power to control the powers of eternal chaos posing a threat to the order of the cosmos. An element of key significance in the assessment of the phenomena of social life, and especially human attitudes and activities, conducted by the Bishop of Merseburg, is the antinomy of the orders of grace (faithfulness to God and good deeds) and sin (service to the Satan and demons, trespasses).

In this perspective, the Slavic religion is basically (and obviously) situated on the side of evil. However, in his work Thietmar sometimes shaped the attitudes and opinions in his own environment while withholding a negative assessment of paganism. This is why the promotion of marital morality inclined him to show Slavic wives who lost their lives in the burial ritual of their husbands as a model of faithfulness. The chronicler mentions that this happened when Mieszko I was pagan ("cum is iam gentilis esset"), but the said practice was not interpreted in categories of sin or stupidity.

Another place in which one can observe a striking lack of negative assessment of pagan cult practice is the description of how the Liutici made an offering of the Polish leader of the stronghold given to them by a Christian ruler, Czech Boleslav, to tutelary gods. This deed undoubtedly deserved condemnation like the one found in the Letter of St. Bruno,[634] yet – as can be conjectured – Thietmar put the good of the Saxons first. They owed their rescue to the Czech

---

634   See above, pp. 107 f.

ruler, and so he did not criticize him (and hence also his pagan allies) for the deed which ordinarily would be disgraceful from a Christian point of view.

Thietmar also refrained from open condemnation of the Liutici in the description of the war in 1017, when they were Henry II's allies in his fight with Boleslav the Brave. Certainly, being convinced that loyalty to the Emperor was a fundamental duty of each member of the Christian community subordinate to him,[635] the chronicler reproves instigators who tried to persuade the participants of an expedition against Poland to abandon it. Thietmar found it hard to accept the said alliance with non-Christians, however, in this case he moderately expressed his emotions. He presented an incident in which one of the Saxons, to show his outrage with the company of the Liutici, destroyed the image, probably the holy banner, of their goddess with a stone, yet first and foremost he morally appreciated Henry II's opponents from the Polish side.

The defenders of Niemcza, besieged by his army, are presented as model Christians. They resisted the Liutici assault by raising a cross against the attackers in confidence that it would bring victory. This scene becomes even more convincingly impressive due to the fact that it takes place in the country whose name was derived by the chronicler, without concealing negative emotions, from a mountain worshipped during the times of the "condemned paganism" (*execranda gentilitas*). In this context, it is hard not to talk about the disgrace of Henry II and the Saxons, because *de facto* they stood out against Christ's cross, and additionally they guaranteed their pagan allies freedom of worship. This was indicated by the attitude of the defenders of Niemcza, to whose land – according to Thietmar – paganism was in its past.

From a historiological perspective the statement that the losses incurred by the emperor and Christian participants of his expedition, as a result of their sins, was of key significance. The Liutici suffered as well, as they lost another "goddess" (after the first one, as was already mentioned, was hit with a stone). In this context it is completely understandable that emphasis was put on the fact that Boleslav the Brave, happy that Niemcza was defended, was described as "rejoicing in the Lord." Hence he was on the side of the good, in a moral and theological assessment, yet it was an exception from Thietmar's recorded treatment of the ruler.

Therefore Thietmar, being a clergyman and a diplomat, respecting the essential dimension of grace or sin in the assessment of his characters' behaviour, respected also the hierarchy of the world he lived in and the wellbeing of his close ethnic community *i.e.* the Saxons. Open condemnation of the Liutici

---

635   This particular role of the emperor as the leader of the Christian community is reflected in his title *vicarius Dei* (see above, p. 50).

THE RELIGION OF THE SLAVS IN THIETMAR'S CHRONICLE 191

and their religion became possible when it did not mean direct criticism of
the emperor or when it did not cast a shadow on the Saxons' benefactors. It
is not accidental that the strongest criticism of pagans appears in the excurse
on Radogošč, which is a separate entity,[636] and also in the description of their
rebellion in 983 and the Obodrite invasion in 1018, in which Thietmar is un-
stinting in hateful words and the most pejorative assessments (*e.g.* "in malo
semper unanimes").

In the literary perspective, they are a tool used by Satan and at the same time
their victory over Christians is treated as heaven's punishment for Saxons' sins.
However, the soothing information that the Obodrite "apostasy" should not be
perceived as a sign of the immediate arrival of the apocalyptic Antichrist directly indicates that the chronicler referred the reflection on the historical role
of returns to paganism to the essence of the Christian historiology. The axis
of his presentation of confrontation between good and evil on the historical
stage is determined by the juxtaposition of God/Christ, St. Peter, the Church
and the Christian faith to Satan, demons, idols, deities/gods, paganism (with
its institutions), and heresy.

Thietmar used notions associated with terminology taken from the Bible
to define the nature of paganism. From his perspective one can even say that
he >>recognized<< particular elements of Slavic beliefs and cults as universal
phenomena embodying *antisacrum* even in the Old Testament. This is why
images of Slavic gods in his perspective are synonymous with idols, demons'
statues, deities, and first and foremost "gods made by hand" (*dii manu facti*),
who in the convention developed by Thietmar combine in themselves the material and the spiritual dimension. By this definition they are made by man, an
object, and yet they envision spiritual power and by doing so they provide real
support to their worshippers.

Even effigies accompanying the Liutici troops, in the narration of Thietmar's
chronicle, become gods and goddesses. Also, the figure named Hennil gains the
name of *domesticus deus*. Using this category of interpretation of gods' representations, Thietmar took into consideration the respect paid to these types of
hierophanies by pagans themselves. To some extent >>he went to their side<<
in interpretation of their *sacrum*, introducing an element of personification of
their idols to the description. It is significant that he attributes irascible personality; human offerings were to tame their "unutterable" (*ineffabilis*) anger
and fury (*ira, furor*).

---

636 Immediately after the end of the excurse about the Liutici cult, there is only enigmatic
information about a lack of balance in the command of the allied Liutici–German forces,
in which one can conjecture an allusion to idols carried in front of the pagan forces.

Hence, in Thietmar's literary convention, pagan gods are bodily present on earth, which hypothetically permits the term *ministri* ("servants") to be used to refer to priests controlling the cult in Radogošč. Typical terms used in such cases, such as *pontifex, flamen,* or *sacerdos,* combine the idea of agents mediating between people and invisible deities or God, while in Thietmar's works idols are incarnated, or rather produced, deities.[637] On the other hand, it is worth taking into account that the Bishop of Merseburg used the term *ministri,* following the *Vulgate,* in which this is the word used to refer to temple servants, meanwhile the term under discussion was used to refer to Radogošč, treated on the pages of the chronicle as the holy city, like the biblical Jerusalem with its famous temple.

Radogošč, holding primacy (*principalis monarchia*) over other temples located in Liutici *regiones,* or possibly those of their neighbours as well ("in his partibus"), according to Thietmar, is the centre of institutional paganism. In this way it took shape bearing a resemblance to the church organization or monarchy. In this context Svarožic resembles the deities of the Old Testament pagan peoples (*e.g.* Baal), whose cult as idolatry was in opposition to worshipping Yahweh-God. Radogošč itself similarly the other Slavonic temples, in this perspective are agencies of the rule of *antisacrum* – demonic powers – in the social and territorial space.

Nonetheless, there is no diabolization of Svarožic (like in St. Bruno's letter to Henry II), and it is doubtful whether Thietmar created this hegemon of the Liutici pantheon as the *princeps* of demons (as was the case later with Redigast in Adam of Bremen's work). Spiritual powers being in opposition to Christ's kingdom are presented also as being manifest in the world without any close relation to objects of idolatry.[638] They haunt some characters, and at the same time manifest their presence in nature, especially in Reinbern's spectacular episode where they inhabit the sea.

The description of the ritual in which they were to be chased away by this bishop does not offer unambiguous premises supporting the opinion that, according to Thietmar, he simultaneously fought against the cult of the sea. However, one should take such a possibility into account, because natural

---

637 However, another possible explanation of the occurrence of the term *minister* and not *sacerdos* or *pontifex,* which does not contradict the ones presented above, can be the taking into account by the chronicler of the difference between the functions of the Christian clergy and Liutici priests.

638 In the case of Hennil's cult, according to Thietmar, the sin of idolatry meant various peculiar manifestations of evil (monsters, spectres led by the Satan) occurring not only in the place where a folk rite related to this fetish was performed but also in the whole surrounding area.

THE RELIGION OF THE SLAVS IN THIETMAR'S CHRONICLE 193

hierophanies, such as Ślęża Mountain, the holy grove (*Zutibure*), or the Glomač spring, are presented by him as Slavic cult objects addressed directly to them. Therefore, similar to the case of idols, Thietmar's view harmonizes the concept of "putting creation above the Creator" (cf. Rom 1:25). In this context it is also worth taking into consideration the respect paid, as a reference, to Radogošč as a holy city by the Liutici.

In reference to the Glomač spring, the chronicler emphasized that according to local people, miraculous events and supernatural phenomena (*mira*) take place there. This remains in agreement with the wider context of this work, in which numerous times he showed special interest (*curiositas*) in various curiosities and unusual events, although not always uncritically.[639] Also in the case of Glomač, he made a reservation that he depended on the testimony of the local community related to prophetic signs, such as blood and ash, which were to show in its water. Perforce, however, he showed that he considered the possibility of the occurrence of miraculous events in the place of a cult with native origin, while he unequivocally assessed the motivation for worshipping such *sacrum* as yielding to "vain hopes" (*spes dubia*).

A more stringent assessment of following pagan religion or "dual-faith" is *superstitio*: superstition occurring in a characteristic expression: *vana superstitio erroris*. It appears in the introduction that the description of Radogošč and together with *inanior executio* (vain, senseless activities) defines the Liutici religion as a whole. Similarly, in the presentation of Bishop Wigbert's activity there is a claim that with his teachings he dissuaded the people from "a vain superstition of an error" ("a vana superstitione erroris,") and next cut down the grove worshipped by them. Both examples of using the said formula refer to phenomena occurring in different social contexts – the Liutici were officially pagan, while *Chutici* were a Christianized community (with potential baptized members) that was controlled by the power of the bishopric.

Thus, the *superstitio erroris* qualification with reference to a particular expression of religious life was not only reserved for the description of paganism. This assessment refers to a trespass of an erroneous choice of the subject of the faith and cult, which is one of the measures of a breach of Church doctrine or discipline, because the term *superstitio* is used in such an extensive meaning of

---

639 For example Thietmar shows detachment when he mentions the story about a wild boar appearing from a lake in Radogošč, to announce a civil war, and it should also be emphasized that *e.g.* the solar eclipse, following Macrobius's views, was considered by him as a phenomenon related to the moon (IV, 15), hence he explained it using rational terms, as much as it was possible given the development of science at that time.

194   CHAPTER 2

the pages of Thietmar's chronicle.[640] Thus by assumption, the Liutici are seen
to have breached Christian faith due to the conviction (from Thietmar's time)
that having access to it, they made the wrong choice and gave it up. There are
only two orders that matter: grace and sin – by not accepting faith, pagans
are automatically doomed to remain in sin.[641] This is an excellent example of
failing to penetrate pagan thought and refusing to start a dialogue with their
religious ideas.

This element of the evaluation of the Slavic religion is visible in the emotional climate of the chronicle's description. An alternative to the chronicler's indifference in this case is a release of negative emotions (*e.g.* "dicere
perhorescam").[642] It is also worth paying attention to an element of terror
which is present in, for example "a reference to the wrath of gods and their
yearning for human offerings", and it is also connected with the weirdness factor, *e.g.* the lake in Radogošč appears frightful ("horribile monstrat"), and the
local temple was to be built on the horns of a beast, or wild animals. Similarly,
the magnitude of Mt. Ślęża and its attributes decided its veneration, and its
exceptional sacral significance was emphasized by the chronicler, who used
epithets to refer to it as typical of holy mountains in model biblical images
(*mons grandis et altus*).

Finally, it is worth paying attention to various ways of expressing the character of the pre-Christian cult and its hierarchy. Worship of divine creatures or
some natural hierophanies treated "as a god" (the holy grove – *Zutibure*) was
distinguished from respect for the prophetic horse from Radogošč worshipped
as sacred (*ut sacer*). Thietmar also shows the hierarchy of cult places, when
speaking about *principalis monarchia* of Radogošč in comparison with other
temples in Polabia.[643] Premises for hypothetical conclusions on this matter
can also be found by observing characteristic ways of using verb forms in the
chronicler's account.

---

640   It is worth indicating the use of the term *superstitio* by Thietmar (VI, 41) to refer to negli-
      gence of duties by a bishop.
641   It should be emphasized that the classical qualification of idolatry as putting the creation
      above the Creator (Rom 1:25), on the pages of the Epistle of St. Paul to the Romans is
      combined with emphasis on the fact that the pagans cannot excuse themselves from sins
      by committing such an offence, as they can recognize the Creator looking at his works (cf.
      Wis 13:1–9).
642   Hatred to pagan Slavs is pejoratively depicted *e.g.* in the expression *avari canes*, but it is
      not reserved only for Slavs.
643   Meticulosity requires to mention also that the Glomač spring was more respected by local
      people than churches, but this is only a vague indication in determination of the intensity
      of this cult, because it is not known if they respected churches at all and if yes then to
      what extent.

THE RELIGION OF THE SLAVS IN THIETMAR'S CHRONICLE   195

The words *colere* and *inmolare*, as well as expressions used to describe bringing down wrath (*e.g. iram placare*), were referred to gods and idols by the chronicler – *dii* (*dii manu facti*), *deae, dii domestici, simulacra demonum* – including above all Svarožic. It is possible to observe here the personalistic treatment of *sacrum*, contrary to the word *venerare*, which refers to very wide notions, such as paganism (*gentilitas*), practicing heresy (*varia demoniacae heresis cultura*), but also holy places (the Glomač spring), time (the month of February) or a holy animal (the horse). The verb *timere* certainly functioned in a similar way with reference to respect or reverential fear of the Glomač spring.

However, the verb *honorare* was used to define worship for the holiest of holies, *i.e.* gods/idols (Svarožic), as well as places and sanctuaries – Mt. Ślęża, the holy grove *Zutibure*, Radogošč. In Thietmar's perspective it is a deified object, a work of humans or an element of nature[644] and – essential in such a case – the expression of attributing to these existences the highest cultic rank by the Slavs was their personification. It is well shown in the greeting (*salutare*) of Radogošč by the Liutici when departing on a military expedition.[645]

Observation of linguistic facts going beyond a basic study of terminology that carry an assessment of the pagan religion – such as *error, idolatry* or *superstitio* – opens an opportunity to give a fuller image of individual characteristics of Thietmar's erudition and his way of conceptualizing sacral phenomena shown in his attitude toward the religion of the Slavs. This direction of reflection completes basic dimensions of research on its interpretation on the pages of the chronicle, *i.e.* theological explanation of the essence of paganism, and also indicates the role played by the hostile to Christians *sacrum* in the events presented on the historical stage.

One should consider the influence of the themes of certain episodes on the accentuation of particular aspects of the Slavic cult. The appearance of the Liutici issue, usually in the context of military actions, resulted in the textual image of Svarožic and the other deities as war patrons. Such narrow specialization, even if it does not constitute historical falsity, constitutes evidence of the

---

644   Hence the holy grove *Zutibure* was worshipped "in omnibus ut Deus" (this expression can also reflect the information about a church built in its place and dedicated to "ad honorem Christi").

645   Thietmar did not use the word *honorare* to refer to worshipping the Glomač spring, which most certainly was the major holiness of the Glomače country, which can weaken the proposed here conclusion related to the rank of *e.g.* Ślęża mountain and *Zutibure*. However, it is worth paying attention to the different character of this aquatic hierophany: in this case miraculous phenomena (*mira*) are of essential significance here, hence the very spring with the flood area, although evoking respect and awe, was not directly considered the highest holiness, and was only the place of its revelation.

chronicler's peculiar sensitivity to the military character of deities combined with indifference to other aspects of mythology related to them. Similarly, emphasis on the triangular shape of Radogošč (*urbs tricornis*) must have resulted from a predilection to accentuate the symbolism of numbers (here number three – connected with divinity) typical of this culture.

In some situations, the chronicler most certainly did not recognize the cult nature of some ceremonies, for example when he described the ritual of entering into a peace agreement by the Liutici with a reference to the symbolism of hair and grass. However, it is hard to identify places in which he would confabulate in the presentation of the general characteristics of native beliefs and cult among the Slavs.[646] In other words, accusations that he departed from the truth when writing about the existence of their temples in the areas located east of the Oder (devastated according to his account about Reinbern) are based on too fragile a foundation to discredit the informative value of the data presented by the chronicler who wrote in this case about contemporary events.

---

646   Some doubts among researchers were raised by the information about inscriptions with the names of idols in Radogošč temple; it was considered as the chronicler's fantasy inspired by *e.g.* the equipment of churches. However, here one can also take into account that this element was a form of copying church interiors by the Liutici who had opportunities to come across them. The very idea of alphabetisation of barbarians, even if on such a small scale, actually raises doubts.

CHAPTER 3

Adam of Bremen on Slavic Religion

1   Introduction: Adam of Bremen and His Work

"A. minimus sanctae Bremensis ecclesiae canonicus"[1] – in this humble manner, Adam of Bremen introduced himself on the pages of *Gesta Hammaburgensis ecclesiae pontificum*, yet his name did not sink into oblivion. We know it thanks to a chronicler, Helmold of Bosau,[2] who had a very high opinion of the Master of Bremen's work, and after nearly a century decided to follow it as a model. Scholarship has awarded Adam of Bremen not only with a significant place among 11th-c. writers, but also in the whole period of the Latin Middle Ages.[3]

The historiographic genre of his work, a history of a bishopric, was developed on a larger scale only after the end of the famous conflict on investiture between the papacy and the empire. The very appearance of this trend in historiography was a result of an increase in institutional subjectivity of the particular Church.[4] In the case of the environment of the cathedral in Bremen, one can even say that this phenomenon could be observed at least half a century

---

1   Adam, [Praefatio]. This manner of humble servant refers to St. Paul's writing *e.g.* Eph 3:8; 1 Cor 15:9, and to some extent it seems to be an allusion to Christ's verdict that his disciples quarrelled about which one of them would be the greatest (see Lk 9:48).

2   Helmold I, 14: "Testis est magister Adam, qui gesta Hammemburgensis ecclesiae pontificum disertissimo sermone conscripsit ..." ("The witness is master Adam, who with great skill and fluency described the deeds of the bishops of the Church in Hamburg ...").

3   The biography and personality of Adam of Bremen are discussed by: Max Manitius, *Geschichte der lateinischen Literatur d. Mittelalters*, vol. 2 (München: Beck, 1923), pp. 398–409; Bernhard Schmeidler, "Einleitung," in Adam, pp. lii–lvii; Werner Trillmich, "Einleitung," in *Gesta Hammaburgensis ecclesiae Pontificum*, ed. Werner Trillmich, in *Quellen des 9. und 11. Jahrhunderts zur Geschichte der hamburgischen Kirche und des Reiches*, (Ausgewählte Quellen zur deutschen Geschichte des Mittelalters. Freiherr vom Stein-Gedächtnisausgabe) 11 (Darmstadt: Wissenschaftliche Buchgesellschaft, 1961), pp. 137–158; Francis J. Tschan, "Introduction," in Adam of Bremen, *History of the Archbishops of Hamburg-Bremen*, trans., introduction and notes Francis J. Tschan, reed. and new introduction Timothy Reuther (New York: Columbia University Press, 2002, pp. xxv–xlvi); Timothy Reuther, "Introduction to the 2002 Edition," in Adam of Bremen, *History of the Archbishops*, pp. xi–xxi; Walter Berschin, *Biographie und Epochenstil im lateinischen Mittelalter*, vol. 4: *Ottonische Biographie. Das hohe Mittelalter. 920–1220 n. Chr.*, part 2: *1070–1220 n. Chr.* (Stuttgart: Anton Hiersemann Verlag, 2001), pp. 212 ff.

4   Schmale, "Mentalität und Berichtshorizont," p. 13.

© KONINKLIJKE BRILL NV, LEIDEN, 2020 | DOI:10.1163/9789004331488_005

before the so-called Concordat of Worms (1122), which is confirmed exactly by the work of Adam of Bremen who was a canon there.

All of Adam's work comprises four books, and the last one, differing from the others in its layout and content, titled *Descriptio insularum aquilonis*, is an excellent geographical and ethnographic description that made him rise to fame as the "Tacitus of the people of the North." Biographical information, essential to have a good understanding of his way of working and his literary achievement, is extremely modest and to a large extent hypothetical. B. Schmeidler, who suggests that Adam of Bremen was born shortly before the middle of 11th c., supported the view that he came from eastern Franconia. However, there were also alternative proposals that he could have come from Thuringia, Upper Saxony, or Lotharingia.[5] The place where the future writer received his education also turns out to be disputable, as according to B. Schmeidler it was either Würzburg or, which seems more certain, the famous school in Bamberg.[6] Nevertheless, one should not forget about an earlier thesis, that it was a school in Magdeburg.[7]

In 1066, or in the following year, Adam came to Bremen to manage a cathedral school at the request of archbishop Adalbert (deceased 1072).[8] A year later he accompanied his supervisor on a trip to visit the king of Denmark Sven Estridsen and, although the journey did not cover the whole Danish state and was related to mainly the king's matrimonial affairs,[9] it turned out to be fruitful for his later work as a chronicler. M. Manitius conjectures that a man with such education as Adam must have continuously accompanied Archbishop Adalbert and must have been his confidant and familiar with the archbishop's plans.[10] However, the chronicler's orientation in political and legal matters was

---

5   Schmeidler, "Einleitung," in Adam, pp. liii ff.; Trillmich, *Einleitung*, [in:] *Gesta Hammaburgensis*, p. 137; Berschin, *Biographie*, pp. 211 f.; cf. Philipp Wilhelm Kohlmann, *Adam von Bremen. Ein Beitrag zur mittelalterlichen Textkritik und Kosmographie* (Leipzig: Quelle & Meyer, 1908); Edward Schröder, "Zur Heimat des Adam von Bremen," *Hansische Geschichtsblätter* 23 (1917), pp. 351–366.

6   B. Schmeidler as above; W. Trillmich as above.

7   Manitius, *Geschichte der lateinischen Literatur*, p. 398.

8   This fact is confirmed in a document from 11th June 1069 (see *Hamburgisches Urkundenbuch*, vol. 1, ed. Johann Martin Lappenberg (Hamburg: Pertehs-Besser & Mauke, 1842), No. 101, p. 97), in which there is Adam's original signature with the title of "magister scholarum". See Schmeidler, as in footnote 5 in this page; Manitius, *Geschichte der lateinischen Literatur*, p. 398, suspected that the reason for entrusting Adam with supervision of the cathedral school was Adalbert's intention to raise its level. See also Trillmich, "Einleitung," in *Gesta Hammaburgensis*, pp. 137 f.

9   Adam, III, 54 (53).

10   Manitius, *Geschichte der lateinischen Literatur*, p. 398.

not rated very highly by scholars.[11] He did not acclimatize well in Bremen: he found the Saxons there semi-pagan, with harsh customs, and regarded patriarchal relations in the environment of the cathedral, where he served as a canon, rather offensive.[12] He died in about 1085.[13]

He was well known as a famous geographer in the early Middle Ages, however one should remember that he had wider interests. He received excellent preparation to start work on the theologically-oriented history of the Hamburg-Bremen Church. Adam was also well-read and followed not only the Bible but also the example of antique writers – Virgil and Lucan, Horace, Juvenal and Ovid. His work was under profound influence of Sallustius, from whom he borrowed whole sentences, which was certainly a custom in his times. It is also difficult to imagine that the *magister scholarum* of Bremen would not have encountered the thoughts of St. Augustine, but the question remains to what degree they influenced him and his work. In this case an important input was provided by the historical and theological thread of dualism present in Augustinian historiology.[14]

It is important to mention, however, that the analyses provided below are introducing a different perspective of research in this field. That is, they take into account the specificity of *civitas terrena* as primarily good, and thus not identifying it with *civitas diaboli*.[15] This corresponds well with the presence in Adam's work of the image of barbarians in societies that cultivate praiseworthy customs. However, if one takes into consideration the universality of the binary model of confrontation of good and evil, the dominion of God and dominion of devil, *etc.* in the Christian thought, as well as the presence of the theological conviction about the primarily good nature of pagans present already in the Bible, it is difficult to prove unambiguously that those models were present in Adam's work directly because of St. Augustine's thought.

Adam's scholarship was also influenced by the medieval historiography and hagiography that he used as sources for the chronicle. One should mention

---

11   Trillmich, "Einleitung," in *Gesta Hammaburgensis*, p. 138.

12   *Ibidem*.

13   *Diptychon Bremense*, ed. Ernst F. Mooyer, *Vaterländisches Archiv des Historischen Vereins für Nieder Sachsen* (1835) [1836], p. 304, gives the day of Adam's death: 12 October, see B. Schmeidler, like in footnote 5 in this chapter; Trillmich, "Einleitung," in *Gesta Hammaburgensis*, p. 139.

14   With the use of this binary model, Carl Fredrik Hallencreutz, "Missionsstrategi och religionstolkning: Till frågan om Adam av Bremen och Uppsalatemplet," in *Uppsalakulten och Adam av Bremen*, ed. Anders Hultgård (Nora: Nya Doxa, 1997), pp. 117–130, has interpreted the place of Uppsala in Adam's work as the capital of paganism.

15   The identifying *civitas terrena* with *civitas diaboli* is an excessive simplification of the conception of the aforementioned Church Father, see *e.g.* Bartnik, *Augustyńska historiologia*.

200   CHAPTER 3

here a group of biographies, such as the *Vita Anskari, Vita Rimberti, Vita Willebrordi, Vita Willehadi, Miracula s. Willehadi* by Rimbert, and *Vita Karoli Magni* by Einhard (Adam I, 13). Adam also used chronicles and annals such as the *Historia Francorum* of Gregory of Tours, the *Gesta Francorum* and *Gesta Anglorum, The Chronicle* of Regino of Prüm, *The Swabian World Chronicle*, and the *Annals of Corvey*. Geographical information, especially useful when writing *Descriptio insularum aquilonis*, was taken – perhaps not directly – from the works by Orosius, Solinus, Martianus Capella, Macrobius, and Beda Venerabilis.[16] His references within his work to diplomas awarded by emperors and popes, metropolitan bishops of Hamburg-Bremen preserved "in scriniis ecclesiae nostrae", *i.e.* in archdiocesan archives, and the *Liber donationum Bremensis ecclesiae* are evidence of a thorough preparation as a historiographer.[17]

Some elements of this written legacy melted in Adam's work into harmonious unity with the oral tradition of the environment of the Bremen cathedral. He sought information from its archbishops and their subordinate suffragan bishops, as well as the accounts of the king of Denmark Sven Estridsen, "who kept all the deeds of the barbarians in [his] memory ..."[18] It was observed, however, that even in the details related to Sven's mother, Adam made some errors.[19] This demonstrates that he had a casual approach to some of the facts. This key subject, as has already been mentioned, was the history of the local Church: the *gesta episcoporum* of the Hamburg metropolis were to build a memorable image of its ordinaries' achievements.

In the historiography of the 20th c., Adam was frequently accused of being partial and biased in the way he presented affairs of his own archdiocese.[20] Yet it seems that this "subjectivity" is present while pursuing the pragmatic goals of his writing (*causa scribendi*). Especially since he declared that he was aware of his responsibility for factual reference of the information he presented: "having truth as a witness that nothing from my heart is prophesised, nothing is thoughtlessly defined, but everything which I am about to putdown I will

---

16   Schmeidler, "Einleitung," in Adam, pp. lxii f.; see also Trillmich, "Einleitung," in *Gesta Hammaburgensis*, pp. 147–149, where a few other, less important works are listed as inspirations for Adam's work.

17   Adam, [*Praefatio*]. See: Schmeidler, "Einleitung," in Adam, p. lxi; Trillmich, "Einleitung," in *Gesta Hammaburgensis*, pp. 143, 148.

18   Adam II, 43: "qui omnes barbarorum gestas res in memoria tenuit ...". Trillmich, "Einleitung," in *Gesta Hammaburgensis*, pp. 139 and 143, decided that Adam did not discuss current political issues with Sven.

19   It was observed by B. Schmeidler, see Adam II, 54, p. 114, footnote 4.

20   *E.g.* Manitius, *Geschichte der lateinischen Literatur*, p. 400; Leon Koczy, "Sklawanja Adama Bremeńskiego," *Slavia Occidentalis* 12 (1933), p. 186.

ADAM OF BREMEN ON SLAVIC RELIGION 201

corroborate with certain testimonies, so if one does not believe me, one would at least give faith to the authority [of those testimonies]."[21]

Adam used concise and prudent language, not always grammatically and stylistically correct, and he did not show any liking for sophisticated rhetorical figures and extensive quotations. Some of his sentences lose clarity due to an atypical selection of words and the breaking of stylistic rules to emphasize the sense of his message. Regardless of the above reservations, the chronicler, admittedly, showed that he was well-read in various types of literature and especially the Bible. He often used phraseology taken from the *Psalms* as well as expressions and motifs from Classical Antique writing.

The literary value of Adam's work does not really lie in its language quality but more in the artful composition of his work.[22] The author likely began his work shortly after archbishop Adalbert's death (1072).[23] Book I is a history of the Carolingian mission to Northern Europe and also the Hamburg Bishopric until the year 936. Its central figures are the emperors Charlemagne and Louis the Pious as well as the clergy and the Apostles of Europe: Anskar and Unni. Among the events described in this part, the establishment of the archbishopric in Hamburg and its later fall and merger into one metropolis with Bremen are of key significance. The subject of Book II is a history of Hamburg and Bremen archbishops from 937–1043. In a description of their missionary attempts, Adam does not ignore the affairs of the Ottonian Empire and the formation of monarchies in the North. He is also interested in Saxony, Slavic lands (especially Elbslavs), and Viking expeditions.

These two historical books – written before the end of 1074[24] – are followed by the third one, more biographical in style and devoted to the times and achievements of Archbishop Adalbert (1043–1072). The book, in which the *magister scholarum* from Bremen showed all his literary and historical talent

---

21   Adam, [*Praefatio*], p. 3: "... testem habens veritatem nihil de meo corde prophetari, nihil temere definiri, sed omnia, quae positurus sum, certis roborabo testimoniis, ut si mihi non creditur, saltem auctoritati fides tribuatur".

22   Trillmich, "Einleitung," in *Gesta Hammaburgensis*, pp. 149 f.

23   For discussion on the content organisation and the time when the chronicle was written see Schmeidler, "Einleitung," in Adam, pp. lii–lxvi.

24   Schmeidler, as above, observed that during writing book II Adam received information about Sven Estridsen's death (the 28th of April 1074); cf. Trillmich, "Einleitung," in *Gesta Hammaburgensis*, p. 139.

202   CHAPTER 3

as well as sometimes – which was rather unusual in the epoch – a critical look at the main character.[25] It was finished before August 1075.[26]

Finally, the fourth book: *Descriptio insularum aquilonis*, as it has been mentioned above, is so much different in its form from the remaining books that sometimes it was treated as a separated work and rewritten leaving out the first three volumes. This description of the "islands of the North" *de facto* referred also to lands which were not islands. It was an excellent work in the field of medieval geography and ethnography. It starts with a presentation of Denmark, and continues with the people living in coastal areas near the Baltic Sea and islands, presents the oceanic lands of Iceland and Greenland after a description of Sweden (Svetjud) and Norway,[27] and finally presents Newfoundland (which in the chronicle is called Vinlandia).[28]

The whole work ends with an epilogue apotheosizing the successor of the above-mentioned archbishop Adalbert on the throne of the Hamburg and Bremen metropolis – Liemar. The first version of the chronicle was ready in 1076. The continuing work of the author mainly consisted of adding glosses and corrections to already written passages, and most probably lasted until the end of his life.

The lack of the original of the work to some extent is compensated by codicological research encompassing 25 manuscripts from the turn of the 11th/12th–18th c.[29] All manuscripts were divided by B. Schmeidler into three groups

---

25   The chronicler's criticism was certainly dictated by the falling through of the plans of
      the would-be patriarch which were considered too bold in the assessment of schol-
      ars (Schmeidler, Trillmich) – Trillmich, "Einleitung," in *Gesta Hammaburgensis*, p. 140;
      Berschin, *Biographie*, pp. 212 ff.

26   Precisely: before the 8th August, when Gottschalk's son Budivoj died – see Schmeidler,
      "Einleitung," in Adam, p. lxvi; Trillmich, "Einleitung," in *Gesta Hammaburgensis*, p. 139.
      Labuda, *Fragmenty*, vol. 3, p. 212, emphasizes that the chronology of events in book III is
      not accurate due to the fact that it was strictly oriented at Adalbert.

27   Adam IV, 7, schol. 111, following ancient science, he thought that Scandinavia was an is-
      land: "Ab hac insula primum egressi sunt Langobardi vel Gothi, et vocatur a historicis
      Romanorum Scantia vel Ganavia sive Scandinavia".

28   *E.g.* Helge Ingstad, *The Norse Discovery of America*, vol. 2: *The Historical Background
      and the Evidence of the Norse Settlement Discovered in Newfoundland* (Oslo/Bergen/
      Stavanger: Norwegian University Press, 1985), pp. 299–305; Grzegorz Witkowski, "Opis
      wysp Północy jako dzieło etnografii wczesnośredniowiecznej," in *Studia z dziejów Europy
      Zachodniej i Śląska*, ed. Rościsław Żerelik (Wrocław: Instytut Historyczny Uniwersytetu
      Wrocławskiego, 1995), pp. 30, 42 f.; F. Donald Logan, *The Vikings in History* (New York:
      Routledge, 2005), p. 93.

29   For manuscripts of Adam's works see Schmeidler, "Einleitung," in Adam, pp. vii–xxxiv;
      Trillmich, "Einleitung," in *Gesta Hammaburgensis*, pp. 150–155.

ADAM OF BREMEN ON SLAVIC RELIGION

with reference to the same number of specimens that were not preserved. According to this concept the first was to be a manuscript written by Adam and under his dictation (A), and the second was its corrected copy given to archbishop Liemar (α). The third specimen (X) is hypothetically manuscript A supplemented with annotations, the so-called scholia (not precisely identified with glosses[30]). On the basis of comparative analyses, it is hypothetically assumed that 141 out of 186 glosses were written by Adam of Bremen.[31] According to the discussed concept specimen X would include a variety of Adam's interjections from an earlier text (some passages were removed, there were also grammatical and stylistic changes), which, according to scholars, decreased the quality of this work.[32]

According to Schmeidler, on the basis of the manuscript (α), the shortest version of the whole work designed in stemma codicum as A1 was made. It is the so-called Vienna Manuscript from the turn of the 12th and 13th c., preserved in the Library of the Imperial Court in Vienna which became the basis of B. Schmeidler's edition. The editor assumed that this version – based on the manuscript corrected and supplied by Adam himself – gave an optimum presentation of the chronicler's original intention. Another version, in the opinion of B. Schmeidler still close to the first (hypothetical) manuscript created with the intention of presenting it to archbishop Liemar, is to be also *Codex Vaticanus* from 1451. The oldest of the manuscripts containing Adam's *Gesta* must be *Codex Vossianus Latinus* from about 1100, kept in the University Library in Leiden, however it contains only a part of Book II and the whole of Book IV.[33]

Regardless of this, Anne K.G. Kristensen[34] postulated to accept this version (*i.e.* A2) as the primary basis in attempts to establish the original content of the chronicle. She was involved in a more extensive polemic with Schmeidler's theses and negated the speculation that the copy of the chronicle made by Adam for Liemar existed at all (*i.e.* α). Thereby Kristensen stated that the shortest of the manuscripts, *i.e.* A1, was not the closest to the original. Moreover, the authoress assumed that the chapters III, 72–78, considered by Schmeidler to be an addition to Book III (and placed in square brackets), should be added to

---

30   Wielgus, *Badania nad Biblią*, p. 22.

31   See Schmeidler, "Einleitung," in Adam, pp. vii–xvii.

32   Trillmich, "Einleitung," in *Gesta Hammaburgensis*, p. 154.

33   Schmeidler, "Einleitung," in Adam, p. xii f.

34   Anne K.G. Kristensen, *Studien zur Adam von Bremen Überlieferung. Die Wiener Handschrift: Erstredaktion oder später verkürzte Fassung?*, (Skrifter udgivet af det historiske Institut ved Københavns Universitet) 5 (København: Københavns Universitet, Historisk Institut, 1975), pp. 11–56.

Book IV. Certainly, this criticism of Schmeidler's views, only signalled here, is of hypothetical nature. However, it abates the power of his findings related to stemma codicum and hence one should take into account a further distancing of this edition of the text of the chronicle – treated as primary for nearly a century – from its original, than from what was assumed by this editor.

In the Middle Ages the work of Adam of Bremen did not enjoy much popularity and was distributed mainly in northern Europe. Editions of the history of the Church in Hamburg are discussed by B. Schmeidler in the introduction to his own edition, and this list should be supplemented with the next editions, starting with W. Trillmich's one from 1961 (with a German translation).[35] The first printed edition was published by Andreas Severinus Vedel (Velleus) in Copenhagen in 1579 on the basis of the manuscript from Sorö.[36]

"It has been laid out to us" – declares Adam in the Prologue addressed to Liemar – "not to please everyone, but you, father, and your church."[37] This statement makes one realize how strongly the genesis of this work was conditioned by current matters of the Hamburg-Bremen metropolis. The reference to Archbishop Adalbert's activity was of key importance here. On one hand it is possible to assume that Adam, even when the archbishop was still alive, had a ready plan of the structure and content of his chronicle and did not express his opinion on his pontificate, as he was rather skeptical about some of its aspects. On the other hand, it should be taken into account that it was exactly the change on the metropolitan throne that stimulated him to review Adalbert's plans on the place of the Hamburg-Bremen archbishopric in the structure of the Roman Church and the Empire, which was expressed in the interpretation of history on the pages of Adam's chronicle.

The archbishopric in Hamburg, established in 834[38] by Louis the Pious, gained in the 11th c. a slightly-falsified tradition created as an element of the implementation of the already-mentioned Adalbert's ambitious plans, in which he made an attempt to subordinate Slavs living in areas reaching the

---

35 Schmeidler, "Einleitung," in Adam, pp. xlv ff.; W. Trillmich, as in footnote 3 in this chapter. And next *e.g.* Czech translation: Adam Brémský, *Činy biskupů hamburského kostela. Velká kronika evropského Severu*, trans. Libuše Chrabová (Praha: Argo, 2009).

36 Schmeidler, "Einleitung," in Adam, pp. xx, lxv.

37 Adam, [*Praefatio*]: "Nobis propositum est non omnibus placere, sed tibi, pater, et ecclesiae tuae".

38 For the sometimes quoted date of 831 (see *e.g.* Witkowski, "Opis wysp," p. 18), possibly it results from adoption of dating the false papal bulla benefitting Hamburg in the same year; see *e.g.* Gerard Labuda, "Hamburg," in sss, vol. 2, pp. 185 f.; Wavra, *Salzburg und Hamburg*, pp. 252, 283 ff.

Peene River. For this purpose – as was shown in B. Schmeidler's research – false papal bulls were attributed to Gregory IV from 831, Agapetus II from 847, and John XV from 989. The content of false documents was influenced by the establishment of the Starigard/Oldenburg bishopric in 968, which was controlled by the Hamburg metropolis and stretched its supervision to Elbslavs reaching the Peene River.

It is noteworthy that the first authentic papal confirmation of Hamburg's rights to the Slavic lands is in the preserved original papal bull of Clement II, issued in the first years of Adalbert's pontificate in 1047. Hence, one should take into account that missionary efforts of the Hamburg Archdiocese were also directed to Elbslavs earlier, perhaps from the very beginning, but only in favourable circumstances was it legalized by this papal document.[39] However, the main goal of Adalbert's efforts was encompassing, with obedience, the kingdoms of Scandinavia – Denmark, Sweden, and Norway.[40] The impetus of these plans was impressive, especially if one remembers the beginnings of the Hamburg diocese, which did not prefigure much success. Regardless of its fervency, St. Ansgar's mission in Scandinavia brought rather limited results. Other members of the Frankish clergy did even less. The invasion by the Danish king Horik I in 845 was a blow which destroyed the young church in Hamburg. The metropolitan seat was moved to the safer Bremen, preserving the continuity of the institution. In practice this meant a union of bishoprics, which was not favoured by everyone at that time.[41]

From the mid-11th c., when Bremen victoriously ended a period of over one hundred years of rivalry with the English clergy for influence in Scandinavia, the pontificate of Unwan (d. 1029) and especially Adalbert (d. 1072) created a need for a tradition of metropolitan splendour.[42] A political action started by Adalbert and its achievements needed propaganda for justification. Bremen, becoming at that time the cultural capital of northern Germany, had to have an advantage over other Church centres to pursue Adalbert's plans. They

---

39   Labuda, *Fragmenty*, vol. 3, pp. 181 f; Wavra, *Salzburg und Hamburg*, pp. 254 f. For more information in this matter see also Scior, *Das Eigene und das Fremde*, pp. 41 ff.

40   Labuda, *Fragmenty*, vol. 2, p. 157; cf. Trillmich, "Einleitung," in *Gesta Hammaburgensis*, p. 140.

41   Labuda, *Fragmenty*, vol. 2, p. 182. Details of the unification of bishoprics are discussed by Wavra, *Salzburg und Hamburg*, pp. 256–258.

42   *E.g.* David M. Knowles, Dmitri Obolensky, *Historia Kościoła*, vol. 2: 600–1500 (Warszawa: Instytut Wydawniczy PAX, 1988) [orig. *Nouvelle Histoire de l'Eglise*, vol. 2: *Le Moyen Age* (600–1500) (Paris: Seuil, 1968)], p. 17.

encompassed a programme of establishing twelve suffragan dioceses which would secure Patriarchate rank for Bremen.[43]

Such a decisive course of action made the number of enemies of the archbishop grow among the powerful Saxons, who were Henry IV's opposition at the same time. For a while the ambitious metropolitan was the counsellor (regent) and teacher of the young ruler, before he started his independent rule in 1065.[44] Among important allies of Adalbert there was the Danish king Sven Estridsen, and especially the Obotrite prince Gottschalk, whose death during the Slavic rebellion in 1066 was an irremediable loss for the metropolitan. Devastation in the Church organization caused by pagans coincided with a financial collapse of the Hamburg-Bremen Archdiocese. In the end, the plans to establish the Patriarchate of the North foundered because of centralist papal policy, in addition to the weakening influence of Adalbert on the young king of Germany.

Archbishop Liemar did not pursue these extremely ambitious plans of his predecessor, and canon Adam supported this trend. However, in this new situation the need to propagate the splendour of the Hamburg-Bremen archdiocese with reference to its oldest history did not decrease. It is worth mentioning that Bremen was separated from the Cologne metropolis, and so references to the Hamburg roots of the Bremen archdiocese were considerably important to defending its metropolitan rights. Adam recognized the main point in Adalbert's plan, namely to encompass the whole of the North with a mission worth continuing,[45] in which one can find reasons which justify the metropolitan status of Bremen on the basis of unity with tradition of Hamburg. Thus, it is not accidental that the chronicler presented this last centre as "an adorable

---

43　Trillmich, "Einleitung," in *Gesta Hammaburgensis*, p. 141; Herbert Ludat, "Die Patriarchatsidee Adalberts von Bremen und Byzanz," in *idem, Slaven und Deutsche im Mittelalter. Ausgewählte Aufsätze zu Fragen ihrer politischen, sozialen und kulturellen Beziehungen*, (Mitteldeutsche Forschungen) 86 (Köln/Wien: Böhlau, 1982), pp. 312–339, esp. 336. Cf. Michael H. Gelting, "The kingdom of Denmark," in *Christianization and the Rise Christianization and the Rise of Christian Monarchy. Scandinavia, Central Europe and Rus' c. 900–1200.* ed. Nora Berend (Cambridge: Cambridge University Press, 2007), p. 95.

44　Adalbert's activity was characterised in detail by Ludat, *Die Patriarchatsidee, passim*; Trillmich, "Einleitung," in *Gesta Hammaburgensis*, p. 140.

45　Establishment of the archbishopric in Hamburg (and Bremen) oriented to the mission among pagans is confirmed by information that Pope Agapetus granted Hamburg a privilege as he was happy with the salvation of pagans (*de salute gentium*) – see Adam II, 3; cf. Adam II, 65. Numerous references to care about the conversion of pagans, *e.g.* Adam II, 72; III, 18; IV, 8. Widely in this matter see Scior, *Das Eigene und das Fremde*, pp. 56 ff.

ADAM OF BREMEN ON SLAVIC RELIGION   207

[and] most fertile mother of the peoples; seat of the metropolis (...) of all the northern nations and capital of its diocese ..."[46]

All activity of the main characters of the chronicle was conducted on the motto *ad gentes!*, which influenced the content of geographical Book IV. In older historiography, a view was expressed that Adam divided humanity into the faithful and unfaithful, *i.e.* Christians and pagans, and he did not distinguish nations and peoples according to their language.[47] However, such an extreme concept cannot be defended. Although the influence of biblical notions on the characteristics of the non-Christian peoples is visible (which is discussed on numerous occasions below), one cannot say that slavish imitation of biblical ideas occurs, especially if one takes into account such basic terms as *gens* or *populus*.

It should also be mentioned that, *e.g.* in the Book of Genesis these terms are connected with a speech community,[48] which corresponds with a maxim that became common in early medieval scholarship: *gentem lingua facit* (Isidore of Seville). However, one language could be used by a few ethnical groups, defined in medieval sources as *gens*,[49] and this was the case in Adam of Bremen's chronicle, where he used this word in general characteristics of both Christian and pagan peoples,[50] observing also that the Slavic peoples do not differ in speech and customs.[51]

The biblical influence on the way the word *gens* functions in Adam's work can be found in the context of presentation of non-Christian peoples as missionary space. The author habitually uses this term or, more precisely, its plural form – *gentes* – as a synonym of the word pagans[52] (also simply called – *pagani*, *gentiles*). However, in the case of the term *populus* this type of theological connotation is not expressed; in the discussed chronicle the term is used with reference to non-Christian communities, or in the context clearly indicating such character, or with appropriate epithet being a signpost in this matter.[53]

---

46   Adam III, 25: "fecundissima gentium mater [...] veneranda"; III, 26: "metropolis sedes [...] omnium septentri onalium nationum et caput suae parochiae ..."

47   Koczy, *Sklawanja*, pp. 187 f.

48   *E.g.* Vulgate, Gen 10:31: "isti filii Sem secundum cognationes et linguas et regiones in gentibus suis"; Gen 11:6: "ecce unus est populus et unum labium omnibus".

49   *E.g.* Zientara, *Świt*, p. 22.

50   *E.g.* Adam II, 22: "Sclavi cum aliis gentibus, Grecis et Barbaris" – see below, pp. 229 f. For Saxons as *gens* see *e.g.* Adam I, 1, p. 4.

51   Adam II, 21.

52   Adam I, 58; II, 26; II, 72; III, 72; IV, 20.

53   *E.g.* Adam II, 5: *gentilium populus*. In the context: Adam I, 26: ".... ut ex eius [*e.g.* Olaf] imperio et populi consensu ...".

208   CHAPTER 3

It is worth mentioning that this otherness of the terms *populus* and *gens*, emphasized by the way Adam used them referring to pagans, corresponds with the juxtaposition *populus Israel* – *gentes*, known from the *Vulgate*. So *populus*, when used to refer to a non-Christian community, required a more precise definition with an adjective indicating their paganism, while the term *gens*, burdened with biblical associations, was in principle related to pagan peoples (*gentes*).[54] Apart from this, the semantic range of both words defining human communities is so limited that Adam replaced one with the other.[55]

The principal division of humankind, from the perspective of the chronicler, is determined by the category of *barbari*. An ancient contradiction of the *imperium Romanum* and *barbaricum* in the Middle Ages found its continuation in the contradiction of the circle of civilization of Christian Europe and barbaric peoples.[56] Hence *barbarus* frequently functioned as meaning the same as pagan, which was confirmed by the canon from Bremen numerous times,[57] however, this notion is not precisely a carrier of a conviction that a given person or community belongs to the pagan circle. First and foremost, it carries information that barbarians are strange, and also expresses an opinion that their culture and social organization are inferior.[58]

This is why even a possible temporary or short-term affiliation with the Christian circle does not mean that they are automatically relieved from the odium of *barbari* attributed to them. This is what happened in the case of the Polabian Slavs[59] in Adam's work, although he mentioned that at the time when Adaldag was the archbishop of Hamburg-Bremen a bishopric was established in Starigard, and he emphasized that in the times of its first bishops (968–988) the Slavs became Christians.[60]

---

54   Johannes Nowak, *Untersuchungen zum Gebrauch der Begriffe populus, gens und natio bei Adam von Bremen und Helmold von Bosau* (Münster: Diss. 1971); see also: Zientara, *Świt*, p. 20; Lech A. Tyszkiewicz, "Uwagi w sprawie wczesnośredniowiecznej terminologii etnicznej," in *Pojęcia "Volk" i "Nation" w historiografii Niemiec*, ed. Antoni Czubiński (Poznań: UAM, 1980), pp. 179–182; Fraesdorff, *Der barbarische Norden*, pp. 69 ff., 191 f.

55   *E.g.* Adam II, 15.

56   Zientara, *Świt*, p. 21.

57   *E.g.* Adam I, 33; II, 26; III, 72; III 77; IV, 1.

58   *E.g.* Lech A. Tyszkiewicz, "Z badań nad narodzinami stereotypów Słowian w historiografii zachodniej wczesnego średniowiecza," in *Wokół stereotypów Polaków i Niemców*, ed. Wojciech Wrzesiński, (Acta Universitatis Wratislaviensis. Historia) 79 (Wrocław: Wydawnictwo Uniwersytetu Wrocławskiego, 1991), pp. 35 f.; Fraesdorff, *Der barbarische Norden*, pp. 280 ff.

59   Adam, II, 43: "[Suein] ... omnes barbarorum gestas res in memoria tenuit ...". Sven Estridsen is mentioned here as an informer about the Slavic rebellion during the pontificate of Libentius. See below, p. 237.

60   Adam II, 26: "quorum tempore Sclavi permanserunt christiani".

ADAM OF BREMEN ON SLAVIC RELIGION   209

In Adam's perspective the subjugation of people and land to the Hamburg-Bremen archbishopric was of key importance.[61] However, in the analyses of this information one should take into account the model of interpretation of mission and conversion in supra-individual categories which functioned on a wide scale, which was also discussed in the analysis of the *Chronicle of Thietmar*.[62] One should not forget that even the very fact that a land was encompassed by the Church organization and that its inhabitants were dependent on the Empire (*e.g.* tributary dependence) was considered inclusion in the Christian circle,[63] which corresponds with the account from Adam's work that out of twenty lands (*pagus*) of Slavs (*i.e. Sclavania*) only three were not converted.[64]

In a similar way – which should be mentioned as an analogy illustrating the way of converting to Christianity mentioned above – the canon from Bremen mentions a political and military action undertaken by Henry I the Fowler on the Slavic land,[65] and next Otto I, who "after subjugating the Slavic people and converting them to the Christian faith, established the famous city of Magdeburg on the banks of the Elbe River, which constituted the metropolis for the Slavs ..."[66]

Let us not forget that at the next stage of Christianization it was assumed that teaching people and leading them to individual conversion would take place, similarly to Adam's narrative in which archbishop of Magdeburg, Adalbert (d. 981), "converted many peoples of the Slavs (...) thanks to his preaching."[67] The chronicler implies that persuasion and teaching are an inherent way to achieve success in a mission. In the case of Scandinavia they even substitute political extortion because missionaries such as Anskar, Poppo or Unni

---

61   Jerzy Kłoczowski, *Młodsza Europa* (Warszawa: PIW, 1998), p. 32, emphasizes that Adam "nearly identifies conversion with obedience to archbishops neglecting any other initiatives or even church decisions", which is a sign – in a historical source and some time ago also a tool in ideological struggle – of rivalry between missionary centres.

62   See above, pp. 79 ff.

63   Adam II, 26.

64   *Ibidem*: "de XX pagos (...) absque tribus ad Christianam fidem omnes fuisse conversos ..."

65   Adam II, 5: Henry having defeated the Slavs in Lunkini (Lenzen) in 929 "... constrinxit, ut tributum et christianitatem pro vita simul et patria libenter offerrent victori, baptizatusque est totus gentilium populus, ecclesiae in Sclavania tunc primum constructae"; cf. Adam I, 56; the Slavs defeated in 929 "regi tributum et Deo christianitatem promitterent."

66   Adam II, 15: "subiugatis Christianaeque fidei copulatis Sclavorum gentibus inclytam urbem Magedburg super ripas Albiae fluminis condidit, quam Sclavis metropolem statuens ..."

67   *Ibidem*: "multosque Sclavorum populos (...) predicando convertit."

210   CHAPTER 3

strived directly to win souls by words and deeds.[68] The chronicler also states
that success of evangelical action is easier to achieve for people sharing the
language and customs with the barbarians.[69]

This essential reflection referring to the missionary practice can be read as
Adam's way of expressing empathy with the barbarians. Thus it is not accidental that in older (especially Polish) research he was attributed with impartiality
in his approach to pagan issues, and in consequence also to the issue of the
Slavs; his joy that resulted from conversion of pagans and indignation directed
to those who challenged these efforts was emphasized.[70] However, considering
this approach as "impartial" seems poorly justified. In this case the intention of
the author for whom the basic criterion used in assessment of pagans or barbarians was their openness to the mission of Christianization is what matters.
It is hard not to notice his negative approach to the Slavs when they turned
against Christianity by trying to lift the Saxon burden by force.[71]

Adam's interest in Slavdom is strictly related to the history of the Hamburg-
Bremen mission on Slavic lands.[72] Hence the chronicler devoted a lot of attention to the Polabian peoples trying to describe their tribal divisions and
presenting a few of their "towns" (*urbs*, *civitas*) as well as their relations with

---

68   Evidence can be found in numerous places in the chronicle, in which missions in
      Scandinavia are shown as verbal persuasion, supported by the authority of miracles and
      holiness of Christianity preachers, but without military force – *e.g.* Adam I, 21: the exiled
      bishop Gaudbert was replaced by Heriger, who "potentia miraculorum et exhortatione
      doctrinae multa paganorum milia salvaret"; Adam I, 26: Anskar arrived in Birka for a
      meeting with Olaf and people: "Quem preveniente misericordia Dei ita placatum invenit,
      ut ex eius imperio et populi consensu et iactu sortis et ydoli responso ecclesia ibidem fab-
      ricata et baptismi licentia omnibus consessa sit."; Adam I, 58: Unni "videns ostium fidei
      gentibus apertum esse, gratias Deo egit de salute paganorum"; Adam I, 59: Unni arrived in
      Denmark and sailed around the islands "euangelizans verbum Dei gentilibus et fideles";
      Adam II, 26: Adaldag appointed bishops from Sweden (Svetjud) "in gentibus legationem",
      including Odinkar, who turned out to be gifted, dedicated, educated and holy, thanks
      to which "et facile barbaris quaelibet de nostra potuit religione persuadere"; Adam II,
      35: bishop Poppo seeing that "barbari suo more signum quaererent", convinced them with
      a miracle with an iron test to "omnem gentilibus ambiguitatem erroris tollere" and "pro
      submovendo illius gentis paganismo" performed another miracle involving the risk of
      burning; Adam II, 58: king Olaf recommended adoption of Christianity not by force but
      out of free will, although he destroyed a pagan temple and built a church.

69   Adam III, 72.

70   Koczy, *Sklawanja*, p. 187.

71   However, it is not a one-sided picture, because the chronicler also blames the Saxons who
      oppressed the Slavs for Slavic rebellions; see below, p. 236.

72   *E.g.* Koczy, "Sklawanja," p. 211. Trillmich, "Einleitung," in: *Gesta Hammaburgensis*, p. 144,
      mentions that information about the political development of missionary areas should
      first of all show obstacles in spreading the faith.

ADAM OF BREMEN ON SLAVIC RELIGION   211

the Germans (Saxons) and the Danes. There were also records about other
Slavic countries and nations, including a few observations about Poles. In his
presentation of the history and geography of the Slavs, Master Adam depended mainly on oral tradition received from King Sven Estridsen,[73] archbishop
Adalbert,[74] and preeminently from merchants and missionaries.[75]

It is striking that Adam privileges a special, less popular word to describe
the Slavdom – *Sclavania*,[76] however, it should be mentioned that this term
occurred over seventy years earlier in the Gospel Books of Otto III. It is one
version of a name of an allegorical female character who personified the
Kingdom of the Slavs (however, the word *Sclauinia* occurs in this context more
often).[77] The fundamental lecture on the Slavic people ("de natura et gentibus
Sclavaniae") was included by Adam in chapters 20–23 of the second book of
his chronicle. It is possible, however, that these passages were not a part of the
original version and were added later, because in terms of content they differ
from the whole structure of Book II.[78]

Although Adam's approach presents some errors, it should be noted that
these are generally not the same errors as the ones which occurred in the earlier cosmography, which he also knew quite well. So it is not accidental that
in the positivist historiography he gained high marks for originality. His work
was well summarized in Leon Koczy's opinion: "The image of Sclavania, as is
presented by Adam in the second volume and partly in some other parts of his
work, is a contemporary picture independent of the Classical literature."[79]

The quoted sentence about the "independence" from the Classical
literature – as will be shown in the studies below – expresses excessive optimism, however it is not worth deploring. In the perspective of studies on the

---

73   Adam II, 26; II, 43.

74   Adam III, 6.

75   Koczy, *Sklawanja*, pp. 207 f.

76   For more information about the notion of Sclavania in Adams' work see Scior, *Das Eigene
      und das Fremde*, pp. 94, 98 ff.

77   Piotr Skubiszewski, *Malarstwo europejskie w średniowieczu*, vol. 1: *Malarstwo karolińskie i
      przedromańskie* (Warszawa: Wydawnictwo Artystyczne i Filmowe, 1973), pp. 192 f.

78   L. Weibull's view discussed by Koczy, *Sklawanja*, p. 211. Similarly one should take into ac-
      count the possibility of incorrect identification of some glosses (*scholia*), as many as 45 of
      them – according to Schmeidler – were not written by the chronicler himself. However,
      taking these scholia which were not written by Adam into consideration means that the
      subject of this research on interpretation of pre-Christian religions encompasses also a
      written debate on this work which took place in the intellectual environment; it is also
      important that this debate took place at the time and in the context of mental culture
      which were not distant from the chronicler.

79   Koczy, *Sklawanja*, pp. 207 f.

interpretation of primary religions in the mental culture of the 11th and 12th c., research on literary infiltration from Classical Antique heritage is an important element in the whole discussion of this problem. A study of stereotypes and cultural topoi conditioning the way strangers were perceived seems equally important in this case in which anthropological inspiration was essential.

"Barbarzyńska Europa" [The Barbarian Europe] (2004), by Karol Modzelewski, is a work that demonstrates that the chronicle written by Adam of Bremen acts as an excellent foundation for such studies. Its findings closely correspond with the method of approaching cultural fact proposed in the first version of this work, which allows these synthetic studies of Modzelewski to be taken into consideration in a harmonious way in the current version of this dissertation. In the undertaken investigations of the interpretation of Old Slavic cults and beliefs in the light of the chronicle of *magister scholarum* from Bremen, the dissertations of Volker Scior[80] and David Fraesdorff[81] turn out to be useful; considering their claims enables a deeper reflection on the chronicler's attitude to the Polabian tribes, perceived as "foreign," and their culture, as well as continuing the discussion on some more detailed issues (see below in this chapter).

However, one should emphasize that the leading theme of historical anthropology in these dissertations was strongly developed also by other researchers of the old Slavdom. Apart from Modzelewski, Christian Lübke is especially notable.[82] It is complementary to the study proposed here on the cultural interpretation of the pre-Christian religion, observed first of all from the perspective that was conditioned by theological rationale.

2 The Religion of the Slavs in *Gesta Hammaburgensis ecclesiae pontificum* – Historiographical Analysis

2.1 *Rethra*
In the excursus devoted to the Slavdom, Adam of Bremen emphasized the leading role of the Redars among the mentioned Polabian tribes and then moved on to present their most famous centre:

"Their best known city is Rethra, a seat of the idolatry. There a big temple was built for the demons, of whom Redigast is the prince. His statue is of gold, [his] bed laid out with purple. That city has got nine gates, surrounded by a

---

80   Scior, *Das Eigene und das Fremde.*
81   Fraesdorff, *Der barbarische Norden.*
82   See above, p. 9, footnote 19.

ADAM OF BREMEN ON SLAVIC RELIGION 213

deep lake from all sides; a wooden bridge offers passage, the way across it is permitted only to those who are to sacrifice or to beseech oracles."[83] This reference is not a borrowing from Thietmar's description of Radogošč,[84] which increases the informative value of this passage of Adam's work. In both sources one can find some details of the community and of the model of the Slavic sanctuary. This reinforces Thietmar's credibility in the matter of Svarožic's cult: after over half a century his information gained partial confirmation on the basis of retrogression.

The discussion about the main capital of the Liutici has become a stable element in studies on the West Slavic religion.[85] The first of the discussed issues is the identification of Rethra with Radogošč, which is usually considered a settled matter. Additionally, Adam gave important information about the location of the stronghold: four days away from Hamburg.[86] Discrepancies between details mentioned by Thietmar and Adam can be explained either by inaccurate information about the cult centre itself or by changes in its arrangement conducted within half a century.

The latter solution leads to the conclusion that the cult stronghold was moved to an island on a lake which was only accessible over a bridge, and according to Adam, only sacrificers and those who came to ask for an oracle had access. Nine gates, instead of three in Thietmar's work, support the idea of the growing splendour of this centre. Although, one should not forget here about a well-reasoned thesis put forward by Roderich Schmidt. He argued that this number is a result of a symbolical interpretation of reality. Adam's account could confirm the view about the growing wealth of the temple as he mentions the use of gold as a material to decorate a statue or the colour purple to cover the bed on which it was placed.

83　Adam, II, 21: "civitas eorum vulgatissima Rethre, sedes ydolatriae. Templum ibi magnum constructum est demonibus, quorum princeps est Redigast. Simulacrum eius auro, lectus ostro paratus. Civitas ipsa IX portas habet, undique lacu profundo inclusa; pons ligneus transitum prebet, per quem tantum sacrificantibus aut responsa petentibus via conceditur".

84　The opposite opinion was expressed by Brückner, *Mitologia słowiańska i polska*, p. 334.

85　For a report of the discussion and literature see J. Strzelczyk, "Radogoszcz," in SSS, vol. 4, pp. 450–451; Stanisław Rosik, "Połabskie władztwo 'księcia demonów'. Teologiczne uwarunkowania opisów pogańskich wierzeń i kultu w przekazach o religii Słowian," in *Studia z historii średniowiecza*, ed. Mateusz Goliński, (Acta Universitatis Wratislaviensis. Historia) 163 (Wrocław: Wydawnictwo Uniwersytetu Wrocławskiego, 2003), pp. 7–21.

86　Dralle, "Rethra," pp. 52 f., estimates that the distance was two hundred kilometers and on the basis of Helmold's data localises Rethra in the border zone between the Redars and the Tollenser. Certainly the distance expressed as "four days" could be shorter than two hundred kilometers.

214   CHAPTER 3

This detail has raised numerous doubts among some scholars.[87] For the hypercritical E. von Wienecke it became a premise upon which he considered the whole description as false and composed on the basis of information about a temple in Uppsala.[88] Nevertheless one should remember that the first source testimony of the existence of statues of deities in Slavdom, provided by Widukind of Corvey, mentions a copper figure of Saturn seized by Saxons in Wagrian Starigard.[89] This increases the confidence in the information that the statue in Rethra was really made using gold (*e.g.* it was covered with metal sheets), taking into account that the temple there was more significant than the Starigard sanctuary.[90]

The use of gold to make a figure of Triglav worshipped in Szczecin is also mentioned in the hagiography of St. Otto of Bamberg in a description of his mission in Pomerania in the 1120s.[91] This information, however similar to the description of the Redigast cult, is discussed as a possible influence of stereotypical images of idolatry based especially on biblical tradition. Such influences are hypothetically recognized in Adam's vision of the Uppsala temple (*e.g.* the motif of golden chain),[92] but on the other hand there is some archaeological data that could be used to support the claim about the reliability of written sources on the subject.[93] Because of the nature of the sources, an unambiguous solution to the problem appears impossible.

The arrangement of the sanctuary in Rethra is another premise supporting the thesis about the occurrence of henotheistic trends in the beliefs of western Slavdom.[94] Additionally, the character of the deity worshipped there is rather intriguing. Thietmar mentions that all gods were equipped with war accessories (meaning also Svarožic), while Adam of Bremen allows a god to be seen in Rethra which primarily personified the royal, sovereign power. This clear

---

87   *E.g.* Urbańczyk, *Dawni Słowianie*, p. 65. However, Słupecki, "Słowiańskie posągi," p. 64, did not see anything surprising in the use of gold and the colour purple.

88   Wienecke, *Untersuchungen*, pp. 24 f. Adam (IV, 26) stated that gold was used to build this temple.

89   Widukind III, 68, p. 82. See above, pp. 54 f.

90   Słupecki, "Słowiańskie posągi," pp. 65; cf. *idem, Slavonic Pagan Sanctuaries*, p. 227.

91   Ebo II, 13.

92   See *e.g.* Anders Hultgård, "Från ögonvittnesskildring till retorik: Adam av Bremens notiser om Uppsalakulten i religionshistorisk belysning," in *Uppsalakulten och Adam av Bremen*, ed. Anders Hultgård (Nora: Nya Doxa, 1997), pp. 9–50.

93   The opinion of Frands Herschend in: Anne-Sofie Gräslund, "Adams Uppsala – och arkeologins," in *Uppsalakulten och Adam av Bremen*, ed. A. Hultgård, Nora1997, pp. 108 f.

94   Łowmiański, *Religia*, p. 203, talks here even about complete domination of Radogost or Svantevit over polidoxy elements.

ADAM OF BREMEN ON SLAVIC RELIGION   215

discrepancy between the sources in the matter of the name of the major deity
of the Redars was explained in a number of ways.

A. Brückner's skeptical views that "only by Adam of Bremen's mistake, a
new deity Radzigost, was imagined!"[95] were supported in Gerard Labuda's
etymological argumentation. This author derived the local name "Radogost"
from two words: "redny" (marshy) and "gozd" (forest),[96] which allows both
a local name and a characteristic of the natural environment in which the
sanctuary was established to be found in this name of the deity mentioned
by Adam. Linguistic research indicates another possibility referring to the
water name, in which it is possible to hear the sound of flowing, stormy water,
and a lake, which is related to the location of the sanctuary on an island or a
peninsula.[97] The "Radogošč" would be a name of a lake, an island, and first and
foremost a town on a lake.

The assumption that the name "Radogost" ("Redigast") was a pseudo-
theonym did not enjoy extensive support among historians of Slavic religion.
The dominant view is that the name mentioned by Adam was Svarožic's sobriquet, which finally occluded the original theonym confirmed by Thietmar.[98]
The very name Radogost is related to the local name Radogošč, which would
indicate that the theonym was coined as Svarožic's local sobriquet. It seems
less probable that Svarožic's worship was eliminated by the cult of a new deity,

---

95   The assumption of Adam of Bremen's credibility in the Rethra issue was fiercely rejected
     by Brückner, *Mitologia słowiańska i polska*, p. 33; in other places there is a whole range
     of negative assessments of Adam's information – *ibidem*, p. 74: confusion; p. 190: fairy
     tales; p. 193: sin; p. 200: fabrication. Brückner derived the name Rethra from the name of
     Redars: "Radegast was not a town like Arkona, it was a poor village with a temple, from
     which the Germans kidnapped only the horse of god, but did not conquer any treasure:
     this is why instead of the name of the place it was enough to use the name of the tribe:
     Redari – Rethra" (*ibidem*, p. 334); cf. Moszyński, *Die vorchristliche Religion*, p. 75. It is
     worth remembering about this position to realise the significance of the development
     of primary source studies over the last century in the assessment of the value of Adam of
     Bremen's work not only in religion history studies, but also the cultural interpretation of
     >>the others<< with consideration for the literary value of the source.
96   See Gerard Labuda, "Mitologia i demonologia w słownictwie, w bajkach, baśniach i leg-
     endach kaszubskich," in *Materiały ogólnej sesji naukowej pt. Świat bajek, baśni i legend
     kaszubskich* (Wejherowo: Muzeum Piśmiennictwa i Muzyki Kaszubsko-Pomorskiej w
     Wejherowie, 1979), p. 13.
97   Moszyński, *Die vorchristliche Religion*, pp. 77 f. See also Ackenheil, *Gottheiten*, p. 7.
98   *E.g.* Gieysztor, *Mitologia*, p. 169. According to Łowmiański, *Religia*, pp. 170 f., "similarly to
     Svarožic sun–Dazbog and Svarožic fire, this Svarožic has got also his personal name –
     Radogost". Urbańczyk, *Dawni Słowianie*, pp. 27, 188, claimed that the name of Svarožic
     was substituted by another alternative one, which eliminated it from use, which was sup-
     ported by a lack of information about Svarožic after Thietmar.

216   CHAPTER 3

strictly related to this particular centre in Radogošč/Rethra.[99] Such a revolutionary change in the sphere of cult bonding raises doubts because the Liutici Federation did not disintegrate.

However, the very dissemination of the theonym Radogost (not necessarily its creation) firstly showed the progress of cult disintegration in Northern Polabia,[100] and secondly could be related to the Redars' ambitions to strengthen their hegemony among their neighbours.[101] By promoting Svarožic's local sobriquet, they would emphasize the importance of the location of the main temple of the Liutici Federation exactly on their territory. This assessment is supported by the fact that Adam used the name Rethra to refer to the centre where the temple was located, and etymologically this exact name is connected with the Redars.

According to A. Gieysztor, the name Redigast also occurs as an epithet related to the name of a tribe.[102] Nonetheless, the name is closer to the word "Radogošč." However, this toponym gained not only an explanation with relation to natural scenery conditions – which has been mentioned above – but primarily as a connection of two words: 'rad' and 'gost', *i.e.* 'kind, willing, happy' and 'guest'. The same explanation is usually given for the name "Radogost".[103] Hence, a god bearing this name, also in its Redigast variant, is one who takes care of guests. It cannot be excluded that the name of the stronghold Radogošč derives from him, although here the opposite direction of the transition of this name is also possible.

---

99   Separating Svarožic and Redigast/Radogost (treated only as a toponym) was supported by Labuda, "Mitologia i demonologia," p. 13.

100   Leciejewicz, *Słowianie*, pp. 193 f. emphasized that in the then Polabia there was "a more general process of adapting the pagan system of religious beliefs to the new social and political reality. The cultural disintegration with the additional lack of a connecting factor in the form of the ruleship system, resulted in quick development of tribal cults". Hence, Radogost would be another, local, name for Svarožic (which is convenient for numerous scholars).

101   Adam II, 21, *expressis verbis* confirms this primacy among the Northern Polabian tribes: "Inter quos medii et potentissimi omnium sunt Retharii". Cf. Jacek Banaszkiewicz, "Jedność porządku przestrzennego, społecznego i tradycji początków ludu (Uwagi o urządzeniu wspólnoty plemienno-państwowej u Słowian)," *Przegląd Historyczny* 77 (1986), pp. 445–466.

102   Gieysztor, *Mitologia*, p. 169. The author stressed the meaning of Rügen analogy in this case, where the god Rugievit (Lord of Rügen) was worshipped.

103   *Ibidem*, p. 129; Urbańczyk, *Dawni Słowianie*, p. 188; Dralle, "Rethra," pp. 54 f.; *idem, Slaven an Havel und Spree. Studien zur Geschichte des hevellisch-wilzischen Fürstentums (6. bis. 10 Jahrhundert)* (Berlin: Duncker & Humblot, 1981), pp. 143 f.; Ackenheil, *Gottheiten*, p. 44. The authors offer also other etymological proposals. See below, pp. 225, 296.

ADAM OF BREMEN ON SLAVIC RELIGION   217

If, since Thietmar's times, there had also been changes in the location, construction, and décor of the central Liutici temple, and there are numerous arguments supporting this view (also the said dissemination of the new name of the major deity), one should then take into account the evolution of the local system of cult and beliefs in the direction of monolatry. This is indicated by information about only one deity worshipped in the sanctuary in which its statue was located.[104] It is essential to mention that the statue was made of gold. The symbolism of this metal is solar, which in the case of the major deity indicates appreciation of the trend to concentrate sovereign power over the pantheon around it.[105] The validity of this interpretation is confirmed by emphasis on the fact that the couch was covered with the colour purple.[106]

This high rank of Redigast remains in agreement with the use in the said description of a calque of the world of demons led by their *princeps*, known from the Gospel.[107] Then the Slavic god and his statue in Rethra in this perspective are an embodiment of this biblical figure.[108] Hence, there is the question of whether demons, mentioned collectively in this passage, are theologically interpreted as particular deities who were worshipped in the sanctuary. It is doubtful. This is supported by the comparison of a description of Rethra with a passage about a temple in Uppsala, in which Adam of Bremen speaks about a miraculous healing of blindness of a priest there after he abandoned idolatry.

According to the chronicler, this priest earlier served demons ("demonibus astare solebat"), however because of the lack of a support of gods ("diis") he lost sight, yet the object of his cult were idols (literally "cultura ydolorum, quam

---

104   Pettazzoni, *Wszechwiedza*, p. 226, wondered whether on the basis of the analogy in descriptions of the seaside Slavic sanctuaries one can assume that Redigast's statue was polycephalic, which would strengthen the hypothesis on the identical arrangement of Rethra and temples with one statue on Rügen or in Szczecin. The existence of polycephalic representations outside the seaside zone in Brandenburg near Brenna is confirmed by Henry of Antwerp; see below, p. 338, footnote 376.

105   This appreciation of the solar element in the Polabian cult furthers the hypothesis on the appearance aspirations to consolidate power in Slavic communities, see above, pp. 364 f.

106   Słupecki, "Słowiańskie posągi," p. 66, finds an analogy to Thor's throne in Uppsala and connected the purple of Redigast's bed with his (hypothetical) elevation as the "god of gods" known from Helmold's work (see below, pp. 345 ff.).

107   The Evangelists present episodes in which Jesus was accused of expelling demons with the power of their ruler, see Mc 3:22: "... dicebant quoniam Beelzebub habet et quia in principe daemonum eicit daemonia"; Mt 9:34: "Pharisaei autem dicebant in principe daemoniorum eicit daemones"; Mt 12:27: "... et si ego in Beelzebub eicio demones".

108   Similarly in the Letter of St. Bruno of Querfurt to king Henry II Svarožic appears as *diabolus*, see above p. 108.

supertitiose venerans") and statues (*simulacra*).[109] In this context, according to the chronicler, gods (*dii*)[110] are a different type of existence than a community of demons, whom the priest served without being aware of this.[111] Thereby one has to accept that in the case of the description of Rethra, there is no sufficient basis to draw conclusions on the number of gods and their images in the local temple merely on the grounds of a premise that it was dedicated to demons. Moreover, taking into account that in the example from Uppsala, Adam gave a specific number of the deities (*i.e.* in triad),[112] the fact that he did the same in the case of the most famous Liutici sanctuary should also be considered.

Even though this is the most probable solution, it is not the only one. In the case of reflection on the organization of sacral space in Rethra, the supposition that there permanently existed a larger number of statues is based on conclusions from analogies, especially in Thietmar's account.[113] Moreover, in neighbouring Scandinavian chief sanctuaries – such as the overmentioned one in Uppsala – several idols were worshipped (however it was possible that only one god was worshipped at the sanctuaries of lower rank).[114] At last it is also worth considering a possibility that there were portable idols in the temple too.

In the analysis of the premise about the dedication of the Rethra temple to demons, it should be born in mind that their presence in a theological perspective corresponded not only with the same idolatry, but also with other cult

---

109   On the issue of Adam's use of the terms *idolum* and *simulacrum* see also: Hultgård, *Från ögonvittnesskildring*.

110   Cf. Adam I, 7, where it is said that pagan cult is addressed to existences which were not gods by nature ("qui natura non erant dii").

111   Adam IV, 28: "Quidam e sacerdotibus, qui ad Ubsolam demonibus astare solebat, nequicquam iuvantibus diis factus est cecus ..." ("One of the priests, who used to assist demons in Uppsala, went blind while the gods were fruitlessly helping him out ..."). On a cult object: "cultura ydolorum, quam superstitiose venerans ..." ("cult of the idols which he superstitiously worshipped ..."). And the successful ending: "... visum reciperet abiectis, quae ante colebat, simulacris." ("... he got back sight after having rejected the images which he had previously worshipped.")

112   Adam IV, 26; for the issue of the temple in Uppsala see *e.g.* Peter G. Foote, David M. Wilson, *Wikingowie*, trans. Wacław Niepokólczycki (Warszawa: PIW, 1975 [orig. *The Viking Achievement.* London: Sidgwick & Jackson, 1973]), pp. 55f., 362 f., 372 f.; Henrik Janson, *Templum nobilissimum. Adam av Bremen, Uppsalatemplet och konfliktlinjerna i Europa kring år 1075*, (Avhandlingar från Historiska institutionen i Göteborg) 21 (Göteborg: Historiska institutionen i Göteborg, 1998).

113   See above, p. 101.

114   See Olof Sundqvist, "Gudme on Funen: A central sanctuary with cosmic symbolism?," in *The Gudme/Gudhem Phenomenon*, ed. Oliver Grimm, Alexandra Pesch (Neumünster: Wachholtz Verlag GmbH, 2011), pp. 63–76, esp. 71 f.

ADAM OF BREMEN ON SLAVIC RELIGION

forms, such as divination, offerings or spells – Adam connected all these activities with demons, emphasizing the presence of their manifestations in a particular man.[115] The very conviction that there was a relation between demons and idols results from *interpretatio biblica* of the pagan *sacrum*.

In this concept deities neither exist nor do their statues have any supernatural properties by themselves, but surrounding them with cult was exactly what introduced an individual man and whole communities into relations with *antisacrum*. This thought found its continuation in patristics – *e.g.* in the writing of St. Cyprian[116] or Augustine[117] – and was confirmed by liturgical practice in church, such as the performance of exorcisms over things.[118] In this doctrinal context Rethra as *sedes ydolatriae* seems to be presented like an apocalyptic *civitas* Babylon in the Bible called *habitatio demoniorum*.[119]

115 Adam II, 57, p. 117: "Nam et divini et augures et magi et incantatores ceterisque satellites Antichristi habitant ibi, quorum pretigiis et miraculis infelices animae ludibrio demonibus habentur" ("For all the diviners, augurs, mages, enchanters, and the other attendants of the Antichrist live there, [and] because of their tricks and miracles the unfortunate souls become a mockery for the demons."); in the context of this passage Adam mentioned, that Olaf, the King of Norway (1015–1030) requested the persecution of the said fortune tellers, magicians and other "antichrist's companions" to strengthen the Christian religion. In assessing results of the forbidden practices Adam agrees here with St. Cyprian (see footnote 116 in this chapter) and St. Augustine – see St. Augustine, *De doctrina christiana*, 20.30–25.38, see: Św. Augustyn, *De doctrina Christiana / O nauce chrześcijańskiej*, Latin and Polish text, ed. and trans. Jan Sulowski (Warszawa: Instytut Wydawniczy PAX, 1989), pp. 82–91. Similarly *e.g.* Herbord III, 24, p. 187: with reference to pagan priests he says "pleni demonibus". L. von Padberg, "Christen," pp. 292–297, presents a Christian image of pagans in the then Middle Ages, emphasizing exactly this "demonization" resulting from participation in cult.

116 Discussing the nature of demons, St. Cyprian, bishop of Carthage (died in 258), claims that "these demons hide in statues and cult images", adding that they guide oracles and divinations of soothsayers of all types and gain control over people's bodies (cf. St. Cyprian, *Quod idola dii non sint*, 8 – see Św. Cyprian, *Pogańskie bóstwa nie są bogami (Quod idola dii non sint)*, introduction and trans. Marek Kondratowicz, *Vox Patrum* 11/12 (1991/1992) 20–23, pp. 444 f.). For more information on St. Cyprian's views on idolatry and demonolatry see *e.g.*: Jeffrey Burton Russel, *Satan, the Early Christian Tradition* (Ithaca: Cornell University Press, 1981), p. 221; Marek Kondratowicz, "Wokół 'Quod idola dii non sint' św. Cypriana Kartagińskiego," *Vox Patrum* 8 (1988) 15, pp. 668 f.

117 St. Augustine in his commentary on the Psalms proves that the worshipper of the statues does not pay attention to the fact that a statue similar to a real body is devoid of an alive inhabitant. In this theological perspective such attitude of people induces demons to occupy statues of pagan gods, and their presence multiplies errors and spreads "deadly deceptions". Cf. Św. Augustyn [St. Augustine], *Objaśnienia Psalmów* (Ps. 103–123), trans. Jan Sulowski, ed. Emil Stanula (Warszawa: Akademia Teologii Katolickiej, 1986), pp. 190 f.

118 See *e.g.* Nadolski, *Liturgika*, vol. 3, pp. 250 f.

119 Cf. Rev 18:2. In addition to this, *simulacrum aurum* of Redigast in Rethra evokes an association with Rev 9, 20: "simulacra aurea et argentea et aerea et lapidea et lignea ...".

220   CHAPTER 3

However, Adam of Bremen went further in his interpretation and associated the place of the Liutici idolatry with the place of eternal damnation. Such a claim based on symbolic and allegorical interpretations was observed in the motif of waters surrounding the cult stronghold, and especially the bridge which allowed access only for those seeking divination or making an offering: "I believe" – explains Adam of Bremen – "that one reason is significant [here], that concordantly the Styx flowing surrounds nine times the perdited souls of those who serve the idols."[120] Hence, participation in idolatric cult activities is presented allegorically as crossing the Styx River, *i.e.* immersion in spiritual death, which embraced the "perdited souls" of people serving idols.[121]

The formulation "congrue novies Stix interfusa cohercet" was taken from Virgil,[122] and additionally the nine waters of the Styx in this case correspond with the number of gates leading to Rethra. This confluence was considered by Roderich Schmidt as an effect of the chronicler's predilection for numerology, which is indicated by a particular place awarded to the number nine in descriptions of the three capitals of paganism (Rethra with its nine gates, Leire with 99 offerings and Uppsala with 72 offerings).[123] Thereby this historian also claimed that some analogies and similarities in Thietmar and Adam's information[124] resulted from the occurrence of a typical thought construction rooted in Christian symbolism (nine is the number of *e.g.* archangels, but also thrones and cosmic powers tamed by Christ, *etc.*), and not a reference to the historical reality of the Slavic cult.

---

120 Adam II, 21: "... credo ea significante causa, quod perditas animas eorum, qui idolis serviunt, congrue novies Stix interfusa cohercet".
121 This view is well located in trends of the theology of that time, in which performance of "ungodly rituals" led pagans to death and was understood as eternal damnation in hell. *E.g.* in the lives of St. Adalbert there is a quotation of a missionary catechesis whose element was freeing from the power of the devil and the abyss of the horrendous hell, to which people were led by the cursed pagan rituals and the cult of idols. See: *Vita Adalberti*, ed. Jürgen Hoffmann, in Jürgen Hoffmann, *Vita Adalberti. Früheste Textüberlieferungen der Lebensgeschichte Adalberts von Prag* (Essen: Klartext, 2005), 28, and Vita Adalberti II, 25; see Wolny, "Z dziejów katechezy," pp. 168 f. The state of potential damnation of pagans, *i.e.* immersion in death is concisely described by St. Bruno of Querfurt in *Vita quinque fratrum eremitarum (seu) vita uel passio benedicti et Iohannis sociorumque suorum auctore Brunone Querfurtensi*, ed. Jadwiga Karwasińska, MPH n.s. 4/3 (1973), 22: *mortui pagani*; see Bylina, *Człowiek*, pp. 34 f.
122 See editor's comments in: Adam II, 21, p. 78.
123 Schmidt, "Rethra," pp. 384 ff. The author shows the occurrence of number three and nine (as a multiplication of three, augmentation) as a characteristic feature of medieval perspective of paganism and consistently analyses these numerical data in Thietmar's description of Radogošč and Adam's description of Rethra as examples of a general trend.
124 *E.g.* 99 offerings in Leire mentioned by Thietmar (I, 17).

ADAM OF BREMEN ON SLAVIC RELIGION 221

However, it is hard not to share in the certain moderation expressed in Jerzy Strzelczyk's views related to such unequivocal assessment of the cognitive value of Adam of Bremen's work: "Schmidt's interpretation (...) can be accused of not taking into account the associative skills of the chroniclers, who – from a theoretical perspective – could resort to Classical comparisons and allegories in relation to real things. The fact that the Styx was to flow its nine currents and that the said quotation of Adam of Bremen referred to 'nine gates' of Rethra, does not by itself undermine confidence in Adam's account of Rethra. Moreover, the Author [R. Schmidt – S.R.] deserves gratitude for pointing out the possibility of allegorical understanding of the controversial text and together with him we agree that only archaeology can help to find the mysterious Rethra."[125]

This opinion was expressed over thirty years ago and the level of optimism related to the possible archaeological success in this search did not grow over that time.[126] Thus, one has to resort to a continuation of the discussion on Adam's writing procedure in the context of the mentality of his epoch. It is true that it is hard to exclude the fact that in the culture of the old Slavdom the numbers 3 or 9 have a symbolical role and could influence the shaping of sacral spaces. Yet, actually taking into account examples indicated by R. Schmidt, it is worth stressing that number 9 used to play an important part in pre-Christian offering rituals in Scandinavia,[127] and this fact could be on the one hand a factor which influenced the formation of the cult neighbouring Slavonic communities. On the other hand, it could also bring the development of stereotypical opinions about an alleged, typical respect by the pagans for this kind of numerical symbolism which could then have influenced the creation of a literary image of Rethra.

---

125 Strzelczyk, "Rec. Festschrift," pp. 200–202.
126 Numerous proposals of Rethra locations, however, hardly verifiable, see Słupecki, *Slavonic Pagan Sanctuaries*, p. 59 (map); Strzelczyk, *Mity*, p. 196 (map). See also: Volker Schmidt, "Rethra, das frühstädtische Zentrum an der Lieps," in *Instantia est Mater Doctrinae. Księga Jubileuszowa Prof. Dr. hab. Władysława Filipowiaka*, ed. Eugeniusz Wilgocki *et al.* (Szczecin: Stowarzyszenie Naukowe Archeologów Polskich, 2001), pp. 201–222; Sven Wichert, "Vademecum Rethram – Eine Revision," *Bodendenkmalpflege in Mecklenburg-Vorpommern, Jahrbuch* 56 (2008) [2009], pp. 103–113. See also pp. 95 f., footnote 261.
127 The importance of number nine in sacrificial context in pre-Christian Scandinavian culture is confirmed by early runic inscriptions (c. 600 AD), see: Olof Sundqvist, "Runology and History of Religions. Some Critical Implications of the Debate on the Stentoften Inscription," in *Blandade runstudier* 2, ed. Lennart Elmevik, Lena Peterson, (Runrön. Runologiska bidrag utgivna av Institutionen för nordiska språk vid Uppsala universitet) 11 (Uppsala: Institutionen för nordiska språk vid Uppsala universitet, 1997), pp. 135–174.

Moreover, one should consider a special way of using symbolic numbers in Adam's work, which introduces harmony to the narration and at the same time makes it more open to further interpretation in the sacral dimension. With reference to the number nine, which is a triplication of the number three which is symbolically related to divinity,[128] the description of Rethra corresponds to the fact that the highest Slavic god was located there. Yet this is only one layer of this complex picture, in which the key message related to the number nine is introduced not earlier than in the Styx motif. In this perspective, nine gates lead to the capital of death and eternal damnation. Thus, the allegorical reference to a sliver of the ancient mythology does not weaken the Christian sense of the commentary of the canon from Bremen. As a result, it arouses a doubt about the extent to which consideration of this place in the categories of *interpretatio classica antiqua* of Slavic beliefs is justified, which is apparently indicated by the letter of the text.

In the assessment of Rethra's place in the textual world presented by Adam of Bremen, the key factor is the religious (and the related political) significance attributed to this place. It was called the "most famous" (*vulgatissima*) town of the Slavdom,[129] which can hardly be explained by any other reason than considering it the "capital of idolatry", which appears here not only as a form of cult addressed to statues but also, in a wider meaning, as denial of worship for a true God.[130] This raises the question of whether or not there were theological reasons to lead to an literary exaggeration of the political role of Rethra in relation to the reality of the Liutici Federation.

At the same time, one should take into account the chronicler's environment where there was a common view of its role as a capital, resulting

---

128 For symbolism of number three see *e.g.* Forstner, *Świat*, pp. 43 f.

129 Koczy, "Sklawanja," p. 229, paid attention to the same issue emphasizing that Rethra turned out to be even more famous than *Iumne* (certainly Wolin), according to Adam, unquestionably the richest centre of Slavdom defined as *civitas opulentissima Slavorum* and *nobilissma*, see Adam II, 22; II, 79, schol. 56 (57). Towns ranked lower than *Iumne* encompassed Demmin – *civitas maxima*, and Starigard – *magna*.

130 Cf. Adam I, 12, on Willehad of Frisia: "ydola confregisse populos ad culturam veri Dei euangelizasse dicitur"; schol. 20: "... rex Haraldus abiecta ydolatria (...) ad colendum verum Deum se convertit". The word *ydola* consistently refers to the antithesis of God – Adam II, 30: "Suein derelictus a Deo, frustra sperans in ydolis suis." Similarly *ydolatria* as a synonym of paganism is juxtaposed with Christianity – see Adam II, 41: "Ipse (*i.e.* Sven – S.R.) igitur mox destructo ritu ydolatriae christianitatem in Nortmania per edictum suscipere iussit"; see also schol. 26.

ADAM OF BREMEN ON SLAVIC RELIGION 223

from church propaganda or commonplace opinions.[131] Scholion 71 provides excellent material for consideration. It includes information about two monks from Bohemia who were tormented to death in Rethra: "Rumour has it that two monks came at that time to the city of Rhetra from the forests of Bohemia. Because they publicly preached the word of God there in the assembly of the pagans, after having gone through torments, as they themselves had wished, they were eventually beheaded for Christ. Their names are indeed unknown among the humans, we truthfully believe, however, that they have been written down in heaven."[132]

The capital character of Rethra is indicated by information about pagans gathering there for a council, and also the very selection of the place in which monks were to expect death when performing their apostolic duties: it is hard to find a better one than the major capital of the pagans.[133] The information is not very specific, as should be the case when one deals with a rumour (*fama*). However, when dealing with hearsay, general stereotypical views should be taken into account. One of them was a conviction that Rethra – enjoying the fame of being the capital of paganism – in the 11th c. was treated as an assembly (*veche*) place.

Adam also placed in Rethra the martyrdom of John Scotus, the bishop of Mecklenburg, which took place during the Slavic uprising in 1066,[134] emphasizing that the beheaded body was left *in platea*. The selection of a translation of this expression as "in the street" would indicate that the chronicler considered the cult centre as an ordinary town.[135] Thus it is possible that the Liutici council convened there,[136] or at least certainly the less numerous convention

---

131   Schmidt, "Rethra," pp. 371 f., indicated an analogy to Adam's image of Rethra, in similarities in the description of Marklo, created as the centre of the Saxon tribes which in pagan times were not yet governed by the royal authority.

132   Adam III, 21, schol. 71: "Fama est eo tempore duos monachos a Boemiae saltibus in civitatem Rethre venisse. Ubi dum verbum Dei publice annunciarent, concilio paganorum, sicut ipsi desideraverunt, diversis primo suppliciis examinati ad ultimum pro Christo decollati sunt. Quorum nomina quidem hominibus incognita, ut veraciter credimus, in celo scripta sunt."

133   Similarly the motif of Christian martyrdom is repeated in the characteristics of the temple in Uppsala, Adam IV, schol. 141.

134   For more information see below, p. 244.

135   Adam III, 51. However, "in platea" can mean on a square, courtyard, *e.g.* in front of a temple.

136   The same *e.g.* Dralle, "Rethra," p. 38, claimed that the mass meeting during which the Bohemian monks lost their lives, was *placitum generale* of the Liutici. See also Zernack, *Die burgstädtischen Volkversammlungen*, pp. 208 ff.

224   CHAPTER 3

of their elders.[137] Regardless, this is not a sufficient basis on which to consider
the reference to such a meeting taking place in Rethra contained in the scholion about the Bohemian martyrs, as credible. This is because it collides with
the earlier statement given by Adam that entry into the town (*civitas*) was possible only for those who were looking for divination or making an offering. It is
doubtful that the Christian monks would be allowed to enter.[138]

Therefore, it seems legitimate to consider the information about the pagan
assembly (veche) in Rethra, which appeared in a gloss to the original version
of the chronicle, as a trace of the dissemination in Germany of the above mentioned commonplace opinion that this centre was the major capital of pagans.
In this situation it was not difficult to assume that this was the place of the
mass meeting.[139] It is also possible to hypothesize that if this type of stereotypical information was circulated, a certain type of simplification could take
place when it comes to the location of the assembly in Rethra itself. It is possible that it took place near the town, but in such a way that the oracle there
influenced its proceedings.[140]

On the other hand however, it is worth taking into account that in the case
of the rumour (*fama*), *i.e.* the story about the Bohemian monks, even the very
common opinion about the capital role of Rethra could prejudge the automatic location in this place of their public activity and martyrdom, without inquir-
ing about detailed circumstances of this event. Regardless of the selection of
a solution to this problem, the content of the analyzed scholion supports the

---

137   Leciejewicz, ">>In Pago," p. 131, emphasized that in towns located at the mouth of the
      Oder, in the 12th c. councils took place near fairs, not near temples. It is worth observing,
      however, that the said early urban centres except for fairs, also had temples with priests,
      whose influence on decisions of the community participating in the meeting is con-
      firmed in St. Otto of Bamberg hagiography (*e.g.* VP III, 8; Ebo III, 15; Herbord III, 17), and
      above, pp. 126 f., and below, pp. 335, 359. See also Jacek Banaszkiewicz, "Otto z Bambergu
      i pontifex idolorum. O urządzeniu i obyczaju miejsca wiecowego pogańskiego Szczecina,"
      in *Biedni i bogaci. Studia z dziejów społeczeństwa i kultury ofiarowane Bronisławowi
      Geremkowi w sześćdziesiątą rocznicę urodzin*, ed. Maurice Aymard *et al.* (Warszawa: PWN,
      1992), pp. 275–284; Rosik, *Conversio*, pp. 255, 456 ff.

138   However, the very presence of the Bohemian evangelisers in Polabia falls within the
      bounds of probability given lively contacts between both countries as early as the 10th
      c. See Łowmiański, *Religia*, p. 194. See also Labuda, *Fragmenty*, vol. 3, p. 187; Ludat, "Die
      Patriarchatsidee," pp. 326 f.

139   See above, p. 223. In this situation "in platea" in the description of the martyrdom of bish-
      op John should be referred to the courtyard or square in Rethra.

140   Similarly to the Wagrian sanctuary of Prowe (see below, p. 335). Such connection of the
      assembly and oracle should be taken into account in the case of the Liutici even on the
      basis of the description of Radogošč in Thietmar's chronicle (see above, pp. 128 ff.).

ADAM OF BREMEN ON SLAVIC RELIGION   225

thesis of stereotypical treatment of *sedes ydolatrie* as the main centre in the whole of pagan Slavdom.

The consolidation or even creation of this commonplace opinion was influenced by the canon of Bremen who used a rather typical template of description in the case of this kind of centre. Jacek Banaszkiewicz emphasized an analogy between the Adam's descriptions of Rethra and Uppsala, the town with the famous temple, located *in medio Suevoniae*. Similarly, since the Redars were hosts in Redigast's sanctuary in relation to the remaining tribes between the Elbe and the Oder, they turned out to be *medii et potentissimi omnium*. In both cases the temple is indicated as the middle point of the domain, and a centre of a politically-organized community.[141]

The primacy of Rethra in this historiographic vision does not accurately reflect the political reality, and at best reflects its general Slavic fame.[142] The chronicler presented this centre as a general capital of paganism on the land between the Elbe and the Oder,[143] without taking into account the accurate reach of the Liutici Federation. However, in this way the capital of the Hamburg archbishops (*Hammaburg metropolis*[144]), aspiring to the rank of the patriarchy of the North and according to Adam *nostra sedis*,[145] found its contemporary antithesis in the form of Rethra as the Slavic "metropolis" (*metropolis Sclavorum*),[146] expressly treated as the "capital of idolatry" (*sedes ydolatriae*).[147]

Finally it should be emphasized that Adam of Bremen does not mention the contemporary expedition of bishop of Halberstadt Burchard to the Liutici land, to which Rethra (*Rheda*) fell prey and which was mentioned in *Annales*

---

141   Banaszkiewicz, "Jedność porządku," p. 447. See also Scior, *Das Eigene und das Fremde*, pp. 117 f.

142   Even at the time of earlier Christianization attempts, the Slavic people could still worship the famous sanctuary, in the name of which sounds the word "advice" (Polish "rada") for "guest" (Polish "gość") – see *ibidem*, p. 448.

143   A convincing argument for it is distinguishing the Redars and Rethra among "numerous Slavic peoples" ("populi Sclavorum multi") listed in this passage and treated as one whole entity living between the Elbe and Oder ("qui inter Albiam et Oddaram degunt"), cf. Adam II, 21.

144   For referring to Hamburg as a metropolis, see *e.g.* Adam I, 15; II, 15, *etc.* (according to the index [in:] Adam, p. 303).

145   Adam IV, 20, schol. 127.

146   Adam III, 50.

147   Pointing at an another bishopric see as an antithesis of Rethra in Adam's view (*e.g.* Mecklemburg because of the martyrdom of bishop John of Mecklemburg in Rethra, see below p. 244) seems to be less justified. According to the chronicler Rethra was a capital of idolatry, and this is why Hamburg-Bremen metropolis as the leading centre of missions in the Barbarian North seem to be the best hypothetical proposal of the discussed antithesis.

226   CHAPTER 3

Augustani (under the year 1068).[148] Even such spectacular success of the suffragan bishop of the Mainz metropolis was not worth mentioning on the pages
of a work devoted to the history of the Hamburg-Bremen metropolis.

2.2   Iumne

After depicting the famous Liutici sanctuary, the chronicler moved the focus
of his attention to the inhabitants of the Oder mouth: "Behind the Liutici,
known also as Veleti, floats the Oder River, the opulentest river in the Slavic
region. In its estuary, where it joins the Scythian Marshes, the famous city of
Iumne constitutes the best-known harbor for the Barbarians and the Greeks
that are around."[149] Then the famous town was located at the "Scythian
Marshes." This element of mythical geography corresponds with the claim
that *Iumne* was populated with "Barbarians and Greeks," where they found the
"most famous" port.

This account – at least what emerges from the chronicler's declaration – was
to limit the expansion of untrue rumours about the "most excellent" town: "For
a praise of the city I have decided that it is kind to mention a few words worth
passing over, as numerous wonderful things are said about it, although they are
hard to believe."[150] Ironically this narration came on the threshold of the birth
of the Vineta legend, the oldest testimony of which can be found in the chronicle of Helmold of Bosau[151] more than a century later. He presented this ancient

---

148   *Annales Augustani*, under the year 1068, p. 128. According to this report, the invaders stole
        a holy horse (see above, pp. 129 ff.), which was not mentioned by master Adam either.
149   Adam II, 22: "Ultra Leuticios, qui alio nomine Wilzi dicuntur, Oddara flumen occurit, di-
        tissimus amnis Sclavaniae regionis. In cuius ostio, qua Scyticas alluit paludes, nobilissima
        civitas Iumne celeberrimam praestat stationem Barbaris et Grecis, qui sunt in circuitu".
150   *Ibidem*: "De cuius praeconio urbis, quia magna quaedam et vix credibilia recitantur, vo-
        lupe arbitror pauca inserere digna relatu".
151   In Helmold's chronicle, the title of chapter 2 is *De civitate Vinneta* (in all existing codices),
        however in other places codices differ from one another – *Iumneta, iumta, iumenta, ui-
        neta, vinneta, ninieta, Immuueta, Vimneta*. The deformed beginning of the name *Iumne*
        in Helmold's work, in all variants can be explained by a paleographic mistake, however,
        a more problematic issue is the explanation for the ending 'ta', which is the same in all
        variants of Helmold's chronicle and did not occur in any earlier writers' works (Adam of
        Bremen, Annalist Saxo). It will have to be explained by Latinisation of the unclear name
        of *Iumne*, which gained wording referring to the *Vinedi*. This view has already been for-
        mulated by Jacobus Langebek, *Scriptores Rerum Danicarum Medii Aevi*, vol. 1 (Hafniae:
        Godiche, 1772), pp. 51–52, footnote h, and it was solidified in historical studies; cf. Ryszard
        Kiersnowski, *Legenda Winety. Studium historyczne* (Kraków: Wydawnictwo Studium
        Słowiańskiego Uniwersytetu Jagiellońskiego, 1950), pp. 41f.; it was not shared by Mikołaj
        Rudnicki, "Odra i jej ujścia," *Slavia Occidentalis* 15 (1936), pp. 67–73, proving the Slavic

ADAM OF BREMEN ON SLAVIC RELIGION   227

and rich town of Slavs and newcomers from other nations as belonging to the distant past. It was to be completely devastated by one of the Danish rulers.

This legend is one of the most mysterious literary and historiographic motifs recorded by medieval authors, which stirred the minds of wide social circles and existed in folklore until the 20th c. The story inspired literature, painting, music, political ideology, and even modern board games. The last two centuries brought attempts at scientific criticism of the legend, which resulted in rich primary literature and proposals of definitive solutions related to its genesis and historical value.[152] It is important, however, that Adam wrote about *Iumne* as a centre that is known and contemporary to him. Did he possibly sense the beginning of the legend in the fame of the centre located on the Oder? This is an excessively cautious judgment.

The chronicler's declaration that, facing the reality of growing popularity of improbable stories, he wanted to say something which would be "worth passing over" ("digna relatu"), is more of a rhetorical game for the reader. The fact that Adam contributed to the creation of this legend himself is confirmed not only in the above mentioned mythization of geography, but also in the further narration about the famous town:

"Indeed, it is the biggest of all cities in Europe and it is inhabited by Slavs and other peoples, Greeks and Barbarians. For even the Saxon newcomers were granted the same rights of inhabitance on the condition that they will not publicly cultivate Christianity while they remain in the city. Since they all still live in the sin of following pagan rituals but besides that, in terms of customs and hospitality, it is impossible to find any other nation that would match

---

  genesis of the name Vineta and its older origin than in the case of *Iumne*. This view is not based on sufficient basis in sources, and first of all it did not take into account the cultural context of the epoch, in which it is not surprising that new names were created to meet the needs of a legend, if only on association basis, whose mechanism is partly explained in the above indicated paleographic findings.

152 The scholarly debate on the legend of Vineta until the mid-20th c. was reported by Kiersnowski, *Legenda Winety*, p. 3–27. *Ibidem*, p. 63–111, where he presented the history of this legend. Lately on this issue see: Monika Rusakiewicz, *Wineta. Korzenie legendy i jej recepcja w historiografii zachodniopomorskiej do XVI wieku* (Wrocław: Chronicon, 2016). A concise study can be also found in Lech Leciejewicz, "Wineta," in SSS, vol. 6, p. 472. Moreover the issue of Wolin-Vineta and basic literature related to it is presented by Władysław Filipowiak, Heinz Gundlach, *Wolin-Vineta. Die tatsächliche Legende vom Untergang und Aufstieg der Stadt* (Rostock: Hinstorff, 1992); Witold Hensel, "Wineta – miasto słowiańskie nad Bałtykiem, niegdyś ludne i opływające we wszelkie bogactwa, czy wytwór baśni o średniowiecznej karze bożej?," *Slavia Antiqua* 40 (1999), pp. 273 f.; Stanisław Rosik, "Wineta – utopia szlachetnych pogan (znaczenie legendy w Helmolda 'Kronice Słowian')," *Slavia Antiqua* 42 (2001), pp. 113–122.

228   CHAPTER 3

their generosity and kindness."[153] A significant factor in the creation of the legend was certainly the consideration that *Iumne* was the largest European town, and a necessary characteristic maintaining its world position was a tolerant attitude of its inhabitants towards newcomers (the only ban was on public Christian cult).[154]

Not for nothing did Adam of Bremen enjoy fame as the "Tacitus" of the peoples of the North. Similar to his outstanding Roman predecessor, he appreciated some barbarian customs, their hospitality, nobility, kindness, and generosity. These stereotypical assessments match one of the main trends in the characteristics of barbarians in the continuation of ancient culture in the Middle Ages.[155] However, there was an alternative to this trend expressed in the emphasis on their savageness and cruelty, but the chronicler decided to only stress that the inhabitants of *Iumne* performed pagan rites.

They are, let us repeat, "Sclavi cum aliis gentibus, Grecis et Barbaris." The Slavs, which is not surprising, are the main element in the city, however it is interesting why all "the other peoples" are locked in the name "Greeks and Barbarians." Even the next sentence about the permission granted to the Saxons to live there,[156] literally clashes with this formula, as they could neither

---

153   Adam II, 22: "Est sane maxima omnium, quas Europa claudit, civitatum, quam incolunt Sclavi cum aliis gentibus, Grecis et Barbaris; nam et advenae Saxones parem cohabitandi legem acceperunt, si tamen christianitatis titulum ibi morantes non publicaverint. Omnes enim adhuc paganicis ritibus oberrant, ceterum moribus et hospitalitate nulla gens honestior aut benignior poterit inveniri."

154   Filipowiak, *Słowiańskie wierzenia*, p. 19.

155   For extensive information about this type of topical assessment of barbarians see Modzelewski, *Barbarzyńska Europa*, pp. 27 ff. The author mentions one-sidedness of this view of the >>strangers<<, not taking into consideration the conditioning of attitudes viewed in this way in the form of customary laws (so called *leges barbarorum*) aimed at guaranteeing security for the whole community. In the case of presentations of the Slavdom, among these stereotypical opinions, hospitality is particularly emphasized, which is a premise that this topos had the best founded basis in the reality of social life (see: Lech Leciejewicz, "Mensa illorum nunquam disarmatur. Kilka uwag o słowiańskiej gościnności," in *Świat średniowiecza. Studia ofiarowane Profesorowi Henrykowi Samsonowiczowi*, ed. Agnieszka Bartoszewicz *et al.* (Warszawa: Wydawnictwa Uniwersytetu Warszawskiego, 2010), pp. 628–633). The occurrence of this kind of stereotypical assessment in medieval literature was conditioned also by meeting particular goals, which were also intentionally supported by the creativity of authors, and this fact is worth emphasizing especially in the analysis of Adam's information about *Iumne*.

156   Lech Leciejewicz, "Sasi w słowiańskich miastach nadbałtyckich w X–XI w.," in *Kultura średniowieczna i staropolska. Studia ofiarowane Aleksandrowi Gieysztorowi w pięćdziesięciolecie pracy naukowej*, ed. Danuta Gawin *et al.* (Warszawa: PWN, 1991), pp. 99–105.

ADAM OF BREMEN ON SLAVIC RELIGION

be placed with the first, nor the second category.[157] It is certainly possible to confine oneself to the statement that the source can be regarded as internally contradictory in this place, and then begin attempts to find representatives of pagan peoples (*e.g.* Prussians, partly Scandinavians) in "barbarians" and Byzantine (Greek) rite followers in "Greeks" who came from Rus'.[158] Another premise to support this interpretation is the fact that Helmold of Bosau, when commenting on the information about Rus' taken from Adam of Bremen's chronicle, stated that its inhabitants in the Church order seem more likely to follow the Greeks rather than the Latins.[159]

In the case of the passage about *Iumne* the cluster *Greci – Latini* was not used. However, the whole expression "cum aliis gentibus, Grecis et Barbaris" corresponds with a phrase from the Epistle of Saint Paul to the Romans: "in ceteris gentibus / Graecis ac barbaris,"[160] which on the pages of the New Testament on the basis *pars pro toto* encompasses all humankind. Therefore, even if some associations with non-Christian people contemporary to the chronicler (as *barbari*) or followers of Eastern Christianity evoked this phrase, it is still a New

---

157 Scior, *Das Eigene und das Fremde*, p. 102, proposed to consider the Saxons a separate category, the so called "newcomers" (*advenae*), in line with the expression "advenae Saxones" used by the chronicler, and thereby excluded from the entirety of peoples representing Slavs and many nations referred to as "Greeks and Barbarians". This inspiring observation related to the way the chronicler viewed the composition of the *Iumne* population and more precisely its migrant element. However, an attempt to claim that the "newcomers" were not included in "other peoples" ("alia gentes") separated from the Slavs, *i.e.* "Greeks and Barbarians" raises doubts. The chronicler mentioned "advenae Saxones" to develop the information that the city is inhabited by "Sclavi cum aliis gentibus, Grecis et Barbaris". This is enforced especially by the expression "nam et", "for/also because", used in a sentence about the Saxons which is connected with the sentence about the "Greeks and Barbarians". Besides even the information that the Saxons had the right to live in *Iumne* allows the expression "quam incolunt Sclavi cum aliis gentibus, Grecis et Barbaris" to be referred to them.

158 This idea can be supported by a testimony available thanks to archaeology offering evidence of contacts between Wolin and Veliky Novgorod or Old Ladoga. The same issue is discussed in *e.g.* Kazimierz Ślaski, "Stosunki krajów skandynawskich z południowo-wschodnim wybrzeżem Bałtyku od VI do XII wieku," *Przegląd Zachodni* 8 (1952) 2, pp. 39, 44; Labuda, *Fragmenty*, vol. 2, pp. 115 ff.; Lech Leciejewicz, "O kontaktach Słowian nadbałtyckich z północną Rusią we wczesnym średniowieczu," in *Viae historicae. Księga jubileuszowa dedykowana Profesorowi Lechowi A. Tyszkiewiczowi w siedemdziesiątą rocznicę urodzin*, ed. Mateusz Goliński, Stanisław Rosik, (Acta Universitatis Wratislaviensis. Historia) 152 (Wrocław: Wydawnictwo Uniwersytetu Wrocławskiego, 2001), pp. 208–214.

159 Helmold I, 1: "Grecos magis quam Latinos imitari videntur".

160 Cf. Rom 1:14.

230   CHAPTER 3

Testament reference which seems to be the most important explanation of its meaning in Adam's work.[161]

In this perspective the phrase *Greci et Barbari* should be treated as a reference to all of humankind.[162] The chronicler would have used it to show the worldwide significance of *Iumne*. A similar formula in the presentation of people in general was included by St. Paul in the Epistle to the Colossians, and it is also worth mentioning that there was a reference to the Scythians in it,[163] who were also earlier referred to by Adam of Bremen, when he wrote about the location of *Iumne* near *Scythice Paludes*.

Therefore, in the narration about *Iumne* the author referred to elements of antique culture, and not merely to Christian antiquity. He mentions that in the town there was the "Vulcanus's pot" (*olla Vulcani*). According to him – in the opinion of the inhabitants – it was to be the so called Greek fire, one of the most dangerous combustible substances used in sea battles and sieges.[164] This motif in the source connects the Latin and Greek element that was present in the culture, which on the one hand corresponds with the emphasis on the worldwide significance of the town and on the other hand indicates a utilitarian meaning of this "pot" of fire. Hence, calling the name of a Roman deity was based here on an allegory and there are no reasons to consider this Vulcanus as *interpretatio Romana* of some Slavic god.[165]

---

161   Nowak, *Untersuchungen*, p. 69; Stanisław Rosik, "Barbari et Greci w Iumne. >>Europa barbarzyńska<< jako koncepcja w studiach nad formowaniem się kulturowego oblicza Kontynentu (wokół przekazu Adama z Bremy)," in *Europa barbarica, Europa christiana. Studia Medievalia Carolo Modzelewski dedicata*, ed. Roman Michałowski *et al.* (Warszawa: DiG, 2008), pp. 191–197 (development the ideas presented in 2000); cf. Rosik, *Greeks and Romans*, pp. 195–201. See also Fraesdorff, *Der barbarische Norden*, p. 284.

162   St. Paul is presented in this place as a debtor, whose duty is proclaiming the Holy Gospel to "Greeks and barbarians" (cf. Rom 1:14). In this way the horizon of apostolic activity in the dimension of all peoples was determined.

163   The motif of Scythians was used by St. Paul in the Epistle to Colossians (Col 3:11), to define their affiliation with the Christian community based on overcoming ethnically, culturally and socially conditioned antinomies: there is no distinction between Greek and Jew, barbarian and Scythian or slave and free. On the matter of Scythians in Adam's chronicle see *e.g.* Fraesdorff, *Der barbarische Norden*, pp. 294 ff.

164   Adam II, 22: "Ibi est Olla Vulcani, quod incolae Grecum ignem vocant, de quo etiam meminit Solinus" ("Vulcan's Pot is situated there, which the inhabitants call Greek fire that Solinus mentioned"). Emphasis on the fact that Greek fire is mentioned by Solinus proves the erudition of *magister scholarum* from Bremen. According to quite popular speculation, this substance was used as fuel for a primitive lighthouse. See: Hensel, *Słowiańszczyzna*, p. 701; cf. Ryszard Kiersnowski, "Kamień i Wolin," *Przegląd Zachodni* 7 (1957) 9/10, pp. 220 f.; Koczy, *Sklawanja*, p. 229.

165   This was proposed by *e.g.* Wirski, "Bóstwo," p. 313, however, he did not take into consideration that it was a kind of fuel (Greek fire) and not a cult object. Similarly, without any

ADAM OF BREMEN ON SLAVIC RELIGION

On a similar basis, Adam then introduced Neptune to the narration, adding that *Iumne* is located on an island: "Neptune divides there into three kinds of nature: for the island is surrounded by three sea waters, one of which is intensively green, the second is whitish, while the third has mad billows and is always turbulent due to constant storms."[166] In this context it is hard to see a substitute for the name of an alleged Slavic god of the sea in mentioning the Roman theonym. Here Neptune is the sea element,[167] which has a triple form of water surrounding the island.

The number three corresponds to typical mythological characteristics of the absolute power of a deity in this case over the sea element. Moreover, Adam's characteristics of water surrounding the island creates a reference to the scenery of the mouth of the Oder. The said sea billows can be hypothetically connected with the Baltic waves and the green waters can be associated with today's Szczecin Bay. The triangular shape of the island especially resembles the outline of Wolin Island. However, it should be noticed that a schematic way of describing whole geographical areas, typical in the geography of the time, is a potential element here.[168]

One way or another, in the discussion on the location of *Iumne*, the predominant proposal for its location is Wolin Island (although Usedom should also be considered).[169] Adam's information about an abundance of goods brought there by merchants from various parts of the world indicates that the city was an impressive emporium.[170] After many generations of scholarly discussion, at

---

grounds – since the literary convention was not taken into account – this author tried to find in the later mentioned Neptune (see below) a Slavic sea god.

166 Adam II, 22: "Ibi cernitur Neptunus triplicis naturae: tribus enim fretis alluitur illa insula, quorum aiunt unum esse viridissimae speciei, alterum subalbidae, tertium motu furibundo perpetuis saevit tempestatibus."

167 In the analysis of this place, it seems very instructive to refer a passage of *Translatio S. Alexandrii* devoted to the Saxons and their religion, which was used by Adam in his work, Adam I, 7. It starts with a cluster of information taken over from Tacitus and the New Testament: "coluerunt enim eos, qui natura non erant dii, inter quos precipue Mercurium venerabantur" – "As they worship those who by nature are not gods, and above all they praise Mercury" (cf. Gal 4:8: "iis, qui natura non sunt dii, serviebatis"). Alluding to the Epistle to the Galatians, in the perception of the erudite from Bremen, certainly evoked additional information from the next line (cf. Gal 4:9) in which pagan gods when faced with the divinity of the Creator, similarly to the opinion of stoics, are reduced to powerless and miserable elements: *infirma et egena elementa*.

168 In a similar way Adam (I, 1) described Saxony as having a triangular shape.

169 Langebek (see below p. 226, footnote 151) located Vineta (*Iumne*) on the north-west cape of Usedom Island.

170 Adam II, 22: "Urbs illa mercibus omnium septentrionalium nationum locupules nihil non habet iocundi aut rari."

232   CHAPTER 3

present there is quite reasonable agreement identifying it as Wolin.[171] The origins of the name of this city, which is still used today,[172] are hypothetically connected with the Wolinian tribe, which most certainly is confirmed by Adam
when he mentions the *Wilini*.[173]

Such clear etymology cannot be indicated in the case of *Iumne*, which is why
until recently it was mostly assumed that the name had a non-Slavic origin and
that it was used in parallel with the native name originating from the name
of the said tribe.[174] However, now the dominant hypothesis assumes a Slavic

---

171   See *e.g.* Bollnow, *Studien zur Geschichte*, pp. 22 f.; Ewa Rzetelska-Feleszko, "Wolin (1)," in
       SSS, vol. 6, p. 561; Lech Leciejewicz, "Wolin (2)," in SSS, vol. 6, pp. 562 f.; Rosik, *Conversio*,
       pp. 238 f.; Jakub Morawiec, *Wolin w średniowiecznej tradycji skandynawskiej* (Kraków:
       Avalon, 2010), pp. 446 f. It is worth mentioning that the concept assuming *Iumne* identi-
       fied with Vineta is Wolin was already put forward by Johann Friedrich Zöllner, *Reise durch
       Pommern nach der Insel Rügen und einem Theile des Herzogthums Mecklenburg, im Jahre
       1795* (Berlin: Maurer, 1797), p. 507; the later rich discussion until the mid-20th c. was report-
       ed by Kiersnowski, *Legenda*, pp. 10 ff., he also supported the identification of Vineta with
       Wolin (*ibidem*, pp. 28 ff., especially pp. 36 ff.). The same view was expressed by Labuda,
       Fragmenty, vol. 2, pp. 129 f. and 184 ff.; Lech Leciejewicz, "Wineta," in SSS, vol. 6, p. 472. The
       wealth of Wolin in the Early Middle Ages, confirmed in archaeological excavations, cor-
       responds with Adam's information about *Iumne*. On the basis of these excavations, it is
       emphasized that strangers (merchants, warriors and craftsmen) coming to this place en-
       joyed significant freedom of action in Wolin. See Leciejewicz, *Słowianie*, p. 143; Władysław
       Filipowiak, "Wollin – ein frühmittelalterliches Zentrum an der Ostsee," in *Europasmitte
       um 1000. Beiträge zur Geschichte, Kunst und Archäologie. Handbuch zur Ausstellung*, vol. 1,
       ed. Alfred Wieczorek, Hans-Martin Hinz (Stuttgart: Theiss, 2000), pp. 152–155; Władysław
       Duczko, "Obecność skandynawska na Pomorzu i słowiańska w Skandynawii we wczesnym
       średniowieczu," in *Salsa Cholbergiensis. Kołobrzeg w średniowieczu*, ed. Lech Leciejewicz,
       Marian Rębkowski (Kołobrzeg: Le petit Café, 2001), pp. 24–39, and recently in an extensive
       monographic study Błażej M. Stanisławski, *Jómswikingowie z Wolina-Jómsborga – studium
       archeologiczne przenikania kultury skandynawskiej na ziemie polskie* (Wrocław: IAE PAN,
       2013). See also below, p. 267.
172   The earliest testimony of this name comes from 12th c. sources, in Ekkehard of Aura's
       (deceased 1126) chronicle, see *Ekkechardi Uraugiensis chronica*, ed. Georg Waitz, MGH SS
       6 (1844), under the year 1125, pp. 263 f., and the hagiography of St. Otto of Bamberg (see
       e.g. Vita Prieflingensis II, 5).
173   Adam II, 18. Earlier most certainly the same people were testified by Widukind of Corvey
       (III, 69) in the record of *Vuloini*.
174   With reference to the said Old Nordic sagas of Jomsvikings based in Jomsborg, *Iumne* was
       considered as sounding similar to *Iom* and thought to be the name of Wolin used only by
       Scandinavians. However, in linguistic research the Nordic origin of the name *Iumne* and
       related names like *Iom* were excluded. This is why the hypothesis of their Baltic prove-
       nience and its dissemination also among the Scandinavians enjoyed some recognition,
       see Labuda, *Fragmenty*, vol. 2, pp. 184–190. It is worth mentioning that most certainly
       Iumne is a deformed form of the original *Iumme – ibidem*, pp. 119, 187 f. For information on

ADAM OF BREMEN ON SLAVIC RELIGION   233

origin of the toponym *Iumne*,[175] and the dissemination of the name "Wolin"
should be related to the social and political changes in the way this centre
functioned in the 11th–12th c., which would also be reflected in its names.[176]

The information about *Iumne* provided by Adam of Bremen is certainly significant in research on the religion of the Slavs.[177] A ban on practicing
Christianity publicly in the town indicates a monopolization of the religious
sphere of the social life by the pagan cult. It is confined to the formula: *paganici ritus*. Although laconic, it bears theological assessment not only because of a
pejorative overtone in the adjective *paganicus*, but also due to a wider context
of this work. It is especially worth recalling here the presentation of the Saxon
religion at the beginning of the work.

The chronicler defined it as superstition (*superstitio*), which in his times was
still practiced by the Slavs performing a "pagan rite" (*ritus paganicus*).[178] He
certainly did not evaluate "pagan rites" in *Iumne* in any other way using the
same words to describe them, whereas the lack of additional pejorative assessment of these rites, which would be quite natural in this context,[179] is exactly
what allows the immediate praise of the local customs to be fully expressed in

---

the earlier discussion on the origin of this toponym, see Ewa Rzetelska-Feleszko, "Wolin,"
in SSS, vol. 6, p. 561.

175   Recently an extensive study on this matter see: Alexandra Petrulevich, "On the etymology
of at Jómi, Jumne and Jómsborg," *Namn och Bydg* 97 (2009), pp. 65–97.

176   In this case the devastation of *Iumne*/Wolin during the invasion of the Danish king
Magnus in 1043 (see Morawiec, *Wolin*, pp. 407–493) is of key significance and it most certainly determined the end of the greatest splendour of this town confirmed by Thietmar,
and possibly half a century earlier by Ibrahim ibn Yaqub, who wrote about a powerful port
of the Weltaba people (Veleti or Wolinians), see: *Relacja Ibrahima ibn Jakuba z podróży
do krajów słowiańskich w przekazie al-Bekeriego*, ed. and trans. Tadeusz Kowalski, MPH
n.s. 1 (1946), p. 50. Thietmar's information (VI, 33) refers to the legation which arrived to
Henry II about 1007 from a "great city" *Livilni*: "... regi pascha Ratisbone celebranti de
Liuticis et ab hiis, qui a civitate magna Livilni dicta missi fuerat." See *e.g.* Labuda,
Fragmenty, vol. 2, pp. 130 f., L. Leciejewicz, "Wolin," in SSS, vol. 6, pp. 561–564, p. 562; *idem*,
"Wolinianie," in SSS, vol. 6, p. 564.

177   The native cult of inhabitants of Volin was incomparably more extensively presented in the hagiography of St. Otto of Bamberg. Additionally, some light is cast on this
problem by results of excavations and their interpretations, see Władysław Filipowiak,
Janusz Wojtasik, "Światowit z Wolina," *Z otchłani wieków* 41 (1975) 2, pp. 82–89; Witold
Hensel, "Wczesnośredniowieczna figurka czterotwarzowego bóstwa z Wolina," *Slovenska
Archeologia* 26 (1978), pp. 13–15; Władysław Filipowiak, "Wolińska kącina," *Z otchłani
wieków* 45 (1979), p. 115; Słupecki, "Słowiańskie posągi," p. 40 f. See also below, pp. 339 ff.

178   Adam I, 7: "quam adhuc Sclavi (...) ritu paganico servare videntur."

179   The same Adam II, 48, where he writes about Bishop Unvanus who requested eradication
of "omnes ritus paganicus, quorum adhuc superstitio viguit". For more information see
below, footnote 206 in this chapter.

234   CHAPTER 3

the subsequent passage of the chronicle. In accordance with this praise, *Iumne* returns in Adam's narrative as a safe haven for the king Harald Bluetooth, driven into exile by his son,[180] and its hospitality for him is surprising.[181]

With reference to this town, one can observe a model for the presentation of barbarians that is far from a hostile and confrontational ideology on the pages of Adam's chronicle.[182] The only vice mentioned was an attachment to the pagan religion, but at the same time a number of admirable, natural virtues were emphasized.[183] These positive traits help the reader to overcome the mental and cultural barriers of his environment that prevent the promotion and implementation of plans to include them in the Christian sphere.[184] Care "for the salvation of peoples" (*de salute gentium*) was one of the leading motifs in the work of Adam of Bremen.[185] He created the historiographic tradition of the archdiocese whose basic activity was the conversion of pagans.

---

180   About 986. Recently this issue was discussed in the context of the Jomsvikings by Morawiec, *Wolin*, pp. 138 f. See also Leciejewicz, "Normanowie nad Odrą i Wisłą," *Kwartalnik Historyczny* 100 (1993), 4, pp. 55 f.; Labuda, *Fragmenty*, vol. 2, pp. 127 f., 191f.

181   Adam (II, 28): "A quibus [*i.e.* Iumne inhabitants – S.R.] contra spem, quia pagani erant, humane receptus" ("By whom he was kindly embraced, against hope, as they were pagans"). This expression indicates that pagans were not expected to treat exiles kindly, humanely – *humane* (cf. Fraesdorff, *Der barbarische Norden*, p. 279; Goetz, *Die Wahrnehmung*, p. 171), and it was thought to be typical of them not to show any mercy – see *e.g.* Adam II, 34: "Is quoniam paganus erat, nulla super exulem misericordia motus est." – "As he [*i.e.* Thrucco Tryggve – it is a mistake as he was dead at that time – S.R.] was a pagan and did not show any mercy towards the exile" [*i.e.* Sven – S.R.]. This context leads to the conclusion that the claim that *Iumne* received the exiled king "against hope" (*contra spem*) in the author's concept is to indicate that in comparison with pagans in general, who treated strangers or Christians in an inhumane way, the inhabitants of this city would be a glorious exception. Adam's striving at emphasizing this fact left political reality, such as a possible alliance between Harald and the Wolinians, outside the centre of attention. To some extent polemizing with the quoted Adam's opinion, Labuda, *Fragmenty*, vol. 2, pp. 124 and 130, emphasized friendly relations between Harald and Wolinians and used this fact to explain the kind reception of the exile. Besides, it is worth observing that in accordance with Adam's information about the customs of *Iumne* inhabitants discussed above, travellers from various parts of the world, and hence also Scandinavians, were in 10th–11th c. regularly hosted in Wolin (see *e.g.* Leciejewicz, *Normanowie nad Odrą*, pp. 54 f.; *idem*, "Obcy kupcy na Słowiańszczyźnie Zachodniej w okresie wielkiego przełomu (IX–XI w.)," in *Cultus et cognitio. Studia z dziejów średniowiecznej kultury*, ed. Stefan K. Kuczyński *et al.* (Warszawa: PWN, 1976), p. 337; Stanisławski, *Jómswikingowie*, pp. 292–298 *et passim*).

182   Also in *Descriptio insularum aquilonis* there is *Iumne* without any references to paganism, see Adam IV, 20.

183   Similarly Adam created the image of Old Prussians, see Adam IV, 18.

184   This comment most certainly does not refer to the most defiant Rans.

185   The care about *salus gentium* was the basic task of the Archbishopric of Hamburg, which is confirmed in papal documents, see Adam II, 3.

ADAM OF BREMEN ON SLAVIC RELIGION

Distinguishing the inhabitants of *Iumne* as a community of world character indicates that this was also the universal reach of missionary plans or aspirations of the Hamburg-Bremen metropolis. In this perspective it is not surprising that the chronicler's delight in recalling Roman (Vulcanus, Neptune) or Greek elements in creating the images of the "largest city in Europe." It is dominated by the Slavs, which in turn corresponds with the emphasis on the fact that it was located at the river mouth, hence "in the gate" (*in ostio*) of the most abundant – according to Adam, of course – river in Slavdom. It was the main axis that connected the social and geographical space of the Slavs. Although *Iumne* itself, located on an island, is characterized as a port open to the world, it acted as a microcosm of the human universum.

2.3   *The Revolt during the Pontificate of Libentius*

Adam of Bremen connected the Slavic rebellion against the empire and Christianity with the crisis of the empire after Otto III's death.[186] After the presentation of these events, he specified that they completed "over seventy years" of Christianity on Slavic land between the Elbe and the Oder.[187] This era fell in the pontificate of the Archbishop of Hamburg and Bremen, Libentius (deceased 1013).[188] However, this part of the narration, along with scholions, indicates that in it there are scraps of memory for a few rebellions of Polabian tribes, starting with the last decades of the 10th c.[189] Most of this information

---

186   Adam II, 40.

187   Adam II, 42: "Omnes igitur Sclavi, qui inter Albiam et Oddaram habitant, per annos 70 et amplius christianitatem coluerunt, omni tempore Ottonum ..." ("Thus all the Slavs that inhabited the lands between Elbe and Oder practiced Christianity for over 70 years, all the Otto's times ...").

188   Adam II, 43. An additional indication here is a premise that at the same time ("eo tmpore") Pope Sergius IV (deceased 1012) solved a conflict with the Bishop of Verden Bernhard II related to the ownership of the town called *Ramsolam*, which is dated to about 1010, see *Hamburgisches Urkundenbuch*, No. 58, p. 69.

189   It should be emphasized that reducing the whole, discussed here, description of the rebellion only to the Obodrite circle does not remain in agreement with Adam's record outlining a wider geographical horizon of events – reaching the Oder. This is why it is hard to indisputably accept G. Labuda's statement (*Fragmenty*, vol. 1, p. 235) that the Bremen tradition, used by Adam, completely disregarded the Slavic rebellions in 983 and 1018. At least the consequences of the last mentioned rebellion could be taken into account in the statement of the fall of Christianity among the Slavs in the Ottonian epoch (especially after questioning the dating of the uprising resulting from the Adam's narrative to the last two years of Libentius's pontificate – see p. 240, footnote 209). On the other hand the rebellion of 983 is evoked by the figure of margrave Theodoric, who was to influence outbreak of described by Adam uprising, according to a scholion added to the original version of the chronicle (Adam II, 43, schol. 31); as he died in 985 and his role in the events which took place two years earlier is testified in Thietmar's work (see above, pp. 76 f.).

236   CHAPTER 3

refers to the Obodrites and Wagrians and in this respect almost certainly during the 990s.[190]

In the information about these events, first Adam and, after nearly a century, Helmold, show symptomatic agreement with Thietmar's earlier account
in the establishment of the reasons for the events which took place in 983:
the Saxons were to blame as they oppressed people subjugated to them.[191] The
rebels led by Mstivoy and Mstidrog looted Nordalbingien and then some Slavic
lands. The description is focused mainly on the consequential ravaging of the
Church, and the person who was the most to blame for the consequences of
the rebellion in Polabia was Saxon duke Bernard 1. It was him who pushed the
Slavs to start the rebellion,[192] and to consequently reject Christianity.[193]

190   The person who is of key significance in the establishment of indicative dating of the
       Obodrite rebellion is duke Mstivoy, and also information from *Annales Hildesheimenses*
       under the year 992 about the destruction of the bishop's capital in Starigard/Oldenburg,
       which additionally corresponds with Adam's information about the martyrdom of the
       clergy in this town during the Slavic rebellion discussed here (see below). See especially
       Labuda, *Powstania Słowian*, pp. 177 ff., in particular 181; *idem, Fragmenty*, vol. 1, pp. 229
       ff., 236 f., 240 ff., 301 f.; vol. 2, pp. 180 ff. The author discredited the view of R. Usinger,
       that Adam's account of the Slavic rebellion was a compilation of two traditions about
       Obodrite rebellions in 983 and 1018. In the earlier discussion other combinations of events
       were also taken into account (two other dates 1002, 1013 were also considered). See also
       Leciejewicz, "Główne problemy," p. 176; Babij, *Wojskowość*, pp. 139 f.
191   Adam II, 42: "Tunc vero et Sclavi a christianis iudicibus plus iusto compressi excusso tandem iugo servitutis libertatem suam armis defendere coacti sunt" ("Then the Slavs that
       were unjustly oppressed by Christian judges shook off the yoke of slavery and were incited to fight for their freedom with arms"); cf. Helmold I, 16. See above, pp. 288 ff.
192   "Bernardus enim dux tam avitae humilitatis quam paternae religionis oblitus primo quidem per avariciam gentem Winulorum crudeliter opprimens ad necessitatem paganismi
       coegit" ("Oblivious to his grandfather's humbleness and his father's fear of God, motivated mainly by greed, duke Bernard oppressed the Winuli [the Slavs] tribe severely and
       thus forced them to turn back to paganism."), see Adam II, 48; Helmold I, 16. Cf. Scior, *Das
       Eigene und das Fremde*, p. 84. Adam (II, 48) reminds also of Bernard's other trespasses: in
       connection with rebellion against the emperor and the civil war in Saxony, he presents
       Bernard as a rebel against Christ and oppressor of churches there; cf. Helmold I, 16.
193   According to an annotation to the original version of Adam's chronicle (see Adam II, 40,
       schol. 28), the pagan reaction was to take place only after Mstivoy was exiled by his own
       subjects, which corresponds with Thietmar's information about the circumstances of the
       death of this ruler indicating that he was a Christian then (see above, p. 87). Mstidrog is
       known only from Adam of Bremen's account, possibly he was the son of the Wagrian duke
       Żelibor, confirmed by Widukind of Corvey, see Christian Lübke, "Mstidrog," in *Lexikon des
       Mittelalters*, vol. 6, *Lexikon des Mittelalters*, vol. 6 (München: Artemis, 1993), col. 882.

ADAM OF BREMEN ON SLAVIC RELIGION

Scholion 28 gives the name of one more culprit in this conflict – the margrave Theodoric.[194] He showed special contempt towards the Slavic dukes. This disdain is exemplified by a story of his offensive treatment of the son of one of them, who remains anonymous in the text, when he was courting a relative of the Saxon duke, Bernard I. Initially the duke accepted their relationship in return for military support provided by the Slavs during his expedition to Italy, but later failed to keep his word. He followed Theodoric's advice not to give his relative to a "dog."[195] This epithet has topical nature, and the premise of its use plainly illustrates the motif of the Saxon guilt for inciting the rebellion; this time it emphasizes their pride, disloyalty and contempt towards the Slavs.[196]

Let us return to the mainstream of the narration of the chronicle. Pointing to the account of Sven Estridsen, Adam outlined a bloody image of pagan reaction: numerous Christians were abducted from Hamburg and later died "because of hatred towards Christianity" ("propter odium christianitatis"). Sixty clergymen including a relative of the Danish ruler, Oddar,[197] were first saved in Starigard, only to be killed later. They were murdered by cutting the sign of the cross on their heads to uncover their brains.[198] It is hard to decide whether the said torture was a kind of religious ritual, or maybe an *ad hoc* idea to ridicule the sacred sign of Christianity. Other martyrs were dragged in Slavic

---

194 Adam II, 43, schol. 31: "Theodericus erat marchio Sclavorum, cuius ignavia eos fieri desertores." ("The margrave of Slavs, because of whose idleness they became apostates, was Theoderic.")

195 Adam, schol. 30: "Sermo est ducem Sclavanicum petisse filio suo neptem ducis Bernardi eumque promisisse. Tunc princeps Winulorum misit filium suum cum duce in Ytaliam cum mille equitibus, qui fere omnes ibi sunt interfecti. Cumque filius ducis Sclavanici pollicitam mulierem expecteret, Theodericus marchio intercepit consilium, consanguineam ducis proclamans non dandam esse cani." ("A rumor has it that a [certain] Slavic duke asked a niece of duke Bernard to be given as wife for his son and she was promised to him. Then the duke of the Winuli [*i.e.* Slavs – S.R.] sent his son with the duke [Bernard] to Italy with nearly a thousand horsemen of whom almost all were killed. And when the son of the Slavic duke expected to be given the promised woman, margrave Theoderic broke the promise claiming that a duke's relative should not be given to a dog.").

196 On the topos of "dogs" (*canes*) in reference to the Slavs see below, pp. 289 ff.

197 Adam II, 43. This Oddar was called *prepositus loci*. According to Koczy, "Sklawanja," p. 223, on this basis he was considered the ruler, head of the stronghold. However, Oddar's affiliation with the group of sixty martyr-priests is confirmed by the word "quorum" starting the next sentence. Hence, in accordance with the Polish translation of this passage as a borrowing from Adam's work to Helmold's chronicle (I, 16), support should be rendered to understanding the term *prepositus* in this place as the 'parish priest' (cf. *Helmolda Kronika Słowian*, trans. Józef Matuszewski, ed. Jerzy Strzelczyk (Warszawa: PWN, 1974), p. 136) or the superordinate of the church in Starigard.

198 Adam II, 43: "Ille cum ceteris tali martyrio consummatus est, ut cute capitis in modum crucis incisa ferro cerebrum singulis aperiretur."

238   CHAPTER 3

towns with their hands tied, until they died of torture.[199] This image of cruelty
is a realization of a stereotypical way of presenting pagans in sources from
that epoch.

A theological explication of these events comes in the next chapter: "Thus
all the Slavs that inhabited the lands between Elbe and Oder had practiced
Christianity for over 70 years, during all of the time of Ottos, in this way cut
themselves off from Christ's body and from the Church, with which they were
previously connected."[200] It is clear from this passage that the chronicler treated the Christianization of the Polabian Slavs as a completed work, hence their
being a part of the Church did not raise any doubts. "Over seventy years" in
Adam's concept uses the symbolism of numbers to emphasize the long-lasting
nature of the relation with Christianity. This time was the whole epoch in the
history of the empire – the Ottonian times.

As indicated above however, these chronological expressions do not match
the details of the presented events. In the chronicle, they are well composed as
an element of the theological interpretation of history. In showing the end of a
certain fortunate epoch, they clearly determine the turning point in the history
of Christianization of the Polabian tribes: "And truly are God's judgements hidden from people, who shows mercy to those he wishes to, and others he makes
obdurate. While we admire his omnipotence, we can observe that those who
were the first to choose Christianity already turned back to paganism, while in
their place converted to Christ those who seemed to be the last."[201] The return
of the Slavs to paganism is read here as their fall and debasement by the power
of God's sentence. They were the people included in the Church earlier than
the Swedish or Norwegians, who were exalted in this situation.

However, the final message of this story about the rebellion of the Polabian
tribes refers to "us," *i.e.* in the chronicler's perspective, the Christians or, more

---

199   *Ibidem*: "Deinde ligatis post terga manibus confessores Dei per singulas civitates
       Sclavorum tracti sunt (aut verbere aut alio modo vexati), usque dum deficerent. Ita illi
       'spectaculum facti et angelis et hominibus' in stadio medii cursus exhalarunt victorem
       spiritum." ("Next, with their hands tied behind their backs, the confessors of God were
       dragged through various Slavic cities (and with whips or in other ways tortured) until they
       died. In this way >>they were turned into a pageant for people and for angels<< and in the
       middle of their lives they gave away their victorious spirits.")
200   Adam II, 44: "Omnes igitur Sclavi, qui inter Albiam et Oddaram habitant, per annos LXX
       et amplius christianitatem coluerunt, omni tempore Ottonum, talique modo se abscide-
       runt ab corpore Christi et ecclesiae, cui antea coniuncti fuerant".
201   Adam II, 44: "O vere occulta super homines Dei iudicia, qui miseretur, cui vult, et quem
       vult indurat. Cuius omnipotentiam mirantes videmus eos ad paganismum esse relapsos,
       qui primi crediderunt, illis autem conversis ad Christum, qui videbatur novissimi"; cf.
       Rom 9:18. Cf. Cf. Goetz, *Die Wahrnehmung*, pp. 113.

ADAM OF BREMEN ON SLAVIC RELIGION   239

precisely, the Saxons.[202] It was for the purpose of punishing their perversity, as an expression of the almightiness and justice of heavens, that the episode of the biblical history of Israel was to happen one more time. It was the episode in which God cleared their way to the Promised Land by destroying seven Canaanite nations, but leaving one – the Philistines. The last ones are compared by the chronicler to the Slavs, turning them into a tool of punishment for the perfidy (*perfidia*) of Christian Saxons.[203]

The activity of Libentius's successor Unvanus (1013–1030) brought reforms and development to the Church network. One of his biggest successes was consolidating the kingdoms of Denmark, Norway, and Sweden under the obedience the Metropolis of the North. Moreover, Unvanus took special care of the mission in Polabia.[204] He managed to make the rebellious duke Bernard pay homage to the emperor, and next helped him to impose tributary dependence on the Slavs. In Hamburg, rebuilt after the devastations of the end of the 10th c., a congregation of canons, "qui populum converterent ab errore ydolatriae," was established by the metropolitan.[205] Their area of activity was certainly not only the superfluously Christianized Saxons, but first of all the Slavs.[206]

---

202   For Adam's identity reflected on the pages of his chronicle see *e.g.* Scior, *Das Eigene und das Fremde*, pp. 38 ff., and above, pp. 198 f.

203   *Ibidem*: God ">>iudex iustus, fortis et patiens<<, qui olim deletis coram Israel septem gentibus Chanaan solos reservavit Allophilos, a quibus transgressi puniretur, ille, inquam, modicam gentilium portionem nunc indurare voluit, per quos nostra confunderetur perfidia." (God ">>a just, mighty and patient judge<<, who once in the face of Israel shattered seven tribes of Canaan and spared only the Philistines, by whom the abominable were punished; I say to you, he [God – S.R.] allowed a small group of pagans to remain obdurate [in paganism] and our perfidy to be deprecated by them."). Cf. Ps 7:62; Act 13:19; Judg 3:1.

204   *E.g.* Jerzy Strzelczyk, "Unwan," in sss, vol. 6, p. 266.

205   Adam II, 49.

206   Adam II, 48, brings a reference to eradication of "pagan rites" from the lives of people living in marshlands near Bremen by Unvanus. "Ille omnes ritus paganicus, quorum adhuc superstitio viguit in hac regione, precepit funditus amoveri, ita ut ex lucis, quos nostri paludicolae stulta frequentabant reverentia, faceret ecclesias per diocesim renovari." ("All pagan rites which had been worshipped in that country until that time he ordered to eradicate; and the groves that our inhabitants of swamps keep visiting with a silly veneration he transformed into churches during restoration of bishopric."). This laconic information about relics of the pagan religion of the Saxons contains a number of terms bringing its theological interpretation. Pagan rites (*ritus paganici*) were described as superstitions (*superstitio*), and they were cherished as a result of a lack of mission in this hardly accessible area because after all they were encompassed in diocese borders. In the chronicler's writing, the cult of groves gained the name of *stulta reverentia*. Substitution of groves by churches falls within canons of the missionary practice in the Early Middle Ages, where people's respect for local pre-Christian cult places was used in smooth transition to a new faith and its practices (attending churches). By analogy this material can refer to details of the Slavic cult of groves known thanks to Thietmar and Helmold, see above, pp. 144 ff. and below, pp. 330 ff.

240   CHAPTER 3

Idolatry – an error that missionaries had to struggle with – in this context was
a synonym (*pars pro toto*) of a pagan religion.

The Christianization of the Slavs, which was entrusted by Unvanus to the
bishop of Starigard, Benno (about 1013–1023),[207] was interrupted by the pagan
rebellion in 1018.[208] Adam remains silent about these dramatic events, but it
cannot be excluded that he transferred its consequences to earlier years, proclaiming the return of paganism among the Slavs "between the Elbe and Oder"
as early as the end of Libentius's life.[209] Thereby Unvanus's pontificate is presented in Adam's work as a time of peace and restoration of the Hamburg-
Bremen metropolis, which at the same time was involved in completion of the
mission among the pagan people. In this context, he emphasizes Unvanus's
cooperation with the Saxon duke Bernard II, and also the organization in
Hamburg of a convention (hypothetically dated to 1025),[210] which was attended by the Danish king, Cnut the Great, and the "satraps" of the Slavs, Uto and
Sederic, all invited by the archbishop.[211] Uto's son was Gottschalk, whose rule
in the Obodrite determines the next growth and then finally the next break in
the wave of Christianization in Northern Polabia.[212]

2.4   *Gottschalks' Times and the Slavic Rebellion of 1066*
The figure of Gottschalk on the stage of history, first in the work of Adam of
Bremen and later in the work of Helmold, was a truly dynamic creation. He
was sent to school in Lüneburg, most certainly around 1029, but when he found

---

207   Adam II, 47: Unvanus "ordinavitque in Sclavoniam (...) Bennonem, virum prudentem, qui
       de fratribus Hammaburgensis ecclesiae electus in populo Sclavorum multum praedican-
       do fructum attulit" ("To the Slavdom Unvanus sent Benno, a man of prudence, who was
       chosen from among the cannon brothers of the Church in Hamburg and whose preaching
       among Slavs was bearing much fruit"). Hence the chronicler highly estimated Benno's
       intellect and his missionary success.

208   It is discussed by Thietmar, who mentions Benno using another version of his name –
       Bernard, see above, p. 186.

209   It should be taken into account that possibly in Adam's narrative in the information about
       the fall of Christianity between the Elbe and Oder, the consequences of Slavic rebellions
       from the two last decades of the 10th c. and the events from 1018 were joined (cf. above,
       p. 235, footnote 189). The argument that Adam connected events with particular pon-
       tificates, hence he would not transfer events from Unvanus's times to Libentius's (*e.g.*
       Labuda, *Fragmenty*, vol. 1, pp. 234 f.), is not convincing, especially when one takes into
       account that the moment of Christianity's fall between the Elbe and Oder indicated by
       the chronicler is at a distance of a maximum of 8 years from 1018, and in relation to 992
       (the fall of the bishopric in Starigard) not less than 18 years.

210   See *e.g.* footnote in: Adam, p. 119; Labuda, *Fragmenty*, vol. 2, s. 183.

211   Adam II, 58.

212   Uto also used the name Pribigniev, see *e.g.* Turasiewicz, *Dzieje polityczne*, pp. 127 f., 132 f.

ADAM OF BREMEN ON SLAVIC RELIGION 241

out that his father had been murdered by a Saxon, he was led by wrath and fury to abandon "the faith and scriptures," and took up arms and joined the "enemies of God." The Slavs helped him to avenge his father's murder by killing "thousands of Saxons."[213] Thus Gottschalk's revenge gained the dimension of a religious fight, and the reference to abandoning not only faith, but also "scriptures" (*cum fide litteris*), makes one aware that – similarly to Thietmar – Adam also saw the living *literati* culture as a legible sign of Christianity.[214]

Gottschalk was eventually captured by the Saxon duke Bernard II who, counting on benefits resulting from acquiring such an ally, concluded an agreement with him and gave him freedom. This was most probably the time of his second conversion to Christianity.[215] After a few years of service for Cnut the Great, which also involved a stay in England, he received the Obodrite throne in about 1043,[216] which after a few years resulted in the revival of the church network in Northern Polabia.[217]

Gottschalk was praised as a supporter of the Hamburg metropolis, which he "worshipped like a mother" ("ut matrem colebat"), and propagator of the faith. Having at his disposal unprecedented power among the Slavs, he decided to force all pagans to accept Christianity, though he managed to convert only a

---

213 Adam II, 66: "ira et furore commotus reiectis cum fide litteris arma corripuit amneque transmisso inimicis Dei se coniunxit Winulis. Ouorum auxilio christianos impugnans milia Saxonum prostrasse dicitur in patris vindictam." ("Deeply moved by anger and rage, he rejected the faith and scriptures, took up arm and after crossing the river he joined the enemies of God – the Winuli [Slavs – S.R.]. With their help he fought against Christians and killed thousands of Saxons to revenge his father").

214 See above pp. 66 ff., where there is more information on that matter. This way of thinking most probably also characterised Helmold – see below p. 294.

215 Helmold dramatized this conversion by an additional episode, see below, p. 294.

216 A disputable date – see Labuda, *Fragmenty*, vol. 2, p. 156; Turasiewicz, *Dzieje polityczne*, pp. 136 f.

217 "Across Elbe and also in Slavdom" – the canon of Bremen wrote about these times – "our matters were going smoothly"; cf. Adam III, 19: "Trans Albiam vero et in Sclavania res nostrae adhuc magna gerebatur prosperitate." See also Scior, *Das Eigene und das Fremde*, p. 51. And after mentioning the duke's marriage and his power among the Slavs (victories and tributes) he adds: "at that time Hamburg enjoyed peace and the land of Slavs [*Sclavania*] was full of churches and priests." ("Qua temporis occasione nostra Hammaburg pacem habuit, et Sclavania sacerdotibus ecclesiisque plena fuit"). See Labuda, *Fragmenty*, p. 157. *Ibidem*, pp. 158 f., more information about Gottschalk's activity until his death at the beginning of the Slavic rebellion in 1066; comp. also *ibidem*, vol. 3, p. 163, 186, 205, 225 ff. See also Władysław Kowalenko, "Gotszalk," in SSS, vol. 2, p. 143; Turasiewicz, *Dzieje polityczne*, pp. 139–157.

242   CHAPTER 3

third of those who, in his grandfather's time,[218] "fell into paganism."[219] From
the perspective of writing the history of the metropolis of the North, it is essential to emphasize that this success was to refer to peoples living in the area
bordered by the Peene River, hence encompassed by the said archbishopric.[220]

Adam emphasizes the duke's personal participation in evangelization.
Monasteries were established in Slavic cities,[221] and bishoprics were re-
established, as a crowning moment for the restitution of local Christianity.[222]
However, extension of the missionary action in Adam's opinion was hampered
by the attitude of Saxons, who were more interested in collecting tributes than
the propagation of Christianity.[223] The chronicler accuses them of greediness
and cruelty, which pushed the Slavs to rebellion and the rejection of salvation.[224]
The pagans' success is treated by him as a fitting punishment for these iniqui-
ties. At the same time, he emphasizes that success in the conversion of the
Slavs would bring them salvation and also peace for the Saxons.[225]

---

218   Mstivoy, see below.
219   Adam III, 19: "omnes paganos ad christianitatem cogere disposuit, cum fere terciam par-
      tem converteret eorum, qui prius sub avo eius [Mstivoy] relapsi sunt ad paganitatem".
220   Adam III, 19.
221   *Ibidem*, 20.
222   *Ibidem*, 21.
223   Adam II, 22: "... mens [scil. Saxonum – S.R.] pronior est ad pensionem vectigalium quam
      ad conversionem gentilium" ("... the minds [of the Saxons] are more likely to provide
      them profits from tributes than to convert pagans"). Adam attributes this assessment to
      king Sven Estridsen.
224   *Ibidem*. See also Scior, *Das Eigene und das Fremde*, p. 84.
225   Adam II, 23: "Nec attendunt miseri, quam magnum periculum suae cupiditatis luant, qui
      christianitatem in Sclavania primo per avariciam turbabant, deinde per crudelitatem
      subiectos ad rebellandum coegerunt et nunc salutem eorum, qui vellent credere, pecu-
      niam solam exigendo contempnunt. Ergo iusto Dei iudicio videmus eos prevalere super
      nos, qui permissu Dei ad hoc indurati sunt, ut per illos nostra flagelletur iniquitas. Nam
      re vera, sicut peccantes superari videmur ab hostibus, ita conversi victores hostium eri-
      mus. A quibus si tantum fidem posceremus, et illi iam salvi essent et nos certe essemus
      in pace." ("And those lamentable [people] do not realize what a great danger they bring
      by their lust. At first, due to their greediness they disturbed Christianity in Slavdom, next
      through their atrocity they made their subjects revolt, and now as, they only demand
      money, they disdain the salvation of those who wanted to believe [in Christ]. Thus we
      can see that by God's fair judgement they predominate over us, [and] with God's permis-
      sion they gained so much strength that our depravity is punished with their hands. For
      indeed, as it is visible, when we live in sin we are vanquished by our enemies, but when
      we convert we will vanquish them instead. If only we insist on them to accept [Christian]
      faith, then they will gain salvation and with no doubt we will be living in peace.").

ADAM OF BREMEN ON SLAVIC RELIGION   243

The programme of such action was implemented by Gottschalk and so it is not surprising that the moral assessment of his defeat during the uprising of the Polabian tribes (1066) is different than in the case of the Saxons in fights against the Slavs. The chronicler started the description of these events with yet more emphasis on the exceptional merits of the Obodrite duke in the propagation of Christianity.[226] He continues by presenting his death that was inflicted by pagans as the beginning of the rebellion.[227] The break of missionary action among Slavs is allegorically explained by the chronicler, again with reference to a biblical story.

This time, however, Polabian tribes did not become the new "Philistines," *i.e.* God's punishment used against Christians, as was the case in the rebellion against the Saxons.[228] They turned out to be the "Amorites," who did not commit the whole measure of iniquity, and thus the time to show them mercy was yet to come. From a theological perspective, this situation has a profound sense of the interpretation of history: such great iniquity must happen to reveal the tried and true faith of Christ's followers.[229] This test turns out to be martyrdom, because this is how the deaths of Gottschalk and other victims of the Slavic rebellion were interpreted.

For the canon of Bremen this duke became "our Maccabee" (*noster Machabeus*), and on the pages of the chronicle he was created as another, after Harald Bluetooth, martyr-king.[230] Thus Gottschalk, or more accurately the literary figure, represents a type of saint created in Anglo-Saxon and Nordic literature, who, being a ruler, follows Christ and dies at the hands of pagans.[231] The duke's death in Lübeck was accompanied by the death of a priest called Yppo, "sacrificed on the altar" ("super altare immolatus est"), and also many

---

226   Adam III, 49, emphasizes that Gottschalk should be remembered for centuries as the originator of the conversion of a large part of Slavdom.

227   *Ibidem*. For the Obodrite uprising against Gottschalk, see *e.g.* Labuda, *Fragmenty*, vol. 2, p. 160; Padberg, *Die Christianisierung*, pp. 163 f.; Babij, *Wojskowość*, pp. 156 f.

228   See above, p. 239.

229   Adam III, 49: "Sed quia nondum >>impletae sunt iniquitates Amorraeorum<<, neque adhuc >>venit tempus miserendi<< eorum, necesse erat ut veniret scandala, ut probati fierent manifesti." ("Since >>the misdoings of the Amorites had not been fulfilled yet<<, >>the time of mercy upon them did not come<< either; it became necessary for offences to be shown, in order to those experienced [in faith] to manifest themselves").

230   *Ibidem*: "Passus est autem noster Machabaeus in civitate Leontia, 7. Idus Iunii ..." Cf. Goetz, *Die Wahrnehmung*, p. 114.

231   Hoffmann, "Beiträge zur Geschichte der Obodriten," pp. 46–48; more information on king-martyrs – *ibidem*, pp. 37 ff.

244   CHAPTER 3

other clergymen and laymen whose death was defined as *passio*.[232] In this context the way of the description of the sacrifice of Yppo seems to be first of all a Christ-typical interpretation of his death as a priest, and not the confirmation of a bloody religious ritual.

However, according to the chronicler, there is no doubt that in the case of the presented martyrdom of John Scotus, the first bishop of Mecklenburg, an offering was made to a pagan deity. He was captured with other Christians in this town and saved for a ritual celebration of triumph. He was taken from one Slavic town to another where he was beaten with sticks, and finally – on the 10th of December, in the "metropolis of Slavs", *i.e.* Rethra – after the cutting off of his arms and legs, he was abandoned "in platea," which means on the street or any other generally accessible square or yard, and his head was stuck on a spear and offered to Redigast.[233]

This is certainly the chronicler's version in which stereotypical interpretations could appear, not only with reference to the location of the place where the events took place,[234] but also in the way pagan cruelty was presented. This is why it was sometimes considered that the cultic character of this execution was Adam's idea.[235] However, it should be emphasized that the making

---

232   Adam III, 50, p. 193: "Passus est autem noster Machabaeus (...) cum presbytero Yppone, qui super altare immolatus est, et aliis multis tam laicis quam clericis, qui diversa ubique pro Christo pertulerunt supplicia. Ansverus monacus et cum eo alii apud Razzisburg lapidati sunt. Idus Iulii passio illorum occurrit." ("Tormented to death was our Machabeus (...) together with priest Yppo, who was sacrificed on an altar with many others, both clergymen and laymen, who for Christ suffered various tortures in many different places. Monk Ansver and others were stoned to death in Ratzeburg. Their torment took place on the first of July").

233   Adam III, 51: "Johannes episcopus senex cum ceteris christianis in Magnopoli civitate captus servabatur ad triumphum. Ille igitur pro confessione Christi fustibus cesus, deinde per singulas civitates Sclavorum ductus ad ludibrium, cum a Christi nomine flecti non posset, truncatis manibus ac pedibus in platea corpus eius proiectum est, caput vero eius desectum, quod pagani conto prefigentes in titulum victoriae deo suo Redigast immolarunt. Haec in metropoli Sclavorum Rethre gesta sunt IIII idus Novembris" ("The elderly bishop John was captured with other Christians in Mecklenburg and kept for a triumph. For his faith in Christ he was beaten with bats, dragged through various Slavic cities for ridicule; as nothing could draw him back from the name of Christ, after his legs and arms were cut off his body, the corpse was left in the street and his decapitated head was planted on a spear by the pagans as a sign of their victory and brought as sacrifice to their god Redigast. This took place in a Slavic metropolis Rethra on the fourth ides of November").

234   See earlier, pp. 224 f.

235   This is why other explanations of the reasons for killing John were proposed, such as a public execution of a captive-Christian or even revenge during fights (see Urbańczyk, *Dawni Słowianie*, pp. 82 f.). Łowmiański, *Religia*, p. 185, considered the execution of bishop

ADAM OF BREMEN ON SLAVIC RELIGION   245

of human offerings to gods by the Slavs also has other testimonies.[236] While
the chronicler's claim in the discussed passage, that the reason for the offering was the celebration of victory, it indicates that in this way they honoured
Redigast's military competency.[237] Nevertheless, the question arises whether
offering only a head to a deity was a general rule in Polabian peoples, or if it
was only incidental.

Adam confirms that in Uppsala there were offerings made of the heads
of male living creatures (including people), whose bodies were abandoned
in a nearby forest.[238] Hence, this type of practice could also be attributed to
Redigast's worshippers as a typical custom of all pagans. The fact that it was
not strange to the Slavs is supported by information that they make offerings
of heads to demons, which was included in a letter written by the Archbishop
of Magdeburg Adalgot in about 1108.[239] Similarly, nearly one hundred years
earlier in a letter written by Bruno of Querfurt to Henry II, there was information about offering a head of a Christian to hosts of demons.[240] This statement
is a metaphor for a threat against the Polish ruler, Boleslav the Brave, because

---

John as a trace of mutual war cruelty and not as a sacrifice. These speculations are not
able to discredit Adam.

236   According to Thietmar's chronicle, Slavic idols needed bloody offerings, which was also
       confirmed in a description of the beheading of the Christian leader of the stronghold
       during the war between Mieszko I and Boleslav the Pious to worship the Liutici tutelary
       deities (see above, pp. 91 f.). Human offerings, according to Nestor's chronicle, were also
       practiced in Rus' (see PVL, under the year 6491 [983]); this information raises some doubts
       because there is a biblical phrase in it, however, it is difficult to question the credibility of
       the source only on the basis of a literary convention. For human offerings of the Slavs see,
       e.g. Szafrański, *Prahistoria*, pp. 375 f., 406, 428; Miś, "Przedchrześcijańska religia," p. 139. It
       should be added that the Baltic peoples also performed ritual killing to worship gods, see
       Žulkus, *Heidentum*, pp. 153 f.
237   Undoubtedly a human offering stresses belligerence of Redigast-Svarožic. Offerings of
       live creatures were made to deities representing power and victory (*e.g.* Indra, Mars); in
       eastern Slavic tribes they would be most certainly made to Perun, see Gieysztor, *Mitologia*,
       pp. 96 ff.
238   Adam IV, 27 – "Sacrificium itaque tale est: ex omni animante, quod masculinum est,
       novem capita offertur, quorum sanguine deos tales placari mos est. Corpora autem sus-
       penduntur in lucum, qui proximus est templo. (...) Ibi etiam canes et equi pendent cum
       hominibus ..." ("And the sacrifice is made as follows: from all living male creatures nine
       heads are given as sacrifice and their blood is to appease those gods. The corpses are
       hung in a grove nearby the sanctuary. Bodies of dogs and horses are hung together with
       humans ...").
239   Text and editing, see Labuda, *Fragmenty*, vol. 3, pp. 233–269; for the text of this document
       see *ibidem*, pp. 234–236. For torture and offering heads to demons see *ibidem*, p. 257. Cf.
       Łowmiański, *Religia*, p. 185.
240   See above, p. 107.

246   CHAPTER 3

of an alliance between the German king and the Liutici. The very selection of
the image, however, certainly corresponds with a popular opinion at that time
and connects it with the way of making offerings by pagans.

Taking into account the symbolic significance of the head or face, it is hard
to consider the idea of offering to gods this particular part of the body (as *pars
pro toto*) as a surprising religious act. The motif of a cut off head had occurred
in the cult of Indo-European peoples since pre-history. It was especially significant for the Celts, whose influence on Slavic beliefs – as a remote tradition –
was sometimes taken into account.[241] However, Aleksander Gieysztor quoted
in his analysis of the information discussed here examples of human offerings made to Mars on Julius Caesar's request in 46 BC.[242] The heads of people
who were ritually killed on the Campus Martius were taken to the Regia building in Rome, and this motif bears similarity to the story of John Scotus's head
being offered to Redigast, *i.e.* to his temple. Certainly, due to Liutici contacts
with the Scandinavian world, special attention should be paid to making offerings to gods in Uppsala as an analogy to the decapitation of the bishop of
Mecklenburg mentioned before and presented by Adam of Bremen.

The very decapitation and the handing of it to personified evil in the case of
a person named John and involvement in conversion of pagans, hence also in
baptizing them, evokes an association with the story of John the Baptist, who
was killed in order to offer his head to Herod's unlawful wife through the hands
of her daughter, Salome.[243] It will remain the chronicler's secret to what extent
he was inspired by this image, to emphasize in his description the way of killing the bishop of Mechlin/Mecklenburg. However, it is worth mentioning that
he outlined a story susceptible to allegorical interpretations referring to the
evangelical episode.

Expressis verbis he provided this kind of interpretation referring to murders
and devastations performed by insurgent Slavs, when he added a prophetic
commentary, or rather a psalmist's lament: "And a prophecy was fulfilled
which said: >>Lord, the pagans invaded your legacy; they profaned your tem-
ple<< and other [misfortunes] that are prophetically lamented on along the

---

241   *E.g.* Jerzy Gąssowski, *Mitologia Celtów* (Warszawa: Wydawnictwa Artystyczne i Filmowe,
      1987), p. 78. See also below, footnotes 98, 336, 378 in the chapter 4.
242   Gieysztor, *Mitologia*, p. 96 f. The basis for using the Roman example in the comparative
      analysis of a decisively later and culturally different phenomenon was inspiration with
      Dumézil's theory.
243   Mk 6:17–29.

ADAM OF BREMEN ON SLAVIC RELIGION 247

destruction of the city of Jerusalem."[244] In this specific historical context it meant that "all the Slavs joined a conspiracy and again surrendered to paganism, killing those who decided to remain in faith."[245] Yet again in Adam's work there is the motif of the "decline into paganism" ("ad paganismum [...] relapsi sunt"), which evokes pejorative association especially as recidivism.[246]

2.5   Rügen

In book IV of Adam of Bremen' work, *i.e. Descriptio insularum aquilonis*, there is a reference to Rügen which attracts attention with respect to the researching of the pre-Christian religion of the Slavs. Rügen and another island, Fehmarn, located in the west, were notorious for being the nest of pirates and robbers. Their exceptional cruelty is shown in the chronicler's statement that they did not even trade the captured travellers but simply murdered them.[247]

Adam presents the inhabitants of Rügen, Rans, as the strongest of Slavic peoples, who could not even undertake any political actions against their will.[248] In this statement – even when it is limited to pagan countries – there is some exaggeration when one takes into account the possibility that there was some lasting political dependence of the Liutici or Obodrite tribes on the island inhabitants. However, Adam's further words show that he means that they had to reckon with the opinion of Rans due to the fear they caused in their neighbours – which is essential – "due to the intimacy with gods, or rather demons, whom they worship more than others."[249]

Thus, the source of fear of the Rans was to be their special intimacy with gods. In this assessment of the perception of the islanders by their neighbours, it is possible to observe the specifics of Adam's work, which strictly connected

---

244   Adam III, 51: "Impleta est nobiscum prophetia, quae ait: 'Deus, enerunt gentes in heredi-tatem tuam; polluerunt templum sanctum tuum' et reliqua, quae prophetice deploran-tur in Ierosolimitanae urbis excidio." Cf. Vulgate, Ps 78, 1. Cf. Goetz, *Die Wahrnehmung*, pp. 113 f.

245   Adam III, 51: "omnes Sclavi facta conspiratione generali ad paganismum denuo relapsi sunt, eis occisis, qui perstiterunt in fide".

246   See *e.g.* Adam, II, 36, where the chronicler mentioned that Eric the Victorious turned back to paganism just after he accepted Christianity: "Hericum [scil. audivi – S.R.] post susceptam christianitatem denuo relapsum ad paganismum".

247   Adam IV, 18.

248   *Ibidem*: "gens fortissima Sclavorum, extra quorum sententiam de publicis rebus nihil agi lex est ..."

249   *Ibidem*: "propter familiaritatem deorum vel potius demonum, quos maiori cultu veneran-tur quam ceteri." It is worth emphasizing that ties with gods were interpreted here theo-logically as a relationship with demons.

248 CHAPTER 3

the political significance of particular pagan communities with religious issues.[250] It was so in the case of Rethra, considered not only as the capital of idolatry but also as the capital of the Slavs.[251] In the times when *Descriptio* was written, the power of the Liutici was most certainly broken,[252] and the hegemony in the circle of the pre-Christian Slavdom was taken over by the Rans, which is exactly confirmed in the discussed reference.[253]

The chronicler next juxtaposed the cruelty of pirates from Rügen and Fehmarn with the attitude of people from the third area, wrongly considered an island, called Semland, which was inhabited by the Sambians or Prussians. These pagans were ultimately praised as "the most humane humans" (*homines humanissimi*), because they helped castaways and pirates' victims, and furthermore – to shame the Christians – they were to despise not only gold and silver but also furs whose "deadly smell poisons the world with the sting of pride."[254]

This praise of the natural attributes of the Barbarians is of topical character.[255] Moreover, on the one hand it allows the attitude contended by the author in his own environment to be stigmatized, and on the other hand it creates a favourable climate to start a mission for the "unputrid" pagans. Thus the chronicler sympathizes with the inhabitants of *Semland*, which is seen in his words comparable with the earlier description of *Iumne*.[256] "Many laudable [words] could be said about the customs of those peoples if only they believed

---

250 This motif was developed by Helmold by attributing a special role in the rule of this community to Svantevit's oracle and his priest (see below, pp. 359, 364 ff.). It is essential that Adam does not confirm this theocratic element in the Rans' political system, and in a gloss added to this chapter there is only information that they are ruled by a "king" ("soli habent regem"), see Adam IV, 18, schol. 121.

251 See above, pp. 222 ff.

252 In the 50's and 60's of the 12th c., see below, pp. 295 ff.

253 Taking over this hegemony can be confirmed by *e.g.* intervention expeditions against the centres of their kinsmen accepting Christianity, Janisław Osięgłowski, "Początki słowiańskiej Rugii do roku 1168 (Zagadnienia etniczne i polityczne)," *Materiały Zachodniopomorskie* 13 (1967), pp. 254, 264; Babij, *Wojskowość*, p. 171. See also below, p. 356.

254 Adam IV, 18: "quarum odor letiferum nostro orbi propinavit superbiae venenum". Cf. Scior, *Das Eigene und das Fremde*, p. 215. See also Goetz, *Die Wahrnehmung*, pp. 193.

255 In this respect medieval authors continued the antique tradition, which was expressed not only in duplicating stereotypical opinions, but also in a lack of understanding of the conditioning of these positive attitudes and characteristics of barbarians, their rights, so as to ensure the well-being of the whole community (*e.g.* not to cause revenge for not rendering help). In the case of contempt for luxurious goods, one should take into account, *e.g.* the significance of manifesting the social position of the host, ostentatious affluence expressed in the generous offering of gifts to strangers (see *e.g.* Modzelewski, *Barbarzyńska Europa*, pp. 27 ff.). See also Goetz, *Die Wahrnehmung*, pp. 187 ff.

256 See above, pp. 233 f.

ADAM OF BREMEN ON SLAVIC RELIGION 249

in Christ, whose preachers they persecute so violently."[257] Therefore the chronicler was prevented from appreciating their customs only by their lack of faith and the fact that they persecuted missionaries.[258]

It is worth remembering that the topos of noble barbarians, related to *Iumne* in the second book of the Adam's chronicle, allowed the eastern range of the missionary area formally subordinated to the archbishops of Hamburg-Bremen, reaching the Oder, at the mouth of which the famous town was located, to be determined. The use of this stereotypical motif in *Descriptio* to refer to the Sambians or Prussians can be then read as a postulate to widen the mission horizon further to the east, outside the Slavic land – certainly with regard for the ambitious new challenges for the metropolis of the North.

3 The Religion of the Slavs in the Historical and Theological Vision of Adam of Bremen

The presentation of pagan Slavs, their history, customs and religion in Adam of Bremen's work was considerably influenced by promotion of the idea of barbarian peoples' conversion. The terms *gentes, naciones,* or *populi* refer to ethnic and political communities, however – especially when they are used in plural form – in the chronicler's perspective they are primarily a missionary space, in accordance with one of the basic tasks justifying the establishment of the Hamburg-Bremen metropolis. Adam, like Thietmar before him, presents the Christianization of barbarians mainly in the dimension of collective life as encompassing whole peoples in both the empire's and the Church's area of influence.

In this context the religion of the Slavs gained a definite pejorative assessment. The Slavs themselves, however, were not perceived in an equally pejorative way. Certainly, they were attributed with cruelty, which was stereotypical in the assessment of barbarians, but in this case, it was strictly connected with their idolatrous practices. On the other hand, in the presentation of these peoples there was a place to include the topos of noble, kind barbarians. It was used to refer to the inhabitants of *Iumne*, who found no equal among other peoples in terms of their customs and hospitality ("moribus et hospitalitate

---

257 Adam IV, 18: "Multa possent dici ex illis populis laudabilia in moribus, si haberent solam fidem Christi, cuius predicatores immaniter persecuntur." Cf. Scior, *Das Eigene und das Fremde*, pp. 215 f.

258 *Ibidem.* In this context there is a reference to the martyrdom of St. Adalbert killed by these barbarians, and also information about the careful watch of cult groves and springs to prevent them from being defiled by Christians setting their foot there.

nulla gens honestior aut benignior"). At the same time it is depicted as the richest and most splendid among Slavic centres, focalizing the whole world like a lens for its openness to visitors from all over the world, which is clearly depicted in topical topical phrase *Greci et Barbari*.

It is worth remembering that its use in the New Testament creates an image of the whole of humankind as the addressee of the gospel, and the presence of this universalist element in the image of *Iumne* is strengthened by Roman associations in the convention of description (names of Vulcanus and Neptune). Moreover, Adam amplifies the significance of the city claiming that it is the "largest city in Europe." The location of this centre in the zone of influence of the Hamburg-Bremen metropolis' missionary plans corresponds with its aspirations to become one of the main capitals of Christianity, worthy of the rank of the Metropolis – may be even Patriarchy – of the North. The key element in the realization of these pursuits was the mission on the Slavic lands, and thus it is not accidental that the chronicler emphasized the location of the city at the mouth of the Oder. This river acted in his narrative as an axis connecting the whole of Slavdom, and its "mouth" in Latin was in fact a gate, *ostium*, to the whole community of these peoples.

Iumne, however, is neither the centre of Slavdom in the religious dimension – in this respect it gives way to Rethra, located on the Liutici Redars land, which was the "capital of idolatry" – nor the geographic one, because it is located on the outskirts of the *ecumene*, near the "Scythian marshes." It is essential that an analogous scheme was used by Adam and is an assignation of significance to particular peoples when he presented three, in his opinion insular, communities living in Fehmarn, Rügen, and *Semland*.

The last of these "islands" was in fact land inhabited by the Prussians or Sambians. It is the farthest located point in relation to >>the observation point<< in Bremen, and it is this place that is the counterpart of *Iumne* according to the scheme. The local Barbarians were *homines humanissimi*, righteous by nature, and were strict yet not contaminated with vices typical of the Christian circle in which the chronicler lived. The Redars, the "middle" tribe which was also the most powerful one, corresponded with Rügen located in the middle of this group of "islands," and it was inhabited by the Rans who were the most familiarized with their gods ("or rather demons"), and simultaneously the most cruel pirates and hegemons in relation to their neighbours.

In the case of stereotypical positive assessments of barbarian customs, one can find an element of fascination with strangeness or indication of models of conduct in the environment of the addressees of this work, or stigmatization of their vices by contrasting them with attitudes of good pagans. First however, it showed that their nature was not completely corrupt by the sin of idolatry,

ADAM OF BREMEN ON SLAVIC RELIGION 251

and hence the postulate of their conversion is such a burning issue. The chronicler unambiguously mentions that the major vice of these noble barbarians is the cultivation of their religion.[259]

In this concept of the presentation of pagans, it is possible to indicate the presence of an analogous thought structure to the one presented in the historiology of St. Augustine by the idea of *civitas terrena* (an earthly state or community). It is initially happy, living in harmony with the Creator, yet in consequence of sin gradually becomes more and more corrupt and subdued to the power of *civitas diaboli*. The last one, *i.e.* the devil's community or state, finds its counterpart in the Slavic world, as it is presented by Adam of Bremen as a place in which the ruleship of the prince of demons with its capital in Rethra is located. However, this is not a strictly spiritual reality, because it also encompasses the peoples practising cult of idols. Therefore, for the Slavs this "capital of idolatry" is the most famous city (*civitas vulgatissima*).

As enemies and persecutors of Christians, these Slavic communities gain the name of "God's enemies" – *inimici Dei*.[260] On the other hand they are the addressees of evangelization, and – importantly in this case – in the light of the tradition referring to (forged) papal documents, their land was to be subordinated to the Hamburg-Bremen archbishopric. Therefore, this metropolis is becoming an antithesis of Rethra, but it is still hard to consider it a counterpart of the Augustinian *civitas Dei*. Its authority exists only in the dimension of the church, and in the case of "God's state" the immanent order was that of the empire (*imperium*). Adam appreciates the role of the imperial factor in supporting the mission, which allows for the realization of the ideal of *civitas Dei* in this cooperation between the institution of the Church and the monarchy. However, it rather refers to the whole empire instead of the metropolis itself.

It should be emphasized, therefore, that accentuation of certain analogies to the historiology of St. Augustine is not to emphasize that there are borrowings from patristic thought in Adam's work, but rather to stress that he referred to a certain archetypical model of interpretation of the mission space (*ad gentes!*), which did not assume only a bipolar juxtaposition of the orders of good and evil, Christianity and paganism, *etc.* The most important aspect in this case was the view that the element of the original good survived in the nature of pagans despite their idolatric practices. Premises for this type of interpretation

---

259 In *Iumne*, according to Adam, being Christian was tolerated and only public practising of this religion was banned.

260 This was the name used to refer to the Christians who were joined by the Obodrite duke Gottschalk during the time of his apostasy.

of history can be found in biblical theology motivating the need to bring salvation to pagans.

The first temporary attempt at Christianizing the Slavs subordinated to the Hamburg metropolis was located by Adam of Bremen as early as the time of Charlemagne. The second time they became Christian took place in the Ottonian epoch, only to return to paganism after the seventy symbolic years. This next moral fall (*relapsio*), according to the chronicler, was a kind of humiliation of the Slavs by God himself, who – for reasons of mysterious judgement – allowed the Scandinavian peoples to supersede them in the "race of faith," although they were baptized later. This situation is explained by the chronicler with a reference to the biblical image of Israel conquering Canaan, where there were Philistines faithful to their idolatry, left as a possible tool of God's punishment.[261]

Overcoming the consequences of this impasse in the mission among the Slavs was later connected by the chronicler with the times of the Obodrite duke Gottschalk, who venerated the Hamburg-Bremen metropolis "like a mother." He taught the people himself and funded churches and monasteries. In the description of his death during the pagan reaction in 1066, he was called "our Machabee" (*noster Machabeus*). Whereas the destruction of the Church network in Polabia in this rebellion was commented on by the chronicler using Psalm 78:1: "Deus, enerunt gentes in hereditatem tuam; polluerunt templum sanctum tuum", which he completed with a punchline: the Slavs rejected the faith killing of those who remained dedicated to it. In the chronicler's perspective this persecution was not a form of punishment for Christians' sins but a time of testing their faith.

Thus, at that moment the rebellious Slavs did not become "like Philistines," but instead donned the comparison to the biblical Amorites. The fiasco of this stage of activities aimed at the conversion of the Polabian tribes is justified by Adam with an allegorical statement that "the iniquity of the Amorites" was not yet full and the time to show them mercy had not yet come. This theological conviction that the final conversion of the Slavs was to be preceded by reaching a full measure of iniquity, somehow sounds optimistic. Deeper and deeper immersion of pagan Slavs in evil – due to increasing waves of apostasy – paradoxically brings the moment of including them in the Church nearer,

---

261   In this particular historical situation Saxons were punished especially for their pride (a prime example here is calling the Slavic duke a dog) and prioritising political and economic benefits over support for the missionary work. According to Adam, the conversion of the Slavs was to stop the rebellion and cruelty devastating the Christian community.

ADAM OF BREMEN ON SLAVIC RELIGION 253

because it did not depend on their virtues, but on the supernatural intervention of Providence in history.[262]

A model of this type of interpretation can be found in the apocalyptics of the New Testament.[263] It is essential that it corresponds with Adam's description of Rethra. There is a certain literary similarity between the presentation of New Babylon in the Book of Revelation to St. John, and additionally the very "capital of idolatry" (Rethra) as a habitat of demons, whose princeps, Redigast, was worshipped there. The dedication of the famous sanctuary – in the chronicler's opinion – to demons remained in agreement with the conviction that the cult of idols, being an alternative to the worship of God, was actually addressed to demons.[264] This is why entering this town, to serve demons, meant immersion in eternal death, which is indicated by the commentary connected with Rethra's description, in the information about the waters of the Styx that surrounded the souls of peoples serving idols. This gloomy place was the place where also Christian clergy were to be murdered.

The information about it – especially the martyrdom of John, the bishop of Mecklenburg – refers to the third rejection of Christianity by the Slavs. In the case of the earlier wave of pagan reaction, dated by Adam to the end of the pontificate of Libentius, the archbishop of Hamburg-Bremen, there is information about dragging martyrs from one Slavic town to another for "the show for people and angels." The fact that Rethra was not distinguished among them was most certainly not accidental. According to Adam, until that time Christianity flourished in the whole area "between the Elbe and Oder," hence Rethra being located there could become the "capital of idolatry" only later, in effect of the return of paganism. It maintained its significance in the times of Gottschalk, who did not manage to complete his work of the reconversion of Slavdom.

In Adam's concept, the primacy of Rethra in the circle of (Slavic) paganism was a situation contemporary to him.[265] Outlining the bipolar picture of

---

262 In scholion 83 it is emphasized that the Slavs rejected the already introduced Christianity three times in a row, in the times of Charlemagne, Otto the Great and the Obodrite Gottschalk: "Haec est Sclavorum tertia negatio, qui primo facti sunt a Karolo christiani, secundo ab Ottone, tertio nunc ab Godescalco principe". The cyclicality of Christianization waves shown here was used by Helmold following in Adam's footsteps in his work, and became the basis to build narration about the conversion of the Slavs which was the main subject of his *Cronica Slavorum* (see below). See also *e.g.* Goetz, *Die Wahrnehmung*, pp. 113 ff.

263 Cf. Rev 18:2.

264 1 Cor 10:20.

265 Possibly this opinion of the chronicler raises doubts in the light of other sources, especially *Annales Augustani*, under the year 1068, about the destruction of Rethra.

confrontation between Christianity and paganism in Polabia, he distinguishes only this "capital" among the cult centres located there. Only with reference to this place, he presents the details of objects in the sanctuary saturating his description with symbolic elements (*e.g.* a gold statue, purple bed, number of gates – 9), allegorical elements (*e.g.* the Styx), and theological ones (demons and their *princeps, ydolatria*, souls' condemnation, *etc.*). Thus, the substrate of historical primary religion in this literary world melted into significant layers of interpretation. On this basis, however, it is hard to discredit the very existence of the famous temple and Redigast, the deity worshipped there.[266]

In the other information about Slavic religion, the chronicler from Bremen did not show considerable interest in the details of the cult, and there is no word about myths. His basic narrative refers to the fate of the Christian circle concentrated around the Hamburg metropolis, shown in the categories of the history of God's people. Necessarily, biblical allegories were critical in the assessment of the historical role of Slavic paganism. The very religion of the Polabian tribes was depicted as idolatry, and the cult of deities worshipped in this way is practically considered as addressed to demons.

However, this is a situational choice of one of the options of pagan gods' treatment accepted by Adam. An alternative is considering them as allegories of elements, which can be observed in references to antique pantheons (*e.g.* in the description of *Iumne*). However, on this basis it is impossible to prove that he treated the essence of Slavic paganism or the antique Roman one differently – *expressis verbis* he considers them the same "error" (*error*) occurring, however, in different cultural areas. In the case of the Slavs, paganism was a determinant of their belonging to the sphere of *barbaricum*, which is

---

266   The conviction on the existence of Rethra corresponds with Thietmar's information about Radogošč or *Annales Augustani* (see above, p. 129). It is also worth reminding that an analogy between the image of Rethra and the presentation of Uppsala in Adam of Bremens' chronicle, taken into account in the discussion so far, was based not only on similarity in creating literary visions of such a capital centre in the context of the role attributed to paganism. On the example of Rethra, it is possible to observe that even a very sophisticated literary interpretation was based on the historical substrate of paganism. Taking into account that it was characteristic of the chronicler's work routines, it is worth taking into account that the image of the temple in Uppsala in Adam's account was also based on the literary interpretation of data about the actual cult centre in this place. By analogy, the case of Rethra can be useful in the discussion on Adam's credibility as an informer about the temple in Uppsala and it can undermine statements assuming the complete fictitiousness of the description, *e.g.* on the basis of assumptions related to pragmatic goals (*i.e.* satirical polemic against the Gregorians) pursued in the chronicler's work (see *e.g.* Janson, *Templum*, pp. 257–320).

clearly visible not only in the occurrence of the above discussed stereotypical assessments of barbarians, but also in recalling literate culture as a determinant of the barrier between Christianity and Slavic religion – the information that Gottschalk abandoned "cum fide litteris" is characteristic in this context.[267]

Finally it is worth emphasizing that Adam's treatment of the "islands of the North" as a separate circle in the *barbaricum* zone was a decisive factor in diminishing the importance of the integral connection between the Rans and the major part of the Slavic pre-Christian communities situated on land on the pages of his work. This situation was changed by Helmold in how he continued the history of the conversion of the Slavs a century later.

---

267   The topos of "dogs" (*canes*) should be added here, it is discussed below, see pp. 289 ff.

CHAPTER 4

Helmoldi Cronica Slavorum on Slavic Religion

1   Helmold and His *Chronicle of the Slavs*

Helmold, although the author of such an outstanding source for the history of the Polabian Slavs as *The Chronicle of the Slavs*, remains rather unknown. Neither the date nor the place of his birth has been established and there is no information about his parents and the environment from which he came. The information about his name was conveyed by Arnold of Lübeck, who undertook to continue Helmold's work which he wrongly treated as unfinished.

B. Schmeidler proposed to treat the expression used by Helmold with reference to the battle of Welfesholz (1115) as the most famous one "in our times" as a premise to consider this date *terminus ante quem* as the chronicler's birth.[1] However, a more convincing argument results from immortalizing Helmold as a witness in a document from September 1150. He had the title of a deacon, which at that time was conferred at the age of at least twenty-five, so consequently the above-mentioned boundary is moved to approximately 1125.[2]

Contrary to an earlier concept from the first half of the 19th c. that he came from Holstein, the current prevailing view is that he came from Central Germany. His ties with the Nordalbings, among whom he happened to work as a priest, are explained by the hypothesis that Helmold's family moved with a wave of emigration to the Harz Mountains after Nordalbingia fell under the rule of the Obodrite duke Kruto (d. 1093). Helmold is the only scribe to mention this event and he gives the number of six hundred Holstein families participating in it. After coming back to the land of his ancestors, already as a priest, he felt disappointed with the austerity of the lives and customs of this faction of his own tribe, which explains his aversion to them.

Counterbalancing this way of thinking is his detailed knowledge of Central Germany, claimed to be a result of contacts with the bishop of Starigard – Vicelin. Thus, the problem of Helmold's homeland remains unsolved: it

---

1   Helmold I, 40.

2   Jerzy Strzelczyk, "Wstęp," in *Helmolda Kronika Słowian*, trans. Józef Matuszewski, ed. Jerzy Strzelczyk (Warszawa: PWN, 1974), p. 15; *ibidem* account of the discussion; cf. Heinz Stoob, "Einleitung," in *Helmoldi presbyteri bozoviensis Chronica Slavorum*, ed. Heinz Stoob, Ausgewählte Quellen zur deutschen Geschichte des Mittelalters. Freiherr vom Stein-Gedächtnisausgabe 19 (Darmstadt: Wissenschaftliche Buchgesellschaft, 1963), p. 3; Scior, *Das Eigene und das Fremde*, p. 139.

© KONINKLIJKE BRILL NV, LEIDEN, 2020 | DOI:10.1163/9789004331488_006

HELMOLDI CRONICA SLAVORUM ON SLAVIC RELIGION 257

is possible that it was Brunswick or Holstein.[3] His aversion to his native Nordalbingian environment could have resulted from its church formation. It should be noted that the chronicler noticed the community of beliefs and lifestyle of the Holzats and their Slavic neighbours which,[4] given the above mentioned juxtaposition of cultural circles: *clerici* (*litterati*) – *illitterati*, must have influenced his own relation to his tribesmen.[5]

Helmold's school age is still a matter of speculation. There are premises that his parents arrived in Segeberg to participate in the construction of this stronghold in 1134, which is supported by an autobiographical note that as a boy he could see some estates of the bishopric in Starigard. There is no agreement on the social status of Helmold's parents or their role in the above-mentioned centre, however, it seems more certain that the place where the future chronicler lived was a monastery in Segeberg. In 1138 it was invaded by the Slavs and the monks had to hide in Neumünster. Helmold probably shared their fate, but in 1139 started his education in Brunswick under the supervision of his future superior Bishop Gerold. Next, he came back to Neumünster (possibly in the summer of 1143; his stay was definitely confirmed in 1147). In 1150, having already been ordained as a deacon as has already been mentioned, he is referred to as a witness of the document.[6]

The chronicler himself mentions in his narration various facts from his life, which allows certain limitation in speculating about his past to be overcome. From 1152 to 1154, accompanied by Vicelin, the bishop of Starigard in his last years (he died in 1154), next in all probability travelled with his successor Gerold to metropolitan Hartwig in Stade (1155). In the winter of 1155/1156 – this is certain – he accompanied Gerold in his inspection of the diocese, collecting on this occasion countless details about the Slavic religion. Before 1163 (it must have been soon after the inspection) he became a parish priest in Bosau, which had a strong economic position in comparison with the remaining part of the diocese; this was also the place where the ailing Gerold finished his life.

Before his death he managed to move the diocese to Lübeck in 1160, and this is why the later part of Helmold's life is confirmed by Lübeck episcopal documents (1170, 1177). Discrepancy in the titles used when referring to Helmold became a reason for more speculations among scholars. Some of them held the view that Helmold spent his last years in Lübeck as a canon or an ordinary

---

3   Strzelczyk, "Wstęp," pp. 15–18. Cf. Stoob, "Einleitung," p. 3; Scior, *Das Eigene und das Fremde*, p. 139.

4   Helmold I, 47, p. 93.

5   In Helmold's eyes Church relations among the inhabitants of Holstein must have left a lot to be desired – Stoob, "Einleitung," p. 2.

6   Strzelczyk, "Wstęp," pp. 18–20; Stoob, "Einleitung," p. 4.

priest. A more convincing thesis claims that until his death (after 1177) he was a parish priest in Bosau.[7]

Despite some grammatical mistakes, his Latin is clear and lively. Although there are frequent repetitions of various phrases which suggest that he did not use it completely effortlessly. B. Schmeidler claimed that this linguistic clumsiness in the *Chronicle of the Slavs* indicates difficulties in translation from German – the language in which Helmold thought and preached – into Latin.[8] H. Stoob paid attention to the fact that due to this stylistic awkwardness, errors and repetitions were not evenly distributed in the work and thus he concluded that although the parish priest from Bosau was well educated, he tried to write in a simple way for the sake of the addressees of his work. Finally, it is hard to decide just on the basis of the chronicle how well he was educated, but there are reasons to believe that he did not lack talent for writing.

On the basis of the joint analysis of chapters 103–104 Stoob showed that Helmold was able to create a clear and well-designed text composition, in accordance with the traditional rhetoric canons.[9] Moreover, on the pages of the chronicle one can find poetic attempts of rather poor quality.[10] His strength is biblical quotations, which is not surprising in this intellectual circle. He frequently decorated his texts with biblical expressions and verses. However, his knowledge of patristics was not so good. He knew the *Dialogues* of Gregory the Great – although it is hard to say if he read them personally – which were certainly useful in his preaching. It should be added that the use of the Bible in the chronicle also has an overtone of pulpit preaching.

In Helmold's chronicle there are also references to Boethius's works: *De consolatione philosophiae* and his not very well known translation of Aristotle's works, later also Sulpicius Severus' *Vita S. Martini* and his letters, as well as the Life of St. John the Merciful (known most probably thanks to the *Golden Legend*), and lastly the anonymous *Disticha Catonis*. The list of Classical authors whose works could have been read by the chronicler when he was still at school encompasses Virgil, Ovid, Sallust, Plautus, Horace, Lucan and Terentius. However, it is hard to decide definitively whether references to

---

7   Hemold's life in 1152–1163 is reflected in the following chapters of his chronicle: 73, 83, 84, 95. See *ibidem*, p. 20–25; Stoob, "Einleitung," pp. 5 ff.

8   Bernhard Schmeidler, "Einleitung," in *Helmoldi presbyteri Bozoviensis Cronica Slavorum*, ed. Bernhard Schmeidler, MGH SSrerGerm in usum scholarum (1937), p. xv.

9   Stoob, "Einleitung," p. 12. The intention to simplify the message by Helmold is supported by omissions of sophisticated details when rewriting some passages of Adam of Bremen's work (see below, pp. 266 f.).

10   Strzelczyk, "Wstęp," pp. 37, 39–40. There one can find a concise discussion on the language of the Chronicle.

HELMOLDI CRONICA SLAVORUM ON SLAVIC RELIGION   259

works discovered in the text, written by the above-mentioned authors, result
from secondary readings (*e.g.* a collection including quotations of famous authors useful at school).

The biggest influence on Helmold's literary creativity was the medieval literary monuments and primarily the *Gesta Hammaburgensis ecclesiae pontificum*
by Adam of Bremen. He also used *Vita Willehadi* and *Vita Anskarii*. Additionally,
he quoted, memorized, or perhaps read in secondary sources fragments of the
Chronicle of the World by Ekkehard of Aura and a few annals such as *Annales S.
Disibodi, Annales Rosenveldenses* and *Annales Palidenses.*[11]

Oral tradition also played an important role in writing the chronicle, with its
decisive dominance in the description of the period from 1066 to about 1115, influencing the section of the relatively poorest historical value of the presented
information. In the case of earlier periods, Helmold had at his disposal narrative sources, while for the later ones (about 1115–1134) he had accounts of
eyewitnesses to finish his work on the basis of up to date observations and his
own experiences.[12]

The Chronicle of the Slavs belongs in the "gesta" genre, and there are two
books in it. The first one must have been finished before the fall of Arkona
(1168). The work, as Helmold declared himself, started under the influence of
Gerold, but the conclusion that it was completed while he was still alive (before 13 August 1163) is not apparent. Such references to suggestions made by
teachers have a topical character. Moreover, some information in Book I refer
to the time after the death of the above-mentioned bishop.[13]

A model for the *Chronicle of the Slavs* was the *Gesta Hammaburgensis ecclesiae pontificum* by Adam of Bremen, which was used by Helmold largely
as historical material, as a composition template, and as a set of ideas that
represented history from a theological perspective. Both clergymen pursued
pragmatic goals commonly set in historiography in this epoch: the promotion
of behaviour patterns, praising God, the people of the Church and rulers, and
moral evaluation of their actions and attitudes over a period of a few centuries.

Following Adam of Bremen, Helmold uses expressions with theological connotations to define peoples treated as pagans, and most importantly, builds a
tradition of splendour of the Starigard/Oldenburg diocese by focusing on their

---

11   For Helmold's literary erudition see Brygida Kürbis, "Helmold," in sss, vol. 2, p. 199; and
      more extensively: Strzelczyk, "Wstęp," pp. 34–40; Stoob, "Einleitung," p. 10 ff.
12   Strzelczyk, "Wstęp," pp. 33 f.
13   The preface of the chronicle confirms that Gerold was no longer alive when this passage
      was written (Helmold did not list him among the people he dedicated his work to), how-
      ever, it is hard to exclude that the preface was not written after finishing the book started
      when the bishop was still alive.

260   CHAPTER 4

evangelization.[14] Helmold sometimes rewrote whole passages from the work
of his predecessor, however their compilation was not a pure reproduction.
He connected clauses with other contexts and additionally he supplemented
borrowed information with his own opinions. This close textual dependence
on the chronicle of Adam of Bremen is visible in Helmold's chronicle in the
description of the events before 1066, but in other the parts of the work he also
used phraseology similar to that of his predecessor.

The first addressee of Helmold's work was the Lübeck cannons (*domini et
patres sanctae Lubecensis ecclesiae canonici*), as already in the first sentence of
his work the author pledges his obedience to them. As the main motif of undertaking his work as a writer, he indicated his will to pay tribute to the Church
in Lübeck, which he calls *mea mater, sancta Lubecensi ecclesia*.[15] Strong ties
between clergymen and their particular church, so important in this epoch,
become visible here.

For Helmold nothing else seemed more appropriate for glorifying the diocese of Starigard-Lübeck than a description of the conversion of the Slavs: missionary activity of clergymen and rulers, and also various obstacles hampering
them in their activity, the existence of which is sometimes only insinuated in
the text. Praise for the people who, thanks to their efforts, lifted the new diocese
to first place in the conversion of the Slavdom (or in fact what remained of it) is
the main programme's assumption of the *Chronicle of the Slavs*.[16] However, for
Helmold the most important thing was not describing outstanding personalities of this epoch but rather their great deeds.[17]

The main character in Helmold's piece was Bishop Gerold, who moved the
bishopric from Starigard to Lübeck. His death must be the decisive moment
for starting the chronicler's work because the concept of the first book which
finished with this moment suggests that Helmold saw in this event the end
of a certain epoch in the Christianization of the Slavs: the conversion of the
Wagrians and Obodrites at that time finally seemed confirmed. Helmold most
likely started the work to pay homage to his teacher and ordinary, and according
to his initial plan he finished the piece with a description of his death. A good
commentary on these observations is found in the words of Arnold of Lübeck,
who described Helmold's literary legacy as "stories about the subjection and

---

14   For notions of *gens, populus* and *natio* in Adam of Bremen's work see above p. 208.
15   Helmold, [*Praefatio*], p. 1.
16   *Ibidem*, p. 2.
17   Stoob, "Einleitung," p. 2.

HELMOLDI CRONICA SLAVORUM ON SLAVIC RELIGION   261

introduction of the Slavs to Christianity, as well as about the deeds of bishops whose persistence strengthened the Church in their region."[18]

Helmold found an urge and model for his literary work in the attitude of earlier writers who, "wished to dedicate themselves to writing and renounced the bustle of everyday life to be able to devote themselves to contemplation in hermitage, to seek the way of wisdom and to place it before pure gold and all jewels. It is them who turned their bright minds to the invisible matters of God and wished to get closer to understanding of His divine mysteries, and who often made efforts above their strength. Others, whose efforts were not as great and did not exceed the boundaries of human abilities, in their chastity enlarged the mysteries of the writings and elaborately described the events from the constitution of the world, telling about the kings and prophets and versatile events of wars, praising the virtues and condemning the vices."[19]

This thought proves that the historiographer did not feel any worse as an author than theologians contemplating matters exceeding the human mind. He sees the mission of a historiographer in the context of theological discipline, which is a description of a holy history aiming to show the history of the world in relation to the Revelation and moral canons. Helmold shows clear affirmation for the value of writing tradition: "For if among the dark and dense haze of this age the torch of the scriptures is not present, darkness will embrace everything."[20] Glorification of the deeds of the people of merit who contributed to the Christianization of the Slavic lands and saving them from oblivion helped consolidate and ennoble the tradition of the young Church in Lübeck, which is based on older Starigard roots.[21]

In the prologue to book II (chapter 96) Helmold supplements his lecture on the goals of historiography: he condemns authors who in their presentation of human actions "depart from the path of truth." He is even able to forgive

---

18   *Arnoldi abbati Lubicensis Chronica*, ed. Johann Martin Lappenberg, MGH SS 21 (1869), Prologus, p. 115: "historias de subactione seu vocatione Sclavorum et gesta pontificum, quorum instantia ecclesie harum regione invaluerunt".

19   Helmold I, [*Praefatio*], p. 1: "propter magnum scribendi studium omnibus negotiorum tumulultibus renuntiarunt, ut in secreto contemplationis otio invenire possent viam sapientiae, preferentes eam auro obryzo et cunctis opibus preciosis; qui etiam extendentes aciem ingenii ad invisibilia Dei et ipsis arcanis aproximare cupientes plerumque supra vires laborare nisi sunt. Alii autem, quorum conatus non fuit tanti, consistentes in suae dispositionis meta, auxerunt et ipsi de simplicitate sua arcana scripturarum, multaque ab ipsa constitutione mundi de regibus et prophetis et variis bellorum eventibus commentantes, super virtutibus laudem, vitiis vero detestationem suis preconiis addiderunt."

20   *Ibidem*: "In huius enim seculi tenebrosa caligine, si desit lucerna scripturarum, ceca sunt omnia". Comments on Helmold's motivation see Strzelczyk, "Wstęp," pp. 27 f.

21   Labuda, *Fragmenty*, vol. 3, p. 199.

those who cowardly hide facts for the sake of their security, but however, he finds no justification for those who lie to gain profits, revile the righteous, or attribute merits to the unworthy. This rather pessimistic introduction can hypothetically be a reply to criticism towards his first journey by a topical "ship of description"[22] on the sea of history, which could take place in the environment of a new bishop. Or, perhaps these words were dictated by the anxiety that by writing about his contemporaries, he would have to pay for his faithfulness to the idea of the Slavic mission with accusations of subjectivity and a fight for human favours.

The motifs described above (*i.e.* referring to models of earlier writers, the obligation to describe missionaries' merits, and the encouragement of his superior) in large part have a topical nature. Hence it is hard to discern to what extent it shows the real intention of the chronicler in these conventional confessions.[23] The general findings related to the topic correspond with Helmold's moralistic complaints about the pride of his contemporaries, who instead of undertaking a description of the immenseness of phenomena occurring by the power of God's judgements, devoted their lives to dangerous, worldly vanities.[24]

A personal factor is equally important in explaining the creation of the chronicle. The work raised the prestige of the parish priest from Bosau in the Lübeck environment. Bishop Conrad – Gerold's own brother and successor – especially in the initial period of his office did not enjoy Helmold's friendly feelings, which must have been a reciprocated attitude. It is possible that Helmold started to write in appreciation of the opinion-forming role of historiography and to contribute to the grandeur of Gerold's times and his achievements in the Christianization of the Slavs. He himself played a role in the described success and, thanks to the dignity of scripture, gained an unquestionable position among the Lübeck clergymen.

It is possible that the full concept of the work was born and shaped when it was being written, however, the clear and well thought over arrangement

---

22 In the preface to book II (Helmold II, 96) the chronicler used such a topos. See Leonid Arbusow, *Colores rhetorici* (Göttingen: Vandenhoeck & Ruprecht, 1963), pp. 97–103; cf. Strzelczyk in: *Helmolda Kronika*, p. 375 (footnote comment).

23 L. Arbusow, as above; cf. Strzelczyk in: *Helmolda Kronika*, p. 75 (footnote comment). An argument supporting the conventional character of the declared reasons for writing (*causa scribendi*) is also the fact that Helmold only very generally referred to the model of earlier writers, while there is no doubt that he borrowed the idea of describing the history of his own diocese and the ways of developing the tradition of its splendour from the work of Adam of Bremen.

24 Helmold I, [*Praefatio*]; cf. Curtius, *Literatura europejska*, pp. 94–96.

HELMOLDI CRONICA SLAVORUM ON SLAVIC RELIGION   263

of the text contradicts it. H. Stoob observed that the initial part of Book I of
the *Chronicle of the Slavs*, heavily dependent on Adam of Bremen's work, in its
form somewhat resembles the three cycles of the Christianization of the Slavs.
A similar rising and falling rhythm of two more waves of Christianization in
Slavdom is used in the construction of the later, more independent narration
of Book I until – one would think – a definitive implantation of Christianity
in the country of the Obodrites and Wagrians took place.[25] A fortunate completion of numerous church and state matters could have actually resulted in
some feeling of stabilization. Meanwhile, the original intention of the chronicler was outdated by a large number of new events to which he could not remain neutral.

    So, the first version of the work, in which on the threshold of the Slavic
mission there was Charlemagne to consider and its completion was being determined by Gerold, needed to be updated. This happened in the Book II of
the chronicle, which reported history as it broke (probably accompanied by
surprise and definitely without an appropriate distance of time necessary to
create a well thought over concept), one may find another sequence of events
following the missionary development and cycles of apostasy from the beginning of the work. The difference is in changing the order of events and the
resulting positive end of this revolution of the historical cycle. It starts with
a description of the uprising of the Obodrite tribe led by Niklot's sons, and is
followed by the intervention of the Saxons in Pomerania, inner German per-
turbations and problems of the emperor in Italy, and finally announces the
definitive victory of Christianity as a result of the conquest of Rugia and paci-
fication of the Obodrite land.[26]

    The small size of book II, finished at the latest in 1172, should not be treated
as a sign that the work is unfinished, as was thought by Arnold of Lübeck and
some other scholars.[27] For in this book there is plainly written, with a dramatic
overtone, the epilogue of the conversion of the last pre-Christian Slavs.[28] One
may go even further in speculations and identify premises that Helmold, when
returning to his chronicler's duties after a certain break, treated this book as a
separate work, although it was related to the previous one.[29] In the exegesis of
the text one should take into account the outlining autonomy of both books.

---

25   Stoob, "Einleitung," pp. 14 f; cf. Strzelczyk, "Wstęp," pp. 30–33.
26   Strzelczyk, "Wstęp," p. 33.
27   Kürbis, "Helmold," p. 199.
28   Strzelczyk, "Wstęp," p. 40.
29   This matter will be discussed in historiography analysis below, pp. 355 f.

264   CHAPTER 4

Even the very structure of the *Chronicle of the Slavs* encourages reflection on the historical and theological method of Helmold's writing. Some facts, especially in the time close to the author and his contemporaries, break the model cyclicality, and the scheme which is quite clear at the beginning of the work is gradually blurred (especially in Book II). However, the regularity and repetition of certain composition structures observed by H. Stoob do not seem accidental. Although an explanation of its genesis should not be searched for in the clearly doctrinal aspect, as it would impute Helmold to such a method of work, this would turn the *Chronicle of the Slavs* into only a theological concept illustrated with appropriately collated historical examples. Such a perspective would be an oversimplification and one should take into account additional factors shaping the image of the past presented in the chronicle.

The order of narration was influenced first and foremost by the chronology of events, which does not change the fact that the perspective of presenting historical information is marked with the extensive use of clichés deeply rooted in the author's mentality. In the Middle Ages, at the time of a particular connection between mentality and the doctrinal system of Christianity, the chronicler entwined dimensions of the theological interpretation of the course of events with their historical account. As a result, the description of events dictated by cycles of fortune and misfortune of the Chosen People, known from the Old Testament, was quite easy for him. Elements in such a cyclical historical drama are also stereotypically constructed literary creations of historical characters. Consequently, Helmold in a way fell into the order of a scheme which he possibly was not really aware of, apart from the material taken from Adam.

Following J. Strzelczyk one should emphasize that "Adam of Bremen encompassed the northern part of Polabia synthetically showing it like a bird's eye view of this area." Yet, "Helmold presented a relatively precise image of the decadent Slavic period in the history of Wagria, which does not have a counterpart on the scale of the whole of Polabia."[30] However, one should not forget that "Helmold was German, a German clergyman and although in his work he presented a lot of precious information about the Slavs and sometimes it would seem he sympathised with them, the *Chronicle of the Slavs* remained a monument of German historiography."[31]

---

30   Jerzy Strzelczyk, "Eschatologia na pograniczu niemiecko-słowiańskim w końcu XII w.," *Roczniki Historyczne* 50 (1984), p. 151. The author adds that "*Gottschalk* and *Vision of Gottschalk* allow for a 'micrographic' perspective on the complex, as one could observe, and difficult cohabitation of the Slavs and the Germans on a scale of a few villages and parishes in the region of Neumünster."

31   Strzelczyk, "Wstęp," p. 25. However, the ethnic question in Helmold's work was on the second place giving way to religious issues – Stoob, "Einleitung," p. 2.

HELMOLDI CRONICA SLAVORUM ON SLAVIC RELIGION   265

The use of Helmold's chronicle in historical research, especially related to the native religion in Slavdom, is hindered because there is no autograph of this monument. Both preserved and unpreserved manuscripts, which were the basis for Latin editions of this work started in 1556, were separated from the original by one or two hypothetical links.[32] Hence one should take into account possible deformations of Slavic names by copyists.

The structure of this presentation of the Slavic religion in Helmold's work may be strictly subordinated to the course of the narrative, bearing in mind that its main plot was the conversion of the Slavs. So, the presentation scheme is determined by the cycles of the missionary activity in Polabia, emphasized by scholars working on this problem, and apart from this by the achievements of particular characters from the period of the definitive success of the mission. The whole presentation is completed with the reference to the last upsurge of Slavic communities against the expansion of Christianity, described in Book II.

It should be noted that the portion of the material borrowed from Adam of Bremen's work will not undergo comprehensive analyses here, because it would mean a number of repetitions from the previous chapter of this work. This method can raise some doubts because in the whole "world of the work" created by the chronicler from Bosau, even unoriginal material gains the quality of an original. It is creative and also plays a modified role. Therefore, to not show disregard for "unoriginal" parts of Helmold's chronicle in the structure of this study, some references to the previous chapter of this study alongside Helmold's inventive moments in using his predecessor's work are emphasized here. In this way, as it can be believed, one may avoid redundant repetitions and at the same time respect the basic postulate of hermeneutics, *i.e.* that the text undergoing criticism should always be treated as an original entity, even when it is a compilation.

2   **The Religion of the Slavs in Helmold's Chronicle (Text Analysis)**

2.1   *Slavdom on the Threshold of the Oeuvre*
Helmold started to implement his literary objectives with a description of the geography, nature, and customs of the Slavic peoples, and also – which is important from the point of view of these considerations – with a presentation

---

32   The matter of manuscripts and their filiation, editions and scientific studies on Helmold's chronicle until 1974 is exhaustingly presented by Strzelczyk, "Wstęp," pp. 45–66; Stoob, "Einleitung," pp. 19–22; Scior, *Das Eigene und das Fremde*, pp. 142 f.

266   CHAPTER 4

of "in how great bounds of errors they had been entangled before [they could receive] the grace of conversion, in order that the efficacy of the divine remedy could be more easily acknowledged due to the great size of sickness."[33] Treating paganism as a captivity in the fetters of errors and a disease allows the Slavs to be seen as people expecting deliverance and healing from Christ. Simultaneously, this is the first clear signal in his work of the ecclesiastical interpretation of their native religion. Next, the chronicler presented a panorama of Slavic peoples determining their location and neighbourhood.

Most of this material was borrowed from Adam of Bremen's work and was also compiled following the example of the fourth book *i.e. Descriptio insularum aquilonis.*[34] Helmold's original contribution in the first chapter was the presentation of the condition of Christianity in Slavdom (*Slavania / Slavia*) and the neighbouring countries. Some of these people are praised, like the Bavarians, and some are reprimanded, like the Poles, whose military forces – although brave – when looting the invaded areas, never saved churches or monasteries and graveyards.[35] Thus, belonging to the Christian circle as such does not mean a positive attitude of the chronicler toward a particular people.[36] Moreover, his moderate favour could be shown to pagans. In the material borrowed from Adam of Bremen, the Prussian thread was mentioned too. According to Helmold's words, although they were devoid of the "light of faith", they were "multis naturalibus bonis prediti" ("endowed with many natural virtues").[37]

Chapter II: *De civitate Vinneta* brings a repetition of the information given by Adam of Bremen on the religion of the Slavs in passages on *Iumne*, Rethra, and lastly Rügen. It is characteristic that when rewriting the information on the Redigast temple, Helmold disregarded a real pearl of *interpretatio Christiana*: the correspondence of nine gates with nine streams of water, which like the Styx were to separate the souls of peoples practising idolatrous cult leading to death. Maybe such sophisticated phraseology was not understood by the

---

33   Helmold I, 1: "quantis scilicet ante conversionis gratiam errorum nexibus impliciti fuerint, ut per quantitatem morbi facilius agnoscatur efficacia divini remedii." This metaphorical assessment pictures the specifics of missionary theology, it is also supplemented by such figurative expressions as "the light of faith" (cf. *ibidem*, p. 6). This aspect of mission theory is discussed *e.g.* by Padberg, "Christen," pp. 303 ff.

34   Cf. Helmold I, 1 (see editor's comments on margins, p. 5–7).

35   *Ibidem*: "homines divino cultui dediti, nec est ulla gens honestior et in cultu Dei et sacerdotum veneratione devocior".

36   *Ibidem*. Helmold even emphasized that the Poles had eight bishoprics.

37   *Ibidem*. Positive characteristics of the Old Prussians by Adam of Bremen with regret that they are pagan is discussed below, see pp. 248 ff. See also Cf. Scior, *Das Eigene und das Fremde*, pp. 215 f.; Fraesdorff, *Der barbarische Norden*, p. 339.

HELMOLDI CRONICA SLAVORUM ON SLAVIC RELIGION   267

parish priest from Bosau. It is also possible that he did not value complex metaphors taking into consideration the abilities of the planned recipient of his
work. Both of these solutions remain only speculations. In a similarly puzzling
way the information about the "Vulcan's pot", *i.e.* the Greek fire, disappeared
from the description of *Iumne* borrowed from his predecessor.[38]

   The most important change in Helmold's chronicle in relation to the text of
the cannon of Bremen is a change of the name of the famous *Iumne* to *Vineta*
and the statement that this town disappeared from the earth. Not having found
the world centre of the Slavs and other peoples in the then-declining and already Christian Wolin (or possibly another nearby centre at the Oder mouth),[39]
the chronicler proclaimed a total devastation of this town by a Danish king
(and there is certainly a grain of truth in this information[40]), thus allowing a
mysterious legend to surround this town.

   The story started to take on its own life in the folk culture of the modern
age as an independent story, developed by its interpreters and adjusted to temporary needs and ideas.[41] A turning point in critical research on the legend,
or maybe only its forerunner, was C.F. Rumohr's idea that the beginnings of
the legend should not be sought after in the Slavic oral tradition but in the
scholarly knowledge of the Middle Ages.[42] Further analyses proved that this
statement was right.

   It is often assumed that the source of this legend was Helmold's ignorance,
which is certainly possible. However, the matter remains unclear. Contrary
to the conviction of Helmold's ignorance on the location of *Iumne*, his own
statement is worth remembering here: "It is said that some king of the Danes,

---

38   Helmold I, 2, p. 8. Cf. Adam II, 21.
39   The said concept of identification of *Iumne*/Vineta with the later Wolin existed even in
      medieval Pomeranian historiography; in the mid-14th c. it was thought to be the most
      probable option by Augustine of Stargard, however, he also took into consideration dif-
      ferent opinions assuming the location of this legendary city on the island Usedom – see
      Augustyn ze Stargardu zwany niegdyś Angelusem [Augustine of Stargard called Angelus],
      Protokół. Kamieńska Kronika-Rodowód Książąt Pomorskich, tzw. Stargardzka Genealogia,
      Latin text and Polish transl., ed. Edward Rymar, trans. Elwira Buszewicz (Stargard:
      Muzeum w Stargardzie, 2008), pp. 44 f.
40   Adam, schol. 56 (57); Arnórr jarlaskáld, *O walce króla norweskiego Magnusa ze słowiańskimi
      korsarzami w Jómie – Wolinie w r. 1043*, in Gerard Labuda, *Słowiańszczyzna pierwotna.
      Wybór tekstów* (Warszawa: PWN, 1954), pp. 305 f., there is also basic information about this
      source. See Labuda, *Fragmenty*, vol. 2, pp. 131, 144 f.; Morawiec, *Wolin*, p. 45.
41   Lately on this matter see: Rusakiewicz, *Wineta, passim*; see also above, p. 227, footnote 152.
42   Carl Friedrich Rumohr, *Sammlung für Kunst und Historie*, vol. 1/1: *Über das Verhältniss
      der seit lange gewöhnlichen Vorstellungen von einer prachtvollen Wineta zu unsrer positiven
      Kenntniss der Kultur und Kunst der deutschen Ostseeslaven* (Hamburg: Perthes & Besser,
      1816), pp. 91–92; cf. Kiersnowski, *Legenda*, pp. 6 f.

268   CHAPTER 4

having oppressed that opulent city with a great fleet, obliterated it from the
foundations. Here up till now are the ancient monuments of that city."[43] The
Danish king mentioned here must be Magnus, who destroyed *Iumne* (probably
Wolin) in 1043, according to Adam of Bremen and the Arnórr jarlaskáld song.[44]
Helmold explicitly states that the remains of this town survived until his times,
which means that he had clear information on the matter.

It is easy to assume that in the rebuilt Wolin and its surroundings there
could be remains of a bigger town settlement. However, the chronicler must
have also seen a lack of continuity in the history of this town which, as it is
known, was called Wolin (*Vulin, Iulin*) in the 12th c.,[45] and no *Iumne*, a name
known to Helmold from in the chronicle of Adam of Bremen, and related in
this narrative to the earlier period in the city's history.[46] Helmold must have
known how the process of Christianization of this area was conducted because
in chapter 40 he mentions the mission of the bishop Otto of Bamberg with an
amiable tone in his account. However, the details of this action and the history
of the nearby bishopric with the capitol in Wolin were not in the area of his
interests.

Helmold generally rewrote with faithfulness whole parts of the text from
the chronicle of Adam of Bremen, but by changing the name of an existing
town, he turned it into a legend reaching – which was his intention – an indefi-
nite past.[47] The motif behind such an effort was probably a need to erase such
a positive model as the inhabitants of *Iumne* in Adam's work from his image of
contemporary Slavs. Then we would be dealing with Helmold's *licentia poetica*,
as he used the motif from his predecessor's work to illustrate, in his opinion,
an outworn tradition of "good" Slavs, changing the original name of their town.
This name transformation may mean the latinization of the previous name.
Yet, its most important advantage was forming a basis for the development of

---

43   Helmold I, 2: "Hanc civitatem opulentissimam quidam Danorum rex maxima classe sti-
      patus funditus evertisse refertur. Presto sunt adhuc antiquae illius civitatis monimenta."
44   See above, footnote 40 in this chapter.
45   *E.g. Ekkechardi Uraugiensis chronica*, under the year 1125, p. 264; Vita Prieflingensis II, 5;
      Ebo II, 1. It is interesting that Helmold showed great intuition or he was simply fortunate
      to break the association between the names *Iumne* and *Iulin*, because they most probably
      have different origins (see above, pp. 232 f.).
46   The name *Iumne* already is attested in Scandinavian sources, though this does not change
      the fact that the name also has a Slavic origin. For discussion on the matter see above,
      pp. 232 f.
47   He added the '-ta' ending, while the beginning '*ium-*', '*win-*', '*uinn-*' could have changed as
      a result of discrepancies in rewriting – see above, p. 226, footnote 151.

HELMOLDI CRONICA SLAVORUM ON SLAVIC RELIGION   269

the medieval etymology: Vineta is the "town of the Vinedes"[48] (*Winithi*), indentified also as Vandals.[49]

Helmold's literary device turned a historical motif into a mythic reality,
which presented a universal message on the nature of the Slavs, which had
already been deprived. In the perspective of Adam of Bremen's work it was a
historical town which in many respects served as an example for Christians;
Helmold – writing at the time of crusades against the Polabian and Pomeranian
Slavs – presented them as barbarians and, even worse, as apostates and blas-
phemers with regard to the true God.[50] In his description written after the devastation of Vineta as the town of good Slavs, the leaders of the Baltic islands are
the Rugians who are the worst of all.[51]

Thus, Helmold's case suggests the birth mechanism of a new literary motif
based on ignorance or – which seems more certain – on his own interpretation
of history dictated by the pragmatic elements of his work. An original contribution of the chronicler from Bosau is a general opinion about the Slavic people,
which was not known from Adam of Bremen's work: "Such are therefore the
peoples of the Slavs spread out across the regions, provinces and islands in the
sea. All that kind of men is dedicated to the cult of idolatry, always wandering
and mobile, who make profit out of piracy, on the Danes on one side, and on
the Saxons on the other."[52] Damage caused to neighbours urged emperors and
the clergy to undertake an effort to make "gentes istae rebelles et incredulae"
recognize "the name of God and the holy grace."

This summary of characteristics seems to reflect stereotypical views on
the seaside Slavs. Idolatry, mobility, and piracy seem to be the markers of
Barbarians identification. Expressions such as *rebelles* and *increduli* are basic
in the topic range of the characteristics of peoples who did not want to accept
German (Christian) supremacy.[53]

---

48   *E.g.* Kiersnowski, *Legenda*, p. 42.

49   Helmold 1, 2, wrote in this case about the inhabitants of the Slavs' province who were
     earlier called Vandals and contemporarily Vinedes (*Winithi*) or *Winuli* ("... qui antiquitus
     Wandali, nunc autem Winithi sive Winuli appellantur").

50   Helmold 1, 6.

51   Helmold 1, 2, Helmold gives short characteristics of the Rans borrowed from Adam of
     Bremen.

52   *Ibidem:* "Hii igitur sunt Winulorum populi diffusi per regiones et provincias et insulas
     maris. Omne hoc hominum genus ydolatriae cultui deditum, vagum semper et mobile,
     piraticas exercentes predas, ex una parte Danis, ex altera Saxonibus infestum."

53   Topoi *rebelles* and *increduli* with reference to the Slavs are discussed by Tyszkiewicz, *Z
     badań nad narodzinami*, pp. 32, 38 ff., and the genesis of *rebelles* with references to the
     barbarians is discussed by Tadeusz Kotula, "Głos (poszerzony) w dyskusji nad referatem
     doc. dra hab. Lecha Tyszkiewicza," in *Wokół stereotypów Polaków i Niemców*, ed. Wojciech

270 CHAPTER 4

2.2   *The First Wave of Christianization*

2.2.1   Charlemagne, Anskar, and the Slavs

A useful bridge leading from the introduction of the Slavic people to the first detailed accounts of their conversion are two chapters in Helmold's work, which present characters and actions which are models in Christianization activity among *gentes*. First, he eulogizes Charlemagne as a distinguished persona among all propagators of Christianity, and states that he deserves to hold the first place among those "who toiled for God in the northern regions. For he himself tamed with sword the most fierce and rebellious people of the Saxons and brought [them] under the Christian laws."[54] Subjugating with a sword and subduing wild and rebellious (*rebelles*) Saxons to God's law determined the beginning of missionary activity, whose success depends on the steps that will follow and is also illustrated with the model example of Charlemagne.

He desisted from collecting tribute from the defeated Saxons so as to avoid excessive repression which could lead to mutiny and make them return to "the errors of paganism."[55] This is what Helmold writes himself, after which he adds, following Adam of Bremen, that the only condition imposed on the Saxons was "in order that, after having rejected the cult of demons, they receive the sacraments of faith and are tributaries and subjects of the Lord God, of all their beasts of burden and their breeding of crops or husbandry they legally present the tithes to the priests, and, having united with the Franks, they form one people. As a result, Saxony was divided into eight dioceses and was subjected to dignified shepherds"[56] and – later continuing his thought – "Therefore the

---

Wrzesiński, (Acta Universitatis Wratislaviensis. Historia) 79 (Wrocław: Wydawnictwo Uniwersytetu Wrocławskiego, 1991), p. 51 f. In the perspective of clerical chroniclers, rebelliousness and unfaithfulness, stereotypical in the characteristics of the peoples who did not want to accept the rule of the Empire, have a religious dimension. It is similar with Saxons (Helmold I, 3), who were converted as *rebelles* – rebels subjugated by the emperor with Christian law enforced on them. Helmold (I, 89) will show his attachment to the topos of *rebelles* in connection with the Slavs subjugated by Albrecht the Bear one more time.

54   Helmold I, 3: "qui pro Deo in partibus aquilonis laboraverunt. Ipse enim Saxonum gentem ferocissimam atque rebellem ferro perdomuit et Christianis legibus subegit."

55   *Ibidem*: "ne forte serviciis aut tributis pregravati ad rebelionis necessitatem et paganismi errores impellerentur."

56   Helmold I, 3: "ut abiecto demonum cultu Christianae fidei sacramenta susciperent essentque tributarii et sublegales domini Dei, omnium iumentorum suorum et fructuum culturae seu nutriturae suae [decimas] sacerdotibus legaliter offerentes et Francis adunati unus cum eis populus efficerentur. Divisa est igitur Saxonia in octo episcopatus et dignissimis pastoribus subiecta."

HELMOLDI CRONICA SLAVORUM ON SLAVIC RELIGION   271

task of [establishing] a new plantation in Saxony was accomplished and confirmed with full force."[57]

The outlined model of Christianization is treated by Helmold as an ideal one. Later in the narration Charlemagne was presented as the initiator of the mission in the area located near the Elbe River and as the author of the idea to establish the Hamburg metropolis, but wars turned out to hamper Christianization. For Helmold, the conferment of the title of emperor on the Frankish ruler is well deserved, and so he completed the justification given after *Vita Willehadi*[58] with the phrase *fidei meritum* located before emphasizing Charlemagne's fame and war merits.[59] Thus, the chronicler's inventions characterize Charlemagne as an ideal Christian ruler, protector of the faith, and conqueror, all of which functioned in reference to the other characters in his work.

Another character, personifying for Helmold a model of a clergyman-missionary, was the Bishop – and next the Metropolitan – of Hamburg, Anskar. He was entrusted with his office by Louis the German, but the establishment of this bishopric, further metropolis of the North, according to the chronicler, was the implementation of the plan of Charlemagne himself to proclaim the gospel to all the barbarians, which did apparently occur: "For thanks to the vehemence of the archbishops of the Church of Hamburg the word of God was spread among all the peoples of the Slavs, Danes, or Normans, and that chilling cold of the North was melted by the heat of the word of God. And so, after so many days and long years and thanks to the labours of doctors among them [*i.e.* those peoples] it was achieved with great effort. For so great was the darkness of errors and difficulty in [getting rid of] the idolatry, that it could have been defeated neither fast, nor easily."[60]

---

57   *Ibidem*: "qui ad imbuendas rudes in fide animas verbo et exemplo sufficerent. Quibus etiam huius vitae stipendia memoratus cesar multo honore, plena denique munificentia providit." All these activities led to the successful final: "Perfectum est igitur in Saxonia novellae plantationis opus et pleno vigore constabilitum".

58   *Ibidem*, p. 12 (Editor's note); also a comment in: *Helmolda Kronika*, p. 94.

59   Helmold I, 3. Cf. Scior, *Das Eigene und das Fremde*, p. 173.

60   *Ibidem* I, 4: "Hic ubi super Hammemburg patris sui comperit votum, communicato statim sapientum consilio sanctissimum virum Anscarium, quem etiam aliquando ad Danos et Suedos predicatorem direxerat, Hammemburgensi ecclesiae ordinari fecit archiepiscopum, statuens eandem civitatem metropolim universis borealibus populis, egatio verbi Dei exinde uberius pollularet in omnes barbaras naciones. Quod et factum est. Nam Hammemburgensis ecclesiae pontificum instantia disseminatum est verbum Dei in omnes Slavorum, Danorum, sive Northmannorum populos, et dissolutum est gelidum illud frigus aquilonis a calore verbi Dei. Multis itaque diebus sive annis maximisque

272   CHAPTER 4

The said "chilling cold of the North" is not neutral in Christian symbolism, but rather it is strictly connected with the area of activity of the impure
spirit.[61] Wars were an additional difficulty in undertaking the mission under
Hamburg's patronage. This summary reflection on the metropolitan goals and
the difficulties in achieving them also refers to the Slavs, which provided an
opportunity to give a theological assessment of their religion (*error, ydolatria*).

Turmoil resulting from war (especially the Danish invasions) during the
reign of Louis the German paralyzed the church network in Saxony. It recov-
ered its operation thanks to the activity of St. Anskar, who joined in his hands
the bishopric of Bremen and archbishopric of Hamburg (thus there was "one
sheepfold and one shepherd").[62] Serving as the emperor's envoy to the King
of Denmark on many occasions, the metropolitan bishop became a respected
authority, and although the king was pagan himself, he did not hamper evangelization of the country. The achieved success gave rise to Anskar's desire to
convert the Svear, where he arrived and managed to obtain the king's agreement for missionary activity for priests sent there with a bishop.

Two countries of the North, evangelized thanks to Anskar's efforts, were to
experience numerous obstacles on their way to Christianity. However – as it
is stressed by Helmold – the undertaking, once begun, was never to be completely destroyed. With this thought, Helmold returns to Slavic affairs: "So,
among all the peoples of the northern nations the sole province of the Slavs
has remained harder than the others and dilatory at accepting the faith."[63]
The connection of the topical toughness (*duritia*) of the Slavs with their resistance to accept Christianity is not the first such case on the pages of medieval
historiography.[64]

---

      doctorum laboribus in gentibus his desudatum est; tanta enim fuit opacitas errorum et
      difficultas ydolatriae, ut nec subito, nec facile potuisset evinci".

61   Forstner, *Świat*, p. 72. See also Fraesdorff, *Der barbarische Norden*, pp. 40 ff., 125 f., 325.

62   Helmold I, 5.

63   Helmold I, 6: "Inter omnes autem borealium nacionum populos sola Slavorum provincia
      remansit ceteris durior atque ad credendum tardior." Cf. Scior, *Das Eigene und das Fremde*,
      pp. 216 f.; Fraesdorff, *Der barbarische Norden*, p. 334.

64   Toughness and stubbornness of the Slavs is a topos in medieval historiography both
      Byzantine and Latin, see *e.g.* Tyszkiewicz, *Slavi genus, passim*; cf. Fraesdorff, *Der bar-
      barische Norden*, p. 334. Even Widukind and Thietmar referred this *duritia* to the tough-
      ness of their lifestyle and laws, however, Cosmas I, 15 – who did not feel culturally strange
      to the Slavic environment as itself – in the Liutici he can see *durissima gens* and their
      duchess Drahomira is perceived by him as "ipsam saxis duriorem ad credendum". Thus
      this characteristic was identified with stubbornness to Christianity, cf. Tyszkiewicz,
      "Slavi genus," pp. 9 f. One may also remember here the opinion of bishop Paulinus of
      Aquileia about Avars and Slavs expressed during the Convention on the Danube (796)
      see: *Conventus episcoporum ad ripam Danubii 796 aestate*, ed. Karl Zeuner, MGH LL 3,

HELMOLDI CRONICA SLAVORUM ON SLAVIC RELIGION   273

It is worth remembering that reliable sources do not indicate that the establishment of the Hamburg diocese was meant for the Christianization of the Slavs. Helmold succumbs here to the falsified Bremen tradition.[65] The inclusion of the Polabian mission in the primary stream of Christianization of the Northern peoples builds the prestige of these efforts. They encountered extremely strong opposition from the Slavs, and attention is drawn to the explanation of their attitude especially in the case of the Rugians – most hardened pagans in Helmold's days.

2.2.2   The Rugians, Svantevit and the Legend of Corvey
The last bastion of public cult in the Old Slavic religion was Rügen. The inhabitants of the island, the Rans,[66] although encompassed in the sphere of Viking influence (they were known for piracy themselves), were very attached to their native gods, in the cult of which a characteristic element turned out to be polycephalic representations and a special (native) way of naming deities using the suffix -*vit*. The first information in the medieval historiography on political activity of the Rans is a description of their participation in the war of the Elbslavs with Otto I in 955, in which they supported the side of the Saxons.[67] This information shows an image of a centralized political organism, pursuing isolationist politics in relation to their kinsmen. In view of the increase of the power of the Liutici federation (after 983) the Rügen inhabitants resigned from their activity on land and became involved in Baltic pirate fights instead. After the fall of Radogošč, the capital of Rügen, Arkona became the most famous centre of the native Slavic cults.[68]

The first attempt to Christianize the island, which was known to Helmold, is depicted in the so-called Legend of Corvey, known also in three other versions (one of which is included at the end of Helmold's chronicle).[69] The

---

Conc. 2/1 (1906), No. 20, pp. 172–176. A similar opinion was expressed earlier by Alcuin. For Alcuin's letter see *Alcvini sive Albini Epistolae*, ed. Ernest Dümmler, MGH Epp 4, Epp Carolini Aevi 2 (1895), No. 111, p. 160. See also below, footnote 479 (about *duritia* of Rans).

65   See above, pp. 204 f.

66   For a discussion on the origin of the name Rügen and Rans see: Jürgen Udolph, "Rügen. Namenkundliches," in *Reallexikon der Germanischen Altertumskunde*, vol. 25 (Berlin/New York: De Gruyter, 2003), pp. 417–421, and also *e.g.* Osięgłowski, "Początki słowiańskiej Rugii," pp. 249 ff.; Franciszek Grucza, "Rugia," in SSS, vol. 4, p. 564 f.

67   Widukind III, 54. Cf. Babij, *Wojskowość*, p. 131.

68   *E.g.* Osięgłowski, "Początki słowiańskiej Rugii," pp. 252–254; Leciejewicz, *Słowianie*, pp. 193, 217.

69   Jacek Soszyński, "Święty Wit a Świętowit Rugijski. Z dziejów legendy," *Przegląd Humanistyczny* 28 (1984) 9/10, p. 136, mentions four versions of the legend: 1) Saxo Grammaticus's (Saxo XIV, 39): invasion of Rügen by Charlemagne and imposition of

274   CHAPTER 4

legend gives an interesting example of the Christian interpretation of a Slavic
deity, which is the identification of Svantevit, worshipped by the Rügen inhabitants with St. Vitus. Helmold located this plot in a presentation of Slavic
peoples, and the background of this story was a conviction that the Rügen inhabitants were converted to Christianity as early as the 9th c. Helmold emphasizes here the Slavs' exceptional resistance (*invincibilis duritia*) to converting to
Christianity.[70] This resistance was so strong that even ardent missionaries did
not become involved in undertaking evangelization, predicting that it would
not be successful. The group that manifested the strongest attachment to paganism was the Rans.[71]

In Helmold's view this situation could be explained by this *antiqua relatio*,
in the light of which the nature of the Rügen idolatry was a departure from
faith in the only God. It was to be implanted by New Corvey monks: "After
having wandered through many provinces of the Slavs, they came to those
who call themselves the Rani or Rugiani and who inhabit the heart of the sea.
There is the kindling and the capital of idolatry. And thus, preaching the word
of God with confidence, they won that whole island. There they also founded
an oratory in honour of our Lord and Saviour Jesus Christ, and in memory of
St. Vitus, who is the patron of Corvey (Corbeia). And afterwards, with God's
permission and due to an [unfortunate] turn of events, the Rani abandoned
faith, and after having immediately driven the priests and the Christians
away, they turned religion into superstition. For instead of God they worship
St. Vitus, whom we believe to be a martyr and Christ's servant, they favour
the creature over the Creator. Under the sky there is no other barbarity which
despises the Christians and the priests more. They pride themselves with the
sole name of St. Vitus to whom they dedicated a temple and a statue with the

---

       tribute to St. Vitus – apostasy; 2) Helmold's II, 108, see below, pp. 360 f.; 3) from the so
       called Lothar' donation: invasion of the island by Lothar – granting it to New Corvey;
       4) the discussed here Helmold's version I, 6. Possible knowledge of Helmold's work by
       Saxo Grammaticus may be of certain significance in the discussion on the history of the
       legend, this view was supported by Inge Skovgaard-Petersen, "Wendenzüge – Kreuzzüge,"
       in *Rom und Byzanz im Norden. Mission und Glaubenswechsel im Ostseeraum während des
       8.–14. Jahrhunderts*, vol. 1, ed. Michael Müller-Wille (Stuttgart: Steiner, 1997), p. 285.

70   Helmold I, 6.

71   Famous for their bravery the inhabitants of this Baltic island became the object of the
       chronicler's attention for the first time in the second chapter of his work, where there is
       information taken nearly completely from Adam of Bremen: "Rani, qui et Rugiani, gens
       fortissima Slavorum, qui soli habent regem, extra quorum sententiam nichil agi de pub-
       licis rebus fas est, adeo metuuntur propter familiaritatem deorum vel pocius demonum,
       quos maiori pre ceteris cultura venerantur." – Helmold I, 2. Cf. above, pp. 247 f.

HELMOLDI CRONICA SLAVORUM ON SLAVIC RELIGION   275

greatest veneration, to whom specifically they attribute the primacy among
the deities."[72]

So a visible sign of a successful completion of Christianization of the island
was the erection of a chapel "to worship Christ and in honour of St. Vitus".
However, the character of the later departure from faith, *i.e.* replacement of
the cult of God with the cult of the saint, is explained by the chronicler with a
biblical idea: *creaturam anteponere creatori*. It was supposed to be done with
God's permission (*permittente Deo*). A clear sign of the apostasy of the Rügen
inhabitants was supposed to be the existence of a splendid temple with the
image of the deity (*templum et simulachrum*). The blasphemous character of
this cult explains particular hatred for the followers of Christ and their priests.

The Rans allegedly boasted of the very name of St. Vitus ("solo nomine sancti Viti gloriantur"), putting it above all other deities (*deitates*). Thus, the saint
was worshipped like or instead of God (*pro Deo venerantur*). This is not the
end of this rich theological commentary: as a result of their trespass the Rügen
inhabitants turned religion (*religio*) into superstition (*superstitio*) and so the
island became *fomes errorum* and *sedes ydolatrie*. Emphasis on the account
that they live in the heart of the sea in a symbolic dimension intensifies the
terror related to this dwelling place of the evil based on associations evoked by
the maritime element,[73] which was most certainly of sacral significance for the
island's inhabitants.[74]

The genesis of the legend is not completely clear.[75] It became known especially thanks to the activity of the Benedictine abbey in New Corvey. At the
beginning of the 12th c., Rügen became the centre of attention of its superiors,
as one may assume, in connection with the expected occupation of the island

---

72   Helmold 1, 6: "... peragratisque multis Slavorum provinciis pervenerunt ad eos qui dicun-
      tur Rani sive Rugiani et inhabitant in corde maris. Ibi fomes est errorum et sedes ydolat-
      rie. Predicantes itaque verbum Dei cum omni fiducia omnem illam insulam lucrati sunt,
      ubi etiam oratorium fundaverunt in honorem domini ac salvatoris nostri Iesu Christi et in
      commemorationem sancti Viti, qui est patronus Corbeiae. Postquam autem, permittente
      Deo mutatis rebus, Rani a fide defecerunt, statim pulsis sacerdotibus atque Christicolis
      religionem verterunt in superstitionem. Nam sanctum Vitum, quem nos martirem ac
      servum Christi confitemur, ipsi pro Deo venerantur, creaturam anteponentes creatori.
      Nec est aliqua barbaries sub celo, quae Christocolas ac sacerdotes magis exorreat; solo
      nomine sancti Viti gloriantur, cui etiam templum et simulachrum amplissimo cultu dedi-
      caverunt, illi primatum deitatis specialiter attribuentes."
73   See above, p. 167.
74   "The sacrum of the see" in the lives of the Rügen inhabitants has been discussed by Miś,
      "Przedchrześcijańska religia," pp. 122 ff.
75   A critical discussion and findings on the origin of the legend of Rügen are presented by
      Osięgłowski, "Początki słowiańskiej Rugii," pp. 254 ff., and Soszyński, "Święty Wit," *passim*.

276   CHAPTER 4

by the Christian side. The basis for claims by the abbey to extend its ownership
of the land to include the island was a document dated 844, which bore the
name of Emperor Lothar as its author. Scholarly criticism of this document,
whose original is not known, assumed that it was false. However, it is possible
to assume that the forgery was used to legalize claims which arose in some
other circumstances.

A result of the energetic activity of Corvey abbot Wibald, participating in
the crusade against the Slavs in 1147, was a confirmation of the alleged establishment of the right to the island in 844 by Pope Hadrian IV in 1155. It took
place at the time when the Legend of Corvey found its lasting place in contemporary awareness, which was confirmed by Helmold (it was also known to a
Danish chronicler Saxo Grammaticus who lived a few decades later). However,
Adam of Bremen, to whom the chronicler from Bosau owed a lot of knowledge
about the Slavs, does not mention it. Similarly, the legend is not mentioned by
Widukind of Corvey, who was the first one to mention the Rans in the whole of
medieval historiography.[76]

The *Registrum Sarachonis*, written by Saracho the Abbot of Corvey, is considered to be the oldest confirmation of the legend. Apart from the above
mentioned chronicles by Helmold and Saxo Grammaticus, the foundational
sources for the discussion on the legend are also the works created in the
Corvey monastery: *Catalogus Abbatum et Fratrum Cobeiensium*, *Chronographus
Corbeiensis*, the letter of Wibald the Abbot of New Corvey written to the bishop of Hildesheim Bernhard, *Annales Corbeienses*, and the above mentioned
false document on establishment of rights to the island by Emperor Lothar for
Corvey.[77]

The key note in *Registrum Sarachonis* is as follows: "The Slavs of the Rügen
island count as a [part of] the patrimony of St. Vitus, but because of the greed
and arrogance of our overseers they have abandoned faith."[78] Admittedly
Saracho died in 1071 and the note is third from last in the list with the number
747, which would allow the information to be dated to the time close to his
death. However, J. Osięgłowski states that the list was only started by the abbot
and it was later continued by his successors.[79] He suggested that the genesis of
the legend was the series of events that took place in 1110–1114. In his opinion
the Corvey Benedictines participated in the invasion by Lothar of Supplinburg

---

76   See above footnote 69 in this chapter; cf. Osięgłowski, "Początki słowiańskiej Rugii,"
      pp. 252 f.

77   For a concise discussion on these sources see Soszyński, "Święty Wit," pp. 133–135.

78   "Rugiacensis insulae Sclaui ad patrimonium sancti Viti spectant, sed ob auaritiam et inso-
      lentiam uillicorum nostrorum a fide defecerunt."

79   Osięgłowski, "Początki słowiańskiej Rugii," p. 260.

HELMOLDI CRONICA SLAVORUM ON SLAVIC RELIGION   277

against Rügen and "they found out more about the island and realised what
benefits would be brought by its ownership. Knowing the language of the Slavs
and a comparison of the main deity of the Rügen inhabitants – Svantevit with
the name of the saint patron of the Corvey monastery – St. Vitus, made them
think of creating a legend, which (...) was very well accepted."[80]

The note from *Annales Corbeienses* (dated 1114 and recorded before 1117),
which informs about the invasion, mentions the dependence of the Rans on
the St. Vitus monastery. The moment, hypothetically indicated by Osięgłowski,
of the creation of the legend thus seems to be quite probable. However, it is
worth trying to move the beginnings of the legend to an earlier period.[81] It is
supported by the fact that after the fall of Rethra, Arkona replaced it as the
main centre of Slavs' paganism according to their German neighbours, and
as a consequence, Svantevit worshipped in the famous temple could become
famous enough to be known even in New Corvey. Helmold confirms such a
possibility: "Also there the oracles are beseeched, and the annual payments are
presented as offerings from all the provinces of the Slavs. However, the merchants, who would venture by chance to those places, are not allowed to sell
or buy until they first offer something precious from their wares to their [*i.e.*
Rugians] god, and only then the commodities are presented at the market."[82]

According to this passage, the Rügen deity gained the highest popularity
among remaining pagan Slavs. Apart from this, information about it could be
spread by merchants who suffered because of payments related to the temple
cult once they decided to trade in Arkona, or also by prisoners of war returning from the captivity of Slavic pirates. J. Soszyński made a hypothesis that the
authors of the legend were New Corvey monks but that they created the legend
long before Lothar's invasion in 1114, during which the legend was of practical
use for the first time. Recalling the matter of tribute to Svantevit during the
capitulation negotiations with the Circipanes, according to this hypothesis, it
was to be used by some monk to teach others that the god of Arkona was in fact
St. Vitus. Hence the price of peace was again undertaking financial obligations
in relation to the patron of New Corvey.

The association of Svantevit with St. Vitus created by a monk in the Corvey
scriptorium, in J. Soszyński's hypothesis, is supported by poor knowledge of the

---

80   *Ibidem*, p. 260 f.
81   Soszyński, "Święty Wit," p. 137, polemised with J. Osięgłowski's thesis, he claimed that
      knowledge of Rügen in Germany even before the beginning of the 12th c. was not scarce.
82   Helmold I, 6: "De omnibus quoque provinciis Slavorum illic responsa petuntur et sacrifi-
      ciorum exhibentur annuae soluciones. Sed nec mercatoribus, qui forte ad illas sedes ap-
      pulerint, patet ulla facultas vendendi vel emendi, nisi prius de mercibus suis deo ipsorum
      preciosa quaeque libaverint, et tunc demum mercimonia foro publicantur."

278   CHAPTER 4

Slavic language of the person who, translating the first part of the deity's name ('*svant-*' into *sanctus*), could not translate the other one, *i.e.* '-vit', which given the medieval tendency for ethymologization resulted in the legendary identification.[83] Its genesis would remain in close relation with the supra-tribal fame of the Arkona deity, and emphasized by Helmold, its exceptional position is shown in the theocratic character of the Rügen statehood: "they revere their priest not less than a king."[84]

A summary of the first report on idolatry of the Rans was a renewed theological qualification of their cult: "So since the time when they first renounced the faith, such superstition has persevered among the Rans up to this day."[85] However, it is worth emphasizing a special character of the interpretation of the Slavic god (his name) in the legend. Namely, at the time when identification of deities with demons from a biblical perspective was rather common, to such an extent that this thinking procedure was considered the essence of *interpretatio Christiana*, in this case a sainted person was identified with a god. Thus, the Rügen inhabitants, who according to Helmold, and repeating Adam's opinion, were known for their intimacy with their gods or one should say demons, in this case surprise us with their cult for a Christian saint.[86]

In research on Christian interpretation of Slavic religion, it is a clear indication to perceive this issue as a complex one. This unbecoming cult of St. Vitus becomes idolatry which in the theological perspective was the sphere of activity of demonic powers. However, an error in the doctrine was the wrongdoing (*superstitio*) of the Rans, who remained unaware of its consequences; they were misled by Satan (for Christians – aware of the consequences of idolatry – the matter is clear). Thus, it is postulated to establish two levels in the reflection of chroniclers-theologians in their approach to the Christian interpretation: 1) an error in cult and doctrine (the case of St. Vitus) and 2) spiritual consequences – openness to *antisacrum* (demons).

The presence of these two dimensions in the view of Svantevit's cult casts light on gift offerings made to him by the Danish king Sven (1146–1157). Did he perhaps make offerings to demons? It is possible to assume that he was

---

83   Soszyński, "Święty Wit," p. 137 f.

84   Helmold I, 6: "flaminem suum non minus quam regem venerantur"; on the basis of this information Kiersnowska, Kiersnowski, *Życie codzienne*, p. 168, claim that the duke of the Rans existed in the shadow of Svantevit and his priests, which seems to be disputable (see below, pp. 302 f., 359, 374).

85   Helmold I, 6: "Ab eo igitur tempore, quo primo fidei renuntiaverunt, haec superstitio apud Ranos perseverat usque in hodiernum diem".

86   Helmold I, 2.

HELMOLDI CRONICA SLAVORUM ON SLAVIC RELIGION   279

aware of the fact that he worshipped St. Vitus[87] with his offerings, who was un-becomingly worshipped by the Slavs (according to the legend ex-Christians).[88] *Superstitio* does not only mean superstition in its contemporary definition – it is a wider notion, which is generally connected with trespassing against faith and cult.[89]

However, explanation of the genesis of the Legend of Corvey does not com-plete the debate over the very name of the Rügen god. Questioning the au-thenticity of events included in this story leaves unanswered questions about the coincidental similarity between the names of the patron of Corvey monks and the Slavic deity. The explanation of the circumstances presented above, in which the legend was born, follows the idea that the legend was circulated to justify the monastery's pretences to ownership of the island. The very rumour could have existed in this or some other form earlier, and it was popularized in a version of such a legend at the moment when occupation of the island by Christians became inevitable.

The origin of Svantevit's name from St. Vitus still had its supporters among scholars in the 19th c.[90] This line of argument became more probable thanks to cases which were known from medieval Rus', where St. Nicolaus and St. Balazs were deified in a pre-Christian way.[91] This fostered acceptance of the whole Legend of Corvey. However, scholarly criticism finally put an end to this view. In this situation the last part of the story to be defended is its basic motif, namely the connection between the Slavic theonym and the name of a Christian saint. The most detailed statement on this matter was provided by H. Łowmiański who, while agreeing with the fictitious character of the Legend

---

87   Saxo xiv, 39, 8; Osięgłowski, "Początki słowiańskiej Rugii," p. 276. However, Saxo
       Grammaticus, who knew the Legend of Corvey, was certain that the king committed a
       religious wrongdoing, which supports the view that the Danish court and church envi-
       ronment did not know the tradition about the motivation related to the cult of St. Vitus
       behind gifts for Arkona, see Saxo xiv, 39, 9: "Suantovitus (id simulacro vocabulum erat)".
88   *Annales Corbeienses*, ed. Georg Heinrich Pertz, mgh ss 3 (1839), under the year 1114,
       p. 8 – Lothar managed to make the terrified Circipanes confess that they used to pay
       rent to St. Vitus of Corvey. Certainly this must have been Svantevit, who functioned in
       Christians' minds as St. Vitus; see Łowmiański, *Religia*, pp. 191 f.
89   See above, pp. 193 f.
90   Franz Miklosich, *Etymologisches Wörterbuch der slavischen Sprachen* (Vienna: Braumüller,
       1886), p. 393. Cf. Moszyński, *Prasłowiański panteon*, p. 171.
91   Urbańczyk, *Dawni Słowianie*, pp. 41. Cf. Wincenty Swoboda, "Kult świętych (2)", in sss,
       vol. 8, pp. 383 f.

280   CHAPTER 4

of Corvey, proposed another explanation of the identification of St. Vitus with Svantevit.[92]

He claimed that this identification must have taken place in the sphere of the Slavic language and excluded Latin as its basis (a decisive piece of evidence for him was a reference to a statement on this matter made by the Slavs themselves noted in *Annales Corbeienses*). Based on the assumption that polydoxy – which was considered the main layer of Slavic beliefs by Łowmiański – is open to accepting a new strange *sacrum*, the scholar concluded that the reception of the Christian saint was a fact.[93] However, St. Vitus was to reach Polabia not on his way from New Corvey but from Prague, where he was worshipped in a Slavic version of his name, as the saint patron of a church erected in the third decade of the 10th c. The intermediate stage on his way to Arkona was to be Brenna (the centre of the Stodorane tribe remaining in contact with Prague), from which the cult was to be moved to Rügen after the stronghold was taken by the Saxons in 940. The element, which was received from the Christians, according to H. Łowmiański, was also Triglav from Szczecin, who was to be a Slavic version of the Holy Trinity. The genesis of the statue of Svantevit, according to this scholar, was connected with an idol with three heads, which on Rügen was given the fourth one – St. Vitus's.

Thus, this reasoning consists of several hypothetical links which actually weaken the strength of the whole argumentation. Similar to ideas related to the genesis of polycephaly, the identification of St. Vitus with Svantevit, which allegedly took place in the Slavic environment and is fundamental to the entire argument, turns out to be questionable.[94] H. Łowmiański did not take into account the possibility that both of these names were identified in the minds of missionaries, who knew the Slavic language to some extent.

The latter hypothetical proposal is an agreement with J. Soszyński's findings, although his assumption that the person who associated Svantevit with St. Vitus knew the Slavic language to such a limited extent that he translated

---

92   Łowmiański, *Religia*, pp. 190–195. The concept was accepted by Moszyński, *Die vorchrist-
      liche Religion*, pp. 61–63, emphasizing additionally that among the Polabian and
      Pomeranian Slavs in the final phase of their native religion, anthroponyms ending with
      "-vit" disappear because the ending was reserved for divine names.

93   The second example of reception of sacrum from the Christian world was – as is empha-
      sized by Łowmiański – the devil who became the "black god". See below, pp. 312 ff.

94   Revival of the idea of Christian genesis of Svantevit was criticised by Witold Hensel, "Jak
      wyglądał posąg arkońskiego Svantevita," *Z otchłani wieków* 39 (1983), p. 124. On the basis of
      research on polycephalism of Pomeranian idols, H. Łowmiański's ideas were considered
      insufficiently justified by Rosik, *Udział*, p. 74. See also Miś, "Przedchrześcijańska religia,"
      p. 107.

HELMOLDI CRONICA SLAVORUM ON SLAVIC RELIGION 281

only the first part of the name of the Rans' deity seems unnecessary.[95] Yet it is highly probable that the translation, which was the basis for the identification, was from Latin in which case translating only the first part (*sanctus*) is fully justified while the name of the saint remained nearly unchanged. Given the contemporary tendency of intellectuals to ethymologize[96] such concurrence was sufficient to identify a character from the Slavic beliefs with a Christian saint by way of "euhemerization."[97]

A solution of the riddle of the cult and the name of Svantevit in relation to his possible non-Slavic roots was sought after by J. Rosen-Przeworska and W. Szafrański, for whom this god was exactly called "Svantevit" (this version of his name is emphasized) and initially was an eponym of the name of the Celtic tribe Svanets, who in the course of their migration were to reach the Oder estuary and Rügen. The name of the Rügen god was to be reminiscent of their stay. Also, the polycephalic way in which Svantevit was presented was known to the Celts and later was to be borrowed from them by the Slavs.[98] However, the Slavic origin of the Rügen god's name gains more substantiation. The discussed meaning of the root "-vit" became the ending of numerous Slavic names (*e.g.* Siemovit).

Slavists' etymological research was conducted in a few directions. Linguists decisively rejected the proposal that two Slavic words: "world" – *e.g.* Polish "świat" and "see" – *e.g.* Polish "widzieć" were heard in the name of the Rans' god.[99] According to a popularized opinion, the first part of his name was the

---

95   Soszyński, "Święty Wit," p. 137. A good example of such a mistake in translation was an explanation of White Mountain given by Thietmar as *Mons Pulcher* (see above, p. 151, footnote 493).

96   *E.g.* Tadeusz Manteuffel, *Kultura Europy średniowiecznej* (Warszawa: Wiedza Powszechna, 1974), pp. 324 ff. See *e.g.* the etymology of the name of Slavic temple "contina", derived by Herbord (II, 31) from Latin "continere", or earlier attempts made by Thietmar (see above p. 151).

97   For "euhemerization" in medieval historiography of the religion of the Slavs see above, pp. 12 f., 31.

98   Szafrański, *Prahistoria*, pp. 414 f.

99   The four-faced idol would actually, symbolically "see" the whole of the world, namely its four sides. Hence the name "śviatovit" or "sviatovid" – derived from "sviat-" (world) and "-vid" (connected semantically to "see") – was reserved for characteristic archaeological findings (see *e.g.* S. Urbańczyk, *Dawni Słowianie*, p. 41), whose best representative was a quadrangular ideographic column with four faces – the so called "Sviatovid" from the Zbruch River; see: Gabriel Leńczyk, "Światowid zbruczański," *Materiały Archeologiczne* 5 (1964), pp. 5–60; Wojciech Szymański, "Posąg ze Zbrucza i jego otoczenie. Lata badań, lata wątpliwości," *Przegląd Archeologiczny* 44 (1996), pp. 75–116 (see also under, p. 365); another finding is a miniature figure from the 9th c. found in Wolin – see Filipowiak, Wojtasik, "Światowit z Wolina," pp. 82–88.

282   CHAPTER 4

root *svęt-*,[100] the same as in the adjective "saint" in the Slavic language (*e.g.*
Polish: "święty"). It initially meant more or less the same as "strong" and its
contemporary meaning appeared later. Following this way of thinking, one
will find A. Gieysztor's explication of *svęt* revealing a term used to describe a
god with "beneficial magic power." Moreover, thanks to the analogy to the Old
Iranian *spenta* and Lithuanian *sventas*, one may conclude that *svęt* was a carrier of information about the remorseless fertility power, able to create life and
natural phenomena.[101]

There was also another idea by which to derive the name of the god of
Arkona from the word 'saint,' (*e.g.* Polish: "święty") in this case similar to 'sick'–
'sickly,' which would make the theonym sound like 'świętowity' (in Old Polish
somebody characterized by sainthood).[102] Linguists however, are more inclined to treat the ending '-vit' as a root of at least a few possible meanings.
Apart from the Indo-European 'vid-' ('see, know') there was an idea to drive
'-vit' from 'witać' (welcome).[103]

G. Vernardsky, on the other hand, defended the idea questioned by
Brückner,[104] in order to identify in "Svantevit" words like 'święty wiatr' (holy
wind) – from Ukrainian 'viter,' Russian 'veter,' and Old Iranian 'vat' (wind). He
found in this god a counterpart of Stribog (ruling the atmosphere) and indicated that the four heads are symbols of cardinal winds and seasons of the
year. Thus, Svantevit would be "Holy Wind" – *i.e.* the "Holy Ghost", which is
supported by information that a priest entering the Arkona temple had to hold
his breath for the time of the service.[105]

---

100   On Rügen the Slavic adjective "saint", *e.g.* Polish 'święty' was pronounced with a nasal "a"
      which led to using the name *Svantevit* in chronicles – Urbańczyk, *Dawni Słowianie*, p. 41.
101   Gieysztor, *Mitologia*, p. 117. Bednarczuk, "W co wierzyli Prasłowianie?," p. 28, mentions
      that – contrary to the consolidated opinion – the adjective "święty" (saint) does not have
      to be an Old Iranian borrowing of the original "shine", "glitter", but it may turn out to be a
      native Slavic word, because in the Baltic region there is also a group of words whose stem
      refers to "svent-", connected to the activity of celebrating.
102   Szafrański, *Prahistoria*, p. 398.
103   Urbańczyk, *Dawni Słowianie*, p. 193.
104   Almost a century ago Brückner, *Mitologia słowiańska i polska*, p. 44 f., rejected the propos-
      al of explaining the word Svantevit as *fortis laetusque*, *validus victor*, or blowing strongly –
      "theomorphosis" of clear and clean air, just like Germanic Wodan or Old Indic Vata/
      Vaju. In Brückner's view Svantevit belongs to a group of names with the '-vit' ending, like
      Siemovit, *etc.*; it is "as if a personal name" and this is why it cannot denote a god of all
      Slavs, it could only be a local one, worshipped mainly on the Wittow Peninsula (hence
      its name).
105   Georg Vernardski, *The origins of Russia* (Oxford: Oxford University Press, 1959), pp. 122 f.
      The information about priests holding their breath when entering the temple in Arkona
      comes from Saxo XIV, 39, 4.

HELMOLDI CRONICA SLAVORUM ON SLAVIC RELIGION   283

The largest number of supporters are in favour of the root '-vit' derived from
Old Slavic 'vit,' which would mean that the word denotes a 'master' or 'ruler.'
Additionally, this root can still be heard in today's Polish 'witać' (welcome)
meaning 'invite.'[106] The collation of '*vitjaz" – 'wiciądz,' 'wojownik,' does not
inspire much respect due to a borrowing from German,[107] although it would
correspond with the militant character of deities of the Rans or Pomeranians.

Most certainly one should see in Svantevit a "strong ruler and lord," which is
in accordance with the position attributed to him in the world of Slavic beliefs.
This name belongs to the younger generation of theonyms and could have become more popular at the time of confrontation with Christianity, concealing
the older ones (*e.g.* Svarožic). These gods' names (such as *e.g.* Iarovit) are clear,
contrary to older names. Their character is functional: Svantevit must play the
role of the 'strong ruler' and maybe he was given this name for a reason, not to
disclose the protected taboo of the highest deity's name.[108]

Apart from this, the term was an ideological reply of the Rans – their theology likely developed in Arkona – to the faith in God preached by missionaries and presented as the only one, the highest and almighty God. It should be
noted that the almightiness of God, which was the key characteristic of God
for his believers in the Middle Ages, would sometimes even remove the idea
of personal relationship to God.[109] The idea of power (almightiness) could especially affect the Rügen inhabitants, as they did not hesitate to include it in
the name of the highest god and lord ('Vit') of the island. Today, the adjective
"saint" in Christianity refers especially to moral perfection. However, the etymology of its Slavic counterpart, *e.g.* Polish "święty" (different also from ancient Hebrew *kadosh*, Greek *hagios* or Latin *sanctus*), leads to the conviction
that among the Slavs it was primarily used to refer to God at the time when
God's almightiness was perceived as his most important characteristic. This
coining Svantevit's name – as a hypothesis of course – could indicate an attempt of ideological Slavic response to the idea of an almighty, divine creature
brought by Christian monotheism.[110]

---

106 Urbańczyk, *Dawni Słowianie*, pp. 41, 193; Miś, "Przedchrześcijańska religia," p. 106.
107 Gieysztor, *Mitologia*, p. 117.
108 The information that the Slavs used a taboo is confirmed by an analogy with the Polish
     word 'niedźwiedź' (bear) as "honey eater". It concealed the original name of this wor-
     shipped animal, whose counterpart is a stem known from Greek '*arktos'. This view was
     expressed by Antoine Meillet (1924), it was accepted by linguists; see *e.g.* S. Urbańczyk,
     Dawni Słowianie, p. 32; Popowska-Taborska, *Wczesne dzieje*, p. 114.
109 Wacław Hryniewicz, "Bóg cierpiący? Rozważania nad chrześcijańskim pojęciem Boga,"
     Collectanea Theologica 51 (1981) 2, p. 9; cf. Rosik, *Udział*, p. 102.
110 Rosik, *Udział*, pp. 100–102.

One should also take into account the possibility that all polycephalic idols – as it is indicated by the organization of the sacral space related to them – may be hypostases of the same highest deity for the Rügen inhabitants, whose concept could have arisen under the influence of contacts with Christianity.[111] The root '-vit' (lord) was to be an identifying sign of the highest Slavic deity. The diversity of names given to his particular personifications would then signify a particular functional aspect of his cult. The significance of matter – contrary to Brückner's opinion[112] – would go beyond the Rans' island: in Havelberg the worshipped deity was Iarovit,[113] whose name in terms of its meaning matches Svantevit, because the root 'jar-' and 'svet-' belong to the same community of meaning for 'strong,' which allows both deities to be identified at the level of their function.[114] Particular tribes could have been attached to the specific personification of the highest deity, which became a tutelary deity for their tribe or territory.

During the discussion about Svantevit and the belief system in the final phase of Slavic religion, the truthfulness of the so-called Legend of Corvey was buried completely.[115] The very identification of St. Vitus with Svantevit in Helmold's work is euhemerism led in the Christian spirit and evaluated as a realization of a topical principle on setting creation over the Creator by the pagans. This leads to the whole array of theological qualifications. The legend also explains that among Rans there was an exceptional bond with a deity – they are apostates: they not so much do not know God (like the Prussians), but they despise this cognition.[116]

The conversion of the Slavs was hampered by special characteristics attributed to them, like the already-mentioned aversion to Christians. In the next two chapters Helmold emphasizes obstacles such as wars, rebellions, and the invasions of the Danes and Magyars. These phenomena were a nuisance in the whole of post-Carolingian Europe, and appropriate rulers came to the rescue in this situation. The parish priest from Bosau sometimes completes the data taken from Adam of Bremen with his own information, compiled in such a

---

111   *Ibidem*, pp. 74–84, 99–104.

112   See above footnote 104 in this chapter.

113   Ebo III, 3, mentioned this deity as *Gerovitus*.

114   Gieysztor, *Mitologia*, pp. 134 f., stated that concurrent military competences and the analogical structure of the names Iarovit and Svantevit do not require acceptance of their identity but more synonymity of both of them to the highest deity, Perun.

115   It is mentioned one more time at the end of Helmold's work, see below, p. 360.

116   Treating the Rügen inhabitants as Christian apostates gained additional confirmation after 1136, when – according to Saxo (XIV, 1, 6–7) – after the Danish invasion of Arkona, a priest or bishop (*antistes*) was established there but he was abolished after the invaders left.

HELMOLDI CRONICA SLAVORUM ON SLAVIC RELIGION   285

way that it would be possible to obtain the dynamics of low and high tides of Christianization. A striking element in this description is a combination of the barbarism of the destroyers of Europe with hatred for Christianity (assassinations of clergymen, devastations of churches and monasteries, jeering at Christian symbols, *etc.*).[117]

A description of the achievements of King Henry I and next Archbishop Unni predict some improvement of these circumstances. Characteristic of Helmold, there is a concept of success of a mission as a result of cooperation between the political and church authorities. The Magyars, defeated by Henry (among others in 933) and the Slavs (in the battle of Lenzen 929), promised a tribute to the king and "baptism to God."[118] Similarly, after Henry's invasion of Denmark ruled by the cruel Gorm, the situation changed there and this prompted Unni to undertake missionary actions in Scandinavia. In the quotation taken from Adam of Bremen's work[119] there is an overtone from the Acts of the Apostles[120] on "opening a door of faith" for pagans, which is an example of historiological interpretation, similar to notes on managing the war by the heavens or success achieved thanks to God's mercy.[121]

2.3   *The Second Revolution of the Wheel of History*
The second cycle of the development and fall of the work of Christianization of the Slavs (chapters 9–16) is presented by Helmold under significant influence of Adam of Bremen's chronicle (especially chapters 9–11). A fragment describing the beginning of the Starigard Bishopric is of great importance in this part of the narrative. Most of it is the original contribution of the author of the *Chronicle of the Slavs* (chapters 12–14).[122] Whereas the later part, presenting a description of the pagan reaction in Denmark (chapter 15) and in the Slavdom (chapter 16), is again strongly influenced by the material from Adam's work, there is also some of Helmold's original material, which is clearly presented by the motif of personal injustice related to the Obodrite duke Mstivoy

---

117   Helmold I, 7–8.

118   Helmold I, 8.

119   *Ibidem*, p. 20: "… misericordia Dei nostri et virtute regis Henrici Danorum Slavorumque pertinaciam esse edomitam ostiumque fidei in gentibus apertum esse …"

120   Acts 14, 26.

121   Helmold I, 7.

122   For information on the establishment of the bishopric in Starigard (Oldenburg) in 968 see *e.g.* Jürgen Petersohn, *Der südliche Ostseeraum im kirchlich-politischen Kräftespiel des Reichs, Polens und Dänmarks vom 10. bis 13. Jahrhundert. Mission – Kirchenorganisation – Kultpolitik* (Köln/Wien: Böhlau, 1979), p. 18 ff.; Scior, *Das Eigene und das Fremde*, pp. 148 ff.

286   CHAPTER 4

in the presentation of the genesis of the Slavic rebellion in the times of the
Archbishop of Hamburg-Bremen Libentius.[123]

Although in this whole part of the text there are no direct references to the
Slavic religion, it is worth drawing attention to supplements added by Helmold
to information taken from the *Gesta hammaburgensis aecclesiae pontificum*. In
these supplements one can observe specifics of the interpretation of the history of the Slavs, which is key in the assessment of their paganism within the
text. The first of these supplements refers to the beginning of Otto the Great's
rule, or more precisely information about the rebellion of the Danes against
this ruler, which was developed by Helmold who added laconic information
about a simultaneous rebellion of the Slavs (most certainly between 936–950).[124]

Next, after the information about Otto I's success in fights with the Slavs
(tribute and accepting Christianity), Helmold added information about the
circumstances of establishing the Hermann Billung March, which cannot be
found in Adam's work.[125] The creation of the march was necessary so as to
ensure durability of the then relations between the Germans, Danes and Slavs
given the emperor's visit to Italy.[126] After the presentation of the Italian matters, Helmold added confirmation of Otto I's ardour in conversion of pagans
and especially Slavs, not mentioned by Adam of Bremen.[127] To sum up, these
additions presented the emperor as a patron of the Slavic mission, ensuring
the right political background for its success.

Next in the writer's focus appear the beginnings of the Starigard diocese
and its bishops, including especially the first of them, Marko, who "bathed the
peoples of the Wagrians or Obodrites in the sacred spring of baptism."[128] In
this way, the pages of Helmold's work presents the culmination of the next
wave of the Christianization of the Slavs in the framework of the organizational scheme of the entire narrative of the chronicle, underlying the general
message that secular authorities establish new political relations which enable
Christianization.

A metaphorical name given to this process, *i.e.* baptism of particular
peoples, the Wagrians and Obodrites, expresses a view from an institutional

---

123   See above pp. 236 f.

124   Helmold I, 9: "Slavi (...) rebellare moliti sunt ..."; see G. Labuda, *Fragmenty*, vol. 1,
      pp. 270 ff.

125   Helmold I, 9.

126   Helmold I, 10. See Labuda, *Fragmenty*, vol. 3, pp. 162 f.; *idem*, "Billungowie," in sss, vol. 1,
      pp. 117 f.

127   Helmold, I, 10: "Reversus ergo in patriam omne studium intorsit ad gentium vocacionem,
      precipue Slavorum".

128   Helmold I, 12: "populos Wagirorum sive Obodritorum sacro baptismatis fonte lavit."

HELMOLDI CRONICA SLAVORUM ON SLAVIC RELIGION   287

perspective at the level of the entirety of societies, thus including whole tribes in the Church, without regard for the progress of individual conversion. This historiological model of interpretation of the propagation of Christianity could have been found by Helmold in Adam of Bremen's work, but one should remember that it was also known by Thietmar.[129] In this case one should take into consideration that the chronicler from Bosau refers to the views which had existed in the circles of German clergy for generations.

Assessment of the attitude of the Slavs at this stage of their Christianization is rather favourable in the pages of Helmold's chronicle. Bishops maintained good relations with the tribal elders, receiving from them means used for the development of the diocese and gaining favour in the eyes of the people.[130] However, some evil characteristics of the Slavs were to appear already in the tenure of Wago, the successor of the first bishop of Starigard. Helmold, when commenting on the deceit[131] attributed to the Obodrite leader called Billug (who was most likely a fictitious character)[132] and planned against the Church in Starigard, claimed that one should beware of the Slavs because "the souls of the Slavs are naturally unfaithful and prone to evil."[133] Only fear of the Saxons was to stop Billug from an open rebellion and rejection of Christianity.

Helmold emphasized that the Slavs started to oppose openly "not only the laws of God but also the imperial orders," at the time when Otto II and Otto III were shaping their Italian policy. Then the remaining power over them was to be held by the Saxon duke Benno, although with difficulty.[134] Regardless of these gradually deteriorating circumstances of the propagation of Christianity, Helmold had no doubt that in the times of the first four bishops of Starigard "the Slavs remained faithful,"[135] and the network of churches and monasteries was to encompass a decisive majority of the *Sclavania* (Slavdom).[136] The chronicler openly referred to the testimony of Adam of Bremen, from whom

---

129   See above, pp. 79 f.
130   Helmold I, 12.
131   *Dolus* – a deceit which was stereotypically attributed to the Slavs in early medieval historiography, see Tyszkiewicz, *Z badań nad narodzinami*, p. 43.
132   Helmold I, 14. For Billug see Gerard Labuda, "Billug," in sss, vol. 1, p. 117. However, Mstivoy is an authentic figure (see: idem, "Mściwój," in sss, vol. 3, p. 325), according to Helmold, he was Billug's son.
133   Helmold I, 14: "Slavorum animi naturaliter sint infidi et ad malum proni"; this is another link in a chain of cliché assessments of the Slavs – see Tyszkiewicz, *Z badań nad narodzinami*, p. 42; Scior, *Das Eigene und das Fremde*, p. 214; Goetz, *Die Wahrnehmung*, pp. 193.
134   Helmold I, 14: "non solum divinis legibus, sed et imperatoriis iussis".
135   *Ibidem*: "Slavi in fide perstiterunt".
136   Cf. Adam II, 24. The author means the partition of the "Slavdom" into 18 regions (*pagus*) of which only three – Adam did not give their names – were to remain unconverted to

288   CHAPTER 4

he also borrowed the information about the pagan reaction in Denmark, and
supplemented it with a report on simultaneous Slavic rebellion.

Helmold commented on all these events in a moralizing manner: they took
place "by the scourge of God due to human sins."[137] In the description of Danish
events, the chronicler refers to a well-known motif from Adam's work related
to the famous city of *Iumne*, however he treated it as Vineta (*Iumneta*), which
was non-existent in his times. King Harald, defeated by his son, was critically
wounded and found shelter in this famous city where, let us not forget, he was
accepted "against hope – as they were Barbarians – in a humane way."[138] So according to the chronicler one did not expect anything good in the "barbarians".
The deceased exile received a halo of a martyr worth a royal position also in
heaven.[139]

The rule of the victorious Sven was characterized by Helmold's rhetorical
zeal with the association to the passage from 1 Maccabees: "Consurrexerunt
omnes iniqui in finibus aquilonis," and so "the all lawless [people] emerged in
the boundaries of the North," rejoicing at an opportunity to vent to their anger
through wars and disorder.[140] The allusion to this biblical phrase could have
been intended to evoke an association between this situation and the biblical
scenery of the invasion of Israel, which in a symbolic interpretation turned
the North into a demonic land of powers hostile to the Kingdom of God. The
northern wind carrying frost and numbness meant evil forces.[141] The appearance of information about wars and riots in this context is in accordance with
Helmold's view that wars and other misfortunes are the works of demons.[142]

The rebellion of the northern Polabian Slavs against the empire and the
consequential fall of Christianity among these tribes, described later in this

---

Christianity. Helmold repeats the same information. For the reach of the "Slavdom" in this
context see pp. 297, 306, 363, 383 f.

137   Helmold I, 15: "permittente Deo propter peccata hominum".

138   *Ibidem*: "preter spem, quia barbari erant, humane". It is worth emphasizing that in this
place one deals with a borrowing from *Gesta* by Adam of Bremen (see above p. 234), however, Helmold replaced *pagani* with *barbari*. Although in Helmold's times both words
were synonyms, the tone of the word *barbari* indicates not only being pagan, but also civilizational inferiority and – as it emerges from the context – the expected rigorous mentality or cruelty. This could be possibly a moralising statement referring to the Saxons: even
barbarians turn out to be humane towards enemies.

139   *Ibidem*. See above p. 243 (about king-martyrs).

140   Helmold I, 15; cf. 1 Macc 9:23: "post obitum Judae emerserunt iniqui in omnibus finibus
Israel, et exorti sunt omnes qui operabantur iniquitatem". See a commentary in: *Helmolda
Kronika*, p. 130, footnote 209.

141   See above, p. 272 and also Fraesdorff, *Der barbarische Norden*, p. 163.

142   Helmold I, 55.

HELMOLDI CRONICA SLAVORUM ON SLAVIC RELIGION 289

book, was interpreted by Helmold according to the conviction that success of Christianization largely depended on the attitude of secular authorities. The successor of the already mentioned Benno was his son, Bernard II, who in the chronicler's opinion turned out to be not only a troublemaker and a rebel against superior authority in Germany, but he also took the blame for the return of the Slavs to paganism. They were supposed to start the rebellion because of his cruel oppression driven by his greed. Another culprit in this situation was Margrave Theodoric, and so Helmold concluded: "For up to this moment the raw in faith pagan peoples, whom formerly the best princes fostered with great leniency refraining from rigour towards those for whose salvation they sought, these [Bernard and Theodoric – S.R.] have assailed with so great a cruelty that in the end, after having shaken off the yoke of servitude, they were forced to defend their liberty with arms."[143]

Helmold based his presentation of these events on Adam of Bremen's account and hence in this case it is hard to date them (it should be generally assumed that they took place in the years 983–1018). The priest from Bosau returns to the plot of a Slavic duke when giving reasons for the rebellion. The duke was refused the hand of a Saxon duchess in an offensive way, namely he was called a dog. A novelty in Helmold's story is the claim that this duke, who was anonymous in Adam's work, was the Obodrite ruler – Mstivoy.[144] The chronicler referred to "common news" as a source of this information.[145] Moreover, he developed a topical, in the assessment of the Slavs, motif of the dogs (*canes*).[146] According to him Mstivoy, outraged after such an offensive refusal, told messengers of the Saxon duke Bernard: "Indeed, there is a need to marry the noble niece of the great prince to an excellent man, surely not to give [her] to a dog. A great favour is returned to us for the service, since we are

---

143 Helmold I, 16: "Rudes enim adhuc in fide gentilium populos, quos optimi quondam principes cum magna lenitate foverant, temperantes rigorem his quorum propensius insistebant saluti, isti tanta crudelitate insectati sunt, ut excusso tandem servitutis iugo libertatem suam armis defendere cogerentur". In this place it is worth emphasizing a particular way of perceiving converted people, they were treated as "pagan", yet at the same time "raw in their faith" – "Rudes enim adhuc in fide gentilium populos ..."; for more information see pp. 76 ff.

144 See Labuda, "Mściwój," p. 325, and above, pp. 86 f.

145 Helmold I, 16: "Sermo igitur est et veterum narracione vulgatum"; cf. Pleszczyński, *Niemcy*, p. 37; cf. *idem, The Birth of a Stereotype*, pp. 35 f.

146 See Lech A. Tyszkiewicz, *Słowianie w historiografii wczesnego średniowiecza od połowy VI do połowy VII wieku*, (Acta Universitatis Wratislaviensis. Historia) 63 (Wrocław: Wydawnictwo Uniwersytetu Wrocławskiego, 1991), pp. 142–146, and also below, pp. 291 f.

already deemed as dogs, not as humans. In such case, if the dog is strong, it will leave many bites."[147]

According to Helmold, the Saxon duke managed to change his opinion and made efforts to reconcile with Mstivoy, but he was not successful in preventing a war.[148] The Obodrite duke set out to the Liutici Rethra, where he convened "all Slavs" living in "the East" and told them about the injustice which happened to him, emphasizing that for the Saxons, Slavs are like dogs.[149] The reply of his audience was composed with reference to the biblical text,[150] and it proves that the chronicler can even put words of reproach for the Saxons in the mouth of the Slavs: "Justly you are suffering – they say – for while rejecting your fellows you honoured the Saxons, a treacherous and greedy people. For this reason, swear to us that you would forsake them, and [only then] we will stand by you."[151] Due to the pragmatic aspect of the discussed message, one should take into account its literary genesis referring not only to the statement attributed to rallying Slavs, but also other details.

Even the very indication that Rethra was the place where Mstivoy looked for help against the Saxons could be only the chronicler's (or his informer's) speculation, based on the conviction that this was the exact place of the "capital of idolatry" already mentioned by Adam of Bremen. It seems even less certain that "all Slavs" living in "the East" were convened to the meeting place.[152] If one is to trust this information at all, it seems more appropriate to believe that there was a council of the Liutici elders in Rethra.[153] Lastly, even the pressure exercized on Mstivoy to take an oath to reject the Saxons, not only due to literary convention but also because of a general view, may be of "inkpot" genesis, shared also by Helmold, according to which for the Slavs oaths were particularly important.[154]

147　Helmold I, 16: "Oportet quidem generosam magni principis neptem prestantissimo viro copulari, non vero cani dari. Magna gratia nobis pro servicio refertur, ut iam canes, non homines iudicemur. Si igitur canis valens fuerit, magnos morsus dabit."

148　The motif of personal offence so strongly emphasized by Helmold raises numerous doubts as explanation for the direct reason for the rebellion, see *e.g.* Labuda, *Powstania Słowian*, pp. 171 f.

149　Helmold I, 16: "Saxonum voce Slavi canes vocentur".

150　Gen 42:21.

151　Helmold I, 16: "Merito haec" inqiunt "pateris, qui spernens contribules tuos excoluisti Saxones, gentem perfidam et avaram. Iura igitur nobis, quod deseras eos, et stabimus tecum".

152　For information on how the notion of Slavdom functioned as a whole in Helmold's work see pp. 266, 363, 368.

153　Leciejewicz, ">>In Pago," pp. 125 f.

154　See below, p. 337.

HELMOLDI CRONICA SLAVORUM ON SLAVIC RELIGION   291

Another striking element here is the appearance of the Saxons'
assessment – they were considered *gens perfida et avara* – developed in accordance with the contemporary stereotypical opinions about the Slavs. It is very
characteristic in this context that the author quotes the source of information
about the Polabian rebellion, taken in fact from *Gesta Hammaburgensis ecclesiae pontificum*):[155] the story of Slavic elders, and not the account of the Danish
king which was referred to by Adam of Bremen.

Thus, the Mstivoy episode allowed a relatively favourable atmosphere for
the Slavs to be introduced to the chronicle, because Helmold intended to
blame the Saxons themselves – their cruel greed, faithlessness, and contempt
for the Slavs causing the Polabian rebellion. The measure of the last of these
characteristics was the use of the word "dogs" when referring to the Slavs. The
earliest confirmation of its use when referring to the Slavs can be found in the
Chronicle of the so called Fredegar (7th–8th c.).[156] It gains interest because of
a play on words in the dialogue between their ruler, Samo, and the Frankish
messenger sent to him, which emphasizes alternative connotations related to
the symbolism of the word dog.

On one hand, this passage indicates "unfaithfulness," meaning remaining
outside the community of the "faithful", *i.e.* Christians, in accordance with a
well-established expression in the early Middle Ages: "pagan dog."[157] On the
other hand, and more than once, there is an indication to the topos of the

---

155   Referring to the authority of the "elders" by Helmold indicates that they were treated as a
      kind of institution in the social life of Barbarians, they were to be the guardians of remem-
      brance and law (cf. Stanisław Rosik, "Dokąd sięgają pamięcią słowiańscy starcy z Kroniki
      Helmolda?," in *Starość – wiek spełnienia*, ed. Wojciech Dzieduszycki, Jacek Wrzesiński,
      (Funeralia Lednickie, Spotkanie) 8 (Poznań: Stowarzyszenie Naukowe Archeologów
      Polskich, 2006), pp. 233–236. A wider context of the discussion about the role of the
      "elders" (*homines antiquissimi*) in barbarian communities is discussed by Modzelewski,
      Barbarzyńska Europa, pp. 60 f. It is worth mentioning here that there was also an alterna-
      tive view on the matter of the elders' knowledge which appeared in historiography in
      11th–12th c, it treated their stories as not worthy of any credit (cf. *e.g.* Gallus Anonymous
      underlined "oblivion of old age" – *oblivio vetustatis*, when regarding to fabulous plots of
      Polish origins, see *Galli Anonymi cronicae et gesta ducum sive principum Polonorum*, ed.
      Karol Maleczyński, MPH n.s. 2 (1952), I, 3; cf. Przemysław Wiszewski, *Domus Bolezlai.
      W poszukiwaniu tradycji dynastycznej Piastów (do około 1138 roku)* (Wrocław: Wydawnictwo
      Uniwersytetu Wrocławskiego, 2008), pp. 162 f.).
156   *Chronicarum quae dicuntur Fredegarii scholastici libri IV cum continationibus*, ed. Bruno
      Krusch, MGH SSrerMerov 2 (1888), IV, 68, p. 154. In this episode Samo's reaction to call-
      ing Slavs – as pagans – dogs by a Frankish messenger, was to claim that they were "God's
      dogs" (*canes Dei*), which will bite unfaithful God's servants (Franks) to punish them. Cf.
      Tyszkiewicz, *Słowianie w historiografii wczesnego średniowiecza*, pp. 138 ff.; Goetz, *Die
      Wahrnehmung*, p. 164 f.
157   Padberg, "Christen," p. 296; *idem, Die Christianisierung*, p. 181.

292   CHAPTER 4

dog as a very faithful animal;[158] the genesis of this stereotype attributing very
positive values to this animal can be found already in the culture of prehistoric
societies.[159]

It is worth mentioning that from the perspective of reflection on Helmold's
mentality, this ambivalence in the use of canine symbolism can be observed
even in the Bible.[160] However, the story about Mstivoy is closer to the previously mentioned episode from the chronicle of the so-called Fredegar because of a

158   See footnote 156 and 160 in this chapter. By analogy one returns here to the earlier dis-
      cussed (see p. 60) motif of a "dumb dog" used by Thietmar with its biblical and patristic
      references, which emphasizes treating dogs as a model of faithfulness and "sheepfold's"
      guardian. Moreover in Thietmar's chronicle a dog is presented as its master's avenger, it
      tears off the killer's arm (Thietmar I, 27). In this context it is worth referring to a custom-
      ary penalty applied in Helmold's times in Germany to offenders and especially unfaithful
      rebels which was public humiliation involving the carrying of a dog on their back as a sign
      of revilement (see Jacob Grimm, *Deutsche Rechtsaltertümer* (Göttingen: Dietrich, 1855),
      pp. 715–718; cf. Tyszkiewicz, *Słowianie w historiografii wczesnego średniowiecza*, p. 143).
      However this form of ridiculing a convict seems to indicate that the evaluation of the dog
      was generally low.
159   In mythologies and rites of prehistoric and ancient societies the dog had a positive
      role, which is shown *e.g.* in burial ceremonies interpreted, among others, as founda-
      tion offerings (see *e.g.*: Małgorzata Andrałojć, "Rola psa w obrzędowości pradziejowych
      ludów Europy Środkowej," in *Wierzenia przedchrześcijańskie na ziemiach polskich*, ed.
      Marian Kwapiński, Henryk Paner (Gdańsk: Wydawnictwo Muzeum Archeologicznego w
      Gdańsku, 1993), pp. 98–109; Tadeusz Makiewicz, "Odkrycia tzw. grobów psów w Polsce
      i ich sakralne znaczenie," in *Wierzenia przedchrześcijańskie na ziemiach polskich*, ed.
      Marian Kwapiński, Henryk Paner (Gdańsk: Wydawnictwo Muzeum Archeologicznego w
      Gdańsku, 1993) pp. 110–117.
160   This is very well depicted in the biblical scene of Jesus meeting the Canaanite Woman,
      a pagan, who pleaded to cure her daughter in whom there was an evil spirit. The initial
      rebuff of help was a pretext to compare pagans to "dogs" (see Mc 7:27; Mt 15:26), which
      in turn was used to develop another image of pagans as "dogs" (pups) which eat scraps
      dropped by children (see Mk 7:28; Mt 15:27). The attitude of the Syrophoenician woman
      was praised by Jesus as showing extremely strong faith and it was rewarded by grant-
      ing her request. The whole pericope shows the New Testament idea of evangelisation of
      not only the circle of Judaism but also pagans. This positive element, associated with the
      topic of the dog (see *e.g.* Mariusz Rosik, "Motyw κυναρια w dialogu Jezusa z Kananejką –
      Syrofenicjanką (Mk 7, 24–30; Mt 15, 21–28). W kręgu biblijnej topiki psa," in *Viae historicae.*
      Księga jubileuszowa dedykowana Profesorowi Lechowi A. Tyszkiewiczowi w siedemdziesiątą
      rocznicę urodzin, ed. Mateusz Goliński, Stanisław Rosik, (Acta Universitatis Wratislaviensis.
      Historia) 152 (Wrocław: Wydawnictwo Uniwersytetu Wrocławskiego, 2001), pp. 429–434,
      was a factor supporting the creation of a positive attitude to the mission among pagans as
      a result of weakening this major negative power of the stereotype of *canes*; for such nega-
      tive symbolism of the dog in this tradition of Christianity and the culture of the Middle
      Ages see *e.g.* Forstner, *Świat*, p. 293 (here there is also a reference to Rev 22:15); Le Goff,
      Kultura, pp. 122, 332.

motif shared by both stories, namely the negative consequences for Christians resulting from showing contempt for the Slavs by making them the equal of dogs. Moreover, referring to this particular way of expressing contempt in Helmold's narrative escalates the Christians' guilt by means of contrast: the Saxons' unfaithfulness, which contradicts the positive connotations of the *canes* topos, becomes even more obvious on one hand, and on the other hand their greed, which is also topically considered characteristic of dogs, becomes even more glaring.[161]

Hence, one can conclude that the Saxon characters in the Helmold's chronicle are not better than Slavs, however it should be emphasized that the latter do not receive a better assessment because of this. According to the chronicler, as it has already been mentioned, they are "faithless and characterized by propensity to evil by nature" and are especially rebellious. So, their "persisting in faith" was possible only under external pressure of a supervisory authority. The stigmatization, therefore, of the custom of referring to the Slavs as dogs arises from promoting the idea of mission among pagans in the chronicle, and the message in this particular episode is the reminder to not waste the first fruit of the mission by the improper attitude of Christian rulers representing the empire.

The very context of occurrence of the word *canes* in Adam of Bremen's chronicle, and later also in Helmold's work, makes one aware of the fact that it indicates not only affiliation with the pagan circle, but also, or even more, affiliation with the ethnic and cultural community, because it was used to refer even to Christened Slavs. This situation shows evolution of the meaning of this topos, which lost its original religious connotations and was used to show hostility and contempt for a "stranger," a barbarian. Thus, even the inclusion of the Polabian tribes in the Christian circle or baptism of their representatives did not mean that this stereotypical assessment of the Slavs would become obsolete among the Saxons.

Topoi of this type conditioned also the attitude of Christian neighbours to the spiritual pre-Christian culture of Slavdom. This is why efforts to eliminate them from social circulation, undertaken by Helmold, was an essential element in attainment of pragmatic goals in his literary work. Fighting against this type of prejudice about the Slavs supported promotion of the idea of their conversion, which was the main reason for the existence of the diocese of Starigard.[162]

161　It is not accidental that Thietmar (III, 17; IV, 25) used the name *avari canes* when referring to Danish or Slavic aggressors and looters.

162　See before, pp. 260 ff.

294   CHAPTER 4

2.4   *From Gottschalk Time Success to the 1066 Rebellion*

The account about the pre-Christian Slavic cult is placed by Helmold in a presentation of the last wave of progress and regress in converting the Polabian tribes inspired by Adam's narrative.[163] According to him, the optimistic view of the beginning of this period was based on the success of archbishop of Hamburg-Bremen Unwan and the bishop of Starigard Benno (chapters 17–18). However, perhaps most of all, the Christian religion in Slavdom was strongly influenced by the conversion of the Obodrite duke Gottschalk (chapters 19–20).[164]

Some attention has been given to this character in the discussion of the chronicle of Adam of Bremen, from whom Helmold took basic information about this Slavic duke. He also used Adam's work to gain the information that Gottschalk, when he was at school in Lüneburg, "fidem reiecit cum litteris" in order to avenge his father, which reflects a conviction that a return to paganism was a simultaneous rejection of the "scriptures."[165] An analogous way of thinking expresses a low assessment of Helmold's compatriots who were thought to be harsh and uneducated, and at the same time accused of maintaining pagan practices.[166]

The episode in the *Chronicle of the Slavs*, which improves the image of the Obodrite duke in the time when he was an apostate of the Christian religion, is a story about an event when he, incognito met a Holsatian complaining about him and moaning about the crimes he committed against the Saxons. Gottschalk admitted who he was and in his confession there is an element of justification – he was his father's avenger – and emphasis on the duke's repentance towards God and Christians whom he would like to compensate for what he did before.[167] This episode stresses the voluntary character of Gottschalk's return to Christianity, which is certainly important for further information – already known by Adam of Bremen – about his capture and release from a Saxon prison to finally – after years of service for the king Cnut the Great – starting his rule of the Obodrites and becoming the protector of efforts to rebuild the church network among them.[168]

---

163   One should remember that according to H. Stoob (see above, footnote 25 in this chapter), it encompassed chapters 17–33. However, it should be stressed that chapters 27–33 do not refer to the history of the Slavs and they are connected with German, church and European issues.

164   For information on Gottschalk see above pp. 252 ff.

165   Helmold I, 19.

166   Helmold I, 47.

167   Helmold I, 19.

168   *Ibidem.*

HELMOLDI CRONICA SLAVORUM ON SLAVIC RELIGION   295

The message of the next story from the *Chronicle of the Slavs* is a reproach
to the Saxons who neglected the evangelization of pagans because of their
greed. Helmold quotes (after Adam of Bremen) information about a civil
war between members of the Liutici Federation (1056/7–1060).[169] The title of
this chapter *Pugna Tolenzorum* solidifies the error regarding two tribes of the
Liutici Federation, the Redars and Tholensi, as one tribe which was to participate in the struggle for hegemony with the alliance of the Circipanias and
Kessinians. Helmold himself is responsible for the propagation of this wrong
identification of both ethnonys. In borrowings from Adam's work, in general
he consistently uses the phrase: *Riaduri atque* (or *et*) *Tholenzi*,[170] however in
his own text he sometimes interprets *atque* or *et* as *sive*.[171]

The same happened in the presentation of the reasons for conflict, which
were not known from Adam's work: "Indeed **Riaduri or Tholenzi** [emphasis –
S.R.] because of their most ancient city and that most famous shrine, in which
the statue of Radigast is displayed, wanted to rule, while they still ascribed to
themselves a unique honour of nobility for such reason that they were visited
by all the peoples of the Slavs for the sake of the oracles and annual payments
of offerings."[172]

On the basis of the information rendered by Thietmar and Adam of Bremen,
it is hard to locate the central temple of the Liutici in any place other than the
territory of the Redars, regardless of whether the name Radogošč or Rethra is
used. Helmold's claim that they had another name, the Tholenzi, means an
actual departure from the division of the Liutici into four tribes, known from
Adam of Bremen's work. However, this division into four peoples is confirmed
by Helmold when he presents the parties of the conflict discussed in this chapter, but simultaneously there is this equation of the names of the said people
by the word *sive* ("or", "that is"): "So, there are four peoples of them who are
called Liutici or Wilzi. It is clear that among them Kycini and Circipani live on

---

169   For information on these events see *e.g.* Labuda, *Fragmenty*, vol. 2, pp. 162 ff.; Babij,
      Wojskowość, pp. 154 ff.
170   Helmold I, 21. Cf. Helmold I, 2.
171   Helmold identified the Tholensi with the Redars for the first time in his presentation
      of the Slavic peoples, see Helmold I, 2: "... occurrit Winulorum provincia, eorum qui
      Tholenzi **sive** Redarii dicuntur ...".
172   Helmold I, 21: "Siquidem **Riaduri sive Tholenzi** [emphasis – S.R.] propter antiquissimam
      urbem et celeberrimum illud fanum, in quo simulachrum Radigast ostenditur, regnare
      volebat, asscribentes sibi singularem nobilitatis honorem eo quod ab omnibus populis
      Slavorum frequentarentur propter responsa et annuas sacrificiorum impensiones."

the other side of the [river] Peene, while Riaduri or Tholenzi live on this side of Peene."[173]

Therefore, in the above quotation one may observe a lack of consistency, which makes one realize that on one hand Helmold showed respect for the authority of his predecessor and so he followed this division of the Liutici into four tribes, but on the other hand he regarded the inhabitants of the Liutici land "before the Peene River" as one people with two names. This way of describing the situation corresponds with the idea that the name of the Redars should not be treated as an ethnic one, but should be explained in reference to the cultural community established around the temple.[174] However, this position does not seem sufficiently justified regarding the strong premises supporting the existence of the Redars tribe in 11th-c. sources.

Helmold did not betray any doubts in this matter either, but the fact that he assumed that they were called *Tholensi* indicates that he did not notice the tribal division of the Liutici community in the area "before the Peene River." This situation, on the one hand, can be explained by the chronicler's poor orientation in the geography of tribal divisions in neighbouring areas, especially that in his times the erosion of old tribal structures took place. On the other hand – as it is indicated by this particular treatment of Adam's information related to the division of the Liutici tribes – it could be Helmold's own invention.

173   Helmold I, 21: "Quatuor autem sunt populi eorum, qui Liuticii sive Wilzi dicuntur, quorum Kycinos atque Circipanos citra Panim, Riaduros sive Tholenzos cis Panim habitare constat."

174   In this concept the Liutici – Redars would be the "assembled people" (literary "the council" – Polish "rada"), who gathered near the temple to rule with the oracle, and their name Liutici would mean the people of a strict or harsh, *i.e.* Old Slavic "luty", god – see Lothar Dralle, *Slaven an Havel und Spree. Studien zur Geschichte des hevellisch-wilzischen Fürstentums (6. bis 10. Jahrhundert)* (Berlin: Duncker & Humblot, 1981), pp. 136–158; *idem*, "Rethra," p. 55. This view, however, disregards clear source data which leaves no doubt as to the ethnic character of the Redars tribe, *e.g.* Adam III, 22, and earlier Thietmar VI, 23–25, who wrote about Radogošč. See *e.g.* Józef Spors, *Studia nad wczesnośredniowiecznymi dziejami Pomorza Zachodniego. XII–pierwsza połowa XIII w.* (Słupsk: Wyższa Szkoła Pedagogiczna w Słupsku 1988), p. 10, footnote 2. The above etymologies of tribal names (or at least the Liutici name) deserve attention, especially if one takes into consideration the information provided by Adam II, 21, schol. 16, that "quatuor populos a fortitudine Wilzos apellant vel Leuticios". Brave, valorous and harsh in the understanding of adjective "luty" are the etymological connotations of Liutici-*Leutici*, and their other name Veleti-*Wilzi*, if it is to evoke this *fortitudo*, certainly must be in connection with the Slavic wolves (Polish "wilki"). Ingenuity of researchers searching for the etymology of the name Redars is sometimes surprising, for example H. Kunstmann, who considered Rethra a name taken from Greek, where the term "ρητρα" occurs in legal and judicial context (*e.g.* law, agreement) – see Strzelczyk, *Tysiąclecie*, p. 260. See also above, pp. 215 f.

HELMOLDI CRONICA SLAVORUM ON SLAVIC RELIGION   297

The main reason for the war, according to him, were the ambitions of the community concentrated around Rethra to execute its superior rights in the Liutici sphere and to do so not only in the realm of cult but also of politics. Representatives of these rights, for Helmold, become one people related to the famous temple. They are connected by the fact that they lived in the same region (*provincia*), the capital of which is Rethra, which is the best explanation for the use of "sive" to refer to relations between the *Redari* and *Tholensi* ethnonyms.[175]

This interpretation finds its analogy in the chronicler's presentation of his contemporary situation in the zone of the late pre-Christian Slavdom, whose centre was to be Arkona on Rügen. There, Svantevit's temple, the place famous for his efficiency in granting oracles, was frequented by the inhabitants of "the whole Slavdom" and was the place where they sent their tributes. Rans themselves, due to the fact that they possessed the famous temple, aspired to extend their power to neighbouring areas.[176] Similarly Rethra, where – as it has already been mentioned – all Slavic peoples were to go because of the oracle and where they sent gifts, had one people as its guardian striving to dominate among its neighbours. It seems, therefore, that in Helmold's presentation of Slavdom there was realized a paradigm in which there was one hegemon of other tribes concentrated around the temple considered its centre.

This is most certainly why he "corrected" the image of the civil war in the Liutici tribes. One should remember that Adam of Bremen described this conflict as a fight between the isolated Circipanians and the other tribes in the Federation.[177] By contrast, Helmold showed that in this fight the "Redars-Tholensi" were isolated and they had to face the other Liutici, so as to present the supporter of the temple primacy as one people aspiring to take control of all other pagan Slavs. In the context of these remarks, one has to assume that the version of events presented by Helmold is most probably an interpretation deviating from the reality of the times he described.[178]

However, appreciation for the conflict over the significance of Rethra in this argument still remains merely a probability. One should pay attention to a proposal to perceive the clash of inter-federation forces as a conflict between the theocracy concentrated in Rethra and the leader of military forces of Circipanian tribe, who wanted to subvert the strong influence of the priests

---

175   Helmold I, 2: "... Winulorum provincia, eorum qui Tholenzi sive Redarii dicuntur; civitas eorum vulgatissima Rethre ..."

176   See further, pp. 322, 364.

177   Adam III, 22.

178   Strzelczyk in: *Helmolda Kronika*, p. 149 (footnote 284); see also Babij, *Wojskowość*, pp. 154 f.

298   CHAPTER 4

on governance.[179] However, taking into account that the basis of their role in politics was their cooperation with the council (veche),[180] it is hypothetically worth extending the field of ideological confrontation and the search for the genesis of the civil war in the aspirations of the Circipanians (and possibly also the Kessinians) to establish the monarchy.[181] The Redars, Tholensi (and maybe also the Kessinians) would definitely oppose this, supporting the traditional role of the council and the temple in Rethra (or Radogošč) as a bonding element of the tribes.

In the light of these findings, the internal war in 1056/7 resulted from attempts to change the political system of the Liutici Federation, which is a premise for the view that the religious factor, represented by the famous temple, was a constitutive element for this supra-tribal community and an indicator of its identity.[182] It is not accidental that the Redars were the main advocates of this order, due to the fact that they had Rethra on their territory. This meant that they enjoyed the condition which was very accurately called "medii et potentissimi" by Adam of Bremen.[183] Hence they would fight to maintain this privileged position among the Liutici.

Helmold, referring to these events and issues after over a century, confirmed the very fact of the political significance of Rethra. However, in comparison with Adam of Bremen's work, he changed the motifs of the Redars' actions. They were by no means defenders of the traditional order, but rather they want to establish a new one at the expense of the freedom of those who opposed them.[184] This fight for imposing hegemony over their neighbours initially was not very fortunate for these "Redars-Tholensi," which allowed Helmold to introduce a key problem from the perspective of his work, *i.e.* the fortunes of Slavic Christianization.

179   Sułowski, *Sporne problemy*, p. 164.
180   On connections between the assembly of the Liutici and the central temple with the oracle in reference to Thietmar's information (VI, 22–25) see above, pp. 126 ff. It is also worth referring to the information provided by Adam of Bremen on *concilio paganorum* in Rethra (see Adam III, 21, schol. 71), although this was probably the meeting of the tribal elders and not a mass meeting of all people – see Leciejewicz, ">>In Pago," p. 131, and also above, pp. 223 f.
181   *E.g.* Labuda, *Fragmenty*, vol. 2, p. 162 (he puts the Kessinians on the side of the Circipanians).
182   For more information see: Lübke, "Religion," p. 83 *et passim*; see also Dralle, "Rethra," pp. 46 f., and above, pp. 225.
183   Adam II, 18.
184   Helmold I, 21: "Porro Circipani atque Kycini servire detrectabant, immo libertatem suam armis defendere statuerunt."

HELMOLDI CRONICA SLAVORUM ON SLAVIC RELIGION   299

The chronicler emphasized that the defeated supporters of the Rethra primacy turned to seek help from the king of Denmark, the Saxon duke, Bernard II, and the Obodrite duke, Gottschalk. Their combined forces vanquished the Circipanians and Kessinians who agreed to a peace settlement. Yet its price was only money – to Helmold's regret – while "there was no mention of the Christianity, neither did they give honour [to the One], who brought them to victory at war."[185] The chronicler blames the Saxons for neglecting religious matters in the course of these events, or more precisely following Adam of Bremen (III, 23) for their insatiable greed (*insaciabilis avaritia*), which resulted in their care only for increased tributes without any care for evangelization.[186] Next in a moralizing tirade, he praises Gottschalk even more as a diligent propagator of the faith, regardless of the pagan period in his life, so as to by contrast accuse the mighty Saxon of laziness in "the work of God," regardless of their origin from Christian ancestors.

Further pages of Helmold's Chronicle (chapters 22–24) bring a description of the falloff of the renewed church organization and the mission among the Slavs as result of the 1066 rebellion. This passage is rich in elements of theological interpretation of paganism. However, the material is not original, and it has been discussed above in the analysis of the chronicle of Adam of Bremen. This was the beginning a break of 84 years in the functioning of the bishopric in Starigard.[187] The fall of Christianity in the lands of the Obodrites and Wagrians was maintained during the rule of Kruto (chapters 25–26). The reasons for such persistence of the Slavs (except for the Rans) in paganism, according to Helmold, was not so much their relationship with deities but rather the attitude of the Saxons, and especially their greed. Helmold argued that tributes imposed by them made the Polabian tribes reach for their weapons and so also destroy the work of Christianization.[188]

2.5   *The Fourth High and Low Tide of Christianization*

The organizational scheme of the narration in the part of the *Chronicle of the Slavs* based on Adam of Bremen's work is also visible in the presentation of events that came later chronologically. Hence this subsequent cycle of high and low tides in missionary work among the Slavs was composed by Helmold within chapters 34–52. The key role in this part of the narration is performed

---

185   *Ibidem*: "de Christianitate nulla fuit mentio, nec honorem dederunt, qui contulit eis in bello victoriam." The quoted sentence combines a borrowing from Adam's work and phrases from the Acts of the Apostles (Act 12, 23).

186   Helmold I, 21; cf. Scior, *Das Eigene und das Fremde*, p. 179.

187   Helmold I, 24.

188   *E.g.* Helmold I, 25.

300   CHAPTER 4

by Gottschalk's son, the Obodrite Prince Henry (deceased in 1127).[189] After the
battle of Śmiłów (Schmilau) probably in 1105[190] – which according to Helmold
led to the fulfilment of God's plans[191] – "all the peoples of the Eastern Slavs"
(most certainly the Warni, Obodrite, Circipanians and Kessinians[192]) became
his tributaries. The Rans were already the unquestionable leaders of pagan
Slavdom at that time.

2.5.1   The Rans' Religion in the Description of Their Struggle with
           Henry the Obodrite Prince
Helmold presents information about the religion of the Rans by describing a
pirate invasion of the Obodrite Lübeck undertaken by the island's inhabitants
in about 1101. It was the beginning of a string of wars between the Rans and their
neighbours (not only wars of revenge), the final result of which was the conquest of the island.[193] Digressing from the main course of narration, Helmold
wove in an independent story devoted to its inhabitants which began with information already known from the pages of Adam of Bremen's chronicle:
    "Rani [Rans], known by others also as Runi, are cruel people. They live at the
heart of the sea, above all devoted to worshiping their idols. They hold the primacy above all Slavic nations, and they have a king and a well-known shrine.
The special veneration of this shrine makes them first among other nations in
terms of respect, and although they enslave many and put them in shackles,
they do not suffer any oppression as they are unapproachable due to the inaccessibility of their dwellings. With weapons they make other people surrender
and they enforce tributes to be paid for their sanctuary. The priest has more
respect among them than the king. They send their army where the lot decides.
When they win, they put the gold and silver in their god's treasury and divide
the rest [of the trophies] among themselves".[194]

---

189   Władysław Kowalenko, "Henryk," in sss, vol. 2, pp. 200 f., presents basic facts related to
      this period in the history of Polabia; see also Labuda, *Fragmenty*, vol. 3, p. 163; Myśliński,
      Polska wobec Słowian, pp. 148 f.
190   A disputable date, see Jerzy Strzelczyk, "Śmiłowe Pole," in sss, vol. 5, p. 569. Turasiewicz,
      Dzieje polityczne, pp. 168 f., 176 f.; cf. Babij, *Wojskowość*, p. 159.
191   Helmold I, 34.
192   J. Strzelczyk in: *Helmolda Kronika*, p. 191, footnote 472. Cf. Łowmiański, *Początki Polski*,
      vol. 5, Warszawa 1973, p. 299 ff.
193   The fights and their reflection in other sources are presented by Osięgłowski, "Początki
      słowiańskiej Rugii," pp. 262 ff., and this study was used in these considerations. See also
      Babij, *Wojskowość*, pp. 171 ff. It is worth mentioning that some scholars moved the date of
      the Rans' invasion of the Lübeck to 1110 – see *Helmolda Kronika*, p. 197, footnote 493.
194   Helmold I, 36: "Sunt autem Rani, qui ab aliis Runi apellantur, populi crudeles, habitantes
      in corde maris, ydolatrie supra modum dediti, primatum preferentes in omni Slavorum

HELMOLDI CRONICA SLAVORUM ON SLAVIC RELIGION 301

In this way Helmold outlined the Rügen theocratic system based on the co-existence of two centres of power: apart from the "king" there was the temple in which the superior priest, acting on behalf of a deity, enjoyed higher authority than the ruler. Hence it is not surprising that in this information the divination of fate had decisive influence on starting military expeditions and that after a victorious return, the seized gold and silver were left in the temple treasury.[195] The ascertainment that the conquered peoples were also to pay annual tribute to the temple, confirms the political dimension of Svantevit's cult.[196] In this perspective the increase of his significance among other Slavic gods was accompanied by the development of the Rügen statehood, the power of which was attributed strictly to the power of the tutelary deity.[197]

The only theological category used in this passage in the presentation of the Rans' cult is its classification as idolatry. Yet, it should be mentioned that the island's inhabitants are devoted to it above all (*supra modum*). This relationship with idols somehow explains the source of their cruelty, and in this context emphasis on the fact that they live in the "heart" of the sea is characteristic, as it is associated with the danger or even presence of anti-sacral powers, especially in this description's climate.[198]

Driven by a desire to dominate the Wagrians and Nordalbingians who were already subdued to Henry, the Obodrite prince – returning here to the main stream of Helmold's narrative – attacked Lübeck, which was successfully

---

nacione, habentes regem et fanum celeberrimum. Unde etiam propter specialem fani illius cultum primum veneracionis locum optinent, et cum multis iugum imponant, ipsi nullius iugum paciantur, eo quod inaccessibiles sint propter difficultates locorum. Gentes, quas armis subegerint, fano suo censuales faciunt; maior flaminis quam regis veneracio apud ipsos est. Qua sors ostenderit, exercitum dirigunt. Victores aurum et argentum in erarium Dei sui conferunt, cetera inter se partiuntur."

195   In the further part of his narration Helmold one more time confirms the existence of the temple treasury and leaving gold and silver there (as long as it was not kept as jewellery for their women). The chronicler takes an opportunity here to emphasize that the Rans did not use coins, but they paid with linen canvas – see Helmold I, 38. For information on Svantevit's treasury see, *e.g.* Łowmiański, *Początki Polski*, vol. 4, pp. 135–138. For paying with shawls see also *Relacja Ibrahima ibn Jakuba z podróży do krajów słowiańskich*, p. 49.

196   Svantevit, or de facto his temple happened to possess some of the prerogatives of ducal power in Rans society, however, it is hard to assume that their god had the same function as a duke, as it was rather unduly proposed by Miś, "Przedchrześcijańska religia," p. 109. The state character of Svantevit's cult is confirmed by the fact that the Danish king – a Christian (sic!) – made offerings to Svantevit. See above, p. 278.

197   Urbańczyk, *Dawni Słowianie*, p. 43.

198   For possible associations with the sea element, see above, p. 167. Helmold emphasizes also that the sea element contributed to the security of Rans, it made their abodes hardly accessible. However, this comment is made in another context describing more practical aspects of their location (cf. footnote 194 in this chapter).

302   CHAPTER 4

defended by the ruler. In the description of these events the spiritual dimension of this confrontation is strongly emphasized and the conflict between
both sides was presented as a struggle between the power of Christianity and
evil forces represented by the pagans.[199] However, the chronicler devotes more
attention to the expedition of Henry to the land of Rans in 1123/4,[200] and its
presentation brings interesting material related to the social and political role
of the priest (most certainly the major priest from Arkona).

"Rugians saw the impetus of that man, >>feared with a great fear<<, and
sent their priest who arranged to talk to him about peace."[201] In this sentence
it is easy to recognise the words from the Bible, for instance from the Book
of Jonah, where sailors were terrified (>>feared with a great fear<<).[202] This
is not all.

The request formulated by the pagan priest and directed to Henry was
composed of crumbs of expressions taken from the Bible:[203] "Ne irascatur dominus noster super servos suos. Ecce terra in conspectu tuo est, utere ea ut
libet, omnes in manu tua sumus; quicquid imposueris feremus" ("Let not our
lord be angry at his servants. Behold, the land is before your eyes, use it as
you please, we are all in your grasp; whatever you lay [upon us], we will bear
it").[204] This compilation of expressions can be analyzed as an instinctive use
of phraseology that the priest from Bosau would have recalled from exercises
at school or even as a result of rewriting biblical phrases. Would it be, however,
proof of insufficient knowledge of Latin? Even if the answer is yes, it is not the
only reason.

If one takes into account the significance of the Bible in medieval works,
one should consider the possibility that biblical references added dignity to

---

199   *E.g.* Helmold 1, 36: "Magnificatusque est dominus Deus in manu Christianorum in die
      illa, statueruntque, ut dies Kalendarum Augusti celebretur omnibus annis in signum et
      recordationem, quod percusserit Dominus Ranos in conspectu plebis suae." ("And the
      Lord God was revered on that day among the Christians, and so they set that every year
      the first of August will be celebrated as a sign and remembrance that the Lord smote Rans
      on his people's eyes").
200   Helmold 1, 38. See: Osięgłowski, "Początki słowiańskiej Rugii," pp. 263 ff. Kowalenko,
      "Henryk," pp. 200 f.; Turasiewicz, *Dzieje polityczne*, pp. 183–185.
201   Helmold 1, 38: "Videntes igitur Rugiani impetum viri >>timuerunt timore magno<< mise-
      runtque flaminem suum, qui cum ipso de pace componeret".
202   Jon 1:10: "timuerunt viri timore magno"; cf. *e.g.* 1 Macc 10:8; Mk 4:40; Lk 2:9.
203   Gen 31:35: Rachel "ait ne irascatur dominus meus" (*i.e.* her father Laban); Gen 16:6: "ecce
      ait [Abram] ancilla tua [Hagar] in manu tua [Sarah] est …", and 1 Macc 1:3: "et siluit terra
      in conspectu eius (*i.e.* Alexander the Great)", the same also in reference to king Demetrius,
      see 1 Macc 11:38 and 52.
204   Helmold 1, 38.

HELMOLDI CRONICA SLAVORUM ON SLAVIC RELIGION   303

the text, emphasized a particular passage, and in this case also added splendour to the character which was outstanding in the author's opinion. Taking into account the importance of the allegorical interpretation of texts, one should consider the possibility that by using such high condensation of biblical phrases, the author wanted to refer to images of the sacred history, in the reflection of which Henry acquired the characteristics of outstanding leaders of antiquity,[205] and features superior to the pagans[206] or rebels.[207] One can speak here about monumentalization and typization of his achievements in the biblical convention.[208]

The very utterance of biblical phrases by a priest who served demons was a particular example of a literary interpretation of paganism on the stage of history. Characteristically, Helmold turns this representative of Rans into a negotiator and advocate of the people who were threatened by annihilation. Because of this, the character does not evoke any association with the sphere of *antisacrum*. In this context, the Rans are mainly rebels and apostates. However, the priest representing them to the outside world, when dealing with the matter of their existence, is actually more significant among them than a prince, as was earlier mentioned by the chronicler. This opinion can certainly raise doubts from the point of view of a positivist historian,[209] and there remains the open question of the extent to which this historiographic image of theocracy, or more precisely hierocracy, of the Rans results from a lack of appreciation or purposeful depreciation of the role of the assembly (veche) by Helmold.[210]

2.5.2   Vicelin – Difficult Beginnings of the Mission
The beginnings of Lothar III's rule was perceived by Helmold as a period of general peace.[211] This was the time when he located the arrival of priest Vicelin

---

205   Like Alexander the Great or Demetrius. See footnote 203 in this chapter.
206   A reference to the allegory of Sarah and Hagar, cf. Gal 4:21–31, shows Henry as Sarah's counterpart (allegorically Israel) who has Hagar, a slave (allegorically pagans). See footnote 203 in this chapter.
207   See footnote 203 in this chapter.
208   See also Helmold I, 38: (Henry) "non credebat eis, eo quod ipse nosset omnes", which refers to the figure of Jesus in the Gospel According to J 2:24: "... Iesus non credebat semet ipsum eis/ eo quod ipse nosset omnes." See *Helmolda Kronika*, p. 203, footnote 512.
209   *E.g.* Wachowski, *Słowiańszczyzna*, p. 128, emphasized that secular people were also Rans' envoys.
210   Possibly it was conditioned by the pragmatics of his work. For further discussion see pp. 359, 374; see also Goetz, *Die Wahrnehmung*, p. 151 f.
211   Helmold I, 51.

304 CHAPTER 4

at Lübeck, the place of residence of the Obodrite prince Henry.[212] Vicelin was a charismatic apostle of the Slavs who, regardless of his posthumous cult, never became as well-known as St. Otto of Bamberg, or the earlier Sts. Bruno of Querfurt and Adalbert. The selection of the town was not accidental because, as it is stressed by the chronicler, it was the only centre of Christianity in the Slavic lands of the Veleti and the Obodrite. The newcomer "was given for salvation of this tribe, to straighten the ways of God among the vicious and deceitful nation."[213] Helmold gave an extensive account (I, 42–46) of Vicelin's life, emphasizing the moment of his arrival in Slavdom with the intention of preaching the gospel and eradicating idolatry (*ydolatriam extirpandi*),[214] only to emphasize finally that these plans were thwarted because of Prince Henry's death and the subsequent wars over his legacy.

Waiting for a better time for his action, Vicelin started preaching the gospel among the neighbouring Nordalbings. This is noteworthy due to the fact that these Saxon peoples did not differ much in terms of religion and customs from the neighbouring Obodrites.[215] Vicelin had to face the challenge of deepening superficial Christianization of this country because the Nordalbings, in the chronicler's opinion, took nothing from Christianity apart from the name and they remained "genus agreste et incultum," ("brood uncultivated and crude") which was expressed in their cult of groves, springs and many other "erroneous superstitions."[216] Hence, it is possible to see in this message a certain

---

212 Vicelin's life and achievement and literature devoted to him are discussed by Strzelczyk, *Apostołowie*, pp. 251–272; *idem*, "Wicelin," in sss, vol. 6, pp. 415 f. See also Scior, *Das Eigene und das Fremde*, pp. 154 ff.; Enno Bünz, "Vicelin," in *Lexikon des Mittelalters*, vol. 8 (München: Artemis, 1997), col. 1622 f.

213 Helmold I, 41: "datus sit in salutem gentis huius, directas facere semitas Dei nostri in natione prava et perversa". The phrase "nacione prava et perversa" refers to Phil 2:15.

214 Helmold I, 46. *Ydolatria* in this place must be a synonym to the whole pagan cult. See below, p. 338.

215 Helmold I, 47: "Tres autem sunt Nordalbingorum populi: Sturmari, Holzati, Thetmarki, nec habitu nec lingua multum discrepantes, tenentes Saxonum iura et Christianum nomen, nisi quod barbarorum vicinam furtis et latrociniis operam dare consueverunt ..." ("There are three Nordalbingian peoples: Sturmari, Holzati, Thetmarki – they do not differ significantly among themselves with behavior, clothing or language, they obey the Saxon laws and name themselves Christians, besides the fact that due to the proximity of the barbarians they got used to thievery and pillage ..."). See also Scior, *Das Eigene und das Fremde*, pp. 196 ff.; Fraesdorff, *Der barbarische Norden*, p. 349.

216 *Ibidem*, I, 48: "Cumque [Vicelinus with his companions] pervenissent ad locum destinatum [to Falder – today Neumünster], perspexit [Vicelinus] habitudinem loci campumque vasta et sterili mirica perroridum, preterea accolarum genus agreste et incultum, nichil de religione nisi nomen Christianitatis habentes. Nam lucorum et fontium ceterarumque superstitionum multiplex error apud eos habetur." See also Fraesdorff, *Der barbarische Norden*, p. 352; Goetz, *Die Wahrnehmung*, p. 204.

HELMOLDI CRONICA SLAVORUM ON SLAVIC RELIGION   305

connection between on one hand the toughness of the people and the primordiality of customs as well as a lack of education, and on the other hand idolatry, which certainly is a reflection of the conviction of the clergy, that attachment to practices qualified as paganism was characteristic of uneducated social groups.

Further lines bring a very enthusiastic description of the effectiveness of evangelization and atonement of this brute people (*gens bruta*). Vicelin visited nearby churches "lecturing the peoples with salutary admonishments, rebuking the wrong-doers, conciliating the backsliders and destroying the sacred groves and all the cursed rites."[217] His example attracted other gospel preachers to him and they created a community of regular canons[218] located in Falder (a region near Wippendorf, now Neumünster).[219] They practiced evangelical recommendations related to their neighbour and they fasted and prayed for the conversion of the Slavs.[220] However, for a long time their prayers were fruitless because "necdum enim completae sunt iniquitates Amorreorum, neque venit tempus miserendi eorum." Thus one can see here an allegory that interprets the persistent native religion of the Slavs in the same way as in the work of Adam of Bremen based on biblical history.[221]

---

217   Helmold 1, 47: "... prebens populis monita salutatis, errantes corrigens, concilians dissidentes, preterea lucos et omnes ritus sacrilegos destruens".

218   There is information about the regular canons only in some of the chronicle manuscripts – see *Helmolda Kronika*, p. 231, footnote 621.

219   In 1330 the monastery was moved to Bordesholm and in 1490 it was reformed and became part of the Windesheim Congregation; it was secularised in 1566. The source documentation, literature and the history of the convent is discussed in *Monasticon Windeshemense*, part 2: *Deutsches Sprachgebiet*, ed. Wilhelm Kohl, Ernest Persoons, Anton G. Weiler, Archives et Bibliothèques de Belgique 16 (Brussels, 1977), pp. 79–94; cf. Thomas Hill, "Bordesholm," in *Lexikon für Theologie und Kirche*, vol. 2, ed. Walter Kasper *et al.* (Freiburg im Breisgau: Herder, 1994), p. 593.

220   Helmold 1, 47; cf. Gen 15:16 and Ps 101:14. Vicelinus's efforts related to the Christianization of the Slavs took him before the emperor whom he prompted the idea of building the Seegeberg stronghold on Wagrian land. According to the chronicler, the missionary was guided by his care for the salvation of the Slavs, however, even during the construction there were voices against "the bald man" (*i.e.* Vicelinus) who was the reason for "all this evil". Helmold observed that the stronghold on the land of the Slavs was – in their opinion – associated with oppression of them. See: Strzelczyk, *Apostołowie*, pp. 263–268; cf. Labuda, *Fragmenty*, vol. 3, p. 191.

221   Helmold 1, 47. See above, p. 243, footnote 229. By no means, however, did the Slavs experience the fate of Biblical Amorites, *i.e.* annihilation – they would experience mercy, which shows a theological idea of the Providence intervening in history, when the measure of iniquity is filled up.

306   CHAPTER 4

2.5.3   On Slavic Rituals: Helmold I, 52

The discussed cycle of the ascent and later fall of the Christianization mission
in Polabia is completed in chapter 52: *On Slavic rituals*. Contained therein is
one of the most precious characteristics of the Slavic religion in medieval his-
toriographies. Its rebirth was supported by dukes Niklot and Pribislav (from
1131) who represented a hostile attitude to Christianity. So: "At that time the
whole Slavdom was full of a multiplicity of idolatry and of errors of superstitions. As except for groves and Penates that filled the fields and settlements,
the most important deities were Prove – god of land of Aldenburg (Starigard),
Siwa – goddess of the Polabians and Redigast – god of land of the Obodrites."[222]
Helmold's "whole Slavdom," as it can be observed here, encompasses an extremely restrained area, because this expression refers only to the Polabians,
Wagrians, and Obodrites.[223]

     The chronicler grouped the entirety of the presented cults within a cluster
of idolatry and superstition (literary "the error of superstitions"), and admittedly there was a rich variety: the cult of groves and also spiritual creatures,
starting with "Penates". Their role was taking care of a homestead and fields,
which allowed the so-called "ubożęta" (tutelary spirits), home spirits and deities, or even ancestors' spirits to be seen in them.[224] Further positions in the
presented catalogue are tutelary goddesses and gods responsible for tribes or
territories. It is highly probable that the sanctuaries of these deities were located in assembly places of tribes united under the rule of one duke.[225]

     None of these deities were distinguished as superior with respect to the
others, which corresponds with the institutional reality of the Obodrite
Federation, in which the main unifying factor was ducal power.[226] However,
one should take into account the ambitions of the leading Obodrites to consider their deity as the most important. It is essential that the chronicler matched
each tribe with one deity, which makes this passage very significant in the discussion on changes in the religion of the Polabian tribes in the 11th and 12th c.,

---

222   Helmold I, 52: "Invaluitque in diebus illis per universam Slaviam multiplex ydolorum cul-
       tura errorque superstitionum. Nam preter lucos et penates, quibus agri et opida redund-
       abant, primi et precipui erant Prove deus Aldenburgensis terrae, Siwa dea Polaborum,
       Redigast deus terrae Obotritorum." Such concept of the "whole Slavdom" is inconsistent
       in comparison with other places in the chronicle, where the Slavic Rans' god Svantevit the
       first to be listed as pagan deity.
223   Urbańczyk, *Dawni Słowianie*, p. 62.
224   Cf. *domestici dii* by Thietmar (see above, p. 161). Images of the creatures can be small idols
       found by archaeologists in the Baltic area; cf. Szafrański, *Prahistoria*, p. 418.
225   Zernack, *Die burgstädtischen Volkversammlungen*, p. 220.
226   See *e.g.* Turasiewicz, *Dzieje polityczne, passim*.

HELMOLDI CRONICA SLAVORUM ON SLAVIC RELIGION   307

and even in the context of the discussion on henotheism in Slavic beliefs.[227] A
lively discussion is also continued in studies on particular creatures listed by
Helmold as deities.

"Siwa" ("Żywa"?) defined as "dea Polaborum" (*i.e.* the so called proper
Polabians, a small tribe using this name) is sometimes connected with "deus
vitae, quam vocabant Zywye" known from Joannes Dlugossius's chronicle.[228]
However, following K. Potkański's argumentation, claiming that if Dlugossius
had borrowed information about "Zywye" from Helmold, then he would move
to his *Olympus* more divine names than only one or two (see below on Podaga),
such direct relation should be questioned.[229] This is why A. Brückner's assumption that Dlugossius created the aforementioned deity only on the basis
of echoes of Helmold's chronicle in later historiography gained recognition.[230]
This view was not accepted by H. Łowmiański, who indicated its inherent difficulties. Also, he understands the convergence of the words "Siwa" – "Żywie"
(similarly to "Podaga" and "Pogoda") as accidental. Thus Siwa, being a local
deity, was not worshipped in territory of Poland.[231]

There is no information about her temple or image. The feminine name
of this deity evokes associations with the Liutici goddesses mentioned by
Thietmar.[232] S. Kulišić assumed that Siwa was a fertility goddess of the Magna
Mater type, which was a relic of the archaic, agrarian, and matriarchal stages in
the development of Slavic societies.[233] Due to Helmold's silence on the matter

---

227   This discussion reaches the earliest testimonies of Slavic beliefs, starting with Procopius
       of Caesarea's information on the Antes and the Sclavenes, in which it is possible to ob-
       serve a division into gods (*theos*) and a group of deities of lower rank (nymphs, rivers,
       daimonia). This model presentation in the case of Helmold's work corresponds with the
       deus – *penates* juxtaposition, for more discussion see below, pp. 308, 376, 380.
228   Urbańczyk, *Dawni Słowianie*, p. 198; Gieysztor, *Mitologia*, p. 195.
229   Karol Potkański, "Wiadomości Długosza o polskiej mitologii," in Karol Potkański,
       Pisma pośmiertne, vol. 2 (Kraków: PAU, 1924) p. 72. Moreover, Potkański assumed that
       Dlugossius's "Żywie" ("Zywye") was one of the "Polish" most certain gods because of the
       existence of "Żywa" among the Polabians and the conviction that Dlugossius did not read
       Helmold – *ibidem*, p. 84.
230   A. Brückner changed his opinion on the sounds of Podaga's and Pogoda's names con-
       vergence: initially he thought it was accidental, however, next he assumed that *Joannis
       de Czarnkow chronicon Polonorum* was an indirect link between them. See Brückner,
       Mitologia słowiańska i polska, pp. 49, 233; *idem, Dzieje kultury polskiej* (Kraków: L. Anczyc
       i Spółka, 1931), p. 139. See also Urbańczyk, *Dawni Słowianie*, pp. 17, 47, 198; Gieysztor,
       Mitologia, p. 197.
231   Łowmiański, *Religia*, p. 183.
232   Possibly the military banners (in sing. so called "stanica"), see Moszyński, *Die vorchristli-
       che Religion*, p. 86; *idem, Staropołabski teonim*, p. 39. See above, pp. 105 , 157.
233   Kulišić, *Stara Slovenska religija*, pp. 42, 197 f.

308   CHAPTER 4

of the Siwa statue, a conviction that she was worshipped just like Prove, in hierophany embodied in nature, was disseminated.[234] However, the silence on the matter of her idol cannot be used as a decisive argument here.

Prove, the god of the Starigard land, has three testimonies in the *Chronicle of the Slavs*. The most extensive one accompanies the description of his sanctuary. Hence his cult will be discussed below on the basis of more detailed data.[235] However, even now it should be emphasized that his position as the major patron of the tribe, in the light of Helmold's work, should not raise any doubts, regardless of the fact that he was not worshipped in a temple and as an idol.[236]

The third of the above-mentioned gods, Redigast, should consistently be identified with Redigast from Rethra with reference to the testimonies of Adam of Bremen and Helmold himself. The dissemination of Redigast's cult among the Obodrite can be confirmed by local names,[237] although it is a double-edged argument because it is possible that a theonim was created from a toponym and not the other way around.[238] Another possibility which should be taken into account is that Redigast's cult came to the Obodrite land from Rethra.[239] From the silence of the sources it is hard to conclude whether in this case he had a temple and a statue, but the Liutici analogy would indicate a positive answer.[240]

---

234   Łowmiański, *Religia*, p. 184. Urbańczyk, *Dawni Słowianie*, pp. 154 and 198, being convinced that more important deities were worshipped with statues, he treats Siwa as well as Prove and Podaga as demons, hence sharing an earlier view of Brückner, *Mitologia słowiańska i polska*, p. 200. In the case of Siwa it was to be a demon of life and growth. This attempt to degrade the said deities does not seem justifiable because Helmold differentiated between gods and goddesses and lower rank supernatural creatures such as "penates". In the assumption of the argumentation questioned here there is a false conviction that idolatry is an inseparable element in polytheism – see also above, pp. 107, 173 ff.

235   See below, pp. 330 ff.

236   See p. 338.

237   According to Łowmiański, *Religia*, p. 171.

238   This argument was rejected by Brückner, *Mitologia słowiańska i polska*, pp. 73 f., (in his polemic with L. Niederle) who treated this testimony of a deity cult as a mistake considered similar to "specious" (in Brückner's opinion) testimony of Adam of Bremen. Moreover, the argument deriving from names is used by Brückner against the existence of the deity arguing that his name was created on the basis of topography by mistake (*ibidem*, p. 74).

239   Łowmiański, *Religia*, p. 184, thought that this cult translation took place after the fall of Rethra, which seems hardly justifiable: it is more probable that the prime of the famous temple can be better explained by possible dissemination of its cult to the neighbours. Such possibility is not excluded by Gieysztor, *Mitologia*, p. 169.

240   Łowmiański, *Religia*, p. 184, claimed that there was no Redigast's statue in the Obodrites, similarly to Siwa and Prove. This way of thinking is a consequence of adoption of a very typical of this scholar theory of the development of the Slavic religion. According to this

HELMOLDI CRONICA SLAVORUM ON SLAVIC RELIGION 309

The three deities discussed above received very disparate qualifications in scholarly debate – from pseudo-deities and demons to major deities. However, Helmold's testimony is unequivocal: they are gods in the strict sense of this word, and at the same time they are patrons of particular tribes. It should also be considered whether in the description the chronicler used a model biblical image, in the light of which particular Elbslavs' peoples each had their own major deity. This would explain a certain untypicality in the names of the major deities presented by Helmold, which according to some scholars would be more appropriate for demons than higher rank creatures. Hence, a suspicion arises that the chronicler, should there be no major deity in some tribe, would fill this actual vacancy with a name of another supernatural creature when building a literary image of the pantheon of the "entire Slavdom."

However, it is enough to notice that the "suspicious" in this case Prove, in the light of further dependable data from Helmold, was a patron of the assembly (veche) place of the Wagrians. His untypical name in comparison with the prevailing double-barrelled ones, in the case of other tribal patrons, gains sufficient explanation in the specifics of his hierophany shaped in the element of nature and related to more archaic levels of Slavic religion. An additional argument supporting the genuineness of his data is the fact that he knew Prove's cult from his own experience.[241] Being a priest himself he had an opportunity to gain knowledge directly from the converted inhabitants of Northern Polabia.

In this context, it is hard to undermine Helmold's credibility in outlining a summary image of the cult of tribal gods, still – what is important – without rejecting the biblical inspiration in the very appreciation of these major deities on the literary stage of history.[242] On the other hand, it is exactly this trend to "henotheize" the tribal *sacrum* that does not allow for a complete resolution of doubts regarding whether the cults of the deities indicated by the chronicler as the major ones had some competitive cults among the tribes attributed to them or not. One obstacle is the resistance to excluding the possibility that in these communities there were more assembly places and sanctuaries, and

---

theory the Obodrites would represent a more archaic level of beliefs and cult than polytheism and idolatry, the evidence for which would be the taking over by the Obodrites of the major deity with a double-barrelled name from the Liutici (not as an archaic one as *e.g.* Siwa). However, this argumentation does not explain the fact that the cult of the idol from Rethra would reach the Obodrites without moving its shape, *i.e.* the statue and the temple, especially that these tribes knew these objects (the example of Podaga).

241 He participated in the devastation of his sanctuary, see below.

242 In this case, however, it is necessary to take into account a wider context of this information, especially significance attributed to Svantevit from Rügen.

310   CHAPTER 4

hence also deities aspiring to a major rank.[243] Therefore this catalogue of three
deities presented by Helmold would have likely been chosen from a longer series of deities.[244]

The goal of the chronicler's presentation was emphasizing the distinctiveness of particular tribal cults, but it also comprises details useful in the research on the changes taking place in the sphere of Slavic beliefs and cults in
the 11th and 12th c. In the case of these investigations, the key significance is
attributed to the problem of the genesis of patron gods of particular tribes or
assembly places, especially in relation to the appearance of double-barrelled
theonyms.[245] Redigast is such a character in Helmold's presentation. Similar to
the earlier confirmed Liutici god with the same name, he was the patron of the
main tribe in the multi-tribal organization.

It is possible that he obtained his name in connection with the topography and natural environment of his sanctuary, as a result of the evolution of
Svarožic's cult, the same as in the case of the Liutici. The name could even

---

243   A certain analogy can be found in the specifics of the Liutici country at the time of Otto
      of Bamberg's mission in 1128. Temples were located in centres quite near to one another
      where there were also assembly places. See Słupecki, *Slavonic Pagan Sanctuaries*, pp. 70–
      94; Rosik, *Conversio*, pp. 418 ff., 456 ff.

244   Siwa seems especially "suspicious" in this respect – the appearance of a female deity lead-
      ing the whole tribal community is a rather exceptional phenomenon. It is possible that
      Helmold, while constructing the pantheon of the "entire Slavdom", decided that a femi-
      nine element should not be missing in it.

245   Pettazzoni, *Wszechwiedza*, pp. 216 f., on the basis of the community of rituals and attri-
      butes, he assumed that the highest god of the Western Slavs was solar and occurred in
      quite a number of variations: Svarožic, Triglav, Svantevit, Rugievit. Similarly Gieysztor,
      Mitologia, p. 116: in Polabia at the time of the political pressure of Christianity, resistance
      meant entire faithfulness to paganism; it ensured cultural identity and politically inte-
      grated the society. "This would explain the appearance in the sources of a number of
      names of deities each of which were worshipped in a different community. Names, but
      not deities, because numerous factors seem to support the substitutory character of these
      new names in the common henotheism of the Slavs; one of the major deities – it was not
      always Perun – was put forward as the patron of the tribal federation, which attributed
      to the deity a special local name." Borrowings from neighbours in the sphere of cult are
      also possible, however, the mythological basis of the cult remained the same as the one
      inherited from ancestors. Similarly Leciejewicz, *Słowianie*, pp. 193 f., considered the emer-
      gence of particular tribal deities as the result of changes in the Slavic system of beliefs
      aimed at adjusting it to the changing social and political reality. According to Leciejewicz
      these tribal deities were the local versions of Svarožic, Perun or Veles, and in the
      11th c. – see *ibidem*, pp. 222 f. – local cults substituting the system of old Slavic mythology
      were developed. Agricultural deities were substituted by war ones. Although A. Gieysztor
      alternatively connected Svantevit and Iarovit with Perun, and Triglav with Veles, there is
      no doubt that cult disintegration as such became a fact and only some functions of gods
      and rituals remained similar.

HELMOLDI CRONICA SLAVORUM ON SLAVIC RELIGION   311

have developed in imitation of their central, supra-tribal cult. This external
influence on the Obodrite religion could anyway be much more considerable.
Namely, even without the participation of the context of natural scenery, the
cult of Redigast could have been moved from Rethra. This idea is more probable thanks to testimonies of Liutici influences among the Obodrites; it is
worth remembering here that the Liutici were the political and military force
that lent victory to the pagan reaction among the Obodrites and the Wagrians
in 1018.[246]

It is not accidental that Redigast's cult developed among the Obodrites who,
similarly to the Redars who kept Rethra under their custody, were the core of
a federation of a few tribes. The Obodrites necessarily aspired to leadership in
this structure, but the cult of Redigast did not play such an important role in
this case as in the case of the Liutici. The institutional conditions, particularly
a long tradition of their monarchy reaching the times of Charlemagne, were
not favourable for this. In this power system in the tribal community there was
no place for "another Rethra."

However, in Helmold's work the absence of mentioning the natural prevalence of the Obodrite cult over the cults of the Polabians and Wagrians in this
context (at least in the assessment of the Obodrites) is worth consideration.
First of all, the schematization of the general image of religion in the "entire
Slavdom" is presented by this author in such a way that one sovereign of all
gods, Svantevit, could appear, which becomes more convincing in further reading of the discussed chapter of the chronicle.

The public character of the cult of the tribal gods is advocated by a description of rituals performed by priests. The deities were widely worshipped,
had priests devoted to them, and had sacrifices made on their behalf.[247]
Celebrations worshipping particular gods started with bloody offerings: "Then,
according to what the lots determine, the priest announces celebrations and
holidays dedicated to particular deities. [After which] men and women with
children come, and to make a sacrifice to their gods they kill sheep and oxen,
and also make human sacrifices of numerous Christians as they claim the gods
are [deeply] fond of their blood."[248]

---

246   See above, pp. 183 ff.
247   Helmold I, 52: "His [deities] dicati erant flamines et sacrificiorum libamenta multiplexque
       religionis cultus." See also above, p. 127, footnote 395.
248   *Ibidem*: "Porro solempnitates diis dicandas sacerdos iuxta sortium nutum denuntiat, con-
       veniunt viri et mulieres cum parvulis mactantque diis suis hostias de bobus et ovibus,
       plerique etiam de hominibus Christianis, quorum sanguine deos suos oblectari iactitant".

312   CHAPTER 4

However, even if one considers it as a topos,[249] taking into consideration the hostility of the Slavs towards the invaders, it is hard to not regard it as probable.[250] The bloody offerings resulted from a need for prophetic divination, which was uttered by a priest who consumed blood.[251] The commentary: "For in the opinion of numerous [people] the deities are easily called by [sacrificial] blood"[252] leaves interpretational freedom in defining who were the "numerous" claiming that it is easier to attract deities and demons with blood.[253] A time for feasting and dancing followed the offerings.[254]

A significant message exists in this context that deserves attention, especially because of its exploitation by the generations of historians of Slavic religion: "There is an astonishing error among the Slavs that during their feasts and revelry they pass a goblet among themselves, into which they articulate words, not of consecration but rather of execration in the names of gods, both the good and the evil one, as it is believed that the good fortune is given by the good god while misfortune comes from the bad one. Thus, in their language they call the bad god 'Diabol' [i.e. Devil] or 'Zcerneboch,' that is a black god."[255]

The ritual portrayed here, during which spells were said above a circulated chalice, was considered a peculiarity by the chronicler, literally a *mirabilis error* ("peculiar error"). So, there was also a theological assessment in this opinion, which gains a special dimension with reference to the words uttered above the goblet: "non consecrationis, sed execrationis" [verba]. This formula[256] shows

---

249   Similar information that pagans claim that their gods rejoiced at Christian blood is a view expressed by Adam of Bremen (IV, 27) regarding to Uppsala. This statement of the chronicler is sometimes treated as an example of the demonization of the Scandinavian religion, see *e.g.* Anders Hultgård, "Menschenopfer," in *Reallexikon der Germanischen Altertumskunde*, vol. 19, ed. Heinrich Beck *et al.* (Berlin/New York: De Gruyter, 2002), pp. 533–546.

250   See *The Letter of Adelgot* published by Labuda, *Fragmenty*, vol. 3, pp. 234–236. Discussion on the source – *ibidem*, pp. 233–269.

251   Helmold I, 52: "Post cesam hostiam sacerdos de cruore libat, ut sit efficacior oraculis capescendis."

252   *Ibidem*: "Nam demonia sanguine facilius invitari multorum opinio est".

253   In another place in the chronicle the expression "multorum opinio" refers to Christians, see Helmold I, 95.

254   Helmold I, 52: "Consummatis iuxta morem sacrificiis populus ad epulas et plausus convertitur". Łowmiański, *Religia*, p. 186, emphasizes that Helmold did not mention sacral orgies condemned by priests from Rus'.

255   Helmold I, 52: "Est autem Slavorum mirabilis error; nam in conviviis et compotationibus suis pateram circumferunt, in quam conferunt, non dicam consecracionis, sed execracionis verba sub nomine deorum, boni scilicet atque mali, omnem prosperam fortunam a bono deo, adversam a malo dirigi profitentes. Unde etiam malum deum lingua sua Diabol sive Zcerneboch, id est nigrum deum appellant."

256   It is mentioned by J. Strzelczyk in: *Helmolda Kronika*, p. 245, footnote 683.

HELMOLDI CRONICA SLAVORUM ON SLAVIC RELIGION   313

the chronicler's aversion to this practice and it is also, due to the antithesis included in it, an allusion to celebration of the holy mass – because of the chalice
motif – and also other possible liturgical formulas of consecrations due to the
expression *consecrationis verba sub nomine*.

The occurrence of these analogies, similar to the figure of the Devil appearing in Helmold's information, favours a view that he could emphasize these
elements of the ritual which evoked an association with church practices familiar to him. It should be taken into account that the chronicler could interpret the significance of the described gestures using measures taken exactly
from the Christian liturgy. It is similar with the very attempt to capture the
sense of rituals with reference to the Latin terminology, including the word
fortuna. Thus, in the perspective of studies on pre-Christian Slavic religious
practices, the content of the quoted passage should be treated with caution.

The mythical sense of the ritual, according to Helmold, is determined by a
conviction of happiness coming from a good god and unhappiness from a bad
one. There is no other confirmation of such rituals practiced by the Slavs and
this leads to an inclination to search for at least partial analogies. It is possible
to indicate here a harvest festival in Arkona described by Saxo Grammaticus:
the priest, having taken a chalice from the Svantevit statue's hand, inspected
the state of the liquid poured into it a year before. After this divination, he paid
respect to the statue by drinking fresh mead and asking Svantevit for multiplication of abundance as well as victories for Rans.[257]

In the discussion conducted on the "peculiar error" so far, the most significant element is Helmold's confirmation of the bipolar structure of *sacrum*,
expressed in such pairs as *bonus deus – malus deus, prospera fortuna – mala
fortuna*. Another important element is the identification of the "bad god" with
the Devil, which according to the source was a work of the Elbslavs. In this
context the question of the genesis of this dualism becomes particularly significant, and especially the influence of the reception of Christian ideas in the
Slavic environment. Making a statement on this matter should be preceded
by a reference to the basic findings in the discussion conducted so far on this
compelling question, which has been debated by scholars for generations.

The supernatural creatures summoned in the ritual seem to have a different nature than the tribal tutelary gods. However, they are also personified

---

257   Saxo XIV, 39, 5. In the discussion on the ritual described by Helmold, it is indicated that
       there was an analogy with magic related to drinking from the chalice confirmed in Rus' in
       The Word of Christolubec. See Gieysztor, *Mitologia*, pp. 240 f.

creatures.[258] Their roles, according to the chronicler, are clearly connected with fate. Since *malus deus* "Czarnobóg" (*i.e.* "black god") is responsible for misfortune, then somehow naturally he should be paired with a "white god," *i.e.* alleged "Białobóg"/"Belbog". However, a mythical character bearing this name appeared in sources rather late and there is no agreement as to whether he was a real Slavic god.

S. Urbańczyk assumed that "Białobóg" is a pseudo-deity, emphasizing that also "the name Czarnobóg is blatantly different from any other divine names, hence it must be Helmold's own interpretation. Helmold probably heard something about the Slavic faith in vicious spirits and in the personification of fate (...), [and] he connected this with Christian images, which could possibly have permeated into Slavic culture."[259] However, the hypothesis of juxtaposition of good and evil in the characters of "Białobóg" and "Czarnobóg" cannot be buried on the basis of this opinion.

The probable authenticity of Białobóg is confirmed by the Slavic lexis. H. Popowska-Taborska ascertains that "the skepticism connected with the existence of the Slavic deity called 'bel bog' is not justified. The name has rich testimonies in Slavic onomastic materials and its traces are also found in Slavic dialect sources." Lastly, in the folklore of the Balkan Serbs there clearly looms the "white god" (*beli bog*) and his antithesis ('black god'), functioning as terms used to refer to good and evil fortune.[260]

According to K. Moszyński even the very word "bog" was translated as: portion, fortune, donor of (good) fate. In this context 'bog' is a term used to refer to mythical creatures personifying good fortune and happiness. It is confirmed in references to the Indo-European language substrate.[261] The most certain

---

258 Helmold emphasizes that prayer over the chalice was said in god's name, which – if it is true – is an additional argument for personal character of the called spiritual power.

259 Urbańczyk, *Dawni Słowianie*, p. 187; cf. *idem*, "Pseudobóstwa," pp. 405 f.

260 Popowska-Taborska, *Wczesne dzieje*, p. 119. See also Moszyński, *Kultura*, p. 708 – compare with the Polish "czarna godzina" (literary: 'black hour' meaning a rainy day). There were also attempts to support this position with the occurrence of two names of mountains in Lusatia: *Czorneboh* and *Bieleboh* (*e.g.* Gieysztor, *Mitologia*, p. 160), however, it is a highly disputable argument. Paul Nedo, "Czorneboh und Bieleboh – zwei angebliche slawische Kultstätten in Oberlausitz," *Lětopis* 6/7 (1963), pp. 9–18, after research on the earlier names of both mountains in the light of written testimonies, concluded that the current names and legends related to them have literary genesis and only at the time of Romanticism they permeated to the general awareness or even folklore (Czorneboh at the end of the 18th c. and Bieleboh as late as the 19th c.). See also Urbańczyk, *Dawni Słowianie*, p. 154.

261 Moszyński, *Kultura*, pp. 708–710; cf. Vernardsky, *The origins of Russia*, pp. 118 f. The original meaning of 'bog' is derived by scholars from the Old Iranian 'baga', and Slavic 'bog' denoted good and abundances, as well as the supernatural giver of "bog" – see *e.g.* Gieysztor, *Mitologia*, p. 74. The same Łowmiański, *Religia*, pp. 223 f.

HELMOLDI CRONICA SLAVORUM ON SLAVIC RELIGION   315

solution will be an assumption that the addressees of the magic spell above the chalice mentioned by Helmold were personifications of fate and fortune, and hence, were its originators. It is possible that they were demons related to the individual existence of the man.

It is also possible that the general human Fate (Slavic "Dola") is in question, known from eastern Slavic folklore with an analogy in a Balkan myth, in which its place is taken by "osud" (fate) or also God. Although Slavic legends related to this theme, in comparison with the Early medieval ones, are rather new,[262] the "great significance of the fate or fortune in the religious life of the Slavs undoubtedly dates back to times thousands of years ago."[263] A related word to fate ("dola"), "deliti," corresponds with the Old Indian "bhajati," from which the "bogu-" descends.[264]

The name "Czarnobóg" most probably refers to (mis)fortune personified in this figure.[265] The use of the term *deus* in his case remains disputable. It can conceal a lower rank spiritual creature or only a supernatural force representing fortune and responsible for fate. However, in Helmold's times the original belief substrate, together with the whole system of myths, could be transformed in such a way that one may speak here about a complete formation of individual divine creatures responsible for fate. It can also be assumed that the divine creatures defined as *deus bonus* and *deus malus* – not related to statues or hierophanies in nature –certainly belonged to the layer of the Slavic religion, whose functioning was a bit shadowed by idolatry or nature cult.[266]

---

262   Łowmiański, *Religia*, p. 189, attacked the view claiming the existence of personified fortune among medieval Slavs, and according to him the evidence for that was no information in these respects in the dictionary of Old Polish, cf. *Słownik polszczyzny XVI wieku*, vol. 5, ed. Maria R. Mayenowa (Wrocław: Ossolineum, 1971). The notion of fortune – fate, in his opinion, developed only under the influence of Byzantium in the south and east of the Slavdom. However, in such a case *ex silentio nullum argumentum …*

263   Moszyński, *Kultura*, p. 700.

264   *Ibidem*, p. 710.

265   Gieysztor, *Mitologia*, p. 160, proposed to assume that another figuration of "Czarnobóg" was 'Ljutbog' – 'ferocious god' in Polabia. The existence of Ljutbog is not confirmed in sources and is only a speculation based on the name Liutici, see above p. 296.

266   This is why in the light of available sources the claim that, Chors, Dazbog and Stribog are aspects of a solar deity, which is called White God (Biełobóg), is too bold, similar to the opinion that for the Western Slavs this god opposing the god of hell Veles, received the names Iarovit, Porovit and Svantevit – see: M. Eliade, I.P. Couliano, *Słownik religii*, Warszawa 1994, p. 197 (an ascertainment based on Marija Gimbutas's studies); comparative material: Mircea Eliade, *A History of Religious Ideas*, vol. 3: *From Muhammad to the Age of Reforms*, trans. Alf Hiltebeitel, Diane Apostolos-Cappadona (Chicago/London: The University of Chicago Press: 1988), pp. 31–37. Similarly, on the basis of Helmold's chronicle, it is difficult to positively verify S. Kulišić's speculation that "Veles's" *Črnobog* would be in

The deities of fate mentioned by Helmold remain in some relation with the dualistic cosmogony – since the microcosm (human being) and macrocosm correspond with each other in belief motifs.[267] This is why in the debate over dualism in Slavic beliefs, emphasized in the discussed passage, a reference to cosmogonic and anthropogonic myths, reported by collectors of Slavic folklore relics and finding their analogies on a universal scale, turned out to be rather important. A characteristic feature of these cosmogonies – apart from the primordial ocean motif, from which the world emerged – turns out to be the dualistic motif claiming that the creation of the world and man was a work of two antagonistic supernatural creatures.[268]

There is a common view that the dissemination of these archaic stories in "Christianized" form in the Middle Ages was influenced by Manicheism-Bogomilism trends.[269] However, Mircea Eliade very accurately emphasized that variants of cosmogonic myths about the creation of the world by the God-Satan pair, occurring in Slavic folklore, are not confirmed in areas of Slavdom influenced by Bogomilism.[270] Therefore, as the sources of dualism present in

---

this perspective a lunar deity; his antithesis in the form of the "white god" was placed by the scholar in the uranic area as a personification of heaven, which he connected with the heavenly god (*deus otiosus*) and Dazbog (*deus dator*), see Kulišić, *Stara Slovenska religija*, pp. 42, 192–194. The notion of 'bog' (parallel to Sanskrit *bhaga*) is of key significance in the proposed connections, and meant good, abundance and the supreme god, a counterpart of *e.g.* Zeus (a precious indicator is the nickname *Zeus Bagaios*), *ibidem*, pp. 153–162.

267 Gieysztor, *Mitologia*, pp. 164 f., shows the dependence of microcosmogony and macro-cosmogony in the Proto-Indo-European myth of the cosmic man, so far confirmed in the Slavdom only once. General information on this matter: Guriewicz [Gurevich], *Kategorie kultury*, pp. 43 ff., esp. 59.

268 The origin of the bipolarity of cosmogony can turn out to be even pre-Indo-European and it could have become more prominent when the Slavs contacted the Old Iranian peoples, and later – which raises controversies – under the influence of the Bogomils. See Gieysztor, *Mitologia*, pp. 156–161. See also Eliade, *A History*, vol. 3, pp. 35 f.; Váňa, *Svět slovanských bohů*, pp. 52 ff.

269 An example of a dualistic myth from PVL (under the year 6579 [1071]): God washed himself in a bath and as he sweated he dried himself with a wisp and threw it out of heaven to the earth. So Satan argued with God about who should make the man out of the wisp. Then Satan made the man and God gave him the soul; cf. Łowmiański, *Religia*, p. 189; see Gieysztor, *Mitologia*, pp. 157 f. *Ibidem*, p. 163, an example of a dualistic myth about keeping order in the world: the devil is in chains from which he releases himself to annihilate the whole world, next he is chained by Christ rising from the dead every year. It is worth mentioning that folklore of Slavs and Balts knows the myth of the fight of the thunder deity (residing on a mountain, in heaven, on the sun or the moon, or the top of a triple tree) with an enemy positioned lowly: under a tree or a stone. The defeated enemy hides in underground waters; while the victorious thunder releases rain (see Gieysztor, *Mitologia*, pp. 98 f.).

270 Eliade, *A History*, vol. 3, p. 35.

HELMOLDI CRONICA SLAVORUM ON SLAVIC RELIGION   317

the discussed cosmogonic myth, one should indicate the Indo-European substrate inherited by the Slavs, which next in folklore acquired an outfit which
was evidently taken from Christianity.

The illustration of the dualism organizing the cosmos can also be seen
in the sculpture of the so-called Sviatovid found in the 19th c. in the Zbruch
River (Ukraine), which has a character of an ideogram.[271] In the lower part of
the obelisk there is a three-headed Atlas-like figure carrying representations
carved on higher parts of the ideogram: they were interpreted as the earthly
sphere and the heavenly one in which there is a four-faced figure. This three-
headed "Atlas" was somehow tamed and was associated with the chthonic
sphere, and thereby with devastating powers and black colour. Hence there
was even an idea to find "Czarnobóg", mentioned by Helmold, in this figure.[272]
However, given such weak premises, it seems safer to accept only that there
was a community of certain characteristics of both figures without identifying
them together.

The view of the nature of the "black god" as chtonic and hostile to man is
supported by a Slavic association of this deity with the devil borrowed from
Christianity.[273] This identification opens another comparative perspective
based on ethnographic material. K. Moszyński observed that: "In the popular
religion of the Polishchuk there are only two types of creatures of some significance, namely these countless chorts and a thunder wielding God, shooting

---

271 In the opinion of scholars (*e.g.* A. Gieysztor, B. Rybakov, Z. Krzak; see below, footnote 381)
     the obelisk is an ideogram of the highest god and *imago mundi*. The image of three-sec-
     toral nature of cosmos joins in him the dualistic opposition of the heavenly ruler of the
     pan-cosmos and the three-headed, certainly enslaved "atlas" from the chthonic sphere.
     The literature discussing this issue is extensive and yet the question of the medieval gen-
     esis of this relic still arises (see below, footnote 381).

272 Rybakov, *Jazyčestwo drevnej Rusi*, p. 241, reminds the forgotten Famicyn's idea that in the
     lowest part of the obelisk there is an image exactly of "Czarnobóg" related in this concept
     with Triglav's triple power over heaven, earth and underworld.

273 Pettazzoni, *Wszechwiedza*, pp. 215 f., associated Helmold's "Czarnobóg" (*deus niger*) with
     "Tjarnaglofi" explained as "Black-headed" known from Knytlingasaga, assuming he was a
     reflection of the Christian devil. Similarly, Łowmiański, *Religia*, p. 187–189, assumed that
     "Tjarnaglofi" was a transformation of "Czarnobóg" taking care of the dead. Filipowiak,
     Słowiańskie wierzenia, p. 22, found possible support for this funeral hypothesis in the
     area of toponomastics and archaeology (a cremation graveyard in the Pomeranian vil-
     lage named Czarnogłowy, *i.e.* "Black-headed"); see also Bylina, *Kultura*, p. 21. Kulišić,
     Stara Slovenska religija, pp. 42, 193, he connects the identification of "Czarnobóg" and
     Tiarnaglofi with Triglav, as a chthonic creature, and like other Indo-European having his
     antithesis (comp. Pluton – Zeus, Vodan – Thor). This etymology is in conflict with the
     findings of Moszyński, *Staropołabski teonim*, *passim*, which, by the way, are worth a sepa-
     rate discussion (see later, p. 75).

318   CHAPTER 4

thunders at this malicious, dangerous and foolish gang; chorts and God – two
contrary worlds of good and evil." However, this Polishchuk faith is very modest and reduced. The Christian outfit of the figures that comprise its subject
seems to conceal the most fundamental layers of religiousness, the ones which
could not be eradicated by Christianization destroying sanctuaries or the elimination of priest-fortune-tellers.[274]

Therefore, the earlier juxtaposition would follow the chorts – Perun line,[275]
but this most certainly was not the initial state. The original antithesis of the
chort was certainly the bies. In terms of type, both of these creatures are clas-
sified as demons (Gr. *daimon*), and the case of a chort it is special, as it denotes
a lame and mutilated bies.[276] A. Gieysztor observed in this pair of hypostasis
of good and evil not personifications but rather primitive notions on which
enriching and specifying beliefs were layered.[277] The proposed model of the
transformation of the primitive juxtaposition of good and evil into supernatural creatures forms a good basis for a hypothesis on the formation of the cult of
bipolar figures: *deus bonus – deus malus.*[278]

A. Gieysztor assumed that Helmold's information discussed here should be
referred to indigenous Slavic beliefs.[279] At the same time he emphasized in
this respect the moment of Old Iranian influences perceivable in the theonym
"Czarnobóg" in the stem '-bog,' which could be the linking element with the
archaic myth. It cannot be excluded that it reached the Slavs already in the
form of a ritual connected with the chalice, whose Slavic name 'chasha' is also
borrowed from Proto-Iranian.[280] It is worth emphasizing this while remembering the universal symbolism of the chalice related to fate ruled by the deities

---

274   Moszyński, *Kultura*, p. 702.
275   H. Łowmiański questioned this position being convinced that a chort is not confirmed in
       sources from Rus' as a demonologic term, and only a bies is (and even he does not fight
       with Perun) and in this situation he assumed that the Polishchuk dualism (God's struggle
       with devils and polarisation of good and evil) were Christian motifs in their worldview,
       similar to the 'black god' of the Polabians. Łowmiański, *Religia*, pp. 66, 354. This position
       should be taken in consideration to carefully approach K. Moszyński's hypothesis and not
       treat it as an optimum one, but only as one possibility.
276   Moszyński, *Kultura*, p. 703.
277   Gieysztor, *Mitologia*, p. 161.
278   If A. Gieysztor's position that fate deities are not "complete personifications" is accepted,
       then it should be indicated that even Helmold's use of the term *deus* to refer to them is an
       expression of cultural interpretation or rather imputation.
279   *Ibidem*, p. 161.
280   Among the Old Iranian borrowings in Slavic languages there is the word chalice: 'chasha' –
       Proto-Iranian '*chashaka*', the word is reconstructed from Armenian and Old Indian con-
       tinuations (see Gieysztor, *Mitologia*, p. 75; Kulišić, *Stara Slovenska religija*, p. 38).

summoned during the rite described in the discussed passage of the *Chronicle of the Slavs*.

This hypothetical path of argumentation is one of the possible illustrations of the fundamental thesis in the conducted research, the thesis which is documented on the basis of the above quoted comparative material relating the bipolar structure organizing the system of beliefs of the Early Slavs, which originates from the archetypical cultural substrate widely disseminated in the Indo-European circle. It is essential that this dualism of good and evil, especially with reference to fate, is not adequate for the antithesis of sin and grace, characteristic of Christianity. It is worth emphasizing this so as to prove that it is hard to connect its occurrence with the influence of Christianity, which in turn has an impact on the explanation of the genesis of the ritual described by Helmold and the related myth.

Meanwhile the same bipolar motif of the juxtaposition of the good and evil gods was sometimes treated as a reflection of an element of Christian beliefs, or more precisely the Christ–Satan antithesis.[281] However in contemporary Church doctrine this juxtaposition did not have any ontological dualism in its nature, so identification of "Czarnobóg" with the Devil has to be considered an effect of a Christian outfit overlapping with the Slavic myth. L.P. Słupecki even assumed that it was done by Christian clergy. He connected this activity with the transformation process of Slavic gods into Christian demons.[282] However, in this situation *bonus deus* would also consistently deserve to be included in the fellowship of demonic powers, while according to the source only the god of evil was considered the Devil.

Thus, it seems more probable that in this case one is dealing with *interpretatio Slavica* of the Christian *antisacrum*.[283] Favourable conditions for such phenomenon had been developed for over two centuries of continuous contacts between the Polabian tribes and Christianity, as well as a few attempts to implant this religion among them. Another significant factor in shaping Polabian beliefs was the cultural contact with Scandinavia that could have influenced the images concerning gods and fate. Unquestionably, there is no doubt that

---

281 Urbańczyk, *Dawni Słowianie*, p. 26; Łowmiański, *Religia*, pp. 188–190. See also Fraesdorff, *Der barbarische Norden*, p. 324.

282 Słupecki, *Einflüsse*, p. 187.

283 However, the thesis that the Christian Devil was considered a deity by the Slavs and only later called "Czarnobóg" (*e.g.* Łowmiański, *Religia*, pp. 188 f.) is doubtful, because he occurred in the context in a pair with a "good god", hence in a heterodoxic constellation for the then Church doctrine. The exponent of this dualism at that time could be the Bogomils, however, there are no proper grounds to assume that their concepts reached Polabia.

the very name "Czarnóbog" (*Zcerneboch*) is Slavic, however, there is a justified presumption that – similarly to Svantevit or Iarovit – it belongs to the generation of theonyms with a relatively late origin, by whose occurrence the high dynamics of changes in religious notions of the Polabian tribes is confirmed.

Resistance against Christianization, or more precisely against the elimination of the native cult organization, acted as the engine of these transformations. By no means did it indicate a questioning of the existence of the Christian *sacrum* by Polabian tribes, which in turn favoured the occurrence of syncretic phenomena or the taking over of particular ideas from the Christian sphere as part of building an effective alternative for this religion.

In the case of the discussed ritual related to fate deities, attention is drawn to the fact that it is not one person who performs the ritual gesture on behalf of the whole community, but rather the chalice over which fortunate or unfortunate fate is besought in the name of gods is circulated among many people. Hence the goal of the ritual was ensuring the participants' good fortune mainly in the personal dimension, which corresponds with the idea of individual salvation or god's providence over particular Christians in their earthly existence. This kind of information was made available as part of basic missionary catechesis, with regard for the hostile role of the devil towards man.

The identification of "Czarnóbog" with the Devil in the Christian environment was fostered by considering both figures as personifications, or sources of misfortunes, as well as their common attribute: the colour black which in the case of the devil evoked chthonic connotations related to him. Thus, a question arises whether the dualistic interpretation of good–evil (god) was connected with the white–black parallel. In other words, is white "by nature" an attribute of a "good god," and finally was he attributed any colours in the Slavic environment, as it is suggested by supporters of the existence of the "white god" ("Białóbog", "Bel Bog")?

For comparison, it is worth observing that in the Scandinavian circle Satan was associated with Odin, who is symbolically associated with darkness. By implication he became an antithesis for Christ, who in turn was attributed with the epithet "White."[284] It is essential that white in the said epithet appeared most probably not due to direct opposition to the evil, Satan, but to emphasize Christ's impeccability and holiness, and at the same time in reference to the

---

284 See *e.g.* Egon Wamers, "Hammer und Kreuz. Typologische Aspekte einer nordeuropäischen Amulettsitte aus der Zeit des Glaubenswechsels," in *Rom und Byzanz im Norden. Mission und Glaubenswechsel im Ostseeraum während des 8.–14 Jahrhunderts*, vol. 1, ed. Michael Müller-Wille (Stuttgart: Steiner, 1997), p. 99.

HELMOLDI CRONICA SLAVORUM ON SLAVIC RELIGION   321

symbolism of baptism.[285] One can thus conclude that the colour white was
associated with Christ without any direct connection to treating them as an
antithesis of Satan/Odin as power of darkness. Similarly, one should take into
account the possibility that the perpetrator of evil presented by Helmold was
associated with black also without relation to the antithesis: white as symbol
of good – black as symbol of evil. So, it seems possible that in the Slavic name
of the originator of good there was no white at all, even if (hypothetically) it
was symbolically associated with him.[286]

Regardless of the solution to this detailed question, it is first of all worth
emphasizing that the example of the diabolization of "Czarnobóg" makes one
realize the occurrence of the trend of "Slavization" of Christian elements in
the spiritual culture of Northern Polabian communities, even at the stage of
attempts to evangelize them. What is more, it should be stressed that among
them it appeared before the final introduction of Christianity in the public
sphere.[287] From this perspective, it would be more accurate to state that it was
not so much "Czarnobóg" that gained the outfit of the devil but more the latter
to be "recognized" in the Polabian environment as a native "god of evil."

To conclude these considerations on the "mirablilis error" of the Slavs in
Helmold's perspective, it is worth emphasizing that the dualistic element in
their beliefs was most certainly of archaic Indo-European heritage, but in the
discussed case, one should take into account the formation of, even if not the

---

285   In this particular context of Old Nordic literature the expression "White" with reference
       to Christ is explained by relation with a white baptismal robe worn by neophytes (see
       e.g. Wolfgang Lange, *Studien zur christlichen Dichtung der Nordgermanen* (Göttingen:
       Vandhoeck & Ruprecht, 1958), pp. 215 f.; commentary of J. Morawiec in: *Saga o Hallfredzie
       skaldzie kłopotliwym*, introd. and trans. Jakub Morawiec (Wrocław: Chronicon, 2011),
       p. 121, footnote 92. For symbolism of white with consideration for baptismal connotations
       (theological significance of washing off sins, receiving eternal salvation) see *e.g.* Forstner,
       Świat, pp. 115 f.
286   This *bonus deus* could have a name related to another characteristic, not the alleged
       white, and an analogy for this can be found in the name Dazbog. In this theonym the
       essential part was the stem "bog" (maybe even without any additional part). However,
       on the other hand, the existence of "Białobóg" cannot in any way be excluded from the
       field of hypotheses. See: Stanisław Rosik, "Jarowit Mars i Czarny Bóg Diabeł. O rozmaitej
       genezie nowych tożsamości słowiańskich bóstw na północnym Połabiu (w kręgu prze-
       kazów z XII wieku)," in *Historia narrat. Studia mediewistyczne ofiarowane Profesorowi
       Jackowi Banaszkiewiczowi*, ed. Andrzej Pleszczyński, Joanna Sobiesiak, Michał Tomaszek,
       Przemysław Tyszka (Lublin: Wydawnictwo UMCS, 2012) pp. 263–275.
287   This situation is not taken into account in the model context of the functioning of the
       so called double-faith in which the occurrence of its phenomena is treated as a response
       of people still attached to paganism to its official abolishment. An analysis of Helmold's
       information supports development of the research questionnaire in the characteristics of
       changes in the religious life of the Old Slavs.

322   CHAPTER 4

ritual itself, then at least the myth related to it, from the 10th–11th c. or the mid-
12th c. at the latest before it was presented in the chronicle. This is supported
by the affiliation of the name "Czarnobóg" (*Zcerneboch*) with the generation
of theonyms created at that time. Soon it was merged into one figure with the
Christian devil by means of *interpretatio Slavica*.

Helmold's intention – continuing the lecture of chapter 52 – was to synthe-
size information on the Slavic cult. After discussing lower-ranking spirits and
tribal gods as well as a pair of deities responsible for fortune, he introduced
to his description a figure which was superior to the aforementioned ones:
"Among multiple Slavic deities Zuantevith, god of Rugians' land, is the greatest
as he is highly effective in his prophecies and in comparison with whom all
other deities are even considered to be semi-gods."[288] It is not the first presentation of Svantevit, the god of the Rans' land, on the pages of the *Chronicle of
the Slavs* as a god which is efficient in granting the oracle. The novelty of this
information lies in the degradation of the other representatives of the pantheon to "semi-gods" (*semidei*).

This exceptional position of the Svantevit was emphasized by Helmold when
he was writing about tributes made to this god: "And from all Slavic provinces
certain amounts of sacrifices were made for him."[289] It should be emphasized
here that these "all Slavic provinces" were an extremely reduced area at that
time, because this remark refers to the followers of the primary religion. "With
an astonishing respect" – the chronicler concludes – "do they treat sanctuaries.
For they do not easily allow to take oaths and do not let the neighbourhood of
sanctuaries to be profaned, even if it belonged to their enemies."[290]

Svantevit's domination over various Slavic deities ("inter multiformia (…)
Slavorum numina") in the perspective of Helmold's narration is not related
to any formal ties inside this pantheon. The significance of the Rans' god resulted from the efficiency of the oracle connected with him ("efficatior in responsis"), *i.e.* the value of hierophany. His supra-tribal authority is confirmed
by tributes coming from "all" Slavic countries. Hence the term "semi-gods,"
referring to all the other deities worshipped there, is a metaphor depreciat-
ing their significance in comparison with the said hegemon and his temple
(this statement is also supported by the appearance of *quasi* before the *semidei*

---

288   Helmold I, 52: "Inter multiformia autem Slavorum numina prepollet Zuantevith, deus
       terrae Rugianorum, utpote efficacior in responsis, cuius intuitu ceteros quasi semideos
       estimabant."

289   *Ibidem*: "Quin et de omnibus Slavorum provinciis statutas sacrificiorum impensas illo
       transmittebant."

290   *Ibidem*: "Mira autem reverentia circa fani diligentiam affecti sunt; nam neque iuramentis
       facile indulgent neque ambitum fani vel in hostibus temerari paciuntur."

HELMOLDI CRONICA SLAVORUM ON SLAVIC RELIGION   323

categorization).[291] The very elevation of the Rans' god to the leading position in the Slavic *sacrum* corresponds with the concept of indicating one "capital of idolatry" for the whole Slavdom borrowed from Adam of Bremen: Rethra and later Rügen–Arkona.

The bloody human offerings made in these main cult centres were, according to sources, the measure of hostility towards Christianity. Helmold mentions that every year one randomly selected Christian was offered to Svantevit in worship.[292] It should be taken into account, however, that this information is possibly based on common opinion about the cruelty of pagans and their hatred for Christianity.

This detailed message corresponds with stereotypical opinion about Slavic cruelty as an innate characteristic (*crudelitas ingenita*)[293] found at the end of the chapter and confirmed by a description of torments inflicted on Christians.[294] The most brutal torture, as is emphasized by the chronicler, was crucifixion. It aimed to jeer and mock the Christian sign of redemption, however he also mentions that this punishment was administered only to perpetrators of the most serious crimes, hence not only to Christians.[295] Thus Witold Hensel claimed that in the case of the Slavs "crucifixion was a customary punishment. Jeering at Christians dying in this way was something secondary,"[296] which seems an optimum solution of the problem discussed here.[297]

2.6   *The Last Ascent and Fall of the Polabian Mission*
The last complete resolution of the cycle of the construction and fall of the Church in Slavdom on the pages of Helmold's chronicle is described in chapters 53–68. Its optimistic beginning is the initiative of Emperor Lothar III,

---

291   One should remember, however, that in further narration Helmold will develop his concepts of the theology of the Slavs and will even find in Svantevit the mysterious "god of gods", see below, pp. 363 ff.

292   Helmold I, 52: "Unde etiam in peculium honoris annuatim hominem Christocolam, quem sors acceptaverit, eidem litare consueverunt".

293   *Ibidem*; cf. Fraesdorff, *Der barbarische Norden*, p. 335.

294   In this description it is possible to find similarity to a list of torments in the letter written by the archbishop Adalgot of Magdeburg from the beginning of the 12th c., calling Saxon lords to fight pagan Slavs; see: *Letter of Adalgot* in: Labuda, *Fragmenty*, vol. 3, p. 235. See also: Pleszczyński, Sobiesiak, Szejgiec, Tomaszek, Tyszka, *Historia communitatem facit*, pp. 189 ff.

295   Helmold I, 52: "Sceleratissimos enim cruci subfigendos autumant."

296   Hensel, *Słowiańszczyzna*, p. 240.

297   The skepticism of Urbańczyk, *Dawni Słowianie*, p. 162, seems excessive, he assumed that human offerings mentioned by Helmold were only public executions of taken hostage enemies. Such offerings and especially with particular attention for Christians in cult centres of Polabians and Rans has more numerous testimonies.

324   CHAPTER 4

who was prompted by Vicelin "to provide a cure of salvation to the Slavs' tribe with divine grace granted him from heaven."[298] In practice the bishop's idea came down to building Segeberg – a stronghold which would ensure peace in the Wagrian country. Also, a church was next built at the foot of the hill on which the fortress stood.[299] In this way Vicelin obtained a missionary outpost and the emperor proved his care for the conversion of pagans. As the founder of the "new cultivation" in the Slavic country he deserved Helmold's special praise.[300]

Lothar's premature death resulted in disorder in the state and unrest in Saxony, which was used by the duke of Wagrians Pribislav to begin the persecution of Christians. His victim was Segeberg and the local missionaries led by Vicelin hid in Faldera.[301] Helmold, to emphasize their missionary vocation and preparation for work among Slavs, quotes a message that even in exile their activity was accompanied by charismatic power (healing and delivering demon-possessed persons) prophesied in the New Testament as signs accompanying the evangelization of the Jews and pagans.[302]

Further narration refers to Saxon matters (chapters 5–58), then the second crusade (1147) and its ideologist, St. Bernard of Clairvaux (chapters 59–61), and finally the Slavic matters. In the centre of Helmold's attention there is the Obodrite duke Niklot and the Saxon expedition against the Polabian Slavs in 1147 (chapters 62–65). Although the crusaders gained prevalence and induced some of the defeated to be baptized, Helmold does not present a positive assessment of the results of this imposed decision. It is emphatically confirmed by the statement that these Slavs were baptized only seemingly: "falso baptizati sunt."[303]

---

298   Helmold I, 53: "Slavorum genti secundum datam sibi celitus potentiam aliquot salutis remedium provideret."
299   *Ibidem.* Cf. Labuda, *Fragmenty*, vol. 3, p. 191; Hoffmann, "Beiträge zur Geschichte der Obodriten," p. 37.
300   Helmold I, 54.
301   *Ibidem*, I, 55.
302   *Ibidem.* The place in the Gospel, *i.e.* Mt 10:8 (see *Helmolda Kronika*, p. 253, footnote 723), mentioned in the editor's comments, one can add also *e.g.* Mc 16:17. A spectacular episode, which was to confirm Vicelinus's spiritual preparation for the mission among the pagans, is a description of an exorcism performed by him – Helmold I, 55. See also Walther Lammers, "Vicelin als Exorzist," in *idem, Vestigia Mediaevalia. Ausgewählte Aufsätze* zur mittelalterlichen *Historiographie, Landes-* und *Kirchengeschichte* (Wiesbaden: Steiner, 1979), pp. 284–302; Strzelczyk, *Apostołowie*, p. 268.
303   Helmold, I, 65. Cf. Kahl, *Heidenfrage und Slawenfrage*, pp. 670–673; Padberg, *Die Christianisierung*, p. 166.

HELMOLDI CRONICA SLAVORUM ON SLAVIC RELIGION   325

In the context of other places in the chronicle in which Helmold affirms the role of secular power as the one that paves the way for mission, it is hard to presume that behind this claim there was a negation of the *ad terrorem, i.e.* military, argument in the propagation of Christianity. It is essential that there was no interest on the side of the Saxon lords in real support for the missionary action among the subdued Slavs. Helmold emphasizes that the crusading ardour incited by Bernard of Clairvaux (chapter 59) was decisively suppressed by economic factors.[304] The war devastated the country and people, who were thought by the Germans to be owned by them.[305] Hence, the very decision of the Slavs to be baptized and allow certain concessions on their side, such as releasing captive Danes, became a sufficient excuse for the crusade participants to finish their military action. This moderate success in Christianization did not satisfy Helmold, and further pages of his chronicle show subsequent obstacles in the development of the missionary work (namely Saxon and Danish problems).

A pessimistic recapitulation of this ascent and fall in the resolution of the wheel of evangelization of the Slavs is a summary presentation of the beginnings of the rule of Henry the Lion (chapter 68), whose expeditions against these peoples, in the chronicler's assessment, were undertaken only for

---

304 For the ideology of the second crusade with a reference to the expedition against the Polabian Slavs in 1147, proclaimed by Bernard of Clairvaux, see Hans-Dietrich Kahl, "Die welweite Bereinigung der Heidenfrage – ein übersehenes Kriegsziel des Zweiten Kreuzzugs," in *Spannungen und Widersprüche. Gedenkschrift für František Graus*, ed. Susanna Burghartz, Hans-Jörg Gilomen, Guy P. Marchal *et al.* (Sigmaringen: Thorbecke, 1992), pp. 63–89. The goal of the crusade in Polabia is outlined very clearly: *ad delendas penitus aut certe convertendas nationes illas*, so until complete extermination or, of course, until the conversion of those nations (*ibidem*, p. 67). See also Padberg, *Die Christianisierung*, pp. 164 ff.; Skovgaard-Petersen, "Wendenzüge – Kreuzzüge," pp. 279 f.

305 Helmold, I, 65: "Dixerunt autem satellites ducis nostri et marchinis Adelberti adinvicem: Nonne terra, quam devastamus, terra nostra est, et populus noster est? Quare igitur invenimur hostes nostrimet et dissipatores vectigalium nostrorum? Nonne iactura haec redundat in dominos nostros?" ("For the servants of our duke and margrave Adalbert spoke among themselves: Is the land that we destroy not ours, and are those people not our people? Then why do we stand as enemies against ourselves and why do we waste our own tributes? Will this harm not reach our lords?"). A lack of conformity between crusade ideals and realistic Saxon politics in 1147 is discussed by Hans-Dietrich Kahl, "Wie kam es 1147 zum >>Wendenkreuzung<<?," in *Europa Slavica – Europa Orientalis. Festschrift für Herbert Ludat zum 70. Geburtstag*, ed. Klaus-Detlev Grothusen, Klaus Zernack, (Giessener Abhandlungen zur Agrar- und Wirtschaftsforschung des Europäischen Ostens) 100 (Berlin: Duncker & Humblot, 1980), pp. 286–296, especially 294 f.; *idem*, "Die welweite Bereinigung," pp. 88 (cf. Skovgaard-Petersen, "Wendenzüge – Kreuzzüge," pp. 282 f.). Kahl emphasizes the existence of spiritual opposition of the crusade: Premonstratensians and Bishop Anselm of Havelberg defied the violence and radicalism of the Cistercians.

326   CHAPTER 4

financial benefits without any attempts to introduce Christianity: "In various expeditions that the young man undertook to Slavdom only money was mentioned but Christianity not even once."[306] While the Slavs "still used to worship various deities and not God, and they violently assault the lands of the Danes."[307]

General information about the Slavic cult is closed here in a biblical formula stating that pagans made offerings not to God but to deities or demons (*demonia*).[308] This theological qualification corresponds with a message about pagan pirate raids of Denmark, and so it is emphasized that neglecting Christianization brings negative consequences, including temporary ones. Simultaneously there appears a topical connection in the presentation of Polabian and seaside Slavs which joins idolatry (*i.e.* the cult of demons or deities) with piracy.[309]

This passage breaks the sinusoid of ascents and falls of the missionary action in Polabia in Helmold's narration.

2.7   *Towards Lasting Success of the Missionary Action*

In the times known to Helmold from his own experience, there was a gradual yet final breakthrough in the Christianization of Northern Polabia which started in the mid-12th c. The end of the story about these events coincides with the end of the first book of the *Chronicle of the Slavs*, which is determined by a reference to the death of the bishop of Starigard Gerold (1163). This was the moment when Helmold originally planned to finish his work and it is essential that it was going to end in an optimistic atmosphere resulting from the author's conviction about achieving the lasting success of the presented mission.[310] The success did not come easily, which was shown by the chronicler focusing on achievements of particular characters, both clerics – archbishop Hartwig and the bishops of Starigard Vicelin and Gerold – and secular ones – Henry the Lion and count Adolf II of Holstein. A lot of the chronicler's attention was devoted to the Slavic duke, Niklot.[311] The presentation of these events brings the richest material in the whole of Helmold's work to conduct research on the religion of the Slavs.

---

306   Helmold I, 68: "In variis autem expeditionibus, quas adhuc adolescens in Slaviam profectus exercuit, nulla de Christianitate fuit mentio, sed tantum de pecunia."

307   *Ibidem*: "adhuc inmolabant demoniis et non Deo et agebat piraticas incursaciones in terram Danorum."

308   Cf. 1 Cor 10:19–20.

309   See below, pp. 328, 372.

310   For the matter of circumstances accompanying the creation of the second book of Helmold's chronicle, see pp. 263, 355 f.

311   See Strzelczyk, "Wstęp," pp. 32 f.

HELMOLDI CRONICA SLAVORUM ON SLAVIC RELIGION 327

2.7.1   Vicelin and Prove's Cult in Starigard
At the threshold of the narrative about the final eradication of the public native cult in Polabia, Helmold devoted his attention to the archbishop of Hamburg Hartwig (1148–1168) who using the coming peace in Slavdom decided to rebuild bishoprics there in Starigard/Oldenburg, Ratibor, and Mechlin/Mecklenburg.[312] They were annihilated by the *furor barbaricus*,[313] however – from the theological perspective of Helmold – this occurred as a consequence of human sins.[314] Bishops appointed in 1149 had to act "in the land of poverty and hunger, where there were the abode of Satan and the habitat of the evil spirit."[315] It is hard not to connect these formulas taken from the Book of Revelation[316] with the stereotypical perception of paganism.

In the creation of the image of Vicelin, the new bishop of Starigard, the image of the country of "poverty and hunger" acquires special significance in the context of stories about economic hardships which had to be faced at the beginning of his pontificate.[317] However, one can already see in this perspective a religious prejudice: the rule of Satan and evil spirits is outlined here as a contradiction of the heavenly, ample, and rich land. It was hard to feel safe in such a land. This image also demonstrates the emotional attitude towards paganism and locates it in the cultural and civilizational context of *barbaricum*.

Hence, when Vicelin reached Starigard he was welcomed by the "barbarian inhabitants of this land." In his presentation of them, the chronicler mentions that their god was Prove.[318] His cult – by default considered as superstition

---

312   For Hartwig see Bernd Schneidmüller, "Hartwig," in *Lexikon des Mittelalters*, vol. 4 (München/Zürich: Artemis, 1989), col. 1947.

313   Helmold I, 69: "quia pax erat in Sclavia, proposuit reedificare episcopales, quas barbaricus furror olim destruxerat in Sclavia". Cf. Scior, *Das Eigene und das Fremde*, p. 212; Fraesdorff, *Der barbarische Norden*, pp. 335 f.

314   Helmold I, 69: "permittente Deo propter peccata hominum".

315   *Ibidem*: "in terram egestatis et famis, ubi erat sedes Sathanae et habitatio omnis spiritus inmundi".

316   Cf. Rev 2:13; 18:2. See also Fraesdorff, *Der barbarische Norden*, p. 323.

317   The Saxon duke Henry the Lion decided that allowing a stipend for the newly appointed bishop would depend on acceptance of investiture from him. Initially under the influence of his metropolitan bishop, Vicelinus objected this request assuming that Henry usurped for himself competences of the emperor himself. However, finally he gave in to the pressure of the duke. Even earlier, however, although he was devoid of tithe, he visited the territory subordinated to him and gave sermons. See Helmold I, 69. Cf. Labuda, *Fragmenty*, vol. 3, p. 192; Strzelczyk, *Apostołowie*, p. 269; Scior, *Das Eigene und das Fremde*, pp. 156, 158 ff.

318   Helmold I, 69: "receptus est a barbaris habitatoribus terrae illius, quorum deus erat Prove".

328   CHAPTER 4

(*superstitio*) – was led by a priest called Mike.[319] This confirms earlier information on the appointment of priests that served particular gods who were patrons of communities or tribal territories.[320] However, the main support of the
local idolatry was first of all a ruler called Rochel, Kruto's descendant, who was
tellingly labeled "ydolatra et pirata maximus."[321] This expression shows a stereotypical connection in the characteristics of the fundamentals of the Baltic
Slavs' attitudes to idolatry with piracy.[322]

In the description of the missionary action undertaken by Vicelin there is information about encouraging barbarians to abandon their idols, in which one
can find a conventional indication of the contradiction of the cult of Christ.[323]
Pagans themselves are shown in this context as rebels. Hence, Helmold blames
the Saxon dukes for the poor results of evangelization as they were not willing to use force to tame the "hearts of rebels."[324] It is not accidental then that
count Adolf II was described with such recognition in the chronicle.

2.7.2   Count Adolf II and the Struggle with Idolatry
In the story about the expedition of count Adolf II of Holstein and the Obodrite
duke Niklot against the Kessinians and Circipanians in 1151, Helmold not only
mentions the devastation of this hostile land by "fire and sword," but also the
demolition of "the sanctuary (...) the most famous with idols and all kinds of
superstition."[325] In the light of this information, the term *superstitio* encompasses all cult rituals abolished with the liquidation of the temple, hence also

---

319   *Ibidem*: "... nomen flaminis, qui preerat superstitioni eorum, erat Mike". It is possible that
       "Mike" is Nicholas, see Urbańczyk, *Dawni Słowianie*, p. 186.
320   Cf. Helmold I, 52.
321   Leciejewicz, *Słowianie*, p. 219.
322   For more information see pp. 326, 372.
323   Helmold I, 69: "Cepit igitur pontifex Dei proponere barbaris viam veritatis, quae Christus
       est, adhortans eos, ut relictis ydolis suis festinarent ad lavacrum regenerationis" ("So the
       God's priest began to reveal the barbarians the way of truth, which is Christ, and en-
       couraged them to give up their idols, and to rush to the bath of regeneration" [*i.e.* to the
       baptism]).
324   Helmold I, 69: "Pauci autem Slavorum applicaverunt se fidei ..." ("Not many among the
       Slavs joined the faith ..."). A certain success mentioned in this place of the chronicle
       was the erection of the wooden church as a missionary centre near a fair frequented by
       crowds of people from Starigard every Sunday.
325   Helmold, 71: "fanum [...] celeberrimum cum ydolis et omni superstitione". J. Strzelczyk in:
       Helmolda Kronika, p. 297, footnote 902, emphasizes that it is not Rethra, hence maybe it
       is Iarovit's temple in Wolgast. However, a more convincing statement was given by Lech
       Leciejewicz, *Miasta Słowian północnopołabskich* (Wrocław: Ossolineum, 1968), p. 63, who
       hypothetically located the fanum of the Kessinians and Circipanians in Kessin.

HELMOLDI CRONICA SLAVORUM ON SLAVIC RELIGION   329

the idol cult. The legitimacy of this interpretation is confirmed by analogy by
the occurrence of the *superstitiones ydolatriae* phrase in another part of the
chronicle – which also praised Adolf for his endeavours to eradicate paganism
and introduce Christianity.[326]

On the basis of these examples, it should be emphasized that in the perspective of Helmold's narration *superstitio* has superior significance in respect
to idolatry, and another thing which must be emphasized is a strong connection between cult of idols and paganism. Idolatry is considered in this case
as an identification sign of pagan religion. Thus it is not accidental that even
to the superfluously christianized Nordalbingia, Helmold attributed only the
"manifold error of the superstitions": the cult of groves, springs, and other superstitions, while he kept quiet about idolatry.[327] Admittedly, the chronicler
managed to see in it more than only respect paid to statues – *e.g. permaxima
ydolatria* means trading on the market instead of going to church on Sunday –
but not in a missionary context.[328]

Regarding the struggle against idolatry, count Adolf is presented on the
pages of the *Chronicle of the Slavs* mainly as an enemy of paganism and a
defender of the Christians. His expedition with Niklot against the Liutici in
1151 resulted in peace in the Obodrite land.[329] Furthermore, in the second of
the above mentioned references about him, he gained the name of a "Lord's
fighter" not only because of the eradication of idolatry, but also as a promoter
of Christianization. He laid down his life in struggle because of his "love for
virtues," gaining the eternal reward (*palma*) as he was faithful to the superior power and defended his homeland.[330] Therefore Helmold created him as

---

326   Helmold II, 101.

327   Helmold I, 47: "Nam lucorum et fontium ceterarumque superstitionum multiplex error
        apud eos habetur." This does not mean, however, that there were no cult of idols there as
        an element of unofficial religiousness following the model indicated in Thietmar's story
        about Hennil, see above pp. 161 ff.

328   Helmold I, 95. As long as idolatry is not only a metaphor here.

329   Helmold, I, 71: "pax in terra Wagirorum, acepitque per gratiam Dei novella plantatio sen-
        sim incrementum."

330   Helmold II, 101: "unus de bellatoribus Domini et certe non infimus in funiculo sortis suae
        utilis inventus est, extirpans ydolatriae superstitiones et faciens opus novae plantacionis,
        quod fructificet in salutem. Novissime peracto boni itineris cursu pervenit ad palmam
        portansque vexilla in castris Domini stetit pro defensione patriae et fide principum usque
        ad mortem." Similarly the efforts of his sons for the conversion of the Slavs were defined
        by the chronicler: "ut suscitaretur cultus domus Dei nostri in gente incredula et ydolatra"
        ("to begin a cult of our God among the infidel and idolatrous tribe"), see: *ibidem.*

330   CHAPTER 4

an achiever of chivalric ideals in the crusade epoch. Furthermore, in a wider
context of this work he appears to be an achiever of the ideal of cooperation
between the secular authorities and the Church, following the model indicated at the beginning of the chronicle by Charlemagne.

2.7.3   Helmold on a Journey with Gerold – a Treasury of Knowledge on
         Polabian Religion

Valuable information about the religion of the Slavs was provided by Helmold
based on his experiences. Travelling with Bishop Gerold and his brother
Conrad, at that time an abbot of Riddagshausen, after leaving the court of the
Wagrian duke Pribislav on 8 January 1156, they headed towards the house of
one of the Slavic magnates called Tesimir and came across a forest (*nemus*).
There, surrounded by the oldest trees, they saw holy oaks dedicated to Prove,
the god of "that land":

> It had happened that on the way we arrived at a grove which was the
> only one it this country as the whole area is flat. This is where in be-
> tween the old trees we saw the sacred oaks devoted to the god of the
> lands, named Prove; these were surrounded by a courtyard [*atrium*] and
> a dense wooden fence into which two gates led. Besides the penates and
> idols worshiped widely across particular settlements, this place was sa-
> cred for the whole country – it had its priest, its feasts and various sacrifi-
> cial rituals. This is also where every Monday the inhabitants of the whole
> country gathered together with the ruler [*regulus*] and the priest to
> hold trials.[331]

---

331   Helmold I, 84: "Accidit autem, ut in transitu veniremus in nemus, quod unicum est in
      terra illa, tota enim in planiciem sternitur. **Illic** inter vetustissimas arbores vidimus sacras
      quercus, quae dicatae fuerant deo terrae illius Proven, quas ambiebat atrium et sepes
      accuratior lignis constructa, continens duas portas. Preter penates enim et ydola, quibus
      singula oppida redundabant, locus ille sanctimonium fuit universae terrae, cui flamen et
      feriaciones et sacrificiorum varii ritus deputati fuerant. **Illic** omni secunda feria populus
      terrae cum regulo et flamine convenire solebant propter iudicia". The word *illic* is in bold
      here as it will be necessary in further analysis, see below, p. 336.

HELMOLDI CRONICA SLAVORUM ON SLAVIC RELIGION   331

Oaks in the Indo-European cultural sphere were a highly attractive hierophany[332] and were related with thunder-wielding heavenly creatures.[333] This evokes an analogy especially to the cult of Slavic Perun. It is worth mentioning that in the so-called Szczecin (Stettin) manuscript of Helmold's chronicle there is an alternative version of spelling the theonym Prove as *Prone*,[334] which is closer to Perun.[335] The occurrence of a different version of this name can be easily explained by a paleographic error.[336] In this situation a hypothetical

---

332   Moszyński, *Kultura*, pp. 527 f., emphasized the priority of the oak over other trees worshipped by the Slavs, which similarly to the cult of trees as such was of Indo-European heritage in their religion, which was ascertained already by James George Frazer, *The Golden Bough. A Study of Magic and Religion* (Abridged Ed. 1922, Adelaide: University of Adelaide, https://ebooks.adelaide.edu.au/f/frazer/james/golden/chapter15.html), chapter 15: *The Worship of the Oak*. For comparison, it is worth mentioning that Herbord (II, 32) confirmed that in Szczecin (Stettin), at the time of Otto of Bamberg's mission, there was an enormous oak with a bubbling spring next to it ("quercus ingens et frondosa, et fons subter eam amenissimus"). The credibility of this information is disputable (see Rosik, *Conversio*, pp. 271–274), however, it is essential that in this case even a very general conviction that the so called barbarians practiced a cult of the oak. The information about the spring in this context evokes a mythical vision of a tree in the centre of the world related also with the notion of a cosmic mountain, see Gieysztor, *Mitologia*, p. 152. Similarly in Lithuania at the time of Christianization in the 15th c., according to Aeneas Sylvius Piccolomini's account, the oldest oak in a forest was considered an abode of the deity, *ibidem*, pp. 89 f.

333   In Rus' according to Old Russian writing, oak forests were to be hierophanies of the thunder deity (Gieysztor, *Mitologia*, p. 91). It is worth mentioning that Perun was worshiped in Veliky Novgorod in the place called Perynia – *ibidem*, p. 53 ff.; Rybakov, *Jazyčestvo drevnej Rusi*, pp. 210, 252–258; cf. Leciejewicz, ">>In Pago," p. 129. Similarly the Balts worshiped the oak as a tree of the thunder deity called Perkun (from 'perk-', 'herk-'; comp. Lat. 'quercus'). Starting the cult fire in Lithuania by rubbing oak trees against grey stones was still mentioned in the 17th c. (see Gieysztor, *Mitologia*, pp. 86 f.). This evokes an association with a conviction well known in old communities that oak wood attracts thunders much better than other types of wood and exactly this characteristic is taken into account as an explanation of the genesis of its cult. On the basis of research on folklore, Moszyński, *Kultura*, p. 528, doubted, however, that the Slavs knew about these properties of oaks.

334   The version *Prone* is contained in the so called Szczecin (Stettin) manuscript of Helmold's work – see a commentary in: *Helmolda Kronika*, p. 244, footnote 678.

335   According to this concept, Prove, worshiped in an oak grove, was the major god which was a mutation or hypostasis of Perun or even identified with him (if one assumes that the *Prone* version is original). See Gieysztor, *Mitologia*, p. 91; Leciejewicz, ">>In Pago," p. 129; Szafrański, *Prahistoria*, pp. 381, 412. Cf. Kulišić, *Stara Slovenska religija*, pp. 68, 163 ff.; Eliade, *A History*, vol. 3, pp. 30 f.

336   Urbańczyk, *Dawni Słowianie*, pp. 115, 186 f.; Łowmiański, *Religia*, p. 219; cf. Niederle, *Život*, p. 98. Moszyński, *Die vorchristliche Religion*, p. 71, assumed that Prove's prototype was

332   CHAPTER 4

attribution of the rule over thunder to the Wagrian deity first of all should be
based on the dedication of sacred oaks to it.

As it seems to result from the quoted passage they grew in an atrium (*atrium*) surrounded by a tight-knit wooden fence, in which there were two gates.[337]
Their front parts were covered with ornaments, whose counterparts were indicated in analogous sacral decorations (also Christian) discovered in the northwest of Slavdom.[338] These ornaments must have not only had aesthetic value
but also symbolized the presence of magical forces that guarded the sanctuary,[339]
which in this case was a fenced cultic grove (*lucus*).[340] Worshipping these
kinds of holy places was confirmed by Helmold in summary remarks about the
religion of the Slavs. An important analogy in this case was Thietmar's information about the "Holy Grove" (*Zutibure*).[341] The cult of groves played a special
role in the religion of the Balts, which should be emphasized due to temporal
and geographic closeness of this analogy.[342]

On the basis of the quoted passage, operationally one should also take into
account the possibility that it was not an atrium (*atrium*) to be surrounded by
a fence (*sepes*), but only the oaks. Then this *atrium* would mean a clearing on
which there was a wooden fence around holy trees. However, the hypothesis

---

Celtic Borvo (cf. *idem*, "Staropołabski teonim," p. 39), however, he did not present any convincing circumstances of this borrowing – see Bednarczuk, "W co wierzyli Prasłowianie?,"
p. 26.

337   See Słupecki, *Slavonic Pagan Sanctuaries*, p. 161.

338   According to Werner Neugebauer, "Der Burgwall Alt-Lübeck, Geschichte, Stand und
Aufgaben," *Offa* 21/22 (1964/1965), p. 223, il. 51, 52, Helmold used this phrase, on the basis
of his experience, associating it with decorations known to him from cathedral doors,
such as the ones discovered in Old Lübeck; the same Hensel, *Słowiańszczyzna*, p. 245.
Ornaments could be anthropomorphic – realistic (like in Behren-Lübchin) or more schematic (like in Gross Raden) – and geometrical ones.

339   See *e.g.* Hensel, *Słowiańszczyzna*, p. 493.

340   Helmold I, 84: "Venientibus autem nobis ad **nemus** illud et profanacionis locum adhortatus est nos episcopus, ut valenter accederemus ad destruendum **lucum**" [emphasis –
S.R.]. Therefore Gerold's companions came to the forest (*nemus*) and "the desecration
place" (certainly due to the pagan cult), and after bishop's encouragement, they started
to destroy the cult grove (*lucus*). Hence the fence determined strict borders of this sacred place, which, by the way, perfectly corresponds with the etymology of the Slavic
word "gaj" (grove) – where one can hear the verb 'gajiti', 'gaić', *i.e.* 'ogradzać' (fence), see
Gieysztor, *Mitologia*, p. 221. Rytter, "O badaniach," p. 133, makes it more precise and claims
that "gaj" was a prat of space in the forest which was ritually extracted as a place where
old ancestors stayed. Cf. Szafrański, *Prahistoria*, p. 321.

341   Thietmar also used the word *lucus* to refer to the holy grove, see above, pp. 145 ff.

342   There are testimonies from the 13th c., of Petrus Dusburg, see: Piotr z Dusburga, *Kronika
ziemi pruskiej*, ed. Jarosław Wenta, Sławomir Wyszomirski, MPH n.s. 13 (Kraków: Polska
Akademia Umiejętności, 2007), III, 52.

HELMOLDI CRONICA SLAVORUM ON SLAVIC RELIGION   333

that there was a fence around the atrium is supported by information found
later in the text about the "fence of the atrium" (*septa atrii*), which importantly
was destroyed by bishop Gerold and his companions after they broke the gates
and entered the *atrium*: "He jumped off the horse and smashed adorned fronts
of the gates himself. Then we entered the courtyard, took down the wooden
fence and piled it up in one place around the sacred trees to form a bonfire
stack ..."[343] Therefore if gates led to the atrium, it seems most accurate to assume that its palisade (*septa atrii*) should be identified with a fence (*sepes*), in
which the gates were assembled.[344]

The grove described by Helmold was probably located four kilometers away
from Starigard on a hill later called Wienberg near Putlos.[345] It was most certainly a religious centre, not only for the region of Starigard but also for the
whole Wagrian territory ("universa terra").[346] This view is supported by an earlier collation of Prove with Siwa and Redigast,[347] who appeared as patrons of
the two tribes: Polabians and Obodrites. The sanctuary was also most certainly
one of the poles of political and religious power in the tribal ecumene, much
like Starigard.[348] This stronghold dominated the flat area surrounding it, as it
was located on a hill which was about a dozen meters high. From the end of
the 7th c. to the 12th c., apart from the duke's abode, there also existed a pre-
Christian cult centre.[349]

---

343   Helmold I, 84: "Ipse quoque desiliens equo contrivit de conto insignes portarum frontes,
      et ingressi atrium omnia septa atrii congessimus circum sacras illas arbores et de strue
      lignorum iniecto igne fecimus pyram ..."
344   This is also why it seems rather improbable that in the opinion of the chronicler there
      were two fences: *sepes* around the oaks with one gate and *septa* around the *atrium*
      with the second gate. Although such ideas were also taken into account, see Leszek P.
      Słupecki, "Sanktuaria w świecie natury u Słowian i Germanów. Święte gaje i ich bogowie,"
      in *Człowiek, sacrum, środowisko. Miejsca kultu we wczesnym średniowieczu*, ed. Sławomir
      Moździoch (Spotkania Bytomskie) 4 (Wrocław: Werk, 2000), p. 42.
345   Leciejewicz, ">>In Pago," 128. For the role of Starigard in the Obodrite land, see *idem*,
      "Główne problem," p. 178; *idem*, *Miasta Słowian*, pp. 51–53, and according to the index.
346   Leciejewicz, ">>*In Pago*," p. 128.
347   Helmold I, 52 – see below, pp. 306 ff.
348   Banaszkiewicz, "Jedność porządku," *passim*; *idem*, *Polskie dzieje*, pp. 414 f.
349   In this place there was also a church erected in the 10th c. and destroyed by returning
      native religion in the 11th c. See: Ingo Gabriel, Torsten Kempke, *Starigard/Oldenburg.
      Hauptburg der Slawen in Wagrien VI. Die Grabfunde. Einführung und archäologisches
      Material*, (Offa-Bücher) 85 (Neumünster: Wachholtz, 2011); cf. Felix Biermann, "Rezension:
      I. Gabriel, T. Kempke, Starigard/Oldenburg. Hauptburg der Slawen in Wagrien VI. Die
      Grabfunde (Neumünster 2011)," *Prähistorische Zeitschrift* 87 (2012), pp. 208–210; and also:
      Ingo Gabriel, "Strukturwandel in Starigard/Oldenburg während der zweiten Hälfte des
      10. Jahrhunderts auf Grund archäologischer Befunde: Slawische Fürstenherrschaft, otton-
      ischer Bischofssitz, heidnische Gegenbewegung," *Zeitschrift für Archäologie*18, (1984) 1,

334   CHAPTER 4

Helmold's claim that the sanctuary with Prove's oaks was related to the place where judgements were made at assemblies taking place "every Monday" has been widely discussed by scholars. According to A. Brückner this information constitutes evidence of a misunderstanding as a result of which the name of the deity was erroneously formed with reference to judgment (law – Slavic 'prawo').[350] This extremely skeptical position did not gain general acceptance of researchers of the Slavic religion.[351] The conflux of the name Prove and the word "prawo" (law) was taken into account as a premise for considering this theonym as a nickname concealing sanctity (taboo), and formed in connection with making judgments near his cult oaks.[352]

It should also be emphasized that the Starigard god appeared on the pages of the chronicle two more times with the same name, which proves that Helmold knew it well. Moreover, he wrote about Prove's cult on the basis of his own experience related to its elimination. The importance of the personal experience of the chronicler in the assessment of his credibility was appreciated by Karol Modzelewski, who assumed that researchers' skepticism related to the information about the deity resulted from prejudice about the substantial value of the discussed passage, which in any case were not groundless.[353]

The information about judgements made during the mass meeting "every Monday" ("omni secunda feria") has often raised doubts. A. Brückner considered this information as "a misunderstanding typical of Helmold,"[354] which

---

pp. 63–80; *idem*, "Starigard/Oldenburg im 11. und 12. Jahrhundert: neue Strukturelemente im Gessellschaft und Kultur," in *Miasto zachodniosłowiańskie w XI–XII wieku. Społeczeństwo – kultura*, ed. Lech Leciejewicz (Wrocław: Ossolineum 1991), pp. 169–188; see also above p. 148, footnote 478. Certainly this cult place should be related to the figure of "Saturn", mentioned by Widukind, and robbed by the conquerors of Starigard in 967 (see above, pp. 54 f.).

350   Brückner, *Mitologia słowiańska i polska*, p. 45; cf. Urbańczyk, *Dawni Słowianie*, pp. 46, 154, 187.

351   See Strzelczyk, *Mity*, p. 165.

352   Łowmiański, *Religia*, p. 183. With literary fervour Ackenheil, *Gottheiten*, p. 33, imagined even an invocation "Oh holy law!", which would provide a substitute name for the god. It is worth paying attention in these investigations that in the 11th and 12th c. in Polabia and Pomerania a new generation of divine names appeared (not necessarily new deities). Except for commonly occurring theonyms ending with "-vit" there was Triglav, whose name was connected with the shape of his statue. It is hard to exclude the possibility that such "deification" was applied to the law, but this is only speculation.

353   Karol Modzelewski, "Omni secunda feria. Księżycowe roki i nieporozumienia wokół Helmolda," in *Słowiańszczyzna w Europie średniowiecznej. Księga pamiątkowa dla Lecha Leciejewicza*, vol. 1: *Plemiona i wczesne państwa*, ed. Zofia Kurnatowska (Wrocław: IAE PAN, 1996), pp. 83 f., 87.

354   Brückner, *Mitologia słowiańska i polska*, p. 200.

HELMOLDI CRONICA SLAVORUM ON SLAVIC RELIGION   335

H. Łowmiański in turn tried to explain using an anachronism: the rituals usual
for the state epoch, that is the alleged regular judgments every Monday, were
transferred to the tribal organisation.[355] However, it is hard to accuse the
chronicler, who maintained good contacts with Polabian people, of imputing them with customs that cannot be confirmed in this case by appropriate
source testimony.[356]

This is why that, in this case, K. Modzelewski's hypothesis deserves special
attention. It is based on the conviction that not earlier than at the time of "the
monarch's jurisdiction," which had at its disposal instruments of social extortion, could it afford to set the date of a trial arbitrarily. Nonetheless "the judicial
system of the tribal epoch had the nature of an assembly (veche), hence it required the presence of a large number of people, who are normally dispersed,
to gather in a certain place and at a certain time. Additionally, it was hard to
send out word every time to call them. Hence not only the place but also days
of these gatherings had to be set in advance, *i.e.* they had to be regular according to the account of time adopted by the society."[357] Assuming that before the
adoption of the Christian calendar the Slavs measured time with the lunar calendar, Modzelewski concluded that by mistake Helmold connected the new
moon (or the full moon) with the expression "lunar day" (lunedi, Montag) used
to refer to Monday in folk Latin and Germanic languages, which resulted in
attributing to Slavs weekly trials conducted on Mondays. Most certainly the
Wagrians had their judgments made after the new or full moon.[358]

Emphasis on the presence of a priest at this meeting indicates a religious
sanction of the order and the peace of the assembly (veche).[359] In the source
there is no information about an oracle, however by analogy one should take
into account its presence in this place.[360] A question also arises of where

355   Łowmiański, *Religia*, p. 183.
356   H. Łowmiański's way of thinking has the "vicious circle" nature (*petitio principii*), because
       there is no confirmation of the proposed speculation related to other premises indicating
       that in the Christian environment in which Helmold lived, judgements were made on
       Mondays apart from the analysed source about this custom attributed to (not Christian)
       Slavs.
357   Modzelewski, "Omni secunda feria," p. 86.
358   *Ibidem*, p. 87.
359   This role of priests at the assemblies is typical not only of the Slavs – even Tacitus,
       Germania, 11, mentioned that among Germanic tribes priests took care of the assembly
       agenda, see Modzelewski, "Omni secunda feria," p. 85; see also Banaszkiewicz, "Otto z
       Bambergu," *passim*.
360   For comparison it is worth mentioning descriptions of oracles in temples in Radogošč,
       Arkona or Szczecin see pp. 128 ff., 277, 361, 364 f., and VP II, 11; Herbord II, 33; see also:
       Rosik, *Conversio*, pp. 268–271.

336   CHAPTER 4

exactly this judicial meeting was held, especially if one takes into consideration a consolidated view in the scholarly debate that it took place in the said atrium surrounded by a fence. However, it is hard to combine this idea with a further claim made by Helmold that access to the so determined sacred space was offered only to priests and people who wanted to make offerings or to use this place as a life-saving asylum.[361] In this situation K. Modzelewski even stated that the deliberations of the assembly were preceded by a collective offering that allowed all the gathered people to enter the sanctuary.[362]

It seems more justifiable to reconsider the validity of a view assuming that the meeting was held in the said *atrium*. In this case the most important issue is the interpretation of the word *illic* in the expression: "Illic omni secunda feria populus terrae cum regulo et flamine convenire solebant propter iudicia," which precedes the information about the limited access to the sanctuary.[363] It is rather probable that the said "there" (*illic*) does not refer to the very cult grove (*lucus*), but to the whole forest (*nemus*), in which it was located. This explanation is fostered by the appearance of the word *illic* earlier in the same passage, and then it refers to *nemus* and, which is essential, also the way the narration was arranged allowed the assumption that this second use of *illic* in this passage also referred to this forest.[364]

The key element in the interpretation of the presented description is the differentiation of meanings of *nemus* and *lucus*, which – especially because of the currently popular Polish translation of the text, in which both terms were translated into one word: "gaj" (grove)[365] – at the current stage of discussion on the topography of Prove's sanctuary is no longer so obvious. As a result, both of these words – *lucus* and *nemus* – in the discussed passage referred to one and the same forest complex. The solution proposed here, however, assumes that judgements were made in the *nemus*, forest, probably on a clearing, near the sanctuary with oaks (*lucus*) surrounded by a palisade. If meetings were connected with offerings, it is possible to assume that access to the sanctuary was allowed only for selected representatives of the assembly.

---

361   Helmold I, 84, p. 159 f. "Ingressus atrii omnibus inhibitus nisi sacerdoti tantum et sacrificare volentibus, vel quos mortis urgebat periculum, his enim minime negabatur asilum." ("Entrance to atrium was prohibited to all except for the priest, those who wished to make a sacrifice and to those who feared for their lives as those were never denied asylum"). Cf. Gieysztor, *Mitologia*, p. 223.

362   Modzelewski, *Barbarzyńska Europa*, p. 375.

363   See above, p. 330 and footnote 331.

364   See above footnote 340 in this chapter.

365   *Helmolda Kronika*, p. 330.

HELMOLDI CRONICA SLAVORUM ON SLAVIC RELIGION 337

The context of the above interpretation is in harmony with the information about asylum granted in the holy space. In this way, a criminal threatened with death or accused of a crime could safely await his sentence passed by the assembly. This is indicated in further words of the chronicler alluding to vile deeds of Christians, such as defiling holy places with crime: "For such respect do Slavs have for their sacred things that they do not allow the neighborhood of the shrine to be stained by blood, even of enemies."[366] Similarly, one can read a later observation of the chronicler as an attempt to stigmatize customs of his own environment by setting an example of the barbarians: "They can hardly agree to take oaths, because for the Slavs taking an oath in a way means perjury as it provokes gods' revenge."[367]

The motif of reluctance to take oaths also occurred in chapter 52 of *Chronica Slavorum*. However, the information about it is not completely compatible with Helmold's claim that the Slavs swore by stones, springs, or trees.[368] Although reluctance to take oaths does not mean that they were completely forbidden, it does lead to a doubt about why Slavs would take oaths at all if it could incur the gods' wrath. It is possible to assume that the chronicler was a bit inconsistent here in his views, but it is worth making an attempt to explain this dissonance by referring to the pragmatic values of the narrative. The information about the gods' wrath (absent when reluctance to take oaths was mentioned earlier) could appear exactly for the purpose of setting an example of the right behaviour for Christians. The chronicler's intention was, most certainly, to show that even the barbarians are moderate about squandering oaths for fear of gods' wrath. It was implied to be contrary to the overuse of ceremonious forms of giving promises that was common among Christians.[369]

It is worth noting the possibility that an element in the Slavic culture which was a pretext for the introduction to the work the view about the said gods' wrath was the very fact that oaths were sworn by stones, trees, or springs.[370] This

---

366 Helmold 1, 84: "Tantam enim sacris suis Slavi exhibent reverentiam, ut ambitum fani nec in hostibus sanguine pollui sinant".

367 Helmold 1, 84: "Iuraciones difficillime admittunt, nam iurare apud Slavos quasi periurare est ob vindicem deorum iram."

368 Helmold 1, 84. The context of the information about these practices is important, namely emphasis on a ban imposed on the converted people, which indicates that they were not rare. See below, pp. 322, 354 f.

369 J. Strzelczyk w: *Helmolda Kronika*, p. 330, footnote 1010.

370 Łowmiański, *Religia*, pp. 235 f., in the discussion on this information, he ascertained that according to the Slavs, their gods showed indifference to human sins; in this imagery, gods were not interested in the fact of breaking oaths, but only in showing faithfulness to gods themselves. This is why the Slavs swore by trees, stones and sources not to offend gods. This association is quite distant from the content of the source.

338   CHAPTER 4

particular selection of elements of nature – and not supernatural creatures –
as guarantors of the given word could be the basis for speculation by either the
chronicler or his informer that according to the Slavs, gods deprecated oaths.

In his following summary, Helmold develops motifs started earlier in chapter 52 of his chronicle: "The Slavs have various idolatry manner as not all of
them agree on one form of superstition. For some of them [*i.e.* deities] are
given sophisticated shapes of divine statues in sanctuaries, such as the idol of
Plön named Podaga, while other inhabit forests and groves, like Prove, the god
of Aldenburg, whose images are never depicted. Some [of the gods'] sculptures
are given two or even more heads."[371] The notion of *ydolatria* occurred here as
a synonym of pagan religion.[372] Moreover, the variety of cults related to statues
was expressed in their polycephalism.

The existence of this phenomenon, sometime earlier in the opinion of
hypercritical scholars such as E. von Wienecke, was a typical pure invention
dictated by Christian interpretation of the Slavic religion.[373] Yet now it is not
contested, especially since there are archaeological testimonies confirming it.
It is worth emphasizing that a polemic with E. von Wienecke's theses was undertaken soon after he announced them, only on the basis of written sources.[374]
The hagiographies of St. Otto of Bamberg are the oldest group of sources that
provide information about the polycephalism of Western Slavic cult statues.
They offer testimony that the cult of three-headed Triglav was concentrated
in the temple in Szczecin.[375] Similarly, in the first half of the 12th c., a statue of
this deity was kept in Brandenburg.[376] Rügen was another important centre of

---

371   Helmold I, 84: "Est autem Slavis multiplex ydolatriae modus, non enim omnes in eandem
      superstitionis consuetudinem consentiunt. Hii enim simulachrorum ymaginarias formas
      pretendunt de templis, veluti Plunense ydolum, cui nomen Podaga, alii silvas vel lucos
      inhabitant, ut est Prove deus Aldenburg, quibus nullae sunt effigies expressae. Multos
      etiam duobus vel tribus vel eo amplius capitibus exculpunt."

372   Cf. Helmold, I, 2; I, 46. See also above pp. 239 f., 304.

373   E. Wienecke assumed that the chronicler's information about polycephalic Slavic statues
      was a rumour resulting from a topographic error related to Szczecin. The three-headed
      Triglav was to be created from words referring to three Szczecin hills, *i.e.* Old Slavic 'głava'
      (head, hill), and so a city on three hills – *'urbs triglavi'* became a city of the deity called
      'Triglous', *etc.* This trend to exaggerate the horribleness of pagan idols was to give rise to
      other numbers of Slavic gods' heads in Christian imagination and exactly this general
      information offered by Helmold on this matter, in the opinion of the German scholar was
      to confirm that there were such rumours around. See Wienecke, *Untersuchungen*, pp. 145
      ff., especially 148.

374   Meriggi, *Il concetto*, pp. 166 f.; Pettazzoni, *Wszechwiedza*, pp. 224 ff.

375   VP II, 11–12; Ebo II, 1; Herbord II, 32–33; cf. *e.g.* S. Rosik, *Conversio*, pp. 258–270.

376   According to Henry of Antwerp (the last decades of the 12th c.) in Brandenburg "idolum
      detestabile tribus capitibus honoratum a deceptis hominibus quasi pro deo colebatur." –

HELMOLDI CRONICA SLAVORUM ON SLAVIC RELIGION   339

polycephalic idols.[377] However, one should not count on finding them – in the light of sources as they were all annihilated.

In polycephalic archaeological findings one should pay attention to a double-headed fragment of a cult figure from Fischerinsel near Neubrande-burg, dated to the 11th–12th c. According to some scholars, it can be a part of a four-headed whole statue.[378] Moreover, some light is cast on the problem of

---

see *Henrici de Antwerpe Tractatus de captione urbis Brandenburgensis*, ed. Oskar Holder-Egger, MGH SS 25 (1880), p. 482. Other information on the matter: *Excerptum chronicae principum Saxonie*, ed. Oskar Holder-Egger, MGH SS 25 (1880), pp. 480 f.; *Chronicae epis-copatus Brandenburgensis fragmenta*, ed. Oskar Holder-Egger, MGH SS 25 (1880), pp. 484 f. The location of the idol is disputable: an open cult space is supported by Th. Palm, a temple by L. Leciejewicz. L.P. Słupecki proposed a location inside the sanctuary on a hill away from the city, although it cannot be excluded that it was located in the stronghold. Elimination of the statue and most certainly many others took place either in 1127 under the rule of the duke of Stodorane Pribislav-Henry (see K. Myśliński, "Przybysław-Henryk," in SSS, vol. 4, pp. 399 f.; Michael Lindner, *Widekind, Meinfried, Pribislaw/Heinrich und andere – das südliche Lutizenland in der ersten Hälfte des 12. Jahrhunderts*, [in:] *Bischof Otto von Bamberg in Pommern. Historische und archäologische Forschungen zu Mission und Kulturverhältnissen des 12. Jahrhunderts*, ed. Felix Biermann, Fred Ruchhöft, (Studien zur Archäologie Europas) 30 (Bonn: Habelt, 2017), pp. 49–67), or later during the actions undertaken by Albert the Bear (1150). For discussion see Palm, *Wendische Kultstätten*, pp. 94–97; Kahl, *Heidenfrage und Slawenfrage*, pp. 565–576 (chapter: "Das ende des Triglaw von Brandenburg. Ein Beitrag zur Religionspolitik Albrechts des Bären"); Leciejewicz, *Słowianie*, p. 222; Słupecki, *Slavonic Pagan Sanctuaries*, pp. 202 f.; Lübke, "Zwischen Triglav," p. 22.

377   See below, pp. 357–359.
378   The discussion on the 65-centimetre long fragment of a cult figure refers to establishing whether these are two twin idols, *e.g.* a pair of divine twins known in Indo-European, *e.g.* Celtic, religions (see Urbańczyk, *Dawni Słowianie*, pp. 66, 68; Rosen-Przeworska, "Celtycka geneza," p. 265), or possibly according to the finders of this relic and its alleged second part Gringmuth-Dallmer/Hollnagel, "Jungslawische Siedlung," p. 229: "das 1.78 m hohe Idol aus Eichenholz zeigt auf einen mehrkantigen Säulenschaft den Oberkörper einer doppelköp-figen Menschenfigur", which seems more probable; cf. *Die Slawen in Deutschland*, p. 312. Witold Hensel, "Jak wyglądał posąg arkońskiego Svantevita," *Slavia Antiqua* 39 (1983), pp. 119–125, assumed that the statue was of key significance in the reconstruction of the Arkona Svantevit, which was to be a double form of this twin representation. An identical idea was presented earlier by the artist Szymon Kobyliński (Marek Konopka, "Światowit z teki Szymona Kobylińskiego," *Z otchłani wieków* 23 (1975), pp. 174 f.). Another image of the Arkona idol was presented by J. Herrman: *Die Slawen in Deutschland*, p. 308. See also Fred Ruchhöft, *Die Burg am Kap Arkona – Götter, Macht und Mythos*, (Archäologie in Mecklenburg-Vorpommern) 7 (Schwerin: Landesamt für Kultur und Denkmalpflege, 2016), pp. 85 f.

340   CHAPTER 4

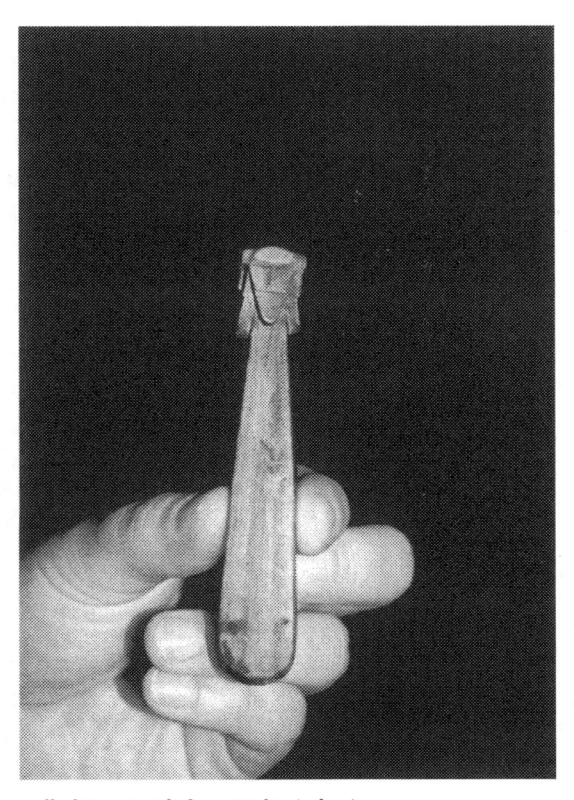

FIGURE 5   The so called "sviatovid" from Wolin (9th c.)
              THE INSTITUTE OF ARCHAEOLOGY AND ETHNOLOGY PAS,
              CENTRE FOR MEDIEVAL ARCHAEOLOGY OF THE BALTIC
              REGION IN SZCZECIN / STANISŁAW ROSIK

West Pomeranian polycephalic idols by archaeological findings of the so-called
pocket deities, especially the famous figure of the "sviatovid" from Wolin.[379]
    It is also important that the phenomenon of polycephalitic idols in the
Polabian and Pomeranian area belonged to a supra-ethnical cultural community determined by the reach of Viking penetration in the Early Middle Ages.[380]

---

379   For "sviatovid" from Wolin see Filipowiak, Wojtasik, "Światowit z Wolina," pp. 85 f.; Hensel,
      "Wczesnośredniowieczna figurka," p. 15. Urbańczyk, *Dawni Słowianie*, pp. 214 f., saw traces
      of a "lower" religion (faith in demons) in small figure findings.
380   Dozens of historical monuments related to the Viking penetration circle (from the British
      Isles to the eastern coast of the Baltic) are accompanied with rich illustration material:
      Jan Peder Lamm, "On the cult of multiple-headed gods in England and in the Baltic area,"
      Przegląd Archeologiczny 34 (1987), pp. 219–231; Janusz Kotlarczyk, "Słonecznego boga
      miejsca kultu," *Z otchłani wieków* 54 (1988), 2/3/4, pp. 159 f., 166; Filipowiak, "Słowiańskie

Another group of archaeological relics, useful in the discussion on the poly-
morphism mentioned by Helmold with reference to Polabian sculptures, are
monuments from East Slavic areas. Among these one should pay attention to
the so-called Sviatovid found in the Zbruch River in 1848, in the area of modern
Ukraine.[381]

The chronicler's information about the specifics of the Polabian idolatry
is in line with the wide comparative context, and not merely the Slavic one.
Regardless of this, the very significance of the polycephalism of idols of the
western Slavs still remains a compelling mystery. For generations there has
been a continuing discussion on its symbolism, for which the only explanation
"from the epoch" appeared in the hagiography of St. Otto of Bamberg by Ebo
of Michelsberg. He gave the opinion of the priests of the Szczecin Triglav who
believed the number of heads indicated power over heaven, earth, and the underworld. This important clue does not resolve the discussion however, especially since three-headedness was only one of the variants of polycephalism.[382]

Hence the concept of a connection between polycephalism and heliola-
try with a characteristic feature of omniscience (ability to see everything),
thanks to a larger number of faces, still remains as up-to-date as it was in the

---

wierzenia," pp. 28 ff.; Andris Caune, "Archäologische Zeugnisse von den heidnischen
Volksglauben in Riga während des 12–13 Jahrhunderts," *Światowit* 40 (1995), pp. 26–42;
Rosik, *Udział*, pp. 34–43.

381   Literature devoted to Sviatovid from the Zbruch is enormous (for an extensive list see
Zygmunt Krzak, "Światowid co i kogo przedstawia?," *Problemy* (1992) 8, p. 30. Basic studies
are presented by Leńczyk, "Światowid zbruczański," and Szymański, "Posąg ze Zbrucza."
See also below footnote 495. The alleged – rather questioned now – initial location of the
obelisk was proposed by Irina P. Rusanova, Boris A. Timoshchuk, "Zbruchskoye svyatilishche." "Sovetskaya Archeologia" (1986) 4, pp. 90–99; *iidem*, "Vtoroye zbruchskoye (krutilovskoye) svjatilishche (po materyalam raskopok 1985 g.)," in *Drevnosti slavyan i Rusi*, ed.
Boris A. Timoshhuk (Moskva: Nauka, 1988), pp. 78–91; Rybakov, *Jazyczestvo drewniej Rusi*,
pp. 236–251; cf. Janusz Kotlarczyk, "Triumfalny słup słonecznego boga," *Z otchłani wieków*
53 (1987) 1, pp. 36–41; *idem*, "W poszukiwaniu genezy wielotwarzowych wyobrażeń
Światowita, Świętowita, Rujewita i innych," in *Wierzenia przedchrześcijańskie na ziemiach polskich*, ed. Marian Kwapiński, Henryk Paner (Gdańsk: Wydawnictwo Muzeum
Archeologicznego w Gdańsku, 1993), pp. 56–64; Słupecki, *Slavonic Pagan Sanctuaries*,
pp. 215–223. It is worth emphasizing that the debate is related to establishing whether
Sviatovid in his upper part (*i.e.* the heavenly one) represents the only highest multiple-
headed god, or a few divine creatures. Cf. Gieysztor, *Mitologia*, pp. 231 ff.; Adam Łapiński,
"Światowid czy model świata?," *Z otchłani wieków* 50 (1984) 2, pp. 128–139; Rosik, *Udział*,
p. 44–48. Other relics from eastern Rus' areas are considered the so-called "stone babas"
and relation to the Slavdom is still discussed. See *e.g.* Włodzimierz Antoniewicz, "Posągi,"
in sss, vol. 4, pp. 241 f.; Leńczyk, "Światowid zbruczański," p. 41; Słupecki, *Slavonic Pagan
Sanctuaries*, pp. 213–215, 221–225.

382   Ebo III, 1; discussion on the matter see Rosik, *Conversio*, pp. 259 f.

342   CHAPTER 4

19th c.[383] On the other hand, a lunar origin has also been considered.[384] The most popular, however, seems to be in this case a reference to a tripartite division of the cosmos.[385] Similarly, four-headedness was related to the symbolism of the four directions of the world, the cardinal winds, and the seasons of the year.[386] Generally, the symbolism of three – and four-headedness was related to the universality of world models of the cosmos and man (psychological aspect).[387]

Moreover, a larger number of faces and heads was justified in regard to mythical motifs[388] or to the development of the numerical symbolism.[389] Referring the shape of images and especially their multi-headedness to various divine roles is a widely accepted possibility. A polymorphic figure in this case would be a counterpart for a few single-headed gods.[390] There was also an idea that the larger number of heads indicated the augmentation of power in the presented gods.[391] Finally, the symbolism of polycephalism was considered as

383   See W. Surowiecki, "Rozprawa o sposobach dopełnienia historyi Słowian," *Roczniki Towarzystwa Królewskiego Przyjaciół Nauk* 8 (1812) 1, pp. 103–105; Ignaz Johann Hanusch, *Die Wissenschaft des slawischen Mythus* (Lemberg/Stanislawow/Tarnow: Johann Milikowski, 1842), pp. 151 f.; Józef Łęgowski-Nadmorski, "Bóstwa i wierzenia religijne Słowian lechickich," *Roczniki Towarzystwa Naukowego w Toruniu* 32 (1925), p. 78; Pettazzoni, *Wszechwiedza*, pp. 217 f.; Kotlarczyk, "Słonecznego boga," pp. 153–168; *idem*, "W poszukiwaniu," pp. 58–63).

384   See *e.g.* Wienecke, *Untersuchungen*, p. 144. The thesis has a larger number of supporters, some of whom foster the lunar-chthonic characteristics not only in the case of Triglav but also Svantevit (see Kulišić, *Stara Slovenska religija*, pp. 40 f., 185–187; Cetwiński, Derwich, *Herby, legendy*, p. 91).

385   A reference to the three-headedness of the oldest layers of Indo-European religiousness encompassing a conviction about a tripartite cosmos (the motif of a cosmic mountain and the tree of life) was found by Joanna Tomicka, Ryszard Tomicki, *Drzewo życia. Ludowa wizja świata i człowieka* (Warszawa: Ludowa Spółdzielnia Wydawnicza, 1975), pp. 67–71; cf. Cetwiński, Derwich, *Herby, legendy*, pp. 69, 157. The view of the three-sector world can be related to the three-headed figure from the underworld of Sviatovid from the Zbruch, additionally, for comparison it is worth emphasizing that the three-headedness is typical of demonic creatures in the southern Slavs (Gieysztor, *Mitologia*, p. 155).

386   See Gieysztor, *Mitologia*, p. 124 f.; Vernardsky, *The origins of Russia*, p. 122.

387   See *e.g.* Krzak, "Światowid," p. 35–37.

388   See *e.g.* Gieysztor, *Mitologia*, p. 130.

389   See *e.g.* Pettazzoni, *Wszechwiedza*, p. 127.

390   See Rudnicki, "Bóstwa lechickie," pp. 414–416; Meriggi, "Il concetto," p. 169; Antoniewicz, "Religia," p. 371; *Die Slawen in Deutschland*, p. 311; Joachim Herrman, *Zwischen Hradschin und Vineta* (Leipzig/Jena/Berlin: Urania 1971), p. 219.

391   See Rudnicki, "Bóstwa lechickie," pp. 414, 416.

HELMOLDI CRONICA SLAVORUM ON SLAVIC RELIGION 343

the result of influences of ideas of foreign religions – for instance shamanism[392] or Christianity[393] – in Slavic spiritual culture.

The wide-ranging scholarly debate was also the genesis of polycephalism of Slavic idols being treated both as native and external.[394] The creditors of the Slavs in connection with the borrowed polycephalism of their statues were sought among: 1) the Asian circle: Hinduism, Buddhism, shamanism of steppe inhabitants who were middlemen in sharing ideas;[395] 2) the Celts;[396] 3) in Southern European cultures;[397] 4) in the community of sea-side civilization encompassed by Viking penetration (Baltic, Northern Sea), which could transfer an older substrate, *e.g.* Celtic.[398] It was even taken into account that there could be an infiltration of the Church doctrine on the Holy Trinity into beliefs

392 Vernardski, *The origins of Russia*, pp. 32, 119, explained multiple faces of statues with the influence of shamanism; see also Włodzimierz Demetrykiewicz, *Altertümliche steinerne Statuen, sog. "Baby" (Steinmütterchen, Becherstatuen) in Asien und Europa und ihr Verhältnis zur slawischen Mythologie*, Extrait du *Bulletin de l'Académie des Sciences de Cracovie* (1910) (Kraków, 1911), p. 115.

393 For the influence of Christian ideas see below, footnotes 399, 400. For a more extensive discussion on polycephalism symbolism see Rosik, *Udział*, pp. 58–63. *Ibidem*, pp. 74 ff. on attempts to find further solutions.

394 Supporters of native genesis of polycephalism in the Pomeranian area are: A. Brückner, *Mitologia słowiańska i polska*, pp. 47, 196; Labuda, "Rec. E. Wienecke," p. 464; Mikołaj Rudnicki, "Bóstwa lechickie," *Slavia Occidentalis* 5 (1926), pp. 414–416; Antoniewicz, "Religia dawnych Słowian," pp. 369–373; Meriggi, "Il concetto," pp. 169 f. In this group of scholars there are also supporters of Christian genesis of polycephalism of statues, claiming that it was the Slavic response to the Church doctrine on the Holy Trinity; see below, footnote 399. For an account of the discussion on the genesis of polycephalic divine images among the western Slavs see *e.g.* Rosik, *Udział*, pp. 52–58; Kotlarczyk, "W poszukiwaniu," pp. 58 f.

395 See *e.g.* Demetrykiewicz, *Altertümliche steinerne Statuen*, pp. 104–115; Władysław Łęga, *Kultura Pomorza we wczesnym średniowieczu na podstawie wykopalisk* (Toruń: Towarzystwo Naukowe w Toruniu, 1930), p. 275; Gąssowski, *Kult*, p. 579.

396 Through Southern European cultures (see *e.g.* Urbańczyk, *Dawni Słowianie*, p. 65) and directly (see Janina Rosen-Przeworska/Włodziemierz Szafrański, "W sprawie policefalizmu bóstw nadbałtyckich," in *Słowiańszczyzna Połabska między Niemcami a Polską. Materiały z konferencji naukowej zorganizowanej przez Instytut Historii UAM w dniach 28–29 IV 1980 r.*, ed. J. Strzelczyk (Poznań: Wydawnictwo UAM, 1981), pp. 255 f.; Janina Rosen-Przeworska"Celtycka geneza niektórych wątków wierzeniowych i ikonograficznych u Słowian zachodnich," in *Słowiańszczyzna Połabska między Niemcami a Polską. Materiały z konferencji naukowej zorganizowanej przez Instytut Historii UAM w dniach 28–29 IV 1980 r.*, ed. J. Strzelczyk (Poznań: Wydawnictwo UAM, 1981), pp. 259–262; cf. Szafrański, *Prahistoria*, p. 232).

397 *I.e.* Dacians, Thracians – according to this concept they had impact through Podolia and from there to Pomerania (see Urbańczyk, *Dawni Słowianie*, p. 71; cf. Szafrański, *Prahistoria*, pp. 255 f.; Krzak, "Światowid," p. 30).

398 See Lamm, "On the cult," p. 230 f.; cf. Rosik, *Udział*, p. 56.

344   CHAPTER 4

of late phase of Slavic religion,[399] however, this view can hardly be defended at
the current state of research. Still, the very influence of Christian beliefs is still
worth being taken into account as a factor which could support the spreading
of the cult of polycephalic figures among the Slavs.[400]

Going back to the Helmold's chronicle, the attention is drawn to the identification of a Slavic deity named Podaga with an idol, which was a way of interpreting the pagan *sacrum* in biblical categories.[401] In historical scholarship,
there were attempts to connect the name of the supernatural character treated
in this way, Podaga, with the "Pogoda" ("The Weather") mentioned by Joannes
Dlugossius. The answer to the question of whether "Pogoda" in the 15th c. is a
misspelt version of Podaga, remains in the sphere of doubtful speculation.[402] It
is thus even more difficult to prove that such a mistake took place in Helmold's
account.

Another direction of hypothetical explications related to the name of a
deity worshipped in Plön was related to the etymology of the root "-dag" explained as "burn."[403] In this context W. Budziszewska indicated a possibility
of interpreting Podaga's function as a domestic fire goddess.[404] Possibly the
same root can be heard in the name Dadźbog (Dażbog)[405] – acceptance of this
solution would locate Podaga in the circle of deities originating from Svarog.
L. Moszyński presented an opposing view. He saw in the name of the idol from

---

399   In the 19th c. *e.g.* A. Kirpichnikow (view quoted after: Niederle, *Život*, p. 150); Brückner,
      Mitologia słowiańska i polska, p. 206; Rudnicki, "Bóstwa lechickie," p. 414; recently the
      most information in Łowmiański, *Religia*, pp. 195 ff.; *idem*, "Zagadnienie politeizmu,"
      pp. 683–685.

400   Detailed criticism of findings related to the Christian genesis of Triglav and Svantevit,
      see Rosik, *Udział*, pp. 66–74. See also Kahl, *Heidenfrage und Slawenfrage*, pp. 80–144; and
      below, pp. 366 f.

401   On this matter see also above, pp. 99 ff.

402   Brückner, *Dzieje kultury*, p. 139, suspected that Dlugossius found Podaga through the
      chronicle of Jan Czarnków, which during his stay in Schwerin where he was a canon, had
      an opportunity to read Helmold's work; cf. Urbańczyk, *Dawni Słowianie*, p. 47. See also
      above, p. 307.

403   Mikołaj Rudnicki, "Polskie Dagome iudex i Wagryjska >>Podaga<<," *Slavia Occidentalis*
      7 (1928), pp. 158 f., he also tried to find a connection between the theonym Podaga with
      the name Dago (allegedly another name of Polish ruler Mieszko I), which did not earn
      recognition in further discussion – see *e.g.* Urbańczyk, *Dawni Słowianie*, p. 47.

404   Wanda Budziszewska, "Wagryjska Podaga i ślady kultu ognia u Słowian," *Rocznik
      Slawistyczny* 44 (1983) 1, pp. 13–15. The authoress indicates that except for the root "dag-",
      there is also a contiguity: "gag-", so in this concept there can occur "Pogaga" as a lection of
      the idol's name known from the Vienna manuscript, which raised doubts in an igneous
      interpretation of deities based on the root "dag", see Urbańczyk, *Dawni Słowianie*, p. 185.

405   Antoniewicz, *Religia*, p. 554. Jakobson sees in Podaga a transformation of the alleged
      "Dabog" – by some identified with Dazbog, for discussion see Gieysztor, *Mitologia*,
      pp. 178 f.

HELMOLDI CRONICA SLAVORUM ON SLAVIC RELIGION   345

Plön the word "potęga" (power), to associate it ultimately with the "mighty god of gods," known from chapter 84 of Helmold's work (*praepotens deus deorum*).[406] This proposal raises doubts because the said chronicler rather suggested that this sovereign of heavens never received worship from people.[407]

A lack of clarity related to the name of Podaga led even to a hypothetical opinion that he (or it) was a pseudo-deity.[408] It is hard to accept this solution, given that Helmold wrote about the times and matters that were important and relevant to him. Most certainly the very name of the deity given in the chronicle is a reflection of some real name, and its possible deformation in the source should not eliminate the conviction of his existence. Taking into account the fact that Podaga was not a patron of a whole tribe – this was Prove's rank – one should assume that the cult of this deity was local, concentrated around a particular stronghold,[409] or a neighbourly territorial community (maybe the so called opole).[410] This corresponds with Helmold's information that the Slavs located their idols in particular settlements.[411]

The most valuable passage in the discussed chapter from the perspective of the synthesis of the Slavic religion seems to be the summary information: "Among the polymorphic shapes of gods that are believed to take care of the fields, forests, sorrows and joys, they do not deny that there exists one god in heaven that commands others. [They believe] this prepotent god is looking after the divine matters only, while the others are his servants, born from his blood and among them all other matters are divided. And the more important one is, the closer one to the mighty god of gods."[412]

---

406   Moszyński, *Die vorchristliche Religion*, p. 78 f.
407   See below, footnote 412.
408   Urbańczyk, *Dawni Słowianie*, p. 187; cf. *idem*, "Pseudobóstwa," pp. 405 f.
409   The same in Wachowski, *Słowiańszczyzna*, p. 65.
410   *E.g.* H. Łowmiański, *Religia*, p. 184, claimed that placing the temple and the statue in the capital of the so called "opole" (*vicinia*), which according to him was Plön, was an unusual phenomenon and it should be connected with the pagan duke Krut, who allegedly initiated this cult in his residence as he wanted it to gain the character of the main political cult of his duchy. In this concept the role of the capital in Starigard (see above) disappears, which in the light of excavations also had cult place with an idol. Moreover Helmold himself confirms the existence of numerous sanctuaries with idols in particular settlements in the Wagrian country (see below, footnote 411), so Podaga's cult can hardly be considered as exceptional as H. Łowmiański would like to it be. About "opole" (*vicinia*) *e.g.* Karol Modzelewski, *Chłopi w monarchii wczesnopiastowskiej* (Wrocław/Warszawa/Kraków: Ossolineum, 1987), pp. 26–36 and 173–192.
411   Helmold I, 84: "... ydola, quibus singula oppida redundabant ..."
412   Helmold I, 84: "Inter multiformia vero deorum numina, quibus arva, silvas, tristitias atque voluptates attribuunt, non diffitentur unum deum in celis ceteris imperitantem, illum prepotentem celestia tantum curare, hos vero distributis officiis obsequentes de sanguine eius processisse et unumquemque eo prestantiorem, quo proximiorem illi deo deorum."

346   CHAPTER 4

A comparison of this schematic image with data from chapter 52 of
Helmold's chronicle shows that among those agrarian deities who took care of
fields one can find "penates," and among those who took care of forests there
are creatures living in them, such as Prove.[413] However, deities responsible
for sadness and joy correspond with the pair *bonus deus* and *malus deus* (the
"Black God"). The "god of gods" remains anonymous here.[414] The key element
in the search for his identity has become a reference to the oldest source referring to the religion of the Slavs, namely the account written by Procopius of
Caesarea about the Antes and Sclavenes in about the mid-6th c.[415] According
to him they practiced a cult of rivers and nymphs, as well as other supernatural
creatures (δαιμονια). However, the first place in their pantheon was to be taken
by the only lord, god (θεος) of rolling thunders. Animal offerings were made to
him, such as oxen, and people in danger called him by taking oaths to make
offerings, which were made after survival.

Speculations that both of these chronicle images of the pantheon centralized around a heavenly sovereign have *stricte* literary genesis – the first one as
an ancient Classical interpretation, and the other one as a medieval ecclesiastical one[416] – do not have sufficient justification.[417] However, it is hard to exclude

413   See the discussion above, pp. 306 ff.
414   In the second book of his chronicle Helmold (II, 1018) used the title *deus deorum* to refer
      to Svantevit, however, it was not a decisive premise in the argument that Helmold, and
      even the Slavs themselves, identified the Rans' god with the mysterious father of gods. It
      was definitely excluded by *e.g.* Rybakov, *Jazyczestwo driewnich slawian*, p. 462. For more
      discussion see below, p. 363.
415   Procopius Caesariensis, *De bellis* 7.14.1; cf. *Testimonia najdawniejszych dziejów Słowian*,
      p. 60 f. There are reservations made by A. Brückner (*Mitologia słowiańska i polska*,
      pp. 46, 173 f.) in the matter of Procopius's credibility as an informer about the Antes and
      Sclavenes, which in further scholarly debate did not gain recognition, see Łowmiański,
      Religia, p. 84; Tyszkiewicz, *Słowianie w historiografii wczesnego średniowiecza*, p. 11.
416   Brückner, *Mitologia słowiańska i polska*, p. 174, speculated that in Procopius's account it
      is possible to observe the image of Jupiter rolling thunders, while in Helmold's vision
      there is a projection of the Christian God. Similarly, H. Łowmiański also emphasized the
      likeness between the supreme Slavic god and his collection of subdued creatures with
      the Christian God surrounded by hosts of angels. Following the earlier historiography
      (A. Brückner, L. Niederle) he claimed that the result of numerous Christianization at-
      tempts interrupted by pagan reaction waves was an adaptation of some elements of the
      Christian beliefs to the sphere of mythological images of the Polabian tribes. However,
      H. Łowmiański assumed that these influences were superfluous, proving that the "god
      of gods" in Helmold's work in a very important respect remained an antithesis to the
      Christian God who intervenes in history (see Łowmiański, *Religia*, p. 186). However, this
      essential difference undermines the sense of proposing such a view that the Slavs took
      over Christian elements to their beliefs just in this particular case of the Heavenly Father
      myth.
417   The same Potkański, "Wiadomości Długosza," pp. 90 f.

HELMOLDI CRONICA SLAVORUM ON SLAVIC RELIGION 347

the very influence of conventions related to the culture of the epoch on the way of presenting this information.[418] An analogy between their content is visible mainly in the domination of the one god over all the other supernatural creatures.[419] Nonetheless, the details of both pieces of information do not favour identification of the "demiurge of lightning (thunder)" with the "god of gods," because the latter one was not supposed to take care of earthly things and no offerings were made to him.

This is a reminder of a synthetic assessment made by Eliade, that the creators of the heavens and the whole cosmos in world mythologies tend to disappear from cult (but not from mythology) to leave space for more dynamic religious forces, among which the sun is frequently mentioned. On the other hand the scholar made a reservation that in some circumstances – for reasons related to agriculture and agrarian religions – the god of heavens gains a new role as the sovereign of the pantheon and simultaneously the god of the atmosphere and thunders.[420] Both of these directions in reflection on the fate of the heavenly father correspond well with the basic trends in the search for the genesis of the "god of gods" mentioned by Helmold.

A. Gieysztor – very cautiously – indicated the possibility that the "demiurge of lightning" was actually Perun, who managed to swallow the competences and functions of the "god of gods." In this case Perun – in accordance with Eliade's conclusions – would either be an updated version of the heavenly sovereign, or the one who ousted him from earthly activity (just like *e.g.* Zeus who superseded Uranus). However, this direction assumes that the routes of Eastern and Polabian Slavdom parted in terms of changes in the pantheon, because the mysterious heavenly father captured in Helmold's work is not a type of *deus otiosus*, who lost his sovereign position in the pantheon, but nor is he Perun's counterpart, because he does not have any earthly roles and does not receive any cult.[421]

---

418 *E.g.* Urbańczyk, *Dawni Słowianie*, p. 22; Kiersnowska, Kiersnowski, *Życie codzienne*, p. 168.

419 Defining the primacy of the heavenly deity captured in both chronicle accounts as henoteism (*e.g.* Urbańczyk, *Dawni Słowianie*, p. 22; Krzak, "Światowid," p. 31) does not have sufficient premises. In the case of Helmold's work the existence of other gods is unquestionable, and calling them *semidei* is a metaphor and not a reference to nature. In the case of Procopius's information, the allegation that there is only one god of the Antes and Sclavenes is based on a conjecture based on the silence of the source.

420 Eliade, *Traktat*, pp. 54–57, 106. Cf. Gieysztor, *Mitologia*, p. 113.

421 Regardless of this, such interpretation of the "god of gods" was considered by Urbańczyk, *Dawni Słowianie*, p. 155; Gieysztor, *Mitologia*, pp. 110–114. Its acceptance means questioning the accuracy of Helmold's information, thus the question arises of why it should not be considered fairy-tale-like in general. For the matter of *deus otiosus* see esp. Eliade, *Traktat*, pp. 50–54; Widengren, *Religionsphänomenologie*, p. 46.

348   CHAPTER 4

In this situation it is worth paying attention to the other track of Slavic beliefs' evolution – marked by Svarog identified with the heavenly radiance.[422] He is the only Slavic god about whom there is information that he was the father of other deities. They were interpreted, in this case, in a solar way: Dazbog, for whom there is testimony in Rus', or Svarožic known in Polabia.[423] In these optics the myth of the "god of gods" presented by Helmold refers to Svarog, and his major position in the cult was next taken by Perun or Svarožic (based in both of these cases on different rules).[424] The progressing disintegration of cults in Polabia was connected with the creation of new forms of major deities after Svarožic, yet memory about the father of gods survived.

Although it was neglected in the editions of the chronicle, it is essential to mention that the reference of the title "deus deorum" to the highest Slavic divinity most certainly is the chronicler's invention. He simply borrowed this title from the Latin (Vulgata) version of Psalm 50.[425] The use of this term in the context which is not related to the Bible – in chapter 84 of the chronicle *deus deorum* turns out to be the main character in theogony – allows, however, one to find the real Slavic deity in *interpretatio biblica* disguise.

However, the chronicler's emphasis on the significance of this heavenly father is an example of using the measure of Christian doctrine in description of the native Slavic beliefs, which is indicated in the way in which this mythical character is presented. The statement that the Slavs "non diffitentur unum deum in celis," hence "they do not deny that there is one god in heaven," indicates that there were attempts to look for traces of monotheism in Polabian

---

422 See above, p. 119.

423 Vernardski, *The origins of Russia*, p. 120; Leciejewicz, *Słowianie*, pp. 113 f. Similarly Łowmiański, *Religia*, pp. 186 f., supporting the view of Slavic prototheism in the Early Middle Ages, claimed that in the light of the discussed source, the Indo-European "god-heaven" had already transformed into a "god functioning in heaven".

424 An alternative for the above mentioned concept developed by A. Gieysztor and assuming that Perun took over the competences of the "god of gods" is an earlier view of Vernardski, *The origins of Russia*, p. 119. On the basis of interpretation of the text of the Rus'-Byzantium treaty from 944 in which an oath was taken by God and by Perun, this author tried to find a mythological model shown by Helmold also in Rus'. Contrary to the conviction that the treaty was guaranteed by divine sovereigns on both sides – the Christian and the Slavic one – Vernardski saw in God an anonymous figure of the Slavic "god of gods", because he assumed that the whole guarantee of this treaty by supernatural forces referred only to one side of the treaty, the Rus'. However, there are no source premises to recognize Perun as Svarog's son, functional analysis does not support this concept either, hence Gieysztor's idea seems better justified.

425 Ps 50:1 (Vulgata: Ps 49:1). This term was used to refer to God by *e.g.* Gallus Anonymous, see *Galli Anonymi cronicae*, Epistola, p. 2. Such titles as the "King of kings" or "Lord of lords" were created analogically; see Rev 17:14.

HELMOLDI CRONICA SLAVORUM ON SLAVIC RELIGION 349

beliefs. It is possible even to make a supposition that behind the said formulation there is a view that pagans originally gained recognition of the Creator, but they abandoned worshipping him as a result of their sins and turned to idols and his creatures.[426]

This theological conviction permeated to the first studies of the religion of the Slavs, and a good example here is the reflections of Joachim Lelewel in the mid-19th c., as the motto of his sketch entitled "Bałwochwalstwo Sławiańskie" [Slavic Idolatry] was simply Helmold's statement: "non diffitentur unum deum," used to prove with eloquence the worth of medieval historiography that the "sprained" human mind lost the knowledge of the initial revelation and started to invent quirky miracles. It departed from the original cognition of the creator.[427] Lelewel's views correspond with the theory of the so-called primeval monotheism in 20th c. religious studies.[428] However, they were based on *stricte* theological premises, which bring them much closer to Helmold's worldview.

In the case of this chronicler, emphasis on the possible survival of traces of faith in the only God, the heavenly Father, among the Slavs would not only be an expression of following a particular theological idea supporting the primeval cognition of the Creator by pagans, but it would also be important in promotion of the idea of missions among them. This would indicate the contact point between their beliefs and Christian ones, which was a very useful motif in missionary catechesis. One should thus take into account especially the selective presentation of Polabian beliefs in the discussed passage of the chronicle, not only due to possible poor recognition of the foreign culture by the author, but also due to a variety of issues conditioning the view of the alien *sacrum* in such a way that it emphasized the content that was especially important from the pragmatic perspective of this work.

After the lecture on Slavic theology, Helmold places a description of the elimination of the said grove which he knew from experience, and the way missionaries acted in this case was striking: the holy oaks survived and only

---

426   Cf. Wis 13; Rom 1:20–25.

427   Joachim Lelewel, *Bałwochwalstwo Sławiańskie* (Poznań: J.K. Żupański, 1853), p. 5. In the same spirit Lelewel explained that a thunder could not be a god, because it was created (*ibidem*, p. 11). The Slavic god-creator was to bear various names: Svarožic, δημιουργος, Redegast, Sviatovid, Bel, Prove, and the others are the said 'semidei' (*ibidem*, pp. 13–18).

428   For the views of the Vienna ethnographic school, especially W. Schmidt, see Eliade, *Traktat*, pp. 43, 59f., 108 ff. (including the bibliography for this issue), and also *e.g.* Włodzimierz Szafrański, "W sprawie tzw. pramonoteizmu w paleolicie," *Światowid* 23 (1960), pp. 151–160.

350 CHAPTER 4

the disassembled fence was burnt down.[429] Hence the very elimination of the border of the sanctuary space meant its annihilation. The object of missionaries' aggression was not the trees, but the cult itself.[430] The key moment in its establishment was manifest in the choice of hierophany, by fencing and desacralization that was conducted analogically – through the destruction of the fence. It is characteristic that the destroyers of the sanctuary were not afraid of demons acting in the profanated place (*locus profanationis*), but of the wrath and stones of its worshippers. Helmold attributed their being saved from misfortune to God's care.[431]

Next the chronicler mentions that he was hosted by the Slavs and still remembered the "bitterness" of their wine, while he saw shackles and various torture devices, as well as Christians suffering in slavery.[432] When, on Sunday, the inhabitants of this country gathered at a fair in Lübeck, bishop Gerold called them "to give up their idols and worship the one God that is in heaven, and by the grace of baptism to break up with their abominable deeds, such as plundering and murdering Christians."[433] One should turn attention to the connection between abandoning idolatry and stopping the persecution of Christians. In reply the Wagrian duke, Pribislav, justified the behaviour of the Slavs who had been forced into piracy and looting Christians (sea merchants and Danes) for the purpose of paying their dues to German dukes. Hence, baptism and the related stoppage of looting created the impossibility of satisfying obligations imposed by the Saxons, and would therefore mean repressions.

---

429 Helmold I, 84: "et ingressi atrium omnia septa atrii congessimus circum sacras illas arbores et de strue lignorum iniecto igne fecimus pyram ..."

430 Gerold acted in a different way than the Bishop of Merseburg Wigbert (1004–1009), who according to Thietmar's chronicle cut down the cult grove (*Zutibure*). In this difference of approach to dendrolatry, it is possible to find a change in approach to nature in the mentality of the 12th c. – see *e.g.* Rosik, *Conversio*, p. 541.

431 Helmold I, 84. Destruction work was conducted not without fear of the missionaries being attacked by exasperated inhabitants, but they survived "thanks to divine protection" ("... non tamen sine metu, ne forte tumultu incolarum [lapidibus] obrueremur. Sed divinitus protecti sumus"). Modzelewski, *Omni secunda feria*, p. 83, emphasized that the "chronicler personally set his hand to this destruction, he was afraid of losing his life and so his story vibrates with the experience of fear".

432 It is not excluded that it was mead called wine.

433 Helmold I, 84: "... ut relictis ydolis colerent unum Deum, qui est in celis, et percepta baptismatis gratia renuntiarent operibus malignis, predis scilicet et interfectionibus Christianorum." This expression "unus Deus, qui est in celis" corresponds with the earlier information that the Slavs "do not deny it that there is one God in heaven". Gerold's missionary catechesis would refer here to images pagans were familiar with and related to the heavenly father defined by Helmold in reference with the *Vulgate* "deus deorum" (see above, pp. 348 f.).

HELMOLDI CRONICA SLAVORUM ON SLAVIC RELIGION   351

In response to this, the bishop quoted another argument, namely that there was nothing strange in the fact that the German dukes "do not believe they commit an offence by attacking those who practice idolatry and live without God."[434] He presented the adoption of Christianity as a way to avoid assaults, showing as examples the Saxons enjoying peace.[435] According to the chronicler, such an explanation persuaded Pribislav, who agreed to accept Christianity and pay tithes as long as he received the right to the land he ruled. It is easy to observe that the statement of the Slavic ruler corresponds with the concept of Christianization of pagans promoted on the pages of the chronicle, which supports an assumption that, being a literary character, he expresses Helmold's opinions rather than his historical counterpart.

Similarly, the opinion related to the Christian notions expressed by Pribislav, as well as to biblical allusions, fosters an assumption that strange elements were imputed to his mentality. This refers especially to the acknowledgement of Gerold's words by the duke as "God's words (...) and appropriate for our salvation."[436] Certainly, it is hard to count on Helmold's quotation of the entire dialogue (if it was not fictitious at all). However, an issue which deserves consideration here is the very attribution of understanding the doctrinal content of Christianity to the Obodrite ruler. Stanisław Bylina claimed that introduction of this motif to the chronicle was an anachronism, assuming that the notion of salvation was strange to pre-Christian Slavs.[437] However, it is still worth taking into consideration the possibility that Pribislav, being a representative of the elite who had frequent contact with Christianity, deviated from the majority of his subjects in terms of his knowledge of its doctrine.

A description of a debate at a convention in Artlenburg, called by Henry the Lion and attended also by Slavic dukes (February/March 1156), is a truly useful resource material for understanding the way in which the *sacrum* was understood by the Slavs. Henry the Lion gave a speech on the matter of the adoption of Christianity, and in reply Niklot, an Obodrite duke, said: "May God, who is in heaven, be your god, and you become our god and for us this will be enough. Worship him and later we will worship you."[438]

The duke obviously interrupted this "blasphemous speech" (*verbum blasphemiae*). A prototype of such deification influencing Helmold's interpretation

---

434   *Ibidem*: "non enim multum se delinquere arbitrantur in ydolatris et in his qui sunt sine Deo".

435   *Ibidem*.

436   Helmold I, 84: "verba Dei [...] et saluti nostrae congrua".

437   Bylina, *Człowiek*, p. 34.

438   Helmold I, 84: "Sit Deus, qui in celis est, deus tuus, esto tu deus noster, 'et sufficit nobis'. Excole tu illum, porro nos te excolemus". The expression "et sufficit nobis", cf. Jon 14, 8.

352   CHAPTER 4

of the cult attributed to Slavs could be the legend of Corvey,[439] but such an apotheosis of the victorious ruler surrounded by a nimbus of a legend finds also its analogy in the deificatiom of King Eric known from the hagiography of St. Anskar.[440] This example was known to Adam of Bremen,[441] and it does not seem to be only an element of the euhemeristic ideas that influenced the composition of a literary vision of paganism.[442]

Helmold's information also provides an image of the relations in the pantheon of Slavs, as long as it encompasses a reflection of the historical reality of their culture: if God who "art in heaven" recognized by them as "deus deorum" neglected earthly matters, he would not be an object of their interest in the perspective of cult, while his representative Henry could seem a perfect candidate for the personification of a divine patron in temporal problems.[443] Justification for such a decision was seen in respect for any surplus of power which was typical of paganism (A. Brückner),[444] or – as an analogy – the similar cult of Roman emperors (L.P. Słupecki),[445] or even the specifics of political relations in Polabia and Pomerania. According to T. and R. Kiersnowski, the

---

439   See above, pp. 273 ff. The possibility of extensive dissemination of the motif of deification of people involved in Christianization by pagans in the epoch mentality (*e.g.* as a test of missionaries' humility), which is indicated with reference to St. Adalbert in the 12th-century hagiography, the so called *Tempore illo* – see: *De sancto Adalberto episcopo*, ed. Wojciech Kętrzyński, in MPH 4 (1884), 12, p. 187 f.

440   *Vita Anskarii auctore Rimberto*, ed. Georg Waitz, MGH SSrerGerm in usum scholarum (1884), 26, p. 56: gods themselves were to announce to the Svear: "Ericum quondam regem vestrum nos unanimes in collegium nostrum asciscimus, ut sit unus de numero deorum". In reply to which the Svear declared that "templum in honore supra dicti regis dudum defuncti statuerunt et ipsi tanquam deo vota et sacrificia offerre ceoperunt." It is worth observing that there is a certain conflux of the names of Henry the Lion and the king of the Svear, because in the Latin text his name was "Hericus".

441   Adam IV, 26: "Colunt et deos ex hominibus factos, quos pro ingentibus factis immortalitate donant, sicut in Vita sancti Ansgarii legitur Hericum regem fecisse."

442   In the earlier literature *e.g.* Stanisław Piekarczyk, *Barbarzyńcy i chrześcijaństwo. Konfrontacje społecznych postaw i wzorców u Germanów* (Warszawa: PWN, 1968), pp. 344 f., expresses a doubt related to the genuineness of Erik's deification, but Łowmiański, *Religia*, p. 245, is not equally skeptical, although he noticed an element of fiction in in the mechanism of its creation. Moreover it is worth to stress, that there are also some premises in the Old Norse poetry and prose indicating that such cases of apotheosis of a famous person really existed (see lately Olof Sundqvist, *An Arena for Higher Powers. Ceremonial buildings and religious strategies for rulership in Late Iron Age Scandinavia* (Leiden/Boston: Brill 2015), pp. 110–140).

443   Łowmiański, *Religia*, p. 244, emphasizes that Niklot was a competent person to make an apotheosis offer, because (at the assembly) being responsible for enforcement of the law and observation the principles of the religion, he was a cult creating institution.

444   Brückner, *Mitologia słowiańska i polska*, p. 342.

445   Słupecki, *Einflüsse*, p. 187.

HELMOLDI CRONICA SLAVORUM ON SLAVIC RELIGION   353

functions of local gods were the same as earthly monarchs, hence substituting them with the Saxon duke was not strange at all.[446]

The arguments presented here to support the truthfulness of the proposed deification of Henry the Lion by the Slavs refer to the information included *implicite* in the text, without taking into consideration the literary convention of the answer ascribed to Niklot by Helmold. Meanwhile, it is hard to define precisely what possible form of worship was offered by Niklot to the Saxon duke, which could be considered divine by the chronicler, having as a model the legendary example of St. Vitus deified by the Rans.

Certainly, the occurrence of forms of religious worship for the outstanding leader when he was still alive lies within the limits of probability and given the close relation between religion and social as well as political life among the Slavs it should not raise considerable doubts. However, casting a living mortal in the role of a god, understood as the highest rank of supernatural creatures, does raise some doubts. The very apotheosis – as is indicated in analogies from antiquity – seems more certain only after the death of a famous person. On the other hand, some attributes of divinity could be worshipped during their lifetime, like in the case of ancient emperors. This possibility can be admitted without much risk in the discussed situation.

The most probable genesis, therefore, of the strict deification of Henry the Lion that should be accepted is the literary one. The Saxon duke, involved in a mission and inspiring respect with his military power, could become one of the figures related to the sacral sphere and could be given the title of "god" as an incorporation – in Slavic eyes – of supernatural power, which in Helmold's understanding was expressed in the term "deus".[447] Even the rejection of this hypothesis will not change the fact that from a theological perspective any worship of man disregarding the Creator was idolatry, which formed a basis for an attribution to the Obodrites an error of: *creaturam anteponere creatori*.

Further pages of the chronicle are devoted to efforts made by Bishop Gerold to save the diocese in Starigard from crisis, and they resulted in another missionary episode related to this centre. Its hero is the devoted Saxon priest Bruno, called from Faldera: "Soon after he arrived in Aldenburg, he committed himself to fulfilling the work of God by summoning the tribe of Slavs to the

---

446   Kiersnowska, Kiersnowski, *Życie codzienne*, p. 169.

447   Moreover, it is worth mentioning here that the chronicler explained 'Zcerneboch' as *deus niger*, which shows that the Slavic 'bóg' ('-boh') was understood by him as *deus*. Meanwhile the word "god" (boh) could be used by Polabian people not only to refer to divine creatures, but also to people considered to be particularly connected with the sphere of sacrum, which can indicate certain analogies. This corresponds with a custom of rural Slavic people, accounted by Moszyński, *Kultura*, p. 707, of calling sorcerers gods.

divine grace of rebirth [in baptism], by cutting out [divine] groves and destroying the sacrilegious rites."[448] In the characteristics of Slavic religion there is, once again, a scheme typical of Helmold: first there is an image of an object or practice related to cult (*lucus, ydolatria, ydolum*), and then a wider category appears, a collective one carrying a theological and moral qualification (*superstitio, ritus sacrilegi*).

The information about the erection, or more precisely, reconstruction of the church in Starigard was saturated with biblical phraseology with references to the fiasco of the earlier Christianization – "And the cult of the house of God was restored among the perverse and abominable nation".[449] This assessment is yet another example of the corrupt nature of the pagans. Count Adolf, who was the protector of this missionary activity, required the Slavs to bury their dead in burial grounds near churches.[450] The Slavic burial rite was maintained among the Christianized people for a long time and the contribution of the secular authority to its eradication was of essential significance.[451]

The consequence of Bruno's pastoral activity, conducted in the language of the Slavs,[452] was that "then the Slavs were prohibited to swear on trees, water springs and stones, and those accused of crimes were brought in front of the priest to face a trial by iron or plowshares."[453] This information about a ban

---

448 Helmold I, 84: "Statim enim, ut venit Aldenburg, aggressus est opus Dei cum magno fervore et vocavit gentem Slavorum ad regenerationis gratiam, succidens lucos et destruens ritus sacrilegos".

449 *Ibidem*: "Et restauratus est cultus domus Dei in medio nacionis pravae et perversae"; cf. 2 Chr 29:35: "cultus domus Domini"; Phil 2:15: "in medio nacionis pravae et perversae".

450 Helmold I, 84: "ut transferrent mortuos suos tumulandos in atrio ecclesiae".

451 It is hard to draw any wider conclusions on the character of Slavic burials on the basis of this information, however, data from other sources can offer some information on this matter. One should especially mention here Otto of Bamberg's account on the first his Pomeranian mission created right after it was completed in 1125 which was recorded by Ekkehard of Aura the next year at the latest, and next in the hagiography of the Apostle of Pomeranians (*Ekkechardi Uraugiensis chronica*, under the year 1125, p. 263; cf. Rosik, *Conversio*, pp. 85 ff., 614, 626 f.). It mentions an order to bury the dead in burial grounds similar to the one mentioned in Helmold's work, adding not to do it in forests and fields.

452 Helmold I, 84. See Scior, *Das Eigene und das Fremde*, pp. 211 f. Łowmiański, *Religia*, p. 268, claimed that Bruno's activity was the first certain case of writing a text in a Slavic language in Polabia using the Latin alphabet (sermons written using Slavic words were delivered when needed) and he considered this fact as exceptional (cf. Labuda, *Fragmenty*, vol. 3, p. 205). The view of common lack of knowledge of the Slavic language among missionaries working there, although became very common in scientific literature, does not seem as justified as it could be suggested by its supporters. For the discussion on this matter see, pp. 72 f., 76.

453 Helmold I, 84: "inhibiti sunt Slavi de cetero iurare in arboribus, fontibus et lapidibus, sed offerebant criminibus pulsatos sacerdoti ferro vel vomeribus examinandos".

HELMOLDI CRONICA SLAVORUM ON SLAVIC RELIGION   355

on oaths – as has already been mentioned above – is in certain opposition
to the earlier information quoted by Helmold that the Slavs rather avoid taking them.[454] The introduction of the so-called God's judgement, just like the
trial of red-hot iron or a ploughshare, does not deviate from the customs of
the German judiciary system of that time. That the Slavs swore by sacred elements of nature such as trees, springs, or stones, is worth emphasizing. This
symbolically indicated a reference to the powers associated with them,[455] and
not necessarily to gods.[456] However, the very swearing of oaths in holy places
was certainly also practiced, for example, during judiciary proceedings near
sanctuaries (such as Prove's grove).[457]

Priest Bruno's missionary work also encompassed dissuading Slavs from
some customary cruelties (*e.g.* crucifying wrongdoers), and in addition to this
it ensured protection for Christians from pagan aggression.[458] This is one of
the essential – apart from *stricte* missionary – goals of the evangelization of the
Polabian tribes. It is also clearly indicated in the last sentence of the discussed
chapter, in which the chronicler emphasized that the Slavs were attached to
"their fathers' sins."[459] These transgressions included the looting and invasion
of the Danes.[460] The whole chapter closed the historiographic depiction of the
conversion of the Wagrians, Obodrite, and so-called proper Polabians, which
was strictly related to cooperation between the secular and church authority.

2.8 *Epilogue: the Final Tackling of Rans and Their Cult*
Helmold's return to the "vessel of description" (*navis descriptionis*) and writing
of the second book of the *Cronica Slavorum* most certainly must have been
incited by the events of 1168 in Rügen. As he was the chronicler of the Slavic
mission, he could not remain indifferent to them. The timeline of Helmold's
chronicle was completed in 1171. A new story started with the appointment

---

454   For the discussion on this matter see above, pp. 337 f.

455   Łowmiański, *Religia*, p. 207, related swearing by stones with worshipping them; the Slavic
      cult of stones is mentioned by Cosmas I, 4; cf. Szafrański, *Prahistoria*, p. 383; Słupecki,
      Slavonic Pagan Sanctuaries, pp. 166 ff. On the stone cult in Pomerania and possibilities of
      its confirmation with a rich set of archaeological testimonies see Filipowiak, "Wierzenia
      słowiańskie," pp. 38–41.

456   For comparison it is worth mentioning Thietmar's description of entering into a peace
      treaty by the Liutici with ritual activities without references to cult places, Thietmar VI,
      25; see above, pp. 142 ff.

457   Such possibility was emphasized by L. Leciejewicz, ">>In pago," p. 131, taking into account
      that an oath was a part of judiciary proceedings.

458   See Helmold I, 84.

459   A biblical reference, *e.g.* 2 Kgs13:6.

460   Helmold I, 84.

356   CHAPTER 4

of Gerold's successor – his brother Conrad (d. 1172). Although a large part of
this book was devoted to characters important on a European scale, like the
emperor or popes, and next to the bishop of Mecklenburg, Berno, the Obodrite
dukes, Pribislav and Vertislav, and finally Helmold's beloved character count of
Holstein Adolf II, Henry the Lion is in the foreground of the story. He was the
first to tame the tribes in the Obodrite Federation, hence he opened the way
for the restitution of Christianity on their lands and he also made expeditions
against the "Troy of the North," *i.e.* Rügen.[461]

The island was the object of Saxon, Danish, and Polish military expansion as
early as the 12th c. Valdemar I of the Danes finally achieved the laurel wreath of
victory. From 1159 he invaded Rügen every year and finally succeeded in forcing Arkona to capitulate in 1168. He was supported by the Pomeranians and
Saxons.[462] At the time of the final struggle with the pressure of the Christian
neighbours, the cult of Svantevit became a guarantee of sovereignty for this last
enclave of Old Slavic religion.[463] It is also represented in the title of the chapter
devoted to the conquest of Rügen, "De Zuantevit Ruianorum symulachro."

The following events remained in the centre of Helmold's attention: the defeated Rans pledged to meet all conditions imposed by the victor in return

---

461   With such an epithet, struggling with its Christian neighbours Rügen entered the pages of
       the 20th c. literature, see Kossak-Szczucka/Szatkowski, *Troja Północy*, esp. pp. 342 ff. – *i.e.*
       the chapter 26: "Troja Północy" ["Troy of the North"].

462   The Rans themselves were not limited in their actions only with defence. The said series
       of wars with neighbours was started by their invasion of Lübeck in about 1101, which re-
       sulted in a retaliatory invasion. Similarly when they burnt down Roskilde, they also insti-
       gated a Danish invasion (1136). Its consequence was temporary subjugation of the Rans
       to the invaders' control and a Christianization attempt. However, internal conflicts in the
       Kingdom of Denmark made it possible for the island to become independent of exter-
       nal political influences and in consequence they brought the missionary work to an end.
       Svantevit's worshippers, famous for piracy, ravaged Denmark again and imposed tribute
       on particular islands. They also became involved in intervention policy towards the Slavs
       accepting Christianity: in about 1128 they attacked Szczecin, which at that time finally be-
       came Christian (cf. Ebo III, 23; Herbord III, 30–31; see Rosik, *Conversio*, pp. 487 ff). In 1147
       they came with successful relief to the Obodrite Dubin besieged by the crusaders. See:
       Osięgłowski, "Początki słowiańskiej Rugii," pp. 262 ff., decisive Danish invasions – *ibidem*,
       pp. 276 ff. The most significant medieval source in the reconstruction of this stage of strug-
       gle (the 2nd half of the 12th c.) is Saxo Grammaticus's chronicle which is richer in details
       than Helmold's one. See also: Labuda, *Fragmenty*, vol. 2, pp. 173 ff.; *idem*, "Waldemar I,"
       in SSS, vol. 6, pp. 298–300; Leciejewicz, *Słowianie*, pp. 217 ff. For basic information about
       Arkona and the events preceding its fall see Władysław Kowalenko, "Arkona," in SSS,
       vol. 1, pp. 47–49; Babij, *Wojskowość*, pp. 171 ff.

463   Cf. Lech Leciejewicz, "Ostatni obrońcy dawnych wartości," *Z otchłani wieków* 52 (1986) 2,
       pp. 62–69.

HELMOLDI CRONICA SLAVORUM ON SLAVIC RELIGION   357

for their lives.[464] Valdemar started his rule over them by toppling the cult of
Svantevit: "And he ordered that very old statue [called] Zuantevith which was
worshipped by all Slavic nations to be taken down, dragged through the middle
of the army in front of the Slavs by a rope tied around its neck, then cut into
pieces and tossed into flames."[465] This spectacular scene in which the statue
was in view of both the conquerors and the defeated to be finally burnt[466] was
not only confirmation of the military triumph, but also a part of a wider context of activities aimed at introducing a new social and political order, hence
also a revolutionary change in the religious sphere.[467]

In the perspective of missionary theology, the ritual toppling of a native cult
is presented as *abrenuntiatio diaboli*, the model for which was Old Testament
images.[468] Similarly, they were intended to show idols' worshippers the pow-
erlessness or the non-existence of gods personified in sculptures. This trend in
interpretation *expressis verbis* corresponds with King Valdemar's order, mentioned by Helmold, given to the Rans to abandon their native cult and accept

---

464   After presentation of forces participating in Valdemar I's expedition the chronicler di-
      rects the description of events using the expression borrowed from 1 Macc 2:47: "pros-
      peratum est (...) opus in manibus regis".
465   Helmold II, 108: "Et fecit produci simulachrum illud antiquissimum Zuantevith, quod
      colebatur ab omni natione Slavorum, et iussit mitti funem in colo eius et trahi per me-
      dium exercitum in oculis Slavorum et frustatim concisum in ignem mitti."
466   Chopping and burning down the idol from Arkona is also mentioned by the Danish
      chronicler Saxo Grammaticus (Saxo XIV, 39, 31–34).
467   Modzelewski, *Barbarzyńska Europa*, pp. 429 ff., esp. 458 ff., says directly that this kind
      of ritual of toppling a native cult was "the end of the world" of barbarians, who were
      shown the powerlessness of their deities in this spectacular way. An antidote for bar-
      barians' trauma caused by destruction of the foundations of their social order was the
      introduction of the cult of Christian God among them as a guarantee of lasting, super-
      natural care of their land and community. Similarly Banaszkiewicz, *Zabić boga, passim*,
      shows the toppling of cult statues and dragging them outside the settlement to pursue
      the idea of taking away the power over the ecumene from earlier gods. The basis for such
      conclusions was Saxo Grammaticus's rapport about the conquest of Rügen, analysed in
      a wide comparative context with a reference to PVL information about Perun's cult in
      Kiev (988). Hence one should take into account the presence of some Slavs' ideas related
      to their gods in the procedure of this kind of public annihilation of their cult. However,
      taking into account that the authors of this spectacle were Christians, including clergy-
      men, it is hard to consider as justified speculations assuming that in some special way
      the procedure of the ritual destruction of idols was adjusted to the features of particular
      divine creatures to whom these statues were dedicated (it was proposed by *e.g.* Leszek
      Wojciechowski, "Trojaka śmierć słowiańskich bogów," in *Christianitas et cultura Europae,
      Księga Jubileuszowa Profesora Jerzego Kłoczowskiego*, vol. 1, ed. Henryk Gapski (Lublin:
      Instytut Europy Środkowo-Wschodniej, 1998), p. 598, with reference to Dumézil's concept,
      or more precisely the three-functional interpretation of pantheons).
468   *E.g.* Is 46:1; 1 Kgs 15:13.

358   CHAPTER 4

Christianity: "And destroyed [Valdemar] the shrine with all the rituals held in
it and plundered the overflowing treasury. He ordered them to give up their
errors in which they were born and to accept the cult of the true God."[469] Thus
the temple was vanquished as well as the cult related to it (*religio*), and they
were replaced on the island by a network of churches.[470]

In this matter cooperation between the Danish king and bishops was
necessary – at least in the consecration of churches. The chronicler emphasized the involvement of Absalon of Roskilde and Berno of Mechlin
(Mecklenburg). The number of established churches, twelve, symbolically indicates that the island was completely Christianized.[471] Apostolic zeal comparable with that of St. Paul was demonstrated by the Rans' duke, Iaromir.[472]
Agreeable cooperation between secular authorities and the clergy in effective
conversion of pagans is a fixed motif in Helmold's work. However, this time

---

469   Helmold II, 108: "Et destruxit [Valdemar – S.R.] fanum cum omni religione sua et erarium
       locuples diripuit. Et precepit, ut discederent ab erroribus suis, in quibus nati fuerant, et
       assumerent cultum veri Dei."

470   Contrary to the revelations announced by C. Schuchardt in 1921 about finding remains of
       the famous Svantevit's temple in Arkona, today there is a view that the place where the
       temple was located was swallowed by the sea. This statement was justified by Ejnar Dyggve,
       "Der slawische Viermastenbau auf Rügen. Beobachtungen zu dem Swantewittempel
       des Saxo Grammaticus," *Germania* 37 (1959), pp. 193–205. A critical study of the results
       of excavation work in Arkona (with regard for the findings of Hansdieter Berlekamp,
       "Die Ausgrabungen auf Kap Arkona 1969–1970," in *Berichte über den II. Internationalen
       Kongress für Slawische Archäologie*, vol. 3, ed. Joachim Hermann; Karl-Heinz Otto (Berlin:
       Akademie Verlag, 1973), pp. 285–289) was presented by Linda Ellis, "Reinterpretations of
       the West Slavic Cult Site of Arkona," *Journal of Indo-European Studies* 6 (1978), pp. 1–18.
       Currently research conducted in Rügen confirms pessimism related to the possibil-
       ity of finding relics of the Arkona temple (see Fred Ruchhöft, *Die Burg am Kap Arkona*,
       pp. 23–29).

471   The introduction of the Christian cult on the island was – one more time in the Helmold's
       narrative – illustrated here in a topical image of establishing the cult of "the house of God
       in the evil and perverse nation" ("ut fundaretur cultus domus Dei nostri in natione prava
       et perversa"). The vocabulary refers to the Bible: *cultus domus* – cf. 1 Chr 23:29 (cf. Helmold
       I, 19, p. 39); *in medio nationis pravae et perversae* – cf. Phil 2:15. See *Helmolda Kronika
       Słowian*, p. 408, footnote 148, 149. See also above, p. 354, footnote 449.

472   Helmold II, 108. It is worth paying attention to the fact that Helmold is not only silent
       about Iaromir's baptism, but also presents him as such a mature Christian that he could
       even start to preach the gospel (*predicatio*). The information that this duke did not keep
       away from using rigorous methods of missionary persuasion, and it is essential that due
       to "innate wildness" (*innata feritas*), indicates that the chronicler still treated him as a
       barbarian (see *ibidem*: Iaromir "qui fungens vice apostoli gentem rudem et beluina rabie
       sevientem partim predicatione assidua, partim minis ab innata sibi feritate ad novae con-
       versacionis religionem convertebat."; cf. Fraesdorff, *Der barbarische Norden*, pp. 350 f.).

HELMOLDI CRONICA SLAVORUM ON SLAVIC RELIGION   359

the previous ruler was involved in the introduction of the new order in the conquered community.

For the duke of Rans, their conversion opened new perspectives in politics. On one hand he could join the elites of the contemporary Christian monarchies, and on the other hand he had an opportunity to strengthen his position in his country. Thanks to the imposed decision on Christianization, which was the consequence of the conquest, Iaromir's personal decision to support the missionary action did not result in a threat of losing the legitimacy of his rule – earlier guaranteed by the assembly (veche) and the temple.[473] Moreover the duke carefully oversaw the new cult organization and this way strengthened his position in society in comparison with the earlier system, which in Helmold's description gained theocratic characteristics.

The chronicler's claim that the king's authority was not as high as that of a priest was a special interpretation of the meaning of divinations and the oracle in the decision process of the ruler and his people.[474] However, it is hard to talk about hierocracy, as at most it was the strengthening of the role of the temple in the political life in comparison with the times of Adam of Bremen, who – let us remember – mentioned only that the Rans were ruled by a "king" (rex).[475]

Hence, in the political system presented by Helmold, both cooperation and certain competition between the ruler and the temple in Arkona were natural.[476] The very expression "rex et populus" emphasizes political subjectivity of the entirety of the community. Thus, one has to take into account the profound significance of the assembly in the rule over the community of Rans.[477] The leading role in this assembly was assigned to the tribal elite, for whom becoming Christian could seem attractive, which is indicated in similarities in

---

473   The ducal power in Pomerania was in an analogous situation earlier, its representative, Vartislav I, could join the action of Christianity propagation in the subdued country only after military subjugation of the said country to Polish Boleslav the Wrymouth, who became a promoter of Bishop Otto of Bamberg's mission in the 20's of the 12th c. See *e.g.* Stanisław Rosik, *Bolesław Krzywousty* (Wrocław: Chronicon, 2013), pp. 196 ff.

474   Helmold II, 108: "Rex apud eos modicae estimacionis est comparacione flaminis. Ille enim responsa perquirit et eventus sortium explorat. Ille ad nutum sortium, porro rex et populus ad illius nutum pendent."

475   See above, p. 248.

476   An expression of the aspiration of the ducal power to maintain certain autonomy from the centre of cult and political power in Arkona unquestionably was "Carentia" (probably Garz or Karenz) and the way it functioned, it was the duke's abode with idols' sanctuaries dedicated to Rugievit, Porevit and Porenut (cf. Saxo XIV, 39, 39–42), and they were presented by the Danish chronicler as "private" (Saxo XIV, 39, 38).

477   Zernack, *Die burgstädtischen Volkversammlungen*, pp. 221–225.

360   CHAPTER 4

the circumstances of the Christianization of Pomerania.[478] In this balance of social forces on Rügen, the chief factor in the defence of their native religion turned out to be – devoid of perspectives due in case of failure – Svantevit's temple.

Creating the second book of the *Cronica Slavorum* as a separate entity, a new story, Helmold discussed this temple and the related cult. He repeated information included in the first book, but he also creatively transformed them. After emphasizing that the Rans are the "toughest" (*gens durior ceteris*) of all Slavic peoples and this is why they remained "in the darkness of infidelity until our times" ("in tenebris infidelitatis usque ad nostra tempora"), he stressed that access to them is prevented by being surrounded by the sea ("omnibus inaccessibilis propter maris circumiacentia").[479] Later he narrated the legend about the first wasted attempt, because of apostasy, to Christianize the island:

"A petty rumor has it that Louis, son of Charles [the Great] has once granted the lands of the people of Rügen to saint Vitus in Corvey as he became the founder of the monastery. It is said that missionaries from that monastery converted the tribe of Rugians or Rans into the Christian religion and founded an oratory of St. Vitus the martyr, who was to be worshipped in that province. Later on, the Rans people, called also Rugians, as a consequence of an unfortunate turn of events withdrew from the light of truth and committed an error even worse than before. We believe St. Vitus to be the servant of God, but the Rans began to worship him as a god, built him a monumental statue and served the creation rather than the Creator."[480]

---

478   In this case for the elites of Western Pomeranian Duchy especially openness to contacts with the European civilization circle and taking over its social life models were essential (see *e.g.* Bartlett, *The Making of Europe*, pp. 269 ff; cf. *idem, Tworzenie Europy*, p. 436; Rosik, *Conversio*, pp. 131, 568 ff.). It is worth emphasizing that even the fact that the Baltic Slavs had to give up piracy after baptism, initially was only theoretical, which is indicated in the last chapters of Helmold's chronicle. Even in the late 12th c. the Pomeranians were accused of piracy (see *e.g. Epistola de leproso per ignem mundato* in: *E codicibus Poznaniensibus*, ed. Wojciech Kętrzyński, MPH 5 (1888), p. 964; cf. Rosik, *Conversio*, p. 436.

479   Helmold II, 108; cf. Scior, *Das Eigene und das Fremde*, p. 216; Cf. Fraesdorff, *Der barbarische Norden*, p. 334. Similarly Helmold I, 6. See also above footnote 72 in this chapter.

480   Helmold II, 108: "Tenuis autem fama commemorat Lodewicum Karoli filium olim terram Rugianorum obtulisse beato Vito in Corbeia, eo quod ipse fundator exstiterit cenobii illius. Inde egressi predicatores gentem Rugianorum sive Ranorum ad fidem convertisse feruntur illicque oratorium fundasse in honore Viti martiris, cuius veneracioni provincia consignata est. Postmodum vero, ubi Rani, qui et Rugiani, mutatis rebus a luce veritatis aberrarunt, factus est error peior priore; nam sanctum Vitum, quem nos servum Dei confitemur, Rani pro deo colere ceperunt, fingentes ei simulachrum maximum, et servierunt creature pocius quam creatori".

HELMOLDI CRONICA SLAVORUM ON SLAVIC RELIGION   361

Calling this story *tenuis fama*, an expression known from Virgil or Boecius,[481] could indicate that it was disregarded and considered an insignificant, not very credible rumour. However, in this context it was significant for the theological assessment of the Rans' religion. In comparison with the version of the legend presented in the first book, the dimension of theological reflections was extended in the quoted passage. Namely the idea of service "to the creature more than to the Creator" (*creature pocius quam creatori*), taken from the Epistle of St. Paul to the Romans (1:25), was preceded by a statement, that when Rans "withdrew from the light of the truth", their error was worse than before.[482]

Therefore, the Rans' religion at the stage of their conversion was a more significant trespass than their original paganism. This corresponds well with Svantevit's exceptionally strong position – the first god in the whole Slavic pantheon, the most famous giver of victories and the most efficient god in providing oracle responses.[483] There is more information about these aspects of Svantevit's cult in a later source written by Saxo Grammaticus,[484] who also mentioned other deities in Rügen. However, also in this wider context – just like in Helmold's work – Svantevit was the major patron of the whole tribe and the main cult centre was located in Arkona.[485]

---

481   *Helmolda Kronika*, p. 408, footnote 153.

482   Helmold II, 108: "a luce veritatis aberrarunt, factus est error peior priore". Cf. Mt 27:64.

483   Helmold II, 108: "Adeo autem haec supersticio apud Ranos invaluit, ut Zuantevith deus terrae Rugianorum inter omnia numina Slavorum primatum obtinuerit, clarior in victoriis, efficacior in responsis".

484   Saxo learnt about the events of 1168 from participants' accounts and first of all from Absalon (maybe even not personally, but from another work which today is lost) – Horst-Diether Schröder, ">>Gesta Danorum<< Saxo Gramatyka jako źródło do dziejów Słowian nadbałtyckich," *Przegląd Zachodniopomorski* 11 (1967) 5, pp. 19 f.

485   First of all Helmold is silent on deities from "Carentia" (Garz?) and the polycephalism of the idol from Arkona. Apart from this, Saxo's *Gesta Danorum* (XIV, 39) brings information about other Svantevit's temples on the island and a detailed description of the Slavic harvest festival, which indicates that this god was not only a war patron, but he also gave good harvest and the resulting happiness (see Urbańczyk, *Dawni Słowianie*, p. 109 f.; Pettazoni, *Wszechwiedza*, pp. 219 ff.). According to Saxo Grammaticus, people gave Svantevit the tithe of the harvest, a third of their war loot and all spoils belonging to the deity of the three hundred horsemen squad. Moreover the chronicler informs about a cult horse as well as beliefs and divinations related to it. As for the temple interior, he mentions that apart from the statue there was a banner, a sword and riding gear. In the light of the Rans' legends these accessories were used by their god during horse night escapades against their enemies. Public character of Svantevit's cult, on the scale of the whole tribe, is indicated by the sending to him of gifts by the Danish king. For a comprehensive study of the Rans' religion, see Miś, "Przedchrześcijańska religia," *passim*. See also above, footnotes 376, 378, 402 in chapter 2, and footnotes 257, 466, 476 in this chapter.

362   CHAPTER 4

FIGURE 6   Cape of Arkona
             STANISŁAW ROSIK

Helmold emphasized the capital role of this centre "on the land of the
Rans."⁴⁸⁶ However he did not mention that this was the place where the temple was located, which would be quite natural given that Svantevit was "deus
terrae Rugianorum." Hence, the chronicler only repeated the scheme consisting indicating one deity as the main patron of a tribe, which offers a sufficient
explanation for why the existence of other sanctuaries and deities worshipped
on the island was not mentioned.⁴⁸⁷ He did not, however, offer a detailed description of this cult as was the case for Prove in the Wagrian land.

    At the same time, it is hard to assume that Helmold did not know about
the location of the major sanctuary of the Rans in Arkona, so disregarding
this fact in his narration indicates that accentuating the very significance of
Svantevit's cult for Slavdom was most important. The Wagrians are noteworthy

---

486   Helmold mentions this at the end of the discussed chapter – see Helmold II, 108: "Urbs
      terrae illius principalis dicitur Archona."
487   The fact that Helmold did not exclude a larger number of deities in the Rans' panthe-
      on is confirmed in information about their "gods" in the history of the Christian priest
      Gottschalk, whose blood was to bring down their wrath – *ibidem*; see also below.

HELMOLDI CRONICA SLAVORUM ON SLAVIC RELIGION   363

here (as the capital of the Starigard bishopric, where Helmold was the priest, was located on their land), as well as their neighbours under the obedience of the Hamburg-Bremen archbishopric. In the historiological perspective of Helmold's work it was not Arkona or even Rans, but their god who enjoyed the power over their neighbours: "Therefore until our times not only the land of the Wagrians but also all other Slavic provinces sent their tributes there, acknowledging him as the god of gods."[488]

In the quoted account there is a characteristic way of viewing "the whole Slavdom" that is typical of Helmold, who treated it as a missionary space under the church control of Bremen or Starigard.[489] Therefore, the ethnic or cultural community of Polabian peoples and Rans is of lesser importance here, while the religious unity among them is prioritized. In this perspective Svantevit's cult is the superior factor tying together "the whole" but *de facto* only pre-Christian Slavdom.

Such ruthless domination of the Rans' god over their neighbours' pantheon seems to originate largely from an "inkpot." Its creation, on one hand, was supported by observation of political relations in Northern Polabia, and on the other hand by a will to create in the world of the text a model confrontation between the power of God and evil powers. Helmold had a ready model in this respect, namely the image of Rethra and Redigast in Adam of Bremen's work, which was inspired by the image of the ruler of demons (*princeps demonum*) well known from the gospel. However, a prototype of the image of Svantevit in the *Cronica Slavorum* was certainly also the biblical motif of *deus deorum* – "god of gods."[490]

Earlier, Helmold (I, 84) had referred this epithet to an anonymous father of Slavic gods, responsible only for the heavenly sphere. Hence it is not possible to identify Svantevit with this mysterious figure due to his roles in earthly matters. There seems to be little probability that Helmold reached some new mythological motifs, which would assume that Svantevit took over functions of the heavenly father. In this situation, an optimum explanation for why the chronicler used the expression *deus deorum* to refer to various deities seems to be not the statement that both existences were identified, but rather that

---

488   *Ibidem*: "Unde etiam nostra adhuc etate non solum Wagirensis terra, sed et omnes Slavorum provinciae illuc tributa annuatim transmittebant, illum deum deorum esse profitentes."

489   Apart from Rans, whose abodes were located not only on the island, the said tributes could be given only by the Obodrite and northern Veleti (Liutici) lands, see J. Strzelczyk in: *Helmolda Kronika*, p. 409 (footnote, commentary).

490   Cf. Ps 50:1 (in Vulgate).

they were joined by a common feature: they are decisively distant from other figures in the pantheon.

In both cases it would happen in a different way: in the first case the basis for the association would be theogony presented by Helmold, and in the other it would be the conviction that Svantevit's cult crossed the borders of the tribe, and as the result of the exceptional authority of his oracle Svantevit is presented in the literary perspective – also in the first book of *Cronica Slavorum* – as a hegemon in the sphere of the whole Slavic *sacrum*.[491] However, it cannot be excluded that the significance of Svantevit was also understood analogically among his worshippers in Rügen. In the 11th and 12th c. the process of cult transformation in the last enclaves of the Old Slavic religion progressed, and one should take into account that priests of native deities created various theologies related to particular cult centres.[492]

In the case of Svantevit, it should be considered that these mythological concepts could have supra-tribal reach, taking into account the exceptional fame of the temple and oracle, and also the range of its worshippers' political influences.[493] Thus a question arises of whether he was initially one of a few local deities on the island, and his brilliant career resulted only from the centre in Arkona and the growth of the Rans' political power, or whether perhaps his cult reached the major deity which was the counterpart of the Liutici Svarožic, and hence was connected with heavenly brightness and fire.[494]

The latter of these possibilities is indicated by Saxo Gramaticus, in whose work Svantevit was depicted as a four-faced idol, which hypothetically could undergo solar interpretation. The presence of this element in the case of the

---

491 Helmold I, 52. See above, pp. 322 f. If one assumes that it was possible that the basis for this statement was a similar assessment of the significance of this cult in the opinion of the Slavs themselves, or at least Rans, one should take into account that this alleged recognition of Svantevit's domination over other tribal deities could take place without the original reference to a theogonic motif. However, this motif could appear even after possible recognition of Svantevit as the hegemon of the whole Slavic pantheon. Such reasoning is essentially only conjecture based on a conjecture – thus it is hard to trust it.

492 Yet another time it is worth recalling the argument supporting the hypothesis on shaping local cults and the related theologies with the occurrence of two-part theonyms – observable in 11th–12th c. sources – such as Svantevit and Rugievit.

493 An expressive example in this matter was the Rans' intervention policy against neighbours accepting Christianity, see above, footnote 462 in this chapter.

494 *E.g.* Gąssowski, *Kult religijny*, p. 583, although he took into account the influence of Christianity on the evolution of the West Slavs' religion, in the case of Rügen he assumed that for internal reasons, Svantevit, "a local deity, most certainly originally without any significance, in the 12th c. started an incredible career, ousting Rans' cults of Rujevit and Porevit, and soon became the most powerful deity on the southern Baltic coast between the Elbe and the Oder."

major deity for a given community corresponds with centralization tendencies in power over it. In the case of the Rans, a possible increase in the significance of the temple and oracle (influencing assembly decisions) could weaken the monarch's position, but to the benefit of the priest, hence it is hard to talk here about decentralization of power over the society. Regardless of this, one should not overestimate the significance of the number of the idol from Arkona's heads, because essentially it was an "added value" to the basic phenomenon of polycephalism in Slavic idols and related ideas.

For comparison, it is worth mentioning the so-called "sviatovid" found in the Zbruch River in 1848 in the territory of modern Ukraine. In the top part of the statue there is a four-faced figure identified with the heavenly sovereign, who maintains rule over figures located in lower parts of the post, most certainly depicting the earthly sphere and the underworld.[495] In the case of this polycephalic figure, the idea of omnipotence (of all seeing) is of key significance. Similarly, Triglav, worshipped in Szczecin, according to priests had three heads to signify that he ruled over heaven, earth, and the underworld.[496] An analogous interpretation should be used in the case of seven-faced Rugievit, although he functioned as an alternative for Svantevit, which should be emphasized taking into account the joining of polycephalism with the expression of divine omnipotence and sovereignty over the world.

An argument which supports this interpretation of the shape of idols is the placement in seaside Slavs' temples of only one polycephalic or multi-faced

---

495   As early as the 19th c. identification of the idol from the Zbruch River with the Arkona Svantevit had numerous supporters (J. Lelewel, T. Żebrawski, Weigel, Bolsunowski, T. Reyman – see Krzak, "Światowid," p. 30). B.A. Rybakov assumed that this four-faced figure was a representation of the major deity in the pantheon of the Eastern Slavs whose name was Rod and he proposed to identify it with Svantevit, see Rybakov, *Jazyčestvo drevnej Rusi*, pp. 236–251, 422 f.; cf. *idem*, "Svjatovid – Rod," in *Liber Iosepho Kostrzewski octogenario a veneratoribus dicatus*, ed. Konrad Jażdżewski (Wrocław: Ossolineum, 1968), pp. 390–394. Despite certain convergence between Svantevit's statue described by Saxo and the ideogram found in the Zbruch, *i.e.* the so called sviatovid, it is hard to share the conviction about such far-reaching community between this finding and the Rans' cult. It would be more accurate to talk about analogies occurring between them: especially four heads and attributes. The key problem in this discussion still remains a doubt, returning like a boomerang, related not only to the Slavic provenience of the "Sviatovid" from Zbruch (he could have been created by nomads invading these lands), but also to its medieval origin – an alternative was a view that it was made during Romanticism as a result of the 19th c. fascination with ancient Slavic motifs. For recent debate on this matter see: Olexiy Komar, Natalia Khamaiko, "Zbručskiy idol: pamiatnik epokhi romantizma?," *Ruthenica* 10 (2011), pp. 166–217.

496   Ebo III, 1.

366   CHAPTER 4

statue, instead of whole pantheons.[497] The initiative to interpret this fact as a
kind of Slavic monotheism or even henotheism, regardless of the premises in
Helmold's text, raises doubts because it seems uncertain that in the awareness
of the Slavs the existence of other deities was negated, including the Christian
God.[498] However, the very influence of monotheism on the evolution of the
beliefs of the Baltic Slavs could result in a trend to present the highest divine
creatures in the form of polycephalic figures as an expression of the view that
this form allows their exceptional power and extensive or even universal capa-
bilities to be shown.

At the time of the decisive struggle with the political and ideological expansion of Christianity, the Rans, similarly to the Pomeranians or Liutici, certainly aspired to create a cult of a sovereign divine existence with universal
powers. This direction of change in the Slavs' religion created an opportunity
for the convergence of the system of their beliefs and Christian ideas in terms
of monotheism.[499] Hence, the process of earlier gods' personalities and gods'
roles overlapping with the figure of the main patron of a tribe led to monolatry
(and this notion seems more appropriate with reference to the Arkona cult
than monotheism). Svantevit turned out to be a more advanced product of this
process. The development of his cult brought analogies with Christian theology: teachings about the only God, ruler of heaven and earth, corresponds with
information about Svantevit – "god of gods" and people.[500]

---

497   *E.g.* Rosik, *Udział*, pp. 96–99.
498   Urbańczyk, *Dawni Słowianie*, pp. 22, 192. See also below, footnote 500.
499   For comparison it is worth emphasizing that this kind of transformation process of the
      pre-Christian religion reached a very advanced stage among the Balts, who – according
      to the words of the Lithuanian duke Gedymin addressed to papal legates in 1324 – were
      to think that they worshipped the only God (certainly they meant the deity of heavens –
      Andajus) practicing their own rite and not needing baptism – see Henryk Łowmiański,
      "Elementy indoeuropejskie w religii Bałtów," in *Ars Historica. Prace z dziejów powszech-
      nych i Polski*, ed. Marian Biskup *et al.* (Poznań: Uniwersytet Adama Miczkiewicza w
      Poznaniu, 1976) pp. 152 f. It is also worth taking into account in the analysis of this infor-
      mation the fact that the Lithuanian and Christian neighbourhood in Gedymin's times
      had already existed for over three centuries, and mutual contacts between both circles
      were rather intensive (the evidence were even dynastic marriages), so the atmosphere
      of the said example of the *interpretatio Lithuana* of the Christian God was supportive.
      Meanwhile for such possible identification of Svantevit in the Rans' mentality there was
      rather no place due to the atmosphere of their political and military confrontation with
      Christ's worshippers. The native cult, its characteristics (expressed also in the polycepha-
      lism of idols), was a guarantee of sovereignty in the face of pressure exerted by all their
      neighbours. Cf. Rosik, *Udział*, p. 103.
500   Transformations of the Polabian and Baltic religion directed to monotheism was taken
      into account by Niederle, *Život*, vol. 2, part 1, p. 179, the same Váňa, *Svět Slovanských*,
      p. 49. Procházka, *Organisace*, p. 155, in ideology transformations leading to the

HELMOLDI CRONICA SLAVORUM ON SLAVIC RELIGION   367

A premise for the existence of many gods in the Rans' mythology, according to Helmold, is the information about making offerings to them in which shedding Christian blood was particularly significant.[501] An offering of a Christian, according to Helmold, was not something regular, but was made only sometimes (*nonnunquam*) to bring gods special joy.[502] This general statement is illustrated by a story "from a few years earlier" about a certain priest from Bardevik, named Gottschalk.

He came to Rügen to a herring fair which took place in November; merchants could attend the fair after payment of a fare due to the "god of this land." In such a large crowd the clergyman was asked to do what was his "duty to God," hence most certainly – as it is indicated in further narration – to celebrate a mass or some other service.[503] Having heard that, the pagan priest informed the "king and the people" that the wrath of the gods can be brought only by blood of a priest who decided to make an offering to "a stranger [god] among them."[504] Terrified barbarians required an offering of the priest made to their god and they even proposed a rather high payment of "100 marks" for

---

establishment of strong and centralised tribal states he saw an incentive for a tribal deity to start to acquire the significance of the exclusive deity, which brings its concept closer to the notions of Christian monotheism. However, it is hard to assume that Rans questioned the existence of other gods, including the Christian God. In this situation it seems more accurate to assume that in their cult there was a trend to establish monolatry, hence the choice of one deity as an exclusive cult object, without denial of the existence of others. The monolatry stage is hypothetically distinguished in the characteristics of the evolution of the deity concept in Old Testament Judaism (Yahwism), *i.e.* evolution from the Canaanite polytheism through (hypothetical) monolatry to monotheism. In the Middle Ages Christian monotheism in a particular way was based on the idea of mediation of hosts of saints interceding with God, which could be used as an analogy in creation of the strong position of the sovereign of heavens in relation to other deities. For maturing Old Testament monotheism going through the phase of monolatry see Lech Stachowiak, "Bóg. II. W Starym Testamencie," in *Encyklopedia Katolicka*, vol. 1, ed. Feliks Gryglewicz, Romuald Łukaszyk, Zygmunt Sułowski (Lublin: Towarzystwo Naukowe KUL, 1973), col. 902–903).

501   Helmold II, 108: "Inter varia autem libamenta sacerdos nonnumquam hominem Christianum litare solebat, huiuscemodi cruore deos omnino delectari iactitans".

502   The custom of specifically choosing Christians as an offering for gods of Rans has its analogy in source data related to the Prussians, see Žulkus, *Heidentum*, pp. 153–155.

503   Helmold II, 108: "Accidit ante paucos annos maximam institorum multitudinem eo convenisse piscacionis gratia. In Novembri enim flante vehementibus vento multum illic allec capitur, et patet mercatoribus liber accessus si tamen ante deo terrae legitima sua persolverint. Affuit tunc forte Godescalcus quidam sacerdos Domini de Bardewich invitatus, ut in tanta populorum frequentia ageret ea quae Dei sunt".

504   *Ibidem*: "Nec hoc latuit diu sacerdotem illum barbarum et accersit rege et populo nuntiat irata vehementius numina nec aliter posse placari, nisi cruore sacerdotis, qui peregrinum inter eos sacrificium offerre presumpsisset".

368   CHAPTER 4

betraying him.[505] If refused, they were ready to use force, but merchants managed to save him, facilitating his escape by boat in the night.[506]

The Rans' hatred of Christianity (*odium Christiani nominis*), exemplified in this story, and also the fact that their "focus of superstition" (*supersticionum fomes*) preponderated over cults of the other Slavs, did not refrain Helmold from praising their virtues: hospitality, respect for parents, or care for the elderly and sick.[507] It is hard not to notice in this information the topos in the characteristics of barbarians modelled on the works of Adam of Bremen.[508] Its occurrence – with the recent introduction of Christianity on the island in the background – fostered a trend in its neighbours' awareness to assimilate recent enemies and treat them as new members of the supra-ethnical, religiously Latin community of *Christianitas*.

3   The Slavic Religion in the "World" of Helmold's Work

The historiological programme of the *Chronicle of the Slavs* remains in close relation with Adam of Bremen's thought. However, it is easy to notice that Helmold creatively developed motifs taken from his work and changed the horizon of interests. In the centre of the chronicler's attention there are the Slavs, or rather the German mission conducted among them, with particular attention on the activity of the Starigard bishopric.

Looking from the comparative perspective of the Christianization of the Germanic peoples, Helmold claims that the "province of Slavs remained stronger and more resistant in accepting the faith."[509] Slavdom – limited in relation

---

505   *Ibidem*: "Tunc barbara gens attonita convocat institorum cohortem rogatque sibi dari sacerdotem, ut offerat deo suo placabilem hostiam. Renitentibus Christianis centum marcas offerunt in munere."; cf. Num 5 8: "ut sit placabilis hostia"; see: *Helmolda Kronika*, p. 410, footnote 158.

506   Helmold II, 108: "Sed cum nil proficerent, ceperunt intentare vim et crastina bellum indicere. Tunc institores onustis iam de captura navibus nocte illa iter aggressi sunt et secundis ventis vela credentes tam se quam sacerdotem atrocibus ademere periculis".

507   *Ibidem*: "Quamvis autem odium Christiani nominis et superstiticionum fomes plus omnibus Slavis apud Ranos invaluerit, pollebant tamen multis naturalibus bonis. Erat enim apud eos hospitalitatis plenitudo, et parentibus debitum exhibent honorem. Nec enim aliquis egens aut mendicus apud eos aliquando repertus est. Statim enim, ut aliquem inter eos aut debilem fecerit infirmitas aut decrepitum etas, heredis curae delegatur plena humanitate fovendus. Hospitalitatis enim gratia et parentum cura primum apud Slavos virtutis locum optinent."

508   See above, pp. 248 f.

509   Helmold I, 6: "sola Slavorum provincia remansit ceteris durior atque ad credendum tardior."

HELMOLDI CRONICA SLAVORUM ON SLAVIC RELIGION   369

to the real one – is understood as a missionary space, which is confirmed by
the way the terms *gentes* or *naciones* in plural forms are used to refer to pagans.
Additionally, he defined their situation as remaining in error (*errorum nexus*)
and enslaved by disease (*morbus*), which needs God's remedy. The salvation
(*salus*) of the Polabian peoples was something the most prominent figures in
the *Chronicle of the Slavs* strove for with all their hearts.

Apart from this, the situation of the Slavs is presented in the evangelical symbolism juxtaposing light and darkness (the Rugians staying "in the darkness of
infidelity they wandered away from the light of truth" – "in tenebris ifidelitatis
a luce veritatis aberrarunt"). *Infidelitas* is a term which makes sense only in the
context of Church doctrine. Northern countries, just like in the symbolism of
the Bible, are the source of all evil and a threat to the People of God, which is
reflected in the chronicle as a memory of the "ice of the north" melting in the
fire of the Word of God (Anskar's mission). In similar spirit it is also said that
Wicelin (I, 69) and his companions were sent to "the land of poverty and hunger, where there were the abode of Satan and the habitat of the evil spirit."[510] In
this quotation there is an annotation from the Book of Revelation of St. John. It
is also worth noting that the Rugians felt sadness when they were requested to
put the Christian priest Gottschalk to death by their priests (II, 109); one may
only assume that according to Helmold story Rans wanted to listen to the Holy
Gospel, however, they were enslaved by their priests – Satan's servants.

A particular type of diagnosis of the Polabian people made by Helmold fits
the logic of the Bible in which people tend gradually to leave God. The image
of natural virtues that the Slavs possessed (hospitality, care for the elderly, *etc.*)
is overshadowed by the progressing decay of their nature: *crudelitas ingenita,*
gentes rebelles et incredulae, naturaliter infidi et ad malum proni. However, the
listed imperfections are not the worst fault of these people, as their return to
paganism filled up the measure of their sin. Helmold certainly does not take
into account the length of the Christianization process, which he understands in the spirit of missionary ideology as inclusion of whole peoples to
Christianity (and along with *e.g.* Bishop Marco "washed" with baptism water
the people of Obotrites and Wagrians).

The history, and also the history of rejecting Christianity, is traced by God;
it is indicated in such expressions as *permittente Deo* or metaphors referring
the described events in Northern Polabia to biblical motifs (*e.g.* "the iniquity of
the Amorites was not yet full"[511]). In this way, even consent to a pagan reaction

---

510   *Ibidem*, I, 69: "in terram egestatis et famis, ubi erat sedes Sathanae et habitatatio omnis
       spiritus inmundi".
511   See above, p. 305.

granted by Providence gains Old Testament sense. The Slavs are the "scourge of God" for Saxons and to some extent they have to exceed the measure of their iniquity themselves, to attribute their accession to Christianity only to God and the Church, and not to their own achievements. However, the chronicler cannot see servants of God in the pagan Slavs. Quite contrarily, wars and any other misfortunes, for him, are demons' acts.

The historical books of the Old Testament and Revelation could have inspired the concept of a cyclical arrangement of the narration of the chronicle following the rhythms of high and low tides of Christianization. Its success or failure depended on a variety of factors: wars caused by the Barbarians, "toughness" of the Slavs, and at last the will of Providence. However, Helmold attributes decisive significance to Saxons' being faithful to God. A lot depends on the religious condition of rulers, which is a clear reference to Old Testament historiology.

In Helmold's chronicle pagan reaction is understood as apostasy after which there is no place for – as it was conventionally called above – "good pagans." Similar to Adam of Bremen's work, this role is taken by the Prussians, and *Iumne* does not play it any longer. In this context the Legend of Vineta does not appear to be a consequence of the author's ignorance, but a purposefully used literary figure aimed at emphasizing a change in the situation of the Slavs (*Vinedi*) in a theological perspective, used by the author as he noticed an alleged lack of continuity in the history of *Iumne* (probably Wolin). The chronicler's attention is attracted mainly to matters related to confrontation between good and evil, whose most clear embodiment is in this perspective the pagan religion. The Slavs, although they did not lose their natural virtues completely, became first of all a tool in the hands of spiritual forces opposing Christ and the Church. This confrontation, similar to the historical books of the Old Testament, is not acted out only in the sphere of human souls or in the spiritual world, but also in the history of whole communities.

The apostatic dimension of paganism in Northern Polabia, and mainly in Rugia, offers additional interpretation possibilities of this phenomenon. Certainly, this situation should be associated with a note about rebuilding worship for the House of God "in natione prava et perversa." The same epithets were attributed to the Christian Nordalbings who worshipped nature. Moreover, in Helmold's typifying perspective the Obotrite duke Henry, son of Gottschalk, being the subduer of the Rugians (1123–1124), bears the characteristics of a "Man of God" (victorious king, Christ), who had to force a mutinous people to return to God. An intercessor of the dissenters is a pagan priest who – sic! – at this moment does not turn out to be the servant of demons, but a zealous, in performing penance, servant of the representative of God (*i.e.* Henry).

This literary device allows the complexity of *interpretatio Christiana* to be realized, which is a logical consequence of treating the holy biblical history as a norm in explanation of history in general.

An important element of the context of medieval interpretation of Slavic religion is character typification. A clear example of the Obotrite prince Henry, the Gottschalk's son, has been mentioned above. Another example is the figure of Vicelin as an exorcist. In Rügen, Prince Iaromir was directly compared to St. Paul. The characteristics of the Apostle of the Nations can also be observed in Gottschalk's literary creation in connection with the persecution of Christianity and next with its propagation. Each of these situations is indirectly referred to as Slavic religion treated as paganism, idolatry *etc.*

In Helmold's views, an element of key significance in missionary activity is guiding pagans to something more than mere formal dimension of accepting Christianity. The chronicler claimed that in 1147, during a crusade against the Polabian tribes, the Slavs "falso baptizati sunt" ("they were falsely baptized") Thus, a category of incorporating whole nations in the Church understood as "baptizing" them, taken from Adam of Bremen (and known also to Thietmar of Merseburg), gains an important supplement: the sacrament taken insincerely does not guarantee its lasting results. This is a clear sign of a move towards an intensification of the spiritual dimension of conversion, which was not only a result of changing standards in how the Church functioned in central Europe at that time in comparison to the reality of 11th c., but also a result of the own reflections of the parish priest from Bosau, who observed the unruly attitude of the Slavs to Christianization.

It is worth noting that Helmold uses the term *barbari* as a synonym of *pagani* (even when rewriting passages of Adam of Bremen's work, he replaced *pagani* with *barbari*). The chronicler's reflection is conditioned not only by factors he was clearly aware of, but also by environmental conditions, namely the sphere of cultural facts reflecting the mentality of its author and recipients. From this perspective, the replacement of the word *pagani* by *barbari* requires closer attention. The consistency with which Helmold uses the stereotypical assessment of *barbari* when referring to the Slavs suggests that this author – and possibly his whole environment – perceived paganism more as a cultural alien phenomenon, and so the aspect of doctrinal confrontation clearly readable in the term *pagani* was attributed to it.

A description of the visit in Starigard, among (*in*) "barbaris habitatoribus" ("the barbarian inhabitants"), clearly indicates that *ydolatria* and *superstitio* are a sign of recognition of the barbarians. In this sense, the propagation of Christianity is also a promotion of Latin culture. Following Adam, Helmold repeated that Gottschalk simultaneously rejected faith and "scriptures." Similarly, the Nordalbings, among whom Vicelin worked, turn out to be Christians only by name. Their austere customs are reflected in such expressions as *gens bruta* or *genus agreste et incultum*, accompanied by information that Vicelin had a lot of work among them, "errantes corrigens, concilians dissidentes, lucos et omnes ritus sacrilegos destruens." Moreover, Helmold creatively developed the *canes* topic in relation to the Slavs. It combines references to cultural inferiority with earlier references to paganism, although it should be noted that Helmold does not seem to share this stereotypical opinion of the barbarians.

The notion of barbarianism contained civilizational and cultural references and, in Helmold's narration, it automatically carried information about the double dimension of the confrontation between Slavs and their Christian neighbours, which shows well the thread of the original reflexion of this scribe combining compilations of Adam's passages: "All that kind of men [*i.e.* Slavs] is dedicated to the cult of idolatry, always desultory and mobile, who make profit out of piracy, on the Danes on one side, and on the Saxons on the other."[512] It is clear that idolatry and piracy in the eyes of the chronicler from Bosau came hand in hand. Also, Rochel, a Wagrian duke, was characterized with the phrase *ydolatra et pirata*. Likewise, in chapter 84 there is an encouragement for pagans to give up their idols and wrong deeds, especially plundering.

The barbarians – as emphasized by Helmold a number of times – were full of hatred for Christianity and the clergy in particular; they showed special penchant for destroying churches; *e.g. barbaricus furror* destroyed the Church organization at the times of Libentius (see I, 69). Nothing good was expected of them and even humane (*humane*) acceptance of the exiled king Harald by the inhabitants of Wolin was to be "preter spem, quia barbari erant" (actually it was not – let us remember – anything extraordinary, given good relations between Wolin and Scandinavia).

The above-mentioned threats put pressure on emperors and the clergy to undertake the effort of Christianization "gentes istae rebelles et incredulae." Vicelin, likewise, worried about the erection of the House of God "in gente incredula et ydolatra" (I, 79). These places in the chronicle clearly show Helmold's historiographic programme: the relation of the barbarians to the Empire and their hostility towards the Church remain inseparable (in the beginning this was referred to the pagan Saxons, see I, 3). Thus, the success of the Slavic mission is not only in the interest of both authorities, it is also their joint task. Stretching political power to the Slavs, in Helmold's opinion, was to accompany Christianization.

---

512   See above, p. 269.

HELMOLDI CRONICA SLAVORUM ON SLAVIC RELIGION   373

The account about the victory of the Obotrite duke Henry, son of Gottschalk, in the battle of Schmilau, where the chronicler clearly sees God's intervention, is a good example of the strong emphasis on the fact that defeated Slavs were obliged to pay tribute and be baptized. Even Henry the Fowler and later Otto the Great in his footsteps – distinctly marked by Helmold – by defeating the Slavs ensured tribute for themselves and baptism for God. According to Helmold's perspective, the first rebels of the Slavs (at the times of Otto II and III) were automatically directed against "non solum divinis legibus sed et imperatoriis iussis" ("not only God's laws but also imperial orders"). Benefits from submission to imperial authority and God's laws were to be experienced by the Slavs themselves, since as idolaters or people "without God" (*sine Deo*) they could be attacked at any time as they were outlaws (I, 84).

The paradigm of cooperation between *imperium* and *sacerdotium* is established at the beginning of the work where Charlemagne and the archbishop of Hamburg, St. Anskar, acts as a prototype. According to Helmold, the emperor is the head of Christianity (although he is not the head of the Church), who fulfils the mission of Constantine the Great. The Franks themselves thus took over the mission of leading Christianity after the Romans and Greeks in a kind of relay of nations; their successors were the Germans. So, the role of Charlemagne in this perspective was taken over by Henry I and more substantially by Otto I the Great, who himself was the emperor and – what was essential for Helmold – also the founder of the bishopric in Starigard. His successors were not equally effective in missionary work. Finally, the role of faith protectors was taken over by laymen who did not have such *de iure* rights as emperors in missionary work, but in practice became its participants.

Gottschalk, his son Henry, count Adolf II, Henry the Lion (according to Helmold, however, interested more in tribute than evangelization), and Iaromir, directly involved in the affairs of Wagria and Rügen, became protectors of missionary actions and propagators of the Christian faith. A conflict between Vicelin and Henry the Lion about investiture proves, however, that Helmold marked the difference in the relations of both of them to the emperor. The heart of the mission at that time turned out to be the clergy. Initially the followers of St. Anskar were missionaries and bishops (Unni, Poppo) and later priests from the bishopric of Starigard led by Vicelin and Gerold. The necessity for cooperation between lay lords and the people of the Church was essential for the success of the mission, which was disturbed by a storm of wars and also by the resistance of the Slavs, escalated by German exploitation.

The pragmatic message of Helmold's work strongly affected the schematization of the literary image of paganism. This does not necessarily indicate a falseness of data, but rather a particular kind of selectiveness and arrangement

374   CHAPTER 4

related to the chronicler's questionnaire about the Slavic *sacrum*. In the composition of this questionnaire the views on paganism in the circulation of contemporary Christian thought was vital.

In Helmold's work, one can observe two tracks of a doctrinal interpretation
of paganism. The first trend is clearly determined by the identification of *dii –
demones* that requires it to be seen in the spirit of direct confrontation between God and Satan. However, the Slavic religion was simultaneously treated
as an error, *i.e.* consequences of the weakness of human nature (*error*, "errores
in quibus nati fuerant"). The latter trend also indirectly refers to Satan, but it is
up to the people themselves and especially their stupidity to take responsibility for existence of this error.[513]

Additionally, paganism is perceived as a spiritual force with a political face.
A characteristic feature of the social and political organization of the Slavs in
the light of Helmold's chronicle seems to be a type of theocracy. Court judgements near Prove's grove were given by a duke, the people, and a priest. In
Rügen, fate read by priests was to have more influence on politics than the will
of the "king" and people. This theocratic hallmark on the system of authority
seems to be undisputable. Still, doubts are raised by its prominent exposure in
the chronicle. Helmold tended to emphasize the divine and priestly element
in the narrative structure.

Writing about the Wagrians (I, 69) the chronicler begins by mentioning
their sanctuary and deity, next their priest called Mike, and only at the end
duke Rochel. As in Rügen, he was mainly interested in Arkona when it was
dominated by priests but remains quiet when it comes to the centre of ducal
power and cult probably situated in Garz. Helmold developed and enriched
Adam of Bremen's data related to Rethra and Rügen. Adam mentions that Rans
are ruled by a king, and according to Helmold the primacy of power is in the
hands of a priest. In a description of an internal war in the Liutici land, the
Redars and Tollenser (by reading Adam's "Riaduri atque Tholenzi" as "Riaduri
sive Tholenzi") in a way become one people defending theocracy.

Fighting paganism is not only the struggle for the souls of particular people, but the destruction of earthly bastions of *antisacrum*. Helmold mentions
devastations of Slavic sanctuaries and statues of various kinds, sometimes
as a prelude to preaching the Gospel and accepting pagans to the Church.
Such dealings are clearly described by the chronicler, who mentions the end
of Rugians' religion – after the public annihilation of the famous statue of

---

513   One should recall here Stanisław Urbańczyk's opinion in which he defined *interpretatio
      Christiana* in a rather laconic way as perceiving paganism as works of the devil and stu-
      pidity (see above, p. 18).

HELMOLDI CRONICA SLAVORUM ON SLAVIC RELIGION   375

Svantevit in fire, King Valdemar "destroyed the sanctuary with all the rituals held in it and plundered the overflowing treasury. He ordered them to give up their errors in which they were born and to accept the religion of the one true God."[514]

From a theological perspective, the sense of such actions was a spiritual struggle against demonic rule. The motif of spiritual confrontation seen with Christian eyes reappears many times in Helmold's descriptions. The Slavs were to make offerings not to God but to demons or idols (statement from the First Epistle to the Corinthians: *immolare demoniis non Deo*). Similarly, pagan Saxons gave up the cult of demons (*cultus demonum*) to accept sacraments of faith. In addition to this, the measure of holiness and preparation for evangelization of nations according to Helmold is the power over evil spirits promised by Christ to his disciples in the Gospel. Vicelin's activity in Faldera, where he acted as an exorcist, was sufficiently convincing that he was prepared for a mission, and obstacles were related to other factors.

Sacrifices of the Christian faithful are a particular sign of hostility towards Christianity. A Christian's death was to make Svantevit especially contented. It is hard to say how much truth there is in this statement about Rans' cult. Scholars discuss the cruelty of wars or customary offerings of people without specifying whether they were Christians, which seems more probable, although not certain. Finding an explicit solution to this problem on the basis of Helmold's chronicle does not seem possible given the diabolizing context of his accounts about Slavic rituals. The estimation of pagan deities' love for human offerings should be discussed in the context of the opinion that demons are attracted to blood (I, 52). Persecution of Christians was presented on the pages of this work in terms of martyrdom, and even the crucifixion practiced by the Slavs was read as a mockery of faith in Christ.

The hallmark of capital bastions of evil on the presented historical stage is the title *sedes ydolatriae*. Rethra, which in a slightly modified literary image still performs the role of this "capital of idolatry" defined for it by Adam of Bremen, as the chronicle action develops is replaced by Rügen.[515] Hence, it

---

514 Helmold II, 108: king Valdemar "destruxit fanum cum omni religione sua et erarium locuples diripuit. Et precepit, ut discederent ab erroribus suis, in quibus nati fuerant, et assumerent cultum veri Dei."

515 The account on Rethra borrowed by Helmold from Adam of Bremen's work indicates a model situation in which the capital and temple have primacy over the Liutici and – after the mutiny at the times of Archbishop of Hamburg-Bremen Libentius – Obodrite tribes. It shows also the prevalence of the capital god, Redigast, over other deities. In the theological perspective Redigast represents the highest spiritual power in the world of Slavic paganism as he is treated as the personification of biblical *princeps* of demons.

was Rethra/Radogošč that was the first centre of spiritual and political powers acting against the spread of Christianity in the Slavdom. When it was defeated an even more dangerous enemy entered the stage of history, which in a way had waited from the very beginning for its time to come.[516] Thus, the missionary phase of the history of the Slavs still lasts when the narrative of the first book ends. New events brought an account written a few years later annexed to the chronicle as the second book. The final episode of the confrontation between Slavic paganism and Christianity in this view was the defeating of Svantevit's cult.

The most detailed information about the world of Slavic gods given by Helmold is connected with the situation after the fall of Rethra and among a variety of embodiments of divinity: (holy) groves, springs, trees and penates, gods (Prove, Podaga, Radogost/Redigast), *malus deus* and *bonus deus*, the main figure turns out to be Svantevit from Rügen, and – in a parallel theogonic motif – the anonymous *deus deorum*. It is striking that, in the first book, Helmold claims that Svantevit is the hegemon of *sacrum*. However, there is no identification of him with the "god of gods." However, it is included in the second book, assumedly under the influence of new information (specifics of the theology of the Arkona cult), or – which seems even more certain – by ignoring the cosmogonic motif and without any reference to the earlier information (I, 84).

Helmold collected embodiments of Slavic deities that he knew into one system and put them in order according to the biblical paradigm: *demones* and their *princeps* as well as God ruling over all supernatural creatures, in a scheme borrowed from the Old Testament of the *Vulgate* where God is called *Deus deorum*, (comp. Psalm 50). The coherence of the motifs of Slavic mythology is of secondary importance here and the chronicler, perceiving Svantevit as a sovereign of the heavenly sphere comparable to Yahweh-God, used a biblical expression when referring to him. It is justified by the fact that Wagria and other Slavic countries sent annual tributes to Arkona, however at this moment a strictly theological cult aspect was equated with its political role, which raises justified doubts when treated as an element of the contemporary historical reality, and seems to be a literary concept of the chronicler.

---

516   A theological explication of this situation is presented in the Legend of Corvey. The Rans' idolatry is not only an *error*, it is *error peior priore* – contempt for the Creator shown through veneration for the creation (St. Vitus). The location "in the heart of the sea" also seems to be a metaphor of being lost in the powers of eternal chaos, and at least terror and demonism which was associated with this unstable element.

HELMOLDI CRONICA SLAVORUM ON SLAVIC RELIGION   377

Another disputable issue is the way Helmold presented tutelary deities of various tribes and territories. In the polytheistic system, which does not know the monotheistic idea of a covenant, it seems unnatural to restrict competences of divine creatures to one territory or tribe (*deus terrae, dea Pelaborum*). In this case it is possible that these are either Christian influences, or a product of the chroniclers' mentality. The latter option seems more probable given that Helmold evidently introduces an artificial hierarchy of Slavic deities in one system. This does not change the fact that the literary vision of tribal theocracy – based on real observation or biblical borrowings – with one divine sovereign being in the lead corresponds with the historiological programme of the *Chronicle of the Slavs*.

The above-mentioned schematization of the image of *sacrum* – of religious institutions and the system of divine creatures itself – as well as a model confrontation between both worlds representing different religions, in fact imitate biblical models. Apart from this, the Bible was the main inspiration for a description of the details of Slavic religion and was the source of theological evaluations and opinions. They are coupled with mental categories drawn from the text.

Helmold refers to the Rugians claiming that "they abandoned their faith (...) and turned religion [of Christians] into superstition."[517] Hence he provides readers with a term comprehensively defining the pagan religion as *superstitio*. A more extensive definition is only the not so rigid *error* (in addition in Helmold's work the expression *error superstitionum* is used a few times). *Superstitio* translated today simply as "superstition" does not adhere to the meaning from the epoch of the chronicler, because it used to mean different kinds of deviation in terms of cult and doctrine.

The heart of pagan religion in Helmold's view is idolatry. On numerous occasions it functions as *pars pro toto* of the whole of paganism (and even – perhaps metaphorically – all divinization of earthly goods). Scholars more prone to scepticism, such as von Wienecke or Łowmiański, took this fact at face value to prove that the notion of idolatry could have appeared in sources even when there was no question of statues. However, studies conducted on Helmold's chronicle prove that in the area of his interest idolatry was commonplace, so such type of argumentation based on the supposed functioning of metonymy loses its sense and in fact is unverifiable.

It is worth noting that Helmold used to compose the Slavic religion's summaries and references at two levels: picturesque facts (sometimes two or even

---

517   Helmold I, 6: "a fide defecerunt (...) atque Christicolis religionem verterunt in superstitionem".

three) – such as *ydolatria, multiplex ydolorum cultura,* groves, priests and offerings – were accompanied by more extensive concepts, paramount to the former ones and carrying comprehensive perspective of the pagan religion, such as *superstitio, error superstitionum, ritus sacrilegus, multiplex religionis cultus.*[518] Thus, the summary information gained dynamics and encompassed all symptoms of *sacrum.* Such images are frequently unsatisfactory in terms of their accuracy, but it is difficult to question in advance the elements appearing in them.

The role of idolatry as a distinctive sign of paganism in such summaries can hardly be depreciated, because it occurs in nearly every report on Slavic cults and beliefs, even more so than when Helmold clearly noted its lack (*e.g.* in Prove's grove or in worship of Siwa). This very special place of idolatry in the textual image of the religious system of the Slavs was influenced by a theological concept of contrasting idolatry directly with the worship of God. The chronicler puts into Henry the Lion's mouth an appeal to the Slavs "ut relictis ydolis colerent unum Deum" ("that they should give up their idols and worship the one God"). This is why spiritual capitals of paganism were called *sedes ydolatriae* and this name was in the case of Rügen supplemented with *fomes errorum.*

It is worth mentioning also that Vicelin came to the Slavs *ydolatriam extirpandi* – hence this expression means *pars pro toto* the whole liquidation of paganism. However, Helmold does not mention idolatry or its absence when writing about the Nordalbings (I, 47), though they were Christian in name only but were encompassed by the bishopric. It can be assumed that in the chronicler's mind the cult of idols was automatically connected with the territories being outside of ecclesiastical authority.

There are other noteworthy definitions of the Slavic cult. Helmold did not try to penetrate the Slavic tribes' mentality to look for the visible–invisible dependencies. He enumerates them in one row, without any attention devoted to putting them in any specific order, spiritual creatures (*dii, deae, deus deorum, penates*) and material embodiments of *sacrum – idolum, simulachrum, lucus, fons.* In the case of some notions it is hard to determine which group they belong to – *e.g. deitates* or *numina* – because Helmold implies that pagans worship both visible and invisible cult objects in a way which is due only to the Creator. The content of chapter 84 is a good example of this. Here the chronicler introduces a kind of gradation of the objects of Slavic worship: penates,

---

518   According to the chapter 3 of the chronicle in the Northern people – the Normans and the Slavs – "opacitas errorum et difficultas silvescentis ydolatriae occurred" (Helmold I, 3).

HELMOLDI CRONICA SLAVORUM ON SLAVIC RELIGION   379

idols, and the highest position which is taken by the Prove's holy grove as *sanctimonium universae terrae*.

"Euhemerization" used by Helmold to justify the cult of Svantevit deserved a separate categorization, and this trend certainly encompasses an attempt to deify Henry the Lion by Obodrites. In the first case there is the cult of the creation, particularly St. Vitus being considered as superior to God the Creator (like in the Epistle to the Romans 1:25), which was clearly attributed only to the Rugians by Helmold. Moreover, he mentioned that the Slavs "do not contradict that there is one god in heaven," but this does not mean that they worship him. The subject of their cult is the group of gods derived from his blood, or – as a result of a bigger error – deified people. In Helmold's view, the mysterious Slavic "god of gods" and the Christian God whose follower was Henry the Lion seem to have a lot in common, although the matter cannot be settled definitely.[519]

Helmold's gods and lower rank deities live in woods, fields, groves, temples, and maybe also in statues and holy oaks and other trees. Some of the deities exist also as *idola*, statues. However, it is only one of equal and parallel categories of description. The same deities are sometimes treated as spiritual and at other times as material. Svantevit is presented on the pages of the *Chronicle of the Slavs* in three versions as: 1) *simulachrum* ("simulachrum illud antiquissimum Zuantevith, quod colebatur ab omni natione Slavorum"), which is most probably not an ordinary representation but *idolum*, which is indicated by giving the statue a name, as in the case of "ydolum, cui nomen Podaga"; 2) deified St. Vitus – a man; 3) a deity of purely spiritual nature, *deus*, which is emphatically confirmed by the identification with the "god of gods."[520] This inconsistency results from using various interpretation templates in the construction of the textual vision of paganism composed of the same element of the historical substrate.

It is tempting to unite all Helmold's views on the essence of paganism into one with the idea: *creaturam anteponere creatori* (cf. Rom 1:25). However, this would be quite an "overinterpretation" because it is easy to observe that various places in the Bible were his inspiration. On the other hand, in the composition of the literary image of paganism, associations with the chronicler's own world and will to have influence on the reader play a significant role. It has

---

519   Even without solving the dispute on Helmold's credibility on the matter of the Wagrian religion, it is easy to notice that he composed a vision of the Slavic theology waving some element of the Christian doctrine in it.

520   Lack of cohesion in the literary motif ascribing the title of *deus deorum* to Svantevit is obvious and indicates that the chronicler rather freely used the Slavic theogonic myth of "god of gods" he knew.

already been mentioned above that in the statement "non diffitentur unum deum in caelis" there is a reference to monotheism. *Mirabilis error, i.e.* a ritual with a chalice to worship the "gods" of good and evil, does not involve consecration (a reference to the holy mass) in the name of gods, but it is cursing, which is flexibly expressed by a word-game *consecratio – execratio*. All this information seems to be marked by elements of Christian culture, although the identification of the "Black God" (*Zcerneboch*) with the Devil is most certainly not Helmold's invention but rather Christian infiltration modifying the Slavic dualism of archaic origin.

A moralistic and didactic trend plays a very important role in the chronicle. The fact that Helmold mentions Slavs' aversion to making oaths seems to admonish the circle of projected readers of the work, the Saxons, who, as one may assume, used to abuse solemn verbal obligations. Similarly, emphasis on the profound respect of the Slavs for holy places (right of asylum, *etc.*) and a customary division of spoils among the Rugians (gold and silver went to the temple treasury and wives) has a moralizing tone, especially in the context of stressed avarice (*avaritia*), which the Saxons were reproached for quite frequently. There are more similar examples. The most interesting ones are certain ways of reproaching the Saxons expressed by Slavic literary characters who sometimes used expressions taken from the Bible.

In situations when pagans speak the language of the Bible it is the easiest to attribute to them notions and views unknown in their religion. Possibly a good example here is a statement made by the Wagrian duke Pribislav that Henry the Lion's speech was "verba Dei (...) et saluti nostrae congrua" ("God's words (...) and appropriate for our salvation"), although it is hard to exclude that in numerous, direct contacts with Christianity, Pribislav had an opportunity to learn the notions of Church teaching. As it has already been mentioned above there were for instance some references to monotheism in the late Slavic beliefs.

On the other hand, there should be emphasised the functioning of some Latin categories, such as *malus deus* and *bonus deus*, as providers of various fortunes (*fortuna*), concealing Slavic notions that could not be precisely translated by the chronicler. Similarly, the notion of *semidei* (semi-gods) does not allow the real significance of these gods in comparison with "the god of gods" to be established, especially considering that in other places Helmold does not hesitate to use the term *dei* when referring to them.

Thus, *semidei* must be an attempt to indicate the special position of the heavenly sovereign and not information about the nature of Polabian deities. The chronicler does not use the notion of demon in any other than a biblical meaning, and so only *penates* may mean spirits of lower rank than gods. In this case it is only a possibility however, as one should take into account

HELMOLDI CRONICA SLAVORUM ON SLAVIC RELIGION 381

an alternative solution, namely that Helmold did not directly refer to the ancient Roman mythology in this case, but only to the very name derived from its circle, which was adopted in the Christian culture and used as a term of household gods. Consequently, the term *deus* in Helmold's narration could encompass not only higher divine creatures but also some categories of lower creatures, as was suggested by some scholars. However, there is no convincing evidence that this happened. It is rather better to assume that the image of the Slavic religion in his chronicle is incomplete.

E. von Wienecke brought attention to the fact that Helmold's vocabulary in his description of a temple cult of Rans resembles the biblical vision of the Temple of Solomon. Actually, the schematic presentation of the Slavic *sacrum* and the vocabulary used in constructing it was quite strongly based on the contemporary literary culture and expressions inherited from the ancient tradition, and especially the biblical one. The interpretation of Slavic religion starts at the level of a word. An example here is a special use of terms which in principle are universal, however, sometimes in a given context of Helmold's writing they may become carriers of ecclesiastical interpretation, *e.g. fides, religio* in phrases such as "religionem verterunt in superstitionem" ("they turned religion into superstition") or "ostium fidei" ("the door of faith") open to pagans. This confirms H.-D. Kahl's opinion that in the Middle Ages the notion of *fides* was restricted to *fideles*, while non-Christian religions were referred to with words such as *consuetudines, ritus* or also *error* or *superstitio*.[521]

A number of concepts of classification have already been mentioned in this summary. In Helmold's use of the language it is hard to observe such consistency as in Thietmar's writings. For example, *sacerdos* and *flamen* are synonyms used to denote pagan priests while the former refers also to Christian priests. Some words have a very wide spectrum of situational meanings – *e.g. error* refers to the whole pagan religion, but it can also mean a particular rite (*e.g. mirabilis error* – a rite with a chalice, see Helmold I, 52); it is similar with *superstitio*.

An interesting case from the point of view of research on *interpretatio Christiana* is the Corvey Legend. This peripatetic literary motif is like a lens focusing two tiers of thought. In an explanation of Svantevit's genesis, the habit of etymologizing that is so characteristic of medieval scholars (based on rather superfluous associations related to consonance of names) converged with a doctrinal explication, based on "euhemerization." Although Helmold is not the creator of the Corvey Legend, he must have mastered the standard etymology

---

521   Kahl, *Die ersten Jahrhunderte*, p. 46.

of his times, which is confirmed first of all by the Legend of Vineta, which was most probably coined by himself.

A certain paucity of means of expression used by Helmold, the simplicity of his language, and foremost its strong saturation with biblical locutions, makes the text of the *Chronicle of the Slavs* – especially in comparison with Thietmar's work – too schematic. This should be taken into account in historical research. Strong dependence of the textual "world" of Helmold's chronicle on the Bible seems to be a blatantly reflected intention of the author, who thanks to this way of literary expression managed to include the described events to the order of the holy history started in Old Testament.

To conclude, it is worth mentioning a psychological element in these descriptions. The Slavs sometimes evoke the chronicler's sympathy and his empathy, although he often conceals the criticisms of the Saxons in such a case. However, the prevailing atmosphere is that of hostility, and these proportions of fluctuating favour can be found in descriptions of the Slavic religion. This religion as such is perceived with hostility, and Helmold's appreciation is limited to only some elements of Slavic religiousness (*e.g.* respect for holy places, aversion to making oaths). Apart from the atmosphere of condemnation and hostility resulting from demonization of *sacrum*, one can observe moments of terror and fear of the cruelty of the Slavic gods, or rather of their followers. However, the polycephalism of idols should not be connected with the monstrualization of gods, but only with a surprise element clearly present in some of the above analyzed descriptions (*e.g. mirabilis error*).

Conclusions

Reaching the completion of this study on the works of Thietmar of Merseburg, Adam of Bremen, and Helmold of Bosau informs the conclusion that the key influence on shaping references to native Slavic beliefs and cults included in those texts was not only a theological assessment of particular religious phenomena of paganism, but also the use of interpretation schemes in history, following or even – in historiological assumption – continuing the biblical holy history in chronicle narrations. Let us first refer to this dimension of the chroniclers' work to later emphases on the specifics of theological and cultural interpretation of Slavic cults and beliefs on the basis of their narratives. With this background, claims will be formulated to assess the usefulness of the conducted analyses in further research on the spiritual life of the Old Slavs, both in terms of source analysis and particular research models.

1 On the Historical Stage

Each of these three chroniclers demonstrated, to various extents, a predilection to create an image of supra-tribal religious unity of pagan Slavdom. This trend to shape a literary vision of relations in Northern Polabia and nearby Baltic islands was fostered by political ties between the people living there. In the light of the chronicles of Thietmar and Adam of Bremen, this unity was to focus around the central Liutici temple in Radogošč/Rethra. However, Helmold copies Adam's concept of Rethra's primacy in the Polabian paganism circle when referring only to earlier times, because when he writes about contemporary issues he accredits the leading religious role in "the whole Slavdom" to Rügen, or more precisely the Svantevit worshipped by its inhabitants.[1] The basic significance in the creation of these visions of supra-tribal religious union is looking at paganism as the antithesis of Christianity, concentrated around one centre or a major deity.

In Helmold's work, paganism even turned out to be one of the determinants of the identity of Slavdom as such (*universa Slavia*).[2] This was due to the fact

---

1 In this way he modified the image presented in the work of his predecessor, who presented the Rans in the circle of the "islands of the North", not emphasizing the influence of their religion on their continental neighbours.

2 Certainly this chronicler uses also the word Slavdom (*Slavia* / *Slavania*) in the ethnic-geographical meaning, and then also to refer to Christian countries and peoples. See *e.g.* Scior, *Das Eigene und das Fremde*, pp. 204 ff.

© KONINKLIJKE BRILL NV, LEIDEN, 2020 | DOI:10.1163/9789004331488_007

384   CONCLUSIONS

that it was treated situationally as a social and geographical missionary space, yet at the same time a pagan community hostile to Christianity.[3] The acceptance of this perspective was accompanied by attempts to create the comprehensive visions of the entirety of cults and beliefs of the Slavs. In their case an indication of one hegemon in this way created – to a great extent "in the inkpot" – a pantheon that turned out to be essential, which in turn was a reference to Adam of Bremen's concept in which he indicated Redigast as the *princeps* of demons, served by pagans in Rethra. Biblical models of the creation of a mystic sovereign in the *antisacrum* sphere or cults hostile to yahwizm were the basis for such a presentation of paganism, which is observable, also in the image of the Liutici religion in Thietmar's narrative.

The antithesis of pagan religion and Christianity was inscribed in the chronicler's reflection on history in the universal dimension (in the theological perspective) of spiritual realities, and at the simultaneous acquisition of moral references. This meant the explicit location of pagans on the side of the evil spiritual powers that were hostile to Christ. It was also a starting point for further interpretations. The most popular of the topoi present in all of the discussed chronicles used to explain the sense of dramatic events in which Polabian tribes participated, was reading their pagan rebellions and invasions as punishment for sins committed by the Christian community functioning in Germany. For Adam of Bremen, an important element was allegorical interpretation of the historical role of the Slavs with reference to biblical peoples. Helmold similarly saw God's judgements in particular events related to pagan activity, like in biblical stories, and he also compared his characters with biblical ones.

In the presentation of the conversion of the Slavs in the perspective of Thietmar and Adam of Bremen, an element of key significance was the institutional dimension referring to whole communities. Encompassing them in the governance of Christian monarchies and the Church network in this perspective determines the limit of their participation in the pagan circle, which in Thietmar's chronicle is well exemplified by events related to Poland. The chronicler emphasized that the cremation rite was binding before Mieszko's times, and similarly he mentioned that the cult of Mt. Ślęża was a phenomenon in the pagan past of the land of the *Silensi* (*pagus Silensi*). Meanwhile, this type of phenomena did not disappear from the social space of the Christianized

---

3 Cf. Stanisław Rosik, "Slavia universa? O współczesnym oglądzie kultury duchowej dawnych Słowian i jego mitologizacji (w nawiązaniu do eseistyki Marii Janion)," *Przegląd Humanistyczny* 53 (2009) 4, pp. 1–17. Similar view see *e.g.* Scior, *Das Eigene und das Fremde*, p. 210.

CONCLUSIONS   385

country with the conversion of its elites. Adopting an analogical perception of
Christianization, Adam of Bremen outlined a vision of over seventy years of
Slavic Christianity "between the Elbe and the Oder" during the Ottonian times.

Consequently, the rebellions of the Polabian Slavs against Christian domination and rule are presented as a return to paganism, based on apostasy, as
they resulted in abolition of the local Church authority. This perspective of religious relations in Slavdom was continued also by Helmold (mainly under the
influence of Adam of Bremen). However, in his narration, in comparison with
his predecessors' texts, the problem of individual conversion and missionary
actions at the level of particular communities in tribes consisting of the elimination of the pagan cult become more significant.

This range of Christianization activity found its legible exemplifications in
Thietmar's narrative, which – in accordance with the above mentioned way of
understanding that whole communities belonged to *Christianitas* – showed
them not as a mission among pagans but as pastoral activity among the people
"entrusted" to the bishops, whose significant dimension was fighting against
superstition, including idolatry. These practices, first and foremost, concealed
still living elements of native Slavic cults. The bishop of Merseburg perceived
them in the theological perspective as signs of evil powers in the world, personified also in the elements (such as the sea in Reinbern's episode), and also
evoked by an individual human sin (*e.g.* Hennil's case).

From the point of view of doctrinal confrontation, the Slavs, due to the fact
that non-Christian, native religious views persisted among them, were considered *inlitterati* – simple and uneducated by Thietmar.[4] This is an example
of interpretation of Slavic beliefs consisting of abandoning religious hostility
to give way for contempt for the cultural and mental condition of a particular
ethnic group representing these beliefs.[5] The creation of this view was supported by contacts between the bishop of Merseburg and his subdued Slavic
people, still attached to their native beliefs and cults. This "diocesional" context neglected Slavdom in *stricte* missionary perspective, which gained essential significance in Adam of Bremen and Helmold's narrations focused on the

---

4   The topical relation between faith and written culture was not strange to Helmold's mental-
    ity, which is supported by the information in Gottschalk's story that he abandoned "writing
    with faith".

5   A similar basis was applied to the topos of dogs (*canes*) with reference to the Slavs and con-
    firmed by Adam and later Helmold; in the light of these narrations it lost its original connota-
    tions related to paganism, and expressed contempt for ethnical distinctness and as a result
    cultural superstitions.

restitution of the church network in Northern Polabia and development of the Christian circle to encompass new peoples.[6]

This comparative outline of categories, which were used in the narrations of these three chronicles to emphasize the role of the native religion of the Slavs on the historical stage, shows that its interpretation in the cultural epoch was conditioned by the particular circumstances in which the authors lived. On one hand, problems concerning the institutions and the environments in which they created their chronicles should be taken into account, but on the other hand there should be consideration for the specifics of how 10th–12th-c. communities of western Slavs functioned. This is especially the case with the groups that resisted Christianity the longest. However, in these interpretations of the past, and contemporary to the chroniclers' Slavic religion, there is also a fundamental theological element, indicating the essence of pagan beliefs and cults with reference to tradition reaching the times of biblical sources of Christian doctrine.

2   The Perspective of Theology and Culture Confrontation

Essentially, references to the paganism of the Slavs in the "world" of the chronicles are determined by their attitude toward God, not merely in a personal dimension, but first and foremost in a collective one. This relationship is usually presented in categories of hatred addressed at God/Christ, saints with Peter the Apostle or St. Lawrence, and also the whole *Christianitas* as a people or as the Kingdom of God. Thus, the essential element of the theological interpretation of the Slavic *sacrum* is connecting it in various ways with the sphere of spiritual powers hostile to God. Pagan sanctuaries and statues are objects used to manifest demonic powers, and sometimes the diabolization of gods takes place (*e.g.* Redigast as *princeps demonum*). The very contact with pagan cult in this context means real danger in the spiritual dimension and it is not accidental that in Thietmar's perspective, alliances with pagans earn a negative assessment, although moderately expressed, and being a transgression they bring misfortune to Christians.

An element of the theological assessment of paganism is included in the very descriptions of events, emotional atmosphere of the narration, and also

---

6   In this context it is worth mentioning the appearance of good barbarians in the works of Adam and Helmold, they were a topical element which allows to create more favourable climate for the promoted idea of the mission.

CONCLUSIONS

the presentations of Christian attitudes towards the strange *sacrum* and particular rituals of pagan cult elimination (*abrenuntiatio diaboli*) with liturgical symbols. First and foremost, however, this assessment is expressed in terminology and theological commentaries, usually laconic and full of clichés. An especially useful topos in the explanation of the sense of paganism in chronicle reflection is the formula of *creaturam anteponere creatori*, putting the creation above the Creator, which is open to various interpretations. This judgment refers not only to the assumed biblical theology of a universal situation in which the original cognition of God is lost, but also to the cases of the return of Christianized – in the optics of medieval sources – Elbslavs to paganism. The selection of gods, idols, nature elements, and also people as cult objects is of key significance here.[7]

The implementation of pragmatic goals faced by historiography in particular situations could influence a reduction[8] of this negative assessment of pagans and their religion.[9] Parenesis was often an important element in such a cases: praising their customs to promote models of conduct to Christian addressees of these works (*e.g.* the topos of Slavic wives' faithfulness in Thietmar's work or praise of noble barbarian customs which can be found in Adam of Bremen's and Helmold's works).

Similar to the occurrence of references to ancient mythologies in chronicle narrations, if it has an allegorical nature (*e.g.* in reference to elements), it is not automatically connected with a pejorative overtone. However, in descriptions of Slavic religion, even these allegorical elements could strengthen the power of its negative assessment (*e.g.* the Styx's motif in the description of Rethra). The same pejorative evaluation concerns also the elements of ancient religion in Thietmar's or Adam's narratives. It is also worth mentioning that in their works, references to Roman or Greek mythology in the presentation of the Slavic world do not function as typical *interpretatio classica antiqua Romana vel graeca* of other people's deities.[10] However, in Helmold's case Slavic "penates" (*penates*) occur, which can but do not have to be an example

---

7   *E.g.* St. Vitus's deification in the legend of Corvey or the proposed apotheosis of Henry the Lion.

8   Its complete exclusion from description cannot be discussed due to pejorative connotation of the very terminology referring to Slavs as pagans, starting with basic terms such as *gentiles* or *pagani*.

9   *E.g.* in Thietmar's narrative when putting emphasis on it would act to the detriment of what was – the superior for the chronicler – good for the emperor or the Saxons.

10 A clear example of *interpretatio Romana* of Slavic deity it seems to be information of Widukind of Corvey about "Saturn" from Starigad.

of Roman interpretation of Polabian cults. This term could be assimilated in the Christian circle to mean tutelary deities without any particular reference to Old Roman mythology.

Linguistic categories certainly are the basic carrier of theological interpretation of paganism. It is worth mentioning here a few terminological groups referring to: 1) cult and beliefs; 2) spiritual creatures; 3) worshipped objects and cult places; 4) priests; 5) pagan communities and their stereotypical assessments. In the case of some words, *e.g. fides* or *religio*, authors reserved them only for the Christian circle, which indirectly also carries a paganism assessment. Moreover, in Thietmar's case an element which emphasizes the categorization of creatures and cult objects (*e.g.* personification) was a special way using verbs expressing worship.

It should be emphasized that, in terms of linguistic pragmatics, there are essential differences between the authors, and hence it is impossible to transfer automatically and without any verification the findings related to the interpretation of paganism from one work to the others. The same terms or phrases sometimes have different meanings, also due to special literary conventions used by particular authors; an excellent example here is the *dii manu facti* motif relating to gods made by a human hand. For Thietmar they are a material composition which gain life in some of the literary situations (*e.g.* they show "speechless wrath"). Such fineness cannot be found in Adam of Bremen's work, or even less in Helmold's. However, the former cannot be denied mastery in operating with symbolic and allegorical motifs.

The presentation of the religion of the Slavs on the Latin basis was also a basic dimension of cultural interpretation of strangers in the intellectual elites of contemporary Germany. Even the pejorative assessment of paganism in a sense meant paradoxically "taming" the Slavs in a Christian intellectual *milieu* by assigning to them a particular, culturally defined – also in terms of values – place in the sphere of collective images of this circle. In this dimension there are some critical stereotypes: on one hand savageness and cruelty of barbarians, connected with their belonging to paganism and intimacy with evil powers, and on the other hand the topos of "noble" barbarians. Legends are an interesting example of the inclusion of the Slavs into the cultural area of their Christian neighbours. The motif of Vineta is worth mentioning in this respect, and especially the so called Corvey legend, for it established a Christian genesis for the cult of Svantevit among the Rans (as the alleged St. Vitus). Using ancient motifs in the presentation of the Slavic world (*e.g.* Vulcanus pot in *Iumne*) would have a similar impact on the chronicles' audience.

CONCLUSIONS   389

3   *Argumentum ex interpretatione ...*

Conducting a study of particular cases of references to the Slavic religion in
chronicle narrations of the 11th–12th c. demonstrated that dependence of the
assessment of the credibility of sources in the fundamental issue of the existence of polytheism and idolatry among the Slavs on particular findings related to *interpretatio Christiana* (or *mythologica*), is groundless. Hypercriticism
in the matter was finally disavowed by archaeological research. Still, in this
case the element of key significance is the conclusion that worshippers of this
overly skeptical position granted primacy to *a priori* assumptions related to
the development of the Old Slavic religion. Hence, they did not conduct a sufficiently profound source studies. Without the archaeological argument the
only possible defense of one of the potentialities of this thesis was to recognize
the inability of full comprehension of the problem as a result of the "contami-
nation" of the chroniclers' descriptions with *interpretatio Christiana.*

Its occurrence should not be a decisive argument, as positive verification
of sources in this case requires additional premises, not only from the basis of
religious studies but also and primarily from studies on the author, the work,
and other contextual information.[11] An element of key significance here is the
hermeneutical inspiration in terms of textual interpretation that further takes
into account the *causa scribendi*. Finally, there is a need to establish potential sources of knowledge of the author of the work and the specifics of his
writing experience. On this basis, one can attempt to assess the usefulness of
the given place in the medieval sources for research on the pre-Christian religion. Frequently one should take into account the determination of a rather
extensive field of multiple hypotheses, and sometimes even the admittance of
"scholarly ignorance" (*docta ignorantia*).[12]

This research has revealed the inability to achieve an uncontroversial solution to the question of whether there had ever been any basic (pre)Slavic
religious system, which would be decomposed at the stage following the epoch
of the most intensive peoples' migration at the beginning of the Middle Ages.
Thus, the creation of religion of the Old Slavs as a whole in historical studies

---

11   On the basis of analogy in Medieval historiography or hagiography and archaeological
       sources as well as comparative research, supported by anthropology or ethnology as well
       as phenomenological inspiration.
12   It is enough to mention that even such a basic term as *deus* or *dea* can refer to supernatu-
       ral creatures of various ranks or even images.

as one compact system turns out to be groundless. One can note, however, the existence of a number of religious systems among the Slavs until the 12th c., between which, in the light of scarce source data, it is possible to see a community of certain elements in mythology and cult. As for some of them, it is impossible to decide whether they belonged to the Early Slavic religious system, or if they are only the heritage of a wider cultural circle, Indo-European beliefs, or even an expression of a universal religious language (archetypes, symbols) functioning on a global scale.

In the case of the analysis of the historiography of the 11th and 12th c. – when the Slavs in Pomerania, Polabia and Rügen still persisted in their native religion, and at the same time remained in permanent contact with their Christians neighbours, as well as the ones who were being Christianized at that time, or had yet to be non-Christian in the Baltic zone – it is important to consider foreign influences on the native Slavic beliefs and cult. Especially in areas where missionary action was conducted for many years, although with breaks, one should take into account the existence of the phenomena of Slavic interpretation (*interpretatio Slavica*) of Christian doctrinal elements, and in the case of lasting church organization in certain communities, the formation of the so-called dual faith that is referred to in some part of the researched source material. Taking into consideration the significance of these external cultural influences (including religious ideas) on the sphere of Slavic cults and beliefs in the 10th–12th c., it is quite difficult to regard as justifiable treating in the strict sense their systems in the categories of primary religion.

Bibliography

Abbreviations

Adam	*Magistri Adam Bremensis Gesta Hammmaburgensis Ecclesiae Pontificum*
Ebo	*Ebonis Vita S. Ottonis Episcopi Babenbergensis*
Helmold	*Helmoldi presbyteri bozoviensis Cronica Slavorum*
Herbord	*Herbordi Dialogus de Vita S. Ottonis Episcopi Babenbergensis*
PVL	*Povest' vremennich let*
Saxo	Saxo Grammaticus, *Gesta Danorum* / *The History of the Danes*
Thietmar	*Kronika Thietmara* [Thietmari Chronicon]
Vita Adalberti II	*Sancti Adalberti Pragensis, episcopi et martyris Vita altera auctore Brunone Querfurtensi*
Vita Prieflingensis	*Die Prüfeninger Vita Bischof Ottos I. von Bamberg nach der Fassung des Großen Österreichischen Legendars*
Widukind	*Widukindi res gestae Saxonicae* / *Widukinds Sachsengeschichte*
SSS	Słownik Starożytności Słowiańskich
MGH	Monumenta Germaniae Historica
MPH	Monumenta Poloniae Historica
n.s.	nova series

Primary Sources

Adam Brémský, *Činy biskupů hamburského kostela. Velká kronika evropského Severu*, trans. Libuše Chrabová. Praha: Argo, 2009.

Adam of Bremen, *History of the Archbishops of Hamburg-Bremen*, trans., introduction and notes Francis J. Tschan, reed. and new introduction Timothy Reuther. New York: Columbia University Press, 2002.

Alcvini sive Albini Epistolae, ed. Ernest Dümmler, MGH Epp 4, Epp Carolini Aevi 2 (1895): 1–481.

Annales Augustani, ed. Georg Heinrich Pertz, MGH SS 3 (1839): 123–136.

Annales Corbeienses, ed. Georg Heinrich Pertz, MGH SS 3 (1839): 1–18.

Annales Magdeburgenses, ed. Georg Heinrich Pertz, MGH SS 16 (1859): 105–196.

Arnoldi abbati Lubicensis Chronica, ed. Johann Martin Lappenberg, MGH SS 21 (1869): 100–250.

Arnórr jarlaskáld, *O walce króla norweskiego Magnusa ze słowiańskimi korsarzami w Jómie – Wolinie w r. 1043.* In Gerard Labuda, *Słowiańszczyzna pierwotna. Wybór tekstów.* Warszawa: PWN, 1954, pp. 305–306.

Augustyn św., *De doctrina Christiana. O nauce chrześcijańskiej*, Latin and Polish text, ed. and trans. Jan Sulowski. Warszawa: Instytut Wydawniczy PAX, 1989.

Augustyn św., *Objaśnienia Psalmów* (Ps. 103–123), trans. Jan Sulowski, ed. Emil Stanula. Warszawa: Akademia Teologii Katolickiej, 1986.

Augustyn ze Stargardu, *Protokół. Kamieńska Kronika-Rodowód Książąt Pomorskich, tzw. Stargardzka Genealogia*, Latin text and Polish trans., ed. Edward Rymar, trans. Elwira Buszewicz. Stargard: Muzeum w Stargardzie, 2008.

Biblia Sacra juxta Vulgatam Clementinam. Editio Electronica, ed. Michaele Tvveedale. London, 2005.

Bogurodzica, ed. Jerzy Woronczak *et al.* Wrocław: Ossolineum, 1962.

Chronicae episcopatus Brandenburgensis fragmenta, ed. Oskar Holder-Egger, MGH SS 25 (1880): 484–486.

Chronicarum quae dicuntur Fredegarii scholastici libri IV cum continationibus, ed. Bruno Krusch, MGH SSrerMerov 2 (1888): 1–193.

Codex Diplomaticus nec non epistolaris Silesiae, vol. 1: 971–1204, ed. Karol Maleczyński. Wrocław: Wrocławskie Towarzystwo Miłośników Historii, 1951.

Conventus episcoporum ad ripam Danubii 796 aestate, ed. Karl Zeuner, MGH LL 3, Conc. 2/1 (1906): 172–176.

Cosmae Pragensis Chronica Boemorum, ed. Bertold Bretholz, MGH SSrerGerm n.s. 2 (1923).

Cyprian św. [St. Cyprian], *Pogańskie bóstwa nie są bogami (Quod idola dii non sint)*, introduction and trans. M. Kondratowicz, *Vox Patrum* 11/12 (1991/1992) 20/23: 437–449.

De sancto Adalberto episcopo, ed. Wojciech Kętrzyński, MPH 4 (1884): 206–221.

Descriptio civitatum et regionum ad septentrionalem plagam Danubii, ed. Bohuslav Horák, Dušan Trávníček. In Bohuslav Horák, Dušan Trávníček, "Descriptio civitatum et regionum ad septentrionalem plagam Danubii (t. zv. Bavorský geograf)." *Rozpravy Československé Akademie Věd* 66 (1956) 2: 2–3.

Die Prüfeninger Vita Bischof Ottos I. von Bamberg nach der Fassung des Großen Österreichischen Legendars, ed. Jürgen Petersohn, MGH SSrerGerm in usum scholarum (1999).

Diptychon Bremense, ed. Ernst F. Mooyer. In *Vaterländisches Archiv des Historischen Vereins für Nieder Sachsen* (1835) [1836]: 281–309.

Ebonis Vita S. Ottonis Episcopi Babenbergensis, ed. Kazimierz Liman, Jan Wikarjak, MPH n.s. 7/2 (1969).

E codicibus Poznaniensibus, ed. Wojciech Kętrzyński, MPH 5 (1888): 961–966.

Ekkechardi Uraugiensis chronica, ed. Georg Waitz, MGH SS 6 (1844): 1–267.

Epistola Brunonis ad Henricum regem, ed. Jadwiga Karwasińska, MPH n.s. 4/3 (1973): 85–106.

BIBLIOGRAPHY

Excerptum chronicae principum Saxonie, ed. Oskar Holder-Egger, MGH SS 25 (1880): 480–482.

Fontes historiae religionis Slavicae, ed. Karl H. Meyer, Fontes historiae religionis 4. Berlin: De Gruyter, 1931.

Galli Anonymi cronicae et gesta ducum sive principum Polonorum, ed. Karol Maleczyński, MPH n.s. 2 (1952).

Gregorii I papae Registrum epistolarum, vol. 2: *Libri VIII–XIV*, ed. Ludwig M. Hartmann, MGH Epp 2 (1899).

Hamburgisches Urkundenbuch, vol. 1, ed. Johann Martin Lappenberg. Hamburg: Pertehs-Besser & Mauke, 1842.

Helmolda Kronika Słowian, trans. Józef Matuszewski, ed. Jerzy Strzelczyk. Warszawa: PWN, 1974.

Helmoldi presbyteri bozoviensis Cronica Slavorum, ed. Bernhard Schmeidler, MGH SSrerGerm in usum scholarum (1937).

Henrici de Antwerpe Tractatus de captione urbis Brandenburgensis, ed. Oskar Holder-Egger, MGH SS 25 (1880): 482–484.

Herbordi Dialogus de Vita S. Ottonis Episcopi Babenbergensis, ed. Kazimierz Liman, Jan Wikarjak, MPH n.s. 7/3 (1974).

Ibn Rosteh, *Kita_b al-A'la_q an-nafi_sa*, the Arabic text and its Polish translation, ed. and trans. Tadeusz Lewicki, in *Źródła arabskie do dziejów Słowiańszczyzny*, vol. 2, part 2. Wrocław/Warszawa/Kraków/Gdańsk: Ossolineum, 1977.

Kronika Thietmara [Thietmari Chronicon], Latin and Polish text, ed. and trans. Marian Zygmunt Jedlicki. Poznań: Instytut Zachodni, 1953.

Magistri Adam Bremensis Gesta Hammmaburgensis Ecclesiae Pontificum, ed. Bernhard Schmeidler, MGH SSrerGerm in usum scholarum (1917).

Magistri Vincentii dicti Kadłubek Chronica Polonorum, ed. Marian Plezia, MPH n.s. 11 (1994).

Monasticon Windeshemense, part 2: *Deutsches Sprachgebiet*, ed. Wilhelm Kohl, Ernest Persoons, Anton G. Weiler, Archives et Bibliothèques de Belgique 16. Brussels: 1977, pp. 79–94.

Ottonian Germany. The Chronicon of Thietmar of Merseburg, trans. and ed. David A. Warner. Manchester/New York: Manchester University Press, 2001.

Povest' vremennich let, part 1, text and translation, trans. Dmitriĭ S. Likhachev, Boris A. Romanov, ed. Varvara P. Adrjanova-Peretc. Moskva/Leningrad: Izdatel'stvo Akademii Nauk SSSR, 1950.

Procopius Caesariensis, *Opera Omnia*, vol. 2: *De Bellis libri V–VIII*, ed. Jakob Haury. Leipzig: Teubner, 1963.

Publius Cornelius Tacitus, *Germania*, ed. and trans. Eugen Fehrle. München: Lehmanns 1935.

Relacja Ibrahima ibn Jakuba z podróży do krajów słowiańskich w przekazie al-Bekeriego, ed. Tadeusz Kowalski, MPH n.s. 1 (1946).

Saga o Hallfredzie skaldzie kłopotliwym, introd. and trans. Jakub Morawiec. Wrocław: Chronicon, 2011.

Saxo Grammaticus, *Gesta Danorum / The History of the Danes,* ed. Karsten Friis-Jensen, trans. Peter Fisher, vol. 1–2. Oxford: Clarendon Press, 2015.

S. Bonifatii et Lulli Epistolae, ed. Wilhelm Gundlach, Ernst Dümmler, MGH Epp 3, Merovingici et Karolini aevi 1 (1892): 215–433.

S. Bonifatii et Lulli Epistolae / Die Briefe von Bonifatius und Lullus, ed. Michael Tangl, MGH Epp sel 1 (1916).

Sancti Adalberti Pragensis, episcopi et martyris Vita altera auctore Brunone Querfurtensi, ed. Jadwiga Karwasińska, MPH n.s. 4/2 (1969).

Testimonia najdawniejszych dziejów Słowian. Seria grecka, zeszyt 2. Pisarze z V–X w., ed. Anna Brzóstowska, Wincenty Swoboda. Wrocław/Warszawa/Kraków: Ossolineum, 1989.

Thietmari Merseburgensis Episcopi Chronicon, Latin and German text, ed. Robert Holtzmann, Werner Trillmich, Ausgewählte Quellen zur deutschen Geschichte des Mittelalters 9. Darmstadt: Wissenschaftliche Buchgesellschaft, 1992.

Vita Adalberti, ed. Jürgen Hoffmann. In Jürgen Hoffmann, *Vita Adalberti. Früheste Textüberlieferungen der Lebensgeschichte Adalberts von Prag.* Essen: Klartext, 2005, pp. 125–159.

Vita Anskarii auctore Rimberto, ed. Georg Waitz, MGH SSrerGerm in usum scholarum (1884).

Vita quinque fratrum eremitarum (seu) vita uel passio benedicti et Iohannis sociorumque suorum auctore Brunone Querfurtensi, ed. Jadwiga Karwasińska, MPH n.s. 4/3 (1973).

Widukindi res gestae Saxonicae / Widukinds Sachsengeschichte, Latin and German text, ed. and trans. Paul Hirsch, Albert Bauer, Reinhold Rau, Ausgewählte Quellen zur deutschen Geschichte des Mittelalters 8. Darmstadt: Wissenschaftliche Buchgesellschaft, 1971.

William of Malmesbury, *Gesta regum Anglorum: The History of English Kings,* vol. 1, ed. Roger Aubrey Baskerville Mynors, Rodney M. Thomson, Michael Winterbottom. Oxford: Clarendon Press, 1998.

Wipo, *Gesta Chuonradi II,* ed. Harry Bresslau, MGH SSrerGerm in usum scholarum (1915): 1–62.

Secondary Sources

Achterberg, Herbert. *Interpretatio Christiana. Verkleidete Glaubensgestalten der Germanen auf deutschem Boden,* (Form und Geist. Arbeiten zur germanischen Philologie) 19. Leipzig: Hermann Eichblatt Verlag, 1930.

BIBLIOGRAPHY

Ackenheil, H.V., *Gottheiten und Kultstätten in und um Oldenburg in Wagrien: archäoglottische Studien über germanisches und slawisches Heidentum*. Hamburg: Fotodruck an der Uni, 1983.

Altaner, Berthold; Stuiber Alfred. *Patrologia. Życie, pisma i nauka Ojców Kościoła*, trans. Paweł Pachciarek. Warszawa: Instytut Wydawniczy PAX, 1990 [orig. *Patrologie: Leben, Schriften und Lehre der Kirchenväter*, Freiburg: Herder, 1966[7]].

Althoff, Gerd. *Die Ottonen. Königsherrschaft ohne Staat*, (Urban-Taschenbücher) 473. Stuttgart: Kohlhammer, 2005[2].

Andrałojć, Małgorzata. "Rola psa w obrzędowości pradziejowych ludów Europy Środkowej." In *Wierzenia przedchrześcijańskie na ziemiach polskich*, ed. Marian Kwapiński, Henryk Paner, 98–109. Gdańsk: Wydawnictwo Muzeum Archeologicznego w Gdańsku, 1993.

Andrén, Anders. *Tracing Old Norse Cosmology. The world tree, middle earth, and the sun in archaeological perspectives*, (Vägar till Midgård) 16. Lund: Nordic Academic Press, 2014.

Anichkov, Evgeniĭ. *Jazyčestvo i drevnaia Rus'*. Petersburg: Tip. M.M. Stasiulevicha, 1914.

Antoniewicz, Włodzimierz. "Posągi." In SSS 4: 241–246.

Antoniewicz, Włodzimierz. "Religia dawnych Słowian." In *Religie świata*, ed. Eugeniusz Dąbrowski. Warszawa: Instytut Wydawniczy PAX, 1957.

Arbusow, Leonid. *Colores rhetorici*. Göttingen: Vandenhoeck & Ruprecht, 1963[2].

Babij, Paweł. *Wojskowość Słowian Połabskich*, vol. 1. Wrocław: Chronicon, 2017.

Banaszkiewicz, Jacek. "Jedność porządku przestrzennego, społecznego i tradycji początków ludu (Uwagi o urządzeniu wspólnoty plemienno-państwowej u Słowian)." *Przegląd Historyczny* 77 (1986): 445–466.

Banaszkiewicz, Jacek. "Otto z Bambergu i pontifex idolorum. O urządzeniu i obyczaju miejsca wiecowego pogańskiego Szczecina." In *Biedni i bogaci. Studia z dziejów społeczeństwa i kultury ofiarowane Bronisławowi Geremkowi w sześćdziesiątą rocznicę urodzin*, ed. Maurice Aymard *et al.*, 275–284. Warszawa: PWN, 1992.

Banaszkiewicz, Jacek. "Pan Rugii – Rugiewit i jego towarzysze z Gardźca: Porewit i Porenut (Saxo Gramatyk, Gesta Danorum, XIV, 39, 38–41)." In *Słowiańszczyzna w Europie średniowiecznej. Księga pamiątkowa dla Lecha Leciejewicza*, vol. 1: *Plemiona i wczesne państwa*, ed. Zofia Kurnatowska, 75–82. Wrocław: IAE PAN, 1996.

Banaszkiewicz, Jacek. *Podanie o Piaście i Popielu. Studium porównawcze nad wczesnośredniowiecznymi tradycjami dynastycznymi*. Warszawa: PWN, 1986.

Banaszkiewicz, Jacek. *Polskie dzieje bajeczne Mistrza Wincentego Kadłubka*. Wrocław: Wydawnictwo Uniwersytetu Wrocławskiego, 1998.

Banaszkiewicz, Jacek. "Źródło Głomacz i jego rajska okolica." In *Viae historicae. Księga jubileuszowa dedykowana Profesorowi Lechowi A. Tyszkiewiczowi w siedemdziesiątą rocznicę urodzin*, ed. Mateusz Goliński, Stanisław Rosik, 407–414. (Acta Universitatis

Wratislaviensis. Historia) 152. Wrocław: Wydawnictwo Uniwersytetu Wrocławskiego, 2001.

Bartlett, Robert. "From Paganism to Christianity in Medieval Europe." In *Christianization and the Rise of Christian Monarchy. Scandinavia, Central Europe, and Rus' c. 900–1200*, ed. Nora Berend, 47–72. Cambridge: Cambridge University Press, 2007.

Bartlett, Robert. *The Making of Europe. Conquest, Colonization and Cultural Changes 950–1350*. London: Allen Lane/Penguin Press, 1993 [Polish transl.: *Tworzenie Europy. Podbój, kolonizacja i przemiany kulturowe 950–1350*, trans. Grażyna Waluga. Poznań: Wydawnictwo PTPN, 2003].

Bartnik, Czesław. "Augustyńska historiologia." *Vox Patrum* 8 (1988): 787–801.

Beck, Heinrich. *Das Ebersignum im Germanischen: Ein Beitrag zur germanischen Tier-Symbolik*, (Quellen und Forschungen zur Sprach- und Kulturgeschichte der germanischen Völker. Neue Folge) 16. Berlin: De Gruyter, 1965.

Bednarczuk, Leszek. "W co wierzyli Prasłowianie? (W świetle badań prof. Leszka Moszyńskiego nad przedchrześcijańską religią Słowian)." *Kieleckie Studia Filologiczne* 10 (1996): 25–32.

Berlekamp, Hansdieter. "Die Ausgrabungen auf Kap Arkona 1969–1970." In *Berichte über den II. Internationalen Kongress für Slawische Archäologie*, vol. 3, ed. Joachim Hermann; Karl-Heinz Otto, 285–289. Berlin: Akademie Verlag, 1973.

Berschin, Walter. *Biographie und Epochenstil im lateinischen Mittelalter*, vol. 4: *Ottonische Biographie. Das hohe Mittelalter. 920–1220 n. Chr.*, part 2: *1070–1220 n. Chr.* Stuttgart: Anton Hiersemann Verlag, 2001.

Biermann, Felix. "Rezension: I. Gabriel/T. Kempke, Starigard/Oldenburg. Hauptburg der Slawen in Wagrien VI. Die Grabfunde (Neumünster 2011)." *Prähistorische Zeitschrift* 87 (2012): 208–210.

Biermann, Felix. "Zentralisierungsprozesse bei den nördlichen Elbslawen." In *Zentralisierungsprozesse und Herrschaftsbildung im frühmittelalterlichen Ostmitteleuropa*, ed. Przemysław Sikora, 157–194. (Studien zur Archäologie Europas) 23. Bonn: Habelt Verlag, 2014.

Bláhová, Marie. *Evopská sídlíšté latinských pramenech obdobi raného feudalismu*. Praha: Karolinum, 1986.

Bogdanowicz, Jadwiga. *Religie w dziejach cywilizacji*. Gdańsk: Wydawnictwo Uniwersytetu Gdańskiego, 1995.

Bogdanowicz, Piotr. "Co można wydedukować z Kroniki Thietmara? Ważny fragment z dziejów panowania Bolesława Chrobrego." *Nasza Przeszłość* 10 (1959): 71–111.

Bogdanowicz, Piotr. "Zjazd gnieźnieński w roku 1000." *Nasza Przeszłość* 16 (1962): 5–153.

Bokszański, Zbigniew. *Stereotypy a kultura*. Wrocław: Wydawnictwo Uniwersytetu Wrocławskiego, 2001.

Bollnow, Hermann. *Studien zur Geschichte der pommerschen Burgen und Städte im 12. und 13. Jahrhundert*. Köln/Graz: Böhlau, 1964.

BIBLIOGRAPHY

Boroń, Piotr. *Słowiańskie wiece plemienne*. Katowice: Wydawnictwo Uniwersytetu Śląskiego, 1999.

Bracha, Krzysztof. *Teolog, diabeł i zabobony. Świadectwo traktatu Mikołaja Magni z Jawora De superstitionibus*. Warszawa: Neriton, 1999.

Brachman, Hansjürgen. "Zur religiösen Vorstellungwelt der sorbischen Stämme an Elbe und Saale." *Studia Onomastica* 5 (1987): 48–59.

Brather, Sebastian, *Archäologie der westlichen Slawen. Siedlung, Wirtschaft und Gesellschaft im früh- und hochmittelalterlichen Ostmitteleuropa*. Berlin/New York: De Gruyter, 2001.

Brather, Sebastian. "Mehrköpfige Gottheit." In *Reallexikon der germanischen Altertumskunde*, vol. 19, ed. Johannes Hoops, 500–505. Berlin/New York: De Gruyter, 2001.

Bruno z Kwerfurtu. Osoba – dzieło – epoka, ed. Marian Dygo; Wojciech Fałkowski. Pułtusk: Wydawnictwo Akademii Humanistycznej im. Aleksandra Gieysztora, 2010.

Brückner, Aleksander. *Dzieje kultury polskiej*. Kraków: L. Anczyc i Spółka, 1931.

Brückner, Aleksander. *Mitologia słowiańska i polska*, ed. Stanisław Urbańczyk. Warszawa: PWN, 1985.

Brückner, Aleksander, *Słownik etymologiczny języka polskiego*. Warszawa: Wiedza Powszechna, 1957.

Brückner, Aleksander. *Starożytna Litwa. Ludy i bogi. Szkice historyczne i mitologiczne*, ed. Jan Jaskanis. Olsztyn: Pojezierze, 1979.

Buchner, Rudolf. "Einleitung." In *Widukindi res gestae Saxonicae / Widukinds Sachsengeschichte*, Latin and German text, ed. and trans. Paul Hirsch/Albert Bauer, Reinhold Rau, 3–15. Ausgewählte Quellen zur deutschen Geschichte des Mittelalters 8. Darmstadt: Wissenschaftliche Buchgesellschaft, 1971.

Budziszewska, Wanda. "Wagryjska Podaga i ślady kultu ognia u Słowian," *Rocznik Slawistyczny* 44 (1983) 1: 13–15.

Burghart, Gottfried Heinrich. *Iter Sabothicum. Ausführliche Beschreibung einiger An. 1773 und die folgenden Jahre auf den Zobten = Berg gethanen Reißen / Wodurch sowohl Die natürliche als historische Beschaffenheit Dieses In Schlesien so bekannten und Berühmten Berges Der Welt vor Augen geleget wird, Mit Kupffern*. Breslau/Leipzig: Michael Hubert, 1736.

Burke, Peter. *What is Cultural History?*. Oxford: Polity Press, 2004. [Polish transl.: *Historia kulturowa. Wprowadzenie*, trans. Justyn Hunia. Kraków: Wydawnictwo Uniwersytetu Jagiellońskiego, 2012.]

Bünz, Enno. "Vicelin." In *Lexikon des Mittelalters*, vol. 8, col. 1622–1623. München: Artemis, 1997.

Bylina, Stanisław. *Człowiek i zaświaty. Wizje kar pośmiertnych w Polsce średniowiecznej*. Warszawa: Upowszechnianie Nauki-Oświata "UN-O", 1992.

Bylina, Stanisław. *Kultura ludowa Polski i Słowiańszczyzny średniowiecznej*. Warszawa: Mazowiecka Wyższa Szkoła Humanistyczno-Pedagogiczna, 1999.

Bylina, Stanisław. "Problemy słowiańskiego świata zmarłych. Kategorie przestrzeni i czasu." *Światowit* 40 (1995): 9–25.

Bylina, Stanisław. "Słowiański świat zmarłych." *Kwartalnik Historyczny* 100 (1993) 4: 73–88.

Cabalska, Maria. "Głos w dyskusji." In *Religia pogańskich Słowian. Sesja naukowa w Kielcach*, ed. Karol Strug, 113–117. Kielce: Muzeum Świętokrzyskie, 1968.

Carp, Richard M. "Material Culture." In *The Routledge Handbook of Research Methods in the Study of Religion*, ed. Michael Stausberg, Steven Engler, 474–490. London: Routledge, 2014.

Caune, Andris. "Archäologische Zeugnisse von den heidnischen Volksglauben in Riga während des 12–13 Jahrhunderts." *Światowit* 40 (1995): 26–42.

Cetwiński, Marek; Derwich, Marek. *Herby, legendy, dawne mity*. Wrocław: KAW, 1989.

Curta, Florin. *The Making of the Slavs. History and Archaeology of the Lower Danube Region, c. 500–700* (Cambridge Studies in Medieval Life and Thought: Fourth Series). Cambridge: Cambridge University Press, 2001.

Curta, Florin. "Tworzenie Słowian. Powrót do słowiańskiej etnogenezy." In *Nie-Słowianie o początkach Słowian*, ed. Przemysław Urbańczyk, 27–55. Poznań/Warszawa: PTPN, 2006.

Curtius, Ernst Robert. *Literatura europejska i łacińskie średniowiecze*, trans. Andrzej Borowski. Kraków: Universitas, 1997 [orig. *Europäische Literatur und lateinisches Mittelalter*. Munchen: Francke Verlag, 1954²].

Dawson, Christopher. *Formowanie się chrześcijaństwa*. trans. Józef Marzęcki. Warszawa: Instytut Wydawniczy PAX, 1987² [orig. *The Formation of Christendom*, New York: Sheed and Ward, 1967].

Dawson, Christopher. *The Making of Europe: An Introduction to the History of European Unity*. London: Sheed and Ward, 1932.

Demetrykiewicz, Włodzimierz. *Altertümliche steinerne Statuen, sog. "Baby" (Steinmütterchen, Becherstatuen) in Asien und Europa und ihr Verhältnis zur slawischen Mythologie*. Extrait du *Bulletin de l'Académie des Sciences de Cracovie* (1910), 104–115. Kraków 1911.

Deptuła, Czesław. "Sakralne wartościowanie morza a problem integracji Pomorza z Polską we wczesnym średniowieczu." *Summarium* 4/24 (1975): 164–173.

Die Slawen in Deutschland. Geschichte und Kultur der slawischen Stämme westlich von Oder und Neiße vom 6. bis. 12. Jahrhundert, ed. Joachim Herrmann. Berlin: Akademie-Verlag, 1985.

Domański, Grzegorz. "Problem plemienia (?) Nice." In *Słowiańszczyzna w Europie średniowiecznej. Księga pamiątkowa dla Lecha Leciejewicza*, vol. 1: *Plemiona i wczesne państwa*, ed. Zofia Kurnatowska, 61–64. Wrocław: IAE PAN, 1996.

BIBLIOGRAPHY

Domański, Grzegorz. *Ślęża w pradziejach i średniowieczu*. Wrocław: IAE PAN, 2002.

Donnert, Erich. "Dannyje niemieckich istočnikov rannego srednevekovja o slavyanach i programma vostocznoj ekspansji u Tietmara mierzeburskogo." *Sredniye Veka* 27 (1965): 26–39.

Donnert, Erich. "Die frühmittelalterlich-deutsche Slawenkunde und Thietmar von Merseburg." *Zeitschrift für Slawistik* 9 (1964): 77–90.

Dowiat, Jerzy. *Chrzest Polski*. Warszawa: Wiedza Powszechna, 1960.

Dowiat, Jerzy. "Krąg uczony i jego instytucje." In *Kultura Polski średniowiecznej X–XIII w.*, ed. Jerzy Dowiat, 252–300. Warszawa: PIW, 1985.

Dowiat, Jerzy. "Normy postępowania i wzory osobowe." In *Kultura Polski średniowiecznej X–XIII w.*, ed. J. Dowiat, 301–374. Warszawa: PIW, 1985.

Dowiat, Jerzy. "Pogląd na świat." In *Kultura Polski średniowiecznej X–XIII w.*, ed. Jerzy Dowiat, 169–192. Warszawa: PIW, 1985.

Dralle, Lothar. "Rethra. Zu Bedeutung und Lage des redarischen Kultortes." *Jahrbuch für die Geschichte Mittel- und Ostdeutschlands* 33 (1984): 37–61.

Dralle, Lothar. *Slaven an Havel und Spree. Studien zur Geschichte des hevellisch-wilzisch-en Fürstentums (6. bis 10. Jahrhundert)*, Berlin: Duncker & Humblot, 1981.

Duby, Georges. *Czasy katedr. Sztuka i społeczeństwo 980–1420*, Warszawa: PIW, 1986 [orig. *Le temps des cathédrales, l'Art et la Société, 980–1420*. Paris: Gallimard, 1976].

Duczko, Władysław. "Obecność skandynawska na Pomorzu i słowiańska w Skandynawii we wczesnym średniowieczu." In *Salsa Cholbergiensis. Kołobrzeg w średniowieczu*, ed. Lech Leciejewicz, Marian Rębkowski, 24–39. Kołobrzeg: Le petit Café, 2001.

Duczko, Władysław. *Viking Rus: Studies on the Presence of Scandinavians in Eastern Europe*, (The Northern World, V) 12. Boston/Leiden: Brill, 2004.

Dumézil, Georges. *Les dieux des Indo-Européens*. Paris: Presses Universitaires de France, 1952.

Durkheim, Émile. *Elementarne formy życia życia religijnego. System totemiczny w Australii*, trans. Anna Zadrożyńska, ed. Elżbieta Tarkowska. Warszawa: PWN, 1990 [orig. *Les formes élémentaires de la vie religieuse. Le systeme totémique en Australie*. Paris: Alcan, 1912].

Dülmen, Richard van. *Historische Anthropologie. Entwicklung, Probleme, Aufgaben*, Köln/Weimar/Wien: Böhlau 2000.

Dyggve, Ejnar. "Der slawische Viermastenbau auf Rügen. Beobachtungen zu dem Swantewittempel des Saxo Grammaticus." *Germania* 37 (1959): 193–205.

Dziewulski, Władysław. *Postępy chrystianizacji i proces likwidacji pogaństwa w Polsce wczesnofeudalnej*, Wrocław/Warszawa/Kraków: Ossolineum 1964.

Eliade, Mircea. *A History of Religious Ideas*, vol. 3: *From Muhammad to the Age of Reforms*, trans. Alf Hiltebeitel, Diane Apostolos-Cappadona. Chicago/London: The University of Chicago Press, 1988.

Eliade, Mircea. *Traité d'histoire des religions*. Paris: Payot, 1949.

Eliade, Mircea; Couliano, Ioan P. *Słownik religii*, trans. Agnieszka Kuryś. Warszawa: Książnica, 1994 [orig. *Dictionnaire des Religions*. Paris: Plon, 1990].

Ellis, Linda. "Reinterpretations of the West Slavic Cult Site of Arkona." *Journal of Indo-European Studies* 6 (1978): 1–18.

Engel, Evamaria. "Der Beitrag der Mediävistik zur Klärung des Rethra-Problems." *Slavia Antiqua* 16 (1969): 95–104.

Engelke, Matthew. "Material Religion." In *The Cambridge Companion to Religious Studies*, ed. Robert A. Orsi, 209–229. Cambridge: Cambridge University Press, 2012.

Fałkowski, Wojciech. "List Brunona do króla Henryka." In *Bruno z Kwerfurtu. Osoba – dzieło – epoka*, ed. Marian Dygo, Wojciech Fałkowski, 179–207. Pułtusk: Akademia Humanistyczna im. Aleksandra Gieysztora, 2010.

Filipowiak, Władysław. "Słowiańskie miejsce kultowe z Trzebiatowa, pow. Gryfice." *Materiały Zachodniopomorskie* 3 (1957): 75–97.

Filipowiak, Władysław. "Słowiańskie wierzenia pogańskie u ujścia Odry." In *Wierzenia przedchrześcijańskie na ziemiach polskich*, ed. Marian Kwapiński, Henryk Paner, 19–46. Gdańsk: Wydawnictwo Muzeum Archeologicznego w Gdańsku, 1993.

Filipowiak, Władysław. "Wolińska kącina." *Z otchłani wieków* 41 (1979): 109–121.

Filipowiak, Władysław. "Wollin – ein frühmittelalterliches Zentrum an der Ostsee." In *Europasmitte um 1000. Beiträge zur Geschichte, Kunst und Archäologie. Handbuch zur Ausstellung*, vol. 1, ed. Alfred Wieczorek, Hans-Martin Hinz, 152–155. Stuttgart: Theiss, 2000.

Filipowiak, Władysław; Gundlach, Heinz. *Wolin-Vineta. Die tatsächliche Legende vom Untergang und Aufstieg der Stadt*. Rostock: Hinstorff, 1992.

Filipowiak, Władysław; Wojtasik, Janusz. "Światowit z Wolina." *Z otchłani wieków* 41 (1975) 2: 82–89.

Foote, Peter G.; Wilson, David M. *Wikingowie*, trans. Wacław Niepokólczycki. Warszawa: PIW, 1975. [orig. *The Viking Achievement*. London: Sidgwick & Jackson, 1973].

Forstner, Dorothea. *Świat symboliki chrześcijańskiej*, trans. Paweł Pachciarek, Ryszard Turzyński, Wanda Zakrzewska. Warszawa: PAX, 1990. [orig. *Die Welt der christlichen Symbole*. Innsbruck: Tyrolia-Verlag, 1977].

Fraesdorff, David. *Der barbarische Norden: Vorstellungen und Fremdheitskategorien bei Rimbert, Thietmar von Merseburg, Adam von Bremen und Helmold von Bosau*. (Orbis mediaevalis / Vorstellungswelten des Mittelalters) 5. Berlin: Akademie-Verlag, 2005.

Frazer, James George. *The Golden Bough. A Study of Magic and Religion*, Abridged Edition 1922, Adelaide: University of Adelaide. Available at https://ebooks.adelaide .edu.au/f/frazer/james/golden/ Accessed 2019 March 20.

Fried, Johannes. "Die Erneuerung des Römischen Reiches." In *Europasmitte um 1000. Beiträge zur Geschichte, Kunst und Archäologie*, vol. 2, ed. Alfred Wieczorek, Hans-Martin Hinz, 738–744. Stuttgart: Theiss, 2000.

BIBLIOGRAPHY

Friedmann, Bernhard. *Untersuchungen zur Geschichte des abodritischen Fürstentums bis zum Ende des 10. Jahrhunderts*. Berlin: Duncker & Humblot, 1986.

Fritze, Wolfgang H. "Der slawische Aufstand von 983 – eine Schicksalswende in der Geschichte Mitteleuropas." In *Festschrift der Landesgeschichtlichen Vereinigung für die Mark Brandenburg zu ihrem hundertjährigen Bestehen 1884–1984*, ed. Eckart Henning, Werner Vogel, 9–55. Berlin: Landesgeschichtliche Vereinigung für die Mark Brandenburg, 1984.

Gabriel, Ingo. "Starigard/Oldenburg im 11. und 12. Jahrhundert: neue Strukturelemente im Gessellschaft und Kultur." In *Miasto zachodniosłowiańskie w XI–XII wieku. Społeczeństwo – kultura*, ed. Lech Leciejewicz, 169–188. Wrocław: Ossolineum, 1991.

Gabriel, Ingo. "Strukturwandel in Starigard/Oldenburg während der zweiten Hälfte des 10. Jahrhunderts auf Grund archäologischer Befunde: Slawische Fürstenherrschaft, ottonischer Bischoffssitz, heidnische Gegenbewegung." *Zeitschrift für Archäologie* 18 (1984) 1: 63–80.

Gabriel, Ingo; Kempke Torsten. *Starigard/Oldenburg. Hauptburg der Slawen in Wagrien VI. Die Grabfunde. Einführung und archäologisches Material*. (Offa-Bücher) 85. Neumünster: Wachholtz, 2011.

Gasparini, Evel. *Il matriarcato slavo. Antropologia culturale dei Protoslavi*, vol. 3. (Biblioteca di Studi slavistici) 12. Firenze: Firenze University Press, 2010. [1st ed. 1952].

Gąssowski, Jerzy. "Archeologia o schyłkowym pogaństwie." *Archeologia Polski* 37 (1992): 137–157.

Gąssowski, Jerzy. "Kult religijny." In *Mały słownik kultury dawnych Słowian*, ed. Lech Leciejewicz, 574–587. Warszawa: Wiedza Powszechna, 1988.

Gąssowski, Jerzy. "Między pogaństwem a chrześcijaństwem." In *Wierzenia przedchrześcijańskie na ziemiach polskich*, ed. Marian Kwapiński, Henryk Paner, 12–18. Gdańsk: Wydawnictwo Muzeum Archeologicznego w Gdańsku, 1993.

Gąssowski, Jerzy. *Mitologia Celtów*. Warszawa: Wydawnictwa Artystyczne i Filmowe, 1987.

Gąssowski, Jerzy. "Schyłkowe pogaństwo na ziemiach polskich w świetle odkryć archeologicznych." *Światowit* 40 (1995): 43–52.

Gediga, Bogusław. "Chrystianizacja i utrzymywanie się przedchrześcijańskich praktyk kultowych na Śląsku." In *Słowiańszczyzna w Europie średniowiecznej. Księga pamiątkowa dla Lecha Leciejewicza*, vol. 1: *Plemiona i wczesne państwa*, ed. Zofia Kurnatowska, 159–167. Wrocław: IAE PAN, 1996.

Gediga, Bogusław. "Monumentalna rzeźba 'mnicha' ślężańskiego w świetle 'sztuki situl'." In *Problemy epoki brązu i wczesnej epoki żelaza w Europie Środkowej. Księga jubileuszowa poświęcona Markowi Gedlowi w sześćdziesiątą rocznicę urodzin i czterdziestolecie pracy w Uniwersytecie Jagiellońskim.* ed. Jan Chochorowski, 187–201. Kraków: Oficyna Cracovia, 1996.

Gediga, Bogusław. *Śladami religii Prasłowian.* Wrocław: Ossolineum, 1976.

Gelting, Michael H. "The kingdom of Denmark." In *Christianization and the Rise Christianization and the Rise of Christian Monarchy. Scandinavia, Central Europe and Rus' c. 900–1200.* ed. Nora Berend, 73–120. Cambridge: Cambridge University Press, 2007.

Geremek, Bronisław. "Umysłowość i psychologia zbiorowa w historii." *Przegląd Historyczny* 53 (1962), 4: 629–643.

Gieysztor, Aleksander, "Bemerkungen zur Apostasie in Zentral- und Osteuropa im 10. und 11. Jahrhundert." *Zeitschrift für Archäologie* 18 (1984): 3–7.

Gieysztor, Aleksander. "Ideowe wartości kultury polskiej w w. X–XI. Przyjęcie chrześcijaństwa." *Kwartalnik Historyczny* 67 (1960) 4: 922–940.

Gieysztor, Aleksander. *Mitologia Słowian,* ed. Aneta Pieniądz, introduction Karol Modzelewski, afterword Leszek P. Słupecki. Warszawa: Wydawnictwo Uniwersytetu Warszawskiego 2006.

Gieysztor, Aleksander. "Przemiany ideologiczne w państwie pierwszych Piastów a wprowadzenie chrześcijaństwa." In *Początki Państwa Polskiego Księga Tysiąclecia,* vol. 2, ed. Kazimierz Tymieniecki *et al.*, 155–170. Poznań: PWN, 1962.

Gilbert, Paul P. *Wprowadzenie do teologii średniowiecza.* trans. Tytus Górski, Kraków: WAM, 1997 [orig. *Introduzione alla teologia medioevale.* Roma: Pontificia Università Gregoriana di Roma, 1992].

Goetz, Hans-Werner. *Die Wahrnehmung anderer Religionen und christlich-abendländisches Selbstverständnis im frühen und hohen Mittelalter (5.–12. Jahrhundert),* vol. 1. Berlin: Akademie Verlag, 2013.

Grabski, Andrzej Felix. *Polska w opiniach obcych X–XII w.* Warszawa: PWN, 1964.

Gräslund, Anne-Sofie. "Adams Uppsala – och arkeologins." In *Uppsalakulten och Adam av Bremen,* ed. Anders Hultgård, 101–115. Nora: Nya Doxa, 1997.

Grimm, Jacob. *Deutsche Mythologie,* vol. 4. Berlin: Ferdinand Dümmlers Verlagsbuchhandlung, 1876[4].

Grimm, Jacob. *Deutsche Rechtsalterthümer.* Leipzig: Dieterich, 1854[2].

Gringmuth-Dallmer, Eike; Hollnagel, Adolf. "Jungslawische Siedlung mit Holzidolen auf der Fischerinsel bei Neubrandenburg." *Ausgrabungen und Funde* 15 (1970): 225–230.

Grucza, Franciszek. "*Rugia.*" In SSS, vol. 4, 564–565.

Grundmann, Herbert. "Litteratus – illiteratus". *Archiv für Kulturgeschichte* 40 (1958): 1–65.

Guriewicz [Gurevich], Aron. *Kategorie kultury średniowiecznej,* trans. Józef Dancygier. Warszawa: PIW, 1976. [orig. *Kategorii Srednevekovoi Kultury.* Moskva: Iskusstvo, 1972].

BIBLIOGRAPHY   403

Halbwachs, Maurice. *The Social Frameworks of Memory*. In: Maurice Halbwachs, *On collective memory*, Chicago, trans. Lewis A. Coser, 35–189. Chicago: The University of Chicago Press, 1992.

Hallencreutz, Carl Fredrik. "Missionsstrategi och religionstolkning: Till frågan om Adam av Bremen och Uppsalatemplet." In *Uppsalakulten och Adam av Bremen*, ed. Anders Hultgård, 117–130. Nora: Nya Doxa, 1997.

Hanusch, Ignaz Johann. *Die Wissenschaft des slawischen Mythus*. Lemberg/Stanislawow/Tarnow: Johann Milikowski, 1842.

Hayes, John H. "A history of Interpretation." In *Mercer Commentary on the Bible*. ed. Watson E. Mills, Richard F. Wilson, 23–52. Macon, Georgia: Mercer University Press, 1995.

Hengst, Karlheinz. "Slawische Sprachstudien im Mittelalter im sächsisch-thüringischen Raum." *Zeitschrift für Slawistik* 37 (1992) 3: 397–406.

Hensel, Witold. "Jak wyglądał posąg arkońskiego Svantevita." *Slavia Antiqua* 39 (1983): 119–125.

Hensel, Witold. *Polska przed tysiącem lat*. Wrocław/Warszawa: Ossolineum 1960.

Hensel, Witold. *Słowiańszczyzna wczesnośredniowieczna*. Warszawa: PWN, 1987⁴.

Hensel, Witold. *U źródeł Polski średniowiecznej*. Wrocław/Warszawa/Kraków/Gdańsk: Ossolineum, 1974.

Hensel, Witold. "Wczesnośredniowieczna figurka czterotwarzowego bóstwa z Wolina." *Slovenska Archeologia* 26 (1978): 13–15.

Hensel, Witold. "Wineta – miasto słowiańskie nad Bałtykiem, niegdyś ludne i opływające we wszelkie bogactwa, czy wytwór baśni o średniowiecznej karze bożej?," *Slavia Antiqua* 40 (1999): 273–274.

Herrmann, Joachim. "Feldberg, Rethra und die wilzischen Höhenburgen." *Slavia Antiqua* 16 (1969): 33–69.

Herrmann, Joachim. "Der Lutizenaufstand 983. Zu den geschichtlichen Voraussetzungen und den historischen Wirkungen." *Zeitschrift für Archäologie* 18 (1984) 1: 9–17.

Herrmann, Joachim. *Siedlung, Wirtschaft und gesellschaftliche Verhältnisse der slawischen Stämme zwischen Oder/Neisse und Elbe*. Berlin: Akademie-Verlag, 1968.

Herrmann, Joachim. *Zwischen Hradschin und Vineta*. Leipzig/Jena/Berlin: Urania, 1971.

Hill, Thomas. "Bordesholm." In *Lexikon für Theologie und Kirche*, vol. 2, ed. Walter Kasper *et al.*, 593. Freiburg im Breisgau: Herder, 1994.

Hiraux, Françoise. "Les vitae des évangelisateurs, schema de projects et de quotidiennetés." In *La vie quotidienne des moines et chanoines réguliers au Moyen Age et Temps modernes, Actes du Premier Colloque International du L.A.R.H.C.O.R. Wrocław – Książ, 30 novembre–4 decembre 1994*, vol. 2, ed. Marek Derwich, 425–438. Wrocław: Institut d'histoire de l'Université de Wrocław, 1995.

Hoffmann, Erich. "Beiträge zur Geschichte der Obodriten zur Zeit der Nakoniden." In *Zwischen Christianisierung und Europäisierung. Beiträge zur Geschichte Osteuropas in Mittelalter und früher Neuzeivol. Festschrift für Peter Nitsche zum 65. Geburtstag*, ed. Eckhard Hübner, Ekkehard Klug, Jan Kusber, 23–49. Stuttgart: Franz Steiner Verlag, 1998.

Holzapfel, Helmut. *Reinbern. Pierwszy biskup Pomorza*, trans. Ignacy Jeż. Koszalin: [Printed] Niepokalanów, OO. Franciszkanie, 1980 [orig. *Reinbern. Pommerns erster Bischof*. Würzburg: Echter, 1975].

Horbacz, Tadeusz J.; Lechowicz, Zbigniew. "Archeologia a poznawanie religii." *Z otchłani wieków* 47 (1981) 3: 177–185.

Hryniewicz, Wacław. "Bóg cierpiący? Rozważania nad chrześcijańskim pojęciem Boga." *Collectanea Theologica* 51 (1981) 2: 5–24.

Hultgård, Anders. "Från ögonvittnesskildring till retorik: Adam av Bremens notiser om Uppsalakulten i religionshistorisk belysning." In *Uppsalakulten och Adam av Bremen*, ed. Anders Hultgård, 9–50. Nora: Nya Doxa, 1997.

Hultgård, Anders. "Menschenopfer." In *Reallexikon der Germanischen Altertumskunde*, vol. 19, ed. Heinrich Beck *et al.*, 533–546. Berlin/New York: De Gruyter, 2002.

Hultgård, Anders. "Runeninschriften und Runendenkmäler als Quellen der Religionsgeschichte." In *Runeninschriften als Quellen interdisziplinärer Forschung. Abhandlungen des Vierten Internationalen Symposiums über Runen und Runeninschriften in Göttingen vom 4.–9. August 1995.* ed. Klaus Düwel, 715–737 (Reallexikon der Germanischen Altertumskunde – Ergänzungsbände) 15. Berlin/ New York: De Gruyter, 1998.

Ingstad, Helge. *The Norse Discovery of America*, vol. 2: *The Historical Background and the Evidence of the Norse Settlement Discovered in Newfoundland*. Oslo/Bergen/ Stavanger: Norwegian University Press, 1985.

Janion, Maria. *Niesamowita Słowiańszczyzna. Fantazmaty literatury*. Kraków: Wydawnictwo Literackie, 2007.

Janowski, Andrzej. *Groby komorowe w Europie środkowo-wschodniej. Problemy wybrane.* Szczecin: IAE PAN, 2015.

Janson, Henrik. *Templum nobilissimum. Adam av Bremen, Uppsalatemplet och konfliktlinjerna i Europa kring år 1075.* (Avhandlingar från Historiska institutionen i Göteborg) 21. Göteborg: Historiska institutionen i Göteborg, 1998.

Jedlicki, Marian Zygmunt. "Poglądy prawno-polityczne Thietmara. Przyczynek do badań nad świadomością prawną wschodnioniemieckich feudałów na przełomie X i XI wieku." *Czasopismo prawno-historyczne* 5 (1953): 39–79.

Jedlicki, Marian Zygmunt. "Wstęp." In *Kronika Thietmara*, Latin text and Polish translation, ed. and trans. Marian Zygmunt Jedlicki, vii–xciv. Poznań: Instytut Zachodni, 1953.

Kahl, Hans-Dietrich. "Compellere intrare. Die Wendenpolitik Bruns von Querfurt im Lichte hochmittelalterlichen Missions- und Völkerrechts." *Zeitschrift für Ostforschung* 4 (1955): 161–193, 360–401.

Kahl, Hans-Dietrich. "Die ersten Jahrhunderte des missionsgeschichtlichen Mittelalters. Bausteine für eine Phänomenologie bis ca. 1050." In *Kirchengeschichte als Missionsgeschichte*, vol. 2: *Die Kirchen des früheren Mittelalters*, part 1, ed. Knut Schäferdiek, 11–76. München: Kaiser, 1978.

Kahl, Hans-Dietrich. "Die welweite Bereinigung der Heidenfrage – ein übersehenes Kriegsziel des Zweiten Kreuzzugs." In *Spannungen und Widersprüche. Gedenkschrift für František Graus*, ed. Susanna Burghartz, Hans-Jörg Gilomen, Guy P. Marchal *et al.*, 63–89. Sigmaringen: Thorbecke, 1992.

Kahl, Hans-Dietrich. *Heidenfrage und Slawenfrage im deutschen Mittelalter. Ausgwählte Studien 1953–2008*, (East Central and Eastern Europe in the Middle Ages, 450–1450) 4. Leiden/Boston: Brill, 2011.

Kahl, Hans-Dietrich. "Wie kam es 1147 zum 'Wendenkreuzung'?" In *Europa Slavica – Europa Orientalis. Festschrift für Herbert Ludat zum 70. Geburtstag*, ed. Klaus-Detlev Grothusen, Klaus Zernack, 286–296. (Giessener Abhandlungen zur Agrar- und Wirtschaftsforschung des Europäischen Ostens) 100. Berlin: Duncker & Humblot, 1980.

Keller, Hagen. "Machabaeorum pugnae. Zum Stellenwert eines biblischen Vorbilds in Widukinds Deutung der ottonischen Königsherrschaft." In *Iconologia sacra. Mythos, Bildkunst und Dichtung in der Religions- und Sozialgeschichte Alteuropas. Festschrift für Karl Hauck*, ed. Hagen Keller, Nikolaus Staubach, 417–437. (Arbeiten zur Frühmittelalterforschung) 23. Berlin/New York: de Gruyter, 1994.

Khamaiko, Natalia; Komar, Olexiy. "Zbručskiy idol: pamiatnik epokhi romantizma?" *Ruthenica* 10 (2011): 166–217.

Kiersnowska, Teresa; Kiersnowski, Ryszard. *Życie codzienne na Pomorzu wczesnośredniowiecznym*. Warszawa: PIW, 1970.

Kiersnowski, Ryszard. "Kamień i Wolin." *Przegląd Zachodni* 7 (1957) 9/10: 178–225.

Kiersnowski, Ryszard. *Legenda Winety. Studium historyczne*. Kraków: Wydawnictwo Studium Słowiańskiego Uniwersytetu Jagiellońskiego, 1950.

Kłoczowski, Jerzy. *Młodsza Europa*. Warszawa: PIW, 1998.

Knowles, M. David; Obolensky, Dmitri. *Historia Kościoła*, vol. 2: *600–1500*. Warszawa: Instytut Wydawniczy PAX, 1988 [orig. *Nouvelle Histoire de l'Eglise*, vol. 2: *Le Moyen Age (600–1500)*. Paris: Seuil 1968].

Koczy, Leon. "Sklawanja Adama Bremeńskiego." *Slavia Occidentalis* 12 (1933): 181–253.

Koczy, Leon. "Thietmar i Widukind (z powodu nowych wydań obu pisarzy)." *Kwartalnik Historyczny* 50 (1936) 2: 656–676.

Kohlmann, Philipp Wilhelm. *Adam von Bremen. Ein Beitrag zur mittelalterlichen Textkritik und Kosmographie*. Leipzig: Quelle & Meyer, 1908.

Kołakowski, Leszek. "Mircea Eliade: religia jako paraliż czasu." In Mircea Eliade. *Traktat o historii religii*, trans. Jan Wierusz-Kowalski, i–vi. Łódź: Opus, 1993.

Kondratowicz, Marek. "Wokół 'Quod idola dii non sint' św. Cypriana Kartagińskiego." *Vox Patrum* 8 (1988) 15: 663–678.

K[onopka], Marek, "Światowit z teki Szymona Kobylińskiego." *Z otchłani wieków* 23 (1975): 174–175.

Korta, Wacław. *Tajemnice góry Ślęży*. Katowice: Śląski Instytut Naukowy, 1988.

Kossak-Szczucka, Zofia; Szatkowski, Zygmunt. *Troja Północy*. Warszawa: Instytut Wydawniczy PAX, 1986.

Kostrzewski, Józef. *Kultura prapolska*. Poznań: Instytut Zachodni, 1947.

Kotlarczyk, Janusz. "Słonecznego boga miejsca kultu." *Z otchłani wieków* 54 (1988), 2/3/4: 153–168.

Kotlarczyk, Janusz. "Triumfalny słup słonecznego boga." *Z otchłani wieków* 53 (1987) 1: 36–41.

Kotula, Tadeusz. "Głos (poszerzony) w dyskusji nad referatem doc. dra hab. Lecha Tyszkiewicza." In *Wokół stereotypów Polaków i Niemców*, ed. Wojciech Wrzesiński, 49–53. (Acta Universitatis Wratislaviensis. Historia) 79. Wrocław: Wydawnictwo Uniwersytetu Wrocławskiego, 1991.

Kowalczyk, Małgorzata. *Wierzenia pogańskie za pierwszych Piastów*. Łódź: Wydawnictwo Łódzkie, 1968.

Kowalczyk, Stanisław. "Filozofia pokoju św. Augustyna." *Vox Patrum* 8 (1988) 15: 831–857.

Kowalenko, Władysław. "Arkona." In SSS, vol. 1, 47–49.

Kowalenko, Władysław. "Gotszalk." In SSS, vol. 2, 143.

Kowalenko, Władysław. "Henryk." In SSS, vol. 2, 200–201.

Kowalenko, Władysław. "Kołobrzeg." In SSS, vol. 2, 447.

Kracik, Jan. "Chrzest w staropolskiej kulturze duchowej." *Nasza Przeszłość* 74 (1990): 181–206.

Krawiec, Adam. "Do czego służą duchy – o pragmatyce niezwykłości w Kronice Thietmara z Merseburga." In *Causa creandi. O pragmatyce źródła historycznego*, ed. Stanisław Rosik, Przemysław Wiszewski, 463–472. Wrocław: Wydawnictwo Uniwersytetu Wrocławskiego, 2005.

Krawiec, Adam. "Sny, widzenia i zmarli w kronice Thietmara z Merseburga." *Roczniki Historyczne* 69 (2003): 33–48.

Kristensen, Anne K.G. *Studien zur Adam von Bremen Überlieferung. Die Wiener Handschrift: Erstredaktion oder später verkürzte Fassung?*. (Skrifter udgivet af det historiske Institut ved Københavns Universitet) 5. København: Københavns Universitet, Historisk Institut, 1975.

Krzak, Zygmunt. "Światowid co i kogo przedstawia?" *Problemy* (1992) 8: 30–39.

Kulišić, Špiro. *Stara Slovenska religija u svietlu novijih istraživanja posebno balkanoloških*, Sarajevo: Akademija nauka i umjetnosti Bosne i Hercegovine, 1979.

Kumor, Bolesław. "Praktyka misyjna Kościoła w X w." *Nasza Przeszłość* 69 (1988): 23–37.

Kürbis, Brygida. "Więź najstarszego dziejopisarstwa polskiego z państwem." In *Początki Państwa Polskiego Księga Tysiąclecia*, vol. 2, ed. Kazimierz Tymieniecki *et al.*, 217–232. Poznań: PWN, 1962.

Kürbis, Brygida. "Helmold." In SSS, vol. 2, 198–200.

Labuda, Gerard. "Billug." In SSS, vol. 1, 117.

Labuda, Gerard. "Billungowie." In SSS, vol. 1, 117–118.

Labuda, Gerard. *Fragmenty dziejów Słowiańszczyzny zachodniej*, vol. 1–3. Poznań: Wydawnictwo Poznańskie, 1960–1975.

Labuda, Gerard. "Hamburg." In SSS, vol. 2, 185–186.

Labuda, Gerard. "Henryk I." In SSS, vol. 2, 201.

Labuda, Gerard, "Mitologia i demonologia w słownictwie, w bajkach, baśniach i legendach kaszubskich." In *Materiały ogólnej sesji naukowej pt. Świat bajek, baśni i legend kaszubskich*, 5–63. Wejherowo: Muzeum Piśmiennictwa i Muzyki Kaszubsko-Pomorskiej w Wejherowie, 1979.

Labuda, Gerard. "Mściwój." In SSS, vol. 3, 325.

Labuda, Gerard. "O wierzeniach pogańskich Słowian w kronikach niemieckich z XI i XII wieku. Glosa do: Stanisław Rosik, Interpretacja chrześcijańska religii pogańskich Słowian w świetle kronik niemieckich XI–XII wieku – Thietmar. Adam z Bremy. Helmold, 'Acta Universitatis Wratislaviensis', nr 2235: Historia CXLIV, Wrocław 2000." In *Monumenta Manent. Księga pamiątkowa dedykowana Profesorowi Tadeuszowi Białeckiemu w 70. rocznicę urodzin*, ed. Adam Makowski, Edward Włodarczyk, 37–57. Szczecin: Wydawnictwo Naukowe Uniwersytetu Szczecińskiego, 2003.

Labuda, Gerard. "Powstania Słowian połabskich u schyłku X wieku." *Slavia Occidentalis* 18 (1947): 153–200.

Labuda, Gerard. "Rec. E. Wienecke, Untersuchungen zur Religion der Westslawen, Leipzig 1939." *Slavia Occidentalis* 18 (1947): 459–470.

Labuda, Gerard. "Wytworzenie się wspólnoty etnicznej i kulturalnej plemion Słowiańszczyzny Połabskiej i jej przemiany w rozwoju dziejowym." In *Słowiańszczyzna Połabska między Niemcami a Polską. Materiały z konferencji naukowej zorganizowanej przez Instytut Historii UAM w dniach 28–29 IV 1980 r.*, ed. Jerzy Strzelczyk, 7–34. Poznań: Wydawnictwo UAM, 1981.

Lamm, Jan Peder. "On the cult of multiple-headed gods in England and in the Baltic area." *Przegląd Archeologiczny* 34 (1987): 219–231.

Lammers, Walther. "Vicelin als Exorzist." In Walther Lammers. *Vestigia Mediaevalia*. Ausgewählte *Aufsätze* zur mittelalterlichen *Historiographie, Landes-* und *Kirchengeschichte*, 284–302. Wiesbaden: Steiner, 1979.

Lange, Wolfgang. *Studien zur christlichen Dichtung der Nordgermanen*. Göttingen: Vandhoeck & Ruprecht, 1958.

Langebek, Jacobus. *Scriptores Rerum Danicarum Medii Aevi*, vol. 1. Hafniae: Godiche, 1772.

Larsson, Lars; Lenntorp, Karl-Magnus. "The Enigmatic House," in *Continuity for Centuries: A Ceremonial Building and its Context at Uppåkra, Southern Sweden*, ed. Lars Larsson, 3–48. (Uppåkrastudier) 10. Stockholm: Almqvist & Wiksell International, 2004.

Le Goff, Jacques. *Kultura średniowiecznej Europy*, trans. Hanna Szumańska-Gross. Warszawa: Volumen, 1994. [orig. *La civilisation de l'Occident medieval*. Paris: Arthaud, 1964].

Leciejewicz, Lech. "Die sozialen und politischen Voraussetzungen des Glaubenswechsels in Pommern." In *Rom und Byzanz im Norden. Mission und Glaubenswechsel im Ostseeraum während des 8.–14 Jahrhunderts*, vol. 2, ed. Michael Müller-Wille, 163–176. Stuttgart: Steiner, 1997.

Leciejewicz, Lech. "Główne problemy dziejów obodrzyckich." In *Słowiańszczyzna Połabska między Niemcami a Polską. Materiały z konferencji naukowej zorganizowanej przez Instytut Historii UAM w dniach 28–29 IV 1980 r.*, ed. Jerzy Strzelczyk, 167–182. Poznań: Wydawnictwo UAM, 1981.

Leciejewicz, Lech. "'In Pago Silensi vocabulo hoc a quodam monte ...'. O funkcji miejsc kultu pogańskiego w systemie politycznym Słowian Zachodnich." *Sobótka* 42 (1987) 2: 125–135.

Leciejewicz, Lech. "Kołobrzeg – siedziba biskupa Reinberna w 1000 roku." In *Memoriae amici et magistri. Studia historyczne poświęcone pamięci Prof. Wacława Korty (1919–1999)*, ed. Marek Derwich, Wojciech Mrozowicz, Rościsław Żerelik, 37–43. Wrocław: Instytut Historyczny, 2001.

Leciejewicz, Lech. "Mensa illorum nunquam disarmatur. Kilka uwag o słowiańskiej gościnności." In *Świat średniowiecza. Studia ofiarowane Profesorowi Henrykowi Samsonowiczowi*, ed. Agnieszka Bartoszewicz *et al.*, 628–633. Warszawa: Wydawnictwa Uniwersytetu Warszawskiego, 2010.

Leciejewicz, Lech. *Miasta Słowian północnopołabskich*. Wrocław: Ossolineum, 1968.

Leciejewicz, Lech. "Normanowie nad Odrą i Wisłą." *Kwartalnik Historyczny* 100 (1993) 4: 49–62.

Leciejewicz, Lech. *Nowa postać świata. Narodziny średniowiecznej cywilizacji europejskiej*, Wrocław: Wydawnictwo Uniwersytetu Wrocławskiego, 2000 (trans. *La nuova forma del mondo. La nascita della civiltà europea Medievale*, trans. Claudio Madonia. Bologna: Società editrice il Mulino, 2004).

Leciejewicz, Lech. "O kontaktach Słowian nadbałtyckich z północną Rusią we wczesnym średniowieczu." In *Viae historicae. Księga jubileuszowa dedykowana Profesorowi Lechowi A. Tyszkiewiczowi w siedemdziesiątą rocznicę urodzin*, ed. Mateusz Goliński, Stanisław Rosik, 208–214. (Acta Universitatis Wratislaviensis. Historia) 152. Wrocław: Wydawnictwo Uniwersytetu Wrocławskiego, 2001.

BIBLIOGRAPHY

Leciejewicz, Lech. "Obcy kupcy na Słowiańszczyźnie Zachodniej w okresie wielkiego przełomu (IX–XI w.)." In *Cultus et cognitio. Studia z dziejów średniowiecznej kultury*, ed. Stefan K. Kuczyński *et al.*, 333–339. Warszawa: PWN, 1976.

Leciejewicz, Lech. "Ostatni obrońcy dawnych wartości." *Z otchłani wieków* 52 (1986) 2: 62–69.

Leciejewicz, Lech. "Sasi w słowiańskich miastach nadbałtyckich w X–XI w." In *Kultura średniowieczna i staropolska. Studia ofiarowane Aleksandrowi Gieysztorowi w pięćdziesięciolecie pracy naukowej*, ed. Danuta Gawin *et al.*, 99–105. Warszawa: PWN, 1991.

Leciejewicz, Lech. *Słowianie zachodni*. Wrocław/Warszawa/Kraków: Ossolineum 1989.

Leciejewicz, Lech. "Wineta." In SSS, vol. 6, 472.

Leciejewicz, Lech. "Wolin." In SSS, vol. 6, 561–564.

Leciejewicz, Lech. "Wolinianie." In SSS, vol. 6, 564.

Leciejewicz, Lech; Rębkowski, Marian. "Uwagi końcowe. Początki Kołobrzegu w świetle rozpoznania archeologicznego." In *Kołobrzeg. Wczesne miasto nad Bałtykiem*, ed. L. Leciejewicz, M. Rębkowski, 299–317. (Origines Polonorum) 2. Warszawa: Trio, 2007.

Leeuw, Gerardus van der. *Phänomenologie der Religion*. Tübingen: J.C.B. Mohr, 1933.

Lelewel, Joachim. *Bałwochwalstwo Sławiańskie*, Poznań: J.K. Żupański, 1853.

Leńczyk, Gabriel. "Światowid zbruczański." *Materiały Archeologiczne* 5 (1964): 5–60.

Lewicki, Paweł. "O psychologii historycznej." *Kwartalnik Historyczny* 82 (1975) 3: 584–592.

Lewicki, Tadeusz. "Obrzędy pogrzebowe Słowian w opisach podróżników i pisarzy arabskich." *Archeologia* 5 (1952/1953): 122–154.

Lindner, Michael. "Widekind, Meinfried, Pribislaw/Heinrich und andere – das südliche Lutizenland in der ersten Hälfte des 12. Jahrhunderts." In *Bischof Otto von Bamberg in Pommern. Historische und archäologische Forschungen zu Mission und Kulturverhältnissen des 12. Jahrhunderts*, ed. Felix Biermann, Fred Ruchhöft, 49–67. (Studien zur Archäologie Europas) 30. Bonn: Habelt, 2017.

Lippelt, Helmut. *Thietmar von Merseburg. Reichsbischof und Chronist*. (Mitteldeutsche Forschungen) 72. Köln/Wien: Böhlau, 1973.

Logan, F. Donald. *The Vikings in History*. New York/London: Routledge, 2005.

Lotter, Friedrich, "Christliche Völkergemeinschaft und Heidenmission. Das Weltbild Bruns von Querfurt." In *Early Christianity in Central and East Europe*, vol. 1, ed. Przemysław Urbańczyk, 163–174. Warsaw: Semper, 1997.

Ludat, Herbert. "Die Patriarchatsidee Adalberts von Bremen und Byzanz." In Herbert Ludat. *Slaven und Deutsche im Mittelalter. Ausgewählte Aufsätze zu Fragen ihrer politischen, sozialen und kulturellen Beziehungen*, 312–339. (Mitteldeutsche Forschungen) 86. Köln/Wien: Böhlau, 1982.

Lübke, Christian. *Fremde im östlichen Europa. Von Gesellschaften ohne Staat zu verstaatlichten Gesellschaften (9.–11. Jahrhundert)*. Köln/Weimar/Wien: Böhlau, 2001.

Lübke, Christian. "Heidentum und Widerstand: Elbslawen und christliche Staaten im 10.–12. Jahrhundert." In *Early Christianity in Central and East Europe*, vol. 1, ed. Przemysław Urbańczyk, 123–128. Warsaw: Semper, 1997.

Lübke, Christian. "Mstidrog." In *Lexikon des Mittelalters*, vol. 6, col. 882. München: Artemis, 1993.

Lübke, Christian. "Pogańscy Słowianie i chrześcijańscy Niemcy. Tożsamości mieszkańców Połabszczyzny w VIII–XII w." In *Bogowie i ich ludy. Religie pogańskie a procesy tworzenia się tożsamości kulturowej, etnicznej, plemiennej i narodowej w średniowieczu*, ed. Leszek P. Słupecki, 73–84. Wrocław: Chronicon, 2008.

Lübke, Christian. "Religion und ethnisches Bewusstsein bei den Lutizen." *Światowit* 40 (1995): 70–90.

Lübke, Christian. "The Polabian Alternative. Paganism between Christian Kingdoms." In *Europe around the year 1000*, ed. Przemysław Urbańczyk, 379–389. Warszawa: DiG, 2001.

Lübke, Christian. "Zwischen Triglav und Christus. Die Anfänge der Christianisierung des Havellandes." *Wichmann-Jahrbuch des Diözesangeschichtsvereins Berlin* (NF 3) 34/35 (1994–1995): 15–35.

Łapiński, Adam. "Światowid czy model świata?" *Z otchłani wieków* 50 (1984) 2: 128–139.

Łęga, Władysław. *Kultura Pomorza we wczesnym średniowieczu na podstawie wykopalisk*. Toruń: Towarzystwo Naukowe w Toruniu, 1930.

Łęgowski-Nadmorski, Józef. "Bóstwa i wierzenia religijne Słowian lechickich." *Roczniki Towarzystwa Naukowego w Toruniu* 32 (1925): 18–102.

Łosiński, Władysław. "Z dziejów obrzędowości pogrzebowej u północnego odłamu Słowian zachodnich w świetle nowszych badań." In *Kraje słowiańskie w wiekach średnich. Profanum i sacrum*, ed. Hanna Kóčka-Krenz, Władysław Łosiński, 473–483. Poznań: PTPN, 1998.

Łowmiański, Henryk. "Elementy indoeuropejskie w religii Bałtów." In *Ars Historica. Prace z dziejów powszechnych i Polski*, ed. Marian Biskup *et al.*, 145–153. Poznań: Uniwersytet Adama Miczkiewicza w Poznaniu, 1976.

Łowmiański, Henryk. "O pochodzeniu Geografa bawarskiego." *Roczniki Historyczne* 20 (1951/1952): 9–23.

Łowmiański, Henryk. *Początki Polski*, vol. 1–6. Warszawa: PWN, 1963–1985.

Łowmiański, Henryk. "Politeizm słowiański." *Przegląd Historyczny* 75 (1984) 4: 655–693.

Łowmiański, Henryk. *Religia Słowian i jej upadek (w. VI–XII)*. Warszawa: PWN, 1979.

Łuczyński, Michał. "*Herberti De miraculis* as a source to the history of religion of western Slavs." *Studia Mythologica Slavica* 16 (2013): 69–77.

Makiewicz, Tadeusz. "Odkrycia tzw. grobów psów w Polsce i ich sakralne znaczenie." In "Wierzenia przedchrześcijańskie na ziemiach polskich," ed. Marian Kwapiński, Henryk Paner, 110–117. Gdańsk: Wydawnictwo Muzeum Archeologicznego w Gdańsku, 1993.

BIBLIOGRAPHY

Malinowski, Bronisław. *Szkice z teorii kultury*. Warszawa: Książka i Wiedza, 1958.

Manitius, Max. *Geschichte der lateinischen Literatur d. Mittelalters*, vol. 2. München: Beck, 1923.

Manteuffel, Tadeusz. *Kultura Europy średniowiecznej*. Warszawa: Wiedza Powszechna, 1974.

Meriggi, Bruno. "Die Anfänge des Christentums bei den Baltischen Slaven." *Annales Instituti Slavici* 6 (1969–1970): *Das heidnische und christlische Slaventum*, vol. 2, 46–54. Wiesbaden: Harrassowitz, 1970.

Meriggi, Bruno. "Il concetto del Dio nelle religioni dei popoli Slavi." *Ricerche Slavistiche* 1 (1952): 148–176.

Michałowska, Teresa. *Średniowiecze*. Warszawa: PWN, 2006.

Michałowski, Roman. "Król czy misjonarz? Rozumienie misji w X/XI w." In *Bruno z Kwerfurtu. Osoba – dzieło – epoka*, ed. Marian Dygo, Wojciech Fałkowski, 129–144. Pułtusk: Wydawnictwo Akademii Humanistycznej im. Aleksandra Gieysztora, 2010.

Michałowski, Roman. "Post dziewięciotygodniowy w Polsce Chrobrego. Studium z dziejów polityki religijnej pierwszych Piastów." *Kwartalnik Historyczny* 104 (2002) 1: 5–39.

Michałowski, Roman. *Zjazd gnieźnieński. Religijne przesłanki powstania arcybiskupstwa gnieźnieńskiego*. Wrocław: Wydawnictwo Uniwersytetu Wrocławskiego, 2005.

Middleton, John. "Magic: Theories of Magic." In *The Encyclopedia of Religion*, vol. 9, ed. Mircea Eliade, 82–89. New York/London: Macmillan Publishing Company, 1987.

Mierzwiński, Andrzej. *Ślężańska układanka*. Wrocław: Chronicon, 2007.

Miklosich, Franz. *Etymologisches Wörterbuch der slavischen Sprachen*. Wien: Braumüller, 1886.

Miller, Daniel. "Materiality: An Introduction." In *Materiality*, ed. Daniel Miller, 1–50. Durham/London: Duke University Press Books, 2005.

Miś, Andrzej Lambert. "Przedchrześcijańska religia Rugian." *Slavia Antiqua* 38 (1997): 105–149.

Młynarska-Kaletynowa, Marta. "Ślęża (2)." In SSS, vol. 5, 564–566.

Modzelewski, Karol. *Barbarzyńska Europa*. Warszawa: Iskry, 2004.

Modzelewski, Karol. *Chłopi w monarchii wczesnopiastowskiej*. Wrocław/Warszawa/Kraków: Ossolineum, 1987.

Modzelewski, Karol, "Omni secunda feria. Księżycowe roki i nieporozumienia wokół Helmolda." In *Słowiańszczyzna w Europie średniowiecznej. Księga pamiątkowa dla Lecha Leciejewicza*, vol. 1: *Plemiona i wczesne państwa*, ed. Zofia Kurnatowska, 83–88. Wrocław: IAE PAN, 1996.

Morawiec, Jakub. *Wolin w średniowiecznej tradycji skandynawskiej*, Kraków: Avalon, 2010.

Moszyński, Kazimierz. *Kultura ludowa Słowian*, vol. 2, part 1. Warszawa: Wiedza Powszechna, 1967².

Moszyński, Leszek. *Die vorchristliche Religion der Slaven im Lichte der slavischen Sprachwissenschaft*. Köln/Weimar/Wien: Böhlau, 1992.

Moszyński, Leszek, "Prasłowiański panteon w słowniku etymologicznym i Lexiconie Franciszka Miklosicha." *Studia z Filologii Polskiej i Słowiańskiej* 31 (1993): 163–174.

Moszyński, Leszek. "Staropołabski teonim Tjarnaglofi. Próba nowej etymologii." In *Tgolí chole Mestró. Gedenkschrift für Reinhold Olesch*, ed. Renate Lachmann *et al.*, 33–39. Köln/Wien: Böhlau, 1990.

Moszyński, Leszek. "Współczesne metody (etymologiczna i filologiczna) rekonstruowania prasłowiańskich wierzeń." *Światowit* 40 (1995): 100–112.

Moździoch, Sławomir. "Społeczność plemienna Śląska w IX–X wieku." In *Śląsk około roku 1000*, ed. Edmund Małachowicz, Marta Młynarska-Kaletynowa, 25–71. Wrocław: Polska Akademia Nauk, 2000.

Mrozowicz, Wojciech. "Początki kultury pisma na Słowiańszczyźnie zachodniej." In *Słowiańszczyzna w tworzeniu Europy (X–XIII/XIV w.)*, ed. Stanisław Rosik, 29–42. Wrocław: Chronicon, 2008.

Myśliński, Kazimierz. *Polska wobec Słowian połabskich do końca wieku XII*. Lublin: Wydawnictwo UMCS, 1993.

Myśliński, Kazimierz. "Przybysław-Henryk." In SSS, vol. 4, 399–400.

Nadolski, Bogusław. *Liturgika*, vol. 1–3. Poznań: Pallotinum, 1989–1992.

Nalepa, Jerzy. "Głomacz." In SSS, vol. 2, 111.

Nalepa, Jerzy. "Głomacze." In SSS, vol. 2, 111.

Nalepa, Jerzy. "O nowszym ujęciu problematyki plemion słowiańskich u Geografa Bawarskiego. Uwagi krytyczne." *Slavia Occidentalis* 60 (2003): 9–63.

Nalepa, Jerzy. "Ślęża Góra na pograniczu wielecko – łużyckim." *Onomastica* 2 (1956): 318–322.

Narbutt, Teodor. *Dzieje starożytne narodu litewskiego*, vol. 1: *Mitologia litewska*. Vilnius: A. Marcinowski, 1835.

Naruszewicz, Adam. *Historia narodu polskiego*, vol. 2. Leipzig: Breitkopf & Hertel, 1836.

Nedo, Paul. "Czorneboh und Bieleboh – zwei angebliche slawische Kultstätten in Oberlausitz." *Lětopis* 6/7 (1963): 9–18.

Neugebauer, Werner. "Der Burgwall Alt-Lübeck, Geschichte, Stand und Aufgaben." *Offa* 21/22 (1964/1965): 125–257.

Niederle, Lubomír. *Život starých Slovanů*, vol. 2, part 1. Praha: Bursík & Kohout, 1924.

Nielsen, Ann-Lili. "Rituals and power. About small buildings and animal bones from late Iron Age." In *Old Norse Religion in Long-Term Perspectives: Origins, Changes, and Interactions: an international conference in Lund, Sweden, June 3–7, 2004*, ed. Anders Andrén, Kristina Jennbert, Catharina Raudvere, 243–247. Lund: Nordic Academic Press, 2006.

Nola, Alfonso M. di. "Slavi." In *Enciclopedia delle Religioni*, vol. 5, ed. Mario Gozzini, col. 1136–1162. Firenze: Vallecchi, 1973.

BIBLIOGRAPHY

Nordberg, Andreas. *Fornnordisk religionsforskning mellan teori och empiri. Kulten av anfäder, solen och vegetationsandar i idéhistorisk belysning.* (Acta Academiae regiae Gustavi Adolphi) 126. Uppsala: Kungl. Gustav Adolfs akademien för svensk folk kultur, 2013.

Nowak, Johannes. *Untersuchungen zum Gebrauch der Begriffe populus, gens und natio bei Adam von Bremen und Helmold von Bosau.* Münster: Diss., 1971.

Oexle, Otto Gerhard. "Obcowanie żywych i umarłych. Rozważania o pojęciu >>memoria<<", trans. Marian Arszyński. In Oexle, Otto Gerhard. *Społeczeństwo średniowiecza. Mentalność – grupy społeczne – formy życia*, 7–44. Toruń: Wydawnictwo UMK, 2000.

Osięgłowski, Janisław. "Początki słowiańskiej Rugii do roku 1168 (Zagadnienia etniczne i polityczne)." *Materiały Zachodniopomorskie* 13 (1967): 239–287.

Otto, Bernd-Christian. *Magie. Rezeption- und diskursgeschichtliche Analysen von der Antike bis zur Neuzeit.* Berlin: De Gruyter, 2011.

Otto, Rudolf. *Świętość. Elementy racjonalne i irracjonalne w pojęciu bóstwa*, trans. by Bogdan Kupis. Wrocław: Thesaurus Press, 1993 [orig. *Das Heilige: Über das Irrationale in der Idee des Göttlichen und sein Verhältnis zum Rationalen*, Breslau: Trewendt & Granier 1917].

Padberg, Lutz E. von. "Christen und Heiden. Zur Sicht des Heidentums in ausgewählter angelsächsischer und fränkischer Überlieferung des 7. und 8. Jahrhunderts." In *Iconologia sacra. Mythos, Bildkunst und Dichtung in der Religions- und Sozialgeschichte Alteuropas. Festschrift für Karl Hauck*, ed. Hagen Keller, Nikolaus Staubach, 291–312. Berlin/New York: De Gruyter, 1994.

Padberg, Lutz E. von. *Die Christianisierung Europas im Mittelalter.* Stuttgart: Reclam 1998.

Padberg, Lutz E. von. "Geschichtsschreibung und kulturelles Gedächtnis. Formen der Vergangenheitswahrnehmung in der hochmittelalterlichen Historiographie am Beispiel von Thietmar von Merseburg, Adam von Bremen und Helmold von Bosau." *Zeitschrift für Kirchengeschichte* 105 (1994): 156–177.

Palm, Thede. *Wendische Kultstätten. Quellenkritische Untersuchungen zu den letzten Jahrhunderten slavischen Heidentums.* Lund: Gleerupska Universitetsbokhandeln, 1937.

Petersohn, Jürgen. "Der Akt von Gnesen im Jahre 1000 und die Errichtung des Bistums Salz-Kolberg. Zur historischen Substanz eines Jubiläums." *Baltische Studien* NF 87 (2001): 24–35.

Petersohn, Jürgen. *Der südliche Ostseeraum im kirchlich-politischen Kräftespiel des Reichs, Polens und Dänmarks vom 10. bis 13. Jahrhundert. Mission – Kirchenorganisation – Kultpolitik.* Köln/Wien: Böhlau, 1979.

Petrulevich, Alexandra. "On the etymology of at Jómi, Jumne and Jómsborg." *Namn och Bydg* 97 (2009): 65–97.

Pettazzoni, Raffaele. *Wszechwiedza bogów*. trans. Barbara Sieroszewska. Warszawa: Książka i Wiedza, 1967 [orig. *L'onniscienza di Dio*. Torino: Einaudi, 1955].

Piekarczyk, Stanisław. *Barbarzyńcy i chrześcijaństwo. Konfrontacje społecznych postaw i wzorców u Germanów*. Warszawa: PWN, 1968.

Piekarczyk Stanisław, "*Religia Germanów.*" *Zarys dziejów religii*, ed. Józef Keller, 497–521. Warszawa: Iskry 1976.

Piskorski, Jan M. *Pomorze plemienne. Historia – Archeologia – Językoznawstwo*. Poznań/Szczecin: Sorus, 2002.

Pleszczyński, Andrzej. *Niemcy wobec pierwszej monarchii piastowskiej (963–1034). Narodziny stereotypu. Postrzeganie i cywilizacyjna klasyfikacja władców Polski i ich kraju*. Lublin: Wydawnictwo UMCS, 2008.

Pleszczyński, Andrzej. *The Birth of a Stereotype: Polish Rulers and Their Country in German Writings, c. 1000 A.D.*, (East Central and Eastern Europe in the Middle Ages, 450–1450) 15. Leiden: Brill, 2011.

Pleszczyński, Andrzej; Sobiesiak, Joanna; Szejgiec, Karol; Tomaszek, Michał; Tyszka, Przemysław. *Historia communitatem facit. Struktura narracji tworzących tożsamości grupowe w średniowieczu*. Wrocław: Chronicon, 2016.

Popowska-Taborska, Hanna. *Wczesne dzieje Słowian w świetle ich języka*, Wrocław/Warszawa/Kraków: Ossolineum, 1991.

Potkański, Karol. "Wiadomości Długosza o polskiej mitologii." In Karol Potkański. *Pisma pośmiertne*, vol. 2, 1–93. Kraków: PAU, 1924.

Potkowski, Edward. *Dziedzictwo wierzeń pogańskich w średniowiecznych Niemczech. Defuncti vivi*. Warszawa: Wydawnictwo Uniwersytetu Warszawskiego, 1973.

Potkowski, Edward. *Książka i pismo w średniowieczu. Studia z dziejów kultury piśmiennej i komunikacji społecznej*. Pułtusk: Akademia Humanistyczna im. Aleksandra Gieysztora, 2006.

Potkowski, Edward. "Problemy kultury piśmiennej łacińskiego średniowiecza." *Przegląd Humanistyczny* 38 (1994) 3: 21–40.

Procházka, Vladimír. "Organisace kultu a kmenove zřizeni polabsko-pobaltskych slovanů." In *Vznik a počatki slovanů* 2, 145–167. Praha: Nakladatelství Československé akademie věd, 1958.

Prucnal, Dariusz. "Władca chrześcijański w Kronice Thietmara biskupa Merseburskiego." *Roczniki Humanistyczne* 44 (1996) 2: 5–36.

Rajewski, Zdzisław. "Pogańscy kapłani-czarodzieje w walce klasowej we wczesnym średniowieczu." *Wiadomości Archeologiczne* 39 (1975): 503–509.

Rajewski, Zdzisław. "Święta woda u Słowian – źródła, rzeki, jeziora." *Slavia Antiqua* 21 (1974): 111–117.

Rechowicz, Marian. "Chrzest Polski a katolicka teologia misyjna we wczesnym średniowieczu." *Ruch Biblijny i Liturgiczny* 19 (1966): 67–74.

BIBLIOGRAPHY

Rechowicz, Marian. "Początki i rozwój kultury scholastycznej (do końca XIV wieku)." In *Dzieje teologii katolickiej w Polsce*, ed. M. Rechowicz, vol. 1: *Średniowiecze*, 17–91. Lublin: Towarzystwo Naukowe KUL, 1974.

Religia pogańskich Słowian. Sesja naukowa w Kielcach, ed. Karol Strug. Kielce: Muzeum Świętokrzyskie, 1968.

Reuther, Timothy. "Introduction to the 2002 Edition." In Adam of Bremen, *History of the Archbishops of Hamburg-Bremen*, trans., introduction and notes Francis J. Tschan, reed. and new introduction Timothy Reuther, xi–xxi. New York: Columbia University Press, 2002.

Ricoeur, Paul. *Język, tekst, interpretacja. Wybór pism*, trans. Piotr Graff, Katarzyna Rosner. Warszawa: PIW, 1989.

Ricoeur, Paul. *Pamięć, historia, zapomnienie*, trans. Janusz Margański. Kraków: Universitas, 2006.

Ricoeur, Paul. ">>Symbol daje do myślenia<<", trans. Stanisław Cichowicz. In Paul Ricoeur. *Egzystencja i hermeneutyka. Rozprawy o metodzie*, ed. Stanisław Cichowicz, 62–80. Warszawa: De Agostini, 2003.

Rosen-Przeworska, Janina. "Celtycka geneza niektórych wątków wierzeniowych i ikonograficznych u Słowian zachodnich." In *Słowiańszczyzna Połabska między Niemcami a Polską. Materiały z konferencji naukowej zorganizowanej przez Instytut Historii UAM w dniach 28–29 IV 1980 r.*, ed. Jerzy Strzelczyk, 257–266. Poznań: Wydawnictwo UAM, 1981.

Rosen-Przeworska, Janina; Szafrański, Włodzimierz. "W sprawie policefalizmu bóstw nadbałtyckich." In *Słowiańszczyzna Połabska między Niemcami a Polską. Materiały z konferencji naukowej zorganizowanej przez Instytut Historii UAM w dniach 28–29 IV 1980 r.*, ed. Jerzy Strzelczyk, 255–256. Poznań: Wydawnictwo UAM, 1981.

Rosik, Mariusz. "Motyw κυναρια w dialogu Jezusa z Kananejką – Syrofenicjanką (Mk 7, 24–30; Mt 15, 21–28). W kręgu biblijnej topiki psa." In *Viae historicae. Księga jubileuszowa dedykowana Profesorowi Lechowi A. Tyszkiewiczowi w siedemdziesiątą rocznicę urodzin*, ed. Mateusz Goliński, Stanisław Rosik, 429–434. (Acta Universitatis Wratislaviensis. Historia) 152. Wrocław: Wydawnictwo Uniwersytetu Wrocławskiego, 2001.

Rosik, Stanisław. "Barbari et Greci w Iumne. >>Europa barbarzyńska<< jako koncepcja w studiach nad formowaniem się kulturowego oblicza Kontynentu (wokół przekazu Adama z Bremy)." In *Europa barbarica, Europa christiana. Studia Medievalia Carolo Modzelewski dedicata*, ed. Roman Michałowski *et al.*, 191–197. Warszawa: DiG, 2008.

Rosik, Stanisław. *Bolesław Krzywousty*. Wrocław: Chronicon, 2013.

Rosik, Stanisław. "Cień wieży Babel na pomorskich kącinach. O niepokornej służbie metafory w badaniach nad początkami Słowiańszczyzny i jej kultury duchowej."

In *Mundus hominis – cywilizacja, kultura, natura. Wokół interdyscyplinarności badań historycznych*, ed. Stanisław Rosik, Przemysław Wiszewski, 401–408. (Acta Universitatis Wratislaviensis. Historia) 175. Wrocław: Wydawnictwo Uniwersytetu Wrocławskiego, 2006.

Rosik, Stanisław. *Conversio gentis Pomeranorum. Studium świadectwa o wydarzeniu (XII wiek)*. Wrocław: Chronicon, 2010.

Rosik, Stanisław. "Dokąd sięgają pamięcią słowiańscy starcy z Kroniki Helmolda?" In *Starość – wiek spełnienia*, ed. Wojciech Dzieduszycki, Jacek Wrzesiński, 233–236. (Funeralia Lednickie, Spotkanie) 8. Poznań: Stowarzyszenie Naukowe Archeologów Polskich, 2006.

Rosik, Stanisław. "Gdy góra Ślęża przerosła Alpy … Uwagi w sprawie recepcji kultury słowiańskiej w kręgu łacińskim (na przykładzie funkcjonowanie etymologii w tekstach do XII w.)." In *Źródła kultury umysłowej w Europie środkowej ze szczególnym uwzględnieniem Górnego Śląska*, ed. Antoni Barciak, 103–114. Katowice: Instytut Górnośląski, 2005.

Rosik, Stanisław. "Greeks and Romans in pagan Wolin. Integrating the Barbarians into the collective memory of the Latin West at the time of the conversion of the Slavs." In *Rome, Constantinople and Newly-Converted Europe, Archaeological and Historical Evidence*, vol. 1, ed. Maciej Salamon *et al.*, 195–201. Kraków/Leipzig: GWZO/Rzeszów: Instytut Archeologii Uniwersytetu Rzeszowskiego/Warszawa: IAE PAN, 2012.

Rosik, Stanisław. "Jarowit Mars i Czarny Bóg Diabeł. O rozmaitej genezie nowych tożsamości słowiańskich bóstw na północnym Połabiu (w kręgu przekazów z XII wieku)." In *Historia narrat. Studia mediewistyczne ofiarowane Profesorowi Jackowi Banaszkiewiczowi*, ed. Andrzej Pleszczyński, Joanna Sobiesiak, Michał Tomaszek, Przemysław Tyszka, 263–275. Lublin: Wydawnictwo UMCS, 2012.

Rosik, Stanisław. "Mons Silensis – axis mundi. Góra Ślęża między historią a fenomenologią." In *Sacrum pogańskie – sacrum chrześcijańskie. Kontynuacja miejsc kultu we wczesnośredniowiecznej Europie Środkowej*, ed. Krzysztof Bracha, Czesław Hadamik, 179–192. Warszawa: DiG, 2010.

Rosik, Stanisław. "O 'rozpoznawaniu' civitas w świecie słowiańskich plemion (tzw. Geograf Bawarski a łacińskie przekazy z XI–XII w.). Uwagi do dyskusji nad kształtowaniem się pojęcia grodu." In *Funkcje grodów w państwa wczesnośredniowiecznej Europy Środkowej. Społeczeństwo, gospodarka, ideologia*, ed. Krystian Chrzan, Krzysztof Czapla, Sławomir Moździoch, 37–42. Głogów/Wrocław: Wydawnictwo Instytutu Archeologii i Etnologii PAN, 2014.

Rosik, Stanisław. "Połabskie władztwo 'księcia demonów'. Teologiczne uwarunkowania opisów pogańskich wierzeń i kultu w przekazach o religii Słowian." In *Studia z historii średniowiecza*, ed. Mateusz Goliński, 7–21. (Acta Universitatis Wratislaviensis. Historia) 163. Wrocław: Wydawnictwo Uniwersytetu Wrocławskiego, 2003.

BIBLIOGRAPHY

Rosik, Stanisław, "Reinbern – Salsae Cholbergiensis ecclesiae episcopus." In *Salsa Cholbergiensis. Kołobrzeg w średniowieczu*, ed. Lech Leciejewicz, Marian Rębkowski, 95–107. Kołobrzeg: Le petit Café, 2000.

Rosik, Stanisław. *"Romanorum prepotens imperator augustus* und *valentior sibi in Christo domnus apostolicus* in der Chronik Thietmars von Merseburg." In *Inter laurum et olivam*, ed. Jiří Šouša, Ivana Ebelová, 373–378. (Acta Universitatis Carolinae – Philosophica et Historica 1–2 (2002), Z pomocných ved historických) 16. Praha: Nakladatelství Karolinum, 2007.

Rosik, Stanisław. *"Rudes in fide gentilium populi* ... Fortdauer der Anzeichen des Heidentums zur Zeit der Christianisierung der Slawen im Lichte der deutschen narrativen Quellen des 11. und 12. Jahrhunderts." *Questiones Medii Aevii novae* 7 (2002): 45–76.

Rosik, Stanisław. *"Slavia universa?* O współczesnym oglądzie kultury duchowej dawnych Słowian i jego mitologizacji (w nawiązaniu do eseistyki Marii Janion)." *Przegląd Humanistyczny* 53 (2009) 4: 1–17.

Rosik, Stanisław. "Sponsae Christi oraz dii manu facti w Kronice Thietmara. Elementy konwencji dziejopisarskiej w służbie historiologii." In *Viae historicae. Księga jubileuszowa dedykowana Profesorowi Lechowi A. Tyszkiewiczowi w siedemdziesiątą rocznicę urodzin*, ed. Mateusz Goliński, Stanisław Rosik, 415–421. (Acta Universitatis Wratislaviensis. Historia) 152. Wrocław: Wydawnictwo Uniwersytetu Wrocławskiego, 2001.

Rosik, Stanisław. "The formation of Silesia (to 1163). Factors of regional integration." In *The long formation of the Region Silesia (c. 1000–1526)*, ed. Przemysław Wiszewski, 41–64. (Cuius regio? Ideological and Territorial Cohesion of the Historical Region of Silesia (c. 1000–2000) 1). Wrocław: Publishing House Wydawnictwo eBooki.com. pl, 2013.

Rosik, Stanisław. *Udział chrześcijaństwa w powstaniu policefalnych posągów kultowych u Słowian zachodnich*. Wrocław: Instytut Historyczny Uniwersytetu Wrocławskiego, 1995.

Rosik, Stanisław. "Wineta – utopia szlachetnych pogan (znaczenie legendy w Helmolda 'Kronice Słowian')." *Slavia Antiqua* 42 (2001): 113–122.

Rospond, Stanisław. "Ślężanie." In sss, vol. 5, 566–567.

Rossignol, Sébastien. "Civitas in Early Medieval Central Europe – Stronghold or District?" *The Medieval History Journal* 14 (2011) 1: 71–99.

Rossignol, Sébastien. "Überlegungen zur Datierung des Traktates des sog. Bayerischen Geographen anhand paläographischer und kodikologischer Beobachtungen." In *Der Wandel um 1000. Beiträge der Sektion zur slawischen Frühgeschichteder 18. Jahrestagung des Mittel- und Ostdeutschen Verbandes für Altertumsforschungin Greifswald, 23. bis 27. März 2009*, ed. Felix Biermann, Thomas Kersting, Anne Klammt,

305–316. (Beiträge zur Ur- und Frühgeschichte Mitteleuropas) 60. Langenweissbach: Beier & Beran, 2011.

Ruchhöft, Fred. *Die Burg am Kap Arkona – Götter, Macht und Mythos.* (Archäologie in Mecklenburg-Vorpommern) 7. Schwerin: Landesamt für Kultur und Denkmalpflege, 2016.

Rudnicki, Mikołaj. "Bóstwa lechickie." *Slavia Occidentalis* 5 (1926): 372–419.

Rudnicki, Mikołaj. "Odra i jej ujścia." *Slavia Occidentalis* 15 (1936): 67–73.

Rudnicki, Mikołaj. "Polskie Dagome iudex i Wagryjska >>Podaga<<." *Slavia Occidentalis* 7 (1928): 135–165.

Rumohr, Carl Friedrich. *Sammlung für Kunst und Historie,* vol. 1/1: *Über das Verhältniss der seit lange gewöhnlichen Vorstellungen von einer prachtvollen Wineta zu unrser positiven Kenntniss der Kultur und Kunst der deutschen Ostseeslaven* (Hamburg: Perthes & Besser, 1816).

Rusakiewicz, Monika. *Wineta. Korzenie legendy i jej recepcja w historiografii zachodnio-pomorskiej do XVI wieku.* Wrocław: Chronicon, 2016.

Rusanova, Irina P.; Timoshchuk, Boris A. "Vtoroye zbruchskoye (krutilovskoye) svjatilishche (po materyalam raskopok 1985 g.)." In *Drevnosti slavyan i Rusi,* ed. Boris A. Timoshhuk, 78–91. Moskva: Nauka, 1988.

Rusanova, Irina P.; Timoshchuk, Boris A. "Zbruchskoye svyatilishche." "Sovetskaya Archeologia" (1986) 4: 90–99.

Rusecki, Marian. *Cud w myśli chrześcijańskiej.* Lublin: Towarzystwo Naukowe KUL, 1991.

Russel, Jeffrey Burton. *Satan, the Early Christian Tradition.* Ithaca: Cornell University Press, 1981.

Rybakov, Boris. *Jazyčestvo drevnej Rusi.* Moskva: Nauka, 1987.

Rybakov, Boris. *Jazyčestvo drevnich slavyan.* Moskva: Nauka, 1981.

Rybakov, Boris. "Svjatovid – Rod." In *Liber Iosepho Kostrzewski octogenario a veneratoribus dicatus,* ed. Konrad Jażdżewski, 390–934. Wrocław: Ossolineum 1968.

Rytter, Grażyna. "O badaniach nad prasłowiańską terminologią religijną." *Slavia Occidentalis* 43 (1986): 129–134.

Rzetelska-Feleszko, Ewa. "Wolin." In SSS, vol. 6, 561.

Schmale, Franz-Josef. "Mentalität und Berichtshorizont, Absicht und Situation hochmittelalterlicher Geschichtsschreiber." *Historische Zeitschrift* 226 (1978) 1: 5–16.

Schmaus, Alois. "Zur altslawischen Religionsgeschichte." *Saeculum* 4 (1953): 206–230.

Schmeidler, Bernhard. "Einleitung." In *Helmoldi, presbyteri Bozoviensis Cronica Slavorum,* ed. Bernhard Schmeidler, SSrerGerm in usum scholarum (1937), v–xxxii.

Schmeidler, Bernhard. "Einleitung." In *Magistri Adam Bremensis Gesta Hammmaburgensis Ecclesiae Pontificum,* ed. Bernhard Schmeidler, SSrerGerm in usum scholarum (1917), vii–lxvii.

Schmidt, Jacek. "Funkcje i właściwości stereotypów etnicznych. Refleksje teoretyczne." In *Wokół stereotypów Niemców i Polaków,* ed. Wojciech Wrzesiński, 5–11. (Acta

BIBLIOGRAPHY

Universitatis Wratislaviensis. Historia) 79. Wrocław: Wydawnictwo Uniwersytetu Wrocławskiego, 1991.

Schmidt, Roderich. "Rethra. Das Heiligtum der Lutizen als Heiden-Metropole." In *Festschrift für Walter Schlesinger*, vol. 2, ed. Helmut Beumann, 366–394. Köln/Wien: Böhlau, 1974.

Schmidt, Volker. "Rethra, das frühstädtische Zentrum an der Lieps." In *Instantia est Mater Doctrinae. Księga Jubileuszowa Prof. Dr. hab. Władysława Filipowiaka*, ed. Eugeniusz Wilgocki *et al.*, 201–222. Szczecin: Stowarzyszenie Naukowe Archeologów Polskich, 2001.

Schneidmüller, Bernd. "Hartwig." In *Lexikon des Mittelalters*, vol. 4 (München/Zürich: Artemis, 1989), col. 1947.

Schröder, Edward. "Zur Heimat des Adam von Bremen." *Hansische Geschichtsblätter* 23 (1917): 351–366.

Schröder, Horst-Diether. ">>Gesta Danorum<< Saxo Gramatyka jako źródło do dziejów Słowian nadbałtyckich." *Przegląd Zachodniopomorski* 11 (1967) 5: 17–30.

Schuchhardt, Carl. *Arkona, Rethra, Vineta. Ortsuntersuchungen und Ausgrabungen.* Berlin: H. Schoetz & Co, 1926.

Schuldt, Ewald. *Gross Raden. Ein slawischer Tempelort des 9./10. Jahrhunderts in Mecklenburg.* Berlin: Akademie-Verlag, 1985.

Schulmeyer-Ahl, Kerstin. *Der Anfang vom Ende der Ottonen. Konstitutionsbedingungen historiographischer Nachrichten in der Chronik Thietmars von Merseburg.* Berlin: De Gruyter, 2009.

Scior, Volker. *Das Eigene und das Fremde. Identität und Fremdheit in den Chroniken Adams von Bremen, Helmolds von Bosau und Arnolds von Lübeck.* (Orbis mediaevalis / Vorstellungswelten des Mittelalters) 4. Berlin: Akademie, 2002.

Sczaniecki, Paweł. *Służba Boża w dawnej Polsce*, Poznań/Warszawa/Lublin: Księgarnia św. Wojciecha, 1962.

Seweryn, Tadeusz. "Figury kultowe." In SSS, vol. 2, 55–56.

Siebs, Theodor. "Beiträge zur deutschen Mythologie." *Zeitschrift für Deustche Philologie* 24 (1892): 432–461.

Sikorski, Dariusz Andrzej. *Kościół w Polsce za Mieszka I i Bolesława Chrobrego. Rozważania nad granicami poznania historycznego.* Poznań: Wydawnictwo Naukowe UAM, 2011.

Sikorski, Dariusz Andrzej. *Początki Kościoła w Polsce. Wybrane problemy.* Poznań: Wydawnictwo PTPN, 2012.

Skonieczny, Tomasz. "Od Wieletów do Luciców. W sprawie zmiany tożsamości plemion wieleckich u schyłku X wieku." In *Populi terrae marisque. Prace poświęcone pamięci Profesora Lecha Leciejewicza*, ed. Marian Rębkowski, Stanisław Rosik, 83–91. Wrocław: Chronicon, 2011.

Skonieczny, Tomasz. ">>Testatur ... si quando his seva longae rebellionis assperitas immineat<< – dociekania nad przekazem Thietmara (VI, 24) o normach regulujących zachowanie ładu wewnętrznego w obrębie Związku Lucickiego." In *Orbis Hominum: Civitas, potestas, universitas. W kręgu badań nad kształtowaniem cywilizacji w wiekach średnich*, ed. Mateusz Goliński, Stanisław Rosik, 61–74. (Scripta Historica Medievalia) 5. Wrocław: Chronicon, 2016.

Skovgaard-Petersen, Inge. "Wendenzüge – Kreuzzüge." In *Rom und Byzanz im Norden. Mission und Glaubenswechsel im Ostseeraum während des 8.–14. Jahrhunderts*, vol. 1, ed. Michael Müller-Wille, 279–289. Stuttgart: Steiner, 1997.

Skubiszewski, Piotr. *Malarstwo europejskie w średniowieczu*, vol. 1: *Malarstwo karolińskie i przedromańskie*. Warszawa: Wydawnictwa Artystyczne i Filmowe, 1973.

Sławski, Franciszek. *Słownik etymologiczny języka polskiego*, vol. 1. Kraków: Towarzystwo Miłośników Języka Polskiego, 1952.

Słownik polszczyzny XVI wieku, vol. 5, ed. Maria R. Mayenowa. Wrocław: Ossolineum, 1971.

Słownik Starożytności Słowiańskich. Encyklopedyczny zarys kultury Słowian od czasów najdawniejszych, vol. 1: A–E, ed. Władysław Kowalenko, Gerard Labuda, Tadeusz Lehr-Spławiński. Wrocław/Warszawa/Kraków: Ossolineum 1961–1962; vol. 2: F–K, ed. Władysław Kowalenko, Gerard Labuda, Tadeusz Lehr-Spławiński. Wrocław/Warszawa/Kraków: Ossolineum, 1964–1965; vol. 3: L–O, ed. Władysław Kowalenko, Gerard Labuda, Zdzisław Stieber. Wrocław/Warszawa/Kraków: Ossolineum, 1967–1968; vol. 4: P–R, ed. Gerard Labuda, Zdzisław Stieber. Wrocław/Warszawa/Kraków: Ossolineum, 1970–1972; vol. 5: S–Ś, ed. Gerard Labuda, Zdzisław Stieber. Wrocław/Warszawa/Kraków: Ossolineum, 1975; vol. 6: T–W, ed. Gerard Labuda, Zdzisław Stieber, Wrocław/Warszawa/Kraków: Ossolineum, 1977–1980; vol. 7: Y–Ż. Suplementy, ed. Gerard Labuda, Zdzisław Stieber. Wrocław/Warszawa/Kraków: Ossolineum, 1982–1986; vol. 8: Suplementy i indeksy, ed. Antoni Gąsiorowski, Gerard Labuda, Andrzej Wędzki. Wrocław/Warszawa/Kraków: Ossolineum, 1991–1996.

Słupecki, Leszek Paweł. "Archaeological Sources and Written Sources in Studying Symbolic Culture (Exemplified by Research on the Pre-Christian Religion of the Slavs)." In *Theory and Practice of Archaeological Research*, vol. 3, ed. Stanisław Tabaczyński, 337–366. Warsaw: IAE PAN, 1998.

Słupecki, Leszek Paweł. "Einflüsse des Christentums auf die heidnische Religion des Ostseeslawen im 8.–12. Jahrhundert: Tempel – Götterbilder – Kult." In *Rom und Byzanz im Norden. Mission und Glaubenswechsel im Ostseeraum während des 8.–14. Jahrhunderts*, vol. 2, ed. Michael Müller-Wille, 177–189. Stuttgart: Steiner, 1997.

Słupecki, Leszek Paweł. "Sanktuaria w świecie natury u Słowian i Germanów. Święte gaje i ich bogowie." In *Człowiek, sacrum, środowisko. Miejsca kultu we wczesnym średniowieczu*, ed. Sławomir Moździoch, 39–47. (Spotkania Bytomskie) 4. Wrocław: Werk, 2000.

Słupecki, Leszek Paweł. *Slavonic Pagan Sanctuaries*. Warsaw: IAE PAN, 1994.

Słupecki, Leszek Paweł. "Słowiańskie posągi bóstw." *Kwartalnik Historii Kultury Materialnej* 41 (1993) 1: 31–69.

Słupecki, Leszek Paweł. "Ślęza, Radunia, Wieżyca. Miejsca kultu pogańskiego Słowian w średniowieczu." *Kwartalnik Historyczny* 99 (1992) 2: 3–15.

Słupecki, Leszek Paweł. "Świątynie pogańskich Pomorzan w czasach misji świętego Ottona (Szczecin)." *Przegląd Religioznawczy* (1993) 3: 13–3 2.

Słupecki, Leszek Paweł. "Wawel jako święta góra a słowiańskie mity o zajęciu kraju." *Przegląd Religioznawczy* (1993) 2: 3–18.

Słupecki, Leszek Paweł. "Wykopaliska słowiańskich świątyń." *Mówią Wieki* (1991) 11: 28–34.

Słupecki, Leszek Paweł. *Wyrocznie i wróżby pogańskich Skandynawów*. Warszawa: IAE PAN, 1998.

Sochacki, Jarosław. "Związek Lucicki – między Polską a Cesarstwem do 1002 r." *Slavia Antiqua* 47 (2006): 17–48.

Sosnowski, Miłosz. "Kilka uwag o chronologii życia i twórczości Brunona z Kwerfurtu." *Roczniki Historyczne* 82 (2016): 63–78.

Soszyński, Jacek. "Święty Wit a Świętowit Rugijski. Z dziejów legendy." *Przegląd Humanistyczny* 28 (1984) 9/10: 133–139.

Spors, Józef. *Studia nad wczesnośredniowiecznymi dziejami Pomorza Zachodniego. XII–pierwsza połowa XIII w.* Słupsk: Wyższa Szkoła Pedagogiczna w Słupsku, 1988.

Staats, Reinhart. "Missionsgeschichte Nordeuropas. Eine geistesgeschichtliche Einführung." In *Rom und Byzanz im Norden. Mission und Glaubenswechsel im Ostseeraum während des 8.–14. Jahrhunderts*, vol. 1, ed. Michael Müller-Wille, 9–33. Stuttgart: Steiner, 1997.

Stabenow, Ulf. "Die Entstehung der Pomoranen." In *Slawen und Deutsche im südlichen Ostseeraum vom 11. bis zum 16. Jahrhundert. Archäologische, historische und sprachwissenschaftliche Beispiele aus Schleswig-Holstein, Mecklenburg und Pommern*, ed. Michael Müller-Wille, Dietrich Meier, Henning Unverhau, 127–148. Neumünster: Wachholtz, 1995.

Stachowiak, Lech. "Bóg. II. W Starym Testamencie." In *Encyklopedia Katolicka*, vol. 1, ed. Feliks Gryglewicz, Romuald Łukaszyk, Zygmunt Sułowski, col. 902–909. Lublin: Towarzystwo Naukowe KUL, 1973.

Stanisławski, Błażej M., *Jómswikingowie z Wolina-Jómsborga – studium archeologiczne przenikania kultury skandynawskiej na ziemie polskie*. Wrocław: IAE PAN, 2013.

Stoob, Heinz. "Einleitung." In *Helmoldi presbyteri bozoviensis Chronica Slavorum*, ed. Heinz Stoob, 1–24. Ausgewählte Quellen zur deutschen Geschichte des Mittelalters. Freiherr vom Stein-Gedächtnisausgabe 19, Berlin 1963.

Storia della chiesa, vol. 4: *Il primo Medievo (VIII–XII secolo)*. ed. Hubert Jedin. Milano: Jaca Book, 1969.

Strzelczyk, Jerzy. *Apostołowie Europy*. Warszawa: PAX, 1997.

Strzelczyk, Jerzy. *Bohaterowie Słowian Połabskich*. Poznań: Wydawnictwo Poznańskie, 2017.

Strzelczyk, Jerzy. "Eschatologia na pograniczu niemiecko-słowiańskim w końcu XII w." *Roczniki Historyczne* 50 (1984): 141–151.

Strzelczyk, Jerzy. *Mity, podania i wierzenia dawnych Słowian*. Poznań: Rebis, 1998.

Strzelczyk, Jerzy. *Otton III*. Wrocław: Ossolineum, 2000.

Strzelczyk, Jerzy. "Radogoszcz." In SSS, vol. 4, 450–451.

Strzelczyk, Jerzy. "Rec. Festschrift für Walter Schlesinger, Bd. II, herausgegeben von Helmut Beumann (Mitteldeutsche Forschungen, Bd. 74/II), Böhlau Verlag, Köln – Wien 1974." *Studia Historica Slavo-Germanica UAM* 5 (1976): 200–202.

Strzelczyk, Jerzy. "Śmiłowe Pole." In SSS, vol. 5, 569.

Strzelczyk, Jerzy. "Thietmar." In SSS, vol. 6, 74–75.

Strzelczyk, Jerzy. "Tysiąclecie powstania Słowian połabskich 983–1983. Naukowe rezultaty jubileuszu." *Studia Historica Slavo-Germanica* 14 (1985): 241–260.

Strzelczyk, Jerzy. "Unwan." In SSS, vol. 6, 266.

Strzelczyk, Jerzy. "Wicelin." In SSS, vol. 6, 415–416.

Strzelczyk, Jerzy. "Wstęp." In *Helmolda Kronika Słowian*, trans. Józef Matuszewski, ed. Jerzy Strzelczyk, 5–69. Warszawa: PWN, 1974.

Sułowski, Zygmunt. "Pierwszy Kościół polski." In *Chrześcijaństwo w Polsce. Zarys przemian 966–1979*, ed. Jerzy Kłoczowski, 17–51. Lublin: Towarzystwo Naukowe KUL, 1992.

Sułowski, Zygmunt. "Sporne problemy dziejów Związku Wieletów-Luciców." In *Słowiańszczyzna Połabska między Niemcami a Polską. Materiały z konferencji naukowej zorganizowanej przez Instytut Historii UAM w dniach 28–29 IV 1980 r.*, ed. Jerzy Strzelczyk, 155–165. Poznań: Wydawnictwo UAM, 1981.

Sundqvist, Olof. *An Arena for Higher Powers. Ceremonial buildings and religious strategies for rulership in Late Iron Age Scandinavia*. Leiden/Boston: Brill 2015.

Sundqvist, Olof. *Freyr's Offspring. Rulers and Religion in Ancient Svea Society*, (Acta Universitatis Upsaliensis. Historia Religionum) 22. Uppsala: Uppsala Universitet, 2002.

Sundqvist, Olof. "Gudme on Funen: A central sanctuary with cosmic symbolism?" In *The Gudme/Gudhem Phenomenon*, ed. Oliver Grimm, Alexandra Pesch, 63–76. Neumünster: Wachholtz Verlag GmbH, 2011.

Sundqvist, Olof. "Runology and History of Religions. Some Critical Implications of the Debate on the Stentoften Inscription." In *Blandade runstudier 2*, ed. Lennart Elmevik, Lena Peterson, 135–174. (Runrön. Runologiska bidrag utgivna av Institutionen för nordiska språk vid Uppsala universitet) 11. Uppsala: Institutionen för nordiska språk vid Uppsala universitet, 1997.

Surowiecki, Wawrzyniec. "Rozprawa o sposobach dopełnienia historyi Słowian." *Roczniki Towarzystwa Królewskiego Przyjaciół Nauk* 8 (1812) 1: 82–119.

BIBLIOGRAPHY

Swoboda, Wincenty. "Kult świętych (2)." In SSS, vol. 8, 383–384.

Szafrański, Włodzimierz. *Prahistoria religii na ziemiach polskich*. Wrocław/Warszawa/ Kraków: Ossolineum, 1987.

Szafrański, Włodzimierz. *Religie światowe i religie Słowian*. (Religioznawstwo) 3. Warszawa: Wyższa Szkoła Nauk Społecznych, 1983.

Szafrański, Włodzimierz. "W sprawie tzw. pramonoteizmu w paleolicie." *Światowid* 23 (1960): 151–160.

Szczesiak, Rainer. "Auf der Suche nach Rethra! Ein interessantes Kapitel deutscher Forschungsgeschichte." In *Siedlung, Kommunikation und Wirtschaft im westslawischen Raum: Beiträge der Sektion zur slawischen Frühgeschichte des 5. Deutschen Archäologenkongresses in Frankfurt an der Oder, 4. bis 7. April 2005*, ed. Felix Biermann, 313–334. (Beiträge zur Ur- und Frühgeschichte Mitteleuropas) 46. Langenweißbach: Beier & Beran, 2007.

Szyjewski, Andrzej. *Religia Słowian*. Kraków: WAM, 2003.

Szymański, Wojciech. "Posąg ze Zbrucza i jego otoczenie. Lata badań, lata wątpliwości." *Przegląd Archeologiczny* 44 (1996): 75–116.

Ślaski, Kazimierz. "Stosunki krajów skandynawskich z południowo-wschodnim wybrzeżem Bałtyku od VI do XII wieku." *Przegląd Zachodni* 8 (1952) 2: 30–45.

Śrutwa, Jan. "Diecezje Pomorza Zachodniego (Diecezja Wolińska a później Kamieńska) między związkami z Gnieznem, Magdeburgiem i bezpośrednią zależnością od Stolicy Apostolskiej." *Szczecińskie Studia Kościelne* 2 (1991): 31–40.

Tarkowska, Elżbieta. "Wstęp do wydania polskiego." In Émile Durkheim. *Elementarne formy życia życia religijnego. System totemiczny w Australii*, trans. Anna Zadrożyńska, ed. Elżbieta Tarkowska, XIII–XL. Warszawa: PWN, 1990.

Todorov, Tzvetan. *Nous et les Autres. La Réflexion française sur la diversité humaine*. Paris: Seuil, 1989.

Tokarev, Sergey A. *Pierwotne formy religii i ich rozwój*, trans. Mirosław Nowaczyk. Warszawa: Książka i Wiedza, 1969 [orig. *Rannie formy religii i ikh razvitie*. Moskva: Nauka, 1964].

Tomaszek, Michał. "Brunon z Kwerfurtu i Otton II: powstanie słowiańskie 983 roku jako grzech cesarza." *Kwartalnik Historyczny* 109 (2002) 4: 5–23.

Tomicka, Joanna; Tomicki, Ryszard. *Drzewo życia. Ludowa wizja świata i człowieka*. Warszawa: Ludowa Spółdzielnia Wydawnicza, 1975.

Topolski, Jerzy. *Metodologia historii*, Warszawa: PWN, 1984.

Trillmich, Werner. "Einleitung." In *Gesta Hammaburgensis ecclesiae Pontificum*, ed. Werner Trillmich, in *Quellen des 9. und 11. Jahrhunderts zur Geschichte der hamburgischen Kirche und des Reiches*, 137–158. Ausgewählte Quellen zur deutschen Geschichte des Mittelalters. Freiherr vom Stein-Gedächtnisausgabe 11. Darmstadt: Wissenschaftliche Buchgesellschaft, 1961.

Trillmich, Werner. "Einleitung," in *Thietmari Merseburgensis Episcopi Chronicon*, Latin and German text, ed. Robert Holtzmann/Werner Trillmich, ix–xxxii. Ausgewählte Quellen zur deutschen Geschichte des Mittelalters 9. Darmstadt: Wissenschaftliche Buchgesellschaft, 1992.

Třeštík, Dušan. *Mýty kmene Čechů (7.–10. století)*. Praha: Nakladatelství Lidové nowiny, 2003.

Tschan, Francis J., "Introduction." In Adam of Bremen, *History of the Archbishops of Hamburg-Bremen*, trans., introduction and notes Francis J. Tschan, reed. and new introduction Timothy Reuther, xxv–xlvi. New York: Columbia University Press, 2002.

Turasiewicz, Adam. *Dzieje polityczne Obodrzyców. Od IX wieku do utraty niepodległości w latach 1160–1164*. Kraków: Nomos, 2004.

Tymieniecki, Kazimierz. "Państwo polskie w stosunku do Niemiec i cesarstwa średniowiecznego w X wieku." In *Początki Państwa Polskiego. Księga Tysiąclecia*, vol. 1, ed. Kazimierz Tymieniecki *et al.*, 261–297. Poznań: PWN, 1962.

Tymieniecki, Kazimierz. *Społeczeństwo Słowian Lechickich*. Lwów: K.S. Jakubowski, 1928.

Tyszkiewicz, Lech A. "Motywy oceny Słowian w Kronice Thietmara." In *Studia z dziejów kultury i ideologii poświęcone Ewie Maleczyńskiej*, ed. Roman Heck, Wacław Korta, Józef Leszczyński, 104–118. Wrocław: Ossolineum, 1968.

Tyszkiewicz, Lech A. "Plemiona słowiańskie we wczesnym średniowieczu." In *Słowiańszczyzna w Europie średniowiecznej Księga pamiątkowa dla Lecha Leciejewicza*, vol. 1: *Plemiona i wczesne państwa*, ed. Zofia Kurnatowska, 45–52. Wrocław: IAE PAN, 1996.

Tyszkiewicz, Lech A. "Podziały plemienne i problem jedności Słowian," in *Słowiańszczyzna Połabska między Niemcami a Polską. Materiały z konferencji naukowej zorganizowanej przez Instytut Historii UAM w dniach 28–29 IV 1980 r.*, ed. Jerzy Strzelczyk 109–132. Poznań: Wydawnictwo UAM, 1981.

Tyszkiewicz, Lech A. "Przyłączenie Śląska do monarchii piastowskiej pod koniec X wieku." In *Od plemienia do państwa. Śląsk na tle Słowiańszczyzny Zachodniej*, ed. Lech Leciejewicz, 120–152. Wrocław/Warszawa: Volumen, 1991.

Tyszkiewicz, Lech A. "Rec. Helmut Lippelt, Thietmar von Merseburg. Reichsbischof und Chronist. Mitteldeutsche Forschungen, Bd. 72, Böhlau Verlag, Köln – Wien 1973, s. 245, 2 ilustr." *Studia Historica Slavo-Germanica UAM* 5 (1976): 203–207.

Tyszkiewicz, Lech A. "Sasi i inne ludy w dziejach saskich Widukinda z Korwei." In (Acta Universitatis Wratislaviensis, Historia) 23: 3–36 (Wrocław: Wydawnictwo Uniwersytetu Wrocławskiego, 1974).

Tyszkiewicz, Lech A. "Slavi genus hominum durum." In *Wokół stereotypów Niemców i Polaków*, ed. Wojciech Wrzesiński, 3–14. (Acta Universitatis Wratislaviensis. Historia) 114. Wrocław: Wydawnictwo Uniwersytetu Wrocławskiego, 1993.

BIBLIOGRAPHY

Tyszkiewicz, Lech A. *Słowianie w historiografii wczesnego średniowiecza od połowy VI do połowy VII wieku*, (Acta Universitatis Wratislaviensis. Historia) 63. Wrocław: Wydawnictwo Uniwersytetu Wrocławskiego, 1991.

Tyszkiewicz, Lech A. "Uwagi w sprawie wczesnośredniowiecznej terminologii etnicznej." In *Pojęcia "Volk" i "Nation" w historiografii Niemiec. Materiały z sesji naukowej zorganizowanej przez Zakład Historii Niemiec IH UAM w dniu 15 V 1979 r.*, ed. Antoni Czubiński, 179–182. Poznań: UAM, 1980.

Tyszkiewicz, Lech A. "Z badań nad narodzinami stereotypów Słowian w historiografii zachodniej wczesnego średniowiecza." In *Wokół stereotypów Polaków i Niemców*, ed. Wojciech Wrzesiński, 27–47. (Acta Universitatis Wratislaviensis. Historia) 79. Wrocław: Wydawnictwo Uniwersytetu Wrocławskiego, 1991.

Udolph, Jürgen. "Der Name Schlesiens." *Jahrbuch der schlesischen Friedrich-Wilhelm-Universität zu Breslau* 38/39 (1997–1998): 15–18.

Udolph, Jürgen. "Rügen. Namenkundliches," in *Reallexikon der Germanischen Altertumskunde*, vol. 25, Berlin/New York: De Gruyter, 2003.

Urbańczyk, Stanisław. *Dawni Słowianie. Wiara i kult*. Wrocław/Warszawa/Kraków: Ossolineum, 1991.

Urbańczyk, Stanisław. "Kapłani pogańscy." In SSS, vol. 2, 371.

Urbańczyk, Stanisław. "Pseudobóstwa." In SSS, vol. 4, 405–406.

Urbańczyk, Stanisław. "Rec. E. Wienecke, Untersuchungen zur Religion der Westslawen der Westslaven. Leipzig 1940. Forschungen zur Vor- u. Frühgeschichte. 1." *Rocznik Slawistyczny* 16 (1948): 40–56.

Váňa, Zdeněk. *Svět slovanských bohů a démonů*. Praha: Panorama, 1990.

Váňa, Zdeněk. *The world of the ancient Slavs*, trans. Till Gottheiner. London: Orbis, 1983 [orig. *Svět dávných Slovanů*. Praha: Artia, 1983].

Vauchez, André. *Duchowość średniowiecza*, trans. Hanna Zaremska. Gdańsk: Marabut, 1996 [orig. *La spiritualité du Moyen Âge occidental VIII–XIII*. Paris: Presses universitaires de France, 1975].

Vernardsky, George. *The origins of Russia*. Oxford: Oxford University Press, 1959.

Wachowski, Kazimierz. *Słowiańszczyzna Zachodnia*. Poznań: Wydawnictwo Poznańskiego Towarzystwa Przyjaciół Nauk, 2000 [1st ed. 1903].

Wamers, Egon. "Hammer und Kreuz. Typologische Aspekte einer nordeuropäischen Amulettsitte aus der Zeit des Glaubenswechsels." In *Rom und Byzanz im Norden. Mission und Glaubenswechsel im Ostseeraum während des 8.–14 Jahrhunderts*, vol. 1, ed. Michael Müller-Wille, 83–107. Stuttgart: Steiner, 1997.

Warner, David A. "Introduction: Thietmar, bishop and Chronicler." In *Ottonian Germany. The Chronicon of Thietmar of Merseburg*, trans. and ed. David A. Warner, 1–64. Manchester/New York: Manchester University Press, 2001.

Wavra, Brigitte. *Salzburg und Hamburg Erzbistumsgründung und Missionspolitik in karolinischer Zeit*. Berlin: Duncker & Humblot, 1991.

Weinrich, Lorenz. "Der Slawenaufstand von 983 in der Darstellung des Bischof Thietmar von Merseburg." In *Historiographia Mediaevalis. Studien zur Geschichtsschreibung und Quellenkunde des Mittelalters. Festschrift für Franz-Josef Schmale zum 65. Geburtstag*, ed. Dieter Berg, Hans-Werner Goetz, 77–87. Darmstadt: Wissenschaftliche Buchgesellschaft, 1988.

Węcławski, Tomasz. *Wspólny świat religii*. Kraków: Znak, 1995.

Wędzki, Andrzej. "Gana." In SSS, vol. 2, 79.

Wichert, Sven. "Die politische Rolle der heidnischen Priester bei den Westslaven." *Studia Mythologica Slavica* 13 (2010): 33–42.

Wichert, Sven. "Vademecum Rethram – Eine Revision." *Bodendenkmalpflege in Mecklenburg-Vorpommern, Jahrbuch* 56 (2008) [2009]: 103–113.

Widengren, Geo. *Religionsphänomenologie*. Berlin: De Gruyter, 1969.

Wielgus, Stanisław. *Badania nad Biblią w starożytności i w średniowieczu*. Lublin: Towarzystwo Naukowe KUL, 1990.

Wienecke, Erwin Von. *Untersuchungen zur Religion der Westslawen*. (Forschungen zur Vor- und Frühgeschichte) 1. Leipzig: Harrassowitz, 1940.

Wirski, Adam. "Bóstwo morskie pogańskich Pomorzan." In *Krzyżowcy, kronikarze, dyplomaci*, ed. Błażej Śliwiński, 309–327. (Gdańskie Studia z Dziejów Średniowiecza) 4. Gdańsk: Wydawnictwo Uniwersytetu Gdańskiego, 1997.

Wiszewski, Przemysław. *Domus Bolezlai. W poszukiwaniu tradycji dynastycznej Piastów (do około 1138 roku)*. Wrocław: Wydawnictwo Uniwersytetu Wrocławskiego, 2008.

Witczak, Krzysztof T., "Ze studiów nad religią Prasłowian. Część 2: Prapolska Nyja a grecka Enyo." *Slavia Occidentalis* 51 (1994): 123–132.

Witkowski, Grzegorz. "Opis wysp Północy jako dzieło etnografii wczesnośredniowiecznej." In *Studia z dziejów Europy Zachodniej i Śląska*, ed. Rościsław Żerelik, 9–43. Wrocław: Instytut Historyczny Uniwersytetu Wrocławskiego, 1995.

Wojciechowski, Leszek. "Trojaka śmierć słowiańskich bogów." In *Christianitas et cultura Europae, Księga Jubileuszowa Profesora Jerzego Kłoczowskiego*, vol. 1, ed. Henryk Gapski, 593–598. Lublin: Instytut Europy Środkowo-Wschodniej, 1998.

Wolny, Jerzy. "Z dziejów katechezy." In *Dzieje teologii katolickiej w Polsce*, ed. Marian Rechowicz, vol. 1: *Średniowiecze*, 149–210. Lublin: Towarzystwo Naukowe KUL, 1974.

Woronczak, Jerzy. *Studia o literaturze średniowiecza i renesansu*. Wrocław: Wydawnictwo Uniwersytetu Wrocławskiego, 1993.

Wrzesińska, Anna; Wrzesiński, Jacek. "Amor et mors – wczesnośredniowieczne groby podwójne." In *Viae historicae. Księga jubileuszowa dedykowana Profesorowi Lechowi A. Tyszkiewiczowi w siedemdziesiątą rocznicę urodzin*, ed. Mateusz Goliński, Stanisław Rosik, 435–444. (Acta Universitatis Wratislaviensis. Historia) 152. Wrocław: Wydawnictwo Uniwersytetu Wrocławskiego, 2001.

Wünsch, Thomas. *Deutsche und Slawen im Mittelalter. Beziehungen zu Tschechen, Polen, Südslawen und Russen*. München: Oldenbourg, 2008.

Zagiba, Franz. *Das Geistesleben der Slawen im Frühen Mittelalter*. Wien/Köln/Graz: Böhlau, 1971.

Zakrzewski, Stanisław. *Bolesław Chrobry Wielki*. Lwów: Ossolineum, 1925.

Zásterová, Bohumila. "Les Avares et les Slaves dans la Tactique de Maurice." *Rozprawy Československé Akademie Věd* 81 (1971): 3–82.

Zernack, Klaus. *Die burgstädtischen Volkversammlungen bei den Ost und Westslaven. Studien zur verfassungsgeschichtlichen Bedeutung des Veče*. Wiesbaden: Harrasowitz, 1967.

Zientara, Benedykt. "Populus – gens – natio. Z zagadnień wczesnośredniowiecznej terminologii etnicznej." In *Cultus et cognitio. Studia z dziejów średniowiecznej kultury*, ed. Stefan K. Kuczyński *et al.*, 673–682. Warszawa: PWN, 1976.

Zientara, Benedykt. *Świt narodów europejskich*. Warszawa: PIW, 1985.

Zoll-Adamikowa, Helena. "Głos w dyskusji." *Nasza Przeszłość* 69 (1988): 182–184.

Zoll-Adamikowa, Helena. "Modele recepcji rytuału szkieletowego u Słowian wschodnich i zachodnich." *Światowit* 40 (1995): 174–184.

Zoll-Adamikowa, Helena. *Wczesnośredniowieczne cmentarzyska ciałopalne Słowian na terenie Polski*, part 1–2. Wrocław: Ossolineum, 1975–1979.

Zöllner, Johann Friedrich. *Reise durch Pommern nach der Insel Rügen und einem Theile des Herzogthums Mecklenburg, im Jahre 1795*. Berlin: Maurer, 1797.

Žulkus, Vladas. "Heidentum und Christentum in Lituanien im 10.–16. Jahrhundert." In *Rom und Byzanz im Norden. Mission und Glaubenswechsel im Ostseeraum während des 8.–14 Jahrhunderts*, vol. 2, ed. Michael Müller-Wille, 143–161. Stuttgart: Steiner, 1997.

Index of Ancient Historical, Biblical and Mythical Figures

Aaron (Arn), bishop of Würzburg (855–962) 60

Abram (Abraham), patriarch   302

Absalon, bishop of Roskilde (1158–1192), archbishop of Lund (1178–1201)   358, 361

Adalbert St. (d. 997)   41, 82 f., 169, 249, 304, 352

Adalbert, archbishop of Hamburg-Bremen (1043–1072)   198, 201 f., 204–206, 209, 211, 220, 325

Adaldag, archbishop of Hamburg-Bremen (937–988)   208, 210

Adalgot, archbishop of Magdeburg (1107–1119)   245, 323

Adam of Bremen, chronicler (d. after 1081)   7, 15, 27, 29, 35, 38, 68, 80, 91, 95, 97, 101, 106, 109, 123, 126, 138 f., 141 f., 192, 197–209, 211–237, 240–242, 245–255, 258–260, 262, 264–266, 268–270, 274, 276, 284–291, 293–295, 297–300, 305, 308, 312, 323, 352, 359, 363, 368, 370 f., 374 f., 383–388

Adolf II of Holstein, count of Schauenburg and Holstein (d. 1164)   326, 329 f., 354, 356, 373

Aeneas Sylvius Piccolomini (d.1464), Pope Pius II   331

Agapetus II, Pope (946–955)   205 f.

Ahura Mazda, deity   130

Al Gardezi, historiographer (11th c.)   115

Albrecht the Bear, margrave of Brandenburg (d. 1170)   270

Alcuin of York (d. 804)   273

Alexander the Great, king of Macedon (d. 323 BC)   55, 303

Andajus, deity   366

Annalist Saxo see Saxo Annalist

Anskar St. (d. 865)   209 f., 270–272, 352, 373

Ansver, monk (d. 1066)   244

Antichrist, biblical figure   186, 191, 219

Aphrodite, deity   116

Apollo, deity   18

Ares, deity   11

Aristotle, philosopher (d. 322 BC)   258

Arnold of Lübeck, chronicler (d. 1211/1214)   256, 260, 263

Arnórr jarlaskáld, poet (d. ca. 1070)   267 f.

Artemis, deity   102, 108

Athanasius St. (d. 373)   144, 188

Athena, deity   11

Atlas, deity   317

Augustine of Hippo, St. (d. 430)   40, 46, 49 f., 58, 76, 79, 82 f., 189, 199, 219, 251

Augustine of Stargard, historiographer (14th c.)   267

Baal, deity   108, 192

Balazs St. (d. 316)   12, 279

Basil St.   15

Bavarian Geographer, conventional name for the anonymous author of *Descriptio civitatum et regionum ad septentrionalem plagam Danubii* (9th c.)   150 f.

Beda Venerabilis (Bede the Venerable), St. (d. 735)   200

Bel, pseudo-deity   349

Belbog (Bel bog) pseudo-deity   314, 320 f.

Belial, biblical figure   16, 108, 110, 145

Benedict V, Pope (964)   52

Benno see Bernard I, Saxon duke

Benno, bishop of Starigard (Oldenburg) (ca. 1013–1023)   240, 294

Bernard I, Saxon duke (d. 1011)   236 f., 239 287, 289

Bernard II, Saxon duke (d. 1059)   240 f., 289, 299

Bernard of Clairvaux St. (d. 1153)   324 f.

Bernhard, bishop of Hildesheim (1130–1153)   276

Bernhard II, bishop of Verden (994–1013)   235

Berno, bishop of Mecklenburg (Mechlin) and Schwerin (1162–1191)   356, 358

Białobóg see Belbog

Bies, mythical figure   318

Billug, alleged Obodrite prince (mentioned
    by Helmold of Bosau) 287
Boethius, philosopher (d. 524) 258
Boleslav the Brave (Chrobry), king of Poland
    (d. 1025) 41 f., 44, 78, 93, 149, 155, 158–160,
        164 f., 170 f., 176, 179–181, 183, 190, 245
Boleslav II the Pious, prince of Bohemia
    (d. 999) 91 f., 189
Boleslav the Wrymouth, prince of Poland
    (d. 1138) 359
Boniface St. *see* Winfrid-Boniface
Borvo, deity 332
Boso, bishop of Merseburg (968–970) 60,
    72–75, 79, 188
Bruno, priest from Faldera (12th c.) 353–355
Bruno of Querfurt St. (d. 1019) 16, 40 f., 48,
    82, 84, 89–91, 104 f., 107–110, 145, 157,
    159, 164 f., 169, 189, 192, 217, 220, 245,
    304
Bruno of Walbeck, bishop of Verden
    (1034–1049) 39
Burchard II, bishop of Halberstadt (1059–
    1088) 129, 225

Ceres, deity 18
Charlemagne, king of Franks and Lombards,
    Roman Emperor (d. 814) 52, 191, 201,
        252 f., 263, 270 f., 273, 311, 330, 360, 373
Charles the Great *see* Charlemagne
Charon, mythical figure 63
Chors, deity 12, 113, 124, 315
Chorts (pl.), Slavic mythical figures 317 f.
Christ, Jesus Christ 45, 49–51, 53, 55, 59, 75,
    79 f., 83–85, 90, 105 f., 108–110, 128, 138,
    145, 158 f., 168–171, 183–187, 189–192,
    197, 219 f., 223, 236, 238, 242–244, 249,
    266, 274 f., 316, 319–321, 328, 366, 370,
    375, 384, 386; Jesus 187, 217, 274, 292,
    303
Clement II, Pope (1046–1047) 205
Cnut the Great, king of England, Denmark
    and Norway (d. 1035) 240 f., 294
Conrad, bishop of Starigard (Oldenburg)
    (1164–1172) 262, 330, 356
Conrad II, king of Germany, Roman Emperor
    (d. 1039) 80
Constantine the Great, Roman Emperor
    (d. 337) 82, 373

Cosmas of Prague, chronicler (d. 1125) 7, 11,
    23, 27, 66, 74, 81, 149, 152, 155, 272, 355
Črnobog *see* Czarnobóg
Cyprian St. (d. 258) 219
Czarnobóg (Zcerneboch), deity 312, 314 f.,
    317–322, 353, 380

Dabog, pseudo-deity 344
Dadźbog *see* Dazbog
Dażbog *see* Dazbog
Dago, alleged name o Mieszko I (*see* below)
Daniel, biblical prophet 168
Dazbog, deity 110–116, 118, 122–124, 215,
    315 f., 321, 344, 348
Demetrius of Ephesus, biblical figure 102
Demetrius I Soter, king of Syria (d. 150 BC)
    302 f.
"Demiurge of lightning", deity (mentioned by
    Procopius of Caesarea) 115, 121, 347
Devil, biblical and mythological figure
    11–13, 15, 18, 25, 32, 80, 104 f., 107 f., 185,
    187, 199, 220, 251, 280, 312 f., 316–322,
    374, 380
Diabol (another name of Czarnobóg, *see*
    above), deity 312
Diana, deity 18
Dion Cato, so called, Latin author (3rd–4th c.)
    46
Dioskouri (pl.), deities 140
Dobrava, Bohemian princess, wife of
    Mieszko I (d. 977) 180
Dodilo, bishop of Brandenburg (968–980)
    86
Dola, deity 315
Drahomira of Stodor, duchess of Bohemia
    (d. after 934) 272
Dziady (pl.), mythical figures 143

Einhard, biographer of Charlemagne (d. 840)
    200
Ekkehard of Aura, chronicler (d. 1126) 232,
    259, 354
Ekkehard "The Red", schoolmaster of
    Magdeburg (10th c.) 40
Emnilda, canoness of Quedlinburg (d. 991)
    40
Eric, king in Sweden (deified according to
    hagiography of St. Anskar) 352

430 INDEX OF ANCIENT HISTORICAL, BIBLICAL AND MYTHICAL FIGURES

Eric the Victorious, king of Sweden (d. ca. 995)
247

Februus, deity   184, 186
Feost *see* Hephaestus
Fredegar, the conventional name for the
anonymous chronicler (8th c.)   292
Frederick, count of Walbeck (d. 1018)   39

Gallus Anonymous, the conventional name
for the anonymous chronicler (12th c.)
27, 291, 348
Gaudbert, missionary bishop in Sweden,
bishop of Osnabürck (845–860)   210
Geddo, schoolmaster of Magdeburg (d. 1016)
40
Gedymin, Grand Duke of Lithuania (d. 1341)
366
Gerold, bishop of Starigard (Oldenburg)
(1155–1163)   257, 259 f., 263, 326, 330, 333,
350, 353, 373
Gerovitus *see* Iarovit
Gisiler, archbishop of Magdeburg (981–1004)
51, 89 f.
"God of gods", (Slavic) deity   12, 30, 114, 120,
217, 323, 345–348, 363, 366, 376, 379 f.
Gonidło, pseudo-deity   162
Goniglis, deity   162
Gorm, ruler of Denmark (d. ca. 958)   285
Goswin, count of Valkenburg (d. ca. 1030)
Gottschalk, prince of Obodrites (d. 1066)
206, 240 f., 243, 251–253, 255, 294, 299,
370 f., 373
Gottschalk, priest from Bardevik (12th c.)
362, 367, 369
Gregory of Tours, historiographer (d. 594)
14 f.
Gregory I the Great, St., Pope (590–604)
40, 46, 59, 61, 69–71, 148, 188, 200, 258
Gregory IV, Pope (827–844)   205

Hagar, biblical figure 302 f.
Harald Bluetooth, king of Denmark and
Norway (d. ca. 986) 222 (as Haraldus),
234, 243, 288, 372
Hartwig, archbishop of Hamburg (1148–1168)
257, 326 f.
Heliogabal, deity   124

Helios, deity   110 f., 113 f., 116, 118, 124, 130
Helmold of Bosau, chronicler (d. ca. 1177)
7 f., 12, 15, 27, 30, 34 f., 38, 56, 68, 72,
75, 87, 99, 103, 114, 122, 126, 136, 141, 143,
147 f., 163, 197, 213, 217, 226 f., 229, 236 f.,
239–241, 248, 253, 255–279, 281–301,
303–339, 341, 343–388
Hennil, deity   161–164, 187 f., 191 f., 329, 385
Henno, deity   162
Henry, count of Walbeck (d. 1004)   39
Henry Gottschalk's son, prince of Obodrites
(d. 1127)   300–304, 370 f., 373
Henry I, the Fowler, duke of Saxony, king of
Germany (d. 936)   44, 52, 56. 209, 285,
373
Henry II, king of Germany, Roman Emperor
(d. 1024)   41, 44, 47, 82 f., 91, 93 f., 107 f.,
110, 145, 149, 157–159, 171, 183, 190, 192,
217, 233, 245
Henry IV, king of Germany, Roman Emperor
(d. 1106)   206
Henry of Antwerp, chronicler (d. after 1227)
217, 338
Henry the Lion, duke of Saxony (d. 1195)
75, 325–327, 351, 352 f., 356, 373,
378–380, 387
Hephaestus, deity   18, 110 f., 113 f., 116, 118, 120
Herbord of Michelsberg, hagiographer
(d. 1168)   16, 100, 331
Heriger, prefect of Birca (9th c.)   210
Hermann Billung, margrave of Billung March
(d. 973)   54, 286
Herod Antipater, tetrarch of Galilee and
Perea (d. after 39)   246
Herodotus of Halicarnassus, historiographer
(d. ca. 425 BC)   178
Hieronymus St. (d. 420)   24, 116
Homer, poet (8th c. BC)   116
Honidlo (Honilo, Honiło) *see* Gonidlo
Horace, Quintus Horatius Flaccus, poet
(d. 8 BC)   46, 199, 258
Horik I, king of Danes (d. 854)   205

Iarovit, deity   110 f., 138, 283 f., 310, 315, 320,
328
Ibn Rosteh, traveller and writer (10th c.)   115
Ibn-Fadlan, traveller and writer (10th c.)   64
Ibrahim ibn Yaqub, traveller and writer
(10th c.)   233

INDEX OF ANCIENT HISTORICAL, BIBLICAL AND MYTHICAL FIGURES   431

Indra, deity   119, 245
Isidore of Seville, scholar (d. 636)   46, 105,
          109, 207

Jan Długosz, chronicler (d. 1480)   10, 18
Jesus *see* Christ
Joannes Dlugossius *see* Jan Długosz
John Apostle St.   40, 253, 369
John Chrysostom, St. (d. 407)   23
John Malalas, chronicler (d. ca. 578)   110–112
John the Merciful, St. (d. 619)   258
John Scotus, bishop of Mecklenburg
          (Mechlin) (1053–1066)   223–225,
          244–246, 253
John the Baptist, St., biblical figure   246
John IV, Patriarch of Aquileia (984–1017)
          105
John XV, Pope (985–996)   205
Jovi (Jupiter), deity   11 f., 18, 121, 346
Juda, Judas Maccabeus (d. 160 BC)   288
Julius Caesar, Roman dictator (d. 44 BC)
          246
Jupiter *see* Jovi
Juvenal, Decimus Iunius Iuvenalis, poet
          (d. after 127)   46, 199

Kave, deity   118
Kruto, prince of Wagrians and Obodrites
          (d. 1093)   256, 299, 328
Kunigunde of Stade (d. 997), wife of
          Siegfried I, Count of Walbeck   39

Laban, biblical figure   302
Lawrence St. (d. 258)   86 f., 89 f., 386
Libentius, archbishop of Hamburg-Bremen
          (1029–1032)   235, 239 f., 253, 286, 372, 375
Liemar, archbishop of Hamburg-Bremen
          (1072–1101)   202–204, 206
Lothar I, count of Walbeck (d. 929)   39
Lothar II, count of Stade (d. 929)   39
Lothar I, Roman Emperor (d. 855)   274, 276
Lothar III of Supplinburg, king of Germany,
          Roman Emperor (d. 1137)   276, 303, 323 f.
Lothar III, count of Walbeck (d. 1003)   42
Louis the German, king of East Franks
          (d. 876)   271 f.
Louis the Pious, Roman Emperor (d. 840)
          201, 204, 360

Lucan, Marcus Annaeus Lucanus, poet
          (d. 65)   46, 199, 258

Macrobius Ambrosius Theodosius, writer and
          scholar (5th c.)   46, 193, 200
Magna Mater, deity   307
Magnus the Good, king of Norway and
          Denmark (d. 1047)   233, 268
Marko, alleged 1st. bishop of Starigard
          (according to Helmold of Bosau)   286
Mars, deity   11, 52, 103, 128, 151, 184, 245 f., 321
Martial, Marcus Valerius Martialis, poet   46
Martianus Capella, writer and scholar (5th c.)
          200
Maurice St. (d. 287)   108, 110, 145, 157
Mieszko I, prince of Poland (d. 992)   39,
          91 f., 176, 179–181, 344 (also as Dago),
          384
Mike, pagan priest of Obodrites (12th c.)
          328, 374
Minerva, deity   11
Mitra, deity   114, 124
Mlada, Benedictine abbess in Bohemia
          (d. 994), sister of Boleslav II the Pious
          66
Moses, patriarch   179
Mstidrog, prince of Obodrites (10th c.)   236
Mstivoy, prince of Obodrites (10th c.)
          85–88, 236, 242, 285, 287, 289–292

Neptune, deity   231, 235, 250
Nestor, chronicler (d. ca. 1115)   7, 15, 24, 28,
          102, 245
Nicolaus of Myra, St. (3–4th c.)   279
Niklot, prince of Obodrites (d. 1160)   263,
          306, 324, 326, 328 f., 351–353
Nikon, Hegumen, chronicler (11th c.)   24, 112
Nyja, deity   65, 71

Oda of Meissen, wife of Bolesław the Brave
          (d. after 1025)   159
Oda of Walbeck, sister of Thietmar of
          Merseburg, wife of Goswin of Valkenburg
          (11th c.)   39
Oddar, relative of Sven Estridsen (11th c.)
          237
Odin, Vodan, Wodan, deity   162, 282, 317, 320 f.

432   INDEX OF ANCIENT HISTORICAL, BIBLICAL AND MYTHICAL FIGURES

Odinkar the Elder, Bishop in Sweden (10th c.)
    210
Olaf, king of Sweden (9th c.)   207, 210
Olaf Skötkonung, king of Sweden (d. 1022)
    210
Olaf II Haraldsson, king of Norway (d. 1030)
    219
Ordericus Vitalis, chronicler (d. ca. 1142)   113
Orosius, Paulus Orosius, theologian and
    historiographer (d. after 418)   200
Otto I the Great, king of Germany, Roman
    Emperor (d. 973)   42, 50, 52, 80, 88, 181,
    209, 253, 273, 286, 373
Otto II, king of Germany, Roman Emperor
    (d. 983)   76, 85, 89 f., 287, 373
Otto III, king of Germany, Roman Emperor
    (d. 1002)   41, 47, 171, 211, 235, 287
Otto of Bamberg, St. (d. 1139)   7, 9, 14 f., 81,
    106, 122, 129, 136, 169, 176, 214, 224, 232 f.,
    268, 304, 310, 331, 335, 338 f., 341, 354,
    359
Ovid, Publius Ovidius Naso, poet (d. 17/18)
    46, 199, 258

Paul Apostle, St.   12, 15 f., 20, 102, 108, 185 f.,
    194, 229 f., 358, 361, 371
Paulinus II, Patriarch of Aquileia (776–802)
    272
Penates (pl.), deities   163, 306–308, 330, 346,
    376, 378, 380, 387
Perkun, deity   331
Persius, Aulus Persius Flaccus, poet (d. 62)
    46
Perun, deity   12, 15, 24, 102, 113 f., 116, 122, 124,
    140, 245, 284, 310, 318, 331, 347 f.
Peter Apostle, St.   52, 80, 83, 85, 187, 191, 386
Petrus Dusburg, chronicler (d. after 1326)
    332
Piccolomini, Aeneas Sylvius see Aeneas
    Sylvius Piccolomini
Plautus, Titus Maccius Plautus, playwright
    (d. 184 BC)   258
Pluto, deity   11, 65, 186
Podaga, deity, idol   307–309, 338, 344 f., 376,
    379, 103, 184–186
Pogoda, alleged deity   307, 344
Poppo, missionary and Bishop of Schleswig
    (ca. 1010–ca. 1016)   209 f., 373

Porenut, deity   139 f., 359
Porevit, deity   139 f., 315, 359, 364
Porovit see Porevit
Pribigniev see Uto-Pribigniev
Pribislav, prince of Wagrians (d. ca. 1157)
    306, 324, 330, 350 f., 380
Pribislav, prince of Obodrites (d. 1179)   356
Pribislav-Henry, prince of Stodorane (d. 1150)
    339
"Princeps demonum"   106, 109, 138, 192, 217,
    254, 363, 375 f., 384, 386
Procopius of Caesarea, historiographer
    (d. after 565)   10 f., 57, 115, 121, 307, 346
Prone see Prove
Prove, deity   56, 127, 136, 146, 175, 306, 308,
    309, 327, 330 f., 333 f., 338, 346, 349, 362
Prudentius, Aurelius Prudentius Clemens,
    poet (d. after 405)   46
Ptah, deity   111

Rarog, mythical figure   119
Redegast see Redigast
Redigast, deity   109, 123, 138, 192, 212–219,
    244–246, 253 f., 266, 306, 308, 310 f.,
    333, 349, 363, 375 f., 384, 386
Radogost see Redigast
Regino of Prüm, chronicler (d. 915)   47, 200
Reinbern, Bishop of Salsa Cholbergiensis
    (Kolberg) (1000-ca. 1013)   164–168, 170,
    172 f., 187, 196
Rikdag, Abbot of Berge (ca. 987–1005)   40
Rimbert, Archbishop of Hamburg-Bremen
    (865–888)   8, 200
Rochel, prince of Wagrians (12th c.)   328,
    372, 374
Rod, deity   365
Romulus, legendary figure   52
Rugievit, deity   107, 110, 139 f., 216, 310, 359,
    364 f.
Rujevit see Rugievit

Sallust, Gaius Sallustius Crispus,
    historiographer (d. ca. 35 BC)   199
Salome, daughter of Herod II and Herodias,
    biblical figure (1st c.)   246
Samo, ruler of Slavs (7th c.)   291
Saracho of Rossdorf, Abbot of Corvey
    (d. 1071)   276

INDEX OF ANCIENT HISTORICAL, BIBLICAL AND MYTHICAL FIGURES   433

Sarah, biblical figure   302 f.
Satan, biblical and mythical figure   11, 18,
       106, 109, 161, 189, 191 f., 278, 316, 319–321,
       327, 369, 374
Saturn, deity   27, 54–56, 185, 214, 334, 387
Saxo Annalist, the conventional name for the
       anonymous chronicler (12 c.)   226
Saxo Grammaticus, chronicler (d. ca. 220)
       7, 27, 107, 129, 140 f., 143, 273 f., 276, 279,
       313, 356–358, 361, 364 f.
Sergius IV, Pope (1009–1012)   235
Siegfried I, Count of Walbeck (d. 990)
       39, 86
Siegfried of Walbeck, Bishop of Münster
       (1022–1032)   39
Siva, (Slavic) deity   306, 310, 333, 378
Sol Invictus, deity   124
Solinus, Gaius Julius Solinus, writer (3rd c.)
       200, 230
Statius, Publius Papinius Statius, poet (d. 96)
       46
Strachkvas-Kristián, prince of Bohemia,
       monk (d. 996)   66
Stribog, deity   282, 315
Sulpicius Severus, hagiographer and
       historiographer (d. ca. 420)   15, 258
Svantevit, deity   12, 110 f., 123, 127, 130,
       137–141, 214, 273 f., 277–284, 301, 306,
       309 f., 313, 315, 320, 322 f., 339, 342, 344,
       346, 356 f., 361–366, 375 f., 379, 383, 388
Svarog, deity   24, 110–120, 122, 125, 134, 137,
       344, 348
Svarožic, deity   32, 101, 104, 106–115, 118–125,
       127, 132, 134 f., 137 f., 141, 152, 192, 195,
       214–217, 245, 283, 310, 348 f., 364
Sviatopolk the Accursed, prince of Turov and
       Kiev (d. 1019)   164
Sven Estridsen, king of Denmark (d. 1076)
       198, 200 f., 206, 208, 211, 237, 242
Sven I the Forkbeard, king of Denmark,
       Norway, and England (d. 1014)   222, 234,
       288
Sven III, king of Denmark (d. 1157)   278
Sviatovid, a four-faced idol, alleged name of a
       deity   281, 317, 340–342, 349, 365
Svitibor, pseudo-deity   146

Tacitus, Publius Cornelius Tacitus,
       historiographer (d. 120)   14, 117, 130, 148,
       181, 198, 228, 231, 335
Tagino, Archbishop of Magdeburg (1004–
       1012)   42, 47
Terentius, Publius Terentius Afer, playwright
       (d. ca. 159 BC)   46, 258
Tertullian, theologian (d. ca. 240)   40, 46
Tesimir, Wagrian magnate (12th c.)   330
Theoderic see Theodoric, margrave of the
       Northern March
Theodoric, canon of Magdeburg, chaplain
       of Walthard Archbishop of Magdeburg
       (11th c.)   43
Theodoric, Margrave of the Northern March
       (d. 985)   76, 235, 237, 289
Thietmar of Merseburg   7, 19, 22, 25, 27, 29,
       34 f., 38–54, 56, 58–63, 65–74, 76–110,
       119, 121, 125–128, 131–139, 141–145, 147,
       149–152, 154 f., 157–167, 169–177,
       179–181, 183 f., 186–195, 213–215, 217 f.,
       220, 224, 233, 235 f., 239–241, 245, 249,
       254, 272, 281, 287, 292 f., 295, 298, 306 f.,
       329, 332, 350, 355, 371, 381–388
Thor, deity   106, 113, 125, 140, 317
Thrucco see Tryggve Olafsson
Tjarnaglofi, deity   40, 75, 317
Triglav, deity   95, 100 f., 137 f., 153, 214, 280,
       310, 317, 334, 338 f., 341 f., 344, 365
Triglous see Triglav
Troian, pseudo-deity   12, 113
Tryggve Olafsson, king in Norway (d. 963)
       234

Unni, Archbishop of Hamburg-Bremen
       (916–936)   201, 209 f., 285, 373
Unvanus see Unwan
Unwan, Archbishop of Hamburg-Bremen
       (1013–1029)   205, 239 f., 294
Uranus, deity   347
Uto-Pribigniev, prince of Obodrites (d. 1028)
       240

Vaju see Vata
Valdemar I the Great, king of Denmark
       (d. 1182)   356–358, 375
Varuna, deity   114, 130
Vata, deity   282

Vele (pl.), mythical figures   63, 65, 143

Veles, deity   11 f., 63–65, 71, 143, 310, 315

Venus, deity   11, 18

Vertislav, prince of Obodrites (d. 1164)   356

Vicelin, Bishop of Starigard (Oldenburg)
(1149–1154)   256 f., 303–305, 324, 326–328,
371–373, 378

Vincent Kadłubek, chronicler (d. 1223)   70

Virgil, Publius Vergilius Maro, poet (19 BC)
46, 199, 220, 258, 361

Vitus St. (d. ca. 303)   12, 274–280, 284, 353,
360, 376, 379, 388

Vladimir the Great, prince of Kievan Rus
(d. 1015)   15, 107, 124, 140, 160, 164

Vodan see Odin

Vulcanus, deity   230, 235, 250, 388

Wago, Bishop of Starigard (Oldenburg)
(974–983)   287

Walthard, Archbishop of Magdeburg (1012)
35, 45, 47

"White God" see Belbog

Wibald, Abbot of Corvey (d. 1158)   276

Widukind of Corvey, chronicler (d. after 973)
27, 46, 49, 52, 54 f., 85, 181, 185, 214, 232,
236, 272, 276, 334, 387

Wigbert, Bishop of Merseburg (1004–1009)
72, 79, 145, 147, 350

Willehad of Frisia, Bishop of Bremen
(787–789)   222

William of Malmesbury, chronicler
(d. ca. 1143)   38, 129

Willigis, son of Siegfried I of Walbeck, prior
of monastery of Walbeck (since 1009)   39

Winfrid-Boniface St. (d. 754)   181

Wipo, chronicler (d. after 1046)   81

Wodan see Odin

Yahweh-God   192, 376

Yppo, priest from Lübeck (d. 1066)   243 f.

Zcerneboch see Czarnobóg

Zeus, deity   119–121, 130, 316 f., 347

Zuantevith (Zuantevit) see Svantevit

Zuarasici see Svarožic

Zuarasiz see Svarožic

Zuttibor see Svitibor

Żywa, deity   307

Żywie see Żywa

Zywye see Żywa

Index of Modern Authors

Achterberg, Herbert   1, 12–14, 16, 33
Ackenheil, H.V.   56, 215 f., 334
Adrjanova-Peretc, Varvara P.   12
Altaner, Berthold   59
Althoff, Gerd   42
Andrałojć, Małgorzata   292
Andrén, Anders   99, 124
Anichkov, Evgeniĭ   12, 20 f., 28
Antoniewicz, Włodzimierz   137, 341–344
Apostolos-Cappadona, Diane   315
Arbusow, Leonid   262
Arszyński, Marian   34
Aymard, Maurice   224

Babij, Paweł   76, 85 f., 89, 91, 93, 123, 157, 183,
   236, 243, 248, 273, 295–297, 300, 356
Banaszkiewicz, Jacek   5, 57, 112, 117 f., 139,
   140, 147, 180, 216, 224 f., 321, 333, 335,
   357
Barciak, Antoni   151
Bartlett, Robert   2, 5, 33, 360
Bartnik, Czesław   49, 50, 199
Bartoszewicz, Agnieszka   228
Bauer, Albert   52
Beck, Heinrich   131, 197, 312
Bednarczuk, Leszek   174, 282, 332
Berend, Nora   5, 206
Berg, Dieter   76
Berlekamp, Hansdieter   358
Berschin, Walter   197 f., 202
Beumann, Helmut   29, 96
Biermann, Felix   77, 96, 125, 151, 333, 339
Biskup, Marian   366
Bláhová, Marie   95
Bogdanowicz, Jadwiga   20
Bogdanowicz, Piotr   93, 145
Bokszański, Zbigniew   36
Bollnow, Hermann   176, 232
Bołsunowski, Karol   365
Boroń, Piotr   126, 142
Borowski, Andrzej   66
Bracha, Krzysztof 149
Brachman, Hansjürgen   58
Brather, Sebastian   55
Bresslau, Harry   81

Bretholz, Bertold   66
Brückner, Aleksander   98, 100, 110 f., 113–115,
   119 f., 134, 136, 138, 142 f., 146, 157, 162 f.,
   181, 213, 215, 282, 307 f., 334, 343 f., 346,
   352
Brzóstowska, Anna   57
Buchner, Rudolf   54
Budziszewska, Wanda   344
Bünz, Enno   304
Burghart, Gottfried Heinrich   154
Burghartz, Susanna   325
Burke, Peter   37
Buszewicz, Elwira   267
Bylina, Stanisław   60 f., 63 f., 69, 179, 182, 220,
   317, 351

Cabalska, Maria   178
Carp, Richard M.   153
Caune, Andris   341
Cetwiński, Marek   132, 342
Chochorowski, Jan   154
Chrzan, Krystian   95
Cichowicz, Stanisław   169
Coser, Lewis A.   34
Couliano, Ioan P.   315
Curta, Florin   6, 9
Curtius, Ernst Robert   66, 262
Czapla, Krzysztof   95
Czubiński, Antoni   208

Dancygier, Józef   2
Dawson, Christopher   2
Demetrykiewicz, Włodzimierz   343
Deptuła, Czesław   166, 168
Derwich, Marek   68, 132, 165, 342
Domański, Grzegorz   93, 149, 153–155
Donnert, Erich   47 f.
Dowiat, Jerzy   66, 76, 98, 134, 137, 182
Dralle, Lothar   96, 104, 126, 213, 216, 223, 296,
   298
Duby, Georges   77
Duczko, Władysław   64, 232
Dülmen, Richard van   37
Dumézil, Georges   5, 27, 140
Dümmler, Ernst   181, 273

Durkheim, Émile   6, 37, 70
Düwel, Klaus   7
Dyggve, Ejnar   358
Dygo, Marian   41, 83, 108
Dzieduszycki, Wojciech   291
Dziewulski, Władysław   26, 74, 162

Ebelová, Ivana   51
Eliade, Mircea   5, 7, 29, 124, 166, 315 f., 331, 347, 349
Ellis, Linda   358
Elmevik, Lennart   221
Engel, Evamaria   96
Engelke, Matthew   153
Engler, Steven   153

Fałkowski, Wojciech   41, 83, 107 f.
Fehrle, Eugen   117
Filipowiak, Władysław   174, 227 f., 232 f., 281, 317, 340, 355
Fisher, Peter   99
Foote, Peter G.   218
Forstner, Dorothea   60, 80, 87, 97, 163, 167 f., 170, 222, 272, 292, 321
Fraesdorff, David   8, 14, 39, 49, 86, 97, 160, 180 f., 208, 212, 230, 234, 266, 272, 288, 304, 319, 323, 327, 358, 360
Frazer, James George   331
Fried, Johannes   171
Friedmann, Bernhard   85
Fritze, Wolfgang H.   76

Gabriel, Ingo   333
Gapski, Henryk   357
Gąssowski, Jerzy   134, 148, 179, 246, 343, 364
Gawin, Danuta   228
Gediga, Bogusław   98, 149, 154, 178, 182
Gelting, Michael H.   206
Geremek, Bronisław   37
Gieysztor, Aleksander   29, 55, 58, 62 f., 78, 81, 95, 110, 113–115, 117–120, 122–124, 129 f., 132, 146, 163, 173, 175, 178, 180 f., 215 f., 245 f., 282, 284, 307 f., 310, 313–318, 331 f., 336, 341 f., 344, 347 f.
Gilbert, Paul P.   51
Gilomen, Hans-Jörg   325
Goetz, Hans-Werner   5, 76, 144, 161, 181, 234, 238, 243, 247 f., 253, 287, 291, 303 f.

Goliński, Mateusz   57, 106, 132, 182, 213, 229, 292
Górski, Tytus   51
Gozzini, Mario   26
Grabski, Andrzej Felix   36
Graff, Piotr   38
Gräslund, Anne-Sofie   214
Grimm, Jacob   142, 162, 292
Grimm, Oliver   218
Gringmuth-Dallmer, Eike   135, 339
Grothusen, Klaus-Detlev   325
Grucza, Franciszek   273
Grundmann, Herbert   66
Gryglewicz, Feliks   367
Gundlach, Heinz   227
Gundlach, Wilhelm   181
Guriewicz [Gurevich], Aron   2, 316

Hadamik, Czesław   149
Halbwachs, Maurice   34
Hallencreutz, Carl Fredrik   199
Hanusch, Ignaz Johann   162, 342
Hartmann, Ludwig M.   148
Haury, Jakob   57
Hayes, John H.   49, 97
Heck, Roman   47
Hengst, Karlheinz   72
Henning, Eckart   76, 172
Hensel, Witold   26 f., 98, 227, 230, 233, 280, 323, 332, 339 f.
Herrmann, Joachim   25, 76, 95, 135
Hill, Thomas   305
Hiltebeitel, Alf   315
Hinz, Hans-Martin   171, 232
Hiraux, Françoise   68
Hirsch, Paul   52
Hoffmann, Erich   56, 243, 324
Hoffmann, Jürgen   220
Holder-Egger, Oskar   339
Hollnagel, Adolf   135, 339
Holtzmann, Robert   39
Hoops, Johannes   55
Horák, Bohuslav   150
Horbacz, Tadeusz J.   26, 173
Hryniewicz, Wacław   283
Hübner, Eckhard   56
Hultgård, Anders   6, 92, 199, 214, 218, 312
Hunia, Justyn   37

INDEX OF MODERN AUTHORS

Ingstad, Helge   202

Jakobson, Roman   119, 121
Janion, Maria   4, 82, 384
Janowski, Andrzej   177, 179
Janson, Henrik   218, 254
Jaskanis, Jan   63
Jażdżewski, Konrad   365
Jedin, Hubert   76
Jedlicki, Marian Zygmunt   39, 43 f., 46, 48,
    54, 77, 87, 92, 126, 143, 146 f., 162, 163,
    183 f.
Jennbert, Kristina   99
Jeż, Ignacy   170

Kahl, Hans-Dietrich   4, 33, 76, 81 f., 93, 181,
    324 f., 339, 344, 381
Karwasińska, Jadwiga   89, 107, 220
Kasper, Walter   305
Keller, Hagen   5, 49
Keller, Józef   117
Kempke, Torsten   333
Kersting, Thomas   151
Kętrzyński, Wojciech   352, 360
Khamaiko, Natalia   365
Kiersnowska, Teresa   98, 104, 125, 127, 144,
    278, 347, 353
Kiersnowski, Ryszard   98, 104, 125, 127, 144,
    226 f., 230, 232, 267, 269, 278, 347, 352 f.
Klammt, Anne   151
Kłoczowski, Jerzy   67, 209
Klug, Ekkehard   56
Knowles, M. David   205
Kóčka-Krenz, Hanna   177
Koczy, Leon   47 f., 85, 200, 207, 210 f., 222,
    230, 237
Kohl, Wilhelm   305
Kohlmann, Philipp Wilhelm   198
Kołakowski, Leszek   29
Komar, Olexiy   365
Kondratowicz, Marek   219
Korta, Wacław   47, 149, 153, 155, 165
Kossak-Szczucka, Zofia   74, 356
Kostrzewski, Józef   65, 365
Kotlarczyk, Janusz   340–343
Kotula, Tadeusz   269
Kowalczyk, Małgorzata   133
Kowalczyk, Stanisław   82

Kowalenko, Władysław   171, 241, 300, 302,
    356
Kowalski, Tadeusz   233
Kozik, Bryan   9
Kracik, Jan   168
Krawiec, Adam   45
Kristensen, Anne K.G   203
Krusch, Bruno   291
Krzak, Zygmunt   317, 341–343, 347, 365
Kuczyński, Stefan K.   80, 234
Kulišić, Špiro   16, 110, 119, 124, 127, 163, 184,
    307, 315–318, 331, 342
Kumor, Bolesław   148, 180
Kürbis, Brygida   47, 259, 263
Kurnatowska, Zofia   93, 98, 135, 140, 154, 334
Kusber, Jan   56
Kwapiński, Marian   134, 292, 341

Labuda, Gerard   8, 16 f., 43, 56, 76, 83–86, 89,
    91, 93, 142, 164, 167, 202, 204 f., 215 f.,
    224, 229, 232–236, 240 f., 243, 245, 261,
    267, 286 f., 289 f., 295, 298, 300, 305,
    312, 323 f., 327, 343, 354, 356
Lachmann, Renate   75
Lamm, Jan Peder   340, 343
Lammers, Walther   324
Lange, Wolfgang   321
Langebek, Jacobus   226, 231
Łapiński, Adam   341
Lappenberg, Johann Martin   198, 261
Larsson, Lars   176
Le Goff, Jacques   66, 83, 87, 292
Lechowicz, Zbigniew   26, 173
Leciejewicz, Lech   4, 54 f., 58, 66, 73, 84, 91,
    104, 126, 135 f., 138, 142, 147–149,
    163–165, 171, 179, 216, 224, 227–229,
    232–234, 236, 273, 290, 298, 310, 328,
    331, 333 f., 339, 348, 355 f.
Leeuw, Gerardus van der   166
Łęga, Władysław   343
Łęgowski-Nadmorski, Józef   342
Leighton, Gregory   9
Lelewel, Joachim   349, 365
Leńczyk, Gabriel   281, 341
Lenntorp, Karl-Magnus   176
Leszczyński, Józef   47
Lewicki, Paweł   37
Lewicki, Tadeusz   177 f.

Likhachev, Dmitriĭ S.   12
Liman, Kazimierz   56, 99
Lindner, Michael   339
Lippelt, Helmut   39–46, 51, 60, 69 f., 92, 181
Logan, F. Donald   202
Łosiński, Władysław   177
Lotter, Friedrich   41
Łowmiański, Henryk   19–23, 26–28, 31,
    54–56, 61–64, 66, 69, 75, 77–79, 82, 100,
    110 f., 114 f., 121 f., 125, 127 f., 133 f., 146,
    151, 162, 172–174, 179, 214 f., 224, 244 f.,
    279 f., 300 f., 307 f., 312, 314–319, 331,
    334 f., 337, 344–346, 348, 352, 354 f.,
    366, 377
Ludat, Herbert   206, 224, 325
Lübke, Christian   5, 9, 72, 74, 77, 80, 84, 149,
    157, 212, 236, 298, 339
Łuczyński, Michał   38
Łukaszyk, Romuald   367

Machek, Václav   119
Madonia, Claudio   4
Makiewicz, Tadeusz   292
Makowski, Adam   8
Małachowicz, Edmund   100
Maleczyński, Karol   150, 291
Malinowski, Bronisław   178
Manitius, Max   197 f., 200
Manteuffel, Tadeusz   281
Marchal, Guy P.   325
Margański, Janusz   35
Marzęcki, Józef   2
Matuszewski, Józef   237, 256
Mayenowa, Maria R.   315
Meier, Dietrich   172
Meriggi, Bruno   17, 69, 338, 342 f.
Meyer, Karl H.   129, 162
Michałowska, Teresa   97
Michałowski, Roman   41, 83, 180, 230
Middleton, John   7
Mierzwiński, Andrzej   149
Miklosich, Franz   110, 119, 279
Miller, Daniel   152
Miś, Andrzej Lambert   26, 110, 125, 245, 275,
    280, 283, 301, 361
Młynarska-Kaletynowa, Marta   100, 149
Modzelewski, Karol   7 f., 29, 36, 142, 212, 228,
    230, 248, 291, 334–336, 345, 350, 357

Mooyer, Ernst F.   199
Morawiec, Jakub   232–234, 267, 321
Moszyński, Kazimierz   60, 62 f., 96, 103, 110,
    115, 119 f., 307, 314 f., 317 f., 331, 353
Moszyński, Leszek   23 f., 31, 75, 110, 116, 118 f.,
    121, 146, 158, 164, 174, 215, 279 f., 331,
    344 f.
Moździoch, Sławomir   95, 100, 333
Mrozowicz, Wojciech   72, 165
Müller-Wille, Michael   50, 55, 130, 171 f., 274,
    279, 320
Mynors, Roger Aubrey Baskerville   129
Myśliński, Kazimierz   76, 91, 93, 300, 339

Nadolski, Bogusław   109, 169, 219
Nalepa, Jerzy   58, 151, 154
Narbutt, Teodor   162
Naruszewicz, Adam   162
Nedo, Paul   314
Neugebauer, Werner   332
Niederle, Lubomír   61, 308, 331, 344, 346, 366
Nielsen, Ann-Lili   99, 176
Nola, Alfonso M. Di   26, 32
Nordberg, Andreas   124
Nowaczyk, Mirosław   62
Nowak, Johannes   208, 230

Obolensky, Dmitri   205
Oexle, Otto Gerhard   34
Orsi, Robert A.   153
Osięgłowski, Janisław   248, 273, 275–277,
    279 f., 302, 356
Otto, Bernd-Christian   7
Otto, Karl-Heinz   358
Otto, Rudolf   5, 166

Pachciarek, Paweł   59 f.
Padberg, Lutz E. von   5, 33 f., 49, 67 f., 75, 80,
    148, 219, 243, 266, 291, 324 f.
Palm, Thede   16, 172, 339
Paner, Henryk   134, 292, 341
Persoons, Ernest   305
Pertz, Georg Heinrich   129, 165, 279
Pesch, Alexandra   218
Petersohn, Jürgen   139, 168, 285
Peterson, Lena   221
Petrulevich, Alexandra   233
Pettazzoni, Raffaele   17, 38, 110, 115, 118 f., 122,
    129–131, 217, 310, 317, 338, 342

INDEX OF MODERN AUTHORS

Piekarczyk, Stanisław   117, 352
Pisani, Vittore   119
Piskorski, Jan M.   172
Pleszczyński, Andrzej   37, 159, 180 f., 289, 321, 323
Plezia, Marian   70
Popowska-Taborska, Hanna   174, 283, 314
Potkański, Karol   307, 346
Potkowski, Edward   35, 62, 67
Procházka, Vladimír   123, 141, 163, 366
Prucnal, Dariusz   50, 77, 87, 180 f.

Rajewski, Zdzisław   25, 127, 131
Rau, Reinhold   52
Raudvere, Catharina   99
Rębkowski, Marian   77, 164 f., 232
Rechowicz, Marian   67, 76, 166
Reuther, Timothy   197, 391
Reyman, Tadeusz   365
Ricoeur, Paul   35, 38, 169
Romanov, Boris   12
Rosen-Przeworska, Janina   132, 281, 339, 343
Rosik, Mariusz   292
Rosik, Stanisław   2, 8 f., 28, 45, 48, 51, 57, 72, 77, 91, 94, 101, 106 f., 110, 117, 122, 129, 132, 136 f., 149–151, 154, 156, 164, 167 f., 175, 182, 213, 224, 227, 229 f., 232, 280, 283, 291 f., 310, 321, 331, 335, 338, 341, 343 f., 354, 356, 359 f., 362, 366, 384
Rosner, Katarzyna   38
Rospond, Stanisław   150
Rossignol, Sébastien   95, 151
Ruchhöft, Fred   339, 358
Rudnicki, Mikołaj   64 f., 226, 342–344
Rumohr, Carl Friedrich   267
Rusakiewicz, Monika   227, 267
Rusanova, Irina P.   341
Rusecki, Marian   59
Russel, Jeffrey Burton   219
Rybakov, Boris   12, 28, 110, 124, 317, 331, 341, 346, 365
Rymar, Edward   267
Rytter, Grażyna   25, 332
Rzetelska-Feleszko, Ewa   232 f.

Šafárik, Pavol Jozef   119
Salamon, Maciej   9
Schäferdiek, Knut   4

Schmale, Franz-Josef   35, 76
Schmaus, Alois   17
Schmeidler, Bernhard   56, 80, 197–204, 211, 256, 258
Schmidt, Volker   221
Schmidt, Jacek   36
Schmidt, Roderich   96 f., 213, 220 f., 223
Schmidt, Wilhelm   349
Schneidmüller, Bernd   327
Schröder, Edward   198
Schröder, Horst-Diether   361
Schuchhardt, Carl   95
Schuldt, Ewald   100
Schulmeyer-Ahl, Kerstin   39, 44, 49, 59, 76 f., 87, 89, 94, 145, 186
Scior, Volker   8, 49, 205 f., 211 f., 225, 229, 236, 239, 241 f., 248 f., 256 f., 265 f., 271 f., 285, 287, 299, 304, 327, 354, 360, 383 f.
Sczaniecki, Paweł   73–75
Seweryn, Tadeusz   163
Siebs, Theodor   162
Sieroszewska, Barbara   17
Sikora, Przemysław   77
Sikorski, Dariusz Andrzej   23, 73, 148
Skonieczny, Tomasz   77, 132
Skovgaard-Petersen, Inge   274, 325
Skubiszewski, Piotr   211
Ślaski, Kazimierz   229
Słupecki, Leszek Paweł   9, 29 f., 55, 57 f., 84, 92, 95 f., 99–101, 104, 107, 127–130, 146–150, 153 f., 158, 172, 175 f., 214, 217, 221, 233, 310, 319, 332 f., 339, 341, 352, 355
Sobiesiak, Joanna   180, 321, 323
Sochacki, Jarosław   77
Sosnowski, Miłosz   41, 107
Soszyński, Jacek   273, 275–278, 281
Šouša, Jiří   51
Spors, Józef   296
Śrutwa, Jan   79
Staats, Reinhart   50, 67
Stabenow, Ulf   172
Stachowiak, Lech   367
Stanisławski, Błażej M.   232, 234
Stanula, Emil   219
Staubach, Nikolaus   5, 49
Stausberg, Michael   153
Stoob, Heinz   256–260, 263–265, 294

Strug, Karol 17, 178
Strzelczyk, Jerzy 29, 41, 43 f., 47, 54, 87, 93,
    95, 97, 104, 110, 115, 119, 132, 135, 138, 142,
    145 f., 148, 151, 162, 167, 213, 221, 237, 239,
    256–259, 261–265, 296 f., 300, 304 f.,
    312, 324, 326–328, 334, 337, 343, 363
Stuiber, Alfred 59
Sulowski, Jan 219
Sułowski, Zygmunt 67, 93, 183, 298, 367
Sundqvist, Olof 131, 218, 221, 352
Surowiecki, Wawrzyniec 342
Swoboda, Wincenty 57, 279
Szafrański, Włodzimierz 55, 57, 70, 98, 118,
    129, 245, 281 f., 306, 331 f., 343, 349, 355
Szatkowski, Zygmunt 74, 356
Szczesiak, Rainer 96
Szejgiec, Karol 180, 323
Szumańska-Gross, Hanna 66
Szyjewski, Andrzej 115, 118
Szymański, Wojciech 281, 341

Tabaczyński, Stanisław 92
Tangl, Michael 181
Tarkowska, Elżbieta 6
Thomson, Rodney M. 129
Timoshchuk, Boris A. 341
Todorov, Tzvetan 37
Tokarev, Sergey A. 62
Tomaszek, Michał 90, 180, 321, 323
Tomicka, Joanna 342
Tomicki, Ryszard 342
Topolski, Jerzy 35
Trávníček, Dušan 150
Třeštik, Dušan 150
Trillmich, Werner 39, 44–47, 54, 90, 109,
    197–206, 210
Tschan, Francis J. 197
Turasiewicz, Adam 87, 183, 240 f., 300, 302,
    306
Turzyński, Ryszard 60
Tvveedale, Michaele 57
Tymieniecki, Kazimierz 17, 47, 61, 78
Tyszka, Przemysław 180, 321, 323
Tyszkiewicz, Lech A. 40, 42 f., 45, 47 f., 54,
    56 f., 91, 106, 135, 147, 154, 181 f., 208, 229,
    269, 272, 287, 289, 291 f., 346

Udolph, Jürgen 150, 273
Unverhau, Henning 172

Urbańczyk, Przemysław 6, 41, 77
Urbańczyk, Stanisław 10, 17–19, 26 f., 31, 56,
    58, 61 f., 65, 69 f., 98, 100, 104, 110, 113,
    115, 119–123, 125, 127, 130, 133, 146, 148,
    162, 174, 182, 184, 214–216, 244, 279,
    281–283, 301, 306–308, 314, 319, 323,
    328, 331, 334, 339 f., 343–345, 347, 361,
    366, 374

Váňa, Zdeněk 25 f., 316, 366
Vauchez, André 49 f., 83
Vedel (Velleus), Andreas Severinus 204
Vernardsky, George 282, 314, 342
Vogel, Werner 76

Wachowski, Kazimierz 125, 135, 303, 345
Waitz, Georg 232, 352, 392
Waluga, Grażyna 3
Wamers, Egon 320
Warner, David A. 39, 45, 51 f., 54, 58 f., 88,
    93, 105, 129, 144, 155, 157, 159, 161, 180,
    184–186
Watson, E. Mills 49
Wavra, Brigitte 33, 80, 204 f.
Węcławski, Tomasz 152
Wędzki, Andrzej 58
Weigel, Max 365
Weiler, Anton G. 305
Weinrich, Lorenz 76
Wichert, Sven 127, 221
Widengren, Geo 6, 347
Wieczorek, Alfred 171, 232
Wielgus, Stanisław 49, 203
Wienecke, Erwin von 1, 10, 13–18, 22, 26, 28,
    31, 54 f., 95 f., 115, 214, 338, 342 f., 377,
    381
Wierusz-Kowalski, Jan 29, 124
Wikarjak, Jan 56, 99
Wilgocki, Eugeniusz 221
William of Malmesbury 129
Wilson, David M. 218
Wilson, Richard F. 49
Winterbottom, Michael 129
Wirski, Adam 30, 230
Wiszewski, Przemysław 8, 45, 91, 175, 291
Witczak, Krzysztof T. 65
Witkowski, Grzegorz 202, 204
Włodarczyk, Edward 8
Wojciechowski, Leszek 357

INDEX OF MODERN AUTHORS

Wojtasik, Janusz   233, 281, 340
Wolny, Jerzy   67, 220
Woronczak, Jerzy   73 f.
Wrzesińska, Anna   182
Wrzesiński, Jacek   1, 36, 182, 291
Wrzesiński, Wojciech   36, 181, 208, 270
Wünsch, Thomas   8

Zadrożyńska, Anna   6
Zagiba, Franz   72
Zakrzewska, Wanda   60

Zakrzewski, Stanisław   183
Zaroff, Roman   129
Zášterová, Bohumila   182
Żebrawski, Teofil   365
Żerelik, Rościsław   165, 202
Zernack, Klaus   126, 223, 306, 325, 359
Zeuner, Karl   272
Zientara, Benedykt   80, 207 f.
Zoll-Adamikowa, Helena   177–179, 182
Zöllner, Johann Friedrich   232
Žulkus, Vladas   130, 245, 367

Printed in the United States
By Bookmasters